THE OTHER GREAT MIGRATION

NUMBER TWENTY-ONE

Sam Rayburn Series on Rural Life,
sponsored by Texas A&M University-Commerce

M. Hunter Hayes, General Editor

A list of other titles in this series appears at the back of the book.

THE OTHER GREAT MIGRATION

The Movement of Rural African Americans to Houston, 1900–1941

~

BERNADETTE PRUITT

Texas A&M University Press
COLLEGE STATION

COVER/TITLE PAGE The United States Army commissioned Sgt. Samuel Countee to design a large painting for a wall in the newly built Black Officers Club at Fort Leonard Wood, Missouri, in 1942. Completed in 1943 or 1945, the "Garden of Eden" celebrated the beauty of Black love, innocence, and hope. The setting: Fifth Ward, Houston, from his mother's front porch. Countee, a native of Marshall and graduate of Houston's Booker T. Washington High School in the 1920s, understood the relevance of the portrait as the Black press's effective "Double V," or "Democracy: Victory at Home, Victory Abroad," campaign for the successful defeat of the racist Axis Forces abroad and of White supremacy in the United States. *(Courtesy Office of Media Relations, Fort Leonard Wood, Missouri, United States Army)*

Copyright © 2013 by Bernadette Pruitt
All rights reserved
Second printing, 2017

Manufactured in the United States of America
The paper used in this book meets the minimum requirements
of the American National Standard for Permanence
of Paper for Printed Library Materials, z39.48–1984.
Binding materials have been chosen for durability.

LIBRARY OF CONGRESS CATALOGING-IN-PUBLICATION DATA

Pruitt, Bernadette, 1965–
The other great migration : the movement of rural African Americans to Houston, 1900–1941 / Bernadette Pruitt. — 1st ed.
    p. cm. — (Sam Rayburn series on rural life ; no. 21)
Includes bibliographical references and index.
ISBN 978-1-60344-948-9 (cloth: alk. paper) —
ISBN 978-1-62349-003-4 (e-book)
ISBN 978-1-62349-609-8 (pbk)
1. African-Americans—Texas—Houston—Migrations—History—20th century. 2. Rural-urban migration—Texas—Houston—History—20th century. 3. Migration, Internal—Texas—Houston—History—20th century. 4. African Americans—Texas—Houston—Social conditions—20th century. 5. Houston (Tex.)—Social conditions—20th century. 6. Community development—Texas—Houston—History—20th century. 7. Houston (Tex.)—Race relations—History—20th century. I. Title.
II. Series: Sam Rayburn series on rural life ; no. 21.
F394.H89N48   2013
305.896'07307641411—dc23
2013017813

*To my grandparents—
Mack Lively and Bertha Juanita Lewis Lively Pruitt,
and Elizabeth and Clinton Pruitt—
thank you for everything.
Your Great Migrations to Detroit, Michigan,
in the last century have molded me
into the woman I am today in this century.
I love you!*

CONTENTS

FOREWORD IX

PREFACE XI

INTRODUCTION 1

ONE
Pulling Up the Stakes
The Great Migration to Houston, 1900–1930   15

TWO
Building a City
Migrant Settlements in Houston, 1900–1941   55

THREE
Beautiful People
Agency in Houston, 1900–1941   95

FOUR
"That Was Their Protection and Safeguard"
Houston's "New Negro," 1917–1941   141

FIVE
In "The Garden of Eden"
The Houston Renaissance, 1900–1941   187

SIX
The Black Economy at Work
Wage Earners, Professionals, Economic Crisis, and the Origins of the Second Great Migration, 1900–1941   213

Conclusion
New Beginnings, New Institutions, New Migrations   277

NOTES   291

BIBLIOGRAPHY   387

INDEX   431

FOREWORD

For sixteen years the Sam Rayburn Series on Rural Life has featured books that present readers with a composite of views pertaining to East Texas and the surrounding regions, revealing the complexities inherent in the history, culture, and people of the area. It is an honor and a privilege to be able to include as the latest volume in the series Bernadette Pruitt's exceptional *The Other Great Migration: The Movement of Rural African Americans to Houston, Texas, 1900–1941*. In *The Other Great Migration* Pruitt deftly combines the diligent research of scholarship with a passion and sensitivity that allows the groups of individuals constituting the core of this book to retain the dignity of autonomous identities instead of becoming reduced to cold statistics and data points. Indeed, Pruitt's keen eye for detail and her descriptive acumen provide contemporary readers with the opportunity to understand factually and emotionally the struggles and triumphs of African Americans who uprooted themselves and their families from, as Pruitt states, "rural communities for small towns, industrialized rural areas, and medium-sized cities throughout the South, including places like Houston that occasionally, over time, mushroomed into major metropolitan centers."

Community serves as an underlying theme throughout *The Other Great Migration,* a constant presence in the book that reminds twenty-first-century readers that individuals band together to exert their influence on their environment by forging and strengthening common bonds. As Pruitt observes, social clubs, the church, and other organizations all provided migrants a distinct sense of common purpose and belonging, all the more important when these women, men and children faced institutional discrimination, poverty and other hardships in the Jim Crow south. Pruitt personalizes her account of "chain migration" by preserving the names and faces of many of those who bravely left their homes to establish or build upon communities, not only seeking a better life but creating one for themselves and those who for generations would benefit from struggles that until now had been under-recorded.

Novelists and poets of color have provided readers from all cultures imaginative accounts of migration and dispersal, leaving the south for cities in the Midwest and east coast. In her novel *Their Eyes Were Watching God* (1937) Zora Neale Hurston focuses on local communities by charting the travails of Janie Mae Crawford, a woman whose quest to establish an independent identity takes her from communities large and small across Florida. Pruitt not only complements the work of some of our nation's most celebrated writers but delves more deeply into these migrations that continue to influence American culture and history by reminding readers that there were quite literally millions of other stories that exist only in familial lore and in the legacies they bestowed upon their descendants and fellow citizens.

Again, it is with great pleasure that I welcome Bernadette Pruitt and *The Other Great Migration: The Movement of Rural African Americans to Houston, Texas, 1900–1941* into the Sam Rayburn Series on Rural Life. Previous books in the series examine an array of subjects and points of history, each shedding new light on the history of east Texas, however broadly one defines the region. This volume stands as an inspiring example that a book series, as with any community, must evolve to nurture and grow.

—M. Hunter Hayes
General Editor, Sam Rayburn Series on Rural Life

PREFACE

Familial bonds and friendships largely inspired this study on the Great Migration to Houston, Texas. Growing up in Detroit, Michigan, in the 1970s and early 1980s, I heard countless stories from family about the South. My earliest recollections of conversations on southern life came from my maternal grandmother, Bertha Juanita Lewis Lively Pruitt, who grew up poor in Memphis, Tennessee, in the 1910s and 1920s. Her chats with friends in the early evenings after dinner caught my attention. While enjoying some of my favorite television shows of all time—*Good Times, The Jeffersons, Little House on the Prairie, The Waltons, Happy Days,* and *Eight is Enough*—I often overheard her fascinating conversations with friends, all of whom either were married or widowed homeowners and devout Christian matriarchs. Grandmama's banters about her childhood, school years, friendships, travails, and treks to the North struck me as incredible.[1]

Even though these women relocated to Detroit during the Great Migrations (1915–1970), they had fond memories of the South's climate, outdoor scenery, kinship traditions, cuisine, social networks, churches, and loved ones left behind. I always wondered why these women set out on this grand adventure for Detroit if their southern communities were in fact so pleasant. Truthfully, life in the South was not always good to these women, particularly to my grandmother, who became a single parent at age fifteen before marrying my grandfather and having my mother years later. Although poverty often followed these working-class southerners turned Detroiters after their settlement in the Midwest, they made do and saw their lifestyles improve slightly.[2]

After my grandmother met and married my grandfather, a truck driver and native Kentuckian named Mack Lively, like most recent Black migrants, the couple settled in a cramped apartment in Detroit's historic

Black Bottom neighborhood on the city's near East Side. Soon the young couple, who were expecting triplets in the fall of 1939, bought a house in an ethnically diverse, working-class community on Detroit's West Side. Tragically, however, my grandfather unexpectedly died not long after the births of the newborns.[3]

His sudden death in the late spring of 1940 devastated the family. Grandmamma, however, survived the ordeal working as a housekeeper, laundress, and washerwoman, and taking in borders to hold on to the house Granddad purchased. In the end, my grandmother kept her small three-bedroom home, eventually paying off the mortgage note before her death in 1984. She lived long enough to see some of the fruits of her labor—her four children finishing high school, marrying and having their own families, entering careers in healthcare, retail, civil service, and the military, as well as proudly witnessing grandchildren and great-grandchildren graduate from high school and enter college.[4]

The human saga of tragedy and triumph in my dad's family intrigued me no less. My dad, a native of Kemper County, Mississippi, and born in 1937, left his rural home as a preschooler in 1941, when his father secured work at Ford Motor Company, which also later became my dad's employer. They too moved to Detroit's West Side, renting a home on Roosevelt Street, only blocks from my mom's childhood home on Tillman Street and Warren Avenue. Tragedy once again devastated my family. In 1955, Grandmother Elizabeth McKenzie Pruitt, once a rural schoolteacher who only finished the eighth grade, died of breast cancer. Granddad probably never imagined becoming a widower at age sixty-three, raising four children, including a seven-year-old son, my Uncle Sheiry. Fortunately, my great-aunt, Granddad's sister, moved in with the family for almost two years, providing the children with a steady female presence.[5]

These two siblings had always depended on one another. With my granddad's support, Aunt Ammonia graduated from high school in Meridian, Mississippi, near their home Collinsville, in Kemper County, in the late 1920s, perhaps the only family member of that generation to do so. My grandfather, a sharecropper and common laborer, often took a third job as an unskilled worker at steel mills in Bessemer and Birmingham, Alabama, to help defray his sister's room-and-board costs. Although she finished high school, my aunt never attended college, a decision she always regretted.[6]

My great-aunt's determination nonetheless inspired others. One of her four children, a daughter, Vera Hayden, became one of the first persons in the Pruitt extended family to hold a doctorate degree. Another cousin, Rome Sherrod, graduated from Meharry Medical College around the same time in the late 1970s. Today, he and two of his sons hold medical degrees. Cousin Vera had advanced degrees in biology and education, ultimately retiring as a biology professor at Alcorn State University in the 1990s. Later, my cousins, Vera and the late Jesse Hayden (a retired mathematics teacher and Korean War veteran), passed on this love for learning to their own children. Jesse and Vera Hayden's daughter, Wanda Hayden Burke, currently an administrator and professor of agriculture and applied science at Southern University in Baton Rouge, Louisiana, earned a doctorate in education from Mississippi State University. Her brother, Jesse Hayden Jr., works as a chemist at Alcorn State University, while younger brother Derwin Hayden graduated with a degree in business administration, from Tuskegee University. Although often ignored, numerous African American southerners like the Haydens remained in the South, persevered, and inspired others to succeed. Inspired by Cousin Vera, my first cousin, the late Sammie Dean Pruitt of Detroit, moved south in the 1970s for college, ultimately graduating from Alcorn State University and then earning a Master of Social Work from Wayne State University, before his untimely death in 2005.[7]

Unlike my Detroit relatives and friends, whose family ties stretched into the rural and urban South, but rarely places in Michigan outside the Detroit city limits (or smaller industrial centers in Michigan), my college classmates in the 1980s had family all throughout eastern Texas (and, on occasions, Louisiana). I found this intriguing. I knew very little about suburban Detroit, much less the small towns and lucrative, diverse farms across the Lower Peninsula of Michigan. My Texas friends, however, were mostly urban and had strong connections to rural communities throughout eastern Texas (and Louisiana). At the same time, a few friends grew up in semirural, small-town environs. One friend, Natalie Brown, today a kindergarten teacher, grew up in San Augustine, a town that once stood as one of the major centers for antebellum slavery inside the East Texas Timber Belt. Other friends grew up in Houston, Dallas, Galveston, San Antonio, and New Orleans, even while having loved ones still residing in the country, family members they visited quite often. I later discovered that most Black Houstonians as well as Dallas and San Antonio residents had family living in the interior hinterlands and were the products of slavery in Texas. Moreover, while they lived in Texas for most of their lives, their experiences did not differ that much from that of my parents' parents, mainly due to close kinship ties, community building, and chain migration networks African Americans depended on. Even some of my college classmates from the Midwest and California (return migrants), including my little cousin, Michael Shawn Stinson, today a real estate appraiser and insurance adjuster who earned a biology degree from Texas Southern University (TSU), traced their slavery or post-Reconstruction roots to eastern Texas. All were the children, grandchildren, nieces, or nephews of internal migrants from the country who took part in the Great Migrations (or the post-Civil War internal migrations to Texas cities).[8]

The people discussed on the subsequent pages took part in the Great Migrations and in doing so, facilitated racial autonomy, institution building, working-class consciousness, social networking, and civil-rights activism. As with my grandparents and other African Americans who left the South in the early twentieth century, these Texans and Louisianans relied on and retained for later generations the kinship patterns of hope, community, and determination, acts that have guided human history for millenniums. Actually, like the millions of African Americans who lived most of their lives in the South, they remained in the region, choosing instead to leave rural and small-town communities for nearby Houston for jobs, schooling, and social justice. It is my hope that these stories spark something wonderful in the mind-souls of the offspring of the internal migrants discussed in this book. Acknowledging and cherishing those small and large sacrifices others have made on behalf of their loved ones, including offspring they would never live to meet, should ferment hope, pride, thankfulness, exceptionalism, and agency.[9]

The author wishes to express her gratitude to a number of people and institutions that helped make this idea a reality. From my years at Texas Southern University and the University of Houston to my postdoctoral fellowship year at the University of Illinois at Chicago and time at Sam Houston State University, mentors have played a profound role in my life and my life's work. Proofreading drafts, holding colloquiums and writing groups and retreats, listening to complaints, providing constructive criticism, taking late-night telephone calls, and cheering their colleague on to the finish line proved quite useful, even when such work interfered with deadlines, classroom lectures, important meetings, and quality family time. Yet, these colleagues and professors etched out quality time to lend a hand. For this reason, I will be eternally grateful. At TSU, from 1984 to 1991, many inspired me to reach for the skies. Naomi Ledé, Merline Pitre, Cary Wintz, Nupur Chaudhuri, Greg Maddox, Howard Beeth, the late George McElroy, the late Robert Giles, Pearlie Fennell, the late Joseph Williams, Gladys Washington (retired), Robert Baker (now at Tennessee State University), the late Hunter Brooks, the late Wolde Michael Akalou, Michael Adams, Sanders Anderson (now at Houston Community College), the late James Race, Billy Turner, Llayron Clarkson, Franklin Jones, Donald Shepherd, and the late John Westbury, among others, provided me with a sound intellectual, spiritual footing.

To my University of Houston (UH) family, thank you. Linda Reed, Joseph A. Pratt, Martin Melosi, Bailey Stone, James Kirby Martin, Thomas O'Brien, Tyrone Tillery, Eric Walther, Guadalupe San Miguel, Gerald Horne, Kairn Klieman, Sarah Fishman, Hannah Decker, and Robert Buzzanco, the University of Houston; Steven Pitts at the University of California at Berkeley Labor Center; Richard Blackett at Vanderbilt University; Joe Glatthaar of the University of North Carolina at Chapel Hill; Emilio Zamora and Steven Mintz at the University of Texas at Austin; were more than professors. They made my time at UH one of the most enriching periods of my life.

My colleagues at Sam Houston State University, beginning with Yvonne Davis Frear (now at San Jacinto College), Howard Henderson, Phillip Sinitiere (now at the College of Biblical Studies-Houston), Glenn Sanford, Don Howard, (now Regional Director of the Troops to Teachers Program at Louisiana Department of Veterans Affairs), Caroline Crimm (retired), Frieda Koeninger, Lydia Fox, Bernice Strauss, Robert T. Cashion, Jeff Littlejohn, Terry Bilhartz, Thomas Cox, Kenneth Hendrickson III, Nancy Baker, Jeff Crane, Rosanne Barker, and James S. Olson, have inspired me in ways they never could imagine. I also want to thank, Charles Heath, Katherine Pierce, Lila Rakoczy, Lindsey Swindall, Wesley Phelps, George Diaz, the late Joan Coffey, Lee and Nicholas Pappas, Brian Domitrovic, David Mayes, Robert Shadle (retired), Joe Rowe (retired), Erin Keenright, Pamela Byrd, Helen Lewis, Suzanne and Andrew Orr, Nancy Zey, Tracy Steele, Brittany Johnson, Kandi Tayabi, Charlann Morris (retired),

Mitchel Roth, Janet and Frank Fair, Cindy Gratz, Kay Raymond, Corliss Lentz, Susannah Ural (now at the University of Southern Mississippi), John Smith, Dominick Fazarro (now at the University of Texas at Tyler), and Robert Bruce (now at Marine Corps University) for their support over the years. Morever, financial support from the department, Office of Graduate Studies, and the Office of the Provost made this journey a doable one.

Friends and mentors have inspired me the most, particularly colleagues in the academy. I must thank Dwight Watson, William Kellar, Demetria and Amilcar Shabazz, Kerry Ann Rockquemore, Benet DeBerry-Spence, Carroll Parrot Blue, Michael Botson, Daniel Walker, Ramona Houston, Sherina Miles-Miller, Antrece Baggett, Amanda Lewis, Tyrone Foreman, Barbara Ransby, Michelle Boyd, Beth Richie, Sonya Ramsey, Nell Painter, Darlene Clark Hine, Charles Robinson Jr., Joel Williamson, Joe William Trotter, Gregg Cantrell, Randolph Campbell, Gretchen Lemke-Santangelo, Kimberly Philips, Earl Lewis, Ernest Obadele-Starks, Eric Arnesen, Albert Broussard, Alexander Tijerina, Jeff Helgeson, Luther Adams, Amrita Meyers, Robert Fink, Jon Wilson, Cory Capers, Helen Jun, Lynette Jackson, Cynthia Blair, Karen Kossie-Chernyshev, David Stovall, Mahdu Dubey, Tera W. Hunter, Steven Reich, Bruce Glasrud, Alwyn Barr, James M. SoRelle, Prudence Cumberbatch, Sharon Holland, and Stephanie Shaw for their support. I will always treasure my time at UIC as a postdoctoral research fellow—undoubtedly the best year of my professional and personal life. In addition, Eric, Alex, Albert, Cary, and Stephanie, especially went out of their way to read the manuscript as reviewers and mentors, providing rich, insightful comments at critical junctures of the rewriting phase of the project. I must thank also Benet, Yvonne, Karen, Rafael Gallo, Kerry Ann, Dwight, Amilcar, Jeff L., Glenn, Phil, Ty, Ken, Tom, Uzma Quraishi and the National Center for Faculty Development & Diversity (NCFDD, formerly BlackAcademic.com) for the outreach, generosity, and love. Benet and Kerry Ann, thank you for being phenomenal mentors during my postdoc year. You are amazing jewels and precious friends! Kerry Ann, your brainchild, NCFDD, made me a book author. God bless you.

I also must take a moment and thank the editorial staffers associated with Texas A&M University Press who helped me complete this project. I must first thank editor-in-chief Mary Lenn Dixon for her patience, support, and guidance these past several years. I am also indebted to TAMU

Press managing editor Thom Lemmons, and project editor Patricia Clabaugh, as well as editorial manager Maggie Casper and copyeditor Jill Pellarin with MPS North America.

To my many students, from alumni to current SHSU students, words cannot describe my appreciation for your acts of generosity through the years, from the rides into Houston to the ways in which you remind me of my calling as a teacher, mentor, and scholar, thank you. I especially need to thank Cynthia Sabbs, Michael Lewis, Chestin Auzenne-Curl, Lecreshia Mack, Ester Kelley, Kimberly Gothard-Ehieze, Ashley Taylor, Stephen Sargent, Dallas Jones, Constance Jones, Trent Jenkins, Julius Michaels, Kirsten Willis, Danielle Brush, Cherval Johns, Jason Morgan, Ashley Baughman, and Raedawn Jiles. To the many others who have been wonderful through the years, thank you and much love.

My parents, the late Clarence Edward Pruitt and Gloria Ann Pruitt, have been in my corner from day one. You have served as a source of inspiration. When times looked bleak, you believed in me. When naysayers shrugged me off years ago, you told me to look to our Lord and Savior. Mamma, you too pattern yourself after love, compassion, hope, and joy. You emulate the kind of glorious beauty God expects of humankind daily: a selfless, unconditional love for God and humanity, as well as unwavering praying wisdom. Thank you, ma'am, for everything through the years. You are my role model. Thank you for understanding the beauty of unconditional love. My late father, too, is my hero. Clarence Edward Pruitt always selflessly put others first, even to his own detriment. Thank you, Dad, for teaching me firsthand God's second commandment.

I must also thank my extended family and spiritual elders for their love and support through the years. To my brother Shawn Scott, your love and devotion never ceases to amaze me. Dad is certainly proud of you and your beautiful, talented daughters. To my many cousins—Michael and Hawa Stinson, Deborah Edwards, James Edwards, Ursula Woodruff, Christina Roche, Brandon and Sharon Perry, Katrina Hamilton, Dwayne Lively, Carol Daniels-Aldridge, Michael Lively, Michelle Lively, Derwin Hayden, Jesse and Donna Hayden, Kim and Vita Pruitt, Debra Price, Christina Scott, Dillard and Crystal Jones, Wanda Hayden-Burke, Pamela Green, the late Keyon DeShore Edwards, the late Sammie Dean Pruitt, the late Fred Pruitt, the late Larry Parks, the late Lanita Pruitt, and the late Jerry Parks—thanks for the unconditional love. I cannot forget about my familial elders. Thank you Aunt Gwen and Uncle James, Aunt Yvonne and Uncle Malcolm, the late Aunt Alice, Uncle Dub and Aunt Machu, Aunt Ruth, Aunt Ruby, Aunt Catherine, Cousin Arnett, Cousins Charlotte and Leon, Cousins Vera and Jesse, Cousin Clarabelle, Cousin Lorraine, Aunt Geraldine, and Cousins Frank and Ethel. My childhood church family, Aijalon Missionary Baptist Church, has remained an intricate part of my spiritual, emotional, and cultural development. Your love and shining light over the years symbolize God's unconditional love for humanity. I also wish to thank my other extended family who has served as guardian angels and role models.

I also want to thank those friends, mentors, and spiritual elders—past and present—who attempted to instill in me a belief that anything is possible "through Christ who strengthens me," God bless you. My dearest friends, including Mary Brown, Jacqueline Donaldson Barber, Benet, Yvonne, Rafael, Antrece, Trudi Wheeler, Louis Jones, Edwina Henry, Pamela Jones, Natalie Brown, Delisa Daniels, Letitia Thomas Williams, LaShunda Hubbard, Ron Julun, Kimberly Brown, Tony Henshaw, the late Marquitta Anderson, Lorinda Jones, Delinsa Maiden, Andre Brown, the late Caroline Stewart, Cassandra Mapusa, Dietra Dumas, Gina Kincaid, London Johnson, Bobbie Williams, Cheryl and Raymond Cockrell, Helen and Raynard Cockrell, Shawna Gant, Irma Gambrel, Lois Owens, Ella Kelly, Joreen Waddell, Deborah D. Davis, Deborah Byrd, Valdine Hackett, Helen and George King, Johnnie and Barbara Walker, Ladonna and Reginald Adams, the late Darryl Crawford, Artresa Johnson, Frieda Spiller, Terry Murray, Belinda Ross, Doris and Billy Murray, Paula Davis, Patra Hayes, Betty Mitchell, Carlos Ross, Pam Williams, Hallie and Lawrence Williams Sr., Doris Pace, Deborah Ross, Barbara Williams, Marjorie Mathis, Laguana Glaze, Marjorie Archie, Carolyn Houston, Earnie Mae Hatich, Shirley and Merlyn Brazille, Charlotte and Elgin Davis, the late Estelle Spencer, and Carlton Green have prayed for me, cried with me, laughed with (and at) me, and celebrated with me. To my entire church family, the Greater Zion Missionary Baptist Church and senior pastor, Michael C. Davis Sr., thank you for your prayers, faithfulness, and love. I also need to thank Pastor Terry K. Anderson and members of Lilly Grove Missionary Baptist Church of Houston; and Pastor Otis Moss III, Pastor Emeritus Jeremiah Wright, and Trinity United Church of Christ of Chicago for their unwavering love. May the Lord continue to bless you as beautiful human souls. I love you all.

What can I tell you, Troy P. Robinson, that you do not already know? Probably nothing but I will attempt to convey how much I treasure you as a friend. When I met you twenty years ago on the campus of the University of Houston, I certainly did not imagine our lives intertwining all these years. Thank you for your friendship, love, and wisdom. You have blessed my life so much. What I respect most of all about you is your love for humanity, particularly African-descent peoples. Tirelessly, you find ways to improve the lot of others around you, as other great leaders, past and present, have. Never give up on the belief that God has a plan in store for us all, one that permeates the lines of demarcation that hold many people hostage. Always love, love always, always love. I love you always.

I wish to thank a few others. Primary care physician Isnardo Tremor; neurologists J. William Lindsey and Jerry Wolinsky; ophthalmologists Paul Salmonsen, Rosa Tang, and Helen Li; optometrists Randy Jose and Nicole Hooper; University of Houston counseling interns; and pychotherapists Connie Vitale and Xyna Bell have provided me with excellent care over the years. In addition, the Texas Rehabilitation Commission donated visual aid tools and eased severe reading and writing discomfort, while SHSU invested in a very expensive visual-aid device that aided me in my research endeavors.

The author also wishes to thank the numerous research libraries, archives, depositories, and digital databases that provided me with data, oral histories, manuscripts, government documents, newspaper collections, and photographs. Local historians Patricia Prather and Naomi Ledé; Madeline Johnson and Lisa May of the Archdiocese of Galveston-Houston; the staffers at the African American Library at the Gregory School, Texas Room and Houston Metropolitan Research Center, and Clayton Genealogy Library of the Houston Public Library (especially Louis Marchiafava, Elizabeth Sargeant, and Aaron Winslow); Charles Frederick Heartman Collection at the Robert J. Terry Library at Texas Southern University; the late Walter Hill and the National Archives and Records Administration branch at College Park, Maryland; M.D. Anderson Library Special Collections; and the Eugene C. Barker Texas History Collection at the Dolph Briscoe Center for American History at the University of Texas at Austin provided me with the bulk of my sources. I must also thank the historians and archivists at Fort Leonard Wood, Missouri, for maintaining the Samuel Countee painting, "The Garden of Eden," and granting me access to this important treasure. I also must thank Steven Smith of the South Carolina Institute of Archaeology and Anthropology at the University of South Carolina, whose scholarship has resurrected the legacy of artist and native Texan Samuel Countee. My mapmakers deserve a shot-out as well. Larry Nierth and the GIS team with the City of Houston Planning and Development Office developed my Texas and Houston maps, while colleague and urban planner Rafael Gallo customized my Louisiana map. Thank you very much for your expertise and kindness. I also need to thank the University of Houston Center for Public History and *Houston History* magazine; and Sage Publications and the *Journal of Urban History* for granting me permission to reprint portions of my 2005 articles for this book. I am also indebted to Ancestry.com and HeritageQuest Online for their excellent online resources. The Newton-Gresham Library on the campus of SHSU has also been a source of delight, as the library's excellent databases have often simplified my digital research in African American Studies. The interview subjects I sat down with and got to know over the course of twenty years as a graduate student and professional historian not only provided me with incredible personal accounts that strengthened my work; these women and men blessed my life with their wisdom, quiet strength, and love for humanity.

In addition, this research would not have been possible without financial resources. Financial resources, like professional research assistance, allowed me to complete the end project. The Texas Southern University Minority Cancer Education Center graduate assistantship, University of Houston African American Studies Graduate Fellowship, and Department of Education Texas Guaranteed Student Loans afforded me with sabbaticals from the classroom, and allowed me to hold on to health insurance coverage as a graduate student, something very crucial for a young woman suffering from Macular Retinoschisis and Multiple Sclerosis. The Institute for African American Policy Research (IAAPR) Summer Stipend Award from the African American Studies Program of the University of Houston and the Murry Miller Alumni Endowed Scholarship from the University of Houston Department of History provided support during summer sessions. The Miss Ima Hogg Student Research Travel Award granted by the Center for American History at the University of Texas at Austin, Mary H. Hughes and Fred White Fellowships with the Texas State Historical Association, Nathan Huggins-Benjamin Quarles Award granted by the

Organization of American Historians, Ottis Locke Award with the East Texas Historical Association, the Alpha Kappa Alpha Sorority Educational Advancement Foundation Scholarship, Sam Houston State University Department of History faculty travel grants, and UIC postdoctoral fellowship supported my research and travel endeavors.

Finally, I must thank the one being truly responsible for this blessing. The Book of Hebrews in the Holy Bible tells us "now faith is the substance of things hoped for and the evidence of things not seen" (Hebrews 11:1). Even when I feared the worst and erred in countless ways, God continued to grant me grace and mercy, even when I did not deserve it. Lamentations 3:22–24 reminds us of how wonderful our Lord is: "Because of the LORD's great love we are not consumed, for his compassions never fail. They are new every morning; great is your faithfulness. I say to myself, 'The LORD is my portion; therefore I will wait for him.'" Thank you, Lord, for your love and blessings each day. Thank you everyone; you are love!

THE OTHER GREAT MIGRATION

Introduction

In 1899, Edward Wilbur Hayes left his home, Big Sandy in Upshur County, Texas, to attend Wiley College, walking sixty-two miles to Marshall, the location of the Methodist Episcopal school. His parents, former slaves and sharecroppers, rarely had enough money to feed and clothe their family. They certainly could not afford a train ticket for their son on the Texas and St. Louis Railway (Cotton Belt Route) or Shreveport line going east. Hayes nevertheless entered Wiley in the fall semester and for the next two years made his family proud, not only earning excellent grades but also putting himself through school. He graduated from Wiley with his teaching certificate in 1901, becoming the four-hundredth Texan to do so. For the next decade, Hayes taught students in a number of rural communities in the East Texas pine belt, including Mineola in Wood County. In Mineola, Hayes met student Marie Fluellen, and later the two married. Hayes also entered the Methodist Episcopal Church (now the United Methodist Church) ministry. Soon Hayes made his living as a schoolteacher and minister, a necessity because of the growing family he had to support.[1]

The family eventually morphed into twelve, including ten children by 1920, with the last being born in Houston in the late 1920s. Like many rural families of color, the Hayes moved around often, from Mineola and Orange in Orange County near the Gulf Coast, to Marshall in Harrison County, and from Marshall to Bellville in Austin County in southeastern Texas, looking for financial security. The family's frequent relocations also reflected Rev. Hayes's responsibilities as a Methodist pastor who, at the behest of the Methodist Episcopal Church, changed congregations every three to four years.[2]

The family nevertheless found it more difficult to make ends meet on Hayes's earnings in rural Texas. Wife and mother Marie Hayes, in the early

1920s, according to son Robert Hayes Sr., decided the family should relocate to Houston. Marie Hayes also believed Houston schools were superior, even to rural White institutions.[3] Robert Hayes remembers his mother's candor on the subject, "'Not a child of mine will grow up in Bellville,' and she must have had some reason [to make such a statement]." Marie Hayes was determined to give her children a better life.[4]

She decided the family would leave Bellville. Like many independent-minded women of color who were secure in their views and had the unconditional support of their significant others, Marie on some occasions made decisions on behalf of the family. She knew the family's time to depart the country had come. For once, according to Marie Hayes, her husband had to wholeheartedly trust her decision and put his family first, even before the church. This was not always easy, especially for a man of the cloth who loved the Lord, but he did listen to his wife. The family packed their bags and moved, even before finding a home, which eventually they did in Third Ward, first on Sawyer Street, then Tierwester Street, and later on Dowling Street. According to Hayes, "We saw a house for rent and we didn't know who owned it. We just moved in."[5] A local congregation came to the aid of the struggling family until Hayes found full-time employment. "Trinity East Methodist Church members . . . heard that a preacher's family had moved in, and the next day they brought food for us . . . and we all joined that church," says Hayes.[6]

Rev. Wilbur Hayes stopped teaching school altogether years earlier, preferring full-time church work as a pastor or associate pastor. To earn additional income, he did seasonal landscaping. The family, not surprisingly, continued to struggle. Hayes points out, "My father's salary [as a Methodist minister] was never over $700 [annually]."[7] With his seasonal job, Hayes brought home $1,000 every year to feed his family of thirteen, which also included a cousin by the late 1920s. Due to long work hours, poor nutrition, and anxiety over caring for the family's needs, Hayes jeopardized his health, eventually dying.[8]

Problems persisted in the wake of the Great Depression, especially after the death of Pastor Hayes, who departed this life prematurely near the Christmas holiday on December 22, 1931. Now a single parent, Marie Hayes cooked and cleaned clothes for White families. The children worked also as domestics, errand runners, porters, kitchen crew, sextons, and so on. The Hayes were determined to survive the Great Depression and live up to the expectations of the late Edward Wilbur Hayes.[9]

Amazingly, the children, even with their responsibilities, remained in school. Marie Hayes was determined to see her children excel academically. They did. The children enjoyed their years at Douglas Elementary and Jack Yates High Schools. According to son Robert Hayes, "The teachers like Mrs. [Hazel] Hainesworth and Mrs. Virginia Miller who taught me Latin . . . were the heroes, nuns of our time. They really made us." Music teacher Hazel Lewis especially made a lasting impression on Hayes, providing him and other Yates students with classical music training. Over the course of the next fifteen years, Marie Hayes watched all eleven children graduate from Jack Yates High School in Third Ward. And six of the children earned college baccalaureate degrees. One went further than the rest, eventually earning an advanced degree. Without the family's move to Houston, this would have been almost impossible.[10]

Between 1890 and 1970, an estimated seven million African Americans uprooted to industrial centers across the country from rural, small town, and urban centers throughout the South, primarily for jobs, but also for a quality education, suffrage rights, and civil liberties. Hundreds of thousands settled southern metropolitan areas like New Orleans, Memphis, Birmingham, and Jackson. Ironically, these figures rarely include the millions more who left rural communities for small towns, industrialized rural areas, and medium-sized cities throughout the South, including places like Houston that occasionally, over time, mushroomed into major metropolitan centers.[11] My study attempts to remedy this error, at least partially.[12]

Drawing from manuscript collections, contemporary pieces, vital statistics, census data, welfare records, newspapers, and oral histories, this book recreates the First Great Migration to Houston, Texas, between the years 1900 and 1941. An estimated thirty-two thousand African American women, children, and men moved to Houston, principally from eastern Texas and southern and central Louisiana, for jobs and self-sufficiency. Please note that this figure—thirty-two thousand—stands as an estimate and not an exact number. The author, a nonquantitative African American urban specialist, who relies on regression tables generated from the decennial censuses of the first half of the twentieth century, realizes her lack of training renders her data questionable and perhaps flawed. Yet, the historian's ability to formulate an estimate for this period does offer readers some degree of evidence that supports the hypothesis laid out in this book. Furthermore, this study does not attempt to provide readers with a general explanation for rural-to-urban internal migration within the entire South. Nor does this book examine all Afro-American internal migrations within the state or Texas–Louisiana region. Nevertheless, by investigating intrastate and regional interstate migration to Houston it places these and other migratory patterns in the twentieth-century South within the context of the larger Great Migrations. The study should also give pause to the absence of studies documenting the internal migration phenomena in the South and stimulate new scholarship in the field.[13]

According to historian Joe William Trotter Jr., perhaps more than any other humanities and social science topic, migration has held a special place in African American life, culture, and history. Since the advent of the African Diaspora and transatlantic slave trade, nearly six hundred years ago, migration has remained a principal theme in African American studies, particularly within the discipline of history. For centuries, as human cargo, runaways, property, and free people, African Americans traveled and settled throughout what ultimately emerged as the United States. Voluntary migrations intensified after the Civil War as freedmen and freedwomen sought loved ones, jobs, land, and autonomy. Most freedpeople moved to nearby or faraway southern farms as tenants and homesteaders. Some moved west as squatters. A few, disillusioned by the state of race relations in the late nineteenth century, fled to the Caribbean and West Africa.[14] Yet, as suggested by Trotter, only with the appearance and spread of big business and industry in the latter nineteenth century did people of African descent, along with other Americans and immigrants from abroad, increasingly abandon their farms and small towns for city life and wage-earning jobs in the United States and elsewhere. These regional treks would birth the Great Migrations of the last century.[15]

The Great Migrations occurred in multiple facets. Several hundred thousand (or several million if one counts those internal migrants leaving rural farms for small towns, rural industrial centers, and medium-sized cities) southerners abandoned their communities in the decades preceding World War I, for light and heavy manufacturing and personal service work in the urban South, West, and North. Railroading, lumbering, longshoring, cotton compressing, and the discovery of oil in Texas, for example, propelled steady entries of people into cities. Industrial work also drove migrants to Birmingham, New Orleans, Charleston, Norfolk, Richmond, Memphis, Nashville, and Louisville. The labor shortage of World War I, however, precipitated their historic entry into the northern industrial workforce. Between 1916 and 1930, an estimated 1.2 million rural farmers relocated to cities, notably to urban centers in the South, Northeast, and Midwest. Notwithstanding the depressed 1930s, which slowed internal migrations from the rural South, heavy internal migrations returned with World War II. The Second Great Migration of 1941 to 1970 brought 4.5 to 5 million people to urban centers, with many making their way to southern cities as well as western and northern points of entry. Since 1970, hundreds of thousands have either returned to the South or followed in reverse order the routes taken by their grandparents while searching for good-paying jobs, an affordable education, and retirement options, thus sparking the New Great Migration.[16]

Although historians and non-historians alike have documented quite well the Great African American Migrations to northern and western cities, they have not adequately explored the steady stream of people into southern towns and cities—perhaps the most understudied aspect of the Great Migrations of the twentieth century. When discussing the interstate and intrastate movements within the South, historians usually identify these migratory patterns as stepwise or temporary settlements that predated migrations to the Northeast, Midwest, and West. Although this is true, contiguous and intrastate migratory patterns within the South sometimes precluded mass exoduses to other regions of the country (table 1).[17]

Take for instance the growth of sawmill towns in East Texas, which confirms this observation. Sawmill communities such as Livingston, Huntsville, Nacogdoches, Tyler, Conroe, and Orange continued to grow in the late nineteenth and early twentieth centuries, even while people increasingly made their way to nearby and faraway cities. Sawmill towns as well as small coastal oil refining communities not only grew as people relocated to the region in search of work, they also served as feeder communities for nearby Houston (see table 1). As these cities grew, Houston's population exploded. Important mill firms like Kirby Lumbering Company relocated their headquarters to Houston and served as anchors for professional, skilled, and unskilled workforces. As Houston's economy took shape, especially in the postwar 1920s, migrations spurred new markets for businesses, developers, school districts, professions, middle-class social advancement, and

TABLE 1. Black population figures for select United States cities, 1900–50 and 2010

Southern Cities	1900	1910	1920	1930	1940	1950	2010
Atlanta	35,727	51,902	62,796	90,075	104,533	124,285	226,894
Austin	5,822	7,478	6,921	9,868	14,681	17,667	129,399
Baltimore	79,258	84,749	108,322	142,106	165,843	225,099	395,781
Birmingham	16,575	52,305	70,230	99,077	108,938	130,025	155,791
Charleston	31,522	31,056	32,326	28,062	31,765	30,854	30,491
Charlotte	7,151	11,752	14,641	25,163	31,403	37,481	256,241
Dallas	9,035	18,024	24,023	38,742	50,407	56,978	298,993
Fort Worth	4,249	13,290	15,806	22,234	25,354	36,933	148,241
Houston	**14,608**	**23,929**	**33,960**	**63,337**	**86,302**	**124,766**	**498,466**
Jackson	4,447	10,554	9,936	19,423	24,296	40,168	137,716
Jacksonville	16,236	29,293	41,520	48,196	61,762	72,450	252,421
Little Rock	14,694	14,539	17,477	19,698	22,103	23,517	81,889
Louisville	39,139	40,522	40,087	47,354	54,060	67,657	163,041
Memphis	49,910	52,441	61,181	96,550	121,498	96,550	409,687
Montgomery	17,229	19,322	19,827	29,970	34,535	42,538	116,524
Nashville	30,044	36,523	35,633	42,836	54,837	54,696	170,747
New Orleans	77,714	89,262	109,930	129,632	149,034	181,775	206,871
Norfolk	20,230	25,039	43,392	43,942	45,893	62,826	104,672
Oklahoma City	1,219	6,546	8,241	14,662	19,344	21,006	86,999
Richmond	32,230	46,733	54,041	52,988	61,251	72,996	103,342
San Antonio	7,538	10,716	14,321	17,978	19,235	28,729	79,644
Shreveport	8,542	13,896	17,485	27,219	35,975	142,169	109,022
Tulsa**	N/A	1,959	8,878	15,203	15,151	17,126	61,137
Washington, DC	86,702	94,446	109,966	132,068	187,266	280,803	305,125

bottom-rung workers, with many relocating from smaller feeder towns and communities, a process that continued well into the twentieth century.[18]

Like their contemporaries who emigrated from the South for industrialized centers in the Midwest, Northeast, and West, internal migrants to Houston sought improved lifestyles and racial autonomy. By relocating to Houston and not Chicago, Detroit, or Los Angeles, they helped transform a coastal town into an international center, even as many of their offspring in later years left Texas for good, traveling instead to Chicago or California.

TABLE 1. *Continued*

Non-Southern Cities	1900	1910	1920	1930	1940	1950	2010
Boston	11,591	13,584	16,350	20,574	23,679	40,057	150,437
Buffalo	1,698	1,773	4,511	13,563	17,694	36,645	100,774
Chicago	30,150	44,103	109,458	233,903	277,731	492,265	887,608
Cincinnati	14,482	19,639	30,079	47,818	55,593	73,196	133,039
Cleveland	5,988	8,448	34,451	71,899	84,504	147,847	211,672
Columbus	8,201	12,739	22,181	32,774	35,765	46,692	220,241
Des Moines	1,676	2,930	5,512	5,428	6,360	8,029	59,186
Denver	3,923	5,426	6,075	7,204	7,836	15,059	63,236
Detroit	4,111	5,741	40,838	120,066	149,119	300,506	590,226
Gary***	N/A	383	5,299	17,922	20,394	39,253	67,446
Hartford	1,887	1,745	4,199	6,510	7,090	12,694	48,331
Indianapolis	15,931	21,816	34,678	43,967	51,142	63,867	226,671
Kansas City, MO	17,567	23,566	30,719	38,574	41,574	55,682	133,338
Los Angeles	2,131	7,599	15,579	38,894	63,774	171,209	365,118
Milwaukee	662	980	2,229	7,501	8,821	21,772	237,769
Minneapolis	1,548	2,592	3,927	4,176	4,646	6,807	71,159
New York	60,666	91,709	152,467	327,706	458,444	747,608	2,088,210
Newark	6,594	9,475	16,977	16,880	45,760	74,965	145,085
Oakland	1,026	3,055	5,489	7,503	8,462	47,562	109,471
Omaha	3,443	4,426	10,315	11,123	12,015	16,311	56,027
Peoria, IL	1,402	1,569	2,130	3,037	2,826	5,777	28,510
Pittsburgh	17,040	25,623	37,725	54,983	62,216	82,453	82,906
Philadelphia	62,613	84,459	134,229	219,599	250,880	376,441	661,839
Phoenix	148	328	1,075	2,366	4,263	5,190	93,608

Houston's population grew from nearly forty-five thousand in 1900 to almost six hundred thousand in 1950, while the African American community rose from fifteen thousand to one hundred and twenty-five thousand. Only Los Angeles experienced greater per capita growth in the twentieth century, with Houston's population reaching two million by 2000. Houston's spectacular growth not only set it apart from other southern cities but also helped explain why it became an important Great Migration destination for African Americans, European Americans, and people of Mexican ancestry.[19]

TABLE 1. *Continued*

Non-Southern Cities	1900	1910	1920	1930	1940	1950	2010
Portland, OR	775	1,045	1,556	1,559	1,931	9,529	36,778
Providence	4,817	5,317	5,655	5,473	6,388	8,304	28,486
San Diego	406	2,296	2,894	3,303	3,789	15,666	87,949
San Francisco	1,664	1,462	2,414	3,803	4,846	43,502	48,870
Seattle	406	2,296	2,894	3,303	3,789	15,666	48,084
St. Louis	35,516	43,960	69,854	93,580	108,765	153,766	157,092
Wichita	1,389	2,457	3,545	5,623	5,686	8,082	42,825
Wilmington, DE	9,736	9,081	10,746	12,080	14,256	17,202	41,081

Sources: Bureau of Census, Negro Population in the United States, 93–104; Bureau of Census, Negroes in the United States, 54–59; Bureau of Census, Sixteenth Census of the United States, 1940, Population, V. 2, Characteristics of the Population, Part 1, 319, 325, 510 & 956; Bureau of Census, Sixteenth Census of the United States, 1940, Population, V. 2, Characteristics of the Population, Part 2, 132, 383; Bureau of Census, Sixteenth Census of the United States, 1940, Population, Part 3, 302, 321, 323, 435, and 569; Bureau of Census,, Sixteenth Census of the United States, 1940, Population, V. 2, Characteristics of the Population Part 4, 306; Bureau of Census, Sixteenth Census of the United States, 1940, Population, V. 2, Characteristics of the Population, Part 5, 265–70, 405, 929 & 938; Bureau of Census, Sixteenth Census of the United States, 1940, Population, 1940, V. 2, Characteristics of the Pop., Part 6, 710, 719, 741, 751, 1026, 1045, 1053, 1061–62 & 1083; Bureau of Census, Sixteenth Census of the United States, 1940, Population, V. 2, Characteristics of the Population, Part 7, 265, 274; US Census Bureau, Campbell Gibson, and Kay Jung, Historic Census Statistics on Population Totals by Race, 1790–1990, and by Hispanic Origin, 1970–1990, For Large Cities and Other Urban Places in the United States (accessed September 16, 2011), http://www.census.gov/population/www/documentation/twps0076/twps0076.html#intro; United States Census Bureau, United States Census 2010 (accessed December 12, 2012), http://2010.census.gov/2010census/#; United States Census Bureau, Sonya Rastogi, Tallese D. Johnson, Elizabeth M. Hoeffel, and Malcolm P. Drewery Jr. The Black Population: 2010 (accessed December 12, 2012), http://www.census.gov/population/race/publications/; and Wikipedia: The Free Encyclopedia (accessed December 12, 2012), http://en.wikipedia.org/wiki/Main_Page. These figures only suggest that the Black populations in these cities increased. One should not assume that these population increases occurred as a result of migration alone. Birthrates, annexation, and in-migration together determine the population increases in these cities. See http://www.census.gov/population/www/documentation/twps0076/twps0076.html#intr.

*In 2010, the Bureau of Census used three categories to define African-origin peoples in the United States. The "Black, African American, or Negro "category refers to African-descent Americans who defined themselves as Black, African American, or Negro. The "Race [Black] in Combination" category describes African-descent Americans who classified themselves as being of two or more of the racial groups listed in the 2010 census—Black or African Americans, White, Asian, American Indian or Alaskan Native, Hawaiian or Other Pacific Islander, and Other Race. In addition, a third category, the "Black Alone-or-In Combination" group combines all African-descent Americans, regardless of their racial combinations and/or ethnicities, including that of Hispanic. According to the Bureau of Census, African-descent Americans from the first two categories totaled 42 million people—the first category, 38.9 million; the second, 3.1 million. In the interest of time, the author chose to use the population figures from the first 2010 census category for African-descent peoples. This means the above 2010 figures perhaps undercount the African-descent population in these cities by perhaps 1 to 3 percent. For more about this topic, see The U. S. Census Bureau website.

**Tulsa's overall population constituted less than 2,500 before 1910; the census did not have figures for the Black population of the city until 1910.

***Data for Gary is unavailable for 1900, as the city only came into existence in 1906.

This study examines those groups that made their way into the city in the early twentieth century as well as the periods that influenced migration streams into the city. It concentrates on four migratory groups. Manufacturing and railroading, from the turn of the century through the early 1910s, influenced widespread internal migrations to Houston. The birth of modern oil refining in the 1900s especially transformed the state's geographic landscape, prompting mass exoduses from rural and small-town communities. World War I ushered in a second period of economic and urban growth as rural migrants relocated to the city for new jobs opening along the Houston Ship Channel, with cotton wharves, shipping firms, and refineries. The city's rise as a regional manufacturing center immediately following World War I prompted a greater period of growth.[20]

The postwar era marked the city's period of rapid expansion, beginning in 1918 through 1930. During this period, newcomers sought better-paying jobs, business opportunities, and a quality education. Black professionals and members of the rank and file found sustainable work.[21] Providing needed services to African Americans, professionals and business owners increasingly worked in their own communities.[22]

The fourth period of migration discussed in this study—that of the 1930s—witnessed some growth as well. However, migrants during the Great Depression also traveled back and forth between the city and country to find both temporary work and relief. Houston, like many cities, witnessed some growth in the last half of the 1930s, prompting what historian Luther Adams calls the onset of the Second Great Migration.[23]

Several factors explain why African Americans felt compelled to move to Houston. Many if not most liked the idea of remaining in the South. Many had already spent time in the city, having worked as temporary laborers in and around the city when not planting cotton. Newcomers, therefore, had some familiarity with manufacturing, longshoring, or wage earning in the service trades.[24]

Most had friends, acquaintances, or family already living in the city, individuals who moved to Houston in the latter nineteenth century as freedpeople or as the offspring of former slaves. Even the one thousand slaves living in the city in 1860 were largely internal migrants from the United States Southeast. Several different migrant groups traveled to the city after the Civil War. Freedpeople through the immediate post-Reconstruction years traveled to the town as they sought to leave behind the harsh reminders of slavery. These Exodusters saw the city as a place of solace, opportunity, and potential. From the late 1870s to the turn of the century, the children of former slaves eagerly left the hinterlands of Texas and

Louisiana in search of opportunities. In many ways, these earliest migrants not only created the impetus for later treks to the city; they also formed the communities later migrants moved to and expanded.[25]

Migrants built and rebuilt communities. The self-help concept of building communities, protecting family, utilizing cultural empowerment, and the art of self-preservation commonly known as community agency, community formation, community building, or agency, at its core involved hope, self-reliance, and racial autonomy. Migrants not only searched for racial autonomy but social justice too. Building on the works of Robin D. G. Kelley and others who place the ordinary actions of individuals and groups in the South within the framework of civil rights, this book defines migration as an invaluable form of protest.[26]

Scholars increasingly have begun to address the issue of humdrum, everyday resistance among the powerless. According to political scientist James C. Scott, these varieties of passive resistance were not without merit. As his studies on Southeast Asia peasants reveal, the timid acts of resistance carried out by Malaysian farmworkers opened the door for increased activism. Supervisors and managers' inability to recognize these actions as threatening or harmful only served to intensify the political resolve of the impoverished peasantry. Even though their actions rarely launched transformation, the peasants' determination remained committed to change and self-reliance. Unlike traditional types of open rebellion or resistance, for example, the Montgomery Bus Boycott, Freedom Rides, and the forming of the Black Panther Party for Self-Defense, everyday forms of disturbance allowed for continuous agitation, and rarely sparked dangerous backlashes. Therefore, for Scott, all modes of resistance equated to resistance, including protest deemed nonthreatening to individuals of authority. This author makes the same argument in this study on the First Great Migration to Houston.[27]

Black community builders found the city's close proximity to the Texas and Louisiana interior attractive as well. Unlike the internal migrants who moved to northern and western cities in the United States, migrants refrained from trips that took them away from their loved ones. This work recognizes internal migration to Houston as a southern regional—contiguous interstate as well as intrastate—alternative to the national movements that took people to other regions of the country. For this reason, people routinely visited loved ones. Houston churches often worshipped with congregations from the country. Because of this reality, newspapers such as the *Houston Informer* chronicled the lives of rural and small-town dwellers as well as Houstonians.[28]

Sometimes African Americans preferred the South to the North or the western United States. Those cultural constructs that identified people as southerners and African American—cuisine, community, music, conversation, dialect and diction, regional identity, historical continuity, and racial autonomy—remained with migrants as they settled in Houston neighborhoods, especially because Houston itself made people reminiscent of what they considered good about the Texas or Louisiana interior. Black migrants remained in close proximity to their loved ones back in the country, always making it a priority to return home for short and long visits. Migrants who settled in Houston hardly saw the South as a besieged place—at least they did not see Houston in this light.[29]

In fact, Houston's migrants moved to the city for the same reasons southerners left the South. They wanted more for themselves and their families. They believed better times lay ahead, especially in cities. They, like the majority of African Americans who remained in the South, had a glimmer of hope in their hearts that their lives would ultimately change for the better. Houston attracted numerous settlers from the Texas and Louisiana interior, who helped make the city the most populated in the South by 1950 and the fourth largest in the country by 1980. Driven by socioeconomic incentives as well as family obligations, internal migrants from the interior steadily poured into the city, eventually paving the way for later return migration and immigration streams, along with a civil-rights revolution. The jobs they took and the communities they settled into reflected their outreach for each other and family and friends left behind. Borrowing from earlier migration schemes, this transformation undoubtedly helped spur the nation's Great Black Migrations.[30]

The work opens examining the push and pull factors propelling migration from the surrounding countryside. Circumstances in rural and small-town communities—customary and legal segregation, disfranchisement, education disparities, violence, and inequities on the cotton farm—stimulated emigration and pushed families and individuals off the farm and out of the town. At the same time, urbanization and industrialization in Houston before, during, and after World War I encouraged immigration and pulled migrants toward better-paying jobs, improved schools for children, and greater social freedoms in African American communities. Amid these and other factors, migrants made the ultimate and conscious decision to leave their places of origin or temporary residency to embark on a new life in budding and industrializing Houston, Texas. Some of the newcomers would eventually demand greater socioeconomic and sociopolitical equities in their new place of residence.[31]

The study also looks at the places people settled. African Americans usually moved into established communities. Sometimes, however, they founded their own communities. After finding homes, migrants put into effect the community-building strategies they had learned to depend on as children and teenagers on the surrounding cotton farms outlying Houston, in the East Texas Piney Woods, and on the cotton and sugar plantations of central and southern Louisiana. These strategies enabled them to forge permanent communities and community alliances in their new city of choice.[32]

The study discusses community agency in detail. The congregations, fraternal societies, clubs, and friendships that stretched from city to farm provided newcomers with the semblance of sereneness and stability. The new relationships that developed between migrants and established residents fostered continued self-help strategies and racial consciousness. African American migrants, utilizing migration as a tool of necessity, helped create permanent communities of agency, activism, and idealism. They opened schools, built churches, formed societies, nurtured relationships, cared for the needy, and carried out key political patterns of activism that helped sustain the larger African American community circles of the period.[33]

Next, the book examines the origins of post–World War I African American political mobilization and the aesthetic conscious in Houston. The Houston Riot of 1917, more than any other event, precipitated a resurgence of activism. Perhaps for the first time since Reconstruction, African Americans looked outward and increasingly advanced the call for social justice and political strength in numbers. Although conservative and moderate in tone, the overwhelming majority of these new political-action organizations focused their efforts on disbanding racial bigotry. Their tone concentrated not on the integration of the races, but rather on human justice.[34]

At the same time, a new generation of artists fostered a concomitant movement. Spearheaded by artists and musicians, a new cultural construct of Blackness began to surface in the Bayou City. This new construct of race acknowledged varying degrees of African American thought. Like the Harlem, Chicago, and Detroit Renaissances of the time, this Houston Renaissance provided the world with a multilayered Houston community. Both climates of political action and cultural consciousness in many ways symbolized the "New Negro" of African America.[35]

From there, the study moves from what scholar Earl Lewis calls the home-community sphere to the workforce sphere. Here the book outlines the work and business patterns of Houston's African American community. Migrants and established residents benefited greatly from Houston's booming economy before, during, and immediately following the Great War. Members of the Afro-American rank and file usually earned as much as three times the wages they held as farmers and farm laborers, even while encountering workforce dilemmas, for example, competition, wage differentials, and union strife. Middle-class professionals and business owners with technical skills catered to and benefited from Houston's changing African American community. Even while the Great Depression altered the lives of migrants, newcomers continued to see the city as a respite from deathly poverty and hopelessness.[36]

East Texas migrants Edward and Marie Hayes sought after practical alternatives to rural poverty and hopelessness. Without question, the offspring excelled, even creating opportunities for others. Robert E. Hayes, the second youngest son of migrants Rev. Edward Wilbur and Marie Hayes, followed his father's dream, becoming an educator and minister. The citywide high school tennis champion entered Wiley College in the fall of 1937. With only $20 in his pocket, the freshman attracted the attention of the school's president, who gave him a job in the kitchen. He told the highly regarded Wiley College president, Matthew Winfred Dogan Sr., he would work for his tuition. Hayes's older brother Leon also attended Wiley but, unlike Robert, had a band scholarship.[37] Robert Hayes worked his way through college as "a dishwasher, pot washer."[38]

The "A" student earned an English degree, with two minors in French and German, in 1941, making himself very marketable as an interpreter, particularly during America's entry into World War II. Hayes then entered Gammon Theological Seminary in Atlanta, Georgia, and put himself through school, waiting tables during the school year and in the summer serving as a Home Mission Council chaplain for Caribbean immigrants working in New Jersey and Connecticut during World War II. His post in the Methodist Episcopal Church probably kept him out of the war. He earned a second undergraduate degree in Divinity in 1945 but wanted to return to Texas. Unfortunately, he could not continue his formal education in his home state: "I couldn't go to SMU; they wouldn't let me in. My son finally went and finished from Perkins [School of Theology] at SMU [Southern Methodist University]."[39] His son, Dr. Robert E. Hayes Jr., has been a bishop with the United States United Methodist Church since 2004 and currently serves as resident bishop at Oklahoma City College.[40]

Hayes, along with his wife, formally Dorothy Dean, a Bethune-Cookman graduate and schoolteacher, whom he married in Palm Beach, Florida, in 1945, moved to Boston in 1947 to attend graduate school. Hayes earned his Master's of Sacred Theology from Boston University in 1949 and an honorary Doctor of Divinity from Wiley College in 1969. He served in a number of capacities in the Methodist Episcopal Church (later the United Methodist Church), as pastor of numerous congregations and later as a provost to a United Methodist Church bishop, the first African American in the United States to do so in nearly two hundred years. As provost in Houston, he spoke and preached at White congregations in eastern Texas in an attempt to prepare White congregants for the merger of the African American and White Methodist Episcopal congregations.[41]

Next, the United Methodist Church asked Hayes to serve as Wiley College's president in an attempt to "give it a decent funeral."[42] The school was nearly $2,000,000 in debt in 1971. To the surprise of many, Hayes later told Wiley's creditors, "I don't plan to close this school."[43] Hayes made the school solvent. He repaid creditors and raised millions of dollars for the private college. Hayes remained president for fifteen years. Hayes Sr., who was born in Marshall in 1920, also sat on the board of the United Negro College Fund. He and wife Dorothy had four daughters and one son, all college graduates. For the Hayes family, migration to Houston led to financial security, intellectual fulfillment, and generational blessings. Although Houston schools for African American children often lacked basic amenities, up-to-date textbooks, and adequate financing, compared to single-room country schools, the city's alternatives offered young people a decent education and a chance at a better life.[44]

ONE

~

Pulling Up the Stakes

The Great Migration to Houston, 1900–1930

Sudden changes in fortunes or circumstances certainly compelled the decision to migrate. Jefferson E. and Ella Collins moved to Houston in 1920 from Trinity, Texas. Like most African Americans in rural East Texas, they rented land as sharecroppers. Although economic challenges prompted their decision, it was more than likely that the recent death of their son Edward ultimately encouraged them to pull up the stakes and start anew in the big city.[1]

Migrant Jefferson Collins learned much from his parents. Jeff Collins was born "in the second year of freedom on August 30, 1865," in Houston County, right outside the town of Crockett in East Texas, two months after Texas slaves learned of their freedom.[2] His parents, Robert and Elizabeth Collins, natives of Mississippi near Vicksburg, "served" as slaves to a farmer named Collins, eventually working on his farm in Houston County. Ambitious, Robert and Elizabeth Collins worked hard in slavery and freedom. Elizabeth, for example, "learned to read and write from the slave owners' children," ultimately teaching these skills to her offspring, including son Jeff.[3] After slavery, the couple secured land in East Texas through Circular 13, a Freedmen's Bureau land incentive program. They also passed down their sense of responsibility and determination to their offspring.[4]

At an early age, Jeff Collins learned the meaning of community building. According to one descendent, "My father [Jeff Collins] was taught to Read-Write and Count."[5] Several siblings finished school and worked as schoolteachers, and others became ministers in the Tauner Spring community of Harrison County. An intelligent man, Jeff Collins "served . . . for fifty years . . . as superintendent . . . and teacher for Sunday [School] and a deacon."[6] Wife Ella Collins, the daughter of a Walker County farmer,

FIGURE 1. Twenty-year-old Jeff Collins, a native of Houston County, Texas, worked at a local lumber mill at the time this picture was taken in Willard, Texas, in Trinity County in 1885. Jeff and his wife moved to Houston in 1920, where he worked for a meatpacking plant before his death in 1936. *(Courtesy Houston Metropolitan Research Center, Houston Public Library, Houston, Texas, Jeff Collins Family Collection, MSS 0184-0002R)*

landholder Muriel Haynes, "to improve his operation of Sunday School & church . . . also served as [a] teacher and [p]resident of the Missionary Society . . . She also learned about responsibility from her father."[7] Not surprisingly, Jeff and Ella Collins "both worked [a number of different jobs] so as to improve our living condition."[8] When not planting or picking cotton, Jeff regularly took temporary work. These fleeting furloughs to sawmill towns, docksides along the Gulf, cottonseed and cotton compress plants, and railroad construction sites introduced Collins and other farmers to wage labor, especially work away from the farm, and prepared them for permanent journeys to Houston. Jeff Collins's wife, Ella, whom he married in 1884, helped on the farm and worked as a housekeeper for White families from time to time. Such part-time work for the Collinses also kept the family afloat.[9]

Soon after the couple married, the Collinses traveled east to Willard, Texas, a small farming and lumbering community in Trinity County. Jeff Collins eventually landed a better-paying job at a local sawmill on the Missouri, Kansas and Texas Railway line in Trinity County (fig. 1). During the golden era of Texas lumbering, from 1880 to 1930, northern investors and nascent regional firms logged almost sixty billion board feet of lumber, garnering billions of dollars over time. At some firms, Collins and other African Americans comprised 30 percent of the labor force. Working ten to twelve hours daily, six days a week, they cut trees, trimmed timber, hauled logs upstream and downstream, and transported finished hardwood by rail. Not surprisingly, they earned less than Whites, faced relentless discrimination in the Brotherhood of Timber Workers, lived in segregated and dilapidated housing, purchased goods on high-interest credit, and sometimes redeemed script notes at company commissaries. Collins thus traveled from mill to mill, looking for better opportunities.[10]

Jeff Collins found stable work at the Thompson Sawmill in Trinity County in the early 1900s. The family most likely traveled to nearby Polk County with the Thompson-Tucker Lumber Company in 1909, when the business moved its operations to the new community of New Willard. Some of the Collins children worked at the company in an effort to help sustain the family. Long hours, low pay, erratic pay periods, and grueling work often overwhelmed sawmill employees, particularly younger African Americans, who earned between fifty cents and a dollar a day.[11]

Job-related injuries took a toll on workers as well. One such on-the-job injury affected the Collins household in 1918. Jeff and Ella Collins's son Edward unfortunately drowned while working at the lumber company. Devastated, Jeff and Ella uprooted their family one last time to Houston. The decline of lumbering in East Texas, beginning in the 1920s, brought about by the eroding supply of timber, also prompted exoduses to Dallas, Ft. Worth, San Antonio, and out of state. Jeff secured an entry-level job at the Houston Meatpacking Company in east Houston near the ship channel.[12] He worked there until his death on April 29, 1936. Ella Collins "lived 19 years after his passing—almost 20 years."[13]

The migration patterns of the Collins paralleled others who moved from place to place as stepwise migrants. Such patterns of movement allowed travelers to relocate from one location to another before settling permanently in a community. For many years, the Collins traveled the East Texas countryside, for work and new opportunities, settling in rural Houston

FIGURE 2. Arma Collins was born in Trinity County in 1905, graduated from Conroe Industrial College, and moved to Houston with his family in the 1920s. For the next four decades, Arma worked at Southern Pacific Railroad, serving as president of the Association of Railway Trainmen, an organization that often embraced the segregationist platform of industrialists. An avid golfer and deacon at Shiloh Baptist Church, Collins, along with community activist Rev. Edwin Harrison, also helped pioneer African American involvement in the Boy Scouts of America. Regrettably, he died suddenly on the job at Southern Pacific on February 22, 1962. *(Courtesy Houston Metropolitan Research Center, Houston Public Library, Houston, Texas Jeff Collins Family Collection, MSS 0184-0023R)*

County, western Trinity County, the sawmill town of Willard in central Trinity County, and New Willard in Polk County, before permanently relocating to Houston. Although often on the road and separated from one another for long periods at a time, the couple ultimately had a large family, raising ten children.[14]

Although some of the offspring remained in East Texas as farmers and schoolteachers, others relocated to El Paso, Dallas, Houston, Los Angeles, Chicago, and Washington, DC, taking careers in nursing, education, manufacturing, transportation, and the federal civil service. One son, Arma, moved to Houston in the 1920s, after completing his studies at Conroe Industrial and Normal School (later Conroe College). Routinely engaging in stepwise migration, "he worked for the Beaumont Paper Co.

FIGURE 3. The granddaughter of Jeff and Ella Collins, Geneva Mae was born in Trinity in 1913. Ultimately, she moved to Fifth Ward with her family, graduating from Wheatley High School in the early 1930s, earning a nursing degree in 1948 from Prairie View. A return migrant, Geneva moved to California for a brief period, eventually returning to Texas to finish school. She worked for the Southern Pacific Railroad Hospital and St. Joseph Hospital, becoming supervisor of the pediatric night unit. She died in 1969 at the age of fifty-six. Here she poses in front of her home in Independence Heights in Houston at 1208 32nd Street in 1927. *(Courtesy Houston Metropolitan Research Center, Houston Public Library, Houston, Texas Jeff Collins Family Collection, MSS 0184-0017R)*

... American flour mills ... and [later] he went to Southern Pacific Railroad."[15] An avid unionist, he became president of the Association of Railway Trainmen, Local 77. In the home sphere, husband and family man, Arma Collins, pushed his nieces and nephews to excel academically. Building on his father's work, he also served his home church, Shiloh Baptist Church, as a faithful member. He loved golf as well (fig. 2). He also helped increase African American involvement in the Boy Scouts of America, serving as a counselor for decades. Although he and his wife, a Prairie View College (now Prairie View A&M University) alumna and schoolteacher, Katie Collins of Sommerville, Texas, never had children of their own, "he was very interested in his family & friends and did whatever he could for his fellow man."[16] He also motivated his family members to excel intellectually. A niece of Arma Collins and the granddaughter of Jeff and Ella Collins, Geneva Mae Justice, graduated from Prairie View College in 1948 and went into nursing (fig. 3).[17]

The Collins story, like that of other African American migrants in Houston, illustrates the heartfelt desire of Texans and Louisianans who sought racial autonomy. Black migration thus served a useful purpose as people found stable work, finished school, opened businesses, and increasingly articulated their grievances. This chapter explores the process of internal migration for those Afro-Americans who moved to the city between 1900 and 1930. A number of factors prompted their decision to emigrate and start anew. Southern poverty and social debasement retarded family stability and financial security. At the same time, Houston, as an emerging industrializing city, provided incoming migrants with opportunities, even while making it possible for newcomers to retain close ties with loved ones left behind. Migrants also reinvented kinships and social constructs that helped foster independence from Whites. Even those affected by natural disasters formed indelible institutions. Houston also provided young people—usually the children of internal migrants from the country—with the means to uproot to desirable places outside the Jim Crow South, notably Chicago, Los Angeles, and the San Francisco Bay region. For the three migratory groups that entered the city between the turn of the century and Great Depression—those of 1900–1914, 1914–1918, and 1918–1930—the city offered people of color a new beginning.[18]

Black migration to Houston both mirrored and differed from other migration streams across the continental United States. Like others who made their way to Chicago, Detroit, Cleveland, the San Francisco Bay area, and other destinations outside the Solid South, migrants abandoned farm communities and small-town tasks for city life. Not surprisingly, problems persisted. Although they benefited from the city's burgeoning economy, migrants found themselves still tied to racial segregation and discrimination. In this sense, their experiences differed somewhat from those of families and individuals fleeing the South. Although racism also permeated cities outside the South, rigid segregation laws and customs distinguished that region from other places of destination in the northern or western United States. Still, for a variety of reasons, newcomers chose the southern city over the farm, small town, western United States and the North.[19]

Like their contemporaries who fled the South, newcomers who made their way to Houston relied on chain migration networks. This safety valve helped migrants reach their temporary and permanent destinations in the

Bayou City (Houston); find sound employment; enroll schoolchildren in area schools; secure part-time work while attending college; join congregations; establish lifelong friendships and attachments; and most of all, extend to others the chain migration links they had come to depend on. These affirming ties served as important first steps in migrants' need to reshape their lives, families, and communities. Even with the emerging lines of demarcation that increasingly separated migrants and established residents in Houston according to socioeconomic class, education, religion, and ethnicity, chain migration networks remained intact. Socioeconomic class self-interests mattered in Houston as they did in other parts of the country. Migrants and established residents in the South, however, all had close ties to the surrounding interior, mainly due to slavery. Migration itself reminded migrants of the past they left behind. Although economic collapse largely fueled migration streams, societal debasement caused migrants to rethink their priorities and head to the big city. In this sense, the Great Migrations tied the racist, impoverished post-Emancipation era to the emerging new innovative century and the chance for socioeconomic betterment.[20]

Origins of the Great Migrations

Although Houston's burgeoning industrial economy provided African Americans with a semblance of socioeconomic freedom, Jim Crow prohibitions and rural and small-town poverty motivated people to abandon their birth homes, familiar family surroundings, and livelihood, and take a chance on the city.[21] Ironically, the period of hope that swept across the South following the Civil War served as the catalyst for the entrenched racism that defined the region for nearly a century. Black Texans and Louisianans in the years between the Civil War and modern Civil Rights Movement lived a fascinating and astringent paradox. On the one hand, they lived as outcasts, deprived of their constitutional civil rights as citizens. Denied the fruits of their labor as indispensable former slaves, farm operators, herdsmen, domestics, unskilled wage earners, manufacturing workers, and skilled laborers of eastern Texas and southern Louisiana, they held little hope in a society that viewed them as nonhuman savages. Paradoxically, African Americans cherished their partial freedoms, believed sturdily in the principles espoused in the Declaration of Independence and Constitution, and with few exceptions, treasured their native American South, perhaps more so than their ancestral homes of West and West-Central Africa. Their sense of worth in many ways came out of slavery and their relationship to Whites instead of their West African and West-Central African cultural beginnings as well as their connection to African-descent people worldwide. In fact, their ability to succeed had to do with their ability to replicate the dominant culture and their inability to progress had everything to do with their connection to Africa, at least in their minds.

Interestingly, as White-controlled institutions, organizations, and groups wantonly stripped them of their political freedoms, dubious economic fortunes, slight educational gains and, often, aspirations, self-respect, and role models, racial autonomy, amazingly, persisted. Perhaps, for no other reason, freedpeople embraced the pathos and negative delineations that defined their existence, therefore, contributing to racist commentary that defined them as American citizens. In some ways, their transition, from slavery to freedom, did little to alter their lack of self-esteem and self-worth as human souls, mainly because of their social conditioning as American slaves.[22]

African Americans following slavery nevertheless carved out communities of hope and self-determination—communities that practiced agency. Utilizing self-help strategies, freed people and their descendants mapped out key survival objectives—notably familial unity, literacy, voting rights, and economic self-sufficiency.[23] One aspiration stood out more than most: landholding. Land, according to historian Darlene Clark Hine, equated to citizenship and democracy. To historian Barbara Blair, property even obscured past transgressions and placed people of color on equal footing with other yeoman-farming Americans. Black Texans and Louisianans procured land at an impressive rate. By 1910, 29 percent of AfroTexans owned land compared to 17 percent of African Americans in Louisiana.[24]

Even while African Americans successfully procured real and personal property, the majority did not. Even while optimistic about their futures as landowners, most fell into debt under the guise of farm tenancy.[25] Under tenant farming, landholders parceled out smallholdings to individual families or individuals. Tenant families usually paid their rent with a portion of the year's crop. The system of course varied depending on a number of factors. Cash tenants leased farmlands for a fee, thus retaining their harvested crops at the end of the planting season. Share tenants usually furnished their own animals and supplies, and paid the fee with a fourth of the yielded crop.[26]

Farm owners mostly classified African American tenants as sharecroppers. Sharecroppers did not have ready cash like rent tenants; nor did they own their own animals and equipment as share tenants. Sharecroppers were willing workers. At the end of the planting season, they usually paid

FIGURE 4. Even with in poor conditions, rural schoolchildren had a passionate zeal for learning excellence. Here in this small community near Edna, Texas, in Jackson County, local schoolchildren, including the older sister of future civil-rights activist Christia Adair—the second from the right in the first row—pose for their annual class picture. This school, typical in the Jim Crow South, comprised one large room that was used to teach multiple grades at once. These overcrowded schools normally relied on one schoolteacher. This school's instructor is standing in the center of the next to last row. Even with these problems, a few students went on to finish the eighth grade and graduate from high school. In the instance of these children, the nearest high school was perhaps located in another county, thus forcing students to leave their families to finish school. A few moved one hundred miles north to Houston. *(Courtesy Houston Metropolitan Research Center, Houston Public Library, Houston, Texas, Christia Adair Collection, MSS 0109-0001)*

their share to owners with one-half of the crop. Tenants mostly purchased food, fabric, ready-to-wear clothes, drugs, toiletries, school supplies, and home amenities on high-interest credit. At the end of the planting season, tenants not only paid owners in cash or with a portion of their harvested crop; they often paid their debts with the remaining crop as payment for all outstanding liabilities. Landless, penniless, uneducated, and completely dependent on tenant farming for their livelihood, African American farmers found themselves tied to the land as paupers with few options short of migration, thanks to the beneficiaries of the new economic order of the post-Reconstruction New South—southern merchants and planters, and northern businessmen and industrialists.[27]

Blacks in Texas and Louisiana lost ground in other areas as well. Tied to economic powerlessness were the implicit and explicit social constructs of paralyzing racial segregation, violence, depoliticalization, and educational depravity. Even while they helped create Texas's first public schools, African Americans rarely finished high school, with most obtaining only a fourth-grade education. The vast majority of Texas and Louisiana African Americans continued leaving school prematurely through the second half of the twentieth century when more families moved to cities (fig. 4).[28]

Disfranchisement also devastated African American dreams. The number of registered African American voters in Texas fell from over one hundred thousand in 1890 to five thousand in 1906. Whites used a number of devices to diminish African American political power, from gerrymandering and intimidation to the poll tax and the White primary. Black tenacity aside, Whites rarely held out hope that African Americans would outsmart their legal maneuvers to maintain political dominance in the state.[29]

These conspicuous acts of racism depended on violence as a form of social control. At least ten thousand African Americans in Texas and Louisiana died at the hands of racists between Reconstruction and the Great Depression. The reasons for these heinous crimes varied but included African American property ownership, education, success in business, political prowess, self-defense, alleged felonies and misdemeanors, and sexual liaisons with White women. Adults and children, men and women, young people and seniors were all vulnerable to the noose of unrighteous social control.[30]

Segregation pervaded every aspect of life and legitimized racial violence, disfranchisement, and educational depravity. Racial segregation, both legalized and customary, dominated southern culture for nearly a century, permeating both White supremacy and African American inferiority. Jim Crow, in the eyes of Whites, correctly rolled back the changes that went into effect due to Emancipation and Reconstruction. Indisputably, for Whites, African American aspirations gave way to social equality. According to historian Grace Elizabeth Hale in *Making Whiteness* (1999), Whites opposed African American advancement on this principle alone. Blacks' desire for education and voting rights as well as self-respect did not sit well with White southerners who were determined to advance a new racial hierarchy to supplant slavery. Nevertheless, African American determination in many ways overshadowed racism.[31]

Migrants' attraction to Houston influenced relocation and nurtured autonomous agency. Many had already traveled to the city to work, visit relatives, attend church, or for leisure. They knew the city well. Houston, to these individuals, offered migrants renewed hope. The city first had to witness its own transformation from a town to a major regional manufacturing center.[32]

Founded August 30, 1836, on a barren edge of the Gulf Coastal Plains by New York City developers, brothers Augustus Chapman Allen and John Kirby Allen, Houston, the first long-standing capital of the Republic of Texas, would ultimately materialize as a magnet for urban sprawl, economic growth, and unfettered possibilities. Located thirty to fifty miles inland from the Gulf of Mexico Sea, at the head of the shallow and partly navigable Buffalo Bayou, Houston formed twenty-five years before the start of the Civil War as a small, commercial terminus for goods leaving the Gulf of Mexico. Boosters, area planters, and merchants, including William Marsh Rice, for whom Rice University is named for, knew the town's success depended on a reliable form of transportation linking the coastal region to the surrounding cotton, sugarcane, and lumbering interiors.[33]

Dramatic economic and infrastructural changes in the coming decades helped transform Houston into a regional transportation giant. With most of the state's railroads beginning in the Bayou City, Houston had already launched itself as a major rail center before the Civil War. After the war, manufacturers linked local and state lines with several major transcontinental lines—Southern Pacific Railroad; Texas and Pacific Railway; and the Atchison, Topeka and Santa Fe—and made railroads the city's largest employer by 1900. With almost twenty railway lines by 1920, the city became a leading rail center in the United States.[34]

Waterway transportation too influenced economic growth. Of the city's surrounding waterways, including the Brazos, San Jacinto, Colorado, Nueces, Sabine, and Trinity Rivers, as well as the Sims, White Oak, Brays, and Buffalo Bayous, only the Buffalo Bayou became a major water terminus in the nation by 1874. The Rivers and Harbors Act of 1899 smoothed the path for the dredging of a twenty-five-foot channel at the bayou. Congress then in 1902 allotted $1,000,000 for the development of a turning basin at the bayou. By the second decade of the twentieth century, seventy miles of railroad track surrounded the new ship channel, making the waterway ripe for business and manufacturing expansion. By the 1920s, the channel already led others around the world in the shipment of cotton. Other businesses followed suit, establishing factories, warehouses, and waterborne facilities along the channel.[35]

A regional transportation hub by the turn of the twentieth century, two events helped trigger Houston's entry into the modern industrial age. Before the Great Storm of 1900, Galveston with its natural harbor dominated the economy of Southeast Texas. The second largest city in the state behind San Antonio in 1850 and 1860, and the largest city in Texas by 1870, Galveston attracted state and national acclaim for its distinctive academic, cultural, and commercial appeal. In addition, the city had become by 1899 the world's largest exporter of cotton. Unfortunately, a Category 3 hurricane struck the island city on September 8, 1900. In what many consider the worst natural disaster in American history, eight thousand people died. An additional three thousand coastal residents from other communities on the island and on neighboring islands also lost their lives when rain and wind gusts of one hundred and twenty miles per hour flooded the city, butchered neighborhoods, demolished buildings, covered area beaches, and drowned residents. The city never recovered, and the disaster precipitated a mass exodus of thousands, including businesspersons who relocated their businesses to Houston.[36]

The rise of the modern Texas oil industry after 1901 propelled Houston's economy as well. On January 10, 1901, Austrian native and engineer Anthony Lucas of the Gladys City Oil, Gas, and Manufacturing Company, with the financial backing of Mellon Company investors from Pittsburgh, Pennsylvania, successfully drilled through a 1,139-foot salt-dome-shaped well, producing seventy-five thousand barrels daily at the Spindletop Oilfield south of Beaumont in eastern Jefferson County. The Spindletop Hill oilfield, which peaked at seventeen million and five hundred thousand barrels in 1902, spurred the modern era of Texas oil refining. It also sparked explorations in the Gulf Coast area, as well as the founding of principle regional and international firms, including J. M. Guffey, which later became Gulf Oil (now Chevron), 1901; the Humble Oil and Refining Company, 1911 (now ExxonMobil); Magnolia Petroleum Company (now ExxonMobil Oil), 1911; and the Texas Oil Company, 1902 (later Texaco Oil).[37] Spindletop also signaled the formation of the Upper Texas Gulf Coast (UTGC) manufacturing region, a one-hundred-mile coastline of factories, from Corpus Christi in the south to Beaumont and Port Arthur in the north, with Houston in the center.[38]

The discovery at Spindletop led to the greatest period of United States oil refining, with the UTGC refining region leading the way with crude oil production of nine hundred thousand barrels daily by 1941. With Spindletop came the liquid fuel age for automobile and airplane fuel, the modern highway system, improved marine and rail transport, mass production, and petroleum-based products, all of which helped propel Houston into a regional manufacturing, organizational giant. Propelled by oil refining, the manufacturing of other goods and trade, and reliable transportation facilities, the number of industries in Houston grew from 78 in 1900 to 429 by 1930. Motivated by an export–import economy based on the shipment of goods for outside markets, Houston and the UTGC manufacturing hub impelled the growth of a prodigious migrant workforce, a metropolis, and an urban state.[39]

The next four to five decades of industrialization, improved transportation, the infusion of investment capital, and migration precipitated Houston's phenomenal rise as one of the world's leading manufacturing centers. In 1930, Houston became the largest city in Texas and the second most populated in the South. Ten years later, in 1940, it would rank twenty-first in the entire United States. In 1950, the city replaced New Orleans as the South's largest metropolitan center and moved up to number fourteen nationwide. The city's population surge of nearly six hundred thousand between 1900 and 1950 would become unprecedented for a southern city. Northeastern and midwestern cities continued to grow in population and size, yet unlike Houston and Los Angeles, much of this increase resulted from suburban sprawl, not annexation or a population explosion within the city limits. Again, Houston's net population growth during this period only ranked second in the nation behind Los Angeles, a trend that would continue for much of the century.[40]

The formation of twentieth-century Houston and the UTGC industrial center, along with other cities, marked the rise of urban Texas and the decline of the rural interior. Dallas emerged as one of the centers of transportation, finance, and business. Fort Worth, already a major distributor, marketer, and transporter of cattle in the late nineteenth century, arose in the early twentieth century to become the chief meatpacking center in the state. Historic San Antonio also emerged as a growing manufacturing and military city in the early twentieth century. In 1900, 17 percent of Texans resided in urban centers. By 1940, this figure had grown to 45 percent, and it rose to more than 60 percent the next decade. Still San Antonio, Dallas, and other cities could not keep up with Houston. Houston's population outdistanced that of all other Texas cities by almost eight times between 1900 and 1940, largely because of manufacturing, a growing labor market, and internal migration.[41]

"He Hopped the Next Train to Houston": The Great Migration to Houston, Texas

Houston's growth helped spark the state's urban revolution. Several factors explain Houston's unusual growth, from 44,633 in 1900 to 596,163 in 1950. Natural births accounted for some of the growth. At the start of the century in 1900, two thousand and five hundred African Americans under the age of ten made up one-fifth of the total African American population of fourteen thousand. In 1910, only four thousand of the city's twenty-four thousand residents of color comprised children under the age of ten—young people who may or may not have been born in the city. In 1930, twelve thousand residents under the age of ten made up a portion (one-fifth) of the city's sixty-three thousand African Americans. Again, these numbers do not tell the whole story, of course. Some children migrated to the city with their parents, whereas others were in fact born in the city. Without complete birth records for Houston residents, it is impossible to determine the actual number of births for these years. Procreation, perhaps, comprised a small proportion of the city's population growth.[42]

Annexation, like procreation, affected the city's rising population. Houston in the late 1920s in particular annexed a number of outlying communities. Independence Heights, a town comprising African Americans, became part of the city in 1929, raising the city's population by several thousand. The city ultimately took over other African American areas later in the century as well: Acres Homes, Highland Heights, Trinity Gardens, and Sunnyside to name some. These new additions brought thousands of people into the city limits in the twentieth century.[43]

Although annexation and procreation were important, immigration and internal migration contributed the most to the city's population explosion. Immigrants from abroad made Houston their home in the first few decades of the new century. A steady stream of immigrants, mostly from Eastern and Southern Europe, but also from the Guangdong region of China near Hong Kong, as well as Japan and the Caribbean, made their way into the city during this period of industrialization. Houston in fact attracted a growing number of upwardly mobile Afro-Caribbean immigrants who were business owners, attorneys, physicians, and educators, with some entering the city after completing their college training in the United States. Even so, the foreign-born Black population in Texas decreased significantly by over one thousand between 1920 and 1930, mainly a result of the Immigration Act of 1924. In 1920, immigrants made up 9 percent of the city's total population. Most moved to Texas to escape massive poverty. Some, like Jewish Russians, the victims of anti-Semitism, found religious freedom and social autonomy in the United States South.[44]

Most immigrants moved from Mexico. Latinos had always lived in the city, especially because the state was once part of Mexico up until the 1830s. People of Mexican origin perhaps remained in Houston after the Texas Revolution in 1836 as prisoners of war. Their numbers, however, remained miniscule, with only one thousand living in the city limits by 1900. Only with the coming of the Mexican Revolution, beginning in 1910, did growing numbers of Mexicans from war-torn Mexico, along with Mexican Americans from West, South, and Central Texas, make their way to Houston for economic opportunities and serene safety. Land reform measures against Mexican President Porfirio Díaz ignited the decade-long rebellion that propelled the mass exodus of 1.3 million citizens who relocated to the United States by 1930. In Houston, Mexican nationals and Mexican Americans of the United States still made up a tiny percentage of the population prior to the second half of the century. In 1940, they comprised twenty thousand residents, or 5 percent of the overall population. They moved to the city for stable jobs. Mexican Americans, like African Americans, worked the worst jobs and faced fierce racism. Increasingly, Latinos and African Americans found themselves competing with one another for jobs in the growing and industrializing Houston.[45]

Internal migrations from the surrounding countryside, not immigration, propelled most of Houston's growth as people of all races, religions, backgrounds, and persuasions migrated to the city for work. Newcomers left the same places individuals and families had abandoned a generation earlier, following the Civil War: surrounding Texas towns and rural communities in the eastern half of the state. Whites made up most of the internal migrants relocating to the city. Like African Americans, native-born Whites sought after better-paying jobs and superior schools for their children. Some, first-generation Americans, left the old countries of Germany, Switzerland, France, Austria-Hungary, and so on, in the mid- and late nineteenth century. These immigrants usually immigrated to rural

Texas for farms. As the boll weevil wrecked havoc on their livelihood, their desire for additional resources spurred their relocation to Texas cities. At other times, second- and third-generation American citizens left the rural and small-town communities their parents and grandparents founded or moved to.[46]

Most of the internal migrants had been third-, fourth-, and fifth-generation Texans whose ancestors—mostly migrants from the Deep South—possibly fought and died in the United States Civil War. These cash-poor farmers and tenants desperately needed to improve their circumstances. More than anything else, the decline of farms influenced their decision to uproot to the city. For these Texans, who largely comprised tenants, internal migration to nearby Houston seemed a logical choice. Although many came to the city with nothing, they found countless job prospects that improved their circumstances. Unlike people of color, they rarely faced social ostracism and ongoing discrimination. Because they benefitted from racism, had more job opportunities, and made up a larger segment of the state's overall population, more made their way into the city.[47]

African Americans, like others, mostly flocked to the city for non-agricultural, wage-earning jobs. Between 1900 and 1930, the city's African American population grew from 14,608 to 63,337, an increase of 65 percent, tripling the city's Black population. Rural-to-urban and small-town-to-city migration, as well as natural births, mostly explained this incredible surge in population. This reflected Afro-Americans' heartfelt desire to improve their lot in life by way of internal migration. In fact, internal migration remained vital to the state's Afro-American population. In 1900, 82 percent of African Americans lived in rural Texas; fifty years later, 65 percent lived in communities defined as cities.[48]

Southerners outside Texas more often than not left their birth state for good. For 1930, 19 percent of Louisiana-born Afro-Americans, 24 percent of Mississippi-born Afro-Americans, and 29 percent of Georgia-born African Americans resided in other states. Black Mississippians, Alabamians, Georgians, Louisianans and others who left southern states, only returned to the South for visits. Most southern states had a shortage of manufacturing jobs that went to African Americans. People also left industrialized areas like northern Alabama, eastern Tennessee, and western North Carolina to escape rigid lines of demarcation that suppressed African Americans as wage earners and human beings. Blacks did seek work in the Birmingham and Bessemer steel mills and Wilmington tobacco mills, but like most birds of passage, returned home after completing several months of intense work. Completely shut out of the skilled workforce throughout the South, these

Figure 5. Perhaps in some circles in Black Houston, the Covington Family—Dr. Benjamin Jesse and Mrs. Jennie Covington, along with their daughter Ernestine Jessie Covington Dent (in the center)—was the community's "First Family." Dr. Covington, one of the city's first Black physicians, graduated from Meharry Medical School in 1901. One year later, he met and married Jennie Belle Murphy, a multiracial former orphan and domestic science student at Guadalupe College. Jennie made clothes and did alterations to pay her tuition at the institution. Clubwoman and social service activist Jennie Covington served as an important bridge builder among the communities. Often overlooked, her mother was Mexican American and possibly taught her Spanish before dying prematurely in the 1880s or early 1890s. After the two moved to Houston in 1903, they found out they were expecting their first and only child. Their daughter was born in the Covington home on Dowling and Hadley Streets. She went on to Oberlin, eventually earning bachelor's and master's degrees in classical music and piano, respectively. She was also one of the first African Americans to earn a scholarship from the Julliard Foundation, securing four $1,000 scholarships in the late 1920s and early 1930s. She later taught piano at Bishop College, eventually marrying hospital administrator Albert Thomas Dent, the future president of Dillard University in New Orleans. *(Courtesy Houston Metropolitan Research Center, Houston Public Library, Houston, Texas, Covington Family Collection, MSS 0170-0015)*

southern out-migrants saw interregional migration as a win–win situation.[49]

Black Texans, on the other hand, remained in Texas. Black newcomers to Houston mostly left a collage of communities throughout eastern Texas.[50] The Collins family left New Willard, an East Texas sawmill town in the 1920s; Oran Williams left Roans Prairie in Grimes County in the late 1920s; Oliphant and Ella Hubbard, schoolteachers, also moved to the Houston area from the sawmill town of Diboll in 1915. Benjamin Jesse and Jennie Covington moved to Houston in 1903, from Yoakum in Wharton

County, where B. J. Covington, a physician, practiced general medicine. His wife, Jennie Covington, was born in Clinton, DeWitt County, in southeastern Texas (fig. 5). Most Texans, prior to World War II, remained in Texas. In 1930, only 13 percent of the native-born Afro-American Texan population lived outside the state. Certainly their smaller numbers in the Texas population would make them less threatening to Whites, to an extent, and perhaps explains their easier accessibility to land and jobs. Motivated by kin and kith ties that stretched from city to country, education, jobs, and business opportunities in nearby Houston, these internal migrants differed to an extent from their southern contemporaries outside the Lone Star state.[51]

Intraregional and intrastate in nature, African American migration originated in eastern Texas and Louisiana. An estimated two-thirds of African American newcomers left farms and small towns in eastern Texas. Blacks have always lived and moved about in the eastern half of the state. According to Texas scholars Alwyn Barr and Randolph Campbell, since the populating of slaves in Texas in the early nineteenth century, 80 to 90 percent of the state's African American population have traditionally lived and moved within the same region of the state.[52] Between 1900 and 1930, almost 90 percent of the state's African American population lived east of an imaginary line that ran northwestward from Matagorda Bay to Goliad and up to Seguin, then northeastward to Austin, Waco, Dallas, Rockwall, Kaufman, and Lamar along the Red River.[53] Particularly between the years 1910 and 1940, Texas African Americans chose intrastate rural-to-urban and rural-to-small-town migration over interstate South-to-North or South-to-West movements. Most others left southern and central Louisiana.[54]

Texas migrants generally moved to Houston from four principle economic areas in eastern Texas: the cotton region of southeast Texas, cotton and timber (mixed) region on the southern edge of the East Texas timber belt, and UTGC (see map 1). Blacks like Roans Prairie native Oran Williams lived in the cotton region primarily and farmed on cotton plantations; those whose lives mirrored Jeff Collins's, resided in the cotton and timber (mixed) region north of the city, grew cotton and corn, and worked at local sawmills. Most East Texas African Americans, like Edward Wilbur Hayes of Big Sandy of Upshur County, living in the timber region, labored as lumber, steel, and refinery workers, but also farmed. Map 1 illustrates the cotton region, cotton and timber (mixed), and timber counties select migrants left. Although people left communities in the UTGC region, the manufacturing area mostly attracted willing workers.[55]

Most of the migrants who made their way to Houston were under

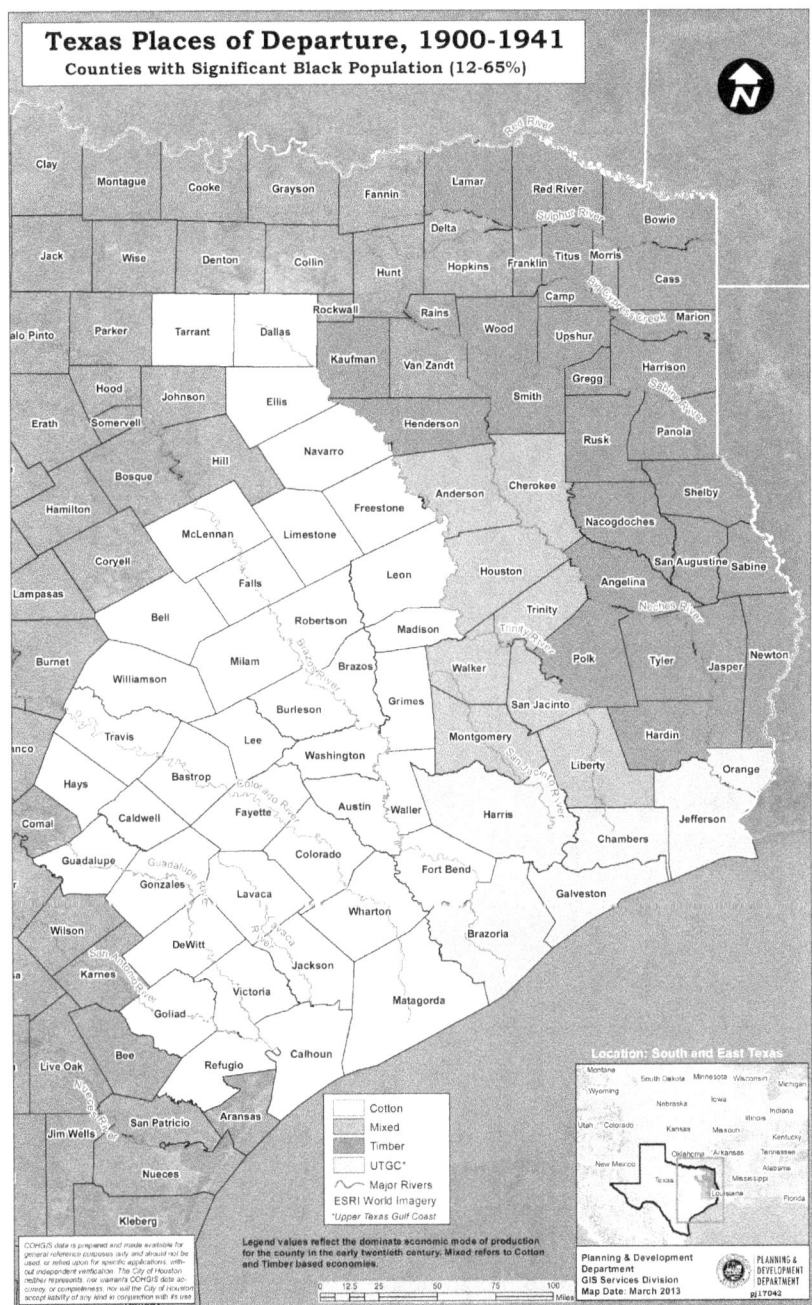

MAP 1. Texas Places of Departure, 1900–1941: Places with Significant Black Populations (12–65 percent)*
Source: Bureau of Census, *Negro Population in the United States, 1790–1915*. 1918 (reprint. New York: Arno Press, 1969), 143. *(Courtesy Larry T. Nierth, GIS Supervisor, GIS Services Division, Planning and Development Department, City of Houston, Houston, Texas)*

TABLE 2. Probable intercensal net in-migration figures among Blacks by age cohort,*** Houston, Texas, 1900–10, 1910–20, and 1920–30

Ages	Males	Females
1900–10*		
5–14	971	1,827
15–24	1,176	910
25–34	579	106
35–44	451	359
44+***	N/A	N/A
	Total	Total
	3,177	3,202
		Grand Total
		6,379
1910–20**		
10–14	88	395
15–19	389	403
20–24	563	170
25–34	421	–91
35–44	81	–339
44–65***	N/A	N/A
	Total	Total
	1,542	538
		Grand Total
		2,080

the age of forty-five. Adolescents and adults under the age of forty-five made up the majority of migrants. Intercensal net migration numbers reveal that individuals between the ages of 10 and 44 made up the largest segment of migrants for the period 1910 to 1930.[56] Table 2 illustrates that younger males represented the greatest segment of the African American migrant community in Houston. It also reveals that for the 1910–1920 intercensal period, male migrants in the 20- to 24-year-old age category outnumbered young female migrants by three to one; those men in the 25- to 34-year-old age cohort group outnumbered women by almost six to one. Although the number of female migrants in these categories for

TABLE 2. *Continued*

Ages	Males	Females
	1920–30**	
10–14	2,218	3,225
15–19	2,561	3,132
20–24	1,349	1,142
25–29	1,141	748
30–34	745	388
35–39	30	−205
40–44	44	−147
45–49	−585	−306
50–54	−241	−122
55–59	−87	−47
60–64	−144	−83
65–69	19	29
70+***	N/A	N/A
	Total	Total
	7,050	7,754
		Grand Total
		14,804

Sources: Bureau of Census, Negro Population in the United States, 205; *Fourteenth Census of the United States, 1920: Population,* V.2., 354; Bureau of Census, *Twelfth Census of the United States, 1900, Population, 132.*
*Cohorts do not include the 1,790 children below 5 years of age who may or may not have migrated to Houston during this period with their parents.
**Cohorts do not include the 14,635 children below 10 years of age who may or may not have migrated to Houston during this period with their parents.
***Incomplete census tabulations prevent further analysis by similar cohorts.

the 1920–1930-period increased, males between the ages of 20 and 34 still dominated.[57]

As the urban population in the state increased, the state's rural population declined. According to census figures, the African American rural population declined sharply between 1900 and 1940. Tables 3 and 4 illustrate the relative population decline among African Americans living in rural counties surrounding Houston. Cotton-region counties both dotted the outskirts of Houston and had the highest percentages of African Americans in Texas at the turn of the century: Fort Bend, Burleson, Waller,

TABLE 3. Black rural-to-urban population growth in Texas, 1900–50*

	Number					
	1900	1910	1920	1930	1940	1950
Rural	501,393	511,185	518,321	525,135	504,281	369,875
Urban	119,329	178,864	223,373	329,829	420,110	608,655
Total	620,722	690,049	741,694	854,964	924,391	978,530

	Percentage					
	1900	1910	1920	1930	1940	1950
Rural	80.78%	74.08%	69.88%	61.42%	54.55%	38%
Urban	19.22%	25.92%	30.12%	38.58%	45.45%	62%
Percent of Total Pop.	19.20%	17.70%	15.90%	14.70%	14.40%	12.73%

Sources: Bureau of Census, *Negro Population in the United States, 1790–1915*, 92; Bureau of Census, *Negroes in the United States, 1920–1932*, 53; Bureau of Census, *Sixteenth Census of the United States, 1940: Population: Characteristics of the Population*, V. 2, 763; Bureau of Census, *Fourteenth Census of the United States, 1920: Population*, V.2., General Report and Analytical Tables, 86; Bureau of Census, A Report of the Seventeenth Census of *Population, Part 43, Texas*, 43-351 through 43-354.

*The population changes in Texas resulted from a number of factors such as out-migration figures and death rates in rural communities, and in-migration figures, annexation, and birth figures in urban communities.

Wharton, Washington, Colorado, San Jacinto, and Walker. This suggests a strong correlation between population declines in the said counties and increase in Houston. However, out-migration alone did not contribute to the African American population decreases in eastern Texas.[58]

Prior to the Japanese attack on Pearl Harbor, death figures for African Americans leaving the rural interior also exceeded out-migration figures. Although little data exists at the Texas Department of Health, Vital Statistics Office, that illustrate this trend before the depression, statistics from the Great Depression corroborate this observation, as thousands of African American Texans died in the 1930s. Vital statistics on Louisiana, on the other hand, do in fact discuss this trend as taking place in the years that preceded World War I. Vital statistics suggest that high mortality rates propelled the population declines in the state prior to World War II, perhaps more so than outmigration.[59]

Although most communities saw no real population declines for the period 1920 to 1930, those that did—Iberville, St. Mary, St. Martin, Iberia, Avoyelles, Beauregard, Red River, Morehouse, Natchitoches—witnessed high death figures that greatly affected the population declines (table 5).

TABLE 4. Black population figures for selected Texas counties, 1900–40*

Counties	1900	1910	1920	1930	1940	1930–40 Death Fig.	1930–40 Death Rates
Freestone	8,302	8,772	9,259	8,776	8,613	955	110.87
Limestone	6,354	9,247	9,099	10,933	9,791	1,138	166.22
Falls	11,985	12,612	11,555	12,515	12,047	1,451	120.44
Leon	6,937	6,878	7,284	8,362	7,515	534	71.05
Robertson	**16,747**	**11,571**	**12,474**	**11,416**	**10,756**	1,590	147.82
Milam	**10,473**	**9,485**	**8,973**	**8,772**	**7,686**	914	127.19
Madison	2,458	2,757	3,127	3,456	3,863	312	80.16
Grimes	**14,327**	**9,858**	**9,810**	**9,700**	**8,814**	1,018	115.47
Brazos	8,815	8,827	9,148	9,064	10,011	1,264	126.26
Burleson	**8,321**	**8,587**	**6,506**	**7,187**	**6,767**	801	118.36
Lee	**4,343**	**4,039**	**4,224**	**3,876**	**3,655**	381	98.57
Fayette	**10,394**	**7,361**	**6,755**	**6,921**	**6,321**	807	127.66
Washington	**16,039**	**12,017**	**11,646**	**9,893**	**9,660**	1,296	134.16
Waller	**7,871**	**6,712**	**4,967**	**4,952**	**4,993**	809	162.02
Austin	**6,193**	**5,018**	**5,059**	**4,852**	**4,398**	561	127.55
Colorado	**9,633**	**7,074**	**6,453**	**5,955**	**5,460**	695	127.28
Lavaca	**4,890**	**4,384**	**3,975**	**3,369**	**3,220**	461	143.16
Fort Bend	**10,814**	**11,422**	**9,996**	**9,787**	**9,110**	1,166	127.99
Wharton	**8,717**	**8,889**	**7,884**	**7,903**	**9,214**	1,187	128.82
Jackson	**2,189**	**2,114**	**2,176**	**1,908**	**1,781**	199	11.13
Matagorda	3,791	4,457	3,974	4,520	4,943	543	109.85
Cherokee	8,196	7,641	9,174	11,565	12,566	1,906	151.67
Anderson	**11,615**	**11,323**	**11,162**	**11,485**	**11,796**	1,550	131.4
Houston	10,342	12,548	10,793	12,374	11,879	1,208	101.69
Trinity	2,813	3,195	3,420	3,181	**3,061**	372	121.52
Walker	8,319	8,362	9,741	8,531	**8,820**	734	83.21
San Jacinto	**5,531**	**5,193**	**5,487**	**5,117**	**4,740**	437	92.19
Montgomery	6,619	7,104	6,358	5,273	7,148	756	105.16
Liberty	2,366	3,401	3,828	5,019	6,075	600	98.76

Sources: Bureau of Census, *Negro Population in the United States, 1790–1915*, 831–34; Bureau of Census, *Twelfth Census of the United States, 1900, Population*, 40–42; Bureau of Census, *Fourteenth Census of the United States, 1920: Population*, V. 3, 990–1014; Bureau of Census, *Sixteenth Census of the United States, 1940: Population: Characteristics of the Population*, V. 2, 792–806; Pratt, *Growth of a Refining Region*, 20; Texas Department of Health, Bureau of Vital Statistics, Texas Mortality, 1930–40.

*The highlighted counties show population losses over the said period. Death rates, birth rates, and out-migration have contributed to the population changes in rural Texas. Although Houston migrants left places in the East Texas timber economic region, this table only concentrates on the cotton and mixed regions because the largest number of Black in-migrants left these two areas.

TABLE 5. Black population figures for select Louisiana parishes, 1900–30*

Parishes	1900	1910	1920 Pop.	1930 Pop.	1920–30 Death Fig.	1920–30 Death Rates	Out-Mig.
Iberville*	17,159	19,145	15,372	12,549	2,501	199.29	322
Pointe Coupee*	19,174	17,147	14,981	12,211	1,839	146.54	429
Saint Landry	26,658	31,234	26,507	29,516	3,716	125.89	N/A
Evangeline**	–	–	5,681	5,772	223	32.92	N/A
Calcasieu	5,966	16,562	8,736	12,112	607	50.11	N/A
Saint Mary*	20,264	21,266	15,174	14,302	2,565	179.34	N/A
Saint Martin	8,883	9,836	7,902	7,545	909	120.47	N/A
Iberia*	14,282	14,474	10,898	10,733	1,762	164.16	N/A
Avoyelles*	11,891	12,039	10,353	9,915	1,242	125.26	N/A
Acadia	4,820	6,546	7,526	8,103	1,175	145	N/A
Lafayette	9,516	10,734	10,811	13,260	1,842	138.91	N/A
Jefferson Davis**	–	–	4,837	4,979	575	115.48	N/A
Beauregard**	–	–	6,105	3,177	489	153.91	2,489
Rapides	21,210	21,445	24,992	25,126	2,563	102	N/A
De Soto	16,903	17,932	17,914	19,215	2,058	107.1	N/A
Caldwell*	3,076	3,465	2,983	2,937	396	134.83	N/A
Red River*	7,471	6,212	7,589	7,551	564	74.69	N/A
Ascension*	12,081	11,255	9,490	7,077	1,351	190.9	1,062
Claiborne	13,827	14,938	14,798	18,042	1,399	77.54	N/A
Bienville	8,240	9,464	8,619	10,624	957	90.07	N/A
Morehouse	12,722	13,971	13,140	13,597	1,792	131.79	N/A
Natchitoches	19,544	20,334	20,697	19,570	2,705	138.22	126

Sources: Bureau of Census, *Negro Population in the United States, 1790–1915*, 812–13; *Fourteenth Census of the United States, 1920: Population*, V. 3, 393–98; Bureau of Census, Bureau of Census, Sixteenth *Census of the United States, 1940: Population: Characteristics of the Population*, V. 2, Part 6, 362–65; Bureau of Census, *Mortality Statistics, 1920*, 91–92; Bureau of Census, *Mortality Statistics, 1921*, 137–38; Bureau of Census, *Mortality Statistics, 1922*, 109–11; Bureau of Census, *Mortality Statistics, 1923*, 99–100; Bureau of Census, *Mortality Statistics, 1924*, 102; Bureau of Census, Mortality Statistics, 1925, 14–15; Bureau of Census, Mortality Statistics, 1926, 14–15; Bureau of Census, Mortality Statistics, 1927, 11–12; Bureau of Census, Mortality Statistics, 1928 and 1929, 83–84; Bureau of Census, *Mortality Statistics, 1930*, 88–89.

For example, St. Iberville's population of color declined from 15,372 in 1920 to 12,549 in 1930, or by 2,823 persons. However, 2,501 of its Afro-American residents died during this same period (table 5). Only an estimated 301 African American residents emigrated from St. Iberville during this ten-year decade. Deaths also contributed greatly to the population decline in Pointe Coupee. The African American population figure for the parish declined by 2,432 for the period under discussion. Only 600 persons left Pointe Coupee, whereas 1,839 died.[60]

Often, death figures exceeded the population total for the ten-year period. Although 1,242 African Americans died in Avoyelles Parish between the years 1920 and 1930, the community's total population declined by 438 persons. This suggests that birth rates and back-and-forth movements to and from the parish contributed to the population change in the parish. Only in Beauregard did the out-migration number exceed the death figure among Blacks. Between 1920 and 1930, 2,439 African Americans left the county, and 489 died. Blacks in Louisiana struggled as well to survive the depressed 1920s and 1930s as the rural economy collapsed. Without good medical care, proper diet, and unending stress, death seemed a probable fact for these residents.[61]

Although death rates greatly affected the African American population changes in Louisiana, Louisiana in-migration played a significant role, nevertheless, in the growth of Houston's African American community. Most Louisiana-born African Americans living outside the state in 1910 lived in Arkansas—25,382—whereas 19,703 resided in Texas. By 1920, most Louisiana-born African Americans were no longer living in the state—34,342 resided in Texas, and represented the largest concentration of Louisianans outside the Bayou State. Their numbers grew to almost 60,000 by 1930. Of the 58,217 Louisiana-born Afro-Americans living in Texas, almost 12,000 (11,880) resided in Houston, which was home to the state's largest single concentration of Louisiana natives of color (see map 2). Thousands of families, like the Knights of Orleans Parish, fled the area in the late 1920s and early 1930s. A sizable number moved to Houston.[62]

Economic need and natural disasters prompted large-scale in-migration to Houston among Louisiana-born Afro-Americans in the 1920s. The year 1927 was especially trying for hundreds of thousands of residents living along the Mississippi River. Much of the southern Mississippi and Louisiana lowlands were flooded after heavy rainstorms flooded the Mississippi River valley. The Great Mississippi Flood of 1927, the worst flood in United States history before Hurricane Katrina, actually began in the

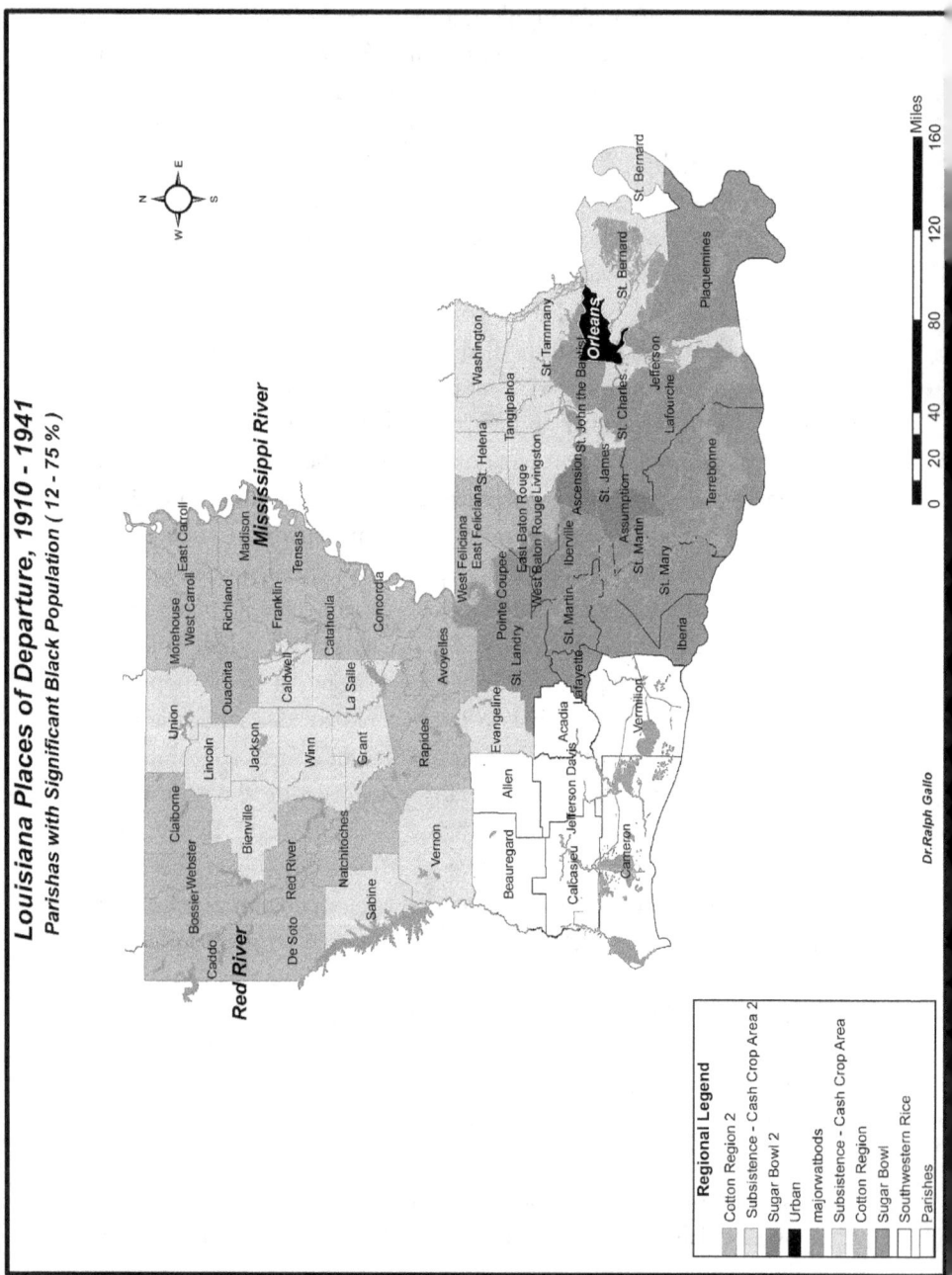

MAP 2. Louisiana Places of Departure, 1900–41: Places with Significant Black Populations (12–75 percent)*

Source: Bureau of Census, *Negro Population in the United States, 1790–1915.* 1918 (reprint. New York: Arno Press, 1969), 140. *(Courtesy Rafael Gallo, urban planner, sociologist, and independent consultant, Houston, Texas)*

summer of 1926 when torrential rains pounded the middle basin of the Mississippi River. By the start of the fall, the river's Iowa and Kansas tributaries had distended to full capacity. The crisis escalated on New Year's Day when the Cumberland River capped Nashville levees at fifty-six feet. The great Mississippi in time burst through its levee system in one hundred and forty-five places, flooding over sixteen million acres of land. Damages reached $400,000,000, and deaths topped 246 in the states of Arkansas, Illinois, Kentucky, Louisiana, Mississippi, and Tennessee.[63]

To stave off a major calamity of Hurricane Katrina proportions, Louisianans decided to dynamite the levee at Caernarvon, Plaquemine Parish. In the end, the act was unnecessary because upstream levee breaks forced water away from the city. The explosion at Caernarvon compounded problems for some of the surrounding communities in the New Orleans vicinity, especially rural places in St. Bernard Parish. The worst, however, was yet to come for the people of southern Louisiana. The Cabin Teele crevasse on the Mississippi, in the end, flooded six million and two hundred thousand acres of land in the state and displaced almost three hundred thousand people. To make matters worse, reports of racial discrimination in Red Cross camps would plague the beleaguered Secretary of Commerce, Herbert Hoover, who headed the relief effort and ignored the accusations of racial injustice. Louisiana African Americans, who lost their homes, land, animals, and total livelihood, felt overwhelmed and frustrated. At least two hundred thousand African American southerners permanently relocated from affected regions in the South, moving mostly to Los Angeles, Chicago, and Detroit. Some tens of thousands moved west to Texas; at least ten thousand made their way to Houston. Louisianans and Texans relied on substantial lines of communication, usually in the form of personal relationships, but also through other means, to aid them in their decision to relocate.[64]

"Unexcelled . . . Opportunities to the Colored Man": Chain Migration

Always, African American families depended on chain migration. Sociologists John and Leatrice MacDonald, as well as historian Earl Lewis, define chain migration as the process by which residents, namely relatives or friends, and former migrants to the city themselves, utilizing their social contacts, introduce potential newcomers to employment options, transportation choices, schools and churches, and afford them initial, temporary housing.[65] This involved multifaceted intertwining elements. Family members often urged their loved ones in letters and during visits to uproot to Houston. In truth, Houston's close proximity to places of origin in Texas and Louisiana usually ensured the latter rather than the former.[66]

Future migrant Luther Stullivan as a boy traveled all the time to the Bayou City to visit loved one Tillie Stullivan of Southern Pacific Railroad. Stullivan's short stints and summer excursions to Houston from rural New Caney, Texas, heightened his love for the southern city. He and his family even lived in Fifth Ward for a year when his father got a job with a construction firm in 1922 or 1923, although they returned to New Caney after that year. Then after his mother's death, he once more came back to the city in 1927 or 1928, after securing a menial job with the Humble Oil Company. Soon afterward, Stullivan sent for his bride. Later, however, he lost his job and returned to the country. Migrants especially sought the assistance of kith and kin for job prospects. Stullivan relocated to Houston a third time in 1934 after securing a stable job with Southern Pacific. A family friend who had been with the railroad for decades recommended the unemployed husband and father for a job.[67]

A number of other factors helped spur migration to the city. Newspapers aided newcomers also as they relocated to Houston. Investigations, feature stories, editorials, and advertisements all influenced migration. Railroad employees, including potential migrants, routinely aided loved ones. Church engagements also introduced Houston to individuals from the countryside. Personal contacts also encouraged farmers to abandon their traditional ways for improved opportunities in Houston. White employers in some instances provided potential migrants with information about job openings.[68]

Often, newspapers bolstered social and political consciousness among country people. The *Houston Informer* especially fostered pride among its readers. Like the *Chicago Defender, New York Age,* and *Pittsburgh Courier, Norfolk Journal and Guide,* the *Houston Informer,* "the South's Greatest Race Newspaper," advocated the "New Negro" ideology of the period.[69] As editor and publisher of the newspaper and later its rival, the *Houston Defender,* Clifton Frederick Richardson Sr. advanced the "New Negro" creed of race pride, intelligent accommodation, economic empowerment, solidarity, and equality. According to some, newspaper editorials and feature stories in the *Informer* about racial violence, voter participation, racial solidarity, and self-help institutions triggered enthusiasm and interest in the city.[70]

FIGURE 6. A fierce defender of Blackness, Clifton Richardson founded his newspaper in May 1919 in response to the tragic Houston Riot of 1917. He created an independent institution that served the city for Houston for nearly a century. Clifton fortunately did not have to rely on outside printers, as he had his own printing press. Civil-rights leader Richardson also served as president of the local branch of the NAACP and president of the Texas Conference of NAACP branches before his sudden death in 1939. At the time of his death, Richardson no longer operated the *Informer and Texas Freeman,* but the *Houston Defender,* which still publishes newspapers each week in Houston. *(Courtesy Houston Metropolitan Research Center, Houston Public Library, Houston, Texas, C. F. Richardson Sr. Papers,* MSS 1457-0003*)*

The son of a working-class couple from Marshall, Texas, Charlie and Bettie Richardson, Clifton F. was born in 1892. He excelled academically and graduated from Bishop College in Marshall, Texas, with a degree in journalism and printing in 1909. The same year he married Ruby Leola Rice, a childhood friend. The next year he and wife Ruby relocated to Dallas, where he worked briefly for the *Dallas Express,* before moving to Houston to take a position with the *Western Star* newspaper in 1911. Several years later, Richardson, along with William N. Nickerson Jr., R. T. Andrews and Campbell A. Gilmore, founded the *Houston Observer,* another fledgling weekly, becoming the newspaper's first managing editor. Eventually he left the paper and founded the *Houston Informer.*[71]

At the time of his death in 1939, the Texan had left a lasting impression on his adopted city. He had founded two successful newspapers that continued to serve the community well into the next century (fig. 6). Along with George Webster, Richardson owned the Webster-Richardson Publishing Company, which printed the *Houston Informer*. Richardson deplored racial exclusion, especially disfranchisement, and regularly shared his thoughts with readers. He also openly denounced racial violence in his newspaper. *Houston Informer* articles immediately following World War I labeled racial violence as "hellish and hunnish."[72] Richardson often mentioned the desire of East Texans to migrate in the wake of racial violence and prejudice: "The colored citizens of Huntsville are all excited and many are anxious to sell out their little belongings and holdings and migrate to more civilized" places like Houston.[73]

Richardson and the *Houston Informer*, along with other journalists and papers, helped endow readers with a sense of racial consciousness. Richardson's public stance against racism stimulated migration among rural and small-town African Americans in eastern Texas. The newspaperman—along with predecessors J. S. Tibbett, Charles Novell Love, and Booker T. Washington's personal secretary, Emmett J. Scott, the founders of the *Texas Freeman,* established in 1893—saw print media as an effective outlet of protest. Subtle, indirect, and often accommodating, these early community papers especially encouraged a spirit of African American autonomy in the larger communities in Houston and throughout the surrounding hinterlands, although Richardson's *Informer* was more direct than indirect. Local editors and publishers also supported in-migrations to the city. African Americans recognized migration as one of the remaining acts of resistance available to them.[74]

Advertisements in the *Houston Informer* about job openings probably became the greatest stimulant for in-migration to Houston. New firms such as the Southern Oil Refining Company advertised in the African American weekly in hopes of securing entry-level workers. Businesses and industries throughout the city, according to the newspaper immediately following World War I, "depended" heavily on African American laborers and encouraged the "exodus" of farmers from the Texas and Louisiana countryside, who sought work on railroads and docks, and in foundries, factories, machine shops, and manufacturing centers.[75]

Civic clubs and business organizations such as the Lincoln League of America and the Chamber of Commerce boosted Houston's appeal for African Americans. Houston, according to these advertisements, offered "unexcelled industrial opportunities to the colored man."[76] Boosters raved about oil and cottonseed companies that employed hundreds of Blacks. Advertisements like these also remarked on Afro-American home ownership, business professionals in the "race" communities, the Carnegie Colored Library, hospitals for African Americans, and Emancipation Park, the first park owned by Blacks, and one of the first recreational parks and playgrounds in the South maintained and operated by the city for Blacks.[77]

In the immediate post–World War I years, the Houston Chamber of Commerce propagated the booster slogan, "Heavenly Houston."[78] For civic-minded African Americans, the slogan and ads highlighted the accomplishments of and opportunities for Houston African Americans. Over the next few decades, many copied the phrase when comparing Houston to other southern cities. While visiting the city in 1930, African American historian Lorenzo Greene remarked to a local Afro-American doctor, "Houston Negroes had the greatest potential for development of any group of Negroes . . . in the South."[79] Houston, according to Jessie O. Thomas, southern field representative for the National Urban League, seemed free of the racial tension that characterized the "average southern community."[80]

Although, in truth, Houston appeared less than "heavenly" to most African Americans living in the city, individuals who saw daily reminders of their inferior status (many, especially businesspersons—Black and White—for economic self-interests) exaggerated the city's alleged congenial race relations.[81] The advertisements, slogans, and studies presented Houston to the world as a subdued community, full of mutual respect between the races and free of superfluous racial strife—excluding the Houston Race Riot of 1917, which did not involve Houston-area African Americans. Such sentiments encouraged African American migration.[82]

In the 1920s and 1930s, the *Houston Informer* also fostered interest for the city among rural subscribers through departments "Passing Parade," "News and Views from Texas Towns," and "The Catholic Circle," cementing bonds between rural and urban life. Stories of race pride, glory, and gossip emphasized church events, high school graduations, banquets, college socials, community events, weather forecasts, deaths, and even divorces. The summer months focused attention on frequent trips to and from Houston. A Miss Lewis returned home to Columbus, Texas, after completing her school year in Houston. Miss Lee of Kendleton in nearby

Fort Bend County and H. Sheldon of Houston had dinner with a friend, Mrs. Ella Brown of Wharton, Texas, a community thirty miles southwest of the city. Miss Diggs of Bellville, Texas, recently returned home for the summer break; before going home, she made a visit to Houston. Three youngsters from Willis, Texas, a small town thirty-five miles north of Houston, returned home to the country after completing another school term in Houston. Although the feature section attempted to bolster respect, dignity, and honor among African Americans in these small Texas communities, the brief write-ups also convinced rural folk that they would not meet resistance and resentment among Afro-American Houston residents. The situation for these internal migrants differed from African American northern migrants, who often experienced a cooler reception from northern residents on their arrival there.[83]

Migrants to northern centers often met persons hostile to the arrival of rural, southern, and often, poorer families. Many of the resident African American families of Chicago, Detroit, Cleveland, Milwaukee, and other places had lived in these communities since the antebellum period. They attended larger middle-class congregations, worked as artisans, sent their children to African American colleges in the North and Upper South, and because of their small numbers, lived for a period in communities where pseudo-congenial relations between the races existed. In their view, the invasion of southern African Americans changed their lives. To them, African American migration strained race relations, encouraged the development of mass ghettoes, and formulated a class divide in the Black community.[84]

Rural migrants to Houston, however, did not witness these occurrences on such a large scale. Resident Afro-Americans—who at one time also migrated to Houston from the country—welcomed their new neighbors. For rural migrants and resident African Americans, Houston became an extension of their abandoned communities. In time, newcomers who regularly visited the country became the new interlocking personal contacts, which linked others to Houston. In many ways, these newspaper stories confirmed to migrants that Houston offered much in the way of opportunity and community solidarity.[85]

Historians have also extensively documented the significance of railroads and railroad workers in the migration episode. Passenger trains frequently stopped throughout the rural southern countryside. Pullman porters and other African Americans employed with railroads regularly conversed with local townspeople about cities. Sometimes, these railroad or Pullman Company personnel relocated to the North from the South. During scheduled stops and personal visits, they discussed the North quite frequently. Potential Houston migrants who worked for railroads as unskilled laborers and porters had the good fortune of living near the urban center. The temporary migrations they used when working off the farm allowed them to see firsthand the benefits offered by the city. Texas railroad employees often visited Houston and found the city attractive and refreshing.[86]

Oran Williams of Roans Prairie in Grimes County worked on the Missouri, Kansas and Texas (MKT or Old Katy) Railroad in the middle and at the end of each cotton season to earn extra money to make ends meet. As a brakeman, he carried out numerous duties: disconnected and connected cars, set couplings, lined switches, performed switching operations, and walked atop rail cars while the train remained in motion in an effort to turn the cars' brake wheels in order to apply the brakes. Being African American, he never received a brakeman's salary.[87] "They didn't pay him a brakeman's wage; they paid him a Black wage. They never would pay a Black and a White man the same thing for the same job. The White got more money for the job than the Black did," says Williams's son Joseph Williams, a retired administrator at Texas Southern University.[88] As a railroader, Oran Williams spent a good deal of time away from the family. Nevertheless, his frequent travels to Houston and employment with the railroad helped him provide for his family. His job also aided him in 1929, when his life was in jeopardy.[89]

A part-time railroad worker, he farmed full-time. Oran Williams dreamed of owning his own land like his father, Moses Williams. Williams, in the early 1920s after marrying Mahala, began farming for an eastern European immigrant, "a White man who would treat him fair."[90] Oran Williams did well as a sharecropper, according to son Joseph Williams: "Because of my grandfather, the man treated him right. . . . He never was in debt . . . he always made money. He didn't just break even . . . he always paid [others] to look after his affairs."[91] Ironically, according to Joseph Williams, this same "fair . . . White man" made a dreadful mistake that almost cost him and Oran Williams their lives.[92] "For several years my father farmed with [for] him and they both made pretty good money until . . . my father got in trouble because this man . . . had a desire for my mother."[93] According to Joseph Williams,

Two things . . . caused us to migrate to leave Roans Prairie and that part of the country. The first one was [that] this Polish White man took a liking to my mother and made it a habit to come around when my father wasn't there. And my father also worked on the railroad while he was sharecropping, so he was really doing better than most of his people. And this man didn't like the fact that my dad was real independent and he kept offering my mother things, and she kept telling my father that he was doing it . . . but she would also tell my father, 'so as long as I can handle it, don't worry about it because you know these ole White people.' Because, she knew daddy wasn't going to take that and she knew that the grandfather and my father might get together and get killed by these White folks. . . . It wasn't healthy for my father to stay there [in Roans Prairie].[94]

One evening in 1929 or 1930, Oran Williams "caught this White man trying to force my mother [to have sex with him]."[95] According to son Joseph Williams,

[My father] came into the house and found him trying to [rape] mother . . . my mother was running from him and fighting. No, my father grabbed him and they had a tremendous fight. . . . [My father] thought he had killed the guy . . . because he wasn't moving. And so that night my father hopped the freight train and told my mother he was going to Houston and when he had got a place for us to stay that he would send for her to come on and the kids. That's how we came to Houston.[96]

His father, Moses Williams, a country preacher, taught his sons to stand up for what they believed in, even respect from Whites. According to grandson Joseph Williams,

He [Moses Williams] demanded his rights . . . He wouldn't let the White people take [his land] . . . Moses Williams carried a six shooter everywhere he went. It was generally known all over Grimes County that he carried his weapon. . . . Moses Williams made it clear that he would die . . . he was perfectly willing to die and kill anybody else he had to in order to maintain what belonged to him. . . . Everybody . . . respected Moses Williams because he demanded it. He wasn't afraid to die or to kill if he had to to protect his family.[97]

Oran took his father's words to heart. He too decided he would kill to protect his wife, Mahala, in 1929 or 1930. He fled his home in Roans Prairie to avert a potential lynching. Regrettably, he had to deal with accusations. Williams's accusers now charged him with attempted murder and theft. "They wanted to get him back there some kind of way," says Joseph Williams.[98] The case eventually went away, he adds. "My father hired a lawyer," who successfully got the charges dismissed.[99] According to Joseph Williams, "My father was told never to come back to Grimes County."[100] Both Williams's attorney and familiarity with railroads saved his life.[101]

Railroads and railroad personnel provided farm families with information about cities. Farmers like Williams and St. Martinsville, Louisiana, migrant Charles Lewis temporarily worked on railroads for extra wages and used trains for their trek across the rural South. People like Oran Williams could safely hide on freight trains to avoid identification, because of the short distance between Houston and Grimes County. When Oran's wife, Mahala, and their five children departed Roans Prairie some sixteen months later, they experienced a safe, short, and cheap train trip. Therefore, the close proximity between Houston and migrant homes—whether in eastern Texas or Louisiana—assured an easy transportation for people traveling alone or with large families. Families looked forward to special occasions, holidays, and church affairs, which allowed for regular reunions with loved ones because of the short distances traveled. Migrant families had long experienced the frustration of temporary separation because sharecroppers, like Williams and Lewis, often worked off the farm for short periods to earn extra money.[102]

Sometimes, newcomers who relied on chain migration networks to ease their transition to city life, later returned the favor by aiding both recent in-migrants and established residents. A mature Luther Stullivan, as a union organizer in the 1930s and 1940s—along with Texas migrant Judson Robinson Sr.—recruited young railroaders for the Congress of Industrial Organizations (CIO).[103]

Fourteen years after his father's controversial 1920 lynching, a determined Lee Coleman of Drew's Landing in Trinity County, Texas, relocated to Houston, settling temporarily in the Third Ward with a cousin, Richard Coleman. Years later, as a Dixon Gun Plant employee, he would invest in rental property. He wanted to provide poor newcomers with affordable and decent housing. Years later, Oran Williams bought a home for his family, also in the Third Ward, and formed a small moving and hauling business for incoming migrants.[104]

As newcomer families trekked to the city to escape ongoing economic contraction or racial discrimination, they commonly traveled separately, not together, with the husband and father relocating first. Most migrants came to the city with little or no money. They scraped by, riding freight trains as hobos, utilizing stepwise movements to earn money to pay for their traveling and settlement expenses, and of course seeking the assistance of loved ones already in the city. The typical movement of men and older adolescents illustrates the significance of binary migratory patterns to Bayou City communities. In each of the above instances, Luther Stullivan, Lee Coleman, and Oran Williams left their wives behind, found work, saved money, and later sent for their families.[105]

This binary movement of African American internal migrants particularly highlights the role of wives, mothers, and older teen girls in the Great Migration melodrama. Women back home in New Caney, Shreveport, Roans Prairie, and other locales near Houston kept the family fires burning by tending to the needs of young children, caring for crops, working odd jobs when available and when time permitted, taking up the slack for exhausted mothers by cooking, washing dishes, sweeping, and feeding smaller children. Interestingly, single mothers generally made the trip to Houston with children. This required sufficient skills in duty delegation, multitasking, and patience.[106]

Jazz musician Milton Larkin of Navasota in Grimes County, a child at the time of his mother's (Ella Larkin) journey to Houston in the 1910s, remembered his older siblings discussing his mother's strong will, tenacity, and even temperament. Crying infants, noisy and playful toddlers, mischievous preschoolers, and rambunctious older children did not always behave in the way mothers wanted them to. Sometimes irate conductors, in an act of frustration and racism, asked families to leave the train at the next stop. Others occasionally threw mothers and children off trains. Even when mothers themselves practiced stepwise migrations with children, relying on the hospitality of kind friends, neighbors, and relatives, the actions of children could generate flare-ups and ill feelings. Occasionally women and men left their children with parents, grandparents, or other extended family members, sending for them once they settled into their new homes. Houston's relatively close proximity to many surrounding Texas and Louisiana communities did in fact help this process along, whereas interregional movements sometimes slowed the pace of family migration.[107]

Occasionally, if not frequently, African American women left the countryside to escape regular bouts of physical and sexual abuse. Harris County Social Service Client Files illustrate the real problem of abuse women suffered at the hands of disillusioned and angry spouses or partners. Sometimes, abuse followed migrants as they made their way to the city. At other times, migrants used out-migration as a weapon against the perpetual cycle of domestic violence. Ethel and George Taylor moved to the Houston area before the start of the Great Depression. George, who attended college for a year, worked briefly as an assistant for a Baytown laboratory until he was laid off. Handsome, charming, and intelligent, George easily enticed and manipulated vulnerable women. Taylor also used his fists to inflict pain and suffering. When wife, Ethel, disagreed with her husband's actions, she faced regular beatings. At some point, Ethel returned to southern Louisiana, probably to escape periods of abuse in the home, which escalated in the erratic 1930s. Ultimately, Ethel, depressed, ill, and out of money, died on an operating table in Jeanerette, Louisiana.[108]

George later married a second woman, Ida Lee. The second wife found out about his abusive tendencies too late; in a fit of rage and anger in 1942, George murdered her. A judge sentenced Taylor to twenty years for the murder. Migration networks usually aided women like Ethel and Ida Lee Taylor as they made their way to the city to sustain a decent livelihood for themselves and their families, although in these two instances, they failed. Despite these realities, in general, chain migration served an important purpose in the lives of newcomers settling in Houston.[109]

An important chain migration network that facilitated migration streams to the city, settlement in temporary homes, school enrollment for children, and job placement, rural-to-urban visits or fellowships perhaps influenced movement more so than anything else did. Houston, unlike Detroit, Chicago, Gary, Milwaukee, Pittsburgh, Philadelphia, Boston, and New York, lacked a local National Urban League office to help facilitate the migration and settlement transition for newcomers. Nor did Houston-area businesses pay labor agents to travel into nearby communities to seek unskilled labor. Advertisements in the *Houston Observer, Houston Informer, Houston Defender,* and *Houston Chronicle* did attract the attention of would-be movers.[110]

Largely, African Americans relied on their weekly, seasonal, or annual visits to the city for temporary employment, church engagements, amusements, family gatherings, graduations, weddings, funerals, parties, concerts, and reunions. Regular visits to and from the countryside on foot, by way of train (even freight train), and occasionally by car provided loved ones with routine, inexpensive links to the big city. City life and culture, music and the arts, schoolwork, community outreach, and church life were often the topics of discussion for individuals entertaining guests or visiting Houston from surrounding small-town and rural communities. Possibly poorer than those friends, family members, church members, and neighbors who left the South permanently, potential migrants to Houston settled on the available bonds that had facilitated relations between kin and kith since the end of slavery.[111]

Individual family histories illustrate as well the inner workings of chain migration. Landowner, schoolteacher, husband, father, and church member Calvin L. Rhone of Fayette County served many years as the La Grange delegate of the Texas Baptist State Sunday School Convention (TBSSSC) an affiliate of the National Baptist Convention. An organization that fostered religious doctrine, cultural pride, self-determination and identity, leadership skills, spiritual growth, and intellectual fervor among Sunday School superintendents and teachers within the Baptist denomination, the TBSSSC regularly convened in Houston. Here, Rhone cultivated long-lasting friendships, including a close relationship with TBSSSC regional secretary W. L. Davis, a longtime friend from his hometown of La Grange and future founder of the National Association for the Advancement of Colored People (NAACP), Houston branch.[112]

Although Calvin Rhone and his wife of over thirty years, Lucia, loved the country life on their three-hundred-acre farm in Fayette County, several of their children—Benjamin, Beulah, and Calvin Jr.—relied on their parents' friendships with Davis and others when they moved away from home, entered college, relocated to nearby Houston, married, and had children. The Rhone offspring later used their own friendships and personal connections at Prairie View and Wiley Colleges, within the International Longshoremen's Association (ILA), school districts where they taught, and in their many affiliations, and continued the cultivation of these relationships through their lifetime. As they bought homes, joined churches, entered their perspective careers, and had families, they aided others. They also extended the chain and offered invaluable assistance to later newcomers—nieces, nephews, godchildren, family friends, and the offspring of former students and classmates—as they relocated to Houston from the country to finish school, find jobs, and escape the degradation of humiliation and despair in Fayette County or other small cotton-based communities throughout eastern Texas.[113]

Conclusion

The First Great Migration from 1900 to 1930 brought tens of thousands of African Americans into the city. Blacks fled discrimination and poverty while formulating new strategies of autonomy. People of color relied on the self-help strategy that helped their ancestors overcome slavery and post-Emancipation violence and abuse: community agency. By way of chain migration, newcomers utilized community agency in an effort to locate homes, jobs, schools, organizations, institutions, and resources. In this sense, immigration and chain migration networks reminded newcomers and established residents alike of the ordeals, prayers, and aspirations that kept their families intact, despite the reality of racial hatred and poverty. The migration saga in many ways bridged the gap between the old world of agricultural slavery and the new century of permanent manufacturing work. Since Emancipation, former slaves and their children relocated to Houston for a fresh new start, finding ways to ward off recurring acts of racial bigotry and rural depravation. In this sense, the Great Migration paved the way for later developments in Houston and elsewhere, particularly the modern Civil Rights Movement. By opening the door for modern-day civil rights, the Great Migration reminded older and newer generations that unfulfilled dreams could in fact find new beginnings, even in the midst of Jim Crow bigotry.[114]

For this reason, the story of internal migration to Houston and other southern cities is essential to understanding the totality of the Great African American Migrations of the twentieth century. Black migration to Houston clearly challenges the prevailing theme in African American urban history that exclusively defines the Great Migrations as a southern exodus. To the contrary, the intrastate and regional interstate migratory patterns to Houston provide evidence that greater movements occurred within the South, the birthplace of the modern Civil Rights Movement. Established residents and newcomers alike forged relationships early on that helped usher in new periods of change. Even the small gesture of finding homes and settling into Houston neighborhoods speaks to the desires and hopes of newcomers and established Houston residents.[115]

FIGURE 7. Joshua Houston Sr. (second row, third from the right) moved to Texas from Alabama when President of the Republic of Texas Sam Houston married Margaret M. Lea of Marion, Alabama, the young slave's mistress, in 1840. For the next two decades, the literate blacksmith, wheelwright, and coachman served the diplomat faithfully. Sam Houston emancipated Houston and his other slaves in January 1863, right before his death. Joshua Houston, a Reconstruction politician, landholder, businessperson, artisan, and institution builder, raised, with the help of each of his three spouses, eight children. Blacksmith Joshua Houston Jr. was born in 1856 (second row, second from the left), married Georgia C. Orviss (second row, third from the left), and they began their life together as man and wife, first in Huntsville, Texas, and later in Houston, moving to the city in 1918. The couple had three daughters. Interestingly, Joshua's and Georgia's siblings, educator Samuel Walker Houston (second row, far right) and Cornelia Orviss, later married, although, regrettably, Cornelia died in childbirth during the birth of the couple's second child, a girl who also died. Samuel Walker Houston did not raise his firstborn, Harold Houston, who was born in 1902. Harold's grandparents and aunts reared the boy. Georgia and Cornelia's father, Rev. George Orviss, was pastor of [the Black] First Baptist Church. A native of Virginia, the biracial minister married the girls' mother, Mary Orviss, another multiethnic/multiracial person of color and of French origin. He married both couples. *(Courtesy Houston Metropolitan Research Center, Houston Public Library, Houston, Texas, Joshua Houston Family Collection, MSS 0437-0006)*

TWO

~

Building a City

Migrant Settlements in Houston, 1900–1941

Unlike most Texas African Americans, Georgia Orviss and Joshua Houston Jr. grew up in prominent Huntsville families, far removed from the mudsills of East Texas poverty. Georgia Orviss, the multiracial daughter of a prominent biracial Virginia minister and a mixed-race mother—Rev. George B. and Mary Orviss—graduated from Mary Allen Seminary in Crockett, Texas, in the 1890s, ultimately becoming an educator. Joshua Houston's father was a civic leader and business owner, Joshua Houston Sr. Once the literate slave of the legendary Sam Houston, he took his former master's name following Emancipation and became the leading spokesperson for people of color in his community. He especially tailored his talks and ambitions toward young people, briefly opening Bishop Ward College for students. His offspring, not surprisingly, soared. Youngest son, Samuel Walker Houston, founded the community's first African American high school, the Houstonian Normal Institute (later the Samuel Houston Industrial and Training School) in 1906. Joshua Houston Jr. also attended school for a period, enrolling in industrial education classes at Prairie View State and Industrial College (now Prairie View A&M University) and eventually opening his own blacksmithing shop (fig. 7).[1]

Initially, Joshua and Georgia Houston welcomed the idea of raising their daughters—Constance and Hortense—in Huntsville. Huntsville, in their estimation, seemed like a good place to bring up children—even African American children (fig. 8). Racism, according to the Houstons, would not stand in the way of their daughters' success. Early on, they attempted to shield Constance and Hortense from racial bigotry. As the girls got older, the Houstons taught them to ignore taunts and racial epithets. Their parents educated them on the quiet but effective ways to resist bigotry. For example, civil rights and women's rights supporter Georgia Houston, who also did beauty consulting in the White community, refrained from using her full name in the presence of Whites; she insisted that her White clients call her G. A. Houston instead. The Houstons wanted their daughters to know they had choices.[2]

Although Whites regularly demeaned children of color, the African American community always reinforced its loving role in the lives of the Houston girls. Strong familial bonds, their faith, and schooling, according to historian Naomi Ledé, afforded daughters Constance and Hortense Houston positive role models, confidence, and vision. Both girls attended their "Uncle Sam ['s]" high school, where they took domestic science classes as well as liberal arts courses. The Houstons also exposed their daughters to operas, classical music, and off-Broadway productions. Constance and Hortense Houston's world differed from that of their peers in Huntsville and East Texas—both Black and White.[3]

The family's successes and directives, nevertheless, obscured the pressures placed on middle-class African Americans to both prosper and remain

FIGURE 8. Although a blacksmith by training, Joshua Houston Jr., like many rural professionals, still farmed. Their home, on Avenue N and 13th Street, was located near downtown. Joshua and Georgia, a Huntsville schoolteacher and hairstylist, had three children. Constance Eloise Houston (Thompson), standing on the far right, was born in 1899; Maxine Elliot, born in 1902; and Hortense Cordelia, 1903. Only Constance and Hortense (standing next to father) survived infancy. Maxine died of cholera six months following her birth. Joshua's wife Georgia stands in the background on the right side of the front porch. *(Courtesy Houston Metropolitan Research Center, Houston Public Library, Houston, Texas, Joshua Houston Family Collection, MSS 0437-0012)*

FIGURE 9. Even with a prosperous blacksmith shop (perhaps his father's), Joshua Houston Jr. made the decision to relocate the family to Houston during World War I. Several factors explain this decision, including growing racial tensions during Red Summer of the immediate postwar period, an unstable economy in semirural/semi-urban Huntsville, and the recent lynching deaths of an entire African American family in the rural community of Dodge in eastern Walker County. He began investing in what became The Houston Place in 1913. According to historian Naomi Ledé, Joshua Houston Jr. spent a good amount of time renovating his new home on 1303 Bayou Street in Fifth Ward. The family moved into the home in 1918, while Hortense was still attending high school. Following Joshua's death in 1928, the family completed the renovations, ultimately making it a bed and breakfast inn for out-of-town guests and Houston locals giving formal affairs. Dignitaries and celebrities such as actor Ethel Walters, jazz great Lionel Hampton, soloist Ella Fitzgerald, Tuskegee Institute President Robert R. Moton, and the insatiable Mills Brothers often stayed at the Cape Cod-fashioned cottage while visiting the city. *(Courtesy Houston Metropolitan Research Center, Houston Public Library, Houston, Texas, Joshua Houston Family Collection, MSS 0437-0015)*

subservient to Whites.[4] The Houstons also worried about racial violence. "We moved to Houston because our mother became concerned—very concerned—after they took a man from the prison in Huntsville and lynched him."[5] The Houstons, frustrated with the town's limitations and dangers, moved to Houston in 1918.[6]

Thinking of their daughters' well-being, Joshua and Georgia Houston moved into a one-story home on Bayou Street in Fifth Ward (fig. 9). The Houstons prospered in Houston. Joshua opened his blacksmith shop on Lyons Avenue, the heart and soul of the Fifth Ward African American business district. Georgia Houston, a lifelong fraternal order member, taught school in Fifth Ward for four decades. Financially stable, Georgia Orvis

FIGURE 10. For over a century, schoolteachers have taken continuing education classes to strengthen their skills and knowledge for the upcoming academic year, to study new subjects of interest, and attempt to earn their degrees and certifications. Prairie View College (currently Prairie View A&M University) offered classes each summer for the state's black teachers. Prairie View, the home of the Colored Teachers Association of Texas (CTAT), which was formed in 1884 by L. C. Anderson, the school's first principal, along with twelve others, occupied a special place in the hearts of African American educators. The only public university for the state's African Americans, the institution, in conjunction with the CTSAT, felt a special obligation to provide the best educational facilities for African Americans. Prairie View College in 1924 also awarded its first baccalaureate degrees to students. Black colleges also slowly moved further from the Tuskegee model of college training, which emphasized industrial education over the liberal arts. In the 1920s, nevertheless, vocational training remained an important staple in the continuing education curriculum. Georgia Houston, her daughters, and other Texas educators of African descent earned 30 to 50 percent less in pay than their white counterparts and worked amid substandard conditions and overcrowding. They accepted their conditions, at the time, but ultimately acted in their interests and the interests of their students. Georgia Houston's class studied industrial and vocational training at Prairie View this summer. Houston, who earned her certification from Mary Allen Seminary in Crockett, Texas, taught school for over forty years. *(Courtesy Houston Metropolitan Research Center, Houston Public Library, Houston, Texas, Joshua Houston Family Collection, MSS 0437-0014)*

Houston, who relied on a domestic to upkeep the household, made provisions for her daughters' future (fig. 10). The girls took music and ballet lessons. The Houstons also put the girls in charm school, affording them the best lifestyle their money could obtain. In addition, the daughters received a quality liberal arts education that prompted their entry into teaching and civic work.[7]

Joshua and Georgia Houston's youngest daughter, Hortense Houston, entered Booker T. Washington High School as a student in the fall of

1918.[8] Founded in 1893, Booker T. Washington High (formerly Colored High School) offered its student body classes in industrial training and domestic science, applied mathematics and science, and the liberal arts, including Greek and Latin. After high school, Hortense enrolled in Fisk University in Nashville, Tennessee, graduating in the mid-1920s with an

FIGURE 11. Hortense Houston, the younger of the Houston daughters born in Huntsville around the turn of the century, taught English at Jack Yates High School. She left Houston in 1927 to marry Milton Young Jr., a first-generation physician from Nashville. The Youngs relocated to Louisville, Kentucky, where he established his practice. In 1936, he became the school physician for the Louisville Municipal College; two years later, he became director of the Louisville Medical Center. A graduate of Meharry Medical College in Nashville, he also earned a Master's Degree in Public Health from the University of Minnesota. Hortense also furthered her education, earning a second bachelor's degree in library science from the University of Illinois, and studying at the Louis Brandeis School of Law at the University of Louisville, becoming the first African American woman to enter the school. She spent the next two decades as a librarian and journalist. Her columns in African American newspapers discussed race relations, civil rights, public health, poverty, and educational disparities among Blacks. The Youngs had two children. Milton Young III also went into medicine, graduating from Meharry and practicing in Louisville. In 1950 or 1951, their oldest, Yvonne Young (Clark), became the first woman at Howard University and possibly the first Black woman in the country to earn a degree in mechanical engineering, and the first woman to earn a graduate degree in engineering management at Vanderbilt in 1972. For five decades, she has taught at Tennessee State University, where she is associate professor of mechanical engineering. She eventually married scientist William F. Clark, Jr., a Meharry Medical College instructor. She is one of eleven women scientists who constructed a storage box for Apollo 11's historic mission. The box allowed the astronauts to transport rocks from the moon's surface. *(Courtesy Houston Metropolitan Research Center, Houston Public Library, Houston, Texas, Joshua Houston Family Collection, MSS 0437-0019)*

English degree. After briefly teaching at the newly built Jack Yates Senior High School, Hortense married C. Milton Young Jr., a first-generation medical doctor from Nashville, Tennessee (fig. 11).[9]

The couple moved to Louisville, Kentucky, where Young established a practice. Both eventually did graduate work at the University of Illinois and had two children—physician C. Milton Young III and mechanical engineer Yvonne Young Clark. Hortense Young was the first African American woman to attend the Louis Brandeis Law School at the University of Louisville in the 1950s. Like her older sister, she supported public housing, election rights, desegregation efforts, and financial security for people of color in Louisville, from the 1930s until her death in 1977.[10]

Eldest daughter Constance Houston entered Prairie View College in 1918 and earned her high school diploma and bachelor's degree in home economics in the early 1920s. For the next twenty years, she taught at Booker T. Washington High School, her sister's alma mater. She obtained a master's degree and later chaired the Department of Home Economics at Texas State University for Negroes (TSUN). A devoted Constance Houston also fell in love (fig. 12), and the schoolteacher soon married tall, handsome, and dark hotel waiter Tracy Thompson (fig. 13). The clubwoman and Young Women Christian Association (YWCA) member also found time for social causes. As a member of the National Council of Negro Women (NCNW), an organization founded in 1935 by Mary McLeod Bethune, Thompson worked with other clubwomen to bring attention to African American slums (fig. 14). Eventually, her efforts propelled the construction of some of the city's and country's first federal housing projects for the poor. Undoubtedly, the underpinnings set in motion in Huntsville and Houston laid the foundation for later success. The Houstons' move to Fifth Ward not only benefited their immediate family but also ultimately helped numerous people, from descendants and extended family to friends, acquaintances, students, and clients.[11]

This chapter examines the settlement patterns of newcomers who relocated to the greater Houston area and explores how migrants like the Houston family created for themselves and others communities of racial independence and interdependence. African American migrants relied on a number of self-help approaches that aided them as they moved into Houston neighborhoods and built new lives. Some moved as singles; others relocated to the city to complete school. Many entered the city limits as

FIGURE 12. The vivacious, charismatic Constance Houston fell in love with Tracy Thompson, a hotel waiter at the Houston Club downtown. The bride and groom, however, came from completely different backgrounds. In contrast to Constance's posh upbringing, Tracy's father sold insurance and gambled; his mother worked as a domestic. The couple, amazingly, put their son through school. Tracy graduated from Houston College for Negroes with a degree in psychology. He also worked as a waiter. Ultimately, he took a full-time position as a waiter, eventually becoming a maître d'hôtel at the Houston Place. He did very well for himself, even traveling across the country to work for special functions. According to Ledé, he served Queen Elizabeth before retiring in the 1980s. The two had their wedding ceremony at Antioch Baptist Church, but took wedding photos at The Houston Place, in October 1928—a bittersweet time for the Houstons, as Joshua Houston Jr. had only died six months earlier from complications due to two strokes. According to historian Naomi Ledé, Constance Houston Thompson's biographer, Georgia Houston did not attend her daughter's wedding. Georgia, gravely ill, did not attend the wedding. In truth, says Ledé, Georgia Houston had not yet come to terms with her husband's death. *(Courtesy Houston Metropolitan Research Center, Houston Public Library, Houston, Texas, Joshua Houston Family Collection, MSS 0437-0020)*

family units, and others built new communities and formed organizations and businesses that benefitted many. Extended family households nurtured these relationships and provided support to newcomers. Black internal migrants of the twentieth century, however, did not move into barren wastelands. To the contrary, most of the migrants moved into neighborhoods formed decades earlier as freedpeople communities of interdependence. Therefore, internal migrants relied heavily on the aid and protection of established residents who had moved to the city in the nineteenth century following slavery.[12]

Prior to America's entry into World War II, African American migrants settled Houston neighborhoods at four distinct periods. Although migrants lived throughout the city, they tended to settle into neighborhoods that surrounded the downtown business district. They usually used the migratory patterns of previous migrants who had made their way from the surrounding interior into the city as freedpeople after the Civil War.

FIGURE 13. After the wedding, the Thompson wedding party took photographs at The Houston Place. The wedding party included "Uncle Sam" Walker Houston (fourth from the right), Hortense Young, the matron of honor (fifth from the right), Constance and Tracy Thompson (center), and best man and physician DeWitt Farris Barclay (fifth from the left). Others in attendance as members of the wedding party or guests include Lucille Breeler, Roby Bedford, Carolyn DeWalt (wife of Lincoln Theater owner and NAACP President O. P. DeWalt), Alice Sheeley, Florence Phelps, Ruby Lucas, Blanch Dogan (the daughter of Wiley College President Matthew Dogan), future Dillard University President Albert Dent, attorney and future *Houston Informer* owner Carter W. Wesley, Richard Ward, and Leon Peacock. Due to Georgia Houston's illness, the Thompsons decided to cancel their reception. *(Courtesy Houston Metropolitan Research Center, Houston Public Library, Houston, Texas, Joshua Houston Family Collection, MSS 0437-0022)*

FIGURE 14. Constance Houston Thompson, on the next to last row on the right side of the photograph, has her face turned to the left, perhaps failing to return to her original pose in time for the shot. Mary McLeod Bethune (front row, eighth from the left) founded the organization in 1935 after stepping down as head of the National Association of Colored Women. Her aggressive determination impressed many philanthropists who donated hundreds of thousands of dollars to her private school for girls in Daytona Beach, Florida (today Bethune-Cookman University). The NCNW served multiple functions as a clubwoman's organization and civil-rights leader. It reminded women of the double burden of being Black and female. Serving as an umbrella organization to twenty-eight groups that sought answers to the multifaceted problems facing African American women, families, and children, the group formed at a time when problems seemed insurmountable. She also served as an advisor to Presidents Calvin Coolidge, Herbert Hoover, and Franklin D. Roosevelt. The Roosevelt Administration formed the Federal Council of Negro Affairs—dubbed the Black Cabinet and Black Brains Trust—an advisory group of forty-five New Deal officials who concentrated their efforts on the special circumstances of African Americans. She served as the unofficial head of the organization, mainly because of her close relationship with Eleanor Roosevelt. Bethune also served as director of the National Youth Administration's African American division. Like Bethune, Constance Houston Thompson (and sister Hortense Houston Young) made it a priority to cater to the needs of her poor students at Booker T. Washington, finding ways for them to continue their education after high school. She also partnered with local groups to improve housing overcrowding and substandard conditions in Houston. One group, the Citizens Committee on Slum Clearance, was headed by White activist Octavia Gunnel. Both groups proved that White and Black women could work together for the common good of all Houstonians. *(Courtesy Houston Metropolitan Research Center, Houston Public Library, Houston, Texas, Joshua Houston Family Collection, MSS 0437-0001)*

Newcomers also followed the advice of temporary migrants who moved to Houston from the farm, for seasonal work. The first migrants of the new century—those individuals relocating to the city around the turn of the century through the start of World War I—moved to each of the city's wards, but they predominated in the Third, Fourth, and Fifth Wards, the communities with the heaviest concentration of African American migrants in the new century (see map 3).[13]

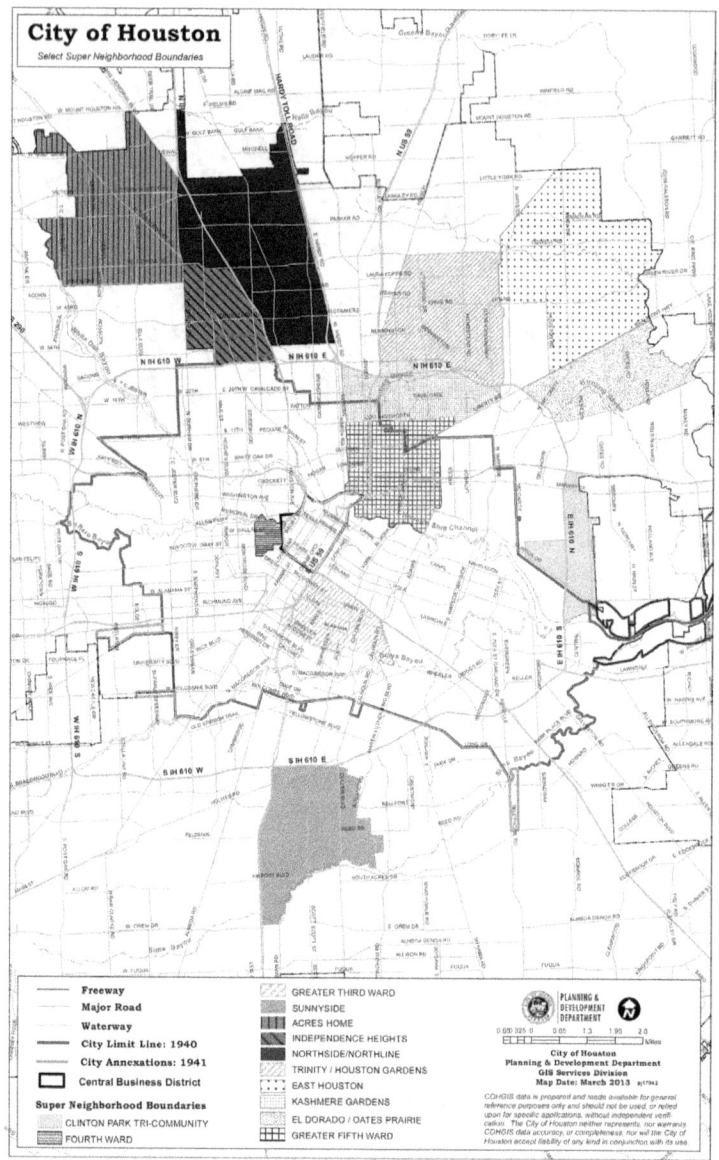

MAP 3. Points of Entry for Houston Newcomers, 1940*
Sources: Bureau of Census. *Sixteenth Census of the United States: 1940. Population: V. 2 Characteristics of the Population. Part 6: Pennsylvania-Texas* (Washington, DC: United States Government Printing Office, 1943), 965, 1045, 1094; Bureau of Census. *1950 United States Census of Population. Houston, Texas: Census Tracts* (Washington, DC: United States Government Printing Office, 1953), 5–13, 50–51; Larry Nierth, City of Houston Planning and Development Department, GIS Services Division, Super Neighborhood Map of Houston, Texas, 2011. *(Courtesy Larry T. Nierth, GIS Supervisor, and Sona Sunny, GIS Services Division, Planning and Development Department, City of Houston, Houston, Texas)*
*The Super Neighborhood boundaries differ substantially from the ward and community boundaries for 1940. This map still provides researchers with useful data regarding the neighborhoods internal migrants settled in the early twentieth century.

With the coming of World War I in 1914, in-migrants increasingly made their way into Fifth Ward, which sat near the industrial corridor along the newly built ship channel, and Third Ward, which surrounded newer affluent neighborhoods along the western edge of the city limits. Newcomers also built homes in outlying areas on the edges of the city or in Harris County. More often than not, these migrants relocated to undeveloped outlying areas, purchased affordable land, and built inexpensive homes in such places as Independence Heights and Acres Homes in Northwest Houston. Others built homes in the new community of Sunnyside along the city's southeastern border.[14]

The interwar period from 1918 to the 1930s increasingly put the spotlight on Third Ward, the new location for the city's African American elite. College-educated Texans as well as ordinary citizens found better-paid work and opened businesses that catered to the city's growing Afro-American population. Many moved into Fifth Ward as well for steady employment and business connections. Migrants from Louisiana, survivors of the Great Flood of 1927, particularly found the ward attractive and affordable. Even as internal migration slowed during the Great Depression, people continued to enter the city from nearby places within the state and elsewhere, especially Louisiana.[15]

The story of migratory settlement into Houston deserves attention for several reasons. Unlike the settlement experiences of internal migrants who headed to Chicago, Detroit, Gary, Milwaukee, and the San Francisco Bay region, newcomers to Houston rarely faced isolation and resentment from established residents. Like recent migrants, older, established residents in the city had ties to the surrounding countryside and therefore welcomed newcomers into their neighborhoods. Blacks, since Emancipation, had long considered Houston a promised land. Even for the newcomers who formed new communities, the Houston area provided them with incentive and hope. Their new or expanded locales also offered a new model for interpreting migrant ambitions. Racism hardly deterred their actions. The close-knit Houston communities of established residents and migrants made good use of their segregated surroundings that propelled autonomous respect and mutual concern. Of course, socioeconomic, ethnic, and religious distinctions existed in Houston as they had in places outside the South. In fact, these demarcations became even more apparent as the African American community increased due to the Great Migration, although in the segregated southern city these distinctions may not appear as obvious.[16]

As migrants made their way into the city, racial segregation increasingly defined residences, racial groups, and city responses to residential needs. Ironically, racial segregation made it possible for African Americans to forge interdependent relationships that challenged the pitfalls of injustice. Blacks lived away from Whites and felt freer to express themselves and their discontent with the racism they encountered. Migrants and established residents also began to foster relationships that would eventually evolve into lasting friendships and community coalitions that effectively challenged White supremacy. Thus, upon their relocation to Houston, migrants learned how the city functioned as a safe haven against bigotry. Although this happened across the country, the southern city remained a place of segregationist oppression. Yet, it provided people with ripe tools to formulate strategies of discontent and disloyalty. Blacks found that the neighborhoods they moved into held the same social and cultural constructs that aided them in the country, thus making it possible to both resist and placate racism.[17]

The city's rising African American population definitely prompted socioeconomic class lines of demarcation among people of color. Increasingly, class defined streets within neighborhoods and households. In some instances, the wealthier classes could rely on these sharp divisions to appropriate fairer treatment from the White masses, especially those groups of comparable means and with similar interests. Still, people of all classes understood their uniqueness as African peoples, especially during the period of increased racial segregation and prejudice. This fact made Houston neighborhoods even more inviting.[18]

Oddly enough, by the interwar period fewer people settled Fourth Ward neighborhoods, once a haven for freedpeople of color after the Civil War. Fourth Ward had initially served as the home to the early African American elite of the nineteenth century. However, by World War I, downtown Houston's westward expansion, as well as the construction of modest homes and middle-class enclaves in or around Fifth and Third Wards, overshadowed the city's initial elite community for freedpeople of color.[19]

Settlement

The Fourth Ward, although not the city's primary commune for African Americans following Emancipation, did in fact hold some of the city's first institutions even before the start of the Civil War. Named aptly for slavery's demise and the spirit of liberation, Freedmantown inside the Fourth Ward, just north of San Felipe Road and west of downtown, especially appealed to newcomers and freedpeople of Houston alike. Freedmen's Bureau schools, religious institutions, benevolent societies, Afro-American–occupied and owned–homes, political institutions, and a joyous excitement of life and liberty attracted newcomers. Situated southwest of Houston's downtown business and commercial district and on the southernmost bank of Buffalo Bayou, Freedmantown continued south to Congress Avenue and west to Main Street. It comprised most of current downtown Houston west of Main, along with neighborhoods on San Felipe (today West Dallas) and Gray Streets, areas that are still almost entirely Black and poor.[20]

Although developed in 1839 as a political district for local council members, the Fourth Ward, after the collapse of slavery, emerged as a center of hope, development, fresh starts, and racial autonomy for freedmen and freedwomen. Former slaves found themselves gravitating to the ward not because of any one attractive measure, but rather because of its close proximity to the Brazos River. Former slaves from the Brazos River Valley plantation communities hiked to Houston on foot, often taking Old San Felipe Road, which ran right into the Brazos River. Others lived east of the city near or in Galveston and Brazoria Counties and along the coast.[21]

A sizable number of those who made Fourth Ward their home purchased homes and made good use of their growing incomes as laboring Americans. Urban historian Cary D. Wintz reiterates this point. Although overcrowding, abject poverty, periods of underemployment, and occasional family pathology often shaped the lifestyles of African Americans in the Bayou City, a good number continued to excel. The number of homeowners grew from 5 percent in 1870 to 12 percent in 1900. The same holds true for a steady rise in business owners and professionals, who increased from 1.4 percent to 9 percent. At the same time, the percentage of men in bottom-rung positions declined from 74 percent to 68 percent, and the percentage of Afro-American women working outside the household even dropped from 78 percent to 64 percent. Ironically, the percentage of skilled artisans dropped from 11 percent to 6 percent for the same period.[22]

Fourth Ward's Black population increased from 1,314 in 1870 to 9,397 in 1920 and then 15,440 in 1940. However, only 12 percent of those Harris County public assistance clients sampled for this study migrated and settled into Fourth Ward. On the other hand, those Fourth Ward residents surveyed from the 1920 manuscript census made up 29.36 percent of the

FIGURE 15. Martha Emma Masterson Sneed and husband Glenn O. Sneed left Galveston in 1909. Fearing another hurricane, the entire family relocated to the Fourth Ward in Houston. A native of Brazoria County, Martha had always known of the dangers of hurricanes. The Galveston Storm of 1900, however, convinced the family to find a home in higher surroundings. Their small children certainly agreed. While living in Houston, Mrs. Sneed helped organize and served on several agencies, from the YWCA to the Married Women's Social, Art & Charity Club. She also worked with social service agencies to help improve the quality of life for Blacks. She died in 1958, but not before seeing her children grow up into community builders themselves, individuals who patterned their actions after their inspiring mother. Martha and Glenn's oldest child, daughter Naomi Bessie Sneed, died during a tonsillectomy at a Houston hospital in 1921. She was seventeen years old. *(Courtesy Houston Metropolitan Research Center, Houston Public Library, Houston, Texas, Sneed Family Collection, MSS 0293-0001)*

total persons used in this study. Still, for years the ward attracted varying segments of the Black community, from the well-to-do to the poor. Clifton F. and Ruby Richardson, for example, lived on Robin Street, located near Antioch Baptist Church.[23]

Another middle-class migrant couple, bartender Glenn Owen Sneed of Travis County and seamstress Martha Emma Sneed, eventually made their way to Fourth Ward (fig. 15). The Sneed family, fearful of experiencing a second hurricane disaster, fled Galveston for Houston right before World War I. The couple and their children first moved to George Street near Fifth Ward and finally settled at 129 W. Gray in Fourth Ward. They had four children, two of whom were born in Houston following their migration from Galveston. The Sneeds soon became a prominent Houston family that served the Black community of Houston in a variety of ways. The family attended Antioch Missionary Baptist Church, also in Fourth Ward. Mrs. Sneed, a native of Brazoria County, served as a member of the Married Ladies Social, Art & Charity Club. The club enabled middle-class, married women like Sneed to regularly meet and showcase their talents in embroidery and playwriting. These women also reviewed the latest works of Harlem Renaissance authors. The club women raised money to maintain parks and playgrounds, visited the sick and shut-in, and aided the poor, especially during the winter months. This group and other African American women's clubs annually celebrated National Club Women's Day. Martha Sneed passed on to her daughters the importance of helping others in the Black community (figs. 16 and 17).[24]

The Sneed children later excelled and followed their mother's footsteps as community builders. Ruth Sneed Jefferson and Martha Francis Sneed Davis Robinson—in later years, stepmother to Houston City Councilman

FIGURE 16. Born in Galveston in 1908, Ruth Sneed Jefferson graduated from Colored High School in 1926. She went on to Bishop College, the University of Colorado, and the University of Denver, eventually earning a degree in literature. She taught at Jack Yates High School as well as James D. Ryan Junior High School. Like her younger sister, Martha, she pledged Alpha Kappa Alpha Sorority and later joined The Links and The Smart Set Club. She talks about some of these issues in the local documentary *In the Name of Colored High, '04* (1993). *(Courtesy Houston Metropolitan Research Center, Houston Public Library, Houston, Texas, Sneed Family Collection, MSS 0293-0014)*

FIGURE 17. Martha Francis Sneed on her wedding day in 1936, at the family home in Fourth Ward. Sneed married Dr. John Davis, a dentist and president of the Charles A. George Dental Society. His civic work included serving on the trustee board at Wesley African Methodist Episcopal Church, maintaining an active role in the Young Men's Christian Association, and serving on the board of Texas State University for Negroes. After Dr. Davis's death in 1960, Martha remarried, entering holy matrimony with Judson Robinson Sr., the labor union activist and real estate developer whose son, Judson Robinson Jr., became Houston's first African American city councilmember since Reconstruction. Martha Sneed Davis Robinson, a Douglass Elementary schoolteacher and later an instructor at Texas State University for Negroes, joined Alpha Kappa Alpha Sorority in college (Bishop College), The Links, and the Smart Set Club. *(Courtesy Houston Metropolitan Research Center, Houston Public Library, Houston, Texas, Sneed Family Collection, MSS 0293-0016)*

Judson Robinson Jr.—also served the community as members of the following service and social organizations: Alpha Kappa Alpha Sorority, Inc.; The Links, Inc.; and the Smart Set Club, organizations that provided scholarships to students and charity donations to the needy (fig. 18). In addition, the nonprofit organizations served as elite social clubs for Black middle-class and upper-class women.[25]

Interestingly, the expansion of the city's downtown commercial district and the rise of Third Ward as the center of African American socioeconomic advancement led to the decline of Fourth Ward's African American community. Far south of Fourth Ward and downtown sat the Third Ward community, another emerging area for African American migrants in the early twentieth century. During the period of the "Walking City" in the mid- to late nineteenth century, members of Houston's silk-stocking community, which included businessman and newspaper publisher Marcellus

FIGURE 18. In 1928, recent Howard University alumna Hazel Hainsworth (Young), along with Lillie Vance Chester, Gladys Davis Simon, Anna Bell Stokes, Marie Viola Butler Taylor, and Erma Sweatt Wallace—the sister of famous Texas plaintiff Heman Sweatt who desegregated the University of Texas in 1950 in *Sweatt v. Painter*—met at Wesley African Methodist Episcopal Church and made provisions to establish the city of Houston's first Alpha Kappa Alpha Alumnae chapter. The organization, which celebrated its centennial in 2008, is the oldest Black Greek-lettered sorority in the United States. With chapters all over the world, the organization, since its inception, has worked to promote community agency and institution building, raising funds to build and refurbish rural schools, and for medical research, scholarships, charities, literacy classes, and adequate health facilities. In this photograph in the front row, Wallace is fourth from the left; Ruth Sneed Jefferson is third from the left; Hazel Young is in the second row and the farthest to the left; Martha Sneed Davis is standing behind Young in the third row and is right in front of door. Others in the photograph include Jonnelle Kelley, a Jack Yates High School librarian standing to the far right on the last row; and Zelda Turner, a Texas Southern University literature professor standing in the front row, third from the right. Today the chapter is home to hundreds of members, circa 1942. *(Courtesy Houston Metropolitan Research Center, Houston Public Library, Houston, Texas, Sneed Family Collection,* MSS 0293-0026*)*

Foster, philanthropist George H. Hermann and attorneys James A. Baker of Huntsville and (Capt.) James A. Baker Sr., lived in the ward. Main Street and Congress Street, two important thoroughfares in the city's downtown business and commercial district, defined the city's original four wards and were west and north of Third Ward. By the early 1900s, African Americans and European Americans had both populated the expanding ward, with the former comprising 31 percent of the ward's total and the latter making up 69 percent. By 1910, Blacks made up 32 percent of the city's total African American population. In the opening decades of the new century, the ward's African American neighborhoods began attracting migrants from surrounding cotton-producing, rural communities south and west of the city, including places in Fort Bend, Waller, Brazos, Wharton Counties, and Grimes Counties.[26]

By World War I, the ward's African American population of 8,000 had surpassed that of the other Black communities throughout the city. Also during World War I, the city began attracting a growing number of Latinos of Mexican ancestry, who lived nearby in Second Ward in and near the city's Eastend community. Developers, by the postwar 1920s, took notice of the changing demographics inside and near the once upscale Third Ward and developed the segregated subdivisions of Riverside, Riverside Terrace, and Washington Terrace, neighborhoods for middle-class and affluent White families; these communities increasingly attracted both Jewish Americans and immigrants from Eastern Europe. As Whites abandoned the Third Ward, the community's neighborhoods became increasingly majority African American communities. The diverse African American population in Third Ward grew from 1,075 in 1870 to 10,382 in 1920, and 25,926 in 1940.[27]

Third Ward not only attracted working-class African Americans like Oran Williams of Grimes County, but members of the posh middle-class elite found the district desirable as well by the 1920s.[28] Third Ward, by the 1930s, replaced Fourth Ward as the premier community for influential African American migrant families such as Lulu B. and Julius White, Carter and Doris Wesley, Jennie and Benjamin J. Covington, and Thelma and Ira Bryant (fig. 19). In 1934, Crockett, Texas, native Ira Bryant and his wife built their two-bedroom, pink-trimmed cottage on Holman Street and Tierwester Avenue. Bryant, a schoolteacher, had just obtained his master's degree from the University of Kansas. His wife, Thelma, a graduate of Howard University and the niece of famed Emmett J. Scott, helped

FIGURE 19. The Clifton and Ruby Richardson family home in Houston on Robin Street in Fourth Ward symbolized the city's growing Black middle class. The bungalow is spacious, charming, and quaint. The one-and-a-half-story bungalow had two to three bedrooms, including an attic the family converted into a spare room. The family had three boys, Clifton Jr., Leon, and Robert, and probably needed more room. Fierce de facto segregationist policies kept middle-class and upscale Black families out of White communities. This would change in the 1940s. In the meantime, homeowners like Clifton and Ruby Richardson maintained their beautifully manicured yards, potted plants, lovely front yards, and clean homes. *(Courtesy Houston Metropolitan Research Center, Houston Public Library, Houston, Texas, C. F. Richardson Sr. Papers, MSS 1457-0007)*

Bryant gather research for his many projects. Graduates of Colored High School, they both continued to travel to and from Houston and California as Bryant completed his doctorate in education at the University of Southern California. He would eventually become principal of his alma mater, Booker T. Washington High School (fig. 20).[29]

Third Ward's lure by the late 1920s was its appeal to both the African American working and middle classes. Home to the modest and working poor as well as the African American elite, the community that remained predominately White through the last half of the twentieth century, Third Ward, appealed to a large gamut within the African American migrant population. Older shotgun homes, along with modest frame houses, dotted the older areas of Third Ward that bordered downtown. Newer homes increasingly went up further south along Holman Avenue, Dowling Avenue, Truxillo Street, Nagle Street, Rosalie Street, Alabama Street,

FIGURE 20. The home of Jennie and Benjamin Jesse Covington served the community in numerous ways. Like The Houston Place, out-of-town guests made the house their home away from home. So prominent were the Covingtons, from the late 1910s to the 1960s, that luminaries such as educators Booker T. and Margaret Washington, contralto singer Marion Anderson, entertainer and activist Paul Robeson, concert tenor Roland Hayes, writer and activist William Pikens and boxing champion Joe Lewis enjoyed the splendor of their stately three-story home on Hadley and Dowling streets while visiting the city. Important meetings regarding issues affecting the Black community went on in the home as well. Covington did not wear his anger and frustration on his sleeve or doctor's coat. Using a multiplicity of subterfuges, the physician found ways to challenge white supremacy. This way, he rarely had to live in fear of being suspected of inciting disruptions. Disruptions, however, did ironically sit well with him, as he knew racial segregation had to end eventually. Lastly, the mere facts that an African American family in Houston had the kind of financial clout that allowed them to purchase an automobile when wealthy Whites first began buying cars; travel across the country and globe, live comfortably without the monetary generosity of others, send their daughter to Oberlin College for the undergraduate and graduate degrees, and live in a stately mansion reminded the world of what African Americans could do and be. *(Courtesy Houston Metropolitan Research Center, Houston Public Library, Houston, Texas, Covington Family Collection, MSS 0170-0001)*

Wheeler Avenue, and Cleburne Street. Businesses also attracted African Americans. Houston Negro Hospital and *Houston Defender* newspaper, Houston Colored Junior College, Franklin Beauty School, the National Association for the Advancement of Colored People (NAACP), Blue Triangle YWCA, and Teal Portrait Studios had offices there. Although Third

Ward increasingly grabbed the attention of African American professionals and poorer people of color alike in the late 1920s and 1930s, another historic ward appealed to aspiring African American migrants as well.[30]

Fifth Ward's close proximity to the ship channel and the east Houston industrial district made it especially attractive to working people. Just east of downtown Houston and bounded by Buffalo Bayou to the south, Liberty Road to the north, Lockwood Drive to the east, and Jensen Drive to the west, the community initially attracted working-class Whites and freed families of the late nineteenth century, with Afro-Americans comprising 50 percent of the residents in 1870. By the 1880s, the ward witnessed a major population boom as Southern Pacific Railroad built several railroad shops in the region. Other manufacturing centers followed suit. People continued to move into the ward as the twentieth century dawned. Native-born European Americans, as well as African Americans, poured into the ward's neighborhoods to find both work and available housing.[31]

Recent immigrants to the city also found the inexpensive homes affordable. Jewish Poles and Russians were among the recent European ethnics to flock to Fifth Ward. Mexicans too moved into Fifth Ward during and after the Mexican Revolution, and continued to pour into the area after the uprising subsided in the 1920s. Latinos of Mexican origin also lived near their jobs along the ship channel and in the Fifth and Second Wards. African Americans, Whites, and Hispanics of Mexican ancestry not only lived in the same ward and worked together but also lived in a potentially integrated setting, at least through the early 1920s. As late as 1920, Mexicans, African Americans, and Whites—immigrants and poorer native-born—lived sometimes in very close proximity to one another on the same street and on the next block.[32]

A desire to work drove African Americans into the ward from the very beginning. After the Civil War, African Americans traveling from nearby Montgomery County farms and East Texas plantations in Polk, Smith, Walker, San Jacinto, and Liberty, as well as from other rural places situated along the Trinity and San Jacinto Rivers, trekked into the sparsely populated community. Blacks, mostly former slaves and unskilled laborers, from the very beginning, formed viable neighborhoods inside the ward. In fact, African Americans created some of the ward's first institutions, including Ashbury Memorial Methodist Episcopal Church (now Ashbury Memorial United Methodist Church) in 1870. Religious and industrious, African American residents bought homes, sent their children to Blanche K.

Bruce Elementary School, opened businesses, and worked hard to provide for their families.[33]

Although industrial fires in the late nineteenth century and early twentieth century devastated lives, particularly a 1912 blaze that destroyed hundreds of Fifth Ward homes, businesses, and institutions, including Sloan Memorial Episcopal Methodist Church, African Americans continued to migrate to the ward, especially in the 1920s. The Black population increased from 578 in 1870 to 9,397 in 1920, to 25,923 in 1940. During the First Great Migration through 1930, African Americans generally moved from the same rural and small-town residences their community slave elders abandoned one or two generations earlier, mainly for work and autonomy. Many, if not the majority of male African American residents in Fifth Ward, worked for one of the manufacturing companies in East Houston and along the ship channel, including railroad shops and yards, oil tool firms, refineries, foundries, cotton compresses and wharves, food processing plants, lumber mills, and paper plants.[34]

Aspiring African Americans particularly made good use of chain migration in their attempt to find jobs and homes. Luther and Louise McBride moved to Houston in 1923. First, they lived at 1315 Schwartz in Fifth Ward; then the couple moved to 1007 Sydnor near the ward. They finally settled on 1015 Bayou in Fifth Ward. Luther McBride was born on a Livingston farm in Polk County; his wife came from nearby Riverside of Walker County. After moving to Houston in 1923, the couple took in Louise's daughter, Bertha Lee Austin, and four grandchildren, all of Groveton in Trinity County, a place not far from Livingston and Riverside. Utilizing chain migration, Bertha Lee Austin abandoned rural life and followed her mother to Houston. Like her mother and stepfather, Luther and Louise McBride, Austin sought socioeconomic opportunity for herself and her family. The McBrides, a typical East Texas Black farm family, settled in Fifth Ward, as did many of their contemporaries from the same region. Even though their overall percentages in Fifth Ward—mainly due to European immigration, internal migration among White laborers, and a heavy supply of work for Whites—right before the turn-of-the-century, Blacks continued to see the area as an acceptable one. By World War I, Black East Texas and Louisiana migrants comprised at least one-third of in-migrants entering Fifth Ward.[35]

Female residents in Fifth Ward and throughout the city, like males, lived near their jobs, or occasionally younger women worked as live-in domestics. Women as residents of Fifth Ward, for example, worked in the Heights, Northline, and Trinity Gardens subdivisions nearby. Women who stayed in Third Ward, for example, worked at either downtown stores or hotels or in the private households of White families of Third Ward or nearby Montrose, Riverside Terrace, Riverside, or Washington Terrace. For men and women, however, commuting to and from one side of town to the other was not unheard of.[36]

Widow Ella Larkin moved to Fifth Ward during World War I or in the late 1910s or early 1920s from Navasota in Grimes County, Texas, with her four small children. Her youngest, a wide-eyed and precocious preschooler named Milton, would, throughout the next few decades, become a celebrated jazz legend (see fig. 40). Recently widowed, Larkin, according to son Milton, followed her sisters to Houston for work. She toiled at several low-paying and menial personal service jobs, working mostly as a domestic, cook, and laundress, before dying prematurely later in the decade. Interestingly, although the Larkins rented their small home in Fifth Ward, they owned land in Grimes County, as the 1920 census lists Navasota and Houston as their residences. Perhaps still in transition, Larkin occupied both residences for a period of time, hoping to stay afloat financially. Certainly, the small cotton farm provided the family with a suitable income and way to pay the mortgage, whereas Houston afforded them more immediate resources, for example, jobs, independent community institutions, better schools, and so forth.[37]

Fifth Ward attracted out-of-state residents, especially Louisianans. Most Louisiana natives relocated to the ward following the Great Flood of 1927. Sisters Sarah Platt and Lena Mouton came to Houston in 1927 as children, after severe floods destroyed their family's crops and drowned irreplaceable livestock. Their parents had lost everything in the flood and opted for migration to Houston after learning of the city's perks—better jobs, shorter work hours, and higher wages—from their relatives.[38]

The family left their farm community south of Lafayette and moved to Frenchtown in Fifth Ward, Houston, a neighborhood developed by Louisiana-born Afro-American Creole settlers of French ancestry in 1922. Initially, Frenchtown comprised four square blocks: Lelia on the south, Gregg on the east, Roland to the north, and Hogg on the west. The first newcomers left St. Martinsville, Lafayette, and LaBeau of southeastern Louisiana, an area known as the Sugar Bowl for its historic sugar plantations and processing plants. The first Frenchtown settlers, including carpenter Albert Chevalier, built their own homes, thriving Fifth Ward businesses, and lasting institutions such as Our Mother of Mercy Church and the Creole Knights of Social Club. They also opened restaurants, bars, groceries, dry cleaners, automobile shops, appliance stores, and so on. The word "Creole," until recent years, exclusively defined Whites of French or Spanish ancestry born in the West Indies or Spanish America, but today it also includes persons of African descent with mixed-race ancestry.[39]

Although many define "Black" Creoles as descendants of "Frenchmen" and African or African-descent women, others give a broader definition that includes all White fathers who lived in Louisiana prior to the Civil War: French or Spanish Creoles or Louisiana natives, French immigrants, Anglo-Americans as well as others of European extraction, and Acadians/Cajuns.[40] Many of the southern Louisiana refugees who fled their state in the wake of economic and natural disasters imprinted onto Houston a rich Catholic and Creole cultural identity. To many of these newcomers and others who eventually made Houston their home, the city and its Afro-American communities served as magnets to the indigent families who were in need of hope and steady incomes. The cultural constructs of Creoles also attracted African Americans to their church services, schools, restaurants, nightclubs, and music.[41]

Creoles of southern Louisiana brought other cultural mores to the city as well. As cooks, Creole housewives transformed Houston's typical southern cuisine. Creole cooking emerges as an important cultural bridge among the group, Houston's African American community, and the city. Creole housewives routinely hosted fundraisers for neighborhood churches and schools by putting together parties and bazaars highlighting South Louisiana foods. Creole women also earned extra money by selling soups, black rice and shrimp creole, crawfish, jambalaya, chicken dinners, boudin, desserts, and beer. Creoles transplanted a delicious cuisine of dishes, including gumbo, a soup dish of seafood and pork; coubeyonne, a fish stew made of fish heads; and boudin, sausages stuffed with pork, liver, rice, and spices. In 1929, Creole families even raised money through dances, parties, and dinners, serving these delicious delicacies for the construction of Our Mother of Mercy Catholic Church. Restaurants and nightclubs like Lavergne's Ballroom in Frenchtown served these dishes to patrons throughout Houston and thus popularized Creole food. The eventual spread of Creole cuisine after World War II led to the establishment of successful restaurant and fast-food franchises, such as Pappadeaux's Seafood Kitchen, Popeye's Chicken, and Frenchy's Chicken, specializing in these southern Louisiana dishes.[42]

Houston's cultural landscape especially changed in the wake of the 1927 mass exoduses out of Louisiana. Charles E. Lewis, a sharecropper in St. Martinsville, married Bertha Marie Thomas, a college graduate from Strait University—now Dillard University. Bertha taught farm children in the rural community of Saint Martinsville—in St. Martin Parish—while her husband struggled as a sharecropper and railroad employee with Southern Pacific. Frustrated by limited and futile options in rural Louisiana—especially as cotton prices steadily decreased throughout the 1920s—the couple decided to migrate to Houston in 1927. After two years of living with relatives and in boardinghouses, the couple bought a home in Fifth Ward on Bleaker Street. Charles Lewis's stable income from Southern Pacific Railroad allowed the family to purchase a modest two-bedroom home. Louisiana migrants like Charles and Bertha Lewis, who moved to Houston for economic opportunities, relied heavily on their families, friends, cultural traditions, and community institutions.[43]

As newcomers from Louisiana and eastern Texas entered Fifth Ward, the African American population in the ward increased from 578 in 1870 to 9,397 in 1920, and 25,923 in 1940. Black in-migration, however, spurred White-out migration. As African Americans from Louisiana and Texas increasingly migrated to Fifth Ward for jobs, Whites, particularly Eastern European Jews and Irish Catholics, abandoned their quaint but decaying neighborhoods for more spacious and racially exclusive areas in and near Third Ward, Fifth Ward, and Northwest Houston. Blacks comprised the majority of numerous Fifth Ward neighborhoods by the 1920s.[44]

One Fifth Ward family built an important resource for African American residents and out-of-town guests. The resourceful Constance and Tracy Thompson, who did not have children, followed mother (and mother-in-law) Georgia Houston's lead and turned their home—the home in Fifth Ward, purchased by Joshua Houston Jr. and called The Houston Place—into a bed and breakfast inn for out-of-town guests and as a gathering place for private parties, weddings, and church functions. Dignitaries and celebrities such as actor Ethel Walters, jazz great Lionel Hampton, soloist Ella Fitzgerald, Tuskegee Institute President Robert R. Moton, and the insatiable Mills Brothers often stayed at the Cape Cod–fashioned cottage while visiting the city. Like established residents who came to the city before her and welcomed her family, Constance helped make people's stay—temporary or permanent—a pleasant one.[45]

Not every newcomer moved into neighborhoods within the city limits. Houston African Americans moved into homes and formed institutions in every section of the city and even outside the city proper. Some built homes in Acres Homes, Independence Heights, Sunnyside, and Barrett Station of neighboring Crosby, Texas, as well as other places on the outskirts of the city's boundaries. In these mostly semirural perspective communities, African Americans usually made up the majority, if not all, of the population. In these places, and unlike the majority of Afro-Americans residing in Houston, residents almost always owned their property and homes. Those who did not own their property were usually long-time renters who still struggled to make ends meet and lived without many of the basic amenities of heating, indoor plumbing, paved roads, and sewers. Usually, the majority of residents entered these unincorporated communities from the country or small towns.[46]

Most of the settlers in Independence Heights were the children of inspiring ex-slaves. Oliphant Lockwood Hubbard left his parents' farm in the East Texas Piney Woods of Weldon to attend Prairie View College in the early 1900s. Oliphant Hubbard graduated in 1909 with a teacher's certificate in primary education. His parents, former slaves Lewis and Victoria Hubbard, made it a point to motivate their children to get an education. They had never learned to read and write as slaves. Only during Reconstruction did Victoria begin reading; Lewis, however, remained illiterate all his life, despite his success as a landowner.[47] According to granddaughter Vivian Hubbard Seals, "They saw to it that all of their children went to public school and some to college."[48] All fourteen of the Hubbard children finished primary school; several finished high school; and a few earned degrees, becoming dentists, physicians, librarians, businesspersons, and educators in Cincinnati, Ohio; East Chicago, Indiana; Crockett, Texas; and the city of Houston.[49]

After college, Oliphant Hubbard met and married educator Ella K. Kyle. Kyle too came from a farming background, having ex-slaves as parents. A native of Woodville, Texas, a sawmill and farming community near the town of Jasper and along the Texas and New Orleans Railroad, Kyle eagerly went into teaching. Ella Kyle graduated from Mary Allen Seminary. For the next few years, the couple taught in impoverished rural communities and thriving sawmill towns alike, including the lumbering settlement of Diboll near the small city of Lufkin. Depressed conditions and poor pay, however, drove them out of East Texas for good.[50]

In 1911, the Hubbards settled in Independence Heights, an African American settlement, established in 1908.[51] White Ohio natives Alfred Alexander and Sarah Wright migrated to Houston in 1905 and later founded the new development. In 1908, Alfred Alexander Wright established the Wright Land Company and offered low-interest loans to African American settlers moving to Houston. Wright sought White business as well, and therefore formed two companies, the Wright Land Company for African American homebuyers and Wright Loan and Security for perspective White buyers. He later formed other African American settlements—Acres Homes, Highland Heights, and several Highland Annexes. Most developers, of course, ignored requests to build quality homes or sell tracts to African American families.[52]

Grateful residents incorporated Independence Heights in January 1915, a half-century after the climax of slavery. The Hubbards and other landholders thus fell in love with the town and symbolic name. Paradoxically, Independence Heights's vast open meadows, spacious pine trees, numerous cotton fields, and sparsely populated neighborhoods took the Hubbards back to the splendor and tranquility of the rural East Texas Piney Woods.[53]

Oliphant Hubbard believed the Houston area offered African American professionals a measure of autonomy and opportunity. He secured a teaching position at the Independence Heights School (now James D. Burrus Elementary School) with the Harris County school district, serving for a period as the school's teacher and principal. Named for the community it served, the school educated the children of twenty or so Independence Heights families. Of course, the school would serve more in the next few years. The small community ten miles northwest of downtown Houston mushroomed quickly from a few dozen families into a town of one thousand by 1920.[54]

For a brief period through 1929, the founders of Independence Heights operated a functional town, formed permanent institutions, created jobs, elected their own public officials, and provided residents with modest city services. The town comprised eight groceries, four restaurants, a taxi service, a blacksmith shop, a meal mill, an electrician, contractors, plumbers, a watch repair shop, a shoe repair shop, a millinery shop, a drug store, and an ice cream parlor. Retired educator, historian, and former resident Vivian Hubbard Seals fondly remembered her childhood home: "I can remember when I used to ride daddy's [Oliphant Hubbard] back to Lindsay's Ice Cream Parlor to buy a 'Say-So,' an ice cream cone."[55]

The Hubbard Family, which included four children by the early 1920s, earned the respect of the entire community. People especially adored wife, mother, educator, and clubwoman Ella Hubbard. Hubbard, like most African American middle-class women of the early twentieth century, continued to work outside the home. Hubbard, like her husband Oliphant, taught school at the Independence Heights School, eventually becoming the school's first female (interim) principal. Hubbard also attended New Hope Baptist Church. She relied on neighbors and church members to house-sit, prepare meals, and care for her children. Most importantly, her community family allowed the Hubbards to serve others.[56]

Oliphant Hubbard, who ultimately left teaching for good, successfully ran for mayor, serving two terms from 1919 to 1923. And city services improved modestly during his tenure in office: water and sewage service, street lighting, plank sidewalks, telephone service, shelled streets, and limited public transportation. Hubbard encouraged residents to take pride in their city: "So let us all try and build up a city that every person who lives here or may come will feel proud of it."[57] Houston finally annexed Independence Heights in 1929.[58]

Although most migrants like the Hubbards usually relied on the help of friends and family to ease their transition, some families moved into the homes of strangers as boarders. Widow Ella Larkin listed two roomers in her Fifth Ward home, interestingly—two 34-year-old widowers who worked as cotton compress laborers. The two men could have been friends from Navasota or acquaintances with Larkin. Commonly, lodgers rented their rooms for an exact fee, one that often included room and board. Harry and Beatrice Hainsworth of Grimes County—although Harry Hainsworth's birthplace on the 1920 census is Alabama—temporarily moved into a boarding house until Harry found permanent work. Christia and Elbert Adair also relocated to Houston in 1925, moving first to a boarding house in Third Ward. Eventually both families bought homes. However, entrenched segregation made it more difficult for African Americans to find permanent housing.[59]

Residential Segregation and Its Effects

Newcomers soon realized the city's drawbacks, with one of the most serious being housing—both residential segregation and overcrowding. Houston, like most southern cities, evolved into a racially segregated community after the Civil War. In Houston and elsewhere, freedpeople of color welcomed the chance to start anew around other African Americans. According to historian Howard Rabinowitz, African American sections of southern cities, for example, Freedmantown in Fourth Ward, often began as free Afro-American communities that dated back to the period before the war and formed independently of White interloping or interference in undesirable areas usually on the outskirts of town.[60]

Even while the practice of de facto or customary segregation defined many Houston neighborhoods in the late nineteenth century, the races still intermingled through the early part of the next century. Those Whites residing near or in the same household units as Afro-Americans generally were either recent immigrants to the United States and business owners of establishments such as neighborhood groceries and commissaries, or working-class native Texans who were content—at least for the time being—with living in close proximity to their places of employment.[61]

The parents of Lullelia Harrison moved to the city in the 1900s from Dayton, Texas, and rented a "little shotgun house" on Saulinier from a kind Italian shopkeeper. According to Harrison, "When I became a toddler and even when I was a baby, he had an adolescent boy named Mauci and that was who played with me, even as a baby. Mauci was my playmate, an Italian boy who had moved from Italy to America."[62] Still, according to historian Louise Passey Maxwell, residential segregation patterns in Houston were evident as early as 1880.[63]

Houston, interestingly, unlike many other southern cities, never adopted residential ordinances that segregated neighborhoods and blocks by race. This perhaps had more to do with the city's opposition to zoning. Houston, a city known for its indifference to zoning or land use laws by municipalities or county districts, differed from a number of cities in this respect in the early twentieth century. Between 1910 and 1917, southern cities enforced both zoning laws and codified (de jure) segregation ordinances aimed at separating the races. Baltimore, Charleston, Dallas, Richmond, Norfolk, Memphis, Nashville, New Orleans, Washington, DC, and others passed laws designed to maintain residential segregation.[64]

These laws—along with restrictive covenants, which emerged in the 1920s—excluded African Americans and other non-Whites from White-majority neighborhoods. Even when the Supreme Court struck down residential segregation in *Buchanan v. Warley* (1917), Whites continued to practice de facto segregation in an effort to resist desegregation. Private neighborhood associations, along with real estate brokers, quickly relied on racial restrictive covenants to separate the races. This practice did not happen across the entire South. In the rural and small-town South, the races segregated customarily, consequently relying less on codified, de jure segregation. Rather, small towns maintained sharp lines of demarcation that separated communities based on the color line. In these places, the races built separate existences, often in different parts of town, and relied heavily on social control as an effective tool to curve integration. In addition, although not readily discussed, residential segregation went on in every region of the country.[65]

Residential segregation in Houston did not differ considerably from patterns in other cities, especially urban centers in the South. White natives to the region, recent European ethnics, people of Mexican origin, and African Americans practiced residential segregation by choice or custom. Groups, not surprisingly, lived with their own kind. Furthermore, working-class Whites, including recent European ethnics, increasingly worked to maintain racial homogeneity in their communities.[66]

Increasingly, Whites as a whole believed African Americans threatened their socioeconomic livelihood and racial hierarchy, although Hispanics, as their numbers increased more so than other ethnics, lived near Whites and Afro-Americans. In Houston, according to historian Robert Fisher, homeowners associations formed restrictive covenants with great speed after 1920 to exclude religious and racial minorities, namely Jewish Americans, Latinos, and African Americans. This method did in fact help to strengthen de facto residential segregation until the Supreme Court struck down racial restrictive covenants in *Shelley v. Kraemer* (1948). Furthermore, the Houston Riot of 1917 frightened many Whites, including the poor, who increasingly supported residential segregation.[67]

The practice of customary segregation had a reverberating effect on African Americans. Because of segregation, African American clustering increased. Large pockets of African American settlements, according to historian James M. SoRelle, dominated areas already populated by African Americans. In Houston, pockets of urban bands formed in several neighborhoods in the Third, Fourth, and Fifth Wards. African American neighborhoods increased in the wards that surrounded downtown. Although Whites predominated in these wards in 1920, specific pockets of African American and poorer enclaves increased. Blacks, even members of the expanding middle class, found themselves unable to escape these communities. Black urban clusters, however, did not reach the level of ghetto formation often associated with places north of the Mason-Dixon Line.[68]

Because of Houston's unusually large size and topography, its African American communities often formed independently of one another and coexisted as separate African American entities. Ironically, like many places in the urban South, Houston maintained and enforced customary residential segregation, which prevented qualified homeowners of color from buying other forms of available housing.[69]

Although Houston African Americans inhabited neighborhoods that hardly resembled the massive urban ghettoes of the northern United States, most, as members of the city's poor and disenfranchised, lived amid unhealthy, horrendous squalor. At the time of the First Great Migration, African American squalor, according to a recent migrant and physician, correlated with poverty, illiteracy, bad diet and poor heath, and ignorance. Suffice it to say, according to physician Henry Lee of Midway, Texas, poverty and racism too contributed to this aura of chaos. Insufficient amenities such as damaged sidewalks, insufficient street lighting, irregular garbage collection, improper sanitation, unpaved streets, and poor sewage services made life difficult for area residents. Residents of Independence Heights ultimately embraced annexation for these reasons.[70]

These problems hardly promoted healthy lifestyles, especially in the wake of continued internal migration. In addition, according to social worker Jesse Thomas of the National Urban League (NUL), Houston's lackadaisical zoning laws contributed to unsafe conditions in the city's Afro-American communities. For example, hairdressers who worked out of their homes commonly washed, pressed, greased, and styled clients' hair in their kitchen, even while preparing and serving meals. Trash, filth, and backed-up sewage inside and outside homes precipitated serious bouts of dysentery, cholera, and typhoid fever, which propelled higher mortality rates among Afro-Americans.[71]

Terrible conditions inside these Houston households equally made African Americans susceptible to unhealthy lifestyles. Absentee landlords especially posed a serious dilemma for Houston's Afro-American neighborhoods. Black and White absentee landlords, says Thomas, housed their impoverished tenants in poorly maintained houses, duplexes, and units.

Poor ventilation in the spring and summer months, insufficient indoor plumbing, contemptible heating sources in the winter months, and inadequate home repairs contributed to this consistent and sad state of affairs. Equally fascinating, many owner-occupied homes lacked basic amenities such as running water and toilets.[72]

Overcrowding crippled African American households. Overwhelmingly, this problem affected renter-occupied households more so than those occupied by homeowners. Sources confirm this observation. Although 1929 NUL findings indicate that Houston's African American households averaged three persons per family, a closer look suggests something else. A substantial number of households housed boarders. One can assume that some Houston households in these communities, especially in the 1920s as migrants streamed into the city, comprised multiple families. A 1943 NUL report suggests that African American owner-occupied households contained, on average, two individuals for every room. For those homes occupied by renters, however, the figure increased to three. Sometimes six to eight family members or individuals occupied two- and three-room houses.[73]

Beginning in the 1920s, some relief came to African American communities. As the city's population doubled between 1910 and 1920, from 138,000 to 292,000, private contractors and developers set out to meet a massive housing demand. Between 1910 and 1930, a number of annexations increased the size of the city. Annexations and migrations combined increased the number of Houston households and stimulated an unprecedented building campaign. No doubt, developers felt confident that profits could be made by providing housing for the city's growing African American middle class.[74]

Investors, therefore, in the 1920s built a number of new developments for middle-class and affluent African American families. Pinecrest Court and the Richardson Addition in Fifth Ward, College Court in Fourth Ward, and Granlin Grove and the Forest Homes in Third Ward catered to well-to-do families. Contemporary homes for African Americans came with indoor plumbing, bathtubs, commodes, and gas and electric energy sources, along with two or three bedrooms. Moreover, some homes came in red brick. These spacious, clean homes differed considerably from the frame-structured, shotgun cottages that housed most residents.[75]

Developers, of course, heeded to customary racial segregation. The alleviation of housing congestion, therefore, did not give way to integration.

Housing patterns thus mirrored the city's disdain for social equality. These new subdivisions, for example, although spacious and up to building standards, were smaller and valued far less than similar middle-class housing developments in nearby Washington Terrace, Riverside Terrace, Montrose, and The Heights. Public and private developers would go further in the 1930s. In 1937, the newly formed Houston Housing Authority would build two housing developments for lower-income families. These projects did offer modest relief for the city's African American community. Interestingly, the growth of the African American community as a whole, including a growing middle class, also propelled the rise of intraracial lines of demarcation.[76]

Stratification

In the wake of population explosion, neighborhood expansion, and community building, Houston Afro-Americans increasingly separated themselves according to socioeconomic class, education, religion, and ethnicity. The intragroup strata that began to define the city's African American community also provided some with the means to marginalize the masses of African Americans, even while remaining embracing and supportive of the poor, homeless, and illiterate. Clubwomen within the community, for example, occasionally worked alongside White women in an effort to curb problems within the larger African American community. By formulating these relationships with Whites, Jennie Covington and other middle-class African American women found ways to self-identify with Whites of the same socioeconomic class and still embrace Blackness. These efforts perhaps prompted people to explore the possibility of integrating into the larger White society and leading the way toward long-standing desegregation and social justice efforts. At any rate, class increasingly separated groups within Houston's African American community.

Class stratification did separate African Americans in the wake of internal migration. The rise of Houston Blacks due to internal migration brought to light the ever-increasing role of stratification in the community. Divisions grew and helped separate people along class lines. Although other demarcation lines divided people around religion, ethnicity, culture, gender, and hue, increasingly, class distinguished the marginal working classes from the educated and business elite.[77]

Ironically, Houston's First and Second Great Migrations blurred and strengthened these lines as, more and more, educated African American men secured working-class jobs in the transportation and the expanding service-sector arena. In addition, the growing number of schools, along with mounting service jobs in medicine, education, public service, business, entertainment, and publishing, raised standards of living. Lastly, people of all occupations lived together as congested housing persisted and racial segregation kept middle-class and upper-class residents outside wealthier White communities. Migrants moving to Houston, like most twentieth-century African Americans, lived in predominately-Afro-American communities, attended all-Black congregations, and sent their children to segregated schools. Racial exclusion on the one hand relegated African American migrants to these communities, lower-paying jobs, and public acts of harassment and humiliation. Although this reality united African Americans around the common theme of racism, it failed to whitewash or blackout substantial differences that existed among varying groups. The homogeneity that arose from racial segregation could not mask the strengthening class distinctions that often defined neighborhoods, churches, families, and leisure clubs.[78]

At the end of the nineteenth century on into the start of the twentieth century, two distinguishable groups comprised Houston's African American community: the working classes and middle-income elites. In some ways, these groups mirrored those in Chicago, Detroit, Cleveland, Milwaukee, New York, and elsewhere in the popular, attractive urban Midwest and Northeast. A few were educated, ambitious, and vigilant leaders, and like their contemporaries across the country, worked with, served, and gave assistance to others within their communities. The rising African American presence in these cities spurred the birth of the new African American elite, one that came of age in the late nineteenth century and turn of the century. The growing demand for African American businesses and enterprises that catered to the Afro-American community in the 1910s and 1920s spurred this rapid transformation.[79]

In other ways, though, Houston's early African American middle-class elite differed considerably from its northern counterparts. People of color in Houston—prior to the Great Migrations—mostly lived their entire lives as slaves before the Civil War. Only a handful—less than twenty by 1860—lived and worked as free(d) African Americans. Although most free(d) people of color earned a decent living as blacksmiths, carpenters, draymen, restaurateurs, or boardinghouse proprietors, none were classified as wealthy. Wealthy or well-to-do free people of color in antebellum American communities outside the South worked as professionals, owned profitable businesses supported by a rich White clientele, and earned their living as exclusive wait staffers and servants. Most of these Afro-American elite lived in the North and Upper South. Fewer lived in the Deep South. In antebellum Texas, the vast majority of skilled African Americans were slaves, not free people of color. Only after slavery did Houston notice an emerging African American elite or middle class.[80]

Prosperous African Americans in Reconstruction and post-Reconstruction Houston, who did in fact invest in real estate, teach school, pastor prestigious congregations, obtain college certificates and degrees, and devote most of their time to service, were only years removed from slavery. People like Rep. Richard Allen, Rev. Jack Yates, Rev. Elijah Dibble, Ella Kyle Scott, Martha Sneed, Jennie Covington, Mabel Wesley, Ina Spivey, and Pearl Lights lived better than most in the African American community. Nevertheless, as these members of the African American middle-class built institutions, cared for the poor, and fought for modest human-rights initiatives, they inadvertently provided solace and support to their own families. They remembered all too well their status as slaves, or the struggles of parents as freedmen and freedwomen, and they passed on these remembrances to their offspring. Without question, the common experience of slavery united African American Houstonians and gave rise to a mutual spirit of cooperation, dedication, and agency-activism. After the Great Migrations, the African American elite still relied on others within the community for their livelihood. Even as they separated themselves along organizational and institutional lines, they considered themselves the guardians of hope and agency, especially as civil rights successes seemed within reach.[81]

Some migrants lived outside the economic security of the African American middle class. Yet, their education, organizational skills, and social mores made them more middle class than working class. These women and men perhaps used benevolence and community-building exercises as tools of opportunity in order to clinch White approval. In this sense, they took up the mantle of Whiteness and even found ways to separate themselves from the masses of working-class Afro-Americans. Most migrants were far from middle class. Still, some members of this group could use their skills to formulate a bridge for the masses of ordinary Blacks and make the American Dream possible for all.[82]

These ordinary workers generally failed in their attempts to secure economic and societal parity with Mainstream America. Most working-class men and women found service jobs as housecleaners, domestics, cooks, washerwomen, laundresses, chauffeurs, draymen, sextons, and porters. Others worked as dockworkers, railroaders, and skilled artisans. Underemployment and occasional unemployment ensured their lowly status as struggling workers. The largest segment in the community, this group ironically varied considerably. Black artisans working for construction teams, railroads, manufacturing firms, grain elevators and shippers, cotton-compress firms, and on docks, comprised one small segment of the working-class or proletariat African American population. As skilled workers, Louisiana migrants who entered the city in the early twentieth century, for example, were classified and paid as *helpers* and not *machinists, electricians,* and so on. Yet, businesses still utilized the skills of these professional artisans and laborers. Blocked from joining established unions like the American Federation of Labor or railroad brotherhoods, they became a vulnerable target for greedy industrialists and White unionists.[83]

Often these members of the Afro-American working class were intelligent, articulate, driven, and college educated, nevertheless. Commonly, college-educated, working-class African American men married teachers, nurses, secretaries, librarians, students, and clubwomen. Schoolteacher Lullelia Harrison Walker, the daughter of a Louisiana artisan-migrant, married a Southern University football star, Alexander Harrison, in 1931. Harrison left school and relocated to Chicago for work. The Harrisons returned to Houston two years later with two sons. Ultimately buying a home in Fifth Ward, Alex took jobs as a hotel waiter, Southern Pacific Railroad redcap, and worker with Sheffield Oil, while wife Lullelia began a four-decade teaching career.[84]

The families of unskilled and semiskilled workers and underpaid professionals topped the working-class pyramid and often blurred the lines between the middle class and working class. Their incomes mirrored that of many working-class Americans; on the other hand, their education, organizational skills, appreciation for respectability, and leadership roles placed them alongside stable, middle-income African American Houstonians. Moreover, one group of laborers, longshoremen, partly due to their reputation as efficient stevedores and because of their success in union organizing, earned wages compatible to middle-class African Americans. Truthfully, only their association with working-class employment placed them in the category. For all practical purposes, they, like elite Afro-Americans, felt they had little in common with the working poor.[85]

Most African American workers made well below the incomes of even these laborers. As unskilled workers, these members of the working poor earned very little money as domestics, service workers, draymen, sextons, and porters. Those engaged in manufacturing usually worked in bottom-rung positions and earned less than Whites. Unskilled laborers comprised the largest proportion of the Afro-American working class. Members of the working poor, most African Americans in Houston labored in the worst sectors of the Houston labor market. They had little schooling or skills outside this basic job segment. Most did not own their homes. Only some owned bank accounts, saved their money, purchased life insurance, and persuaded their children to remain in school. They worked long hours and earned little in wages. Increasingly, the working poor spent little to no time with wealthier Afro-Americans. They often attended more spirited churches, enjoyed blues clubs and juke joints, often substituted good health with poor diet and, occasionally, substance abuse, and sometimes engaged in self-destructive behavior that cost them their families.[86]

Lastly, marginalized Afro-Americans, individuals who experienced constant underemployment and unemployment, found themselves on the verge of poverty and homelessness. Sometimes these members of the working poor did seasonal work, laboring four to six months out of the year as cotton-compress laborers. They also found themselves still tied to the country as cotton pickers or sugarcane workers during the summer and fall months. For the most part, they found themselves hired and fired more regularly than other groups. Often too poor and vulnerable to keep decent, bottom-rung jobs, they also lived back and forth between neighbors, church members, homeless shelters, relatives, and love interests.[87]

Some working-class migrants, in spite of their many difficulties, worked hard to maintain stable families. Nathaniel and Mary Harper left Baton Rouge, Louisiana, in 1926 or 1927. The couple moved to Acres Homes, Texas, a semi-farming community northwest of Houston. Acres Homes, with its tall grasses, stoic pine trees, dirt roads, tiny row houses, and slender bayous, reminded the couple of their Baton Rouge community. The couple could also rely on the tiny community's kith and kin networks of friendships, church members, coworkers, neighbors, and relatives.[88]

Nathaniel, a high school graduate, worked as a laborer, mostly at tire and auto-repair shops, earning $60 a month; his much younger wife,

Mary, reared the family's six children, ages two to twelve. An old-fashioned Nathaniel Harper, almost fifty, more than likely had considerable reservations about Mary working outside the home. The family even purchased a modest home in the community of Acres Homes. Like most Acres Homes homeowners, the family did not have indoor plumbing. Heavy flooding in the fall and summer months also made living conditions deplorable. Unfortunately, hard times in the upcoming years would force husband and father Nathaniel to seek public assistance. For the Harpers, temporary public assistance seemed a logical option for the time being. Whether Mary Harper later worked outside the home is unclear. More than likely, she did eventually work outside the home as a domestic. Higher costs of living in postwar 1940s made it almost impossible for working-class families to live on the income of just one wage earner. Like most recent settlers in the city, the Harpers remained hopeful that their city of choice offered them and their children respite from painful racism and poverty.[89]

Conclusion

Relying on chain-migration networks, migrants made their transitions into Houston neighborhoods. Established residents—family, friends, acquaintances, and employers—directed newcomers to homes, schools, churches, entertainment, and jobs. Most migrants moved in with family and friends upon their initial arrival, only later securing their own homes. Sometimes migrants entered the city without their families, only sending for loved ones after finding permanent housing arrangements. Often migrants lived with strangers; as boarders, some developed new relationships and saved up to purchase homes. Occasionally these newfound friendships blossomed into lifelong partnerships.[90]

As migrants comfortably settled into their new Houston communities, they remembered those who aided them. Internal migrants, regardless of their circumstances, never forgot their humble beginnings. In the process of making new homes, migrants sustained the close familial and friendship relations that stretched from the country to the city. In doing so, newcomers created or inculcated the important familial and friendship connections that helped them reaffirm the close-knit bonds that supported their survival in the big city. They even extended the chain and reached out to others living in the country or small-town communities. More often than not, the communal ties that grew out of or sustained migration evolved out of slave communities and post–Civil War agency that defined the freedom commune. Without doubt, their experiences differed considerably from their contemporaries who left the South for openly hostile segregated neighborhoods of color that reluctantly welcomed their arrival.[91]

Not everyone settled in Houston communities as a permanent solution. Of course, for some, migration to Houston represented a temporary solution; permanent relocation to the Midwest or western United States would occur in later years. For the time being, Houston represented a practical choice. Migration, however, did not improve the lives of all who made their way into the city. Poverty withstood the transition from country to city and often sparked continued instability and increased delinquency and crime, as *Houston Informer* headlines in the 1930s imply.[92]

For these reasons, the middle class gradually built a wall between themselves and the masses of working-class African Americans. We see this even among working-class Louisianans who believed their distinctiveness qualified them and their children for special privileges as perhaps honorary Whites. Nonetheless, by formulating such self-help tasks, they laid the groundwork for more concrete social, economic, and political changes that would transform their communities—in the city, in the small town, and on the farm—in later years to come. Migrants also helped older residents create and expand the city's Afro-American organizations and institutions that gave people of color needed shelter and protection against the winds of racial segregation. For this reason, Afro-American settlement into Houston represented a new beginning, not only for the resettled newcomers but also for the larger African American community and city as a whole. This new settlement would benefit greatly from the community building exercises and civil-rights euphoria that would make its way into the city in the years to come.[93]

THREE

Beautiful People

Agency in Houston, 1900–1941

Born in 1881, in the town of Clinton, a tiny farm community west of the Guadalupe River, just ninety miles north of the Gulf Sea in DeWitt County, Texas, Jennie Belle Murphy—known to friends and family as Ladybelle—was raised by relatives, sometime after the death of her mother, Rachel Thomas. The multiethnic, multiracial teenager of West African and Mexican descent, with a passion for sewing, gardening, and service, left home at the turn of the century to study domestic science at Guadalupe College, a private Baptist school for African Americans, located in Seguin, Texas. Already a sought-after seamstress, Murphy worked to help defray tuition and board costs, even on occasion doing alterations for the spouse of the school's president, David Abner Jr., who later served as the director of the National Baptist Convention Theological Seminary. Her studies and work duties fortunately did not get in the way of her personal life.[1]

Murphy, possibly while still attending Guadalupe College, fell in love with and married Benjamin Jesse Covington of Falls County, a recent Meharry Medical College graduate. Born in 1869, in tiny Marlin, Texas, a cotton-farming community twenty-four miles south of Waco and one hundred and twenty-one miles south of Dallas, in the middle of the Blackland Prairie region in central Texas, the studious, attractive, chocolate-complexioned son of former slaves was bedazzled by the caring, lovely, tall, fair-skinned beauty. The couple married on September 30, 1902, in Seguin, perhaps following the completion of the bride's studies, and settled briefly in Wharton and Yoakum, near Jennie Covington's hometown, before moving to Houston in 1903.[2]

Covington, who described herself as "a plain woman from the country," no longer struggled to make ends meet, being the wife of one of the most recognizable professionals in the city of Houston.[3] So prominent were the Covingtons from the late 1910s to the 1960s that luminaries such as educators Booker T. and Margaret Washington, contralto singer Marion Anderson, entertainer and activist Paul Robeson, concert tenor Roland Hayes, writer and activist William Pikens, and boxing champion Joe Lewis enjoyed the splendor of their stately two-story home on Hadley and Dowling Streets while visiting the city. A concerned Covington used her connections to draw attention to the plight of the poor, especially African Americans. The privileged, empathetic woman made it her life's mission to care for others as her aunt and uncle, Jane and Will Jones, had provided for her. For the next sixty-five-years, the upper middle-class homemaker from the country worked to improve the lives of thousands.[4]

Civic leader and humanitarian Jennie Covington, along with other migrant women, helped establish interracial coalitions, women's clubs, social service agencies, and community centers that reached out to African Americans in need. Although Covington and other migrants rarely protested White privilege and racism in public, they came to the aid of African Americans through charitable means. Jennie Covington; Martha Sneed, a Brazoria County native; educator Mary L. Jones, who moved to the city from Huntsville around the turn of the century; and others who migrated to the city before the 1920s wave of internal migration, founded the Blue Triangle Young Women's Christian Association (YWCA) branch in 1920, with the assistance of the local and national board of the YWCA. Through the years, the branch provided Houston African Americans, especially women and girls, with an employment office, cafeteria meals, a travelers aid program for recent migrants in need of assistance, public aid to families in need, recreation facilities for children, and a camp retreat as well as educational and Christian conferences. Because of the generosity of Covington and other newcomers to the city, the Blue Triangle YWCA, during its existence from 1920 to 1998, served over 30,000 people.[5]

Covington's concern for Afro-Americans, especially young people and the poor, motivated others to get involved, including family. In later years, Covington, an advocate of racial justice, planted seeds of ferment in her offspring, including grandson Thomas Dent, the eldest child of Ernestine Jessie Covington Dent. Ernestine, the only child of Dr. and Mrs. Covington, was a classically trained pianist and music teacher who married New Orleans hospital administrator Albert Dent, the future president of Dillard University. Award-winning writer and activist Tom Dent, who founded the scholarly periodical *Callaloo* in 1969, like his grandmother, Jennie Covington, earnestly sought after racial liberation for people of color, becoming a major grassroots and national leader in the modern Civil Rights Movement. At the same time, Covington and others who had the means to work closely with Whites on interracial commissions and social welfare agencies still perhaps found themselves self-identifying as distinctive, better suited, or important liaisons for the Black communities. Perhaps they desired the complete integration of the races and progress for all; some possibly desired full-fledged social acceptance for themselves in the larger society. And some, even while embracing certain concepts of superiority that mimicked White supremacy, ultimately moved closer toward real social equality for all. Migrant Jennie Covington, once a Booker T. Washington accommodationist, in later years endorsed Du Bois integrationists such as Dr. Martin Luther King Jr. and grandson Tom Dent, believing the time had come for real change.[6]

Whether as an accommodationist or integrationist, Covington desired the beautiful splendor of social equality for the race and showed it through her actions. "Beautiful people," a phrase my late father used to describe family and members of the community he admired and respected for their positive deeds and positions as spirited role models, aptly defines the migrants discussed in this chapter.[7] Migrants and veteran Houstonians in the African American community made inroads favoring social autonomy, self-respect, and racial integrity. Through community agency, the internal migrants in this chapter found ways to initiate hope and shepherd change. In time, their actions, which mirrored the community building that emerged decades earlier in slave quarters and in freedom communities before the Great Migration, would propel bolder moves toward social justice and racial change. Therefore, this chapter assesses the varied community-building strategies available to African Americans at this time. The Black elite, for example, used community-building concepts that reflected their cautious nature and mutual alliances of self-interest with Whites and other Black elites. Some people in power desired improved conditions for all African Americans, whereas others looked at achieving amenable goals that would lead to later victories. Members of the rank and file, particularly churchgoers, also found ways to better the lives of those around them. All sought ways to fight structural racism in all facets of society. Many define these acts of self-help as agency.[8]

The Conceptualization of Agency

Covington's evolution as a community activist reflects the multilayered dimensions of Houston's migrant community in the first half of the twentieth century, especially with respect to "agency," a term with multiple and often contradictory meanings. Agency, the notion of autonomous self-help and community building, involved intergroup relationships, intraracial coalitions, cross-cultural alliances, and, sometimes, interracial relationships for the purposes of self-improvement and liberation. Black migrants of varying age groups, class stratums, and education levels partook in agency. People approached agency differently, of course, depending on who they were and their lifestyle interests.[9]

Many advocated self-help intervention that did not involve upsetting the racial status quo, but others, prompted by a host of problems and issues, promoted immediate racial equality and/or integration. Most newcomers, if not all, however, supported some form of community-building effort that involved the establishment of institutions and programs that promoted social betterment and racial autonomy. Recent migrants like Covington not only benefitted from the assistance of others but also, through community agency, they themselves built neighborhoods, institutions, and organizations that aided the masses. They had to—for themselves, their families, and the survival of their communities.[10]

Still, as discussed by historian Walter Johnson, agency often meant different ideas to different individuals or groups. Perhaps, as assessed by Johnson, historians feel the need to cultivate labels that do not necessarily correctly define the actions of historical groups. Slave celebrations, although an exercise in Blackness, possibly, according to Johnson, had more to do with an exercise in humanity than resistance or liberation. In the same vein, migrants and established residents in Houston perhaps thought less about formulating change than proving their ability to adapt for the purpose of mutual and group social acceptance. African Americans who did not advocate radical stances that would upset the status quo or propel White backlashes perhaps looked at self-preservation as a reliable means to an end. Perhaps they saw themselves less as agents than as perpetuators of survival in a racist world. Although this was true, the migrants and established residents still engaged in some form of agency. For any victory or success among African Americans, according to historian Grace Elizabeth Hale, equated to a formidable threat to White supremacy in all its forms.[11]

The efforts of African American migrants like Jennie Covington hastened enormous changes for the city's Black community. New schools, business ventures, churches, nightclubs, social clubs, and political organizing efforts signaled the birth of a new era. Throughout the first half of the century, African American migrants, utilizing community building, craftily challenged the institutions, employers, and laws that relegated them to a debased position in society. To the outside world, agency provided people of color with their own subservient institutional outlets and agendas that adhered to Jim Crow racism.[12]

Cleverly, however, community agency allowed for multiple strategies that included generational activism. By building the institutional resources that aided future community activists, migrants planted seeds of protest that reverberated into a clearer denouncement of racial bigotry in later years. Ironically, this process did not first materialize in the twentieth century. To the contrary, agency served as a lifeline to both West African societies and slave communities in the Americas. Black migrants to Houston, therefore, utilized the community concepts they had learned in their rural or small-town settlements that formed during slavery or following the Civil War, cultural constructs that were also distinctively African in origin.[13]

Twentieth-century migrants did not do the heavy lifting alone. Black migrants and established residents found common ground and avoided some of the intraracial dissent that divided groups of color outside the South. The common denominators of southern culture and slavery drew people together in an effort to combat real problems. Virtually all of the city's Afro-Americans—recent migrants and established residents—could trace their lineage to slavery and freed communities throughout Texas and Louisiana. This experience alone shaped the self-help ideas and actions of both groups, who intermingled together at church, on the job, in school, in nightclubs, at meetings, on the residential streets, and in the country or small towns. Migrants and older residents, who made their way into the city as freedpeople or as the offspring of former slaves in the nineteenth century, adopted quiet agency as the strategy of choice in their war against racism and poverty because anything else would have certainly instigated an immediate backlash. The self-help concept of agency not only looked to the future; it allowed these southerners the chance to reflect on the beauty of their rural, small-town beginnings and the first recollections of community building that protected them and their ancestors from oppression and deadly self-destruction.[14]

Nor did recent migrants build Houston's first Afro-American institutions. Rather, they added to the institutions others before them—nineteenth-century Black migrants—had created before and after the collapse of slavery. From bondage to liberation, Houston African Americans sought agency as a tenet of solace and legitimacy. Largely the products of the Transatlantic Slave Trade, domestic slave trade, and occasionally the illegal trafficking of Africans, slaves and ex-slaves found succor in community building. Slave Elias Dibble, with the help of White Methodists, formed the African Mission of the Houston Methodist Church in 1847, and later in 1865 established Trinity Methodist Episcopal Church, the first African American congregation in the city. Another minister and former slave from Virginia, John Henry "Jack" Yates, who came to Houston by way of Matagorda County after the Civil War, served as the first resident pastor of Antioch Baptist Church and helped establish the first Baptist Association for African Americans in Houston. Yates also encouraged members to purchase land near the church. In 1872, with the help of Elias Dibble, Yates purchased what would become the city's first Afro-American park, Emancipation Park, in Third Ward. Later in 1885, he founded Houston College, or Houston Baptist Academy, a forerunner of Houston Colored Junior College, which later became Texas Southern University.[15]

Others were no less determined. Politician and contractor Richard Allen, a former biracial slave, originally from Virginia, also promoted socioeconomic development and civil rights among people of color, even supporting the Exodus of 1879. He, along with Dibble and Yates, also supervised the Gregory Institute, the first school for Afro-Americans, originally established in 1870 as a training school for Afro-American teachers. Allen's son-in-law, John Brown Bell, a grocer and philanthropist, also gave back to the community. A native of Macon, Georgia, Brown, whose parents named him for the radical antislavery martyr, bought his first grocery store in 1882. Perhaps the wealthiest Afro-American in the city, he regularly reached out to the community. As a National Negro Business League (NNBL) board member, he funded numerous projects. He also served as Antioch Baptist Church treasurer and held membership in the Masons, Knights of Pythias, and the United Brothers of Friendship. Over the course of his life, Bell donated and loaned thousands of dollars to Houston's Afro-American community. Another former slave from Virginia, Mariah Sharkie, helped form the Women's Convention auxiliary of the state's Afro-American Baptist Church in 1886. In Houston, Sharkie and other women established churches, formed kindergartens, and donated to the poor.[16]

The children of former slaves and migrants relied on community outreach too. Emmett Jay Scott, the son of South Carolina and Rosharon, Texas, slaves, was born in 1873. He attended Wiley College and later worked for the *Houston Daily Post* as a janitor, errand runner, and copyeditor. In 1893, he helped establish the *Texas Freeman,* the city's first African American newspaper, ultimately catching the attention of Booker T. Washington and politician and educator Norris Wright Cuney, who both hired him as their personal assistant in the 1890s.[17]

These early acts of community agency among freedpeople and their direct descendents would influence an entire century of activism in the African American community, dating back to the early 1900s. Twentieth-century migrants, therefore, saw firsthand the organizations, associations, and friendships that evolved around southern social constructs, particularly the family. Both working-class and middle-class settlers noticed the churches, schools, lodges, social service agencies, and, later, healthcare agencies that catered to the community. Black migrants, who also used their own familial and community constructs to build in the city, took delight in knowing what awaited them and what they could contribute to the betterment of their adopted city. The city's African American community comprised a society of community builders, self-made men and women, and determined "laborers of love" on behalf of African Americans.[18]

Self-Help Benevolence

Some of the oldest self-help institutions in the African American community—fraternal orders, secret societies, benevolent groups, and mutual aid societies—attracted numerous settlers in the early twentieth century. They had already for centuries provided invaluable assistance to members and nonmembers alike. In some ways, fraternal orders originated centuries before the onset of African slavery in the Americas. This is especially true of benevolent societies, perhaps the first African American institutions to exist in British North America and the United States. Influenced by West and West Central African secret societies and societal customs; early radical, autonomous voluntary associations that followed the American Revolution; early conservative, segregated, predominately White fraternal lodges; slave communities; and postbellum rural and small-town cultural constructs, Houston's multilayered African American community formed benevolent societies, fraternal lodges and/or mutual-aid associations that catered to the community. Important as well to Houstonians were female auxiliaries and independent female lodges that provided services to women.[19]

Both service-oriented and recreational in nature, these organizations generally served as the only means of civic and political organizing outside the church, following Reconstruction. Some Houston lodges were national in scope, whereas others formed as local and regional organizations. Black migrants formed both segregated chapters of predominately White fraternal orders and African American–controlled orders. Texans and Houstonians in the late nineteenth century established the Prince Hall Masons, Grand United Order of Odd Fellows, and Grand Lodge of the Knights of Pythias. Some organizations like the Young Men's Benevolent Club and Freedmen's Aid Society served as community charities, whereas others centered on building on the work of fraternal lodges.[20]

Black migrants not only joined national lodges; they also formed their own fraternal societies and mutual aid associations. Members of the African American community in 1882 formed the Ancient Order of Pilgrims. Educator Henry Cohen Hardy, a Jamaican national, established the city's first Houston-based national lodge for African Americans. With thirty-one chapters in the surrounding Houston area as well as across the United States by 1915, the order emerged as one of the most influential organizations in the city. Members not only provided health benefits and life insurance for policyholders but also owned real estate that provided office space for African American professionals and businesses. In the early twentieth century, the Pilgrim's four-story building (fig. 45), located across the street from Colored High School on San Felipe (later West Dallas) and Bagby, in Fourth Ward, housed physician practices, law offices, drug stores, groceries and commissaries, and dental offices; it also held parties and dances for the general public, thereby providing relaxing enjoyment for young people. The organization's assets, valued at $200,000 at the start of the Depression, comprised real estate, liquid capital, and individual business establishments. The organization always aided people in distress, and it also raised tens of thousands of dollars for the larger African American community.[21]

Other lodges and mutual-aid societies in Houston included the

Knights and Daughters of Tabor, Heroines of Jericho, the United Brothers of Friendship, Sisters of the Mysterious Ten, the Household of Ruth, Grand Court of Calanthe, Woodmen Union, Sons and Daughters of Mercy, Daughters of Czar, Wonderful Workers of the World, American Woodmen, and Loyal Friends of America. These organizations, although multidimensional as social clubs, voluntary associations, and, on occasion, life insurance and benefits firms, often formed to meet a particular task. In 1907, seven African American educators, including post-Reconstruction migrants and recent newcomers to the city, led by Alabama native and Fisk College graduate E. O. Smith, formed the Pilgrim Congregational Church and Library Association to raise public awareness about the need for an African American library (see fig. 21). In 1909, a temporary library facility with three hundred volumes opened inside the city's African American high school. With the support of other community leaders—Houston native and Booker T. Washington confidant Emmett J. Scott, along with Washington himself, the city's civic community, and Julia Ideson, director of the Houston Lyceum and Carnegie Library—the association procured $15,000 from philanthropist and industrialist Andrew Carnegie for the Colored Carnegie Library.[22]

FIGURE 21. The Carnegie Colored Library Board *(Courtesy Houston Metropolitan Research Center, Houston Public Library, Houston, Texas, Covington Family Collection, MSS 0170-0050)*

The Colored Carnegie Library, completed in 1914, brought together an ensemble of Houston's best and brightest—educators, ministers, professionals, fraternal leaders, and business people—for the common good of the community. Recent migrants to the city, along with other members of the fraternal society, played a pivotal role in the completion of the project. They chaired boards, reached out to the civic community for funds and resources, and persuaded members of the community to give, as well as donated and loaned thousands of dollars for numerous charitable causes. Perhaps the first real business entity in the community since Emancipation, lodges in many ways shaped the ideals of the city's first group of African American business owners. Many, if not most, African American business owners, belonged to an established fraternal lodge or mutual benevolent society in the early half of the last century. Lodges and fraternal orders certainly afforded African American men useful leadership skills that would become essential in later years to come.[23]

Although men principally developed and dominated these important organizations in the community, they alone did not operate them. Women, in fact, regardless of their socioeconomic status, employed a host of self-help approaches in their fraternal societies, clubs, churches, homes, and political affiliations to reach out to others in need. Black women found lodges appealing, mostly because the organizations provided an important outlet for political creativity, socioeconomic independence, and business development. In some instances, these women successfully created thriving institutions that functioned independently of male orders. In Texas and Houston, some of the most successful fraternal societies were those headed by women. Women's fraternal societies, like male lodges, provided needed services to the community. First, they offered loans, life insurance policies, and health benefits to members. Second, these female-run establishments operated professionally, promoted integrity, and provided employment opportunities to women of color. Third, the organizations endorsed the concept of group economy among women of color. Lodges increasingly opened doors of opportunity for African American women with clerical skills, accounting experience, college degrees, and exceptional leadership qualities.[24]

In 1895, African American women and men established an organization known as Hermione #4, the sister organization to the Grand Lodge of the Knights of Pythias, and among other endeavors, highlighted self-reliance and institution building. Three years later in 1898, a group of Houston women affiliated with Hermione opened the Grand Court Order of Calanthe, of Texas. The organization did more than establish insurance policies and insurance benefits for its female members; the groundbreaking fraternal order also invested in real estate, government bonds, and the free-enterprise stock market.[25]

Mostly, the all-female lodge invested in its members. The organization, which had a sizable income of $600,000 in 1930 and assets totaling $250,000 by 1950, provided an important service to eligible members. The Grand Court, the wealthiest African American female fraternal society in the country, gave beneficiaries $100 at the turn of the century. The Grand Court also provided business training and employment opportunities for talented women. As one of the few female-owned organizations of its time in African American communities, it showcased the financial savvy of African American women, whose talents were both ignored and misused in male-dominated businesses and institutions like the church. The organization also did something else: It brought together migrant women from differing socioeconomic backgrounds, professions, and education levels. Domestics and laundresses attended meetings, socials, teas, and church services with Elmo, Texas, native and civil-rights leader Lulu White as well as other members of the African American elite. Unlike similar African American organizations of the twentieth century, it did not limit its members to the well-to-do. Members included maids, chambermaids, housewives, high-school dropouts, entertainers, schoolteachers, businesspersons, physicians, clubwomen, and activists. The fraternal order, whose members included migrants Lulu B. White, Jennie Covington; physician and Huntsville, Texas, native Thelma Patton; and educator Mary L. Jones Johnson, whose mother came to the city by way of Huntsville, made substantial donations and loans to others as well.[26]

Annually, donations went to local and national organizations and charities. Women—and men—in their lodges, clubs, churches, and exclusive societies—gave to the Community Chest, shelters, hospitals, and schools. In the 1930s, local branches loaned $40,000 to Paul Quinn College for the construction of a building. The organization also allowed members to borrow money to pay taxes and purchase homes. Women of various backgrounds in the Grand Court, Order of Calanthe and other female associations benefited from the economic security these organizations brought. During the Great Depression, when many, if not most, African American fraternal societies went bankrupt, some female-operated associations prospered because of sound business decisions.[27]

The Gospel of Giving According to Women

Collective and individualized women's activism reached new heights in the city as African Americans increasingly moved to Houston and joined voluntary associations and lodges, clubs, literary societies, sororities, churches, and charities. The women in these organizations reached out to young people, gave to the indigent, clothed the homeless, ministered to the faithless, and inspired the desperate. Historian Audrey Y. Crawford has written extensively on African American clubwomen in Houston. These women, according to Crawford, fostered a spirit of activism, self-help, bravery, community devotion, and camaraderie. Racism forced women in the community to take an active role in charity and self-help support. Disciplined and committed as institution builders, these women provided numerous services to African Americans, improved countless lives, and made Houston, like Atlanta, Chicago, Detroit, New Orleans, Gary, and other cities, a viable and vital option of progress. As their fathers, brothers, husbands, friends, and lovers fell victim to political exclusion and economic polarity, and as White women's organizations—for the most part—shut them out of mainstream social welfare agencies and formalized social work, these women formed their own identifiably African American self-help institutions and worked for the advancement of the race.[28]

Again, internal migrant Jennie Covington comes to mind as a tireless community builder. A reformer, Covington worked as an unpaid social worker, gave back to her daughter's school, labored in her church, and did her part as a clubwoman. In fact, the efforts of progressives like Covington helped inspire more formalized social welfare organizing efforts for people of color. Progressives in 1904 orchestrated a carnival to raise funds for their charitable work, ultimately forming United Charities, a formal philanthropic group. In 1915, these efforts helped chart the Houston Foundation (currently The United Way), a permanent philanthropic agency that administered funds to local social welfare groups and charities.[29]

The next year, the city created the Social Service Bureau, which facilitated the creation of varied programs, from public health and childcare to welfare and relief. Social welfare advocates expanded these efforts. In the 1920s, prior to the Great Depression, the Houston Community Chest, a philanthropic agency comprising thirty-three separate agencies, distributed monetary resources to Houston-area charities. In 1928, the group administered almost $400,000 to local charities, with tens of thousands going to organizations either serving all Houstonians, regardless of race, or African Americans exclusively.[30]

Covington worked closely with these groups, even those that segregated their facilities. Most charities segregated their services or offices, or barred African Americans completely. Black women, nevertheless, put the needs of others first. Houston's most successful social service agencies within the African American community—the Blue Triangle YWCA, Bethlehem Center, Darcus Home for Delinquent Girls, and Boy Scouts of America—were those operated and staffed by well-off middle-class women (and men), including African American migrants like Jennie Covington. Concerned advocates ultimately opened the Darcus Home, another facility for African Americans. Moreover, homeless mothers, schoolchildren, the poor, and the unemployed benefited from Covington's volunteer efforts at the Houston Settlement Association, Bethlehem Center, C. W. Luckie Elementary School Mothers' Club, Antioch and Bethel Baptist Churches, and Married Ladies Social, Art & Charity Club. Covington helped make social welfare a practical, sustainable solution for African Americans. For example, as a Bethlehem Center volunteer, Covington headed the center's Social Service Advisory Committee, a group that investigated family welfare matters in the African American community. Covington, who also worked with coalitions that promoted interracial harmony, and other migrant women used their networks, organizations, and passion to make a difference.[31]

Black women migrants like Covington always enjoyed their multiple affiliations and did their part for the community. Organizations like Zeta Phi Beta Sorority; Alpha Kappa Alpha Sorority; the Smart Set Club; Sigma Gamma Rho Sorority; Delta Sigma Theta Sorority; Ethel Ransom Art and Literary Club; the Married Ladies Social, Art & Charity Club; and The Links, Incorporated, became important community-building institutions in the city. Some organizations like Sigma Gamma Rho Sorority began on college campuses; others initially formed as social gatherings for housewives, only to later shape into self-help charities and political forums. These and other local organizations played a major role in uplifting the poor, sick, and downtrodden in the community. At the same time, the important vestiges of friendship, mutual respect, and discipline reinforced notions of racial identity, societal advancement, and collective consciousness. Although these organizations often exposed hierarchical elitism, intra-color conflict, class divisions, and rivalries, they all admonished the erroneous worldview regarding so-called African or African American laziness, irresponsibility, inferiority, and savagery.[32]

Most groups, even those that began as social clubs, formed a collective consciousness around the crucial issues of social welfare, racial autonomy, cultural concerns, and gender bias. In 1902, educator Melissa Price, along with friend Mary Crawford and twelve others, organized the Married Ladies Social, Art & Charity Club (fig. 22). The exclusive club of upstanding African American women focused on agency, institution building, and aesthetic expression among members. Members read contemporary and historic literature, canvassed local and out-of-town events, painted, and discussed extensively women's issues, along with African American life and culture. In time, the group of fourteen women began addressing serious issues plaguing the African American community, such as poverty, lack of educational opportunities, and gender inequity.[33]

The organization limited its membership to "respectable" married

FIGURE 22. In 1902, educator Melissa Price and domestic Mary Crawford, as well as twelve others, organized the Married Ladies Social Art & Charity Club. The exclusive club of upscale African American women focused on agency, institution building, and aesthetic expression among members. Today the one-hundred-year-old organization limits membership to married women living with their spouses. *(Courtesy Houston Metropolitan Research Center, Houston Public Library, Houston, Texas, Covington Family Collection, MSS 0170-0003)*

wives of prominent husbands.³⁴ The women's organization, which grew to seventy members at any given time, considered itself privileged and felt the city's most prominent women within the African American community could effectively help bridge the gap between the rich and poor and across the racial divide. The exclusivity and elitism that permeated the city's African American community did in fact create walls of exclusion and degrees of separation between the well-to-do and poor. For this reason, other middle-class groups like the 1906 Art and Literary Club, which sponsored a 1908 lecture given by National Association of Colored Women (NACW) President Margaret Murray Washington, the third wife of Booker T. Washington, followed the doctrine of the founders of the NACW and developed other local, grass-roots organizations. Still, middle-class in nature, the 1906 Art & Literary Club, which ultimately affiliated with the NACW, never attracted the majority of migrant women. The majority of women migrants entering the city utilized another self-help tool to reach family and friends in need.³⁵

Numerous other women's organizations formed in the city. Some, like the Cinderella Bridge Club and Chat-an-Hour Coffee Club, concentrated on cultural outlets and brief excursions from real life. The Ethel Ransom Art and Literary Club, named for the Fort Worth African American civic activist and nurse, began as a social organization for middle-class Afro-American women in Houston. Like many of its predecessors, the group moved in the direction of community service. In 1927, the year of its founding, the club joined the Texas Federation of Negro Women's Clubs, an association made up of different African American social and service women's clubs throughout the state.³⁶

Houston clubwomen, like their contemporaries across the country, always worked in multiple organizations and with multiple groups in an attempt to provide the best possible service to African Americans in need. These women's clubs, along with philanthropic organizations, occasionally worked with local White groups, focused their time and effort on lynching crimes, opened kindergartens and day-care centers, joined Mothers' Clubs, founded community centers, and served on settlement-house boards, boards of orphanages and nursing homes, and active church axillaries. Commonly, busy women made time for multiple groups in an effort to do their part in the world and at the same time utilize release valves of pleasure and fun in an often challenging world for dedicated activists of color. Sometimes, the children of migrants carried on the work of their

FIGURE 23. Educator, civic leader, and civil-rights activist Lullelia Harrison (far right) pledged Zeta Phi Beta while she was an undergraduate student at Wiley College in the late 1920s. She would quickly move up the ranks of the organization, which had already cemented an excellent reputation among college students at HBCUs. According to the organization's website, Zetas recruited on the campuses of HBCUs, whereas the others, which did as well, spent a lot of time recruiting on predominately White campuses as well as the larger, popular HBCUs. Zeta Phi Beta created this sister organization in an effort to collaborate with the larger African American community on a number of issues. In the Houston area, the two sister-groups retained a strong bond. One of the members of the sister organization is Christia Adair, who is standing next to Harrison. *(Courtesy Houston Metropolitan Research Center, Houston Public Library, Houston, Texas, Zeta Amicae Records, RGE 0050, Box 3, folder 1)*

parents. Zeta Phi Beta Sorority national president, schoolteacher, wife, and mother Lullelia Harrison, whose parents settled Fourth Ward in the 1900s or 1910s from southern Louisiana and Dayton, Texas, pulled double duty to complete her roster of regular activities that mostly benefited others; at the same time, Harrison, like other active women, had children to raise, a husband to tend to, and other family responsibilities awaiting at home every evening (fig. 23). Still, institution building and agency for these women never waned and usually began in the familiar church setting.[37]

Spirited Church Work

Black women and men usually began their nonfamilial community building efforts in the church. Since Emancipation, the church and church work, more than any other forum, has embodied agency. Religion worked as a chief agent of liberation for people of color. At the same time, churches provided African Americans with important community-building resources that allowed for civic work, fundraising, political activism, and self-help sufficiency. Churches therefore filled an important void in the African American community and had done so since the days of slavery.[38]

The need to provide people with spiritual insight for daily living led to the massive growth and scattering of African American congregations in the late nineteenth and early twentieth centuries, particularly in the wake of the Great Migrations. Church growth symbolized African Americans' need for solace, support, and autonomy. Churches especially expanded in the twentieth century as internal migrants flocked to African American communities throughout the city. In 1915, almost fourteen thousand people had memberships at thirty-two Baptist and Methodist African American congregations. In 1929, ninety-five churches held worship services in African American neighborhoods across the Houston area. These ninety-five churches represented well over thirty thousand people, although of these, only seventeen thousand attended church regularly.[39]

The city's ninety-five African American congregations comprised a gamut of Christian faiths and denominations. Baptist, Methodist Episcopal, African Methodist Episcopal, Christian Methodist Episcopal, Roman Catholic, Church of God in Christ, Congregational, Presbyterian, Episcopalian, Christian, Church of the Living God, and Seven-Day Adventist churches represented the city's growing, rich diversity within the African American community. Some nineteen thousand of the city's thirty thousand African American church members were Baptist, with Baptist congregations comprising 65 percent of the city's African American churches. The city's seventeen Methodist congregations made up the city's second largest body of African American churches, being 15 percent of the city's total. As Houston's African American population grew, especially in the 1920s, wealthier, established churches like Trinity Methodist Episcopal and Antioch Baptist increasingly catered to working-class and middle-class African American families, whereas younger, smaller congregations spoke for one class of congregants—the struggling working poor (fig. 24). The city's newer churches included marginal, storefront, shotgun-house congregations that held services in dreadfully dreary and desolate structures. Still, regardless of their socioeconomic means, these churches had one issue in common: the celebration and worship of a loving, embracing Creator.[40]

One of the most noteworthy of these new storefront and working-class churches was the Church of God in Christ (COGIC) Pentecostals, the largest African American Pentecostal (AAP) or holiness sect in the United States. According to historian Karen Kossie-Chernyshev, Pentecostalism, a religious movement that emphasizes the spiritual baptism of Christian

FIGURE 24. According to historian Craig Wilder, the close bonds that exist between pastors and their deacon boards are reminiscent of the fraternal orders that existed in West Africa prior to the outbreak of the transatlantic slave trade. A village chief could always rely on his entourage for protection. Antioch Baptist Church, founded in 1866, is the city's oldest African American Baptist congregation. Rev. Jack Yates, the congregation's first permanent African American pastor, still has descendants who attend Antioch. Antioch remained a symbol of Black success and vision. The deacon board took this picture with the pastor on August 9, 1936. Those individuals standing are William Hagan, Walter Smith, Andrew Cruise, Zack Sally, V. C. Henry, William Townsend (southeastern Texas), W. L. Mosley, and G. S. Johnson. The front row of seated men includes Harry A. Hainsworth, J. T. Collins, Pastor T. J. Goodall, L. H. Spivey (Bryan, Texas, native), and J.D. Collins. Harry Hainsworth (originally from Alabama, is the father of Latin instructor Hazel Hainsworth. Harry Hainsworth, a postal carrier, put all three of his children through Howard University; he also saw his son finish law school. *(Courtesy Houston Metropolitan Research Center, Houston Public Library, Houston, Texas, Mary L. Jones and General and Mary L. Jones Johnson Collection, MSS 0119-0014)*

believers through glossolalia, or the "speaking in tongues," had roots in Houston and helped expand COGIC churches across the country. Black Louisiana native William J. Seymour moved from Cincinnati to Houston around 1905, during the first phase of twentieth-century migration, where he learned the teachings of holiness ministers. In Houston, he attended an African American holiness congregation pastored by woman of color Lucy F. Farrow, a former servant of Charles F. Parham, the White leader of the Apostolic Faith movement (later the Pentecostal Movement) that originated at the Bethel Bible School in Topeka, Kansas, in 1901. Seymour publicly rejected both racial segregation and gender inequality in the Pentecostal church. Parham relocated to Houston and held regular revivals, eventually establishing another bible school. Seymour attended the school, sitting outside the classroom, and accepted the teachings of the baptism of the Holy Ghost through the conversing in tongues. Seymour relocated to Los Angeles in 1906, to pastor a small congregation where he played a role in the famous Azusa Street Revival, eventually influencing Charles H. Mason, the founder of the COGIC body.[41]

The first COGIC congregation in Texas, Center Street, formed in Third Ward, Houston, in 1909 and propelled the birth of later churches. The number of AAP congregations in the city grew to thirty-one by the early 1930s. The Great Migrations and their emphasis on African American agency accelerated the growth of these congregations. In Houston, ministers like H. W. Falls of New Iberia, Louisiana, and Houston resident William "Billie" Johnson formed churches in Fifth Ward "shotgun" houses that grew into six-hundred-seat edifices.[42] COGIC row houses and storefront churches like Third Ward Church of God in Christ on McGowen and Live Oak grew among the poorer working-class migrant population. Many observers like National Urban League field worker Jesse Thomas commented that established African American churches in the Houston area did not do enough to welcome incoming migrants into their church families. Migrants simply remedied the problem by creating their own churches. The southwestward migration of AAP aided the growth of these congregations. The simple, yet inspiring and spiritual messages of hope, liberation, opportunity, and spiritual separation mesmerized followers who heard these ministers in the country and city. Black Protestants of all sects relied on their faith and each other for spiritual comfort and hope.[43]

For thousands of others, the Roman Catholic Church symbolized both spiritual equality and racial autonomy. Houston's first African American

FIGURE 25. Houston's first African American Catholic Church, St. Nicholas in Third Ward, first opened as a school in 1887 on the corner of Chenevert and Lamar. The Afro-American Sisters of the Holy Family took over the instructional duties of the White Sisters of the Incarnate Word in 1905, and served two hundred students at the school. *(Courtesy Photograph Collection, Archives of the Archdiocese of Galveston-Houston, Archdiocese of Galveston-Houston, Houston, Texas)*

Catholic Church, St. Nicholas of Third Ward, first opened as a school in 1887 on the corner of Chenevert and Lamar (fig. 25). The Afro-American Sisters of the Holy Family took over the instructional duties of the White Sisters of the Incarnate Word in 1905 and served two hundred students at the school. Under the direction of the Society of St. Joseph (The Josephites), St. Nicholas Parish and School drew hundreds of congregants and students in the new century. Laypeople also played a role in the church's success. New Orleans migrant Albert E. Woodley, along with his family, moved to Houston in 1913, during the first phase of twentieth-century migration, and made St. Nicholas his home. He established a chapter of the Knights of Peter Claver in 1916. The lodge, together with the Ladies Auxiliary of the fraternal order, created a new enthusiasm among church members and nonmembers. Outings, dinner parties, dances, and festivals brought people together under the Catholic Faith and made St. Nicholas a popular place of worship. In 1929, the new parish on Bell Avenue and St. Charles boasted of three thousand members.[44]

During the third phase of the Great Migrations to the city, the Great Flood of 1927 brought even more African American Catholics to the city, with most settling in Fifth Ward, even while attending St. Nicholas in Third Ward. The next year the Diocese of Galveston-Houston purchased two city blocks in the 4000 and 4100 blocks of Sumpter Street. The Josephite Society paid for the new church. Builders, including Fifth Ward residents, broke ground on April 28, 1928. Completed in the spring of the following year, Bishop Byrne blessed the new edifice on June 9. Contractors also completed the rectory, convent, and school. Our Mother of Mercy of the Fifth Ward, a church that would become home to 50 percent of the city's African American Catholic parishioners, played a leading role in the educating of some four thousand African American Catholics and non-Catholics in the city by World War II. Like St. Nicholas in the 1920s, Our Mother of Mercy would later serve as a feeder church to new parish communities in nearby Trinity Gardens as well as faraway Acres Homes and Sunnyside (fig. 26). Even as people left the city in later years for surrounding suburban enclaves north and west of the city, Houston's African American Catholic community would continue to grow.[45]

Some of the reason for the church's growth had to do with the

FIGURE 26. The Great Flood of 1927 increased the African American Catholic population by substantial numbers. With the assistance of recent Louisiana migrants and the Society of Saint Joseph of the Sacred Heart (The Josephites), the Roman Catholic Church built Our Mother of Mercy Parish for Fifth Ward residents who did not want to travel three miles to St. Nicholas Parish or attend the segregated Our Lady of Guadalupe Parish. The church, located on 4000 Sumpter Street, opened in 1929 for mass to Frenchtown residents, becoming a parish one year later, with the school opening for students in August 1930. *(Courtesy Insurance Surveys (circa 1936), V. 4, Archives of the Archdiocese of Galveston-Houston, Archdiocese of Galveston-Houston, Houston, Texas)*

organization's public stance on racial bigotry. Around the country, for example, people made mention of the growth of African American priests, suggesting Catholics, unlike Protestants, sincerely believed in a sincere measure of equality. White Catholics' public crusade to end racial bigotry especially touched African Americans. *The Houston Informer and Texas Freeman,* for example, recognized the efforts of the Catholic Church in the 1930s, and emphasized, "the straight-forward attitude" of "Catholic leaders . . . on the question of the mistreatment of the Negro in America" is encouraging and therefore the church is "entitled to the credit for it."[46]

Whether Catholic or Protestant, migrant women churchgoers wielded influence in their new Houston churches. Although often dismissed by their male counterparts as unimportant, Christian women of color exercised monetary power, operated business offices, and swayed pastoral staffs and male-dominated committees. Black women also used their organizational powers to speak out against issues facing the community, including sexism. Historian Elizabeth Brooks Higginbotham argues that National Baptist Convention members' focus on matters of race, for example, lynching crimes, often reflected their discontent and disillusionment with gender prejudice within their congregations and denomination. Black women, according to Brooks Higginbotham, sought a double victory that ended racism and sexism both within and outside the church walls. Perhaps because women influenced their pastors, members, and communities so greatly, it became a crucial priority to remind them of their subordinate place within the church body. Still, amid gender politics and exclusion, according to Kossie-Chernyshev, African American Christian women carved out niches of liberation, sexual identity, and spiritual strength. Spiritual love, most of all, defined these women and their actions.[47]

Often the unsung champions of racial autonomy and spiritual expediency, these Christian women stood as amazing institution builders in the Bayou City. Kathleen Evans Stewart was one such individual. Born in the Piney Woods of Teague, Texas, in the early twentieth century, Kathleen Stewart would later follow her parents to La Porte in eastern Harris County near Galveston Bay, where her father, like so many men, found work in the community's booming oil-refining economy. There in La Porte, she met and married W. H. Stewart, also a common laborer working to make ends meet. The couple moved to Houston in 1938, joining St. John's Baptist Church on Dowling St. in Third Ward, where for the next forty years, she worked as an ardent supporter of disability rights.

Because of her overwhelming generosity toward the listening disabled, St. John's soon developed a reputation as a safe oasis for the hearing impaired. Growing up with a hearing-impaired sibling gave Kathleen Stewart a compassionate temperament often absent in the minds and hearts of others. At a young age she also learned sign language.[48]

When Kathleen Stewart joined St. John's her sister understandably felt somewhat out of place. Stewart later inquired about the church hiring an interpreter for Sunday worship. Her pastor told her to find an interpreter. Stewart would become a dedicated signer for the hearing impaired, even establishing a "Silent Department" that prioritized the needs of this important body. Without formal college education, Stewart became one of the most visible persons in Houston's religious community, always, until her death in 1981, promoting the welfare of the hearing disabled and faithful community building. For Stewart and other dutiful newcomers to the city, this exercise in faith did not begin and end in the church house.[49]

The Search for a Quality Education

Spirit-filled community cooperation came in many forms. Many, for example, advocated intellectual development and formal education for recent migrants from the country. Thousands of transplants moved to the city for this reason. Houston's schools, the largest in the South and, according to Columbia University Teacher's College, one of the strongest systems in the nation, aroused enthusiasm in the African American community it served. The school system grew from 6,380 students in 1900 to 26,015 students in 1920, with African Americans generally comprising at times almost one-third of all students attending schools and at other times a quarter of the school system's student body. For parents, the city's segregated school system offered young people a better selection of classes. Like many southern schools at this time, course listings combined industrial training with a handful of liberal arts classes. Even while Houston's Afro-American schools fared poorly when put up against White institutions of learning, when compared to other African American schools in the South, they ranked, according to historian William H. Kellar, number one.[50]

African American transients found the Houston Public School System, established in 1876, attractive, but they faced enormous obstacles that precluded their children from having an education that matched that of Whites. Since day one, city officials maintained two separate and unequal school systems for its students. Unfortunately, as the city's population and economy burgeoned in the first decades of the new century, expenditures for Afro-American students, classroom buildings, equipment, and salaries remained unequal to that of Whites. In 1918, Texas officials, for example, allocated $9 for each White child and $6 for each Black student. In 1929, the per capita cost for African American students, $25, differed greatly from that of $47 for every White child. The disparities, according to C. Richardson, only worsened as the postwar 1920s rolled on.[51]

The city's schools actually discriminated against two debased groups, although this fact was often ignored. According to education scholar Guadalupe San Miguel, Mexican-origin children, since the turn of the century, had a noticeable and growing presence in the city's schools. Most of the earliest schools for Mexican-descent youths evolved from White elementary schools in the city's barrios in and around Second Ward, Denver Harbor, and the near Northside. And only after World War II did Mexican Americans enter high school in significant numbers, with most attending Jefferson Davis High, John H. Reagan High, Charles H. Milby High, and Stephen F. Austin High. Whites comprised the majority at these schools through the second half of the twentieth century, when more Whites increasingly moved to the city's more exclusive Westside communities or suburbs. White flight, insensitive faculty, language laws, poverty, illiteracy, sickness and disease, crime, and substandard housing characterized Latino communities and schools in the early twentieth century, despite Mexican Americans' desire to learn and their love for the United States. As with African Americans, institutionalized racism in district policy, curriculum, and teacher attitudes typically characterized the Mexican American educational experience during this period. Reform initiatives also ignored the plight of people of color—Black or Brown.[52]

When the city formed the Houston Independent School District in 1924 and hired Indiana native Edison Ellsworth Oberholtzer as its first superintendent, the situation, according to historian Karen Benjamin, worsened. The district's new $11,000,000, child-centered curriculum and cosmetic makeover benefited Whites only. Expanded curriculum, new classrooms and laboratories, technology-driven campuses, and athletic facilities prompted immediate changes for the district's White student body. Fifth-graders, for example, scored above the national average in spelling, arithmetic, and reading in 1926. Unfortunately, the reforms excluded African Americans. Black teachers relied on outdated textbooks, dingy science labs, classrooms without chalkboards, outdated and boring curriculum, and insufficient school supplies. Principals in these poorer schools faced similar challenges. Dangerous flooding, fire hazards, unsanitary conditions in kitchen lunchrooms, weedy school grounds, dilapidated buildings, overcrowding, and glaring disparities between White and African American schools, according to newspaperman Clifton Richardson Sr., retarded African American learning and performance. In 1926, only after criticism did the district allocate $600,000 for Afro-American schools, ultimately tripling the district's building capacity for Afro-Americans. Still, the district discriminated against people of color. For the same year, the total value of the city's school buildings, equipment, and property for White students totaled nearly $25,000,000; for African Americans, the total value of all school properties was only almost $5,000,000.[53]

Racial discrimination also had a visible hand in the city's higher education. "The strange career of public higher education in Houston, Texas," according to scholar Amilcar Shabazz, echoed the problem of race in the United States.[54] Oberholtzer developed the idea for Houston Junior College (HJC) for Whites in the early 1920s. Professional development courses as well as baccalaureate training would enhance the reputation of the school district, regardless of race. The school district created HJC in March of 1927; amid the concerns of a special committee of prominent African Americans, the district a few months later established Houston Colored Junior College (HCJC). Even though both schools offered continuing education programs for educators pursuing credit toward certification and the obtaining of the undergraduate degree in education, school board officials, along with Texas Higher Education Coordinating Board members, felt uneasy funding another public college for African Americans. HJC (now The University of Houston) remained the dominant institution, whereas HCJC, which in 1934 became a four-year college called Houston College for Negroes (now Texas Southern University [TSU]), remained in name, funding, and curriculum the subordinate school.[55]

Equally glaring, African American educators earned less pay. For example, high school principals with master's degrees, such as Navasota, Texas, native James D. Ryan and Alabama-born Ernest O. Smith, earned a maximum salary of $2,750, whereas their White peers with the same credentials made $4,500, a difference of 65 percent. The same principle applied to faculty: Black high-school instructors with master's degrees earned $900 less than their White peers in 1929. Although common in the South, this practice did not occur everywhere. In San Antonio, for example, schoolteachers, regardless of their race or ethnicity, earned equal pay. Tulsa, Oklahoma, where Oberholtzer came from, also practiced salary parity. Only in the 1940s, after African American educators threatened lawsuits, did pay inequities within the Houston school district end.[56]

For African American educators, including recent migrants from the country, the overt discrimination served as a real reminder of racism's piercing effects—glass-ceiling barriers at the workplace, a lower standard of living, compromised learning potential, social inequities, underemployment, and so on. Black educators had few alternatives outside Houston. Former Houston Independent School District (HISD) educators Thelma Scott Bryant, Hazel Hainesworth Young of Navasota, and Lullelia Harrison argue that African American schoolteachers had few choices. Black educators could not readily express their frustrations with the administration; nor could they hold public forums with parents to discuss alternative options. They essentially had few options outside the cloak of public accommodation. Taking other teaching positions in surrounding areas meant taking a reduced pay cut. They could not risk retaliation from an already oppressive institution. Their only alternative, at least prior to World War II, was insular self-help.[57]

In fact, racial discrimination allowed African American educators and parents the chance to rely on themselves, each other, and a growing African American migrant community. Drawing from the examples set forth by late nineteenth-century newcomers, recent internal migrants found ways to coexist in their racist professional world. The school district's limitations or faults only translated into self-reliance and community interdependence. Thelma Scott Bryant recalls the dedication of her schoolteachers at Douglas Elementary School, then on 3000 McGowan, "The teachers were very dedicated . . . I had an English teacher, Miss R. H. Pendleton, who was so good that really what I learned in high school and college never surpassed what she gave us in the elementary school." The distinguished list of HISD alumni substantiates this claim, a list that includes future St. Louis Urban League President Fredda Crawford (Witherspoon), who ultimately married Robert Witherspoon. Witherspoon was the attorney who precipitated a series of events that ultimately propelled a major Supreme Court victory with *Shelley v. Kraemer* (1948), which overturned the national policy of courts upholding residential restrictive covenants based on race (fig. 27).[58]

Beneath the pretense of accommodation, James D. Ryan, like so many

FIGURE 27. Dr. Fredda Crawford (Witherspoon) was born in 1923 or 1924 to caterer Vanita Crawford and Missouri Pacific Railroad employee R. E. Crawford. The family lived on Andrews Street in Fourth Ward. Mother Vanita Crawford moved to Houston with her family in 1911 and joined Antioch Baptist Church in 1913, remaining a faithful member until her death in 1992. Vanita and R. E. Crawford saved for their daughter's well-being, especially her education. At the age of fourteen Fredda graduated valedictorian from Booker T. Washington High School. She went on to Bishop College, graduating four years later with a baccalaureate degree. An accomplished young woman, she earned a business degree from Hughes Business School after completing undergraduate school, and later three master's degrees in psychiatric social work, psychology, and guidance and counseling from the University of Chicago. She later earned her PhD in guidance and counseling from Washington University, making St. Louis, Missouri, her home by World War II. She eventually married Robert Witherspoon, a local attorney, one of the instigators behind the push to desegregate the neighborhood of Lewis Place, a scheme that ultimately led to the striking down of restrictive covenants in the United States in *Shelley v. Kraemer* (1948). The Witherspoons were the parents of two children, including California attorney Vanita Witherspoon. Fredda Witherspoon had a fruitful life as an educator, social worker, and community activist, teaching for nearly thirty years at Saint Louis Community College. According to Witherspoon, it was a necessity to put her intellectual creativity and skills to use in the community. She served as the president of the Missouri Conference of the NAACP, vice chair of the Saint Louis Urban League, first African American president of the Saint Louis YWCA, national president of the Iota Phi Lambda Sorority, children's youth director at West Side Baptist Church. Her motto speaks to her community service and dedication to teaching: "Everyone should do all the good she can as she passes along life's highway; time is fleeing and life is too short to be unkind or thoughtless; we pass this way but once." She died in August 1996. *(Courtesy Houston Metropolitan Research Center, Houston Public Library, Houston, Texas, Vanita E. Crawford and Antioch Baptist Church Collection, MSS 0192-0007)*

other internal migrants, especially post-Reconstruction and first- and second-wave twentieth-century newcomers, cultivated a form of cautious self-help. Born in Navasota in Grimes County on October 25, 1872, James Delbridge (Professor Jimmie) Ryan completed his initial education at Prairie View College in 1890. That same year, at the age of seventeen, the recent migrant began teaching mathematics for the Houston school system. A decade later, he began a long career at Colored High School, first as a math instructor. In 1912, he became the school's principal. He later earned a master's from Wiley College and became principal of the new Jack Yates High School in Third Ward in 1926. The racial inequities were obvious to Ryan. He discussed them at length at a Colored Teachers State Association of Texas convention. However, he never challenged White peers, administrators, or city officials to reform African American schools, pay equal salaries, and eradicate racial disparities.[59]

Instead, "Professor Jimmie," as many beloved students called him, used his own resources to fund programs, purchase school supplies, and finance the careers of skillful teachers. James D. Ryan persuaded mail clerk Will J. Jones in 1912 to form choral clubs at African American schools for a modest fee, which Ryan himself paid. Jones, a former student of music at the reputable New England Conservatory of Music in Boston, loved teaching music. Regrettably, the school system did not pay the salaries of African American music teachers in the early decades of the century. Will Jones served African American HISD children for twenty-two years before the district officially recognized him as a music teacher. By the 1930s, African American schools, largely because of generous benefactor James D. Ryan, enjoyed choirs, music departments, bands, and music textbooks.[60]

Ryan, along with others, formed other programs as well. He was also instrumental in the development of athletics in African American high schools. Before 1925, Ryan purchased uniforms and equipment for the Colored High School football team, and R. G. Lockett and YMCA secretary H. P. Carter volunteered as head coaches. Community builders definitely addressed the needs of school children. An accommodating James D. Ryan used his resources to implement programs, provide resources, and help initiate future policy. The actions of Ryan, Smith, and other accommodationists paid off. With the help of extracurricular activities, many of their students at Booker T. Washington, Jack Yates, and Phillis Wheatley went on to have fruitful and lucrative careers in medicine, dentistry, nursing, accounting, library science, mortuary science, music, journalism, business, higher education, and teaching.[61]

FIGURE 28. Crockett, Texas, native Ira Babington Bryant, graduated from Colored High School in 1922 and went on to earn an undergraduate degree at Fisk University, a master's from the University of Kansas, and a doctorate in education at the University of Southern California. He eventually became principal of his alma mater, Booker T. Washington, in 1938. Later he served as principal of the new Kashmere Gardens High School in the 1950s and 1960s. *(Courtesy Houston Metropolitan Research Center, Houston Public Library, Houston, Texas, Thelma Scott Bryant Collection, MSS 0013-0005)*

Later generations also enhanced public education for African Americans. Ira Babington Bryant, a native of Crockett, Texas, moved to Houston in 1920 from Caldwell near College Station and Bryan; there his father served as the principal of the Caldwell Colored School and his mother was a schoolteacher (fig. 28). He was held back a year at Colored High School, a decision made by Principal James D. Ryan, who concluded the young boy was behind his classmates; however, Bryant would go on to earn an undergraduate degree from Fisk University in 1926, a master's degree in sociology from the University of Kansas in 1934, and a doctorate in education administration from the University of Southern California in 1948. He began his teaching career at Wheatley High School in 1929 and later became principal of Booker T. Washington in 1938 (fig. 29).[62]

During this time he wrote numerous case studies and monographs, including the pioneering *The Development of Houston Negro Schools* in

FIGURE 29. Called "Old Colored High" by alumni who graduated before 1926, when its name changed to Booker T. Washington High School, the school is possibly the oldest public high school for African Americans in the South, outside Washington, DC, of course. Even with overcrowded conditions and incomplete resources, the school had a mixed curriculum that comprised vocational training and liberal arts. Hazel Hainsworth Young told the interviewer years earlier that Howard University classmates from all across the country were surprised at her mathematics, science, and language arts skills. Colored High School remained the only secondary school for African Americans until the district built Jack Yates High School. She majored in Latin and went on to teach Latin at Jack Yates and Phillis Wheatley High Schools. Originally built in Fourth Ward, the district later constructed a more modern building in Independence Heights. Today the school has a magnet component that specializes in engineering. *(Courtesy Houston Metropolitan Research Center, Houston Public Library, Houston, Texas, HMRC Photograph Collection, MSS 0114-0823A)*

1935. According to historian Willie Lee Gray, Bryant formulated an African American studies curriculum for students, modeling his work after John Hope Franklin's *From Slavery to Freedom*. He later headed the new Kashmere Gardens High School from 1957 to 1968 when he retired from the district. He continued teaching at Dillard University, Texas State University for Negroes, Bishop College, and Prairie View College. Although Bryant loved education, the NAACP board member opposed vocational training, particularly for ex-convicts, arguing the curriculum could never substitute a traditional liberal arts education. On the other hand, he encouraged primary-based research and sociological methodologies among high school students, developing with the assistance of Wheatley High students, for example, a study that mirrored Du Bois's *The Philadelphia Negro* (1896) and examined poverty, substandard housing, and segregation among Houston African Americans. He was the first African American inducted into the Alpha Epsilon Chapter of Phi Delta Kappa Professional Education Association in 1946. Bryant as well as other educators saw education as an effective weapon in the ongoing war against White supremacy.[63]

More than any other group, women as educators and parents worked to improve the needs of Houston's African American student body. One Jack Yates High School teacher, church member, and writer, Mary L. Jones

FIGURE 30. Third Ward students entered Yates High School in 1926 (today the location of James D. Ryan Middle School). Hazel Hainsworth (front row, third from the right) had only graduated from Howard University a year earlier. She taught Latin at Yates and Wheatley, but later became dean of girls at both institutions. The owner of the photograph, Mary L. Jones Johnson, featured in the front, sitting, on the far right side, wrote "deceased" in multiple places on the photograph, noting those colleagues that no longer lived. Most believe that Hazel Hainsworth Young, who died July 2008 at the age of 103, was the sole surviving member of the Jack Yates High School first faculty. The sister of plaintiff Heman Sweatt, Erma Sweatt (Wallace), and the daughter of internal migrants from eastern Texas, is to the right of Hainsworth (Young). The man seated in the middle is the "eccentric" James D. Ryan, a native of Navasota and the school's principal, who began his teaching career as a mathematics instructor. Although accommodating, Ryan found ways to improve the conditions of his student body. The first Jack Yates High School building is named James D. Ryan Middle School in his honor. Also noticeable is the fact that women outnumber men. *(Courtesy Houston Metropolitan Research Center, Houston Public Library, Houston, Texas, General and Mary L. Jones Johnson Collection, MSS 0119-0015)*

Johnson, wrote a brief history of her beloved Yates in the 1930s, after the school district refurbished and added to the original high school (fig. 30). Her recollections of the school's beginnings and expansion in the 1920s and 1930s reveal an amazing spirit of racial pride and agency. Completed in 1926, the high school opened to sixteen faculty and hundreds of students in February 8, 1926. The faculty, either migrants or the children of migrants, included Johnson, Fisk University alumnus Hortense Houston Young, recent Howard University graduate Hazel Hainsworth (prior to her marriage to Howard Young), Mary Holden, Josie Taylor, Virginia B. Miller, Ellie Walls Montgomery, John Grigsby, Viola Calvin, Nellie Holmes, Jewel Ledson, and Erma Sweatt, sister of famous civil rights plaintiff Heman Sweatt. Johnson, whose mother, migrant and Antioch Baptist Church member Mary Jones, helped found the Blue Triangle YWCA for Afro-Americans and Mothers' Club branches in African American schools, highlighted the institution's potential and progress during these first decades.[64]

Yates, like Wheatley and Washington High Schools, served as a multipurpose facility, housing junior and senior high school students and programs. The continued growth, according to Johnson, served as an indicator of progress and encouraged officials to add new additions to the original school, today the site of James D. Ryan Middle School. On top of the auditorium, cafeteria, and nineteen classrooms in the original school building, bond monies supported the building of a gymnasium, industrial shop, girls' gymnasium, several sewing rooms, a laundry, and science laboratories. The school's curriculum, which varied from Western Civilization, United States history, biology, chemistry, trigonometry, plane and general geometry, industrial arts, cooking, sewing, kinesiology, health, general science, and general mathematics, was designed to prepare students for both manufacturing labor and college. The author also revealed to readers the schools' influence on Third Ward in the 1920s and 1930s.[65] According to Johnson, "Local conditions began to change and within a few years a new community had grown up around the school, a hospital[,] landscaped gardens, businesses, parks, new homes and amusements."[66] For Johnson, the school represented more than an institution of learning; it became the heart and soul of a new and thriving African American community, one that bypassed abrasive and painful interracial interaction for Black love.[67]

Migrant women particularly brought with them to the city lessons of self-help consciousness from their rural upbringings. Julia C. Hester, a graduate of Spelman Institute's (now Spelman College) teaching certification program, migrated around the turn of the century to Houston from Dublin, Georgia, with her husband. Mrs. Hester taught school and actively participated in fraternal, religious, and social activities. As a member of Payne Chapel African Methodist Episcopal Church, she worked tirelessly to improve life for Fifth Ward children, who would ultimately make their way to Phillis Wheatley High School (fig. 31). She welcomed children into her home and offered recreational entertainment for them. Upon her death during World War II, church members and community leaders formed the Houston Negro Community Center in 1941, later renaming it the Julia C. Hester House in her memory. The Fifth Ward community center continued her traditions by providing children with extracurricular

FIGURE 31. One of the nation's biggest kept secrets has been the Phillis Wheatley High School jazz program. Created in the early 1930s by music teacher Percy McDavid, Wheatley's jazz program focused on the evolution of jazz, from blues to the rise of bebop in postwar 1940s. Percy and Russell McDavid trained numerous students, including two of the leading jazz artists of the day—Illinois Jacquet and Arnett Cobb. So impressive was Wheatley's jazz instruction that legendary Duke Ellington visited the school in 1935. The school's jazz ensemble has continued to stir creativity, imagination, philosophy, and passion in the minds and hearts of its students. Non-musicians did well at Wheatley as well. Perhaps Wheatley's most famous alumna is not musician Illinois Jacquet, who actually left school before completing his studies, but future attorney and US Rep. Barbara Jordan. The above photo, which dates back to 1940, does not show any male faculty. By this time, the McDavid brothers had relocated to Kansas City, Kansas. Faculty member Mary L. Jones Johnson, who was also one of the first teachers at Jack Yates High School in the 1926–27-school-year, later joined Wheatley's faculty and is standing third from the right. *(Courtesy Houston Metropolitan Research Center, Houston Public Library, Houston, Texas, General and Mary L. Jones Johnson Collection, MSS 0119-0013)*

FIGURE 32. Music teacher Corrilla Rochon earned a living teaching piano to Houston African Americans. Her most successful student, Ernestine Jessie Covington (Dent), went on to Oberlin in 1924, eventually earning a bachelor's degree in classical music and a master's in piano, and earning four Julliard music fellowships. Rochon, a serious perfectionist, worked with dozens of young people, including Ernestine Covington and Thelma Scott (Bryant). Rochon also put together a women's orchestra that performed regularly at special functions. Featured in the Ladies Symphony Orchestra are (standing left to right) Miss Jennie Covington (Dent), Mrs. Virgie S. Cornish, Mrs. E. M. Johnson, Mrs. B. F. Barlow, Mrs. Milton Griffin, Mrs. M. E. Isaac, Mrs. Frank Martinere, and Miss Corine Wright; as well as (seated left to right) Miss A. E. Butler, Miss Daisy McGee, Mrs. B. J. Covington, Madame Corrilla Rochon, director, Mrs. J. L. Blunt, and Mrs. R. O. Smith. Both Ernestine Jessie Covington parents played music. Her father played the trumpet in college. *(Courtesy Houston Metropolitan Research Center, Houston Public Library, Houston, Texas, Covington Family Collection, MSS 0170-0033)*

activities, ranging from basketball leagues, boxing classes, arts and crafts classes, book review clubs, and choral clubs.[68]

Louisiana native Corrilla Rochon, a music teacher who had previously lived in Galveston, moved to Houston in 1902 or 1903. Although a trained pianist, Rochon could not secure a teaching post with the school district. A multiracial woman of French, and Jamaican or Haitian ancestry, "Madame Rochon," as her students called her, made her income by teaching piano to Houston African Americans. Her most successful student, Ernestine Jessie Covington (Dent), went on to Oberlin in 1924, later earning undergraduate and master's degrees in classical music and piano, respectively. Rochon, a serious perfectionist, worked with dozens of young people, including Ernestine Covington, Thelma Scott (Bryant), and Thelma Hainsworth (Young). Rochon also put together a women's orchestra that performed regularly at special functions. The Ladies Symphony Orchestra included violinists Ernestine and Jennie Covington (fig. 32). Rochon rented a home on Dowling, sharing it with longtime friend Bessie Osborn, a librarian with the Colored Carnegie Library, who lived with Rochon for decades as a roomer.[69]

Parents did their part as well. A group of African American mothers established in 1909 Mothers' Clubs (now Parent Teacher Associations [PTAs]) at several Houston schools to address a series of problems that plagued African American schools. In its first six years, the club raised $4,000 for schoolchildren and classrooms. More than anything else, overcrowding compromised the learning of Afro-American pupils. Mothers' Clubs, PTAs, concerned church members, and individual educators raised thousands of dollars, purchasing school equipment for industrial and domestic science classes, musical instruments, phonographs, kitchen utensils, desks, tables, bookshelves, and projection slides. The clubs also cleaned school grounds and replanted trees on the premises. Parents and educators alike often paid the salaries of nonsalaried instructors who taught in the schools for years without pay. Their commitment to fairness and racial equality in the classroom persuaded a reluctant school board to build new schools and repair old ones. This zeal mirrored the community's commitment to quality healthcare.[70]

The Push for Quality Healthcare

Healthcare or lack thereof affected every segment of the city's African American migrant population and required enormous amounts of resources and time. Migrants, like established residents, faced a number of medical quandaries in the early twentieth century. Black Houstonians suffered disproportionately from sickness and disease. Poverty, educational disparities, poor housing, and racial discrimination largely explained this crisis. This plight only worsened as transients flooded into the city.[71] Migrant H. E. Lee discussed the crisis in the *Red Book of Houston*. According to the Tillotson College (now Huston-Tillotson University) and Meharry Medical College graduate, "Since life and health depend so much upon proper housing, wholesome food and sanitation, one can readily see the gravity of the situation regarding the Negro immediately after emancipation and even now, for that matter."[72] Annually, according to Lee, fifteen hundred people in the city's African American community lived every year with serious illnesses.

Of these, seven hundred to eight hundred usually died. Sadly, according to Lee, the community could have avoided 45 percent of the deaths.[73]

Poor diet and sanitation, along with inadequate housing contributed to this alarming health calamity. Housing overcrowding, especially, bred tuberculosis, typhoid fever, and other communicable illnesses. Poverty, underemployment, and families' inability to own homes largely explained why African Americans found themselves in this situation. Absentee landlords also contributed to this nightmare. Minimal health codes made the poor—regardless of race or ethnicity—vulnerable to conniving property owners who cared very little about the well-being of their indigent tenants. Poor city services equally contributed to this bad situation. As discussed in chapter 2, poor drainage and sewer systems in Afro-American communities caused serious health risks. Torrential rainstorms always led to heavy flooding; and inadequate drainage and sewer systems always prompted periodic flooding, dirty well water, and festering bacteria and fungus underneath and inside the home. Regrettably, food prepared, preserved, and cooked in bacteria-infected water supplies caused instant illness and sometimes death. Food itself caused a great deal of concerns. Often, unscrupulous grocers in these communities sold customers spoiled meat, stale bread, and spoiled canned vegetables and fruits.[74]

Lee made several suggestions. First, Houston African Americans needed to concentrate their efforts on home ownership. Home ownership, according to Lee, represented the best form of treatment for unnecessary communicable diseases and ailments. Black homeowners, according to the writer, rarely faced these health challenges. Education too served as a springboard for improved health and lifestyle choices. Those African Americans with high school and college diplomas made better choices with regard to their eating habits and living arrangements; more than likely, they owned their homes; and by seeing their physician regularly, they practiced preventative health more often than others. Moreover, Lee, like most African American physicians of the early twentieth century, relied on self-help.[75]

Only people of color could solve these ailments plaguing their communities, according to Lee. Blacks could not depend on others to address these problems. He particularly noted that African Americans with influence, charisma, dedication, and formal education must be on the forefront of this community enterprise. Blacks could no longer afford to involve themselves in intraracial antagonism and feuds over wealth, power, religion, physical attributes, and gender. The health crisis plaguing people of African descent during the start of the First Great Migration could destroy the entire community, according to Lee. Without a resolution, the group faced extinction.[76]

Individual and collective immorality equally contributed to these challenges. Women in particular, according to the general practitioner, had a responsibility to raise their children, especially their sons; as males, God could sanction to find solutions to these overwhelming problems. Sexual promiscuity, he contended, made matters worse. Unmarried women, rambunctious young men, adulterers, and child killers or abortionists all caused discord and disharmony in the African American community. Without righteous moral character, men could not save their communities. Interestingly, Lee, who moved to the city around the turn of the century, like most African American males in leadership positions, saw women as guardians of male births; objects of male sexuality; occasionally, pariahs for community disarray; and simple caretakers of the community. Houston women in nontraditional roles such as medical professionals, scientists, authors, and educators seemed to these men absurd.[77]

Worth noting is that a mildly chauvinistic Lee, like most accommodationists of the period, failed to mention racism's role in this quagmire. Not once did he discuss structural racism's role in creating the city's health crisis. Ironically, Lee and other male civic leaders rarely compared their lot with that of women. In other words, they generally failed to correlate racism with sexism. When he did discuss Whites, he usually spoke with praise and admiration. For example, Lee argued that slaveholders, regardless of their motives, fed, cared for, and nursed their slaves to adequately maintain health because they could not allow their chief investment to fall victim to premature death. Thus slaveholders kept slaves alive in time to secure their freedom. The descendants of slaves now had to do their part by ensuring the continued productivity of the race. Only through self-help, love, and a spirit of agency-activism, could the race press on, conquer chronic illnesses and infections, and increase its life expectancy.[78]

Fourteen years later, as the African American migrant population grew in the city, another study substantiated Lee's findings. The National Urban League's study of Houston African Americans, headed by field secretary Jesse O. Thomas, found African Americans more vulnerable to tuberculosis and syphilis. Looking at the city's annual vital statistics report, 3,402 individuals died in the year 1928. Of these, 30 percent, or 1,036, were African American. Blacks at this time only comprised 22 percent of the population; however, they made up 42 percent of the city's tuberculosis deaths and 42 percent of all syphilis deaths for the same year. Jesse Thomas in this study points to several factors contributing to African Americans' poor state of health in the late 1920s.

Unlike Dr. Lee, Thomas vocally discussed racial discrimination. According to Thomas, racial segregation in particular prevented African Americans from receiving quality preventative healthcare and treatment. Although African Americans comprised 22 percent of the city's population, they made up a smaller proportion of the Houston Tuberculosis Sanitarium's patients. The city's Mexican residents, only 7 percent of the city's total population in 1929, made up a larger proportion of the patients at the hospital than African Americans. All the city's major hospitals segregated their African American patients. Of these, only Hermann Hospital, according to NUL findings, treated its African American patients with respect and common courtesy. In his summation, Thomas suggested that the White clinics and hospitals hire African American physicians and nurses to care for African American patients, foster a greater sensitivity toward African Americans in general, and find additional space for the housing of African Americans during their stay.[79]

Jesse Thomas mostly discussed the state of Houston Negro Hospital, completed in 1926. The hospital's beginnings as well as the medical establishment's commitment to quality healthcare for its White citizenry speak to both the dichotomy of race in Houston and the endurance of African American agency. Houston's first twentieth-century Afro-American physicians included Benjamin Covington, Henry E. Lee, T. Bryant, O. C. Garrett, J. H. T. Lindsay, E. O. Durham, Charles Jackson, and R. F. Ferrell, and with few exceptions they moved to the city either from the surrounding countryside or right out of medical school. They, along with other medical professionals such as dentists J. L. Cockrell and C. A. George; pharmacist P. W. Watts; and practical nurses Louvenia Burr, Dona Foster, Annie Hagen, and Bessie Johnson, could not teach or practice clinical medicine in the city's hospitals.[80]

Excluded from hospitals, refused entry into the state's health-science training programs, and dismissed as inept, stupid, and lazy, these medical and health professionals relied on themselves and the benevolence of their communities' limited resources. They looked inward as they opened practices throughout the Houston area. In the wake of Houston's spectacular growth in the twentieth century, these health professionals slowly saw their practices bloom. Their chief concern, however, centered on quality care for the critically ill, especially individuals in need of surgery. Their dream of offering African Americans quality medical care soon turned into a reality.[81]

Central to this task was pulmonary specialist Benjamin Jesse Covington, who reorganized the Lone Star State Medical Association (established in 1882 in Galveston and currently the Lone Star Medical, Dental, and Pharmaceutical Association) in the early 1900s. Covington was a self-taught pulmonary surgeon, who, during the city's influenza outbreak of 1918, developed a treatment vaccine that medical officers used overseas to treat soldiers. The son of ex-slaves, Covington worked his way through school, initially laboring as a janitor and bell ringer and ultimately graduating from Hearne Baptist Academy in 1892 with his high school diploma. Three years later, the schoolteacher and bookkeeper entered Meharry Medical College, graduating in 1900 as a general practitioner. He relocated to Houston with his wife three years later.[82]

Motivated in part by local efforts to build a charity hospital—Hermann Hospital, which opened in 1924 and eventually became the gateway to the Texas Medical Center—but also by racial bigotry in the medical profession, and with the support of civic leaders, doctors founded four medical facilities for African Americans. They established the People's Sanitarium in 1911 on Andrews Street; Union Hospital, a six-bed and single surgical area facility, in 1918 on Howard and Nash; and Union-Jeremiah Hospital, an eleven-bed facility, on Andrews and Genesee in 1923, all in Fourth Ward. African American doctors in the mid-1920s petitioned the city to provide adequate medical care for African Americans. They particularly felt flustered by the steady growth of private and public hospitals in the city, including Hermann Hospital in 1925, Methodist Hospital in 1924, and Jefferson Davis in 1924, health centers that refused the services of African American physicians. Even hospitals that catered to the well-being of African American patients refused African American doctors and nurses. However, an unlikely benefactor donated the funds for the construction of a new facility for African Americans. In 1925, Houston oil tycoon and philanthropist Joseph S. Cullinan, the founder of Texaco Oil, donated $80,000 for the construction of the Houston Negro Hospital on Ennis Street and Elgin in Third Ward, in memory of his son, Lt. John H.

FIGURE 33. For nearly two decades, African American physicians attempted to meet the needs of Black Houstonians, forming sanitariums, clinics, and small hospital facilities. They still needed additional resources to provide their patients with the kind of health care well-to-do Whites received in the city's expanding medical center. In 1925, Houston oil tycoon and philanthropist Joseph S. Cullinan, the founder of the Texas Fuel Company (later Texaco Oil), in memory of his son, Lt. John H. Cullinan, who died in battle in 1918 in World War I, donated $80,000 for the construction of the Houston Negro Hospital on Ennis and Elgin Streets in Third Ward. The city gave the hospital three acres of land to build the facility. Completed in 1926 and opened in 1927, the hospital had a full medical staff and room for sixty-one adult patients and sixteen infants. *(Courtesy Houston Metropolitan Research Center, Houston Public Library, Houston, Texas, Maurice J. Sullivan Papers, MSS 0054-0001)*

Cullinan, who died in battle in 1918 in World War I. The city gave the hospital three acres of land to build the facility.[83]

The hospital, completed in 1926, opened in May 1927 (fig. 33). For the city's twenty-five African American physicians, the new facility represented a new chapter in medical history. One of eleven southern hospitals open to African American medical professionals, the hospital allowed new doctors the opportunity to work closely with experienced practitioners. The city also attracted top physicians from around the country. George Patrick Alphonse Forde came to Houston to practice medicine at Houston Negro Hospital. A native of Barbados, Forde graduated at the top of his class at Meharry in 1913. Houston Negro Hospital, which cost $6,000 annually to maintain, cared for sixty-one adult patients and sixteen infants. The Community Chest paid the hospital's operating costs annually. Even though discord among the White advisory board, African American board of directors, and African American medical staff damaged public confidence in the institution, and although half the city's African American residents preferred the overcrowded, segregated facilities and White hospital staffers to Houston Negro Hospital, the community's ability to create and operate such an institution speaks to the legitimacy of community agency.[84]

Although not always apparent, Houston Negro Hospital broke glass ceilings for African American women, including physicians (fig. 34). Huntsville, Texas, native Thelma Adele Patten Law, the first African American female to practice medicine in Houston, was on the hospital's medical staff. Law was also one of the first African American obstetricians/gynecologists in the state. Born in Huntsville, Texas, in 1900, to schoolteachers

FIGURE 34. Members of the Lone Star State Medical Association (established in 1882 in Galveston and currently the Lone Star Medical, Dental, and Pharmaceutical Association) placed this holiday greeting on the front page of the *Houston Informer*, Christmas 1926. The twenty-four-member professional organization of physicians, dentists, and pharmacists would usher in 1927 with a new, modern medical facility—the Houston Negro Hospital. The group also shattered an important glass ceiling with the membership of the first woman physician, Huntsville, Texas, native Thelma A. Patten (Law), the first Black OBGYN in the city of Houston and one of the first in Texas. A graduate of Howard University and a member of Delta Sigma Theta Sorority, the young physician was also friends with another Black woman physician, Dr. Carrie J. Sutton. The two had been friends since their childhood, and both attended Howard, even pledging the same sorority. Even with the gender breakthrough within the medical profession, sexism continued. One group conspicuously missing is African American nurses. *(Courtesy Houston Metropolitan Research Center, Houston Public Library, Houston, Texas, Houston Informer, December 25, 1926)*

Mason Barnett and Pauline B. Garza Patten of San Antonio, Thelma Patton (Law) moved to Houston in 1905 or 1906, residing in northern Fourth Ward. Father Mason Patten found work as a railway postal clerk, while mother Pauline cared for their growing family. Thelma, the oldest, graduated valedictorian from Colored High School in 1917 and immediately entered Howard University with childhood friend Carrie Jane Sutton (Brooks) of San Antonio. While attending Howard, both women pledged Delta Sigma Theta Sorority's Alpha Chapter, completed their undergraduate studies, and entered medical school, graduating in 1923. Interns at Freedman's Hospital in Washington, D.C., the pioneering women earned their medical licenses in obstetrics and gynecology in 1924.[85]

One of ninety-two African American women physicians in the United States in 1929, Patten Law had returned to Houston five years earlier, where she established a practice with general practitioner Charles Whittaker Pemberton of Marshall, Texas. Facing numerous challenges, the practice took off, in spite of clients' preconceived prejudices toward women doctors. As a woman physician, Thelma Patten Law, who married educator and coach James Law in the 1930s, experienced two forms of discrimination: racism and sexism. Black women were only 2 percent of all African American medical doctors in the United States in 1929. Scholar Darlene Clark Hine argues that even though Afro-American male physicians held private practices, more often than not, African American women did not. Black male colleagues deemed them less intelligent, and African American patients felt uneasy seeing women doctors of any race.[86]

Patten Law, a pioneering physician, overcame these obstacles. For one, Dr. Patten Law largely worked with indigent patients in public clinics. Law, who became president of the Lone Star Medical Association in 1940, when Houston hosted the National Medical Association's annual meeting, worked at Houston Negro Hospital, St. Elizabeth Hospital, Prairie View Hospital, Jefferson Davis Hospital's outpatient pediatrics clinic, and Maternal Health Center, the forerunner to Planned Parenthood. As a volunteer, Law headed the Negro Health Clinic at the Maternal Health Center, improving the lives of hundreds of women and children in the twenty-five years she worked with the organization. In 1955, Law became the first African American to join the Harris County Society (now the Harris County Medical Society), the professional association of Harris County physicians.[87]

Patten also influenced others around her. Law, a return migrant to the city, would mentor several African American women physicians, including Catherine J. Roett, the daughter of Houston Negro Hospital founder and physician Rupert Roett of Barbados and the city's first African American pediatrician, and Edith Irby Jones, the first African American graduate of the Medical School of the University of Arkansas and first female president of the National Medical Association. Law also mentored and respected medical colleagues who did not hold degrees in medicine. Nurses in particular respected Patten for her fairness toward them.[88]

Medical doctors, public health centers, and patients relied heavily on nurses—both untrained and licensed. Black women since slavery had earned a living as untrained or practical nurses, nursing wounds, caring for the sick, and healing as well as delivering babies. In addition, nurses performed domestic duties. Hospitals also hired out nurses and retained their pay through the early twentieth century. The professionalization of nursing during World War I and the successful outreach of the National Association of Colored Graduate Nurses ushered in slow changes for nurses, as board certified, licensed, college-educated professionals replaced the unskilled. The numbers of Houston nurses increased dramatically after World War I as licensed and unlicensed nurses moved to the city for work. Between 1920 and 1940, the number of untrained nurses only grew slightly, from 107 to 123. On the other hand, the number of trained nurses in the city tripled, from 20 to 63.[89]

A miniscule number of professional nurses earned their living exclusively as clinical staffers or faculty at private practices, hospitals, public health centers, and nursing schools. Austin native Juanita Clarke had a successful career as a nurse. A graduate of Virginia State Medical and Prairie View Colleges, the Austin, Texas, native also did graduate work at Howard University. Clarke worked as an educator and public health nurse in Anderson County and at Bishop College in Marshal, before moving to Houston with her husband, a high school teacher, in the late 1930s. A public health nurse for the state, she especially worked to raise awareness about tuberculosis and other communicable diseases facing African Americans.[90]

According to historian Peggy Hardman, African American nurses like Clarke benefited from the expansion of public health programs, private hospitals, and the professionalization of the nursing profession, more so than physicians, who increasingly found themselves shut out of segregated hospitals and clinics. Ironically, Darlene Clark Hine argues that Afro-American nurses faced the same challenges other health professionals of color experienced, even as more nurses entered the medical profession. Although they helped desegregate hospitals and clinics, secured stronger credentials, and increasingly trained other nursing professionals, they still faced fierce racism. Their obstacles only motivated them to work harder as professionals and community activists. Third-wave internal migrant Juanita Clarke, a member of Good Hope Baptist Church, helped pave the way for other changes. Clarke, along with her contemporaries in medicine, education, the clergy, and those involved in clubs and fraternal orders, as with the first generation of migrants, also set in motion new sociocultural and sociopolitical constructs that placed greater emphasis on race relations and racial justice.[91]

Conclusion: Giving Back

The first generation of migrants who made their way into the city from the surrounding environs in the 1900s and 1910s saw insular racial autonomy and quiet resistance to racism as effective measures of racial progress. Taking notice of the agency performed by their predecessors, who relocated to the city immediately following slavery or decades afterward in the nineteenth century, they placed greater emphasis on self-help strategizing and community building from the inside out. They established institutions and organizations that helped facilitate racial success. These early migrants, along with established residents, gave back to their communities in numerous ways. In doing so, they offered African Americans alternative solutions to pressing problems and challenges facing their families, neighborhoods, and the larger society. Interestingly, these institutions and self-help programs created by early twentieth-century migrants and established residents did something else. They created the impetus for civil rights.[92]

Increasingly those who moved to the city during and after World War I did more than join self-help organizing efforts. They formed catalyst groups that forced Whites to reconsider racial exclusion as the appropriate guise of citizenship. They precipitated the rise of an articulate, educated, and somewhat pseudo-militant group of race leaders who, through quiet and moderate political action, combated racial oppression. Political action more often translated into confrontation. The emerging direct assault on White hegemony would differ considerably from the accommodating posture of Old Guard elites like James Ryan, John Brown Bell, Mabel Wesley, and E. O. Smith, men and women who generally believed that direct confrontation had unpleasant consequences for African Americans individually and collectively. Ironically, as the new moderate militants came on the scene, many of their views mirrored those of the Old Elite. In fact, even within the ranks of this new Houston militancy, differing viewpoints, class bias, and sexism threatened an untied assault on White supremacy. Motivated in part by a brief episode of interracial violence and turmoil, this new generation of migrants put in motion historic changes for the city and its African American community.[93]

FOUR

"That Was Their Protection and Safeguard"
Houston's "New Negro," 1917–1941

Against the wishes of local Whites, commissioned officers, military officials, and African American troops themselves, the United States Army ordered the segregated Third Battalion—Companies I, K, L, and M of the Twenty-fourth Infantry—to Houston for a tour of guard duty at the construction site of Camp Logan (now Memorial Park). Located three miles west of downtown and named for Mexican War and Civil War veteran Maj. John A. Logan, the isolated, forested training facility cost the War Department nearly $2,000,000 to complete. It served as one of sixteen temporary cantonments for the war effort, specifically for the training of national guards units entering active duty. Army officials saw Camp Logan and Ellington Field, an aviation school built the same year and just south of the city, as ideal training centers, mainly because of their proximity to Houston. Houston's comfortable climate, dependable transportation facilities, location to the Gulf of Mexico, and the Gulf Sea's propinquity to the strategically important Panama Canal all influenced the War Department's decision to construct the Army National Guard cantonment.[1]

Generating an estimated $1,000,000 in revenue for the city each month, the camp pleased Houston's civic and business elite, even after learning of the army's decision to deploy African American troops to guard the construction site. To be sure, many were outraged. Some suggested the presence of the soldiers would spur violence against the city's African American population. Most felt Houston Whites would never respect the men as professional soldiers under any circumstances. In the end, protests were of no avail. Secretary of War Newton Baker, although aware of the potential powder keg that awaited the regiment on their arrival in Houston, felt racial norms had no place in military directives. Besides, argued Baker, African Americans were indispensable to the United States Armed

Services and had been since the Revolutionary War. This was especially true of those in uniform in the last half-century, including members of the Twenty-Fourth Infantry who would invigorate Houston's African American community, who truly desired civil liberties, economic security, and social acceptance.[2]

"We'd Seen Black Men in Captains' Uniforms!"

World War I provided African Americans with the prospect to prove their allegiance to their country. In 1918, scholar-activist and NAACP *Crisis* magazine editor W. E. B. Du Bois urged people of color to "close ranks" and, at least for the time being, support the Allied Forces in their effort to defeat the Central Powers of Europe.[3] Blacks did just that: An estimated four hundred thousand wore uniforms; almost one million worked as wartime factory personnel; and many more, as loyal supporters of the war effort, rallied behind the United States. Some 380,000 men served in the Armed Forces during World War I, of which 367,710 were drafted, serving primarily in the American Expeditionary Force's Services of Supply (SOS) units—stevedore regiments, engineer service battalions, butchery companies, pioneer infantry battalions, and labor battalions. Black troops served in professional capacities and as chaplains, clerks, intelligence officers, surveyors, attorneys, drafters, and physicians, as well as in other capacities, and over one thousand earned commissions as officers. In addition, forty-two thousand men fought in the Ninety-Second and Ninety-Third Combat Divisions, serving in the French Army. France awarded members of the Ninety-Third Division more than 500 Croix de Guerre, Distinguished Service Cross, and Legion of Honor medals for their service. Still, in the end African American patriotism and valor did little to diminish racial hatred abroad and at home. This was especially true in the South.[4]

Most White Houstonians resented the presence of armed African American soldiers in their city. People particularly loathed what they perceived as recalcitrance and arrogance within the military outfit. Although the city's three major newspapers, the *Chronicle, Post,* and *Press,* praised the experienced infantry for their past military victories and superior marksmen skills, editorials, and stories also kept in the news negative incidents involving the battalion—drunkenness, disorderly conduct, and resisting arrests. Clergy reminded Houstonians of the need to pass a prohibition ordinance, especially in light of the men's proximity to White neighborhoods. Houstonians also expressed consternation over the War Department's decision to send three thousand African American Illinois National Guardsmen to the camp for training. White officers, fearful of another Brownsville Raid, ordered troops, including military police, not to carry their firearms off base. Still, many in the city saw the soldiers as a nuisance.[5]

Soldiers saw the situation differently. Although many of the men grew up in the South, they expected fair treatment as dedicated servicemen. Those soldiers born in the North or the Caribbean noticeably expressed angst at what they saw as outrageous racism. Soldiers, in fact, demanded equal treatment for all African Americans. They protested the way Whites treated local Afro-Americans, especially women, on the city streets, in public places, when aboard streetcars, at places of business, and on the job. Black Houstonians generally appeased Whites to maintain their jobs and lifestyles. Their ability to reshape, reinvent, and influence their own communities was, at least to them, more important. Afro-American Houstonians relied on patience and restraint, but the soldiers, as temporary second-wave migrants to the city during the war, influenced by their personal successes and an emerging national trend called the "New Negro" Movement, demanded more of African American Houstonians and their temporary home, Houston, Texas.[6]

No event shaped Black protest in the early twentieth century more than the "New Negro" Movement. The term "New Negro" derived from earlier and contemporary periods of protest in the 1890s and during World War I but was commonly associated with the postwar 1920s and 1930s, the sociopolitical commentary of St. Croix native and socialist Hubert H. Harrison, and the iconic Alain Locke anthology, *The New Negro: An Interpretation*, published in 1925. Inspired by several events, a period of cultural self-expression, intellectual creativity, and political mobilization took shape. Black Houstonians, including recent newcomers to the city, also adopted the "New Negro" ideology of racial radicalism, economic independence, cultural consciousness, and prudent constructionalism. Before the Houston Riot, frustrated African Americans taunted Whites in hiding only; after the rebellion, people increasingly and more openly opposed racism. This chapter examines the "New Negro" Movement in Houston. Whether in court, on institutional boards, with the use of song lyrics (discussed in chapter 5), during sermons, in editorials, or as members of the military, "New Negroes" cautiously, but often boldly, fought back.[7]

"New Negroes" differed in their perspectives, of course. Some demanded immediate equality; others opted for fairness and equity within the segregated arena. Conservative "New Negroes" still appeased Whites. Ironically, the more "New Negroes" demanded fairer treatment, many, including anti-accommodating "New Negroes" themselves, retreated to the politics of appeasement when direct protest seemed too threatening. Nevertheless, escalating racial discrimination and hostility, whose roots stretched back to the transatlantic slave trade and slavery, convinced many that accommodation no longer worked as a prudent strategy.[8]

The mutineers certainly agreed. The Houston Riot took the lives of twenty people and sparked disconcertion on the part of Houstonians, including recent migrants from the surrounding interior. Whether instigators of political coalition building, or initiators of cultural construction, migrants, with the unknowing support of the Houston rioters, put into motion the "New Negro" Movement. The immediate catalyst for change was the Houston Riot of 1917, an event that triggered interracial negotiation and limited civil-rights pursuits; it also came with dramatic consequences.[9]

The disrespect members of the 24th Infantry encountered daily from Whites contrasted with the admiration they garnered from African Americans. Hazel Young, a preteen attending Antioch Baptist Church in 1917, remembers vividly the warm reception the infantrymen received from the community. According to Young, the enlisted men were courteous and kind. Young goes on to say, "I know they were handsome, well-groomed, polished, and I know they came to Antioch."[10] Some of the soldiers, particularly some Chicagoans, visited Antioch regularly and attracted the attention of women congregants who ultimately courted the enlisted men. A few couples announced their engagements in the weeks leading up to the riot. Female companions, churchgoers, as well as adolescents from the community, also spent time with the soldiers on base. Some curious teens, perhaps sexually active, found the confident men fascinating; those who were engaged to be married, who may or may not have been sleeping with servicemen, enjoyed spending intimate time with their partners; and occasionally, missionaries held prayer meetings and bible studies on the base in hopes of spurring genuine repentance.[11] Antioch and other churches as well as civic clubs treasured the soldiers and "had planned a reception for the men."[12] This, of course, never came to be.[13]

On August 23, around two in the afternoon, Pvt. Alonzo Edwards of Company L came to the aid of Fourth Ward resident Sara Travers. Earlier around eleven, officer Lee Sparks chased after a group of African American teens playing dice in an alley. After breaking up the game, Sparks began shooting at the teens, chasing them into a Fourth Ward neighborhood. Indifferent to African Americans, the veteran officer from nearby Fort Bend County barged into residences and interrogated families, eventually coming to the Travers home. Travers, a wife and mother of five, was home ironing when Sparks demanded that she reveal the whereabouts of the assailants. Outraged by the officer's gall and disrespect, the woman threatened to report Sparks. The officer dragged Travers, who was wearing underwear, an old skirt, and a flimsy blouse at the time, outside her home. Young gave her version of the account, "There was a Black woman being mistreated by a White policeman and the Black soldier resented the way in which she was being treated." Edwards, following procedure, politely asked the police whether he could be of assistance. Sparks responded in his usual way, hitting the soldier in the face with the butt of his revolver.[14]

Police arrested the infantryman and attacked him for a second time in jail. Later that day, responding to Edward's treatment, Cpl. Charles Baltimore of Company I, one of twelve military policemen in the division, went to the scene of the incident to inquire about the soldier. After an argument between the military police (MP) and police ensued, police officers hit Baltimore in the head with a gun butt. The soldier ran, but he was shot at and hunted down by officers, eventually apprehended and arrested. Later released, Baltimore returned to the cantonment.[15]

Black Houstonians felt uneasy and feared the worst. Away from the base, "the rumor had gotten out that the soldiers were going to shoot up the ward. . . . My godmother was afraid to stay out there all night."[16] Lena Robey, the sister of record producer Don D. Robey recalls, "My mother and father had separated, and I lived with my mom on Sadlier Avenue, which was in Fourth Ward right where all the confusion started . . . on West Dallas. My mother was real light and . . . afraid to go out on the street, so she sent me and my brother to the store [that evening to buy something for dinner].[17]

Apparently, false rumors of the MP's beating death circulated to the battalion's barracks. From that point on, the situation rapidly deteriorated. According to eyewitness testimony, between 8:00 and 8:30 in the evening, frazzled and angry soldiers reported hearing supposed gunshots outside the barracks, with Pvt. Frank Johnson decrying, "The White mob is coming!"[18] Even after learning of Baltimore's safety, the obstinate soldiers revolted.

Then, chaotically, infantrymen, mainly servicemen from Company I, including Cpl. Baltimore, but also men from Company L, seized weapons and, against the orders of their commanding officer, Maj. Kneeland S. Snow, left the camp.[19]

In what most witnesses and investigators considered an orchestrated mutiny, one hundred or more armed militiamen marched onto the streets along Buffalo Bayou, with one group heading north toward downtown into a working-class suburb, the Brunner Addition, and another traveling east, entering a predominately White neighborhood in the Fourth Ward, randomly firing on innocent Whites. The heinous killing spree claimed the lives of unarmed teenagers, individuals stepping off trolleys on their way home, people in bed, armed residents in self-defense, servicemen, and police. Seeking revenge for the alleged murder of a fellow soldier, the rioters marched in the direction of the Houston Police Department headquarters. The riot left sixteen Whites and Hispanics dead. Among these were eleven civilians, four police—including possible instigator Rufus Daniels—and one soldier from the Second Illinois Field Artillery. In addition, four Black soldiers involved in the insurrection died, among them Sgt. Vida Henry, the possible mastermind in an alleged staged coup, who potentially took his own life. It was several hours before National Guard troops and police foiled the rebellion.[20]

Three separate court-martial tribunals indicted one hundred and eighteen enlisted servicemen, mostly of Company I; one hundred and ten were found guilty. The wartime tribunals sentenced twenty-nine to death (although President Wilson overturned ten of the sentences) and handed down sixty-three life sentences in federal prisons. The tribunals found others mentally incompetent. Two of the White commanding officers were also court-martialed, but later released. Prosecutors never charged White civilians or police officers with inciting the vigilante incident. Both the media and an independent panel overlooked the role racism played in potentially triggering the events that culminated in the deadly mêlée. Houston Whites felt some vindication, whereas African Americans expressed remorse for the infamous battalion.[21] According to Young, "[the riot] was a tragedy that could have been avoided had the Army used more common sense."[22]

On the surface, the mêlée did little to alter race relations. Thelma Scott Bryant said the following about race relations in the city: "As far as the riot was concerned, it was a short [hiccup in our lives]. Later . . . we settled back in our place. As long as you knew your place, you stayed in it. Only when you [left that place did] you get into trouble."²³ Perhaps only a few thousand African Americans left the city behind the disturbance and aftermath. According to historian Garna Christian, editorials applauded the city's Afro-Americans for their efforts to bring about peace. The deadly assault exposed the spectacle of defiance among the nonconforming African American militia in comparison to the more docile civilian population. Beneath the topsoil, however, Afro-Americans in Houston and across the country increasingly protested racism. According to historian Robert V. Haynes, the riot "ignited race consciousness" in the African American community.²⁴ Influenced by the Houston rioters, Black Americans increasingly drew on their core emotional instincts with respect to interracial conflict. Red Summer 1919, for example, exposed a new turn in race relations, one that saw African Americans abandoning accommodation while embracing racial radicalism. Black migrants in Houston thus increasingly inculcated agency and recalcitrance. Accommodationists, nevertheless, would not make this transition an easy one.²⁵

From an "Old Negro" to a "New Negro": The Birthing of a Movement

Blacks in the 1900s and 1910s generally followed the political leanings of Booker T. Washington. For two decades until his premature death in 1915, Washington's political ideology of accommodation challenged notions of Black social justice. Rather, he publicly endorsed the platform of pseudo-racial reconciliation and the delay of African American social equality and political attainment.²⁶ According to Washington, in a speech at the Atlanta Cotton Exposition in 1895, "In all things that are purely social we can be as separate as the fingers, yet one as the hand in all things essential to mutual progress."²⁷ African Americans, according to Washington, would only attain the sought-after measure of social justice "after severe and constant struggle rather than artificial forcing."²⁸

In retrospect, accommodation began not with Booker T. Washington, but rather in the slave community, which since day one had utilized hidden disobedience as a tool of survival. It is here where glimpses of racial constructionalism or appeasement emerged. Blacks in slavery simply masked their real thoughts with smiles, compliance, and docility. Beneath the surface, and unknown to Whites, a veiled, independent slave community flourished, one that nurtured harmless self-preservation on the one hand and self-contained racial resistance on the other. Resistance in hiding remained a cornerstone of Afro-American life well after slavery's death. From the depths of self-preservation and quiet resistance came Black agency or community building. For this reason, African Americans survived slavery and rebuilt their lives shortly thereafter. Unresolved feelings of angst, nevertheless, remained with people of color. Even as African Americans created viable institutions that outlived forced servitude, they retained subliminal and obvious messages of self-hate and social inferiority, making accommodation simple as a lifestyle choice.[29]

As racial segregation replaced slavery in the late nineteenth century, accommodation strengthened. Codified or de jure racial segregation followed and nurtured the construction of racial inferiority on the part of Afro-Americans and racial superiority on the part of Whites. Between 1876 and 1965, Texas established and maintained segregated schools, prison populations, public carriers, public places, and hospitals; increased the African American prison population; and passed vagrancy laws designed to curtail the movement of people. Houston followed suit, segregating streetcars, public facilities, parks, and work floors between 1903 and the late 1920s.[30]

Many African-descent Houstonians, including recent migrants to the city, embraced segregation, at least publicly. *The Red Book of Houston* editor, Emmett J. Scott of Tuskegee Institute, discussed segregation candidly: God fostered the social doctrine of segregation, which involved more than physical separation. This society dictate allowed for African American business development, self-help, and spiritual healing, according to Scott. African Americans needed to provide for themselves and prove their worthiness to God as moral defenders of racial autonomy and interracial cooperation: "Every individual owes it to his race to remain true to the racial lines and traditions and to work up, through the mediums offered, to the best life possible under the conditions."[31]

Scott, along with contributors, identified with the rhetoric of Washington because, for no other reason, segregation benefitted the community's elite financially and politically, as well as propelled racial autonomy, even while possibly endorsing the theory of Afro-American inferiority. As mentioned in chapter 2, scholars refer to such persons as Old Elite professionals, who, in the North, earned their living servicing Whites; these included, for example, barbers, artisans, contractors, and butlers and headwaiters. In the South, however, older established elites, generally migrants and former slaves or their children (people like Scott), with few exceptions, usually, served the growing African American community. Educators, attorneys, longshoremen, businessmen, medical professionals, ministers, and others in the African American community solicited their business from within the community, but remained, for the most part, conservative in tone when it came to race relations. Sometimes, southern migrants such as freedman John Brown Bell catered to Whites as well. This was especially true of those who serviced White clients and professionals, as well as civic leaders dependent on White approval. This early Afro-American elite thus benefitted from the politics of accommodation.[32] Scott also encouraged readers to remain in the South: "Despite the carpers of both races, the Afro-American race fares better among the Whites of the southern states than anywhere else in the world."[33]

The city's most prominent White civic leaders certainly agreed. From attorney James Addison Baker Sr. (Capt. Baker) and *Houston Chronicle* founder Marcellus Foster, both of Huntsville, Texas, and progressive mayor H. Baldwin Rice to Pennsylvania native and oilman Joseph S. Cullinan and Texas governor and newspaper publisher William P. Hobby of Moscow, Texas, to millionaire politician and Tennessee native Jesse H. Jones, White powerbrokers supported both African American accommodation and White hegemony. Only in this milieu did the races interact. Only in this instance did Whites support Afro-Americans, from conservative ministers and business owners to accommodating educators and artists.[34]

When African Americans and their non-Black allies did not abide by this sociocultural precept, however, White civic and business leaders made their feelings and actions known. Following the horrific beating of a northern White civil-rights activist in Austin in 1919, Governor Hobby telegraphed Mary White Ovington of the national NAACP office in New York City, saying, "[NAACP executive secretary John R.] Shillady was the only offender in the matter. . . . Your organization can contribute more to the advancement of both races by keeping your representatives and propaganda out of Texas."[35] Most Houston African American migrants and established residents, thus, in the early twentieth century stayed clear of both the NAACP and frontal assaults on racial segregation. Anything outside appeasement certainly prompted swift and dangerous consequences.[36]

Segregation and accommodation therefore inspired interracial cooperation, although such mutual relationships placated the racist status quo. Like accommodation, interracial cooperation derived from slavery, when the races knew their clearly defined places. When these carefully constructed lines of demarcation disappeared after the Civil War, groups developed new rules of etiquette, communication, and cooperation. Political partnerships, business arrangements, employment prospects, philanthropy, and reform initiatives created short-lived and lifelong affiliations built on constructive accommodation.[37]

For example, early Houston Public Schools educator Mamie Wesley, a native of Montgomery County, Texas, and the mother of World War I officer, attorney, and newspaperman Carter Wesley, finished normal school at the Gregory Institute in the late nineteenth century before beginning a forty-year career as a schoolteacher and principal. Although she commented privately about racial disparities, she never publicly criticized Whites for their refusal to provide equal funding to African American schools, choosing instead, for example, to purchase sewing machines and accessories out of pocket for her Crawford Elementary School students in Fifth Ward. This kept tensions minimal, while promoting community agency. Still, by World War I and the 1920s, a growing number of migrants to Houston, mainly but not exclusively younger African Americans, reconsidered Washington's mantra of passive activism.[38]

Booker T. Washington's death in 1915 helped position southerners who disagreed with accommodation in principle. Increasingly, younger migrants, including those twentieth-century business leaders and labor activists who relied less on White patronage or approval, publicly attacked racism and formalized accommodation.[39] In his typical fashion, migrant and *Houston Informer* editor Clifton Richardson Sr. protested acts of discrimination in his newspaper. "The *Informer*," according to Richardson, "does not believe in condoning crime, not even when perpetrated by a Black man, but when police officials resort to undue methods and high-handed methods to prevent a thorough and impartial investigation of alleged crimes from all angles, they simply increase rather than diminish crimes, and also create additional contempt and disrespect for law and order, thereby becoming *particeps* criminals."[40]

Criticisms such as this marked the start of the "New Negro" Movement in the city. A vigilant "New Negro" crusader, Richardson formed the newspaper in 1919 in response to the riot. The Houston Riot and its outcome struck a nerve with individuals like the newspaperman and motivated them to act. On the heels of the Houston Riot, increased racial violence and intolerance, and indifference to racial appeasement, a new period of protest defined Houston's African American migrant community.[41]

The "New Negro" protest initiative that took shape in cities, at workplaces, on farms, and during active military duty postulated a new beginning in the African American political, intellectual, and cultural imagination, one that had broad implications for the city and nation in the coming decades. Several events spurred revolution. Not surprisingly, World War I sparked much of the change, influencing behavior among Afro-American soldiers, opening up doors of opportunity to wage earners, and propelling the largest transregional population shift among Afro-Americans since slavery. The Great Migration opened economic, social, and political doors once closed to people of color. Living in close proximity with other Afro-Americans and increasingly away from Whites, migrants cherished the newfound social and political freedoms that gave them hope. Blacks certainly enjoyed their voting privileges outside the South. Political mobilization efforts like Marcus Garvey's Universal Improvement Association and African Communities League, established in 1914 in Kingston, Jamaica, influenced adjustment as well. With a following of two million, Garvey's appeal stretched to Texas; on city streets, in *Negro World* editorials, and in arenas, he promoted racial autonomy and Pan-Africanism, the concept of uniting African-descent peoples worldwide as an effective weapon against colonialism, racism, and economic exploitation.[42]

Another organization, the NAACP, attracted a large spectrum of the community. The birth of the NAACP reflected a growing mood in America, one that demanded an immediate resolution to both racism and racial appeasement. Members of two groups helped to birth the organization. The Niagara Movement, mostly African American professionals, met annually from 1905 to 1907, to discuss the state of race relations in the United States. Along with prominent Whites who were disgusted by the heinous Atlanta, Georgia, and Springfield, Illinois, riots of 1906 and 1908, respectively, they founded the NAACP in 1909 in New York City. The success of the organization, which grew from nine thousand in 1914 to ninety thousand in 1920, evolved from effective litigation, direct protests, and lobbying campaigns, as well as its reliance on influential Whites, coalition building, fundraising, Supreme Court victories, and its national magazine, *The Crisis: A Record of the Darker Races*. The magazine, which was read by thirty thousand weekly, was edited by Du Bois, and challenged its African American readership, spoke to sympathetic White allies, and influenced public policy. The fledgling organization optimistically formed a number of branches in the South during the war as well.[43]

Influenced by these national and local events and organizing efforts, Houstonians, including internal migrants, forged alliances to fight racial oppression. In doing so, they set the stage for a new political direction, one that both challenged traditional, conservative leadership and rallied around the platform of immediate racial justice, especially in light of the riot. Although African American Houstonians first entertained the idea of forming a local NAACP branch in 1915, the Houston Race Riot of 1917 served as an important catalyst for change. The NAACP itself saw an urgent need to form a local branch to better address racial problems in the city. While she was in Houston investigating the riot, NAACP fieldworker Martha Gruening expressed to NAACP Executive Secretary James Weldon Johnson her interest in establishing the local branch. According to Gruening, Houston, with its large African American middle class and its politically conscious community, seemed the perfect locale for the growing national organization. Houston seemed an excellent venue for a new political consciousness or a "New Negro" Movement.[44]

Houston's "New Negro"

Not since Reconstruction had African Americans been so actively engaged in politics. Building on this historic tradition, the emerging African American leadership of the period, which mostly comprised migrants from the surrounding region, fueled greater political interest in the years that followed the riot and World War I. The Texas Federation of Colored Women's Clubs, NAACP, Lincoln League, Negro Voters Civic, Independent Colored Voters Leagues (ICVL), Progressive Voters League (PVL), Civic Betterment League (CBL), Harris County Negro Democratic Club (HCNDC), Third Ward Civic Club (TWCC), NNBL, Negro Chamber of Commerce (NCC), and the Interdenominational Ministerial Alliance (IMA) allowed for limited spirited political activity. So too did African American churches, fraternal orders, women's clubs, businesses, and newspaper headlines and op-ed pieces propel political and civic engagement within the community.[45]

Sometimes affluent African Americans, usually political conservatives, worked alongside White allies, from radical liberals and moderate liberals to liberal conservatives and moderate conservatives. Immediately following World War I, Progressive-era reformer and New Dealer Jennie Covington and other respected members of the African American community—all migrants from the surrounding countryside—collaborated with White liberal segregationists on the Texas Commission on Interracial Cooperation (TCIRC) in an effort to improve relations between the races. Reformer Jennie Covington worked with White and Black educators, clubwomen, ministers, physicians, and businesspeople on the TCIRC, eventually serving as its state director in the 1950s. Covington also served as cofounder and first head of the Houston Commission on Interracial Cooperation, the affiliate of the state commission.[46]

Whites founded the first Commission on Interracial Cooperation in Atlanta in April 1919 as a response to the turbulent postwar racial climate. Statewide commissions with local committees sprang up across the country, especially in the South over the next few years, with the Texas commission forming in 1920. The commission addressed lynchings, inequitable healthcare and diseases, prison reform, police brutality, improvements in education, racial intolerance, and cooperation between the races. In Texas, Covington and other African American commission members perhaps had an extended agenda, one that promoted interracial cooperation and racial equality.[47]

The presence of Covington, Prairie View College administrator W. R. Banks, and other members of the African American elite was noteworthy, but the African American commission members rarely spoke openly about their true views on racial equality. Even those TCIRC commissioners with affiliations in the NAACP and other organizations that promoted Afro-American democracy or equality rarely made their opinions known. Black TCIRC members mostly adopted the persona of conservative, accommodating Huntsville educator Samuel Walker Houston and patterned themselves after racial constructionalist Booker T. Washington.[48]

Blacks did not want to upset Whites on the commission, including women's rights advocate and TCIRC state director Jesse Harriet Daniels Ames of Georgetown, Texas, who ultimately relocated to Atlanta in 1929, establishing the Association of Southern Women for the Prevention of Lynching. Ames, considered a White liberal to most, typified White liberal conservatives who supported improved rights for African Americans, even while opposing racial integration. Ames's Association of Southern Women for the Prevention of Lynching (ASWPL), for example, never publicly affiliated itself with African American women's clubs, including the National Association of Colored Women (NACW) and National Council of Negro Women (NCNW), even while collaborating with the latter in an effort to deter racial violence. Although the anti-lynching group opposed racial violence, it would not endorse the Costigan-Wagner anti-lynching bill of 1935. However, the organization always supported modified racial segregation. Other White TCIRC members, including conservative moderate Joseph Lynn Clark, chair of the History and Government Department at Sam Houston State Teachers College, opposed social equality and integration outright, although he influenced subtle improvements for segregated facilities within the African American community.[49]

Moreover, within the interracial coalition, deference to social custom often made ongoing dialogues about racial equality difficult. The interracial commission, for example, held separate meetings for Blacks and Whites, although the general body met together during the group's annual meetings each November. Occasionally, though, Black and White members challenged their peers to adopt different strategies when it came to integrated commission work. At the annual statewide meeting held November 1926 at the Presbyterian Church in Houston, women made several recommendations. Mrs. N. E. Hunter said, "White and colored women can help each race better understand each other by making it possible for men and women of both groups . . . to come before groups of the opposite race."[50] Mrs. Dyson stated, "Get a few together from the two groups and start with a definite program of things to be done, discussing an inter-racial commission."[51] Another Black speaker presented a different perspective. Miss A. Bowden, perhaps as a way to discourage integration within the commission, said, "The needs [of Blacks] can be known only through the Negro groups."[52]

Members certainly avoided radical stances such as condemning racial segregation, the White Democratic primary, and the concept of White privilege. In the 1930s and 1940s, the NAACP successfully took state universities to court in an effort to desegregate graduate and professional schools, mimicking other southern states. In response to these desegregation efforts, the Texas legislature passed legislation, awarding scholarships to African American residents who had been accepted into out-of-state graduate and professional schools, in an effort to avoid school desegregation or integration. The commission not only endorsed the measure but also recommended dozens of prospective students for the program. According to the 1940 annual report, no one questioned the motives of the legislature, at least not publicly.[53]

The commission certainly did all it could to discourage desegregation as well as distinguish itself from the unpopular NAACP and other organizations that were determined to desegregate society. TCIRC Secretary S. W. Johnson, an African American from Houston, said in her 1926 report on commission activities, "At first the outlook seemed a bit discouraging, but the men who began to work took hold with undaunted courage and began to look about for men who were thoughtful, foresighted and conservative."[54] In the report, which incidentally ignored the role of women commission members, Johnson also praises the local police, district attorney, school superintendent, business community, and public carriers for their commitment to improving the conditions of African Americans.[55] By the late 1920s, members felt strongly that the organization remove specific references to the "women's division and men's division and that both terms be dropped from our official literature," as women played a dominant role in lobbying legislatures, meeting with groups in local communities, and orchestrating diverse coalitions, as well as etching out long-term plans for the organization.[56] Nevertheless, other Houston residents—Afro-Americans, of course—made different claims as they criticized public servants, industrialists, politicians, and educators for their continued pattern of racism in the city.[57]

To be sure, the conservative, conciliatory TCIRC helped thousands of African Americans in the state, even raising bail money and attorney fees for individuals wrongly accused of crimes. The organization investigated alleged wrongdoing involving city officials, police, hospitals, businesses, and civic leaders. The commission also successfully lobbied for the opening of an African American tuberculosis hospital. Members also appealed to civic leaders in an effort to raise money for the state's hard-pressed private HBCUs during the depression. The group's Black members adopted gradualism as a suitable approach to challenging racism, hoping this would ultimately prompt widespread support for civil rights in the future.[58]

White members disagreed with this line of thinking completely, particularly those conservatives who embraced the "separate but equal" principle as plausible. Some commissioners believed the state's systemic racial problems had less to do with White hostility than with "misunderstandings" between the races, as well as ineptitude on the part of people of color. The organization, for example, never discussed racism as a contributing factoring affecting African American progress or lack thereof. Covington eventually realized the sobering fact that White Texans, for the most part, cared very little about toppling racial injustice. Still, in her own way and in her numerous organizations Covington was determined to improve the lives of others.[59]

Disillusioned and frustrated, Covington, in later years, publicly denounced the pro-segregationist platform of Texas politicians, civic leaders, and businesspeople: "I will say that these [segregationist] bills are a travesty of justice, conceived in iniquity and designed to crush and subdue the spirit of the Negro."[60] Like NACW founder Mary Church Terrell, Covington, as a grey-haired senior, grew frustrated and angry. Racial bigotry, according to Covington, remained the most perilous challenge in the South, largely because of intolerance on the part of Whites and inaction on the part of African Americans.[61]

Although interracial coalitions helped pave the way for later civil-rights victories, most "New Negroes" worked inside grassroots, intraracial organizing efforts. Migration, the growth of the African American middle class, community building, and politicalization in the age of the "New Negro" during and following World War I all worked to improve conditions for some African Americans, making it easier to challenge White racism. Sometimes, however, clashing views, even among African Americans, made real improvement difficult. Political dissention threatened the establishment of the important NAACP branch, formed in 1918. When it became apparent that community momentum favored the creation of an NAACP branch, conservatives eagerly worked to gain control of the organization. Turf wars ignited between "Old Guard" constructionalists and members of the emerging "New Negro" order. Alabama native and educator E. O. Smith founded the CBL shortly following the riot in an effort to repair the city's growing racial rift. The nineteenth-century migrant challenged individuals like Bryan, Texas, native and postal railway unionist Henry L. Mims (also a nineteenth-century newcomer) and newspaperman Richardson, radical CBL members who vehemently opposed racism and appeasement.[62]

The conservative faction of the CBL used character assassination, lies, deception, and manipulation in an attempt to secure the charter. For Smith and other conservatives, racial reconciliation through appeasement seemed the prudent approach to rectifying racial divisions.[63] Actually, according to historian Jon Wilson, Smith and educator and newspaperman William Leonard Davis, originally from Lavaca County, Texas, opposed forming a civil-rights organization altogether. Alabama native E. O. Smith and Lavaca County, Texas, native W. L. Davis, who incidentally also served as the secretary of the executive board of the Negro Division of the Federal Food Administration in 1918, perhaps wanted to use the proposed NAACP branch to expand their political base in the city. Smith and Davis possibly worked alongside Whites, potentially carrying out their directives to thwart organizing efforts, says Wilson. Only after their failed attempts exhausted their finances did the constructionalists concede.[64] A relieved Walter White later commented to Smith, "I trust that your spirit of subordinating your own claims to the greater good, [sic] will be duly appreciated by every citizen of Houston, so it is by the national office of the N.A.A.C.P. and by the Secretary in particular."[65]

This was not the first time "New Negroes" waged war against enemies. Mims, who first inquired about an NAACP charter in 1915, helped found the National Alliance of Postal Employees (NAPE) in Chattanooga, Tennessee, in October 1913. According to Mims:

> The Colored Railway Postal Clerks of this division are now organized at the several railway centers, and have requested me to ask the clerks of the country to attend a National Conference at Chattanooga, Tenn., Oct. 2, 3 and 4th [1913]. . . . It is thought that this is the proper time to organize a National movement among the colored clerks, and to this end it is desired that each Railway center send [a] representative. . . . There is no reason why we can not [sic] be men and make suitable provisions for our wives and dependents, nor should we be without means to effectively present our grievances and petitions to the Department whenever in our judgment it becomes necessary to do so.[66]

The organization, perhaps the first industrial union in the United States that catered to the needs of people of color, sought to protect the rights of African American railway postal clerks who became the targets of organized attacks from White unionists, who increasingly branched off into the area of railway clerking as safer steel railcars replaced wooden boxcars. The Texan served as the national body's first president. A fierce follower of Du Bois and the NAACP, Mims and other newcomers to the city had only recently abandoned the political ideology of Booker T. Washington. For him and other postal railway employees, only aggressive protest challenged the racial polarity of the city. The Mims group, which advocated women's rights as well as racial equality, ultimately secured the local charter in August 1918.[67]

Unfortunately, multiple problems ensued for the new chapter for several decades to come. Rivalries, initially between the Mims–Richardson faction and the Smith–Davis contingency, but also among progressive "New Negroes," persistently plagued the organization. Migrants Davis and Smith, according to historians Wilson and James SoRelle, eventually gained control of the young chapter by 1919 and urged members to take a delayed, conciliatory approach to local racial matters. In return, newspaperman Richardson gave little to no coverage to chapter events and affairs. Richardson stepped down as secretary and left the organization in 1919 after accusations of misappropriation of funds surfaced. Problems remained nevertheless, even after "New Negroes" regained control of the chapter in the 1920s. The organization also struggled to retain members after 1919. By the mid-1920s, the ICVL, PVL, and TCIRC competed with the NAACP for members. In addition, not everyone supported the NAACP. Many prominent Afro-Americans like the Covingtons avoided the NAACP altogether, preferring less vocal groups or interracial coalitions instead.[68]

Other challenges threatened the NAACP as well as the African American community. Racial violence after World War I posed a serious problem for "New Negroes." The Houston branch of the NAACP, like offices across the state, experienced a fierce White backlash after World War I. Texas branches, which grew from four in 1918 to thirty-one in 1919, had some of the highest numbers nationwide and led the country with the number of local NAACP offices. Moreover, according to historian Steven A. Reich, Texans from across the state increasingly identified with the protest schemes of the young organization that called attention to the state's woeful neglect and abuse of its African American citizens. From farm tenants and wage earners to businesspersons and college-trained professionals, Afro-Texans sought wage increases, pay equity, better schooling, social equality, electorate rights, and an end to racial violence. Whites, of course, for the most part saw these demands as outlandish; and many, if not most, considered the NAACP the state's number one nemesis. White anger routinely turned into violence and mayhem: The brutal lynching of Will Stanley in Temple in 1915, Jesse Washington's lynching death in Waco in 1916, the hanging of a Galveston man in 1917, the mass murder of the Cabaness family in Huntsville in 1918, the Joe Winters lynching in Conroe in 1922, the Longview Riot of 1919, the near-death beating of NAACP executive secretary John Shillady in Austin in 1919, the murder of Robert Coleman in 1920 in Shepherd, and George Hughes's lynching death in Sherman in 1930 readily come to mind. Texans lynched almost four hundred people between the years 1889 and 1942, with 80 percent of victims being African American. Escalating racial violence in the state unfortunately drove thousands out of the NAACP by 1923. Intimidation, beatings, rape, and murder persuaded many to rethink the value of direct protest.[69]

The Second Ku Klux Klan (KKK) and other terrorist groups also intimidated Houston African Americans. Wartime violence and D. W. Griffith's release of the iconic *Birth of a Nation* (1915), a film based on Thomas Dixon's novel *The Clansman* (1905), catapulted the rise of the Second Ku Klux Klan. Nationwide membership rose to five million by the mid-1920s, with Texas, Oklahoma, and Indiana having the largest membership rosters.[70]

The Houston Riot touched off a tailspin of fear, anger, hatred, and racism. Billie Mayfield, the publisher of *Colonel Mayfield's Weekly*, expressed his contempt for society's moral disintegration, blaming the alleged moral decline on Jewish Americans, Roman Catholics, Latinos, recent European ethnics, Asian immigrants, and African Americans. In Houston, police officers, public officials, educators, ministers, college students, professionals, homemakers, and businesspersons endorsed and/or joined the terrorist group in an effort to curtail what they saw as the immoral degradation of society.[71]

Not every White Houstonian endorsed the Klan. From business leaders and politicians to ordinary law-abiding citizens, some saw the terrorist organization as a nuisance. Joseph Cullinan, founder of Texas Oil Company (later Texaco Oil), publicly denounced the actions of the group; so did Huntsville, Texas, native and *Houston Chronicle* publisher Marcellus Foster, whose editorials criticizing the KKK helped Miriam Ferguson win her gubernatorial race in 1924, when she campaigned as a Republican and anti-Klan candidate. In addition, this period saw the formation of the Texas Citizenship League, an organization that openly challenged the KKK. Members included Cullinan; timber and oil executive John H. Kirby of Tyler, Texas; and former Texas secretary of state and American General Life and Accident Insurance Company (now VALIC) founder John Lee Wortham.[72] The organization's flyer stated that the organization supports "the principle of equal justice to all."[73]

A suspicious NAACP member responded to the flyer, writing "Bull" next to the group's equality mandate.[74] The critical NAACP branch member, perhaps branch secretary John M. Adkins, whom the organization wrote to in 1923, concluded the Texas Citizenship League, like the KKK was a "political organization . . . for Whites only," looking out for its own [White] interests. The city's civic elite, including these men, wholeheartedly supported racial segregation. They simply believed the Klan's actions tarnished the city's reputation and risked alienating Houston from business investors and the national civic community. Nevertheless, Houston's civic leadership ultimately helped lead the way for the KKK's downfall in the mid-1920s.[75]

In the meantime, African Americans remained the Klan's as well as other hostile groups' number one target. Several heinous acts in the 1920s confirm this observation, including the castration of dentist John Lafayette Cockrell, possibly from Louisiana, and the tarring of physician R. H. Ward, two African American doctors who allegedly had regular sexual liaisons with White women.[76] According to Thelma Scott Bryant, "They took him [John L. Cockrell] out and tarred and feathered him. Did you ever hear of tarring and feathering? . . . And cut off his private parts. . . . Of course he left town after that."[77]

In 1928, three days after the shooting death of a police officer by Afro-American assailant Robert Powell, Whites kidnapped and lynched the young man, who was healing from gunshot wounds.[78] In 1924, a group of White youths stoned to death a "colored girl" because "she got off the [Houston Heights streetcar] 'ahead of Whites.'" According to the *Informer,* "The alleged culprits were turned loose under a nominal bond; and there has not even been a wave of protest from any source."[79] No doubt, ongoing threats and acts of violence affected the stability of the Houston NAACP branch, motivating members to eschew interracial controversy and racial unity, especially if the latter could bring about one's death.[80]

Racists also went after civic leaders and businesspersons. Not everyone respected Independence Heights Mayor Oliphant Hubbard, for example. Sometimes Oliphant Hubbard's spirited speeches on racial autonomy, self-help, education, and self-defense upset local Whites, including members of the local Klan. Members of the Houston Ku Klux Klan saw the mayor as someone who advocated social equality. Mostly Mayor Hubbard advanced the notion of racial autonomy. Klan threats continued and convinced residents to guard the Hubbard home. Oliphant Hubbard took precautions too, sometimes greeting visitors with a loaded 30–30 shotgun.[81] "They threatened my father all the time, says daughter Vivian Hubbard Seals . . . and wanted him dead."[82] After Hubbard left politics for good and the residents voted to annex the city in 1929, the death threats ended.[83]

As referenced in chapter 1, civic leaders often exaggerated race relations in the city, suggesting people got along quite well, in hopes of influencing internal migration into the city. In truth, Houston did not shield African Americans, including the outspoken newspaper editor and NAACP branch founder Clifton Richardson, from racial antagonism, the threat of injury, or violence.[84] According to observer Thelma Scott Bryant, "You had C. F. Richardson who was the real first editor of the *Houston Informer* . . . but C. F. Richardson was the great fighter . . . and they were always beating him up as he went from one little town to another making a big talk about the NAACP, and they would catch him coming through some of these little small towns, give him a beating and turn him loose."[85] Richardson's vigilance against the Houston Ku Klux Klan in the 1920s led to several death threats, including a sign nailed to his door that read, "Nigger, leave town. Don't let the sun go down on you."[86] In truth, White supremacists attacked Richardson on several occasions. According to son Clifton Richardson Jr., "My father was active in . . . [going after the Klan]." His outspokenness and civic engagement made him a target. In 1928, according to Cliff Richardson Jr., "[a] cop stopped him and took him downtown for having a defective headlight. But actually they whipped [him] for what he was writing about the Klu Klux Klan. He went to his grave with a V-neck scar right here where [doctors stitched a massive laceration with] thirty-five stitches in his head."[87]

The KKK also planned to execute Richardson, according to his son Cliff Jr.:

> They did have a plan to kill him. They had two plans. One of them . . . officers in Wharton were gonna [sic] arrest him and when they walked across the courthouse square, some sniper was supposed to shoot him down. Then there was another one [that] was hatched here and that also goes to show you, you just never know. Of course the Whites that were hatching this plan had a Negro waiter and he overheard the Klan, but [they] thought that he was one of those same [accommodating] Niggers [they could control] and they discussed anything in front of him. But a lot of people that they call safe are only safe because they have to be. . . . [He] called my father and told him that the plan was to lure him up to an office in one of the buildings downtown on Main, [I believe, but] I don't recall. They were gonna [sic] kill him and cut up his body and each one of them was gonna [sic] take a piece of it away so that he would disappear without a trace. But he got in the wind of that. Of course he had a lot of problems. They vandalized his office several times. They

blocked . . . him [from borrowing money and establishing credit in the city]. He could more or less live with that.[88]

Unlike Richardson, most residents of color felt more at ease living with segregation than publicly challenging Whites, even when it came to obvious injustices. Even social worker Jesse Thomas, who spoke favorably about Houston as a southern city in his 1929 National Urban League (NUL) piece, admitted the pseudo-congenial race relations between the races resulted from several factors. Away from the job and busy city streets, the races rarely had social contact with one another. When the races did in fact meet on the job—in the homes of Whites, on streetcars, in public places, and while commuting to and from work on downtown streets—the groups adhered to racial segregation and customs.[89]

By all means, institutionalized racism angered African Americans, including the silent, compliant majority. According to Thelma Bryant, "Most of us realized it was just a way of life in the South. We knew we had our place and had to stay in it, as the White people would say . . . [however] I didn't like that at all."[90] Even during vacations, the second-class citizenship never disappeared. For instance, on entering the last stop that preceded the train's entry into the South, railroad conductors announced "that all Negroes had to get in another car."[91] Furthermore, according to the former biology teacher:

> They had a special car for us in the South. That was another thing that bothered me. The locomotives in those days burned a lot of coal. The windows were up on the train. The car that they assigned to us was always right behind the engine and all these cinders were coming back into the Negro car. If you were on one of the last cars, you didn't get as much of that as you got on the first. So when you arrived at your destination, you were just as dirty as you could be. I didn't want to accept it [Jim Crow Segregation] but I am nothing but a child [in the 1900s and 1910s] and can't do anything about it."[92]

Most felt powerless to act in defense of their families and communities. Furthermore, White supremacists groups, such as the Ku Klux Klan, White vigilante mobs, and law enforcement officers did not hesitate to use violence and intimidation to ensure compliance and subordination among African Americans.[93]

Despite the threats, local NAACP leadership remained committed to battling racial bigotry. The NAACP branch, with the assistance of the TCIRC, successfully freed a young Houston man wrongfully accused of raping a White woman in March 1922. The district attorney sentenced to death Texas native Luther Collins, an African American, for the crime. The local NAACP kept the case in the news, raised funds, and successfully argued the case in court. After four unsuccessful trials, the Harris County district attorney dismissed the case in 1926.[94] In addition, Lincoln Theater owner O. P. DeWalt of Polk County, Texas, served as chapter president in 1924 and remained an outspoken defender of social justice until his shocking murder by a disgruntled employee in 1931.[95]

The organization nevertheless found it difficult to survive DeWalt's death and ongoing challenges. Clashing personalities, conflicting ideologies, possible cronyism, corruption allegations, accusations of sexism, and ongoing conflicts with the national office plagued the Houston branch and affected membership. Although the local NAACP branch had over four hundred members in 1918, from 1922 to 1937, the chapter struggled to survive due to poor fundraising and membership drives. In the 1930s, more accusations of unethical dealings and the misappropriation of funds riddled the branch, leading executive secretary Walter White and others within the national office to consider the disbandment of the chapter.[96]

The 1930s, though, saw important new developments that helped transform the struggling NAACP into one of the nation's largest branches by World War II. So too did the world witness a heightened vigilance on the part of Houston Blacks, including those not necessarily involved in the NAACP. As the Great Depression raged on, activists more readily focused on economic and educational disparities as indicators of racial bias. Pay inequities among the middle class, especially schoolteachers, brought this to the forefront. Black frustration over disfranchisement also propelled increased activism, especially among radical migrants seeking immediate change.[97]

Richard Randolph Grovey, a civil rights and labor activist, was born in Brazoria County, Texas, in 1890, the son of landowners Thomas and Nellie Grovey (fig. 35). The oldest of four children and the only one to finish high school, he graduated from A. J. Moore High School in Waco, Texas, in 1910. He then earned a degree from Tillotson College in Austin, Texas, in 1914. After a brief stint as a school principal, in 1916 Grovey married a Prairie View College student, Ethel Nathan of Brenham, Texas, in Waller

FIGURE 35. Richard Randolph Grovey was born in Brazoria County, Texas, in 1890. The son of landowners and the oldest of four children, Grovey graduated from A. J. Moore High School in Waco, Texas, in 1910. He then earned a degree from Tillotson College (now Huston-Tillotson University) in Austin, Texas, in 1914. After a brief stint as a school principal, Grovey in 1916 married a Prairie View College (now Prairie View A&M University) student, Ethel Nathan of Brenham, Texas, in Waller County. In 1917, after the birth of their first child, a son, the Grovey's moved to Houston. To them, the city's close proximity to their hometowns, schools, and economic opportunities made their decision a practical one. *(Courtesy Richard Randolph Grovey Family, Houston, Texas)*

County. The next year, following the birth of their son, the family embraced the Great Migration and moved to Houston. They considered Houston a good place to raise a family, despite the drawbacks of segregation and the tumultuous Houston Riot that engulfed the city that same year.⁹⁸

To be sure, the couple in some ways identified with the soldiers of the Twenty-fourth United States Infantry, who had taken up arms during the August 1917 Houston Mutiny. They too hated racial segregation and inequality, resisting daily. Relying on what historian Robin D. G. Kelley calls "infrapolitics," the Groveys, for example, conducted business transactions and signed documents using their first and middle initials, followed by their last name, thereby never disclosing their full names and risking humiliation.⁹⁹ According to daughter Nell Cole:

[B]oth of my parents adopted their initials ... my father always went by R. R. Grovey. He did not allow anyone to deal with his name.... My mother had that attitude; my mother was E. T. Grovey.... That was their protection and safeguard for not being demeaned by somebody calling them by Richard or Ethel.[100]

Grovey's protest imagination went further. Tired of taking orders and feeling undervalued, in the 1920s, he left a skilled job as a boilermaker's helper at Houston and Texas Central Railroad and enrolled in barber school, ultimately opening a barbershop in Third Ward on Dowling Street. Grovey soon used his barbershop as a meeting place for the community, especially the working poor.[101]

In the late 1920s, motivated by ongoing conversations at his shop about the perpetual racial divide, Grovey founded a political-action organization, the Third Ward Civic Club (TWCC), one that intersected civic reform with labor organizing. The organization protested wage differentials, poor city services, crime, police brutality, and segregation, and led labor strikes. Grovey also sought to unite African Americans across class lines, believing that a well-executed united front in the community could mean the start of a concerted civil-rights agenda.[102]

Racial exclusion in politics particularly frustrated many, including Grovey. Since the days of Reconstruction, White Texans had sought the complete disenfranchisement of Blacks, although third-party movements and political agendas such as the Greenback Party, Populism, and Prohibition had hampered their actions. Politicians ultimately reached their goal during the Progressive Movement. Led by statesman and lawmaker Alexander W. Terrell, the Twenty-seventh and Twenty-eighth Legislatures passed the poll tax statute of 1902 and the Terrell primary election laws of 1903 and 1905, respectively. Although the former targeted poorer Texans of all races and ethnic groups, the latter laws required that county party executive committee chairs ban Blacks from voting in primary elections. So too did Whites use these statutes to bar Mexican Texans in South Texas from voting in primary elections. A 1912 law also required that voters pay their poll taxes before voting in primary elections, although sometimes the statute did not block all African Americans from exercising their constitutional right to vote.[103]

Occasionally, county chairpersons permitted African Americans to vote, particularly potential voters holding poll-tax receipts, residing in cities. By the early 1920s though, county officials adhered to the wishes of White Democrats and refrained from giving ballots to African

Americans. Undeterred, migrant Houstonians fought back. For example, when the Harris County Democratic Executive Committee (HCDEC) barred African Americans from voting in the February 1921 primary election, newspapermen and southeastern Texas natives Charles N. Love and W. L. Davis, along with others in *Love v. Griffith* (1922), unsuccessfully sued the local Democratic machinery in the Court of Civil Appeals for the First District of Texas, charging racial exclusion. Two years later in *Love v. Griffith* (1924), the United States Supreme Court upheld the lower court decision.[104]

Influenced by earlier court decisions as well as the pleas of White Democrats determined to bar African Americans from participating in local primaries, in 1923, the Thirty-eighth Texas Legislature passed the White Democratic Primary law, explicitly prohibiting African Americans from voting in local, statewide, and national primary elections. Like other former Confederate states, Texas had a single, functioning political party—the Democratic Party. Interestingly, other southern states used Democratic political machines, which many considered private organizations and outside state control, to disfranchise Afro-Americans through implicit means. The state's White Texans, paradoxically, frustrated with what they considered a growing Black political threat—continued voting privileges in local elections, the rise of the NAACP, and direct challenges to White hegemony, including resistance to violence—adopted a maneuver that explicitly violated the constitutional rights of Blacks. When the courts declared the initial law unconstitutional in 1927, White Texans went to work constructing a meatier statute.[105]

Black Texans, unabashed, took the state to court in response to numerous election laws. In *Nixon v. Herndon* (1927) and *Nixon v. Condon* (1932), the Supreme Court ruled that two White primary laws were unconstitutional. Both the 1923 and 1927 laws, according to the Supreme Court, violated the Fourteenth-amendment rights of Black Texans, largely the amendment's "equal protection" clause. The latest Texas statute, passed weeks following the *Herndon* decision, granted the Democratic Party's executive committee the power to determine voting eligibility in primary elections. Black Texans, from Houston to El Paso, challenged the new law in the federal courts. Although the Supreme Court once again ruled in favor of physician Lawrence Nixon of El Paso, many recognized that a different political maneuver defining the party as a private club could sway jurists of the High Court. Shortly after the *Condon* decision in 1932 and the passage of a new statute that invalidated the previous law, the Democratic Party, a private

FIGURE 36. Tired of taking orders and feeling undervalued at the Houston and Texas Central Railroad in Houston, Grovey in the 1920s left a skilled job as a boilermaker's helper. He enrolled in barber school and subsequently opened a barbershop on Dowling Street in Third Ward. Grovey soon used his barbershop as a meeting place for the community, especially the working poor, establishing the Third Ward Civic Club (TWCC) in the late 1920s or early 1930s. His leadership skills attracted the attention of other civil-rights activists, who recruited him to form an aggressive organizational assault on the White Democratic Primary. The TWCC worked with Independent Colored Voter's League, formed in 1927, and, later, the Harris County Negro Democratic Club (HCNDC), established in 1932, to create effective opposition to the architects of the white primary—The Texas Legislature and Democratic Party. On this KTRH Radio broadcast, Grovey (left) and another member of the HCNDC discuss their cause with mainstream (Houston-area, especially Whites) listeners. *(Courtesy Richard Randolph Grovey Family, Houston, Texas)*

organization, according to the state, took responsibility for determining eligibility for its primary elections in the state. Black Texans, many of them recent migrants to cities, undaunted, continued their fight.[106]

Grovey and the TWCC joined forces with several political action committees in an attempt to orchestrate real change. Grovey worked with the ICVL, an organization founded in 1927 that sought ways to address the statewide election abuses. The following year, Grovey and the TWCC joined forces with attorneys Jasper Alston Atkins of North Carolina, James Nabrit of Alabama, Houston native Carter Wesley, and native Texan and businessman Julius White, forming the HCNDC in 1932, in an attempt to unite African Americans against a common foe. The organization staged mass demonstrations and boycotts, published editorials in newspapers, and held debates on local radio programs (fig. 36).[107]

Black Texans got behind the political activists. Women's clubs held fundraisers, and ministers in the pulpit advocated continued defiance. The group, as supporters had done previously, also launched lawsuits against political officials who upheld the biased White primary. Julius White, the husband of Houston civil-rights activist Lulu B. White, also a migrant from eastern Texas, filed a suit against the local Democratic Party in an attempt to force the local political establishment to uphold the Supreme Court decisions. His attorneys, including newspaperman Wesley, filed an *amicus curiae* brief with the *Nixon v. Condon* case, as well as a writ of mandamus in federal district court against local Democrats; ultimately, however, the plaintiffs in *White v. Lubbock* (1930) failed in their efforts.[108]

Local Whites, in fact, adopted the Huggins Plan, a resolution named for *Houston Chronicle* editor and Harris County Democratic Party Executive Chair Judge William O. Huggins, who publicly adopted the recent disfranchisement scheme, limiting voting privileges to White Harris County Democrats. This declaration, ironically, only invigorated the state's African American community. In El Paso, San Antonio, Fort Worth, Tyler, and Beaumont, Blacks filed lawsuits, charging the state's Democrats with civil-rights infringements. Nixon, for example, once again ignored the actions of White Democrats and attempted to vote in the 1932 primary elections, but was ultimately refused a ballot. Once more, he went to court. In *Nixon v. McCann* (1934), the first White primary case victory won by Texas Blacks at the federal district court level, the judge ruled that the state indirectly controlled the Democratic Party, as the White primary statute prompted the actions of the voluntary association (Democratic Party). Not surprisingly, though, nothing changed. So too did the "opinion" of gubernatorial candidate James G. Alfred, endorsing circumscribed voting rights for African Americans in 1934, give further credence to the newest resolution of the Democratic Party. Black Texans still refused to give up hope.[109]

Black Houstonians especially remained optimistic. Grovey, determined to make history, filed a lawsuit in 1932 against election judge Albert Townsend, charging the official with violating his constitutional rights when he refused to issue him a ballot. In what many considered a controversial move, with the financial backing of local Houstonians but without the assistance of the national NAACP, Grovey took the case to the US Supreme Court. The national office expressed some apprehension about the suit, fearful a negative verdict could reverse the organization's efforts. A loophole—suing for damages under $20—allowed the attorneys to forego the Texas Appellate and High Courts and take the case directly to the United States Supreme Court.[110]

Unlike the previous cases involving Nixon, this time the Court in *Grovey v. Townsend* (1935) ruled in favor of the defendant, arguing that the Democratic Party as well as other political organizations were in fact "voluntary associations for political action . . . not the creatures of the state . . . [with] . . . power to determine . . . membership and . . . [eligibility] . . . in the party's primaries."[111] Many, according to historian Darlene Clark Hine, compared the devastating ruling to the Supreme Court's Dred Scott decision of 1857 and blamed the defeat on Grovey and his attorneys. Determined to rewrite history, the NAACP and Houstonians, including plaintiff Lonnie Smith, a local dentist originally from Marshall, Texas,

FIGURE 37. Possibly patterned after the Third Ward Civic Club, Fifth Ward residents, immediately following the *Smith v. Allwright* decision of 1944, formed the Fifth Ward Civic Club in an attempt to increase political awareness among Fifth Ward residents. Phillis Wheatley High School alumna Helen Perry (second from the left in black dress) remained politically active for much of her adult life. Perry's other memberships included the NAACP, Heroines of Jericho and/or Order of the Eastern Star, and United Negroes of America. Perry, who later bought a home in Clinton Park/Fidelity Park in the late 1940s or early 1950s, earned her living as a vocational nurse and worked at Hermann Hospital. Migrant Texans or Louisianans in Fifth Ward, Houston, felt the impact of the White Primary Law and assertively formulated ways to promote political involvement. Ultimately, this would lead to real results in the Fifth Ward/Clinton Park area. These same women and men, as well as their children, would elect Fifth Ward resident Barbara Jordan—the daughter of Texas migrants—to the Texas Senate in 1966 and United States House of Representatives in 1972. *(Courtesy Houston Metropolitan Research Center, Houston Public Library, Houston, Texas, Helen Perry Collection, MSS 0276-0019)*

continued their assault, eventually invalidating the White primary with the *Smith v. Allwright* decision (1944), arguing that the law violated Texans' Fifteenth Amendment rights (fig. 37).[112]

Anger over the *Grovey* ruling lingered for years, nevertheless. Embarrassed by the negative publicity as well as disillusioned by the 1935 defeat, Black Houstonians turned on Grovey and his attorneys. Middle-class professionals in particular resented how Whites verbally attacked Afro-Americans on the city streets, in the print media, and on the radio. Blacks, in return, threatened Grovey, verbally attacked the family, and stopped patronizing his barbershop. Teachers, according to daughter Nell Grovey Cole, even demeaned the Grovey children in school. NAACP members especially branded the activist a troublemaker. One attorney in particular despised Grovey. According to Cole, future Supreme Court Justice Thurgood Marshall "disliked my father" with impunity and blamed him alone for the defeat. Hardly phased by the community's pretensions, Grovey continued fighting for the rights of others.[113]

Obviously, this political shift involved middle-aged migrants like Grovey. Young people born at the turn of the century or after 1900, nevertheless, comprised a large segment of the city's new activist segment in the African American community in the 1930s. Younger migrants, mostly from eastern Texas, along with the young adult children of earlier migrants, felt comfortable working for the African American liberation struggle. Younger moderates and moderate militants who supported the immediate disintegration of disfranchisement and racial segregation also made up a larger proportion of the African American population, compared to the middle-aged and elderly founders of the NAACP who battled a large constituency of accommodationists during World War I. By the interwar period, younger African Americans increasingly joined the NAACP, NUL, and other groups as a way to do their part for the movement.[114]

The new direction represents a generational shift as well as an organizational restructuring that placed greater importance on economic ills, even while remaining true to political mobilization. Younger second- and third-wave internal migrants of the twentieth century, who entered the city as adults during and following World War I, felt comfortable challenging segregation. Sometimes activists like attorney and newspaperman Carter Wesley, who was born to migrant parents and grew up in Houston, took a stronger position on the race question, one that differed from that of their conservative, accommodating parents. These young women and men, most being two generations removed from slavery, ardently and openly opposed racial discrimination. Unlike physician B. J. Covington, individuals born after 1900 sought to dismantle the systems of segregation and racism as opposed to working within them. Although they knew their supposed place in the Jim Crow South, they found ways to use subterfuges to survive and to conspire against southern racism at the same time.[115]

Increasingly, younger civic leaders spoke out publicly and privately about the racial divide, even while remaining true to traditional community building. Born in Brazos County, Texas, in 1909, Moses L. Price was the son of sharecroppers, Rev. Britain and Alice Price. His parents, though poor and uneducated, pushed their children to succeed. M. L. Price attended the Wilcox School, a one-room shack, through grade six; soon thereafter, he entered Bryan High School, Colored, ultimately transferring to Guadalupe College in Seguin and graduating with his high school diploma in 1931. He went on to earn an undergraduate degree at Samuel Huston College (SHC) in Austin in 1933, graduating summa cum laude. Price later obtained a graduate degree from Houston College for Negroes (HCN). In college, he took theology classes and entered the ministry, preaching some of his first sermons in the early 1930s in San Antonio, Beaumont, and Houston; more than likely, he commented in the pulpit about the state of race relations during the Great Depression.[116]

After graduation, Price moved to Houston to pastor the Greater New Hope Baptist Church. Then in 1938, he became pastor of the Greater Zion Baptist Church on Trulley Street in Third Ward, where he served as pastor for forty-six years. His knowledge of the Bible, spellbinding sermons, and statewide prominence helped propel him to numerous ministerial positions in the state and nation. Price served as moderator of the Lincoln District Association, first vice president of the National Baptist Convention of America, and president of the Missionary Baptist General Convention of Texas. He promoted foreign missionary work, Christian cooperation, and familial love among Afro-American Christians (fig. 38).[117]

Price loved the African American community. An outspoken proponent of higher education, he felt Afro-Americans had a responsibility to support Historically Black Colleges and Universities (HBCUs),[118] and he supported the establishment of a private university in Texas. "We can build a Baptist university . . . in Houston. . . . As the association's leader, I will not be satisfied until every church becomes a regular contributor to the Bishop College drive."[119] Black colleges, in Price's viewpoint, would serve

FIGURE 38. Rev. Moses Price, a native of Brazos County, Texas, became pastor of the Greater Zion Baptist Church (now Greater Zion Missionary Baptist Church) in 1938 and served in this capacity for nearly a half-century. During this period, he worked with NAACP organizers in a relentless attempt to defeat the White Primary Law of Texas. Unlike most African American ministers of the twentieth century, Price spoke openly about structural racism in the United States. He challenged his members to fight back as New Negroes. He later became the first vice president of the National Baptist Convention of America. The recipient of an undergraduate degree from Sam Huston College (now Huston-Tillotson University) and a master's degree from Houston College for Negroes, Price also promoted higher education for Blacks. He even attempted to open a Baptist College for African Americans in Houston, circa 1940s. *(Courtesy Houston Metropolitan Research Center, Houston Public Library, Houston, Texas, Rev. Moses Price Collection, MSS 0277-0000)*

an important role in the ongoing civil-rights struggle by educating the movement's future leaders.[120]

Pastor Price not only pushed the community to support African American colleges but also courted the notion of political mobilization for people of color. He joined the NAACP in the 1930s and encouraged church members to do the same. Like his friends and colleagues Rev. Albert A. Lucas and Rev. Lee Haywood Simpson, Price believed African Americans could effectively challenge racial segregation. He became a prominent member of the organization for decades.[121]

In addition, the migrant supported other civic causes. Price sat on the board of Riverside National Bank (now Unity National Bank), the

Standard Savings Association, Texas Southern University (TSU), the Eliza Johnson Home, and Bishop College. His activities also extended to the Young Men's Christian Association, American Woodmen, the Progressive Pilgrims, and Phi Beta Sigma Fraternity (PBS). These African American organizations allowed Price to formulate policies for the interest of people of color. He believed in the idea of racial self-preservation, understanding that African Americans themselves would inspire the community and bring about collective and individualized change. Pastor Price helped shape civil rights, Baptist theology, and instruction in higher education in Houston and Texas for decades. He continued to work in the church and community until his death in 1984.[122]

For Price, appropriate male leadership provided the community with the affirming values and qualities deemed suitable to the civil-rights cause. Civil-rights groups, like churches, relied almost exclusively on African American men as community activists. Not surprisingly, the NAACP and other civic groups represented male dominance and the perspective that only men could appropriately address the social ills facing people of color. Organizations heavily compensated for the lack of African American male involvement in mainstream politics and the citywide economy. The absence of Afro-American men in business, commerce, banking, higher education, science and engineering, and the skilled crafts made their presence in religious and civic groups more important.[123]

These organizations gave men multiple platforms and celebrated manhood in important ways. African American institutions compensated for those White-controlled establishments that ignored educated, successful, professional, confident Afro-American men. As well, male-oriented activities provided African American men with strong role models that attempted to cultivate future generations.[124]

Social justice was a prevailing theme in male-dominated congregations. Rev. Albert Anderson Lucas, one of the most successful protest pastors of the twentieth century, according to historians Darlene Clark Hine and Merline Pitre, became the pastor of Good Hope Baptist Church in 1935. A native of the Dabney Hill Community of Burleson County, Texas, Lucas, who was born in 1886 or 1887, graduated from Conroe College in the 1900s or 1910s in theology studies and headed several churches before arriving in Houston sometime thereafter. The pastor's oratorical, organizational, and fundraising skills served usefully in eliminating Good Hope Baptist Church's $8,000 debt, eventually increasing the congregation, and constructing a larger sanctuary.[125]

Before long, in the late 1930s, local NAACP leadership began taking notice of Lucas's oratory and fundraising skills, electing him president in 1939. Under his leadership and direction, the membership grew from several hundred in 1939 to nearly two thousand a year later. In his sermons, he urged African Americans to join the NAACP and fight racism. God desired this of all African American Christians. Utilizing churches, civic groups, and keen organizational strategies, Lucas also solicited the support of White liberals, PBS Fraternity, the Progressive Voter's League (PVL), the Interdenominational Ministerial Alliance (IMA), the *Houston Informer,* and area congregations in an effort to dismantle the White primary (fig. 39).[126]

FIGURE 39. Born in Burleson County in the late 1880s, Albert A. Lucas attended Conroe College and in the 1930s relocated to Houston to pastor Good Hope Baptist Church (now Good Hope Missionary Baptist Church). The young pastor's oratorical, organizational, and fund-raising skills helped Good Hope raise $8,000 to pay off their church mortgage. He eventually increased the size of the congregation and built a larger sanctuary. The NAACP asked Lucas to serve as the organization's chapter head in 1937. His potent leadership abilities helped increase the chapter's membership, even attracting White supporters, like communist labor lawyer Arthur J. Mandell, by World War II. He, like Price, inspired his members to join the organization and pay their poll taxes. Lucas believed the Christian leadership within the community had a responsibility to lead the political fight to destroy the White primary of Texas. *(Courtesy Houston Metropolitan Research Center, Houston Public Library, Houston, Texas, Rev. Moses Price Collection,* MSS 0277-0007*)*

Ironically, male dominance in politics and civic practices challenged gender fairness. Most male-controlled groups during the period of the "New Negro" never gave gender equity a passing thought. Nor did men generally care. Although they did not believe in the inequality of the races, they regularly practiced gender discrimination. In the same way that Whites upheld racial segregation and White supremacy, African American men saw gender exclusion as a moral and spiritual mandate. Moreover, women cheered on their men. With few exceptions, they did not work alongside them in the political and civic world. Even educated, professional women labored in certain spheres of influence and generally refrained from working directly with men in the civil-rights struggle. Only in a handful of instances did women challenge this pretense. Even though women did begin to play a role in the fight for social justice, their paltry numbers did little to break down gendered inequality.[127]

Occasionally, "New Negro" activists transcended race, gender, and class.[128] Lulu Belle White, a Prairie View College graduate from Kaufman County, Texas, and the wife of businessman and alleged racketeer Julius White of Victoria, Texas, brought together varying segments of the African American community when she summoned women's groups—Grand Court Order of Calanthe, Eastern Star, YWCA, and the Metropolitan Council of Negro Women—to support the *Grovey v. Townsend* (1935) case. They raised money; held mass demonstrations, went door-to-door soliciting support, and attended meetings, asking people to support migrant R. R. Grovey and his impending trial against the state. According to Lulu White biographer Merline Pitre, by organizing Houston women in the community around the cause of civil rights, the schoolteacher-turned-activist introduced them to the assertive dual cause of racial-gender equality.[129]

Although African American clubwomen like Jennie Covington acknowledged racial and gender discrimination, they rarely adopted unpopular approaches publicly to eradicate these practices. For example, as a TCIRC board member Covington could not convince fellow White board members to support racial equality. Women hardly worked outside the traditional women's spheres of influence such as the church, school, women's club, and neighborhood.[130]

On the other hand, White became a bridge between women's groups and the male-dominated civil-rights struggle. She aligned with women and women's causes in churches, benevolent societies at community centers, and in social and charity clubs, giving money and time to noteworthy causes.

She did more for women and civil rights: She would go on to serve as head of the Houston branch's Youth Council and branch executive secretary, as well as becoming president of the statewide office of branches, being one of a handful of women garnering such political influence in the state.[131]

Not all "New Negro" migrant women activists agreed with White's methods. A few, like Covington, preferred working alongside Whites. Born in Victoria, Texas, in Leon County, in 1893, Christia Daniels Adair grew up in nearby Edna in Jackson County, where her father, Handy Daniels, took over a hauling business. Ada, Christia's mother, worked as a washerwoman. The Daniels also had a farm. The Daniels made sure their four children respected authority, revered the church, and understood the politics. Each night after supper, Handy and Ada gathered the children around the dinner table to discuss issues facing people of color.[132] "It would be boring," says Christia Adair in an interview before her death, "but we had to listen."[133] Mostly, Handy and Ada Daniels wanted their children to excel academically. Christia earned her high school certificate in home economics from Prairie View College in 1914.[134]

Adair used her education to serve others. She taught school in Edna, earning $35 a month. Students in her fourth- and fifth-grade class included Benjamin M. Jordan, the father of future attorney and lawmaker Barbara Jordan. In 1918, after Christia married Elbert Adair, a brakeman for the Missouri Pacific Railroad, she quit teaching. According to Adair, "I had his encouragement and support in whatever field I chose of [to] volunteer [in]—community, church, and civic services."[135] The couple moved to Kingsville and Victoria, where Adair championed interracial progressive reform. Perhaps because of her father's reputation in Edna, her strong recommendations from godfather and educator J. W. Frazier and instructors, or due in part to her fair complexion, Adair successfully built coalitions with Whites around similar interests. In the Victoria area, the women shut down gambling houses and campaigned for women's suffrage. Adair later felt betrayed when Texas counties banned African American women from voting in primary elections.[136]

By 1920, her civic work shifted to civil rights after the Texan faced racism firsthand. On learning that presidential candidate Warren G. Harding's train had planned a stop in Kingsville, she and ten schoolchildren met the train, along with others from the community. She situated her students near the observation deck area, so Harding could recognize the group.[137]

This did not happen. Harding "reached over" the African American youths and shook hands with the White schoolchildren.[138] The humiliating experience destroyed her respect for the Republican Party: "I became upset and decided at that moment that I would become a Democrat."[139]

In 1925, the Adairs left Kingsville for Houston, where Elbert remained employed with the railroad as a brakeman. They failed to find a home right away. According to the 1930 manuscript census, the couple resided in a rooming house, perhaps because of the strengthening onset of the economic crisis, although sometime later they moved into a home in Third Ward.[140]

Adair's volunteer work continued in the Bayou City. She worked closely with the Methodist Episcopal Church, National Association of Colored Women's and Girls' Clubs, and NAACP. Lulu White took her under her wing, hiring her as a secretary in 1943. When White chaired the statewide office, Adair became executive secretary of the Houston branch of the NAACP. Often she disagreed with the direction of the local and statewide branches, especially the confrontational tactics of White. Ironically, while she clashed with NAACP leadership, she got along well with Whites, at least on the surface. The first African American woman in the country, according to sources, to serve on a United Methodist Church board, Adair felt at ease with Whites. Adair also found employment opportunities in areas often closed off to African American women, working as a secretary for the Harris County Agricultural and Home Demonstration Service after her husband's death in 1943. Regardless of her affiliations, she never swerved from her love for social justice (see fig. 24).[141]

Coming from all walks of life, "New Negro" teachers, attorneys, physicians, barbers, railroad workers, steel millers, ministers, and businesspersons built a social protest community based on social equality, racial uplift, and cultural solidarity. Observers have painted interesting portraits of this protest initiative. Historian James M. SoRelle has argued that most "New Negro" leaders rarely challenged segregation and institutionalized racism. Their passive and accommodating approach, according to SoRelle, differed very little from that held by Booker T. Washington. "New Negro" contemporaries agreed with this assessment.[142] Clifton Richardson, in editorials, criticized "pussyfooting pulpit pimps" for playing down White racism. According to Richardson, "Any reputed colored leader who issues the statement in the press or utters it from the platform or pulpit, [sic] that there is 'no cause for complaint' on the part of the colored race in Dixie is either a dyed-in-the-wool pussyfooting biped or a fit subject for an insane asylum."[143]

Although SoRelle and Richardson's analyses are appropriate, they dismiss too quickly the diverse protest strategies—which included accommodation—within the community. In earnestness, "New Negro" leaders challenged White racism in a variety of ways. SoRelle himself points out that these responses often represented a practical solution and not an endorsement of institutionalized racism. Some "New Negroes," as SoRelle charges, presented a public posture that appeared accommodating, perhaps to ward off White criticism or even violence. Richardson—who had been threatened numerous times by the Ku Klux Klan and Houston Police Department—knew all too well the real threat of danger, including death, for challenging Whites. Certainly, civil-rights leaders were agents of change. Through multilayered agency, these activists sought to eradicate White supremacy on their own terms.[144]

Some leaders, like Kendleton, Texas, native Richard Guess and Tennessean C. W. Rice, understood race relations as Booker T. Washington had, emphasizing hard work among African Americans while publicly acquiescing to the White power structure. Others, like Wesley, supported economic solidarity and racial segregation. Militant moderates, like migrants Richard Randolph Grovey and Lulu White, supported direct confrontation and immediate integration and equality. Migrant ministers, like A. A. Lucas and M. L. Price, believed in both racial autonomy and Divine intervention. The time for deliverance, according to the pastors, had come for people of color. Many, as discussed in chapter 3, chose insular work in the community over direct challenges to White racial hegemony. "New Negro" leaders often differed on how to best promote African American progress, but most supported the principle of racial equality and the elimination of White supremacy—their sanity demanded this of them.[145]

Older conservatives, such as B. J. Covington, opposed racism, and in a conversation with historian Lorenzo Greene in 1930, Covington compared race relations to a "volcano."[146] "One never knows when an eruption will occur," said Covington.[147] Usually, Dr. Covington and other seniors spoke out behind closed doors, although on rare occasions they publicly denounced the actions of Whites. When Cullinan appointed an all-White board to supervise Houston Negro Hospital in May 1927, Afro-American medical staffers as well as community leaders, both conservatives and moderate radicals, criticized the plan. The hospital's bylaws, approved by Cullinan, called for a White advisory board to approve the decisions of the Afro-American hospital board of directors, which delegated responsibilities to hospital administrators. At the very least, according to Richardson, the city should have established an integrated board of directors to supervise the facility.

Richardson and other Black board members took matters into their own hands. In 1928, the Black board revised the hospital bylaws, more importantly, calling for a more independent board of directors. In response, the White advisory group nullified the Black board's ability to govern. The Black hospital trustees, who comprised civic leaders and medical staffers, ultimately resigned in outrage. The White advisory board also hired White physicians, who replaced some of the Black doctors. Cullinan supported the White advisory committee's decision. The creation of a new board the next year did little to rectify the matter. This ongoing problem continued well into the next decade, although the White advisory board eventually disbanded in the late 1930s after Cullinan's death.[148]

Black physicians expressed resentment toward the hospital's superintendent as well. Many believed Murfreeboro, Tennessee, native Margaret H. Bright, who earned her credentials from Tuskegee Institute Hospital and Lincoln Hospital (currently Lincoln Medical and Mental Health Center), undermined the integrity of the hospital in her negative reports to the White advisory board and Joseph Cullinan.[149] In a letter to the hospital's board of directors and advisory committee, the medical staff recommended that the hospital terminate Bright immediately, calling her a "tyrant and despot," "bearer of tales," "harsh and unsympathetic," and "deficient in tact and diplomacy."[150] According to Lee, Covington and other physicians, the entire city blamed her for the hospital's quandaries. On the other hand, Bright especially criticized hospital chief of staff Herbert Lee, who in earlier years often blamed the Black poor for their health problems, dietary concerns, and housing challenges. Bright, who stepped down as superintendent of nursing at Prairie View to take the staff position at the hospital, had a good deal of credibility within the White Houston medical establishment. She even referred Black patients to White hospital staffers or White-staffed hospitals. According to Houston Negro Hospital records, she possibly had legitimate concerns, for example, accreditation issues, noncompliance of hospital policies and procedures, absences, and competency concerns.¹⁵¹ Chief-of-staff Herbert Lee, perhaps a conciliatory Black in some circles, aggravated the White hospital board who desired that the physician "fall in line" or face termination. This quandary perhaps reflected both Black medical staffers' refusal to acquiesce to Whites and African Americans' inability to come together as one for the sake of their community, the latter being perhaps an consequential impossibility due to the social dictates of White supremacy and Black inferiority.¹⁵²

Ironically, the majority of African Americans, through the end of World War II, chose not to utilize the services of the hospital. African Americans, though cognizant of the racial realities of the day, which catered to White supremacy, still patronized the very same racist institutions that demeaned them, perhaps to simply accommodate Whites. "New Negroes" themselves often believed the myth of African American and African inferiority.¹⁵³

However, not everyone believed African American physicians lacked the skills and training of Whites. According to Thelma Bryant,

> Another thing that bothered me was when we went to the doctor's office and the doctor had a special little room for the Black folks, you know, if you were a White doctor. But you see, all my [adult] life I have gone to the Black doctors and the Black dentists, and I am not in for all this giving my money to the White doctors, but, of course, my mother came up in that environment and had a White doctor, and I was just dragged along as a child, you know, so I resented the fact that when she went to the White doctor, that she had [sic] pushed off into a special little room, and they had to call her by her first name, even though it was a nurse: "Alright, Ella, come on in here." No one called her Mrs. Scott, see; that bothered me. So I guess when I got grown, I really have taken on many of my husband's prejudices. He hated White people and I almost hate[d] them too.¹⁵⁴

Although segments of the migrant middle class, business owners, professionals, and unionists pursued the eradication of the White primary and racial segregation in the courts, through mass demonstrations, boycotts, and labor organizing, most did not, at least not publicly. To be sure, most African Americans considered voting a privilege afforded to others. Whether due to apathy, illiteracy, disinterest, financial distress, or fear, Afro-Americans considered formal politics unnecessary. And while they supported the idea of racial justice, they knew having regular wages and minimal housing, at least for the time being, meant more. The masses of

Afro-American Houstonians understood the risks of standing up to "The Man," "Mr. Charlie," or "Miss Emma." Looking inward and not outward, they opted out of public protest schemes and adhered to White hegemony. Community building, churches, fraternal orders, dances, concerts, and family reunions allowed them to survive the misery of racial exclusion. This suited Whites fine.[155]

Railroader Luther Stullivan of New Caney, Texas, made the following observation: "You control the Negro when you . . . got him on his knees [praying]. When you're on your knees all the time and then [in] a honky-tonk, the White man ain't worried about you. But if you're going over here having a meeting somewhere else, he want [sic] to know what you're talking about."[156] In other words, according to Stullivan, religion and casual contact in nightclubs prompted Afro-American apathy, passiveness, and the racial status quo. God, through the Holy Bible, orders Christians to wait on their just reward in heaven. Through the Christian mantras, God's children must ignore vengeful ideas, love their enemies, and reverence government officials.[157] As the hymn by Washington Phillips says, "If you trust and never doubt, He will surely lead you out. Take your burdens to the Lord and Leave it [sic] there."[158] According to Romans 12:19: "Dearly beloved, avenge not yourselves, but rather give place unto wrath: for it is written, Vengeance is mine; I will repay, saith the Lord." In other words, God will punish the guilty, especially those who harm His children. Ministers, missionaries, and matrons repeated these statements weekly in classes, meetings, and sermons. These Christian principles undoubtedly protected jobs, saved lives, and allowed for other forms of release.[159]

Ironically, according to Stullivan, these ideas also promoted segregation, disfranchisement, educational disparities, wage differentials, poverty, and systemic racism. Furthermore, wealthier African Americans could rely on their accomplishments, accolades, education, skills, wealth, and influence to offset racism. For example, migrant B. J. Covington rarely traveled with his family on streetcars. He did not have to because he had a car and could avoid racial unpleasantness. Poorer African Americans, however, did not have this luxury. They had to work to provide the basic essentials. Anything that threatened their basic livelihood seemed irrelevant and foolhardy. In some ways, traditional politics became increasingly less important to the masses of African Americans—churchgoers as well as non-churchgoers. Disfranchisement schemes such as the poll tax and White Primary discouraged many, as did the real threat of violence. Others, if not the majority of African Americans, using pragmatism or realpolitik, considered formalized politics unimportant and a distant second to material needs such as a home, job, food, and clothing.[160] *Houston Informer* editor Clifton Richardson, in an October 1927 editorial, expressed to readers the following: "The *Informer* is of the opinion that the Negro of Texas should wake from their [sic] political lethargy and apathy and organize their [sic] forces for the reclamation and retention of their full potential and political rights."[161]

Politics, in truth, had multiple meanings for African-descent migrants and established residents in Houston. Although most preferred not getting involved in formalized protest initiatives, they did engage in topical debates and express opinions about the state of race relations daily. Their early morning conversations with God, late night discussions in clubs, and talks at church picnics validate this observation. Although hard to believe, actually, as scholars Kelley and Scott have pointed out in their works, the working-class masses did more than talk; they resisted in numerous ways. The working poor in the community spent their leisure time at home, in church, in salons and barbershops, at fraternal meetings, enjoying sports, dancing, drinking, cooking, gambling, fighting, making love, and expressing their disgust for racism, as well as mocking White America.[162]

Alternatively, working people lashed out at one another, for example, murdering, arguing, robbing, raping women, molesting children, or engaging in habitual use of drugs, perhaps to provide coping mechanisms against daily racial oppression. The heinous rape and murder of twelve-year-old Ernestine Mae Bailey of Independence Heights in January 1926 shocked many Houstonians and illustrates a growing, alarming trend in the city—Black-on-Black crime. Although only representing 4 percent of the total police arrests in 1928, Houston African Americans made up a high proportion of alleged criminals guilty of murder, assault to murder, swindling, and theft of an individual. In cities across the country, crimes committed by African Americans against African Americans—usually lower-income, established residents and recent migrants—rose as the Great Migration continued to bring southerners to cities. And although difficult to prove, perhaps violent crimes reflected a warped reaction to poverty, gender inequality, family dysfunction, overcrowded conditions, racism, and powerlessness. People could not take out their anger on Whites without consequences, but they could hurt other African Americans. Besides, they too believed the hype that Afro-Americans were worthless savages, nothing more and nothing less.¹⁶³ Scholar and activist Du Bois, in his study on African American Philadelphians, even said, "Negro crime in the city . . . was natural. . . . Crime is a phenomenon of organized social life, and is the open rebellion of an individual against his social environment. . . . Since the beginning . . . [this is] the Negro."¹⁶⁴ Still, not everyone believed the hype. Again, we look to Thelma Scott Bryant: "They [social pathologies] were current, but not as numerous [as they are today]. Now it was only occasionally that you hear of a girl having a baby out of wedlock. I think parents had a tendency to make these men marry these girls . . . You didn't have a lot of crime like robberies, burglaries, and killings. . . . We didn't have all that."¹⁶⁵

Although most people rarely resorted to criminal activity, the sense of hopelessness, apathy, and rage remained. Most civic leaders concluded that the masses of African Americans cared very little about political mobilization or anything else outside the realm of dysfunction. Working-class political thought did in fact exist within these politically conscious realms, albeit often couched in the cultural aesthetic or satire. Scholars rarely recognize the daily actions of the working class as political or activist in nature. Social scientists in recent years, however, have begun to rethink this assessment. According to Kelley, the terrain of covert politics allowed for nuanced resistance in the Afro-American community. The ability to appear ignorant, lazy, crazed, and stupid provided African-descent people options in the depressing world of racial exclusion. For example, often people emotionally detached themselves from the world of their employers. Reflecting on a time when the Grovey family struggled to make ends meet during the depression, Nell Cole remembers her mother putting herself through school as a housekeeper. Cole said, "My mother worked in service, and that was something she didn't want either of us to do. . . . I remember her telling me how sometimes she could be hungry, but she refused to eat [the food she prepared for her White Jewish employer]. . . . My mother would say, 'I'd never take anything.' She was adamant that my sister and me [sic] would not have that need [employment as domestics]." This served a useful purpose in a world that devalued African Americans daily.¹⁶⁶

In truth, quite often the Black working classes aligned themselves with the Black elite in an effort to save lives, avert violence, avoid police arrests, eschew job firings, and protect reputations. As Clifton Richardson Jr. points out, those individuals Whites perceived as "safe" often wielded a good deal of power, as they found ways to warn Blacks of possible arrests, firings, police visits, and beatings.[167] These people often warned Blacks at great sacrifice to their own personal safety. Luther Stullivan reminds readers that bellhops, waiters, porters, servants, maids, union members, and so on, always looked out for their friends and Blacks in general in an effort to protect the race, even if they could do little else to bolster the "New Negro" cause. Stullivan certainly did his share for the race: "I'd sit in front of that station . . . and the Macatee Hotel was over here, the Turnman Hotel, over there. Police would be in the parking lot. . . . We'd get up and get on the phone—we known [sic] those bellhops—and tell them, the police is out here watching yall [sic]. . . . And I'd seen a many bellhop get beat so bad." The bellmen often arranged meetings between prostitutes and their respective clients. According to Stullivan, "That's how the bellhops made their money."[168] As well, the Black masses embraced the concept of the "New Negro."

Thus, even while the masses refrained from publicly denouncing Jim Crow segregation and structural racism, they never completely acquiesced to White hegemony, even if their quiet protests seemed minimal or inconsequential. Blacks perhaps ignored their inner tears or felt disconnected from organized political machines, but certainly voiced their views on race in America. Although many Whites compared African Americans to grateful children, they were not privy to the whole story. Even those Afro-Americans who publicly criticized other African Americans while paying tribute to Whites made good use of political theatrics and private emotions. Sometimes the main topic of discussion, while at other times inescapable thoughts, the topic of race relations prompted internalized oppression and determination, especially among the ordinary masses. This may explain the growing number of African Americans who to this day suffer disproportionately from mental illness as well as other diseases and ailments, including cancer, heart disease, lupus, HIV/AIDS, and so forth. Therefore, even while people enjoyed themselves on the dance floor or in the church house, they expressed their discontent and sorrow, and hoped for a better day on earth and in heaven. Interestingly, an emerging cultural resurgence within the African American community would provide working-class people with more opportunities to protest. In the years following the Houston Riot, working-class notions of political consciousness initiated and imitated a rising cultural revolution that encouraged debate, dialogue, and integration.[169]

Conclusion

The changing cultural and political milieu of Afro-Americans during the Great Migration suggests a growing consciousness surrounding radical Black thought. African Americans felt compelled to challenge racist thought and society through the courts and cultural milieu. They increasingly understood their role in achieving equal treatment and racial autonomy. Houston Afro-Americans, largely due to their economic status as employed laborers, professionals, and business owners, would continue to embark upon this journey of Black liberation and equality.[170]

Ironically, Houston African Americans, unlike others in the South, did not engage in radical forms of behavior. Their political ploys, offensive to Whites, nevertheless did not lead to riots in the streets. Houston sources do not give credence to a localized Marcus Garvey following. Although Garveyites lived in Houston, they were probably underground and unimportant even to the mainstream African American media. Blacks nevertheless relied on daily subterfuge to survive racism. Still, African Americans used their political clout, economic power, increased numerical strength, and growing cultural diversity to pursue the cause of social equality. Cultural expression, like politics, found a home in Houston and prompted renewed thoughts of social equality.[171]

FIVE

~

In "The Garden of Eden"
The Houston Renaissance, 1900–1941

Politics alone did not drive Houston's "New Negro" Movement. Migrants also relied on coded expressions of protest, such as the use of literature, political satire, music, dance, visual arts, as well as sports, in their efforts to break free of White supremacy and embrace Blackness. Houston especially created a culture of expression for musical entertainers. Saxophonist Tom Archia, born Ernest Alvin Archie Jr., in November 1919, in Groveton, Texas, in Trinity County, just northeast of Huntsville and 120 miles northeast of Houston, learned a good deal about Black consciousness from his parents and grandparents. Both sets of families and grandparents, the McDades and Nathan and Virginia Archie, farmed in Waller County at the turn of the century, with the Archies owning a lucrative watermelon farm. Both sets of families taught their descendants to appreciate their past as well as plan for the future. Also important to the former slaves and landholders was education. Their children especially learned early on the value of a college education, with Archie's parents becoming professional educators in the era of the "New Negro."[1]

The "New Negro" Movement influenced the Archies in a variety of ways. Ernest Archie Jr.'s parents, for example, attended college, taught school, with his father, Ernest Archie Sr., graduating from Prairie View College in the early twentieth century. For the young couple, Henrietta and Ernest Archie Sr., teaching afforded them the opportunity to influence young people as well as share with others a level of social consciousness. According to Tom Archia biographers Robert L. Campbell, Leonard J. Bukowski, and Armin Büttner, Ernest A. Archie Sr. even aspired to a level of social consciousness that set him apart from members of his extended family. For example, the schoolteacher changed his surname from Archie to Archia in the early twentieth century, perhaps during college, suggesting his father,

Nathan Archie, used an incorrect spelling. This action, however, possibly stems from a viewpoint that concluded African-descent Americans were better off rejecting immediate reminders of slavery and Jim Crow oppression, with names being a chief reminder. Other evidence supports the observation that Archie had cultivated other ways to reject Whiteness for Blackness. On his 1917 World War I draft registration card, thirty-year-old Ernest A. Archie defined his race as "African," not "Colored" or "Negro," terms more readily used by Americans at the time. The Archies [Archias], at the time of Ernest A. Archia Jr.'s Groveton, Trinity County, birth, in November 1919, aspired to the doctrine of the "New Negro" and found solace in the belief that better days were on the horizon for African peoples around the globe.[2]

In truth, Ernest and Henrietta's new life in the country and in Houston had already begun symbolizing this dawning of the "New Negro" age, especially for their talented offspring. Ernest Archia met his wife Henrietta in the all-Black community of Sunny Side (or Sunnyside) in Waller County, a small town ten miles south of Hempstead, Waller County, where Henrietta was a student. Henrietta probably attended Prairie View, which was also in Waller, as she taught school for several decades, even earning a higher salary than her husband. Using stepwise migrations, the couple eventually taught school and farmed in Waller and Trinity Counties, in Milam County further west, and in Baytown, just east of Houston, where Ernest A. Archia Sr. served as a school principal. Rural schoolteachers of color generally traveled from place to place in search of steady work and farmland to occupy. Sometime around late 1919 or in the early 1920s, the couple and their newborn son, Ernest Jr., relocated to Houston from Rockdale in Milam County. The couple lived on 4519 Lyons Avenue and across the street from St. Elizabeth Hospital in Fifth Ward in Houston, although they later bought a home in the rural community of Pelly just east of Houston, where they taught at the "colored school." Other members of the extended family lived in Fifth Ward also, even selling watermelons, no doubt from the family farm, at a stand on Lyons and Hill Street (now Jensen Avenue). Having an extended family in Fifth Ward aided the Archias, allowing their two children the opportunity to study music at Wheatley High School in Houston and not attend the segregated high school in Pelly or Baytown.[3]

The Houston area afforded Ernest A. Archia Jr. (Tom Archia) and his little sister Richie Dell Archia the opportunity to train as budding music students and professional musicians. Sister Richie played the piano, even playing in high school for the Wheatley jazz band, before going on to study piano and classical music at Prairie View. Ernest began playing the violin as a young boy, only to learn the saxophone as a teenager. Their musical training began in the country, when the family visited loved ones each summer, and before the death of grandmother Virginia Archie in 1932. Fortunately their interest grew, especially as their parents got them formal training in the city. In high school, the pair studied jazz and blues with future jazz artists Illinois and Russell Jacquet, Arnett Cobb, George Haynes, and Calvin Boze, and under the direction of future Los Angeles public schools music head Percy McDavid.

After graduating from Wheatley in the 1930s, the Archias entered Prairie View. Tom, only wanting to appease his parents, decided to earn a teaching degree in 1939. In earnest, he wanted to play the sax professionally. He played in the school's Collegians jazz band, which also featured Wheatley High School classmate Boze and chemistry major and future jazz artist Tony Russell (Charles) Brown. Graduation almost did not happen because Archia spent more time enjoying the company of jazz bands than studying. After college, he taught school. According to cousin Johnnie Mae Walton, Archia taught school and directed a small-town school band in East Texas for one year, again, only to appease his parents. Ultimately leaving his job, he joined the Milton Larkin band, which formed at the Aragon Ballroom in Houston in 1936. Undoubtedly, as a "New Negro," the jazz artist had decided to live a different life from the one etched out by his parents who were also of the "New Negro" persuasion. For the next forty years until his death in 1977, the spirited Archia cultivated a bluesy jazz sound that attracted bandleaders and record producers nationwide, from Houston to Chicago and Los Angeles to Washington, DC Although nicknamed "Sonny," Archia soon took the name "Tom," as producers considered the pseudonym more appealing to jazz and blues audiences as well as nightclub promoters.

After a long run with Larkin's band, Archia recorded his solo, entitled "Jump Through the Window," with the Roy Eldridge "Little Jazz" Orchestra in 1943, right before Larkin's band's seven-month stay at Joe Louis's Rhumboogie Club [Café]. He then played with the Carroll Dickerson band, an unpopular group that included a young Charlie "Bird" Parker. After being fired from the band in the late 1940s, Archia played with the Bill Pinkard quartet in Chicago. He also spent time in Los Angeles, recording and playing with brothers Illinois and Russell Jacquet, Howard McGhee, and Helen Humes and Her Allstars, the latter being part of Norman Grantz's famed

Jazz at the Philharmonic (JATP) series, which also featured a young Dizzy Gillespie as well as artist Coleman Hawkins. By this time his little sister Richie Dell Archia, who graduated from Prairie View in 1942 and taught music in Port Arthur, Texas, had relocated to Los Angeles during the war and worked as a musician. When Archia returned to Chicago in 1947, he recorded a number of instrumental tunes on the Aristocrat label.[4]

By this time, the unconventional Tom Archia had his own band, "Tom Archia and His All Stars," often a trio or quartet that played as the house band at the Macomba Lounge on South Cottage Grove Avenue in Chicago. The jazzy blues band also recorded for Chicago-based Aristocrat Records (later Chess Records), which mostly recorded blues. In 1947, Archia contributed to an Aristocrat recording of "Bilbo is Dead" with a rising star in on the blues scene, seventeen-year-old Mississippi transplant Andrew Tibbs. The song, which celebrated and mourned the death of Mississippi politician and racist Theodore Bilbo, made Tibbs a star and helped catapult Archia's career. Archia saw a change in his personal life as well, as he started a family. In 1949 he met his future wife, Fredda Kelln, a native of Winnipeg, Manitoba, Canada. An avid jazz lover, Kelln moved to Chicago with friends in the 1940s to become better acquainted with bebop jazz, the new sound that combined improvisation, scatting, fast-beat rhythm & blues (R&B), and swing. Eventually she fell in love with Archia. Hard times fell upon the musician, making their union far from harmonious. Archia, like many Chicago musicians, according to music historians, began to see a relative decline in the number of professional musical engagements he secured at clubs in the late 1940s and 1950s. He often got into disputes with musicians, agents, club managers, and union locals for violating union policies. Unions especially disliked members taking musical gigs during their off-nights and engaging in jam sessions with fellow artists, as these performances could be misconstrued as professional performances for pay. Many considered these events unethical since musicians often found themselves playing or jamming at clubs they did not have contracts with. He not only lost work for violating these policies. The couple's interracial relationship, which produced three children, probably did not sit well with many Chicagoans and put an added burden on their family. His constant drinking affected his family life also. By 1960, Archia and his common-law wife had separated. Fredda married someone else, and Tom never had contact again with two of his three children. He continued to work, however, by now as a lesser-known billed performer. He continued to struggle financially, as rhythm and blues and rock and roll grew more popular among American audiences. By 1964, the musicians Local 208 erased him from the membership list, probably for failure to pay dues. He returned home to Houston in the late 1960s, continued to play in local clubs, and died in January 1977 at the age of fifty-seven. Archia lived life on his own terms, as a rebel and, yes, as someone who inherited the "New Negro" mantra from his parents and refused to accept second-class citizenship in the United States. Instead, his music made him an artistic trailblazer and someone who loved the culture of Blackness he shared with the world. His defiance toward the establishment as well as his relationship with his White spouse speaks of someone who refused to abide by the tenets of even life in Houston, the city that introduced him to jazz.[5]

For the working-class and elite, cultural awareness defined Houston's period of Black self-rediscovery. An important conduit of racial autonomy and consciousness, the Black aesthetic influenced ideas and attitudes, bridged socioeconomic lines of demarcation, and brought African American influences into the popular mainstream. Prompted by a national movement in the Black arts, people of African descent promulgated a new period of artistic, intellectual genius. Although Harlem emerged as the center of this gift, the "New Negro" Movement penetrated other parts of the country, including the Midwest, Northeast, California, and places in Texas. Because of heightened human-rights quandaries in Haiti, Ethiopia, and other places around the globe, it propelled international interest in the literary, philosophical, and artistic brilliance of United States African Americans. The fine arts served as more than a backdrop of tranquility in the real-life stage of racism. As stated in the Holy Bible, the Garden of Eden provided, for a short while, a peaceful coexistence between woman and man; so too did literature, music, art, photography, athletics, and satire succeed at bridging gaps and drawing people of different persuasions toward a particular talent, even as the artist's motives made good use of both performance and protest. The arts solidified the spiritual union between Black autonomy and talent, with the latter becoming the means to ending African American injustice. This brief chapter reconstructs the "New Negro's" creative endeavor in Houston. Through written expressions and opinions, music, and the visual arts, Black Houstonians in the first four decades of the twentieth century formed the impetus for their own artistic Edenic gardens of tranquility, enjoyment, and autonomy. And while some artists learned their artistic creativity in the city, many made the real decision to uproot from the city, largely for the same reason Blacks left small towns and rural farms for Houston: better jobs and new avenues of social freedom. The southern city simply could not compete on the same stage as Chicago, New York, or Los Angeles. Internal migration and city life in Houston, nevertheless, opened minds and creative proclivities that stayed with artists until the end of their lives. The city offered hope to these talented women and men. The city also gave these artists sound formal training in some instances. It is this real truth that makes the Houston artistic creations of the day, whether literature and journalism, music and visual arts, or sports and satire, true representations of a renaissance or rebirth of Blackness, one that celebrated Black, southern identity—Black Texas or Louisiana identity. Of course some artists became successes in Houston after relocating from the country. These individuals helped promote Blackness as well as the artistic world they helped shape in the city.[6]

Satire

In Houston, migrants used the African American media to stimulate cultural and sociopolitical consciousness. Because the races never discussed race relations with one another, the Afro-American media provided people of color with ways to express their frustrations. Editorials and commentaries explored race relations, while feature stories and human-interest topics allowed individuals to connect with African American heroes. Often, news stories and commentaries garnered a good deal of enthusiasm and support from the African American masses. Clifton Richardson hired Simeon B. Williams, possibly a schoolteacher, to edit and write a regular column in the *Houston Informer*. Williams's column, "Cimbee's Ramblings," won over its audience easily.[7]

Using heavy African American vernacular, the column discussed the news stories of the day and provided people of color, particularly the uneducated masses, with an odd-looking character they easily identified with. Cimbee, whose clothing and appearance made him look like a gruff European dressed in Late Middle Ages or Early Modern period clothing, held ongoing conversations with the fictional "Gus." In these dialogues, Cimbee relied on satire, humor, and broken English vernacular to probe the minds of his readers. In a September 9, 1919, commentary, Cimbee talked about an Austin minister who felt African Americans complained too much "'bout [sic] our treatment":

Our fore parents . . . made the white man feed us and clothe us for 200 years. That's where the saying arose: "White Man's Burden." About this time . . . some rabid abolitionists . . . got up a great big army and made our friends quit feeding us. The "doc" sure got eloquent along here, and pictured to me what a good time our folks were having. Nothing to do cept [sic] a little plowing and hoeing and chopping and cooking and picking cotton, which didn't keep them busy but a little 108 hours a week. Even now . . . our folks reap the benefits . . . [8]

Clearly, Cimbee wanted the reader to ponder what he considers absurd, ludicrous notions of inferiority and accommodation among members of the pulpit. If anything, according to the writer, Blacks should reconsider these anachronistic ideas for a "New Negro" consciousness that honestly and openly acknowledges the burden of racism in America. On the other hand, the fiction often promulgated in churches and among other African American leaders only dispels the truth about what W. E. B. Du Bois, in 1903, called the number one problem facing Americans—the problem of "the color line."[9]

Famed folklorist John Mason Brewer, a native of Goliad, Texas, believed African American Texas folklore reminded the world of the consciousness and spirit of an American people. Without it, people would only have partial accounts of Texas's history. Scholar Lorenzo Thomas calls this literature historiography, not the brutish savagery defined by many journalists, intellectuals, and observers of the early twentieth century. Black folklore also provided people of color with an interesting means of commentary. Hardly seen as defiant, folklore allowed for persuasive criticism or commentary of American society, as seen in the work of S. Williams's "Cimbee's Ramblings." A useful type of historical writing, folklore paved the way for other genres of literature in the century. The *Houston Informer* introduced a new feature in 1935, "Dreamship," comprising poetry, commentaries, and satire. Again, the weekly provided a useful outlet for individual and collective critiques of society. Another feature, the "Junior Informer Club," allowed youths to enter poetry, essay, and art contests in an effort to showcase and cultivate young talent as well as give adolescents a voice to express themselves. Most of these works, not surprisingly, addressed race relations or African American identity.[10]

Music

Although literature largely characterized the Harlem, Detroit, and Chicago Renaissances, music dominated the Houston (and Dallas) artistic scenery, despite the popularity of print media. In the late nineteen and early twentieth centuries, African Americans created new sounds of hope, passion, praise, and heartache. Their American musical creations, from gospel, blues, and ragtime to zydeco and jazz, provided purposeful solace in the hardening world of poverty, violence, racial segregation, and depoliticalization. These musical genres, though North American in origin and borrowing from European rhythmic and instrumental styles, had their roots in the melodic sounds of West African drumming, singing, shouting, and dancing. This music also drew from slave spirituals, ring shouts, and call-and-response work songs, which served as useful instruments of survival for African indentures, slaves, and their descendants through the collapse of slavery.[11]

After slavery, African Americans continued to rely on music as a formidable mode of self-help. Music brought nourishment to freedpeople and their descendants. As a form of community agency following Reconstruction, the music aesthetic advanced a type of self-discovery and resistance that provided musicians with a platform or voice against self-hate and personal tragedy as well as reoccurring acts of racial injustice. Whether on the farm, railroad construction crew, or dock at sea; in the steel plant, the sawmill, or the cotton compress; or elsewhere in the South, African Americans used music as a necessary respite or source of spiritual, psychological rejuvenation.[12]

Music mimicked internal migration. Black musical genius, in fact, drew from migration. Like internal migration, music provided individuals with an emotional and spiritual escape hatch from suicide, murder, or insanity, allowing people to retool or restart. It provided hope for individuals thrown off course because of poverty and discrimination. When musical artists traveled from country to country, country to city, or southern city to northern/western city in search of work options, they planted new roots and affirmed the beauty of Blackness, this time, of course, through rhythmic sound. Even when musicians traveled up the road or into the next county to earn additional cash for the family or raise funds to support the neighborhood school or church, they utilized temporary migrations as mechanisms of protest. Itinerant musicians and ballad songsters, blues artists, religious quartets, zydeco personalities, and jazzmen who traveled to and from the country and city, and from the South to the North and West, shared their life stories with the world in an attempt to earn livings and express emotions. Ultimately, they helped redefine the nation's fledgling cultural landscape.[13]

Perhaps one of the most inventive musical genres born in the United States, blues, gave birth to later forms of popular music as well as an American cultural identity. Three distinct blues sounds graced the American landscape before and during the First and Second Great Migrations. In the Appalachian Piedmont, blues artists made their way to the Northern Atlantic Seaboard, bringing with them a fascinating blues sound. In the Mississippi Delta, artists such as "Big" Walter Horton brought to Memphis, Chicago, and Indianapolis a unique southern blend of blues and country-western. And in East Texas, blues combined ragtime with other melodic sounds from the lumberyard, railroad bend, and cotton field. The latter also helped pave the way for internal migrations to nearby Houston.[14]

For these Texas musical artists, including blues greats Henry "Ragtime Texas" Thomas, Huddie "Leadbelly" Ledbetter, Beulah T. "Sippie" Wallace, Victoria Spivey, Blind Lemon Jefferson, Sam "Lightnin'" Hopkins, and Mance Lipscomb, migration to and from Houston (and Dallas) allowed for reprisals from debilitating racial atrocities—physical, emotional, and spiritual—as well as sociopolitical and socioeconomic liberation.[15]

Navasota, Texas, native Mance Lipscomb used dinner parties, Juneteenth festivals, holiday carnivals, weddings, and, of course, temporary migrations as opportunities to perfect his art—blues. He traveled quite frequently and temporarily worked on other farms, railroads, and with other small industries. This made him readily available as a musician to groups at gatherings throughout eastern Texas.[16] Mance Lipscomb, like his father before him, used his music as a vehicle of expression and reaction to his circumstances. The following lyrics to Lipscomb's *"Big Boss Man"* accurately describe the pain, anger, and resistance of African American men like those living on Navasota cotton farms:

> Told my wife this mornin' [to] just pack her things
> And go. Ain't gonna work for the mean boss man no more
> 'Cause he's the Mean Boss Man,
> Don't You hear me call,
> "Ain't so big. You just tall—

That's all."
Early this morning, children, an' it won't be long
My boss man's gonna call me,
Yes, I'll be gone
'Cause he's [the] Mean Boss Man. He won't treat me right.
Work me so hard,
Keep so I can't sleep at night.[17]

The pain of racism and poverty ironically offered African Americans a spiritual cleansing, healing, joy, reflection, peace of mind, and faithful respite. For a few, these new, emerging sounds also offered financial benefits away from the farm, railroad crew, sawmill, and sugarcane house.[18]

Blues also helped inspire a new musical genre, jazz, which dated back to the 1910s. A confluence of African, African American, and European American musical styles, jazz relies heavily on improvisation, syncopation, polyrhythmic sound, blue notes, and shuffle notes to construct a creative musical sound. Jazz originated in New Orleans, Chicago, and North American ragtime circles around the turn of the century. It blended West African musical traditions, the music of European brass bands, and African American spirituals, along with other American folk music, including ragtime and blues; it also had roots that stretched into the East Texas blues country. Like its southern cousins—blues, zydeco, and itinerant music—jazz also made good use of the protest imagination, self-reflection, and internal migration, therefore, making Houston an important center for jazz.[19]

For two reasons—internal migration and the success of Phillis Wheatley High School's jazz program—Houston would launch the careers of a number of jazz artists in the early twentieth century. Navasota native Milton Larkin pursued the same dream as his violinist father and vocalist sister (who moved to Detroit, Michigan, in the 1920s) by studying music. He graduated sometime between 1927 and 1929, but while at Phillis Wheatley High School, he probably traveled in the same circles as, and possibly played with, Percy McDavid, who also performed throughout the Houston area while in high school and visiting Houston when away from college in Prairie View. Mentors as well as friends at the school realized Larkin's potential and offered him encouragement. After graduating from high school, Larkin began his professional career as a trumpeter, trombonist, violinist, and "territory band" leader, forming a band in 1936 at the Aragon Ballroom in Houston. In a career that spanned six decades the orchestra leader best known for his rendition of the bluesy Texas sounds of "big-foot swing" and "honking," captivated audiences across the globe.[20]

The term "territory bands" defines those bands and orchestras that mostly performed regionally without the recognition and fame of the beloved mainstream groups, for example, the Tommy Dorsey Orchestra, Duke Ellington Orchestra, Louis Armstrong Orchestra, and Count Basie Orchestra. Although territory bands rarely received the national media coverage of the more internationally recognized groups, they did nevertheless maintain noteworthy and exemplary reputations for their innovative and supreme musical styles, vocalists, leadership, and sidemen. Larkin—without question, a "New Negro"—refused to record for labels during his prime years, arguing that the lower wages paid to African Americans insulted his intelligence. Larkin enjoyed performing before live audiences that appreciated his skills, perhaps more than he cared to make money for recording companies that, in his opinion, devalued African American musicians.[21]

Although Larkin only recorded a few records in his lifetime (1910–1996), usually with other solo musicians and groups, and largely performed in New York, Chicago, and Houston, he retained a reputation around the world as a superior, first-rate musician and orchestra leader. Territory bands especially grew as Blacks increasingly made their way to cities for financial stability and social opportunities. Big and small territory bands in cities across the nation helped African Americans generate income for their families, record albums, and postulate new kinds of musical art forms in the United States. According to Lorenzo Thomas, members of the Count Basie and Duke Ellington orchestras, while visiting Houston, made it a point to carefully study the Larkin band during their midnight set. Interestingly, members of the Larkin Band included former Wiley College music students or band members under the direction of Bernard Adams. These Texas artists included bebop drummer Roy Porter and guitarist Sonny Boy Franklin.[22]

A jazz genius, Larkin developed his craft in Houston. With the help of teachers, club owners, along with White and Black friends who were artists, Larkin found music to be an amazing outlet. A Black male in the Jim Crow South, Larkin, like so many others, including the immortal John Coltrane of North Carolina, found his musical abilities and insightfulness crucial to his social development (fig. 40). Larkin following his service in World War II, became director of the Apollo Theater Band, and only permanently

FIGURE 40. A native of Navasota, Texas, Milton Larkin graduated from Phillis Wheatley High School in the late 1920s or early 1930s. After graduating from high school, Larkin began his professional career as a trumpeter, trombonist, violinist, and "territory band" leader, forming a band in 1936. In a career that spanned six decades, the orchestra leader best known for his rendition of the bluesy Texas sounds of "big-foot swing" and "honking," captivated audiences across the globe. Here Larkin (back row, standing fourth from the right) poses with other members of the 375th United States Army Band during World War II. After the war, Larkin worked at the Apollo Theater in Harlem as the theater's band director. *(Courtesy Houston Metropolitan Research Center, Houston Public Library, Houston, Texas, Milton Larkin Collection, MSS 0252-0123)*

resettled in Houston on his retirement in the 1970s. The city especially allowed for imagination, creativity, inventiveness, and interracial collaboration. Whites, for example, ignored social customs and often played at the Eldorado Ballroom and Bronze Peacock, popular nightspots for African Americans. For artists such as Larkin, the urban experience, especially during and following the Great Migrations to cities, allowed for cultural and intellectual growth; it also ignited heightened protest on the part of artists.[23]

Migrant musicians, such as bandleader Milton Larkin, transformed Houston as they did other cities across the country. The city, through its music, reflected the anguish and hope of people of color, while at the same time serving as a laboratory for up and coming artists in the making. This was particularly true of jazz musicians who studied Larkin and his work.[24] One such artist, Illinois Jacquet, would eventually leave the Bayou City to work with the likes of Duke Ellington, Lionel Hampton, Cab Calloway, Lena Horne, Lester Young, Nat King Cole, and migrant Houstonian Milton Larkin of Navasota. The parents of Jean-Baptiste "Illinois" Jacquet left rural Broussard, Louisiana, in 1922. At the time, Illinois, only six months old and the youngest of six children, had no idea of how much his simple life would change.[25]

His mother, Sioux Nation descendant Maggie Jacquet, like many African American parents in the rural South, wanted more for her children than a life of rural poverty. To Maggie Jacquet, Broussard, Lafayette Parish, a sugarcane community in southern Louisiana, offered her children nothing short of poverty, ignorance, and racial bigotry. She convinced her husband that growing Houston offered their family real prospects for success. Gilbert Jacquet, the family patriarch, agreed. He knew his wife's hunches were usually correct. He worked many years as a railroader and sugarcane worker to make ends meet. Yet to no avail, the Broussards continued to struggle. He wanted a new start as well. The family boarded a train for Houston in April or May of 1922.[26]

The Roman Catholics left Broussard by train and settled in Sixth Ward, Houston, a community northwest of downtown. Gilbert Jacquet found work immediately. Like many Houston African Americans of French ancestry from southern Louisiana, Illinois's father worked full-time as a skilled artisan at Southern Pacific Railroad. Of course, he hardly earned what White craftsmen made in the industry. Skilled Black railroaders, on average, earned 25 percent less in pay compared to their White peers. In the 1920s, people of color suffered from industry-mandated wage differentials, on-the-job and closed-door antagonism from White peers, and government inaction. Still, railroader Gilbert Jacquet had reliable work. Jacquet, a man used to doing more, worked a second job.[27]

Additional work tided the family over from month to month and paid for important incidentals like parochial school for the boys. Fortunately for Jacquet, part-time work came in the form of a popular pastime— music. The hardworking engineer's helper loved music, especially zydeco, an admired fast-tempo, bluesy, piano accordion and rub-board-based folk music indigenous to southern Louisiana. In Houston and southern Louisiana, he played in bands to raise additional dollars for his family, often playing in zydeco clubs in Fifth Ward.[28]

Always putting his family first, Gilbert Jacquet worked hard as a musician and railroader to give his children the best. He particularly wanted his children to have the opportunities that were not afforded to him, such as attending a quality Catholic school. He therefore pushed his sons to excel in their studies. For this reason, the Jacquets enrolled their children in the city's only private educational institution for African Americans before 1930, St. Nicolas Catholic School in Third Ward. For the most part, the boys worked hard. They did their chores, ate their meal, and then studied their lessons, although Jean-Baptiste sometimes fell short.[29]

Hardly studious, Jean-Baptiste often studied the least. Fun and friends usually came before homework. Popular as a student, he loved the girls, easily made friends, and lived for the music of the day. Peer pressure often influenced his many decisions. Jean-Baptiste, probably as a teenager, took the name "Illinois," a term that derives from the American Indian word *Illiniiwek*, which means "superior man." Jacquet increasingly saw his Catholic, Creole birth name as unpopular and corny in Protestant Houston, Texas. He also increasingly studied his favorite course and hobby, music.[30]

Gilbert Jacquet introduced his offspring to music before they could read or walk. The Jacquet boys loved music, especially jazz. Jean-Baptiste Jacquet danced as a toddler, sang as a preschooler, and played the drums while in elementary school. Illinois and his brothers also studied music at Wheatley, enrolling in the 1930s. At Wheatley High, they studied several musical genres, including jazz and classical music (fig. 41).[31]

Jacquet soon began playing the saxophone in high school. His years at Wheatley were filled with self-discovery and revelations about himself, his family, and community. The Jacquet family's decision to uproot to Houston represented a clear turning point for young Illinois. Although Illinois Jacquet and other jazz students experienced racism firsthand in clubs across town, on the city streets, and in their community, they—unlike musicians, such as Mance Lipscomb, who lived most of his life in the rural South and remained tied to the land as a sharecropper—found greater opportunities for self-expression in the city.[32]

These opportunities helped establish their careers in education, entertainment, business, and as part-time musicians. They also received excellent training from Wheatley High School music teachers. Musician and music instructor Percy McDavid, who was often compared to Chicago's famed music teacher, Walter Henri Dyett of DaSable High School, had much to do with the school's success. A third-generation educator, music teacher Percy McDavid loved his students. Houston native Percy McDavid was the son of migrants, a schoolteacher and physician, Amanda of Navasota of Grimes County and Fountain L. McDavid of Bastrop County. Like many upper-middleclass African Americans around the turn of the century, he grew up in Fourth Ward.[33]

FIGURE 41. While most African Americans in the city in the first half of the century danced to the music of blues, jazz, and zydeco, which collectively helped produce contemporary genres of music, including soul, rhythm and blues (R&B), and hip-hop, a few enjoyed classical music. Fewer students, however, studied the classics. One young woman, a native Houstonian, the daughter of migrants Benjamin and Jennie Covington, Ernestine Jessie Covington (Dent), embodied the "New Negro." Her experience as a concert pianist, without question, challenged notions of African American savagery and inferiority. As one of the first professionally trained pianists of color in the United States, the young woman paved a path of distinction for later generations of artists. The Houston Colored High School valedictorian entered Oberlin Conservatory of Music in the fall of 1920 at the age of sixteen. She described Oberlin as "a fine school" and "simply beautiful to be there." At Oberlin, where she majored in classical music as an undergraduate and piano, as a graduate student, while minoring in violin, Ernestine Jessie Covington Dent studied music theory, musicianship, music appreciation, and musicology. Her graduation recital, which she performed with the conservatory orchestra, was the Saint-Saens Concerto in G-minor. After earning her bachelor's degree in 1924, she applied for a one-year $1,000 fellowship with the Julliard Musical Foundation. She won four in a row and worked with Olga Samaroff and James Friskin, but did not receive a graduate degree, which the school rarely awarded at the time. She returned to Oberlin to earn the master's degree after getting married and having her first son, Tom. She earned the master's in piano in 1934. She also taught at Bishop College for several years before the birth of her first child. After completing her education in Oberlin and New York in the 1920s and 1930s, Ernestine Jessie Covington Dent continued her performances, touring cities and colleges across the South, exclusively to African American audiences. *(Courtesy Houston Metropolitan Research Center, Houston Public Library, Houston, Texas, Covington Family Collection,* MSS 0170-0038*)*

Possibly sheltered from much of the brutality of racial segregation, Percy and his brothers had role models who motivated them to pursue their dreams. The McDavid brothers learned to read music as children and began performing professionally while attending Booker T. Washington High School and at Prairie View (Percy) and Huston College (Russell), garnering reputations before beginning their teaching careers. Pianist Percy McDavid, along with his older brother Russell, who was also a music teacher in the school district, taught music at Wheatley High School for five years, mentoring their music students before relocating to Kansas City and Los Angeles, respectively, beginning in the late 1930s. At Wheatley, McDavid cultivated the talents of young artists, as well as motivated youths to remain in school, study music, form bands, invest in instruments, and soar in their careers. While at Wheatley, Percy McDavid, according to *Houston Press* music critic John Lomax, was one of the few music teachers in the nation who taught jazz to their orchestra students.[34]

By the end of the 1930s, school districts outside the South sought after McDavid, no doubt influencing his decision to eventually leave Houston. McDavid, who taught in the Kansas City, Kansas, schools for a decade, earned a master's degree from the University of Southern California in 1941. McDavid, who also became supervisor of music for the Los Angeles Independent School District, and helped integrate [along with pianist–arranger–law school alum Marl Young] two locals of the American Federation of Musicians union in Los Angeles in the 1950s, had a lasting impact on his schools and students, from Houston's Illinois Jacquet to Kansas City, Kansas, to Los Angeles's Horace Tapscott, until his death in 1975. Internal migrant McDavid especially taught his students the value of self-preservation as well as racial autonomy. By way of example and through music, McDavid reminded his students that ultimately racial exclusion had no power over their thoughts and desires. While Jim Crow certainly retarded African American mobility, it could not destroy Black faith. Music especially provided these students with resources—both spiritual and intellectual—that would help some challenge White hegemony. People all over the country understood Percy McDavid's special gift to Wheatley students.[35]

So popular was Wheatley's jazz program under McDavid's direction that Duke Ellington visited the school in 1935, probably while in the city doing a concert. According to music student Riche Dell Archia in a 1998 interview, "[Duke Ellington's] visit was our first from a [famous] person. . . .

[Luckily,] the band knew all his tunes."³⁶ This kind of exposure certainly helped shine a national spotlight on Wheatley, her teachers, and gifted students like Jacquet. Community events and social functions also allowed musicians to display their talents outside their communities, influence White philanthropy, fuse differing musical genres like blues, and motivate slight social change. Illinois Jacquet did just this. Unfortunately, as an unfocused student, Jacquet dropped out of Wheatley before graduating. An impatient Jacquet left school in 1939 at the age of sixteen to begin a successful sixty-year career in entertainment.³⁷

Three years after leaving Houston, the high-school dropout would go on to record with the Lionel Hampton Orchestra the most celebrated version of Benny Goodman and Lionel Hampton's "Flying Home". The vivacious tenor saxophone solo of Jacquet catapulted the nineteen-year-old to international stardom. Known as a pioneer of sax screeching and honking, the jazzman was also a skillful melodic improviser. Occasionally, he played the double-reed woodwind instrument, the bassoon, as well. After leaving Hampton's orchestra in 1943, he joined the Cab Calloway Band, recording with the legendary bandleader the soundtrack of the timeless 1944 classic *Stormy Weather*. Jacquet and brother Russell, along with a young Charles Mingus, in the mid-1940s formed a small band in Los Angeles, a move that reunited him with former Wheatley music teacher, Percy McDavid. His immortal appearances also included the Academy Award–nominated short film *Jammin' the Blues* (1944) and the debuting Jazz at the Philharmonic (JATP) concert in the same year. The JATP celebrity and former Wheatley High music student by the 1940s had matured musically and politically.³⁸

It was during a Jazz at the Philharmonic concert in his hometown of Houston in 1955 that he; Ella Fitzgerald; Fitzgerald's assistant, Georgina Henry; and Dizzy Gillespie were arrested for allegedly gambling in the dressing room between performances. Angry over the artists and the decision of their Jewish-American producer, Norman Grantz, to demand that the Houston Music Hall, where the jazz concert was held, open to an integrated audience, police staged a raid on the artists' dressing room.³⁹ According to Jacquet in reference to an earlier issue involving discrimination at the Rice Hotel in downtown Houston, "If no one say[s] [or does] anything, nothing [changes]."⁴⁰ By the time of the next JATP concert one year later, the city had desegregated the audience and had done so without any rancor or violence. Nearly a half-century later in 1993 at the presidential inaugural ball, he and amateur saxophonist President Bill Clinton performed "C-Jam Blues." Internal migration to Houston, along with his years of musical training at Phillis Wheatley High School, without question, changed Illinois Jacquet's life for the better.[41]

Urban life and culture undoubtedly helped musicians develop an important brand of activism. Although music, on the surface, rarely challenged White supremacy, intuitively it helped spearhead antiracist civil-rights agency. Jacquet and other musicians, like writers and artists, constructed their own devices of protest. Melodic tones, high-pitched notes, improvisation, and edgy lyrics all masked intuitive messages of racial protest, social injustice, and human rights. This was especially the case for musicians living in the city. Both African American and White-oriented establishments in the music world understood and welcomed this phenomenon. Black sound undeniably drew crowds and sold records, and sometimes earned artists decent livings. At the same time, the urban community blanketed musicians and singers from unflattering criticism, harsh rancor, and economic boycotts, at least until these artists directly challenged the racist, hegemonic status quo, as Jacquet, Fitzgerald, Gillespie, and Grantz did in 1955.[42]

The segregated city and independent African American community throughout America fostered these geniuses and their incredible work, thus, allowing for inventive mechanisms of protest agency. Increasingly, people, through music, challenged legal segregation, racial violence, and degradation. Again, the city allowed for this subtle change. For this reason, the Great Migrations to cities helped popularize American music and culture.[43]

This transformation did not happen overnight, but in spurts through the popularity of African American jazz artists and dances, as well as other artists. In Houston, Black youth in the early 1920s primarily attended dances at house parties. Thelma Bryant, however, remembers when dance halls began opening in the city. "Just about the time we came out of college, we started getting dances at halls and places especially for dancing."[44] During the start of the jazz age in the 1920s, Blacks held dances at the American Mutual Benefit Association building, downtown, Odd Fellows Temple, also downtown, and by 1926 or 1927, the Pilgrim Temple. The four-story Pilgrim Temple, which was located right across from the original Colored High School, attracted partygoers, sororities, fraternities that gave dances by invitation only, wedding receptions, and business groups, all of which sponsored concerts featuring Duke Ellington and Cab Calloway. Perhaps as many as *one hundred* nightclubs catered to Blacks in the first half of the last century, with most being jazz clubs.[45]

The Bronze Peacock nightclub also validates this point. Established in 1940 and located in Fifth Ward, the Bronze Peacock nightclub not only showcased local and popular artists, but equally served as a meeting place for Fifth Ward neighbors. The club's music brought about pleasure and enjoyment; its atmosphere equally provided patrons and artists with a venture of choice for venting. Again, working-class Afro-Americans, in particular, found an entryway that allowed them to ponder their daily encounters with Whites as well as their perceived state as docile, subjugated people. Their ability to openly express their discontent and frustration allowed them to survive Jim Crow. The nightclub scene, as with the church house or fraternal order, perhaps made it easier for patrons to mask their true identity, thoughts, and even hopes. Protest, of course, took place in an atmosphere of pleasure while enjoying dinner as well as dancing to blues, bebop, or zydeco.[46]

The club's owner, native Houstonian Don D. Robey, knew African American patrons needed downtime. Owner Don D. Robey, a Houston native whose parents moved to the city in the nineteenth century, also formed a successful record label, Peacock Records of Houston. These types of multipurpose ventures became increasingly popular in the city compared to in the farm community and small town. So successful was Robey that he built an empire that laid the foundation for his family's wealth. One of his children, Louis R., ultimately entered medicine, becoming a surgeon in the Houston area, as did a number of other Robey offspring, mainly due to the foresight of record producer and Bronze Peacock owner Don D. Robey.[47]

As the Bronze Peacock courted Houston's Fifth Ward with live music and good food, another club dazzled club goers in Third Ward. Migrants Clarence and Anna Dupree opened the Eldorado Ballroom in 1939 (fig. 42). According to historian Leigh H. Cutler, the couple established a classy venue that mirrored Harlem's Savoy Ballroom, home of jazz music and dance fads. Located on the corner of Elgin and Dowling across from Emancipation Park, the club served as an important undertaking for the Duprees. On most nights, the club billed the leading musicians of the day, from Louis Armstrong and Duke Ellington to Cab Calloway and Lionel Hampton. So too did audiences enjoy homegrown jazz musicians Arnett Cobb, Milton Larkin, Illinois Jacquet, and Conrad Johnson. In later

FIGURE 42. The "home of happy feet," the Eldorado Ballroom, located on Dowling and Ennis Streets in Third Ward, opened in 1939 when developers Clarence and Anna Dupree, migrants from Louisiana and eastern Texas, respectively, created a business center for local residents. The club, which catered to young audiences, featured some of the top-billed entertainers of the 1940s, 1950s, and 1960s, including Duke Ellington, Lionel Hampton, Cab Calloway, Illinois Jacquet, Milton Larkin, B. B. King, and Ray Charles. *(Courtesy Houston Metropolitan Research Center, Houston Public Library, Houston, Texas, Milton Larkin Collection, MSS 0252-0141)*

years, Della Reese, Fats Domino, B. B. King, and Ray Charles entertained patrons.[48]

The club's high ceilings, neon lights, and spacious dance floor reflected the sensibilities of the owners, who wanted to give their patrons more than a good time. The beautiful splendor of what was called [the Houston] "home of happy feet" dazzled two generations of music and dance enthusiasts. The fashionable club did more, however. Schoolchildren entered talent shows and band competitions, and even enjoyed sock hops. Social clubs such as fraternal orders and fraternities also rented the space for parties and galas. The Eldorado Ballroom catered to the African American community on multiple levels as migrants and established residents, their children, and later their grandchildren sought and celebrated Black beauty. The club also symbolized the Houston Renaissance's ability to embody the cultural beauty that made the period spectacular and important.[49]

As pointed out by Cutler, "It was a source of freedom, an escape from problems, and a way to express one's soul." Black nightclubs, music, and musicians from multiple backgrounds and walks of life symbolized the Houston Renaissance.[50]

Visual Arts

The visual arts, like music, challenged White supremacy and notions of African American degeneration as well. The work of Laura Wheeling Ware, Jacob Lawrence, Lois Malilou Jones, Aaron Douglas, Archibald Motley, and Palmer Hayden, for example, challenged mainstream images of Blackness. Increasingly, after World War I, African American intellectuals and artists challenged White supremacy in their many works on many levels, highlighting Black creativity, intelligence, protest, and economic independence, even in the Lone Star state. By the mid-twenties, the Harlem Renaissance had reached Texas. Young artists in public schools and on college campuses refined their traditional trajectory and developed new cultural constructs in their music, writings, paintings, sculptures, films, and theatrical productions. These constructs more readily identified with Afro-American life, celebrated unique vehicles of self-expression, and challenged racist depictions of African Americans.[51]

Beginning in 1930, Houstonians got the opportunity to observe African American art. The Harmon Collection featured paintings, sculptures, and sketches and was shown at the Houston Museum of Fine Arts in September 1930. Despite the inconvenience of the strict enforcement of segregation, which limited the number of African American patrons able to visit the museum, the exhibit showcased the beauty and dignity of Blackness in America. Other exhibits followed, including those displaying artwork at churches, schools, and community centers within the African American community. The exhibits, as well as the actual artwork, challenged the negative constructions of Blackness, perhaps making it possible for people to resist in new ways in the near future.[52]

The grandson of Rev. Jack Yates, Samuel Albert Countee, contributed a great deal to the national "New Negro" Movement (fig. 43). Born in Marshall, Texas, in 1909, to laborer and businessperson Thomas Countee and schoolteacher and dormitory matron Nannie Salina Yates Countee, Sam Countee emerged as one of the nation's most inspiring young artists of the 1930s, developing his passion for painting and sculpting as a

FIGURE 43. The grandson of Rev. Jack Yates, Samuel Countee, loved art. Born in Marshall, Texas, in 1909, Countee emerged as one of the nation's most inspiring young artists of the 1930s and 1940s. His work eventually attracted the attention of the mainstream art community in Houston. Emily Langham of the Art Museum of Houston trained and mentored Countee for years, introducing him to the established New England art world. He later earned a scholarship to study at the Boston Museum of Arts. By the late 1930s, his paintings and sculptures portraying African American life were part of exhibits at Howard University, Atlanta University, Smith College, the American Negro Exposition, Hall of Negro Life at the Texas Centennial Central Exposition in Dallas in 1936, and Institute of Modern Art in Boston. During World War II, the United States Army commissioned the Staff Sargent to create a large painting for the wall of the new African American officer's club at Fort Leonard Wood, Missouri. His creation became "The Garden of Eden." *(Courtesy Houston Metropolitan Research Center, Houston Public Library, Houston, Texas, Rev. Jack Yates Family and Antioch Baptist Church Collection, MSS 0281-0065)*

child. While a student at Houston's Booker T. Washington High School, from 1924–28, he began to garner a reputation as a gifted young artist. Largely influenced by the Harlem Renaissance, Countee's work displayed the heartfelt passion for African American self-reliance, sensuality, and spirituality.[53]

Countee continued his training at Bishop College. A year after graduating from high school, he entered Bishop College, majoring in art and paying his way through school as the portrait artist of faculty and administrators. A promising artist, he was named artist in residence at Bishop

College in 1933, a title of distinction made possible by the prestigious William E. Harmon award. Between 1933 and 1935, he presented his work at numerous exhibitions around the country, including one sponsored by the Harmon Foundation in 1933 that featured the piece "Little Brown Boy", a painting critics called a monumental achievement "deserving" of the coveted distinction. He graduated from Bishop College in 1934.[54]

His work also attracted the attention of the White mainstream art community in Houston. Emily Langham of the Art Museum of Houston trained and mentored Countee for years, introducing him to the established New England art world. He continued to win prizes for his work. In 1934, he earned a scholarship to study at the Boston Museum of Arts (currently the School of the Museum of Fine Arts, Boston), even serving as an artist in residence. He also trained for a brief time at Harvard University, probably in a summer workshop as an in-resident artist or fellow.[55]

By the late 1930s, his paintings and sculptures portraying African American life could be seen at Howard University, Atlanta University, Smith College, the American Negro Exposition in Chicago in 1940, the Institute of Modern Art in Boston, and the Hall of Negro Life at the Texas Centennial Central Exposition in Dallas in 1936. Countee's work was among several murals, paintings, photographs, books, essays, reports, and studies on display at the Hall of Negro Life. A historic tribute to African American culture and life in Texas as well as in the United States, the exhibit marked an important first for people of color worldwide. It featured the works of artists, scholars, poets, physicians, military heroes, scientists, reformers, former slaves, and other dignitaries of influence. Countee's exhibit particularly dramatized African American cultural history. "My Guitar" celebrates the popular instrument's treasured reputation in African American folk life and music, especially as an instrument of autonomy and resistance. Noted Harlem Renaissance philosopher Alain Locke recognized Countee in his *The Negro Genius* (1937), referring to the emerging artist as someone who "bears watching."[56]

His genius continued through World War II. Drafted into the United States Army in 1942 and ultimately receiving a promotion, S. Sgt. Samuel Countee of the 436th Engineer General Service Dump Truck Company was commissioned the next year by the US Military to create a large painting for the wall of the brand new African American Officers' Club at Fort Leonard Wood, Missouri. The painting of a young African American couple enjoying each other's company while picnicking, has been called a subliminal portrait of Adam and Eve in the Garden of Eden. A celebration of Black love and beauty, the painting also challenges the widely held notion of White superiority and Black inferiority.[57]

After the war, Countee, who settled in Long Island, New York, earned a respected reputation for his portraits of the African American elite and entertainers. He also earned a living as a private instructor. Artist Countee never forgot where he came from and routinely recognized his art instructors at Booker T. Washington and Bishop. He also taught art classes at Narcotics Anonymous meetings in the New York City area.[58]

Countee himself found love, marrying Mary Miner in 1955, four years before his untimely death on September 11, 1959, the result of complications from cancer. Students of his work have suggested that his time in World War II, including service in the Persian Gulf, possibly contributed to his growing stress, illness, and death. His legacy to the art world, on the other hand, will live on, as the quiet Countee through his visual art has forced the world to come to terms with its erroneous generalizations of African Americans.[59]

Black artists, through photography, neutralized denigrating images, viewpoints, and stereotypes as well. Photography, like music, art, folklore, scholarship, athletics, and political involvement, reached large circles of people and sought to inculcate an appreciation for African American life and culture. Perhaps the most famous African American photographer, James VanDerZee (1886–1883), captured the diversity of Harlem in the first half of the twentieth century through his creative mix of photographic images and hand-tinted, retouched negatives. From funerals and weddings to clubwomen, religious figures, and politicians, African American New Yorkers found photography an inviting tool of resistance. VanDerZee therefore provided hope with his ability to empower his clients with self-preservation and self-determination.[60]

Through the medium of photography, African American Houstonians also challenged the degrading daily images that were spewed in newspapers, magazines, album covers, advertisements, postcards, and department store display windows. As early as Reconstruction, African American photographers or individuals knowledgeable in photographic printing provided services to the city. However, only in the early twentieth century did the city list African American photographers of the period, in city directories, souvenir booklets, and special cultural publications like *The Red Book*.[61]

Interestingly, according to curator Dannehl M. Twomey, many, if not most, photographers relocated to the city from the country, usually a place in eastern Texas or Louisiana. Although most worked sporadically, usually advertising in the city directory for one to five years, a few garnered fine reputations as photographers. This was not an easy feat, even in the segregated South. Many African American patrons preferred White professionals, assuming the quality of the work or service would be superior. Black photography businesses failed for other reasons as well—financial strain, poor location, personal squabbles, and other job obligations.[62]

Fortunately for Elnora and Arthur Chester Teal, these everyday realities had no bearing on their four-decade business. The couple began dating in Waco, where A. C. Teal worked. After marrying, they settled in Houston, more than likely near the end of World War I. Teal Studios opened in the city in 1919 on Andrews Street in Fourth Ward. The pair for a long time operated several studios at once.[63]

The career of Elnora Teal, according to Kendall Carlee in *The Handbook of Texas Online,* is particularly noteworthy. The United States Bureau of Census in 1920, according to Carlee, listed only one hundred African American female photographers out of a total number of 34,867 nationally. In 1930, women comprised 15 percent of all African American photographers nationwide (eighty-five out of five hundred and forty-five). By the late-1920s, Elnora Teal operated one of the studios. After her husband's death in 1955, she took over the Teal's School of Photography for at least a decade. Clients appreciated her flair for detail so much that they often preferred her to her husband.[64]

The business specialized in studio portraitures, but A. C. Teal traveled regularly throughout eastern Texas, photographing various African American institutions. Doing group portraits, publicity stills, event shots, candid photos of citywide and group events, the studio captured the essence of Texas's "New Negro." Like contemporary James A. VanDerZee, the couple politely challenged mainstream notions of African American savagery. The company regularly did touch-ups on request and invested in the best photographic equipment and materials utilized for the processing and printing of photographs, garnering a reputation of excellence throughout the city. The results were magnificent. Many, if not most, of the thousands of photographs in the African American–oriented manuscripts throughout Houston—photographic and oral history collections in various Houston area archives—were Teal portraits. The photographs, which highlighted the totality of the city's African American community, have remarkably stood the test of time. The photos also represent the transformations that slowly took place at the time of the "New Negro" Movement.[65]

Conclusion

For these migrant artists, the arts revolution reinforced the notion of racial autonomy and equality. The ability to influence change, even minimal, challenged racial exclusion. Whites, perhaps for the first time, bought African American art, trained students of the arts, purchased African American music, and admired possibilities of cultural integration. These artists, though successful, were not immune to racial bigotry, as in the case with A. C. Teal, who in the 1940s suffered a police beating that law enforcement officers blamed on Teal's public intoxication while driving and resisting arrest. Nor were entertainers and artists immune to negative views of self. The popularity of hair conking among men, for example, gives credence to this argument. Illinois Jacquet, Miles Davis, Little Richard, Tom Archia, James Brown, and other artists popularized the straight look for Black men in the first half of the twentieth century, eager to alter the chemical makeup of their tightly curled locks, hair deemed unattractive to many, including perhaps most Afro-Americans at the time and even today. And yet, these artists recognized their ability to empower themselves and others through their talent and commentary. Certainly, these artists used these experiences to shape their work and better resist White supremacy, making use of sublime portrayals of Blackness. Although a cultural statement, the Houston Renaissance had political implications as well. As a representative of the "New Negro" era, African American artists forced a southern city and a nation to take notice of authentic Blackness. The Houston Renaissance thus provoked enormous possibilities, perhaps more than any other aspect of the "New Negro" Movement. Although their music and artistic expressions rarely challenged Whites directly, as members of the city's booming workforce, those artists who stayed in the city remained faithful agents of change. Their dollars, whether large or small, played an important role in the "New Negro" fight for social equality.[66]

SIX

~

The Black Economy at Work

Wage Earners, Professionals, Economic Crisis, and the Origins of the Second Great Migration, 1900–1941

Regardless of their political views, cultural preferences, or birth homes, African American migrants settled in Houston primarily for jobs. Tillie Stullivan grew up in New Caney, Texas, a farm and sawmill town thirty miles northeast of Houston, in the late nineteenth century. The offspring of former slaves, he and his eleven brothers and sisters grew up poor and never finished school. Instead, they raised cotton on the John Robertson plantation in eastern Montgomery County. Tillie and his brothers also drove cattle some fifteen miles from the fork of the San Jacinto River to New Caney.[1]

Isam Stullivan, Tillie's father, ultimately bought a small farm in the neighboring community of Willis—probably before the Panic of 1893. Although he passed away before paying off the note, his children stepped in and helped their widowed mother Lucinda pay off the mortgage in the twentieth century. This milestone motivated other family members to work toward owning their farms, but most of the offspring lived their lives as sharecroppers, seeing landownership as a lifelong inconsequential impossibility.[2]

An ambitious young man, Tillie Stullivan would avoid tenant farming altogether. A generation removed from slavery, he knew he had other options, especially in cities. Houston seemed a good place to start over. Tillie appreciated the city's booming economy—one that provided work to industrious African Americans. A childhood friend of Stullivan's father recommended that the young man apply for an entry-level job at Houston's SP Railroad, one of the city's largest employers in 1900. He put in an application and the railroad hired him immediately.[3]

The new century ushered in unprecedented industrial growth, especially in the area of transportation. Railroads, the largest employer in the city before World War I, employed over two thousand workers, including hundreds of African Americans, and paid out several million dollars annually in wages and salaries in the early 1900s. With eighteen railway lines, the city grew into a major railroad hub by 1920. The job at the SP Railroad's Englewood Shop particularly appealed to Tillie because of its close proximity to African American neighborhoods in Fifth Ward, the working-class district in northeast Houston, not far from the city's eastern manufacturing and shipping district. The railroad shop's location on Liberty Road in Fifth Ward made it possible for SP Railroad employees to commute to and from their jobs.[4]

Tillie and other unskilled Afro-American shop workers did menial tasks as maintenance crew, sextons, and porters. The semiskilled and skilled jobs generally went to White males prior to the mass migration of southern Louisiana African American Creoles in the 1920s. Even then, SP classified and paid these artisans as "helpers" and not specified skilled wage earners. Stullivan's entry into Houston's unskilled workforce nevertheless signified a major departure for thousands of rural and small-town African Americans living in Texas and Louisiana. On migrating to Houston, newcomers usually found stable, low-end wage-earning jobs—at least through the onset of the Great Depression—assuring the economic survival of their families and communities.[5]

The workplace remembrances of Tillie Stullivan and other internal migrants help scholars better understand Houston's Afro-American community in the four decades preceding World War II. Railroads between the turn of the century and World War I propelled unprecedented internal migration into the city, and Houston's wartime and postwar economic booms following World War I stimulated even greater migratory streams thereafter. African Americans, like others in previous decades, permanently moved into the urban, industrial-commercial wage-earning sector. They secured jobs as sextons, compress workers, teamsters, chauffeurs, landscapers, servants, stevedores, porters, unskilled industrial laborers, domestics, laundresses, and artisans. Although most migrants labored as unskilled laborers, a select few found work in other circles as teachers, nurses, physicians, and civil servants. A smaller pool of migrants created their own business enterprises within the African American community, often providing stable jobs to others.[6]

Even while African-descent laborers earned more money and better provided for their families, they faced serious challenges to their financial well-being. Both employers and White unionists discriminated against African American workers with impunity. Moreover, people of Mexican origin, who comprised 5 percent of the city's overall population in 1940, increasingly competed with African Americans for low-skilled work, especially during the Great Depression, when employers often preferred them and out-of-work Whites over Afro-Americans. Furthermore, unemployment and underemployment affected African Americans more so than many others, putting tremendous strain on families as children dropped out of school to help support parents, women labored outside the home, and men toiled long hours for little pay, even leaving the family for long periods of time to find additional work. In the wake of adversity, these migrants nevertheless remained hopeful and steadfast in their efforts to succeed. This chapter discusses the jobs migrants held in Houston, the businesses they birthed, the barriers they encountered at the workplace, the devastation of the Great Depression, and the community's resilience to these economic challenges.[7]

Origins of Houston's Black Workforce

Historians trace the origins of Houston's African American workforce to antebellum slavery. The responsibilities held by slaves—and to a smaller extent, free people of color—undoubtedly contributed to Houston's prosperity and impetus for continued economic growth. Although they rarely worked for wages, slaves enjoyed a greater degree of freedom as hired help or bondservants to Houston residents. Those that did in fact earn wages did so primarily to purchase their freedom and property. Slave (and free or freed African American) laborers hauled cotton, lumber, and other freight by way of wagon, riverboat, and rail; cultivated staple crops such as cotton, sugar, and occasionally tobacco; produced potatoes, corn, tomatoes, peas, peppers, onions, and other foodstuff for the household and open market; and raised and slaughtered livestock. Others cooked meals, washed laundry, cleaned rooms, and cared for and waited on others in private homes, stores, restaurants, and hotels.[8]

As the city and its economy boomed in the 1850s and early 1860s, the responsibilities of slaves grew. Some constructed single-family homes, stores, and office buildings; swept and scrubbed chimneys; drained and cleaned sewer ditches; built and repaired roads; and laid railroad tracks. Others labored as dressmakers, draymen, teamsters, wheelwrights, blacksmiths, carpenters, and stevedores. Always, their work took precedence over their own family obligations. On average, slaves worked from sunrise to sunset six days a week. When grieving, as expectant mothers, as frail seniors and small children, without personal fulfillment, often begrudgingly, while engaged in sabotage, and at great personal sacrifice, slaves carried out their duties. Although their work differed very little from that of small-scale White farm families in Texas and Louisiana, their identity and status as distinct laborers or chattel placed them at the bottom of an unchangeable caste system. Even during the Civil War, many, if not most, remained partially loyal to their slaveholders, at least through the end of the conflict.[9]

Blacks continued to contribute to Houston's economy after the war, mostly as unskilled laborers, tenant farmers, and domestics. As their numbers grew in the latter nineteenth century, according to the research of historian Robert Zeigler, Houston African Americans formed the nucleus of the city's bottom-rung workforce, and along with others, comprised an essential component of the city's expanding labor force. According to Zeigler's findings, in 1870, 82 percent of African Americans labored in the unskilled and personal-service workforce divisions. This figure climbed to 84 percent in 1880. Due to underemployment, between 1865 and 1880, African American women comprised 40 percent of the Afro-American workforce, compared to White women, who made up only 8 percent of the overall White labor force. For the same fifteen-year period, White men held almost 50 percent of all skilled jobs.[10]

This trend changed very little as the city entered the new century. Only a few African Americans worked in occupations outside the traditional wage-earning labor force as educators, physicians, and ministers. Eleven percent in 1870 owned businesses or relied on special skills in blacksmithing, carpentry, barbering, or tailoring. Disappointingly, the proportion of these skilled workers declined from 11 percent in 1870 to 8 percent in 1890, largely because of the growing influx of internal migrants from the surrounding countryside and immigrants (to a lesser degree) of European extraction who increasingly entered the semiskilled and skilled workforces. These general figures went largely unchanged in the early twentieth century.[11]

Regardless of these challenges, African American workers sought after equity and respect from their White peers, supervisors, and employers. Whites, on the other hand, with very few exceptions, wanted neither. Black aspirations collided with White intolerance. According to Wintz and Zeigler, despite their unifying national slogans, the National Labor

Union (NLU) and Holy and Noble Order of the Knights of Labor, for example, discriminated against African Americans with impunity. And while African Americans joined NLU chapters in Houston, they never associated with White affiliates, which generally discouraged biracial unionism. Despite official policy that banned racial discrimination, the union affiliates in Houston and throughout the country caved in to White pressure and practiced racial segregation and exclusion.[12]

Trade unionism especially posed a problem for Houston African Americans. Since the days of slavery, the presence of skilled African Americans upset Whites. Whites, beginning in the 1840s, passed legislation, formed trade associations and benevolent societies, joined national unions, and used intimidation in an effort to bolster their own financial standing and at the same time thwart African American entry into the area of skilled crafts. Mainly due to its incredible growth as an urban-industrial enclave, Houston, as a southern city, witnessed the birth of an unusual number of trade associations. Labor and benevolent organizations such as the Houston Typographical Union Number 87; Workingmen's Club, Lone Star Division Number 139; Ancient Order of United Workmen; Brotherhood of Locomotive Engineers (BLE); and the umbrella organization, the Houston Labor Council, banned African American membership in the late nineteenth century. The arrival of the radical, groundbreaking Texas State Federation of Labor (TSFL), the state's affiliate of the American Federation of Labor (AFL), in 1900 did little to reverse this trend.[13]

Racial exclusion hardly deterred African American migrants, especially in the 1900s, when manufacturing and commercial growth propelled wage labor. The new century saw further economic growth as people continued to migrate to the city for jobs. In 1890, sixty-four firms with a net worth of $720,000 employed almost six hundred workers, earning $160,246. By 1910, nearly 250 manufacturers employed 6,300 people. With an aggregate capital of $16.5 million, these firms distributed $4.2 million to workers in annual salaries and wages. Male workers—mostly recent immigrants or migrants from the surrounding countryside with wage-earning experience—especially played a leading role in the city's transformation from a small commercial center to a regional industrial center.[14]

Perhaps the most noticeable stimulus influencing lifelong wage earning in Houston among African American migrants between Emancipation and the Great Depression, temporary migrations shaped both their permanent entry into Houston's transformative economy as well as their resilience to constant urban havoc—racism, contempt, poverty, and futile educational success. The learned arrangements on cotton and sugarcane farms, in small towns, and in African American households produced monetary and social means of support. During down periods on the farm, from late May through July or early August right before the harvest season, and again in the late fall and early winter months, African Americans found work alternatives that suited family relations, individual needs, collective hopes, and job demands. For this reason, young men and male adolescents, in particular, reached out to nearby cotton compress towns and cities, coastal wharves and docks, lumber mills, railroad gangs, and flour and corn mills for brief wage-earning work, occasionally as the dominant labor force. Largely because of the pitiful wages and the seasonal nature of the work, but also because of the dependability of African American males, year after year, cotton compresses, for example, employed impoverished men of color at a dollar a day. Younger women and teenage girls, especially those unmarried, also worked in growing numbers away from home as live-in domestics, private nurses, washerwomen, and cotton-compress cotton pickers, often earning a quarter to thirty cents an hour. These jobs often provided poor farm families with their entire livelihood, at least until the start of the busy harvest season.[15]

These work experiences blurred the worlds of agriculture, light industry, and urban manufacturing in a number of ways. Temporary work experiences and migrations provided people of color with colorful hopes and possibilities outside the humdrum cycle of rural poverty. Additional cash helped families settle accounts with employers or pay off encroaching debts at mercantile stores; prepare for special occasions like church picnics, homecomings, and holidays; and sometimes gave individuals the incentive to open small businesses and organizations—salons, barbershops, juke joints or night clubs, restaurants, and fraternal order societies. Undeniably, temporary migrations to cities and manufacturing towns offered men and women practical workforce experience—operating mechanical devices, performing routine tasks, formulating concepts, and comprehending mass production. These temporary migrations from the farm then laid the groundwork for more permanent treks to nearby towns and cities, as well as interstate, interregional, and international migrations to the Midwest, West Coast, or from the Caribbean and West Africa.[16]

White employers and planters regularly endorsed the reality of African American mobility. Historian William Cohen notes that plantation owners entered into arrangements with industrialists in nearby towns and cities in an effort to direct migration flow to particular businesses and manufacturing firms, of course, for a financial incentive. Often planters worked with labor agents, hired by area business firms, to direct mobility among their tenants and laborers. Black mobility from afar during mid-seasons in the summer, or following harvest time, therefore did not generate a great deal of controversy because laborers and tenants had little to do on the farm, especially in the fields.[17]

Planters, on the other hand, would not endorse African American mobility during periods of intense work demand. At these times, in the spring and late summer months, as well as during the fall harvest season, planters often utilized the services of state and local officials who welcomed involuntary servitude in multiple forms. Politicians passed laws that outlawed mobility among people with outstanding debts; other laws forbade movement of any kind; some discouraged and outlawed intercounty mobility; and then others outlawed vagrancy and other forms of perceived criminal misconduct.[18]

Moreover, both Texas and Louisiana developed convict-labor laws with planters, railroads, and manufacturers in mind. These new penal codes would imbue anti-Black notions of social control, provide states with inexpensive and safe maintenance of convicts, and allow for a needed service for planters and industrialists, especially railroad builders. Perceived criminals, including African Americans charged with the petty crimes of chicken and pig thefts, vagrancy, and insubordination, as well as debt-ridden tenants who dared to abandon their preexisting arrangements with unscrupulous landholders, were subject to convict leasing, as well as fines and penalties for petty crimes such as vagrancy. Sixty percent of Texas's prison population by the late 1870s comprised African Americans. As William Cohen reiterates in *At Freedom's Edge,* a fear of Blackness of any form and construct—prosaic or openly critical of White supremacy—represented a fundamental problem for the South.[19]

African Americans, needless to say, still utilized mobility, especially travels in the form of temporary migrations, as a vehicle of empowerment, resistance, and self-reliance. Historians Peter Gottlieb and Kimberly Phillips both interpret the importance of temporary movements on the farms, from farm-to-farm, and to small-towns, coastal cities, industrial communities, and interstate metropolises in the lives of ordinary and extraordinary African Americans. Blacks, who eventually made their way to Pittsburgh and Cleveland, found good use of chain migration networks and kith and kin experiences to and from the city and farm that reverberated in both directions lasting spiritual highs. Blacks made good use of emotional strength, intellectual gratification, prayers, tenderness, sisterhood, cultural consciousness, community continuums, political idealism, and economic empowerment, however small.[20]

In Texas and Louisiana, as throughout the South, these cultural mechanisms began on the farm. Continuing the agency and survival skills constructed in slavery and redefined in the Reconstruction years, they manufactured ways to carve out safe havens of economic self-reliance and sociopolitical self-sufficiency, eventually abandoning rural work for good. Young people, in particular, saw migration as a form of practicality and as an opportune time to venture out on their own.[21]

Franklin Pierce Walker, a southern Louisiana adolescent, routinely left his family's tenant farm to attend school and work in nearby towns and cities. Although most African American men in the South performed bottom-rung jobs at ship-channel docks, cotton gins, sawmills, in mines, in refineries, and on railroad and construction teams, many southern Louisiana teens like Walker worked regularly with machinists, tailors, barbers, blacksmiths, and carpenters—both skilled African American and European American Louisianans. Of note, Walker, who routinely worked odd jobs away from the tenant farm he grew up on, welcomed the prospect of heading west to Texas to work as a journeyman for relatives. Before the turn of the century, Walker, after the death of his father and at the age of fourteen, left his home of Verdunville, Louisiana, in Evangeline Parish, to study blacksmithing under the tutelage of an uncle in Liberty, Texas. His uncle, Sylvester Walker, had migrated to Liberty, a tiny farming community twenty-five miles east of Houston, from Louisiana years earlier.[22]

Young Franklin Pierce Walker moved on in another few years. He later left Liberty and moved to nearby Dayton, again for work. While in Dayton, the young man opened his own blacksmithing shop. He also fell in love and married sweetheart and Dayton native Etta Day, the possible granddaughter of slaveholder Isaiah Day, whom Dayton is named for. By the 1910s, Franklin, utilizing stepwise migration routes that allowed him to travel to several destinations before permanently settling down, relocated one last time, to Houston from Dayton in Liberty County. The newlyweds settled in Fourth Ward, with Franklin Pierce Walker, like others, finding sustainable work as a blacksmith in the expanding industrial city.[23]

Men at Work in the New Century

According to census data and select local welfare documents, migrants from the surrounding interior, like Franklin Pierce Walker, and their children comprised the majority of individuals employed in the city in the three decades that preceded the Great Depression. Even while they brought with them semblances of rural and small-town lifestyles, their prior experiences in southern manufacturing and commercial enterprises, as well as their transition into mainstay wage earning, helped them to bolster the causes of the city's African American wage earner. Unlike southern migrants who abandoned the South altogether for the North and West, these migrants remained in the South. Upon their arrival in Houston, they worked those jobs they had previously held while supplanting their farm income at different times during the year. These migrants thereby faced perhaps a relatively smooth transition into the permanent wage-earning sector when compared to their contemporaries who trekked to Pittsburgh, Chicago, Detroit, and the San Francisco East Bay Area. Black newcomers also transferred many of their rural and temporary industrial workforce habits and strategies to the city. Diligence, stamina, workplace amusement, repetition, and submission, along with prior work experience, afforded them long-standing laboring opportunities in the Houston area—at least through the start of the early 1930s. Employers even recommended agricultural workers for work in the city—work that occasionally became permanent.[24]

Regrettably, these transferred work experiences could not protect African American newcomers from workforce impediments to their economic stability. Job competition, racial exclusion, underemployment along with the city's dual workforce, and the economic crisis of the 1930s caused a series of flows and ebbs in the African American labor force. For decades, African American men dominated the city's menial labor force, comprising at least 80 percent of the Afro-American workforce, compared to 50 percent for White males. Although this propelled underemployment, their strong footing as menial workers ensured them stable employment options, with increased competition notwithstanding.[25]

The 1920s witnessed the introduction of the Latino worker as a competing group within the unskilled labor force in Houston. Although fewer than five hundred Mexicans resided in the city in 1900, their numbers had grown to two thousand by 1910, and to fifteen thousand by 1930. Due to World War I, industrial growth, and the Mexican Revolution (1910–1920), thousands of mostly unskilled, but also skilled and professional, Mexican laborers traveled to the city for the same work options that rural African Americans, European Americans, and Latino Americans had. Latinos, like African Americans, worked the railroad lines and in the railroad shops, at foundries, for cotton compresses, and for oil refineries in Mexico. Mexicans also labored as dishwashers, cooks, barbers, waiters, and peddlers.[26]

To some within the African American community, the growing Mexican *colonia* in Houston severely weakened job opportunities for African Americans. Jesse Thomas of the NUL argued that Afro-Americans in the late 1920s lost their footing in the labor market due to Mexican-origin immigration and migration. He went on to say that some employers—like Central and East Texas planters—preferred dependable Mexican and Mexican American workers to African Americans. Some Black workers even believed Latinos worked for less money.[27]

Houston's industrial and business boom provided bottom-rung employment for both African American and Spanish-speaking workers. To be sure, a small number of Latinos worked for community-based businesses as tailors, barbers, clerks, shopkeepers, neighborhood storeowners, and street peddlers of tamales, candy, and chili. Still, people of Mexican ancestry often worked near their homes for the growing oil refining industry, along Houston Ship Channel, for area railroads, as well as other manufacturing and nonmanufacturing firms in Second Ward, Fifth Ward, and suburban communities like Magnolia Park. The increasing Mexican population in the unskilled and semiskilled job market thus understandably concerned African American newcomers and established Houston residents who customarily secured employment easily in the unskilled job market.[28]

The greatest obstacle to African American advancement at the workplace was not the influx of Mexican-origin workers, but rather racial hatred. Blacks, as did Mexican and Mexican American workers, witnessed daily abuses by those who feared the growing numbers of non–European Americans at the workplace would disrupt White privilege. For obvious reasons, this unstated rule first took shape in the rural antebellum South and continued in postbellum rural life. The polarity of Black–White relations dictated the rural work culture of African American farmers in Texas and elsewhere in the South. In other words, Texas Whites invoked the color line through legal and extra-legal means in their social, political, and economic relations with African American farmers. Black farmers who uprooted to Houston in the early twentieth century understood their subordinate place in the

Jim Crow South. The established racial hierarchy of southern life extended to the city. Extenuating circumstances in the city, however, often confused rural newcomers. As permanent workers, they soon realized mechanization and modernization through urbanization defied their nonthreatening role as menial laborers in the urban South.[29]

The urban South, in many instances, affronted White plurality and domination. The city provided African Americans with increased social resources and freedoms—more self-help institutions, residential neighborhoods outside the influence of Whites, improved schools, and greater intraracial diversity. Moreover, the city stirred greater political consciousness among people of color who sought social and economic equality. The city, perhaps unknowingly, in many ways invalidated the dichotomy of race. For instance, the expanding African American middle class of professional lawyers, physicians, journalists, principals, teachers, and entrepreneurs demanded—implicitly and explicitly—courteous treatment from Whites, especially poorer or less influential ones. The growing African American workforce, including recently arrived migrants, took note of these irregularities. Most outwardly conformed, but others did not, especially those workers affiliated with organized labor.[30]

For Houston dockworkers, strength in numbers seemed advantageous. Racial segregation in the workplace made it possible for African Americans to dominate certain arduous, mostly but not exclusively bottom-rung and semiskilled jobs such as baseline dock work, adding an aura of solidarity within the African American community that often crossed lines of stringent demarcation—class, education, ethnicity, religion, culture, and skin tone. Black dockworkers in Houston outnumbered Whites by three to one. Dock work, arduous and grueling, did not attract large numbers of White men after World War I, for one simple reason: White males earned more money at oil refineries, steel foundries, construction companies, and in other segments of the transportation area. Because of their reputation as excellent laborers and their numbers, stevedores, foremen, shipping agents, brokers, shippers, and employers preferred African Americans. Whether as deepwater screwmen who earned $5 to $7 a day, or as coastal pier men who earned $2 daily, Afro-American dockworkers were considered invaluable by employers and supervisors.[31]

Black dockworkers also successfully unionized. After the construction of the Houston Ship Channel in 1914, the ILA organized European and African American dockworkers in separate unions. The union, which formed in the Great Lakes in the 1890s, soon adopted the Fifty–Fifty Plan, which guaranteed equal work for each group—White and Black. African American longshoremen also held bargaining power within the segregated Gulf Coast District Council, which headed Gulf of Mexico ILA locals in the United States, although industrialists, especially in the 1930s, often exploited racial/ethnic tensions among African Americans, European Americans, and Mexican Americans in an attempt to incapacitate the ILA. Blacks fought back in numerous ways, including successful unionizing. Still, the success of African American waterfront workers was the exception to the rule, even though men of color refused to give up on the potential benefits of organized labor.[32]

Realizing this, White workers aligned with unions, politicians, and industrialists to enforce racial supremacy on the job. White employees, with few exceptions, did not support the promotion of qualified African Americans to better-paying wage scales. White employers regularly entered into contractual agreements with White workers, honoring job discriminatory practices against African American laborers. Mostly, Whites endorsed segregated unions that ignored African American pleas for redress on the job. In an attempt to regain what they considered dominance—perhaps numerical dominance—at the workplace, White peers and supervisors, with the help of management, relegated the growing African American workforce to marginal jobs that paid poorly and impeded their social and monetary security. The result was a biased, unethical workforce that ensured African American underemployment and social debasement.[33]

Ironically, the source of this racist antagonism was the concept of White paternalism and Social Darwinism, which bolstered the ideology that African Americans, impoverished Latinos, Asians, recent European ethnics, Native Americans, and working-class Whites belonged at the bottom of the socioeconomic hierarchy. In other words, this view placed wealthy Whites in charge of others. Racial/ethnic sabotage and depressed wages for all workers provided the best way of maintaining this fallacy. Most migrants who left the countryside in search of jobs in the South, West, and North desired a degree of permanent socioeconomic stability and even mobility—the latter, in many ways, being a misnomer, especially in the South, where upward mobility for all wage earners seemed tenuous, at best.[34] Regrettably, African American wage earners in Houston and in other southern cities instead received little of what they desired in the new century—socioeconomic equality with others.[35]

The migrants who made Houston their home realized the sobering fact that the Bayou City's uneven workforce structure made African Americans more vulnerable than Whites to constant layoffs, job competition, and negative changes in the economy. The city's labor force structure also revealed the material gap among the racial and ethnic groups. Whites, regardless of socioeconomic class standing, held the highest paying jobs in Houston industries. They worked as the engineers, carpenters, bricklayers, boilermakers, and supervisors. On the other hand, Houston industries primarily employed people of color as unskilled workers. Blacks also fared poorly in professions outside industry and trade. In 1920 and 1940, White men held 97 percent of the city's male clerical positions. For the same years, they occupied 93 percent of the male professional positions (tables 6 and 7).[36]

This material gap between Whites and people of color, coupled with White hostility toward interracial labor union solidarity, exposed the existence of a two-tier labor system that relegated African Americans (and people of Mexican ancestry) to less pay and fewer economic freedoms for their families. Again, one of the most telling signs of this dual workforce was the importance of child and female labor in the African American community. The NUL reported in a 1943 study that the median grade level completed by Houston African Americans was seven, compared to eleven for Whites. Young people regularly dropped out of school to help support loved ones.[37]

Census data, according to historian Earl Lewis, provide the most useful analysis on African American labor and the many challenges African American workers faced daily. Like their contemporaries in Norfolk, Virginia, and other southern port cities, African American Houstonians, for the most part, faced unique economic challenges that precluded their ability to reasonably care for their families. The general rate of job participation in the Houston workforce among Afro-American men describes both their easy accessibility to certain jobs and their overall vulnerability to underemployment, even as their numbers grew. The employment participation rate of African American males rose immensely due to rural-to-urban migration. The African American male workforce rose from 12,538 in 1920 to 21,543 in 1930, an increase of almost 60 percent (see tables 6 and 8). Table 7 shows that for the year 1940, over 23,000 men constituted the Afro-American male labor force. Of the 21,543 Afro-American male workers living in Houston at the time of the 1930 census, possibly an estimated one-third (7,050 males; see table 2) moved to the city in the 1920s.

TABLE 6. Houston work force engaged in occupational divisions, 1920

Houston Males	Total 48,749	Whites 36,186	Blacks 12,538	Others 25
Agriculture, forestry, and animal husbandry	568	375	193	–
Extraction of minerals	670	629	41	–
Manufacturing and mechanical industry	17,819	12,593	5,226	–
Transportation	7,060	4,345	2,715	–
Trade	9,178	7,616	1,561	1
Public service	1,074	932	142	–
Professional service	2,508	2,195	312	1
Domestic and personal service	3,714	1,531	2,160	23
Clerical occupations	6,158	5,970	188	–

Houston Females	Total 17,181	Whites 9,437	Blacks 7,738	Others 6
Agriculture, forestry, and animal husbandry	30	6	24	–
Extraction of minerals	1	1	–	–
Manufacturing and mechanical industry	2,083	1,312	770	1
Transportation	687	666	21	–
Trade	1,380	1,309	71	–
Public service	17	15	2	–
Professional service	1,596	1,317	279	–
Domestic and personal service	7,986	1,466	6,516	4
Clerical occupations	3,401	3,345	55	1

Source: Fourteenth Census of the United States, 1920, V. 4, Population: Occupations, 1114–16.

TABLE 7. Houston workforce engaged in occupational divisions, 1940

Houston Males	Total 113,957	Whites 90,446	Blacks 23,394	Other 117
Professional and semi-professional	8,193	7,679	511	3
Farmers and farm managers	138	117	21	–
Proprietors, managers, and officials	15,284	14,717	533	34
Clerical, sales, and kindred workers	24,025	23,395	615	15
Craftsmen, foremen, and kindred workers	19,821	18,369	1,450	2
Operatives and kindred workers	20,141	15,321	4,805	15
Domestic service workers	1,769	156	1,607	6
Protective service workers	1,729	1,637	92	–
Service workers (except dom. and prot.)	8,896	3,544	5,312	40
Farm laborers and foremen	230	142	87	1
Laborers (except farming and mining)	12,665	4,575	8,090	–
Occupations not reported	1,066	794	271	1
On public emergency work separate from above)	2,131	1,526	604	1
All unemployed males (experienced and new workers)	14,767	9,562	5,185	20

Houston Females	Total 49,204	Whites 31,426	Blacks 17,769	Others 9
Professional and semi-professional	5,082	4,418	663	1
Farmers and farm managers	17	13	4	–
Proprietors, managers, and officials	1,836	1,672	162	2
Clerical, sales and kindred workers	14,480	14,255	223	2
Craftsmen, foremen and kindred workers	362	333	29	–
Operatives and kindred workers	4,141	3,039	1,101	1
Domestic service workers	14,923	2,006	12,916	1
Protective service workers	18	18	–	–
Service workers (except dom. and prot.)	7,503	5,111	2,390	2
Farm laborers and foremen	21	15	6	–
Laborers (except farming and mining)	333	185	148	–
Occupations not reported	488	361	127	–
On public emergency work (separate from above)	1,252	981	271	–
All unemployed females (experienced and new workers)	4,372	2,431	1,939	2

Source: Sixteenth Census of the United States: 1940, Population, V. 3: The Labor Force (Washington, DC: Government Printing Office, 1943), 506–11.

TABLE 8. Houston work force engaged in occupational divisions, 1930

Houston Males	Total 99,709	Whites 73,570	Blacks 21,543	Others 4,596
Agriculture	870	468	309	93
Forestry and fishing	29	21	3	5
Extraction of minerals	1,068	991	45	32
Manufacturing and mechanical Industry	37,262	26,172	8,784	2,306
Transportation	13,618	7,729	4,825	1,064
Trade	20,176	17,411	2,415	350
Public service	2,168	1,850	279	39
Professional service	5,503	4,825	610	68
Domestic and personal service	8,298	3,605	4,097	596
Clerical occupations	10,717	10,498	176	43

Houston Females	Total 37,689	Whites 22,531	Blacks 14,395	Others 763
Agriculture	56	24	20	12
Extraction of minerals	3	3	–	–
Manufacturing and mechanical Industry	3,299	2,279	699	321
Transportation	1,047	1,025	19	3
Trade	3,631	3,391	167	73
Public service	46	43	3	–
Professional service	4,141	3,558	570	13
Domestic and personal service	17,819	4,658	12,839	322
Clerical occupations	7,647	7,550	78	19

Source: *Fifteenth Census of the United States: 1930, Population, V. 4: Occupations, By States* (Washington, DC: Government Printing Office, 1933), 1593–96.

Potentially, 25 percent of the 1940 African American male workforce (3,673 men; see table 9) moved to the city in the 1930s.[38]

Although represented in each general workforce division, African American men more often than not found themselves occupying unskilled jobs. Black men comprised almost 70 percent of the unskilled industrial male workforce for the decennial years 1920 and 1930. An examination of the 1920 Houston manuscript census also points to this claim. Nearly 60 percent of the African American males surveyed for this study—persons listed in the 1920 manuscript census—worked in the unskilled labor division. Unskilled male workers represented 67 percent of the sample taken from Harris County welfare applications. Black unskilled laborers worked in four different areas: industrial, transportation, trade, and personal service. Harris County welfare applications also validate this argument. For the years 1920 and 1930, those men employed with manufacturing and mechanical firms constituted 40 percent of the African American male

TABLE 9. Probable intercensal net in-migration figures among Blacks by age cohort, Houston, Texas, 1930–1940*

Ages	Males	Females
1930–1940		
10–14	1,590	2,770
15–19	2,419	2,833
20–24	1,057	770
25–29	620	299
30–34	225	–176
35–39	–368	–648
40–44	–515	–492
45–49	–811	–596
50–54	487	–303
55–59	3	271
60–64	–104	–57
65–69	44	70
70+**	N/A	N/A
	Total	Total
	3,673	4,741
	Grand Total	8,414

Sources: Bureau of Census, *Sixteenth Census of the United States, 1940 Census of Population,* V.4, 2, 1044.
*Cohorts do not include the 11,537 children below 10 years of age who may or may not have migrated to Houston during this period with their parents.
**Breakdowns for these later age-cohort groups prevent further analysis by similar cohorts.

workforce. Although the number of African American males employed in Houston industries increased steadily after World War I—from 5,226 in 1920 to 8,784 in 1930, to 14,000 in 1940—they mainly worked as unskilled laborers.[39]

This held true for all African American males employed in the Houston labor force.[40] For the most part, Afro-American males in the transportation arena worked for paltry wages. Most of the African American transportation employees worked as menial workers, draymen, teamsters, porters, and sextons. Black oil refinery workers, steelworkers, construction crew, cotton compress laborers, and railroad track repairmen rarely worked as semiskilled and skilled workers. When they did, as in the case of Louisianans employed at Southern Pacific Railroad, employers paid them less money even when they performed the same tasks as Whites. In this instance, industrialists used job classifications to ensure separate pay grades for European Americans and African Americans doing the same kind of work. Employers named skilled African American boilermaker railroad workers "boilermaker's helpers"; African American plumbers became "plumber's helpers," and so forth. African American (and Mexican and Mexican American) male laborers found themselves limited to low-paying jobs, jobs historically held by people of color, whereas Whites worked in better-paying occupations reserved for Whites.[41]

Outside manufacturing firms and transportation-related companies, African-descent men primarily worked in the commerce arena as deliverers in retail shops, drug stores, and groceries; as lumberyard laborers; and as porters or helpers in stores. Due to heavy in-migration streams in the 1920s, their numbers grew from 1,561 in 1920 to 2,415 in 1930. Black men also worked in the personal service and domestic job category as porters, butlers, caddies, waiters, and chauffeurs. In 1920, 2,160 persons comprised 18 percent of the total Afro-American male workforce, and for 1930, 4,097 men made up 19 percent of the Afro-American personal service labor force (see tables 6 and 8). Their increased numbers in these categories between 1920 and 1930 suggests that they, like unskilled laborers in the manufacturing and transportation divisions, lost jobs outside these menial labor categories. As more of these men gained employment as menial industrial laborers, store porters, and servants, fewer found work outside the minimum skill and pay labor force.[42]

Only in a few small instances, where men earned enough money to support the entire household, did African American families rise above the cycle of underemployment and poverty.[43] The story of Harry Hainsworth, a Navasota, Texas, migrant, illustrates how African American males outside the menial workforce provided for their families and secured a better future for their children. Harry and Beatrice Hainsworth migrated to Houston from Navasota in 1909. Public schoolteachers, the couple believed Houston would offer much to their family, especially the children, Hazel, Robert, and Mae Frances, the youngest of whom was born in 1913, after the family settled in Houston. The family settled in Fifth Ward on Davis Street, only after living for a period of time as boarders, and eventually bought a home. Harry Hainsworth worked at a furniture store before securing employment as a mail carrier with the United States Post Office. Amazingly on a monthly salary of $175 in the 1920s and 1930s, postal worker Harry Hainsworth put his three children through college.[44]

The Hainsworth children all graduated from Colored High School (later Booker T. Washington High School) of Houston and Howard University and became productive members of society. Hazel Hainsworth (Young), who became one of the first faculty members of Jack Yates High School in 1926, remembers working throughout the summer months to earn extra money to help offset her tuition costs. She later became Dean of Girls at Yates and Phillis Wheatley High Schools. Howard University Law School alumnus and attorney Robert Hainsworth Jr. founded the Black Lawyers Association in Houston and unsuccessfully fought to integrate courthouse restaurants in the city in the 1950s. Mae Frances Hainsworth (Hutson) taught one year at the Burrus Elementary School in Independence Heights, before moving to Oakland, California. Hutson worked many years as a civil service employee with the United States Air Force. Although the Hainsworths struggled and sacrificed much in order to help their children complete their studies at Howard University, they did better than most African American families in Houston.[45]

Black men like Harry Hainsworth, in small numbers, provided for their families as clerical personnel, professionals, and public servants. For 1920, only 188 men worked in clerical occupations and 312 worked as professionals; and for 1930, 176 and 610 worked in clerical and professional careers, respectively (see tables 6 and 8). The number of African American males engaged in professional exploits nearly doubled between 1920 and 1930, but the increase was not substantial compared to the growth of the entire Afro-American male job force. Table 7 confirms that due to unemployment and underemployment, the number of Afro-American professionals dropped substantially, to 511 in 1940. Those African American males who entered into middle-class professional positions worked as ministers, teachers, musicians and music teachers, physicians, attorneys, dentists, and journalists. Still, regardless of their position in society or income level, they usually relied on the assistance of women in the household, particularly spouses, as co-wage earners.[46]

Working Women in the Home and Work Spheres

Black men could not alone sustain their families and communities on their incomes. They needed the aid of their wives and sometimes, unfortunately, their children. As wives, siblings, nieces, cousins, and daughters, African American migrant women supplanted the meager incomes of males within their households. As on the farm, they often worked outside the home, earning extra money for the family's survival. The city, unlike the farm, allowed these women greater access to jobs, better schools for their children, and educational opportunities that sometimes allowed their entrance into the middle-class job arena. These women, along with African American men, in their own way challenged White hegemony on the job and engaged in race consciousness, for example, by serving as church fundraisers, community outreach neighbors, caretakers, fraternal order members, and astute observers of socioeconomic ills. They also asserted a large degree of power within the African American family as breadwinners. Occasionally, they found themselves to be the only working parties in the household. Because of the stigma attached to the work they could get, women of color held jobs without significant competition during these times, at least through the start of the Depression. According to census data as well as other sources, women in the African American community, more often than White women, lost their husbands prematurely to death, permanent illnesses, disagreements that sparked family breakups, and short-term separations, as husbands frequently traveled to the country for work during the planting and picking seasons. Black women as co-wage earners also maintained their responsibilities in the home as wives, mothers, and homemakers, cooking, cleaning, ironing, washing, tending to sick loved ones, caring for husbands and small children, and enrolling older youths in school. These migrants, as co-wage earners or sole providers, greatly shaped the lives of their families and communities by ensuring the economic and social survival of their households and institutions.[47]

The Houston census reports for 1920, 1930, and 1940 point to the importance of African American women in the home and work spheres. Although the percentage of Afro-Americans living in Houston declined as the twentieth century progressed, due to increased rural-to-urban migration streams among Whites, the group represented a higher proportion of the Houston labor force because of the high numbers of African American women in the workforce. Black women entered the job market in Houston and other places in disproportionate numbers compared to White females. In 1920, African American women made up 25 percent of the Houston female population but 45 percent of the Houston female workforce; in 1930, they constituted 22 percent of the entire female population in Houston but 38 percent of the Houston female labor force. In 1940, they comprised 23 percent of the female population in Houston but 36 percent of the overall workforce for women. They were also an integral part of the African American labor force in the city. In 1920, they made up 38 percent of the entire African American workforce for the year; and in 1930, they comprised 40 percent of the complete Black job force. For 1940, they equaled 43 percent of the total African American workforce. The number of Afro-American women in the overall African American workforce rose to almost half of the total Afro-American labor force by 1940.[48]

Black females in Houston, therefore, ensured the durability of their families and communities in tough times. Actually, according to historian Jacqueline Jones, twentieth-century African American women simply continued the arduous, painstaking, and often proud work traditions their foremothers established in Africa and America centuries ago, whereas most White and Mexican women in Houston only entered the wage-earning workforce at the onset of World War I. Black females in the city and nation, most of whom worked in the personal service labor sector, helped lead the way for working women in the twentieth century.[49]

White women, on the other hand, had more lucrative job choices in the expanding industrial, secretarial, sales, and professional job markets almost as soon as they entered the workforce, with most growth coming from the clerical and sales professions—secretarial, retail sales, and telephone/telegraph operations. They also constituted the majority of professional working women in Houston (see tables 6–8). White women primarily gained access to newly created jobs that reflected the city's budding economy. White women certainly earned more money and aided their families' rising standard of living. The division of labor along racial lines also kept most White women outside common labor occupations and thus ensured them greater pay and upward mobility.[50]

Black women almost always remained employed in the bottom sector of the workforce—domestics, laundresses, washerwomen, chambermaids, seamstresses, and low-skilled cotton compress workers. A sample profile of African American female residents of Independence Heights, Third Ward, Fourth Ward, and Fifth Ward in 1920 illustrates that African American women mainly labored as personal service employees and domestics. Sixty-seven percent of the women sampled from the Houston 1920 manuscript census worked in the domestic and personal service job sector. The author's research findings show that 72 percent of the Afro-American females identified in the Harris County Social Services files labored in this division.[51]

Census reports for the entire city also suggest that African American women comprised the majority of workers in the personal service and domestic division of labor. Black women in 1920 comprised 82 percent of the females employed in the personal service and domestic labor force division; in 1930, the group made up 72 percent of the female personal service and domestic labor force (tables 6 and 8). Table 7 illustrates that in 1940 they constituted 87 percent of the total female workers in this area. The percentage dropped by 1930, but the Depression left Blacks at the bottom workforce sector among women.[52]

Although Afro-American males faced growing competition from Mexican-origin workers, African American women did not, at least until after World War II. Mexican women in Houston did not work outside the home in large numbers. Those working women who made a supplemental income worked in mercantile stores, retail shops within the Mexican community, and as laundresses. Many single Mexican females, however, worked outside the home. A growing number of Latinas valued the importance of women working to sustain the home, as did African Americans. Nevertheless, with little competition and earning only meager wages, the personal service and domestic workforce for the most part ensured stable employment for African American women throughout the first half of the twentieth century.[53]

The personal service and domestic jobs provided African American women with wages; nevertheless, the low-level labor division compromised the stability of the Afro-American family. It reinforced the unequal relationship between White and Afro-American women and fostered notions of docility and debasement. According to Jones, as society increasingly associated wage labor with the time-oriented manufacturing of commodities and goods, the African American wet nurse, private nurse, cook, laundress, and maid remained an anachronism in the twentieth-century labor force. Moreover, the relationship between the domestic and employer seemed reminiscent of a time when African American women—at least to their White female employers—were servants first and family members second.[54]

Black women often spent more time at the job than at home caring for the needs of their families. They left home before daylight and returned at night. A small number of scholars have made a correlation between the increased absence of both parents in the household and the rise of juvenile delinquency in the early twentieth century, particularly among African Americans. Although delinquency often followed poor young people of color, especially urban dwellers, overburdened, overworked Afro-American women, as best they could, held firm to their commitment to family and community. Older, married women, thinking of their children and spouses, refused to work as live-in help. As Jones points out, they devised other ways of putting family first. When domestics came to work late, White employers excused the behavior as inept, irresponsible, and proof of their innate inferiority. Black women simply focused on their families' needs and took children to school, combed their daughters' hair, or cooked breakfast for the family. Black women also demanded time off for church events such as revivals, out-of-town engagements, and Sunday School district meetings. Houston domestics also thought of their families when they found employment in nearby White neighborhoods. This allowed them to either walk to work or spend less time riding streetcars. For example, Alice Guillory, a twentieth-century migrant from Church Point, Louisiana, worked for a White family near her Third Ward home. The White family she worked for resided on Texas Avenue, near the central downtown business district. Her welfare application does not indicate whether the maid walked to work or took the streetcar, but Alice Guillory's close proximity to her job allowed her to easily do both.[55]

Black women experienced other difficulties as well. The low wages of domestic work jeopardized the economic and emotional security of women. Some women domestics who graduated from high school and attended college could not find employment outside the domestic field. The racialization of the female employment sector in the period of Jim Crow basically limited African American women's chances of upward mobility for themselves and their families.[56]

High school graduate Ruby Smith, the eldest of five daughters from Brewster and Silsby, Texas, just west of the city, pleaded to social workers for work, insisting that she had to care for her ailing mother and younger siblings. Before moving to Houston in the late 1930s, Ruby worked as a domestic, earning only $3 weekly. Ruby's testimonial proves that women had little problem working for the good of the family. Although institutionalized racism assured their economic and social debasement in the Houston job market, these migrant women believed their limited employment options did at least assist their families in the midst of adversity. In times of economic crisis, White women, however, for the most part, generally refused employment in the stigmatized field of domestic labor. Although most Afro-American women in Houston worked as domestics and personal service personnel, a significant number worked in other areas of the growing economy.[57]

Black women migrants, especially during World War I and the 1920s, found a number of jobs in Houston outside the personal service arena as boarding-house managers, semiskilled laundresses, hairdressers, librarians, and teachers. They especially moved into the unskilled and semiskilled labor forces with more intensity, working primarily as cotton pickers at compresses, laundry workers at laundries and cleaners, and at home as seamstresses or dressmakers. In the growing number of cotton compresses and warehouses along the ship channel, African American women employees examined bales for dirty or burnt cotton and removed the bad cotton from the bales. Cotton picker personnel—primarily women and African American—earned the lowest of wages among cotton compress employees, making only a quarter to thirty cents an hour. As laundresses and seamstresses at home, they often earned what their poor African American clients could afford and what their wealthier White clients chose to give them.[58]

Not all African American women worked at home or outside the household as wage earners to help support the family. African American women who labored as homemakers did so for a variety of reasons. Frenchtown wives and mothers mostly worked as housewives and stay-at-home mothers. Receiving little or no allowance, these housewives and mothers did laundry, cooked meals, and cared for small children and elders. These migrant women also fulfilled their role as community caterers and cooks, serving people in the neighborhood and church at social functions. Their spouses often earned better wages as semiskilled or skilled artisans at SP Railroad and other industries. Frenchtown residents emphasized their distinctiveness instead. Their full-time duties as homemakers, like their religion and ethnic diversity, set them apart from the larger African American community. Ironically, many if not most African American Catholic homes in Fifth Ward could have benefited from the additional cash working wives would have brought in. Although they prided themselves on those indicators that distinguished them monetarily from other African Americans (and Protestants), mostly because of wage differentials, they struggled to make ends meet. Most, for example, like other people of color, lived in shotgun houses without indoor plumbing.[59]

Other women like Beatrice Hainsworth, an Anderson, Texas schoolteacher, left their careers and concentrated on their families, especially their children. Black housewives' focus on family was even more so. In rare instances, woman worked as housewives and research assistants to their spouses. Housewife Thelma Scott Bryant quit her teaching job in the mid-1930s after marrying migrant educator Ira Bryant of Crockett, Texas, in Houston County. Throughout their marriage, Thelma Bryant worked as her husband's researcher during his tenure in graduate school. She traveled with him on research trips and gathered data for his projects, copyedited his work, and typed his dissertation and manuscripts. Thelma Bryant aided her husband in the completion of numerous case studies, scholarly articles, papers, and monographs, including three self-published books: *Texas Southern University—It's Antecedents, Political Origins and Future* (1975), *Barbara Jordan from the Ghetto to the Capitol* (1977), and *Andrew Young—Mr. Ambassador* (1979). Still, the majority of African American women worked outside and in the home, accepting what they could for the betterment of the family.[60]

Black women, like Huntsville, Texas, native and physician Thelma Patten Law, in small yet visible numbers worked as social workers, musicians, medical doctors, attorneys, dentists, schoolteachers, college instructors, librarians, and trained nurses. In 1920, Afro-American women comprised almost 18 percent of the professional female workforce; and the group constituted close to 14 percent of that same labor force in 1930. By 1940, African American women made up 13 percent of the same labor force. Teaching constituted the largest field among these professionals in Houston. Of the 279 African American female professionals in Houston in 1920, 199, or 71 percent, worked as teachers. Of the 570 African American female professionals in 1930, 413, or 72 percent, earned their livelihood as teachers. Teachers in 1940 comprised 72 percent, or 480 of the 663 total, of the African American female professional workforce.[61]

Teaching attracted African American women for several reasons. For one, other professions barred them, which made teaching a practical substitute for intelligent, college-degreed women of color. Moreover, more people of African descent graduated from college with degrees and certifications in teaching than any other field in the nation in the early twentieth century. Black professionals trained in education often found lasting employment in Houston-area schools. According to educator Ira Bryant, who became principal of Booker T. Washington High School in 1937, 70 percent of the 306 African American Houston Independent School District (HISD) teachers had college degrees. By the mid-1930s, a sizable number had enrolled in graduate schools. The establishment of the Afro-American branch of the HJC in 1927 allowed local educators to earn degrees in education without disrupting their teaching careers. The rise of the African American population in southern cities like Houston also inspired the demand for African American teachers to teach in Afro-American schools. Migrants and established residents also demanded that school districts hire African Americans to teach their children.[62]

African Americans felt Afro-American educators, particularly women, would respect, nurture, and educate their children. Vacated teaching spots among men increased the supply of jobs for qualified African American women. The teaching profession became increasingly female as the century progressed, even as administrative areas became increasingly, but not exclusively, male dominated. Of the twenty-six African American schools in HISD in the 1934–35 academic year, eleven, or 42 percent, had female principals and head teachers.[63]

Although educators assumed the large pool of women in the teaching profession would assure school districts that teachers and parents would remain largely silent and content on matters of low pay and racial injustice, African American teachers worked tirelessly in the community as political and social activists. Yet women educators of color earned low salaries compared to Whites (including White women who also felt the burden of gender bias) and African American males. Victims of racial and gender discrimination, African American women were met with challenges daily. These professionals faced hostile White-controlled school districts that refused to distribute funds fairly. At the same time, Afro-American male supervisors as well as White peers reminded them of their hierarchical status in the professional world of Jim Crow. Nevertheless, they remained committed to their responsibilities as professionals in the business world.

Often these women took their lead from women and men in the business world who made their living offering goods and services to the city's growing, diversifying African American community.[64]

Black Business at Work

The owners of the Nobia A. Franklin Beauty School in the Odd Fellows Building on West Dallas in Fourth Ward come to mind as businesspersons devoted to both financial success and African American empowerment. The largest African American cosmetology college in the South, before the desegregation of the industry gave African Americans access to White-owned beauty colleges, Franklin Beauty School improved the livelihood and self-esteem of thousands, especially women, for several decades. The rise of the beauty industry in the early 1900s immediately shaped the lives of women of color. Black women, according to scholar Julia Blackwelder, usually as high-school graduates, found ways to offset careers in domestic help and poverty, first as traveling beauty consultants, then as unlicensed but apprenticed hairdressers, and later as licensed cosmetology professionals. Black women as clients also found solace in the new enterprise of the turn of the century. The beauty business, a multimillion-dollar industry for African American women, helped transcend the proverbial attitude surrounding notions of Blackness and attractiveness.[65]

The Franklin Beauty School story, according to Blackwelder, intersects business history, beauty culture, race, and gender. Black women, since the days of the transatlantic slave trade, fought back attacks on their natural loveliness, from their rich skin tones and their succulent lips, to their voluptuous bodies to tightly-curled, wool-like hair strands. The new industry, although embracing stereotypical notions of non-African attractiveness, repackaged African female physicality and subtly challenged White supremacy.[66]

Nobia A. Franklin opened a salon in her San Antonio home in the early 1910s. Modeling her business after beauty moguls Sarah Breedlove Walker, Sarah Spencer Washington, and Annie Tumbo Malone, Franklin sold self-manufactured hair tonics, creams, oils, and shampoos. She then opened a shop in San Antonio in 1917, before moving her business to Fort Worth and Houston. Eventually, she relocated to Chicago and hired someone who would become her successor. James Jemison, Franklin's eventual son-in-law and employee, who took the helm of the fledgling college in the

1930s, made the school into a regional success and indirectly opened doors of influence that remain ajar for African American women, civic leaders, and businesspersons in the twenty-first century.[67]

Nobia Franklin's daughter and son-in-law, Abbie and James H. Jemison, inherited the business in 1934. James Jemison, a native of Mississippi, graduated from Wendell Phillips High School on Chicago's South Side in 1927, eventually becoming an apprentice of Madame N. A. Franklin. Unlike many men in the industry of cosmetology, he remained active in hairdressing while moving in the direction of management. After Franklin's death in 1934, the Jemisons relocated the Franklin Beauty School to Houston. Jemison restructured the business, emphasizing the beauty college. The move benefitted the Jemisons during a time when cosmetology schools increasingly trained aspiring beauticians as licensed practitioners in cosmetology. The Franklin Beauty School, though not the only one in the state, grew to become the largest in the South by World War II.[68]

In the public eye, the Jemisons advanced the notion of African American beauty culture, focusing foremost on the process of hair straightening and maintenance. The couple understood the relevancy of beauty culture among African American women, who found solace in hair and grooming at a time when White society defined Blackness as hideous. Even while deferring to perceptions of White beauty, African American cosmetologists consciously undertook the challenging task of reinventing White beauty to fit African American definitions of glamour. Although hair straightening and facial bleaching suggested African American's willingness to choose concepts of Whiteness over Blackness, African American women, more so than other groups of women, found spiritual release and pleasure in the sisterhood of hairdressing, style, and glamour, and continued to promote and celebrate their unique African sensuality. They therefore recognized and celebrated their African beauty and autonomy, perhaps in ways they were unaware of at the time. Community builders and shrewd business owners, the Jemisons and their descendants continued to train thousands of beauticians well into the next century. Interestingly, the Jemisons and the Franklin Beauty School did a good deal more for the cause of Blackness.[69]

In the private sector, beauty college mogul J. H. Jemison helped propel civil rights (Abbie Jemison retreated from public life in the 1940s). An ardent member of the YMCA, PBSF, Democratic Party, NUL, Business and Professional Men's Club, and GHBC, he welcomed the opportunity to give back to the community and propel moderate civil rights. Jemison lobbied the Texas Board of Hairdressers and Cosmetologists to hire an African American beauty-salon inspector in the 1940s and 1950s. A racial moderate, Jemison was, to a degree, respected by individual White business leaders, local politicians, and state officials. In his reserved and quiet way, he urged African Americans to pay their poll taxes, vote, and vigorously campaign for social equality. Jemison helped finance lawsuits involving groups that sought to dismantle legal segregation, as in a 1952 suit involving public golf courses. Politically astute, he supported a number of desegregation efforts, even financing rallies, radio broadcasts, and forums that fostered ways to challenge White supremacy. Preoccupied as he was with business, Jemison still made time for civil rights.[70]

Although some scholars argue that Houston's African American business elite only played a minor role in civic affairs and civil rights, nothing could be further from the truth. Although not always vocal and visible to others the community's business elite, who had mostly migrated to the city from the surrounding countryside in the late nineteenth century or early twentieth century, or were the children of internal migrants, helped shape civic affairs, economic growth, and civil rights for years to come. Many, like club owners and philanthropists Anna and Clarence Dupree of Carthage, Texas, and Plaquemine, Louisiana, respectively, donated to important charitable causes and formed viable nonprofit agencies and enterprises in the community. Others, like the Jemisons, who established the City-Wide Beauticians Association for licensed beauticians, helped form professional societies that promoted the interests of both African American businesses and the community as a whole. Those professionals that held private practices and offices—individuals like physician Benjamin Jessie Covington—also created professional associations for peers. Some, like Fifth Ward pastor Simpson, invested their resources in institutions for the community. Rev. Lee Haywood Simpson, a Calvert, Texas, migrant, along with the Central District Association of Texas (an affiliate of the NBC), built a nursing home for seniors in New Waverly in western Walker County near the city of Huntsville. A few, like newspaper moguls Carter Wesley and Clifton Richardson Sr., shaped African American thought and identity through their media outlets, editorials, and community involvement. Although most of these business owners (perhaps with the exception of a few like Richardson and barber R. R. Grovey), rarely publicly challenged the city's caste system and certainly benefitted from racial segregation, they did work behind the scenes to improve the lifestyles of their parishioners,

FIGURE 44. Houston's African Americans at the upstart of the twentieth century faced challenges, namely racial segregation and underemployment, but found ways to survive racism and poverty. Black businesses played an important role in ensuring the survival of the race. In Houston, African Americans created business districts that housed the majority of African American businesses. The city's first major business district was located in Fourth Ward on San Filipe (later West Dallas) and housed barbershops and beauty salons, boutiques, groceries, drug stores, restaurants, filling stations, car repair shops, law and medical offices, churches, and schools. Standing third from the left is Stafford Harrison, a schoolteacher and barber, whose multiracial grandson Edwin Harrison will finish college at Prairie View College, play semiprofessional football in Puerto Rico, and later return to Houston and take a lead in labor union organizing, civil rights, and integration will become the father of retired Texas Southern University Professor of Sociology Cecile Harrison. Stafford and the other men on the photo attend Trinity Episcopal Methodist Church in Fourth Ward and sing in one of the church's singing groups. Relaxed, handsome, and certainly engaged with their surroundings, Harrison, who died in World War I reaffirms the view that African American men took pride in their community and race. *(Courtesy Houston Metropolitan Research Center, Houston Public Library, Houston, Texas, MSS 0182-0079)*

clients, patrons, and neighbors. Most supported desegregation efforts as well, even if they failed to make their viewpoints known to Whites.[71]

A look at the history of African American business enterprises in the city points to a long tradition of community agency and civil-rights involvement. Black businesses in the city grew out of the aftermath of slavery and continued to prosper in the next century, even while a handful of businesses catered to slaves and free people of color in the antebellum era.

African Americans in different parts of the city opened restaurants, blacksmith shops, commissaries, icehouses, retail shops, and barbershops during the period of Reconstruction. In the late nineteenth and early twentieth centuries, Black businesses sprouted throughout the city, from the traditional wards to the outlying enclaves populated by African Americans. The Great Migration especially propelled the growth of businesses in Black Houston. In Fourth Ward, businesses had offices on West Dallas, with some renting space in the Odd Fellows building. The Pilgrim Building, from the 1920s until the 1930s, maintained office space as well for African American professionals as well as proprietors in the historic ward (fig. 45).

FIGURE 45. Jamaican immigrant Henry Cohen Hardy formed the Ancient Order of Pilgrims in 1882 in Houston. As the fraternal order grew in size, it took a leading role in Houston's Black community, providing office space for prospective tenants by 1927. The Pilgrim's four-story building, located right across the street from Colored High School on San Felipe (later West Dallas) and Bagby in Fourth Ward in the early twentieth century, not only housed physician practices, law offices, drug stores, groceries and commissaries, and dental offices but also boasted a ballroom for parties and dances for the general public. The organization's total assets by the opening of the Great Depression were $200,000. *(Courtesy Houston Metropolitan Research Center, Houston Public Library, Houston, Texas,* MSS 1248-3022*)*

Prior to the 1930s, Fourth Ward boasted the overwhelming majority of Afro-American businesses.[72]

To the far northeast, in Fifth Ward, business owners generally used Lyons Avenue as a central commercial strip, while in the self-contained, productive community of Independence Heights, businesses dotted Houston Avenue (now North Main) in northwest Houston. Aside from traditional businesses such as restaurants and groceries as well as auto mechanic shops and barbershops and beauty salons, Fifth Ward was home to a number of jazz, blues, and zydeco clubs, with several dozen featuring local and international celebrities. In addition, southern Louisiana cuisine made up a significant portion of the menu items at a number of food establishments in Fifth Ward and elsewhere. Third Ward's business strip, located principally on Dowling Avenue, catered to various types of consumers. Serving from one-half to two-thirds of the African American community, these businesses provided insular protection against venomous racial bigotry and also trained later generations of business owners and professionals. They created viable institutions that benefitted the community while advancing the notion of creative, self-help interdependence. So too did the hundreds of businesses in Independence Heights, Sunnyside, and Acres Homes nurture self-reliance, hope, and racial autonomy, even while members of the community increasingly sought after White-controlled business establishments.[73]

Business leaders, however, did much more than provide services and products for residents. All the while, businesspersons like grocer and realtor John Brown Bell spearheaded societal change, for example, by establishing business associations, churches, schools, fraternal orders, political leagues, and donation drives. As African American Houston grew, so too did these independent enterprises in the community—both traditional retail shops as well as social organizations. Internal migrations fueled business growth as the twentieth century arrived. The 1900–01 Houston city directory listed a number of self-employed individuals, including African American draymen, carpenters, blacksmiths, tavern owners, grocers, real estate developers, movers, bootblacks, hucksters, basket makers, yardmen, junk collectors, and teamsters. African Americans found creative ways to make money, despite growing competition from White establishments.[74]

The Great Migration propelled unprecedented business growth. Once again the historian consults *The Red Book of Houston*. African Americans in 1915 owned at least 370 businesses in the city. These businesses ultimately influenced further expansion in the African American community in the twentieth century. Fruit stands, dry goods mercantile establishments, groceries, ice cream stands, and restaurants offered African Americans courteous, individualized service. Boardinghouses, cottages, and private homes provided lodging accommodations to individuals and families. Nightclubs, dancehalls, and theaters gave African Americans entertainment. Pharmacists, optometrists, physicians, dentists, realty companies, attorneys, and accountants offered specialized services to clients. Life insurance firms and benevolent organizations provided members with insurance coverage at a time when others did not. Barbers, beauticians, and manicurists offered individualized services to clients. Filling stations and automotive specialty shops, plumbing and electrical contracting, blacksmitheries, hardware stores, and painting businesses; tailoring and clothing stores; funeral homes; media firms such as newspapers, publishing houses, and radio stations; the music trade; stationary and office goods; and photography shops catered to an exclusively African American clientele. These business firms gave African Americans greater access to wealth and influence; ultimately, people of color used these vestiges of independence to challenge their second-class state.[75]

As discussed earlier in chapter 3, the Great Migrations gave life to Afro-American economic growth and community agency as former slaves and their descendants moved to the city and worked together to resurrect African American hopes in the wake of Houston's population explosion of the early twentieth century. Although this trend happened outside the South, northern communities expressed some dismay at the decline of certain African American businesses that catered exclusively to White clienteles while witnessing a growth in the overall African American population due to internal migration from the South. This explains why historian Cary D. Wintz argues that segregation, in the end, benefitted African American Houstonians—recent arrivals and established—who opened businesses that catered to a community that was completely ignored by others in the city. The city's burgeoning economy also spurred African American business vitality as economic growth, for some at least, translated into real wealth. Houston did, however, experience a decline in the number of Afro-American businesses in the city by the late 1920s and 1930s, probably a result of the economic crisis of the day. Still, even as the Great Depression saw a decline in African American businesses, Houston was home to one of the largest Afro-American business communities in the nation, according to the Bureau of Census.[76]

A 1929 Bureau of Census publication estimated that 259 African American retail shops served the community in 1929. Despite having fewer African American businesses in the country (the city ranked thirteenth in the nation among cities with fifty thousand people or more), Houston ranked second, only behind Detroit, in the monetary dollar value of sales of these businesses per capita in select United States cities. The city also ranked third in per capita sales among African American businesses, only behind New York and Detroit, with sales in 1929 totaling $1.3 million. The city's incredible urban and industrial growth, which African Americans benefited from, largely explained the success of these business establishments. Many different types of businesses succeeded, including lodging, hauling and shipping, manufacturing, construction, laundries and cleaning, tailoring and dressmaking, food, and service. Restaurants and eating establishments comprised the majority of these retail shops (table 10).[77]

Perhaps the most successful African American businessperson in the city was Hobart Taylor Sr. A native of Wharton County, Texas, Taylor was born in 1890. His father, freedman Jack Taylor, a former Washington County slave, invested in real estate, making shrewd purchases in Fort Bend and Wharton County. Hobart's father, Jack, a handsome, dark-chocolate-complexioned man, stood up to segregationists and bigots, routinely inciting agitation and attacks from White members of his community of Kendleton in the post-Reconstruction 1880s. Fort Bend, with its predominately Afro-American population, witnessed numerous racial skirmishes during and following Reconstruction. Jack Taylor, unmoved by such threats, taught his son the importance of racial progress and economic independence. Hobart Taylor, who graduated from Prairie View College as a baseball star, would take his father's wisdom to heart. He took a job as an insurance salesman at Standard Life Insurance Company of Atlanta, Georgia. Soon the young agent would become one of the first salespersons to write policies that totaled $1,000,000. Taylor later took a management position at the National Benefit Life Insurance Company in Washington, D.C., before returning to his home state.[78]

He subsequently returned to Texas and in 1932 established a taxi service in Houston. A cunning businessperson, Taylor petitioned the Chrysler Motor Corporation to develop an automobile that could withstand the terrible city streets in Houston's African American neighborhoods. The automotive maker padded the taxis with extra cushions and designed them to allow greater airways for automobile motors. Taylor's company soared after World War II, as the city's African American middle class grew and

TABLE 10. Houston Black retail business endeavors on the eve of the great depression, 1929*

Type of Business	Stores	Proprietors/ Firm Mem.	Employees Full	Employees Part-time	Payroll	End of the Year Stocks	Net Sales Amount	Net Sales Percent Total
Total	259	272	259	22	$155,511	$82,000	$1,343,588	100
Food group	73	74	22	2	$12,652	$22,420	$357,914	26.64
Candy and confectionary stores	8	8	4	1	$3,284	$1,430	$24,120	1.8
Grocery stores (without meats)	21	21	6		$2,400	$4,480	$90,533	6.74
Grocery stores (with meats)	28	28	8	1	$4,544	$14,430	$147,961	11.01
Fruit stores and vegetable markets	11	11				$1,570	$50,900	3.79
Meat markets (with seafood)	2	6	4		$2,424	$510	$44,400	3.3
Other food stores	3							
Automotive retailers	22	25	21	3	$12,602	$3,490	$143,833	10.71
Filling stations								
Filling stations (gasoline and oil)	5	6	3		$2,120	$810	$33,688	2.51
Filling stations (tires and accessories)	6	6	8		$5,580	$1,200	$10,750	5.27
Filling stations (with other merchandise)	3	4	5		$3,128	$210	$28,645	0.8
Garages and repair shops	7	9	5		$1,774	$1,270	$156,348	2.13
Other automotive businesses	1						$123,296	
Apparel stores	12	14	19	9	$17,945	$24,600	$156,348	11.64
Women's accessories	3	3	12	6	$14,226	$23,260	$123,296	9.18
Other apparel stores	6	8	5	3	$3,319	$1,040	$29,002	$2.16
Shoe stores	3	3	1		$600	$300	$4,050	0.3

TABLE 10. *Continued*

Type of Business	Stores	Proprietors/ Firm Mem.	Employees Full	Employees Part-time	Payroll	End of the Year Stocks	Net Sales Amount
Furniture and Household	1	(X)	(X)	(X)	(X)	(X)	(X)
Restaurants and eating establishments	113	117	160	4	$86,317	$8,320	$466,624
Restaurants, cafeterias, and lunchrooms							
Cafeterias	1	50	63	3	$32,368	$4,590	$180,746
Lunchrooms	50						
Restaurants with dining facilities	18	20	62		$30,965	$1,280	$124,590
Lunch counters and refreshment stands							
Lunch counters	22	58	30	1	$21,344	$1,540	$124,545
Refreshment stands	16	16	5		$2,036	$610	$29,318
Beverage stands	6	6				$300	$7,425
Other retail establishments	38	72					$218,869
Cigar Stores with Cigar Stands	1	(X)	(X)	(X)	(X)	(X)	(X)
Coal and Wood Yards	11	11	6		$3,312	$1,020	$31,550
Ice dealers	3	3				$250	$4,324
Drugstores/ pharmacies							
Pharmacies without Fountains	3	3	3	3	$2,000	$1,950	$16,780
Pharmacies with Fountains	12	13	16	$10,586	$8,770	$89,556	$89,556
Jewelry stores	1	(X)	(X)	(X)	(X)	(X)	(X)
Miscellaneous retailers	7	9	10	1	$7,517	$7,260	$65,177

Source: Bureau of Census, *Negroes in the United States, 1920–1932*. 1935. Reprint. New York: Greenwood Press, 1969, 5

*The Census Bureau has omitted the dollar totals to avoid disclosing the proprietors' operational and personal finance

used more of its expendable wealth on varying services like taxis. Unlike many African American businesses that catered exclusively to people of African descent in the Jim Crow era, Taylor competed well with White-owned cab companies. By the 1970s, Hobart Taylor was a millionaire, perhaps the first African American millionaire in the state. His family's property in Wharton and Fort Bend also brought the Taylor Family wealth and prosperity, and included oil reserves. An advocate of racial equality, he and Victoria native and nightclub owner Julius White financed the *Grovey v. Townsend* case as well as other lawsuits brought by Houstonians of the 1930s and early 1940s.[79]

A good friend of and campaign contributor to Lyndon Baines Johnson, he would set the course for his son, also a graduate of Prairie View College. After undergraduate school, Hobart Taylor Jr. earned a master's from Howard University and later a J.D. from the University of Michigan. President John F. Kennedy appointed attorney Hobart Taylor Jr. executive vice chairman to the Equal Employment Opportunity Commission (EEOC). He later served as special counsel to President Johnson. Hobart Taylor Jr. helped Johnson formulate Executive Order 11246, which Taylor Jr., along with other Kennedy administration officials, coined "affirmative action."[80]

Hobart Taylor Sr. instilled in his son the importance of community agency, something he himself took very seriously. Hobart Taylor gave back in many ways. He taught Sunday School at Wesley Chapel African Methodist Church in Third Ward and gave religiously to the United Negro College Fund (UNCF), serving as one of the agency's strongest national contributors. For Taylor, individual economic success meant collective racial progress.[81]

According to historian James M. SoRelle, who has written extensively about the Houston African American business elite in the early twentieth century, African American business owners, since the end of World War I, had profited from segregation in the city; however, they still suffered from the social constraints brought about by structuralized racism. Truthfully, most businesses fared poorly as compared to HT Taxicab Co. Although booster campaigns of the 1920s in the *Houston Informer* promoted racial autonomy and economic exclusivity in the community, striking a nerve with readers, a good percentage of the population adamantly opposed patronizing African American businesses. These discussions urged people to invest in African American businesses over those owned by Whites, Jewish merchants, and the Chinese. Racial advocate Richardson also suggested that African American business owners provide quality services to clients. Still, many ignored these pleas, as many Blacks embraced White supremacy, even at the expense of their own mutual well-being.[82]

Black business associations formed in the 1920s and 1930s in an attempt to promote economic cooperation and racial unity in the African American community as well. Regrettably, lack of preparation and poor management hurt these businesses, including that of the Negro Chamber of Commerce, founded in the early 1930s. The chamber hoped to encourage increased support for African American businesses in the community and promote better relations between the Negro Chamber of Commerce and the mainstream Houston Chamber of Commerce. Unfortunately, the chamber and booster campaigns failed to capture the minds and hearts of the vast majority of African American residents, many of whom frequented non–Afro-American business establishments that catered to people of color.[83]

Many argued African American establishments charged too much for services; others claimed the quality of services fared poorly compared to others; then some admitted that they saw African American professionals and businesspersons as inferior to others, especially Whites. As might be expected, the same individuals who ignored African American businesses rarely spoke out against the ongoing acts of discrimination they encountered daily. Moreover, business associations rarely acknowledged the success of female-oriented enterprises like the Franklin Beauty School and thus gave the impression that women did not fit into the scope of African American business empowerment. In many ways, self-hate and racial passivity prevented the continued success of a good number of Afro-American–owned businesses. Nevertheless, migrant women and men, mostly the children and grandchildren of former slaves, opened business enterprises and relied on the innate resources of their communities for their livelihood and a sense of racial progress. Unlike many businesses, a handful of business owners like the Jemisons, Taylor, the Duprees, and Wesley not only survived the daunting crisis of the 1930s, they also managed to expand their business operations during the stressful ordeal of the Great Depression.[84]

The Great Depression and the Origins of the Second Great Migration

Black business owners, professionals, artisans, and unskilled workers, most of whom moved to the city from the surrounding countryside between the late nineteenth century and the late 1920s, found themselves vulnerable to the economic downturns of the 1930s. The worst economic crisis in United States history, the Great Depression affected all aspects of African American life and culture. From business failures and unprecedented unemployment figures to racism and family disintegration, African Americans, on the whole, fared poorly. Although the discovery of Texas oil fields prompted Houston firms to expand their operations, a move that ultimately bolstered the city's static economy by the end of the 1930s, as the world's demand for petroleum goods grew in the wake of a new European war, Houston's African American community suffered. Recent migrants to the city, who in better times sought economic relief from the relentless brutality of rural poverty, faced further deprivation and devastation in the years that followed the October 29 stock market plunge in 1929.[85]

Martha Williams certainly knew hard times. A homemaker from rural Louisiana, the young woman occasionally worked as a washerwoman or domestic to earn extra cash and make ends meet. Her husband, Charlie Williams, like many African American men from southern Louisiana, earned his living as a tenant farmer and artisan. Frustrated with their marginal existence in the Bayou State, the pair relocated to the Houston area not long after the outbreak of World War I. More than anything else, the heightened call for cotton and petroleum goods during and after the war stimulated unprecedented migration streams from the surrounding countryside into the more urban, industrial centers along the Gulf Coast.[86]

Charles and Martha Williams, like many newcomers to the greater Houston industrial region, hoped the area would offer them and their unborn children economic and educational opportunities, as well as greater access to racial equality. In this sense, their decision to relocate to Alief, Texas, then a small town just west of Houston, reflected a desire to find real economic progress for the family as tenants. Typical stepwise migrants, the Williams family eventually moved on to the Fifth Ward in Houston in the early 1920s after the births of their first two children. In the decade following World War I, the family's conditions improved, and they eventually rented a home in the increasingly Afro-American–occupied ward.[87]

Regrettably, the family faced hard times during the Great Depression. The nation's worst economic calamity devastated the working poor, especially African American families like the Williams. Within three years of the stock market crash, thirteen million Americans—25 percent of the workforce—lost jobs. Charlie Williams soon lost his job. Ultimately, he lost a great deal more. The Depression took a heavy toll on the family, which included four more children by the early 1930s. Martha and Charlie Williams, overwhelmed, burdened with debt, conscious of the growing rift that loomed over their relationship, soon separated. Charlie Williams, like many unemployed and frustrated men of color during the period, left his family, went from odd job to odd job, and traveled to and from the countryside in search of temporary work.[88]

His young wife, accustomed to working as co-wage earner or housewife, had to now support a family of seven on the meager earnings of a laundress. Williams and her children left their home on Cage Street and moved in with neighbors. The single mother worked on and off at a bag factory and as a cook for an affluent White family. Unfortunately, like many African American domestics alive during the period, Martha routinely found herself out of work. Williams and other domestics of color in Houston and around the country increasingly found themselves competing for personal service work with Whites, Latinas, and other out-of-work African Americans, including clerical staffers, schoolteachers, social workers, librarians, medical professionals, secretaries, sales consultants, and housewives.[89]

During her periods of unemployment, single mother Martha Williams applied for and received public assistance from the Harris County Department of Public Welfare (HCDPW) and the newly formed Federal Emergency Relief Administration (FERA). Despite her trying circumstances, wife, mother, and migrant Martha Williams remained proactive, steadfast, and determined to care for her family. Like other African American newcomers to the city, migrant Martha Williams relied on her inner strength and community outreach to keep her family together. She depended on many forms of assistance—kith and kin, Houston's expanding and fluctuating labor market, and the power of her God. Public assistance and charity also kept her and her family off the streets. With purpose in the face of travails, and a sincere resolve to conquer discrimination and overarching poverty, Williams retained her sanity. Through force of will and hard work, she made a home for her family in Houston.[90]

Although the Williams family relocated to the Houston area during better financial times, financial strain, mechanization, illness, and even death helped to drive African Americans out of the Texas interior. Noteworthy is the fact that death rates contributed greatly to the population declines in Texas counties right before World War II. During the Great Depression decade, most cotton region counties surrounding Houston witnessed African American population declines. Death figures, however, not out-migration totals, accounted for most of the decrease. For example, the African American population in Limestone County between 1930 and 1940 declined by 1,142 persons; of that number, 1,138 persons suffered deaths. In Leon County, the African American population declined by 847. Deaths—534—largely accounted for the decline. Deaths sometimes exceeded the population change. Whereas Robertson County had a total population decline of 660 Afro-Americans in the 1930s, 1,590 of its African American residents died.[91]

The nearby mixed-region counties also saw little out-migration among the Afro-American residents (table 11) for this same period. Houston County, the birthplace of migrant Oliphant Lockwood Hubbard, saw an African American population decline of 495 during the Depression. However, 1,208 African American residents died during the same period. San Jacinto County, the birth home of Lee Coleman, a migrant who moved to Houston in 1934, also saw a small population decline compared to its death total among African Americans. Some 437 Afro-Americans died in the county, which had a total population decrease of only 377.[92]

Several factors possibly explain this. Aside from birth figures, in the mixed-region counties, African Americans often found temporary jobs at lumber mills in Trinity, Huntsville, and New Waverly. Still, their numbers declined in mill towns just as manufacturing firms altogether shut down their operations. More importantly, during the Great Depression, African Americans routinely moved back and forth between the city and country in search of work. Some returned to the farm in the early 1930s, after employers laid them off. The temporary migration patterns of jobless African Americans searching for farm work perhaps altered greatly the population figures for rural and small-town communities surrounding Houston in Texas (see table 11). Poverty as well as poor ventilation and sanitation, along with unhealthy diet and stress probably explain the high death rates for eastern Texas African Americans, especially during the trying 1930s. With jobs and welfare hard to come by in 1930s Houston, some rural residents simply died trying to improve their standing.[93]

Louisianans too continued to relocate to Houston during the Great Depression and in the wake of economic instability brought on by the Great Flood of 1927. Table 12 substantiates the instability. Although many Louisiana parishes continued to grow, mainly due to births, the high death figures suggest family instability brought on by poverty, Agricultural Adjustment Administration (AAA) policies, farm mechanization, separation, sickness,

TABLE 11. Black population and mortality figures for select Texas counties, 1930–40*

Counties	1930	1940	1930–40 Death Fig.	1930–40 Death Rates
Freestone	8,776	**8,613**	955	110.87
Limestone	10,933	**9,791**	1,138	166.22
Falls	12,515	**12,047**	1,451	120.44
Leon	8,362	**7,515**	534	71.05
Robertson	11,416	**10,756**	1,590	147.82
Milam	8,772	**7,686**	914	127.19
Madison	3,456	**3,863**	312	80.16
Grimes	9,700	**8,814**	1,018	115.47
Brazos	9,064	**10,011**	1,264	126.26
Burleson	7,187	**6,767**	801	118.36
Lee	3,876	**3,655**	381	98.57
Fayette	6,921	**6,321**	807	127.66
Washington	9,893	**9,660**	1,296	134.16
Waller	4,952	**4,993**	809	162.02
Austin	4,852	**4,398**	561	127.55
Colorado	5,955	**5,460**	695	127.28
Lavaca	3,369	**3,220**	461	143.16
Fort Bend	9,787	**9,110**	1,166	127.99
Wharton	7,903	**9,214**	1,187	128.82
Jackson	1,908	**1,781**	199	11.13
Matagorda	4,520	4,943	543	109.85
Cherokee	11,565	12,566	1,906	151.67
Anderson	11,485	11,796	1,550	131.4
Houston	12,374	11,879	1,208	101.69
Trinity	3,181	**3,061**	372	121.52
Walker	8,531	**8,820**	734	83.21
San Jacinto	5,117	**4,740**	437	92.19
Montgomery	5,273	**7,148**	756	105.16
Liberty	5,019	6,075	600	98.76

Sources: Bureau of Census, *Sixteenth Census of the United States, 1940: Population: Characteristics of the Population,* V. 2, 792–806; Pratt, *Growth of a Refining Region,* 20; Texas Department of Health, Bureau of Vital Statistics, Texas Mortality, 1930–1940.

*The highlighted counties show population losses over the said period. These population figures result from out-migration, death rates, and birth rates. Birth rate figures for Texas counties are only available for the years after 1930. Although Houston migrants left places in the East Texas timber economic region, this table only (as table 5) concentrates on the cotton and mixed regions because the largest number of Black in-migrants left these two areas.

TABLE 12. Black population figures for select Louisiana parishes, 1930–40*

Parishes	1930	1940	1930–40 Death Fig.	1930–40 Death Rates	Out-Mig.
Iberville	12,549	14,171	2,194	154.82	N/A
Pointe Coupee	12,211	13,556	1,683	124.15	N/A
Saint Landry	29,516	33,815	3,574	105.69	N/A
Evangeline	5,772	6,999	278	39.71	N/A
Calcasieu	12,112	14,452	788	13	N/A
Saint Mary*	**14,302**	**14,242**	2,071	145.41	N/A
Saint Martin	7,545	9,651	794	82.27	N/A
Iberia	10,733	13,447	1,801	133.93	N/A
Avoyelles	9,915	10,556	1,095	103.73	N/A
Acadia	8,103	8,319	933	112.15	N/A
Lafayette	13,260	14,098	1,815	128.74	N/A
Jefferson Davis	4,979	6,015	604	100.41	N/A
Beauregard***	**3,177**	**2,593**	301	116.08	283
Rapides	25,126	26,890	2,360	87.76	N/A
De Soto	19,215	20,114	1,411	70.15	N/A
Caldwell	2,937	3,496	313	89.53	N/A
Red River	7,551	7,987	593	74.24	N/A
Ascension	7,077	7,948	1,066	134.12	N/A
Claiborne*	**18,042**	**17,083**	1,069	62.57	N/A
Bienville	10,624	11,491	780	67.87	N/A
Morehouse	13,597	16,129	1,687	104.59	N/A
Natchitoches	19,570	19,946	2,440	122.33	N/A

Sources: Bureau of Census, *Fourteenth Census of the United States, 1940: Population,* V. 3, 393–98; *Fourteenth Census of the United States, 1920: Population,* V. 3, 393–98; Bureau of Census, Bureau of Census, *Sixteenth Census of the United States, 1940: Population: Characteristics of the Population,* V. 2, *Part 3, 366–76;* Bureau of Census, *Mortality Statistics, 1930,* 88–89; Bureau of Census, *Mortality Statistics, 1931 and 1932,* 10; Bureau of Census, *Mortality Statistics,* 1932, 10; Bureau of Census, *Mortality Statistics, 1933 and 1934,* 91–92; Bureau of Census, *Vital Statistics of the United States, 1937,* 50–51; Bureau of Census, Bureau of Census, *Vital Statistics of the United States, 1938,* 50–51; Bureau of Census, *Vital Statistics of the United States, 1939,* 50–51; Bureau of Census, *Vital Statistics of the United States, 1941,* 79–81.
*Parishes show a population loss over the 10-year period.
**The state formed these counties after 1910.

and death wrecked havoc and misfortune on the people of Louisiana. In fact, by glance, the death figures for Louisiana, at least for some parishes when compared to Texas counties, seem particularly troubling. Of the twenty-nine Texas counties surveyed for this study, eleven had death figures that were one thousand or higher, making up almost one-third of the places chosen. For the selected Louisiana parishes, however, the thirteen that have death figures that range in excess of one thousand comprise a larger percentage of the total selected places. Furthermore, considering the patient–doctor ratio in the rural South compared to cities, these staggering figures seem practical, and certainly compelled survivors of illnesses to flee to the city.[94]

Families such as the Williamses sometimes utilized back and forth movements to meet their financial obligations. Migrants—previous ones from the late nineteenth century as well as those groups entering the city in the first decades of the next, along with recent newcomers from the surrounding interior—during the Great Depression traveled back and forth between the city and country to find both temporary work and relief. Often, migrant families separated briefly after making the trip to Houston to accommodate family members earning extra cash, working as farm laborers. These re-step, or return, migrations allowed families to remain in the city while male (and sometimes female) loved ones temporarily returned to the farm. Instead of living on the farm and migrating to larger plantations, small towns, or nearby cities in search of wages, they ironically left the city in search of short-term work on farms. This process of internal migration, only in reverse, also influenced continued rural-to-urban migration as return migrants continued to refer to themselves as Houston residents. In this sense, recent migrants sought to find ways to supplant their traditional earnings until federal relief or jobs became available, ultimately influencing others from the country to relocate to the city.[95]

Not surprisingly, the Great Depression magnified return migrations to and from the country. Willie Shives left his family in 1932. He found work on a farm outside Houston. Shives, a native of Mississippi, provided for his family, including his wife, Rosie Lee, their children, and his elderly grandmother, by working mostly as a farm laborer and unskilled common worker. He did the best he could under the circumstances and remained hopeful that a better day would soon come.[96]

Another migrant, Archie Boyd, also decided to return to the farm. In 1920, Boyd and his large family moved to Houston from Bremond, Texas, in Robertson County near College Station. His wife Emily was born and reared in Wharton, Texas, just south of Houston. They also raised their children in Wharton before moving to Houston. The family managed to get by until the Depression hit Houston. Due to unforeseen circumstances, Archie saw continuous layoffs in the Great Depression years. Events worsened to the point of Archie bagging groceries at the Farmers Market to put food on the table. His wife Emily took a laundry job. The family, however, needed more money; Archie returned to the farm and temporarily worked as a farm laborer in Rosenberg in Fort Bend County. Houston's close proximity to surrounding farms allowed for the return of many farmers to the hinterland for the good of the family.[97]

Thousands of African Americans in the Houston area also fled to California and the Midwest during the Great Depression, ultimately influencing tens of thousands to leave Texas during and after World War II. Historian Gretchen Lemke-Santangelo, in her groundbreaking study *Abiding Courage: African American Migrant Women and The East Bay Community* (1996), tells readers that although a large contingency of newcomers to the West Coast came from working-class backgrounds, large numbers held high school diplomas and college degrees, with a few coming from more affluent backgrounds. Music teacher Percy McDavid fits this model, as did his older brother Russell, a graduate of Huston College. The McDavids' departure represents the migratory upstart of middle-class African Americans in 1930s as emerging Black Urban Professionals (BUPPIES) seeking greener pastures outside the Depression's and segregation's chokeholds. Many others, including physicians, attorneys, educators, musicians, and civil servants, abandoned their birth or migrant homes.[98]

Nevertheless, even while the McDavid brothers and other younger Houstonians, more often than not the children of internal migrants, left the city permanently, others tried to find ways to make do in their—or their parents'—adopted Houston, even in the midst of financial instability. In the depression-ridden 1930s, African American males made up the majority of migrants. Young men such as Luther Stullivan of rural New Caney, Texas, found work at SP, along the Houston Ship Channel, on construction teams, and with industrial firms looking for menial laborers. At the same time, some men, like Oran Williams, traveled alone to Houston in search of work and left their families behind. Occasionally, female migrants outnumbered their male counterparts. Only in the 10–19-year-old age group did African American female migrants outnumber males for each intercensal period. This suggests that teenage girls and younger women, usually unmarried with no children, sought out and found jobs as domestics and housecleaners. Older women in the 20–44 age categories migrated to Houston less often. Moreover, teens such as Cleopatra and Wallace King of rural Bastrop, Texas, also dominated these migration categories because their parents often sent them to Houston to complete their schooling. Only for the 1930 intercensal period did the in-migration figures for young adults decline because of return migrants traveling back and forth between Houston and the country in search of work (table 9).[99] The population numbers certainly confirm this observation, as the city's African American community grew from 63,000 to 86,302 between 1930 and 1940. The estimated population growth shows a potential net increase from eight thousand to ten thousand people during the 1930s.[100]

Still, a wide spectrum of Americans, both recent migrants and established residents, lost stable jobs. One University of Texas study, published in 1942, suggested African Americans suffered disproportionately from constant layoffs, racial bias, and discouragement. Using individual surveys and census data, the study made several findings. The city's unemployment rate fluctuated from 37 percent in 1928 to 32 percent 1934. In the period from 1937 to 1938, unemployment fell to 31 percent. Black unemployment figures, however, according to the findings, topped 40 percent. Of the city's fifty-eight census tracts, African Americans made up the majority in nine. Unemployment rates in these census tracts—neighborhoods in Third Ward, Fourth Ward, Fifth Ward, and Independence Heights—varied from 46 percent in 1928 to 56 percent in 1934. Several years later, from 1937 to 1938, the figure dropped slightly to 45 percent. Other sources made analogous claims. According to one *Houston Informer* piece, African Americans made up the vast majority of jobless residents in 1931. Perhaps an oversimplification, the observation certainly sheds light on a real problem facing Houston and the nation.[101]

Additional Bureau of Census statistics, although more conservative, tell a similar story. According to a 1930 Census Bureau statewide report on unemployment, twenty-four hundred African Americans—7 percent of the almost thirty-six thousand employable persons of color in the city—reported being without work, with males comprising 69 percent of all individuals reporting unemployment. This included both unemployed individuals looking for work as well as underemployed workers recently laid off. More than likely, many of those claiming employment worked seasonal jobs and took on temporary work where and when they could find it and spent equal time in the countryside as migratory farm workers. Still, at the same time, census enumerators made some allowances for these explanations in the special unemployment bulletins published in 1931. In other words, these figures may or may not speak more to the accuracy of unemployment in Houston's African American community in the early 1930s when compared to other groups.[102]

Although perhaps somewhat misleading or conventional, these findings shed light on the dire situation for people of African descent. Already vulnerable to racism, seasonal workforce fluctuations, underemployment, and as undervalued jobholders, African Americans—especially men—lost firm economic footing with the coming of the Great Depression, for several reasons. Worker layoffs essentially exacerbated poverty and deprivation in the community. A chain reaction sometimes devastated family relationships, precipitating dislocation, family dysfunction, higher high school dropout rates, stress, depression, illness, and even death.[103]

Black business growth halted, forcing many to cut jobs, foreclose on property, and lose millions of dollars in capital. Blacks lost jobs within the African American community, as when the Grand United Order of Odd Fellows (GUOOF) and Progressive Order of Pilgrims, as well as several other fraternal-aid societies that often sold life, burial, and health insurance policies to its African American members, went into bankruptcy. The closing of these businesses had a far-reaching effect on the group. The Odd Fellows and Pilgrims, for example, owned office buildings in or near downtown and housed a number of professional offices as well as businesses. When they foreclosed on their property, people not only lost jobs and office space, but members also saw their policies lapse. Although perhaps difficult to prove, African Americans per capita potentially made up a larger proportion of all jobless residents in the 1930s. Consumer spending also dropped as individuals and families lost sustainable financial ground.[104]

Not surprisingly, employers laid off an excessive number of African Americans, often in an effort to provide jobs for other unemployed groups. In an effort to make do, unemployable Whites, normally sustainable as wage earners, took jobs that normally went to men and women of color. As aforementioned, some preferred Latinos to Afro-Americans. Hispanics, however, had their own troubles in the 1930s—unemployment, underemployment, deportation and repatriation schemes, and a noticeable rift between Mexican nationals and Mexican Americans.[105]

Blacks, almost 22 percent of the city's residents in 1930, saw mounting devastation. The general causes of the Depression—declining farm profits and rising debt, overproduction of American goods, speculation and margin buying in the stock market, small business decay, weakened consumer confidence, constant layoffs, and bank failures—destroyed segments of the African American economy, especially businesses. African Americans thus lost crucial jobs in their own communities, even in the last half of the 1930s. Etta Caffey, a widow, left California and moved to Houston with her small son in the early 1920s. With a college education, Caffey secured a job with the GUOOF, a fraternal-aid society that sold life, burial, and health insurance policies to its African American members. She worked at the company for nearly a decade as a typist, earning $63 a month. Caffey's salary allowed her son, John, to complete high school in the late 1930s.[106]

Unfortunately, the family soon experienced hard times in the wake of the Great Depression. The single mother lost her job in 1937 or 1938, in the midst of what economists called a recession that followed a brief period of New Deal economic recovery in the mid-1930s; by this time, the Depression had already taken a toll on African American businesses. Like many establishments, the Odd Fellows relied on its member-client bases to retain policies. The loss of steady employment, however, made it difficult for African Americans to continue many of their affiliations; this loss of consumer spending made it impossible for small businesses to survive. The depression therefore forced the GUOOF into bankruptcy. Racial divisions in labor kept Caffey out of the clerical positions she deemed qualified to have. For the remainder of the 1930s, she worked as a cafeteria helper at a Houston school. Her income dropped from $63 a month to $5 a month. This greatly compromised her integrity and financial security. By the end of the decade, Etta Caffey faced severe underemployment, only earning one-twelfth of her salary at the Odd Fellows. The Great Depression essentially retarded African American mobility.[107]

Private and public relief efforts, regrettably, did little to improve conditions for Houston African Americans before the creation of the New Deal. The history of social services in the city possibly explains the failure of volunteerism for African Americans prior to the New Deal. Progressives in 1904 orchestrated a carnival to raise funds for their charitable work, ultimately forming United Charities, a formal philanthropic group. In 1915, these efforts helped chart the Houston Foundation (currently United Way), a permanent philanthropic agency that administered funds to local social welfare groups and charities.[108]

The next year the city created the Social Service Bureau (SSB), which facilitated the creation of varied programs, from public health and childcare to welfare and relief. Social welfare advocates expanded these efforts. In the 1920s, prior to the Great Depression, the Houston Community Chest (HCC), a philanthropic group comprising thirty-three separate agencies, distributed monetary resources to Houston-area charities. In 1928, the group administered almost $400,000 to local charities, with tens of thousands going to organizations either serving all Houstonians, regardless of race, or African Americans exclusively. Racial segregation dictated what programs would aid people of African descent, with most ignoring the group completely. Almost 22 percent of the city's population in 1930, Blacks sometimes received aid at proportionate levels, although this only sustained some very briefly as unemployment rose to nearly 50 percent among the group.[109]

Although African Americans in 1931 made up a large bulk of those unemployed, they constituted only a small fraction of those who received private and public relief at the local level. The SSB provided the most help for African Americans. Unfortunately, in 1929, African Americans constituted only 17 percent of the bureau's Family Department cases, whereas 22 percent of the agency's aid went to Afro-Americans. The agency's small annual budget of $37,000 simply could not meet the needs of the African American population and entire city together. The agency also dispensed aid first to White families and tended to the needs of others last. Other HCC agencies ignored the perilous and depressed condition of poor African Americans altogether.[110]

To make matters worse, city officials did very little to aid Afro-Americans. In 1930, Mayor Walter E. Montieth's Houston Unemployment Aid Committee remarked that African Americans could alleviate their burden by returning to the country in the summer months to work on the cotton farms. Social Service Bureau Chief Walter W. Whitson, in 1931, commented that in his estimation White unemployment topped that of African Americans at a ratio of four to one. When criticized by the *Informer* and social worker Jesse Thomas, Whitson fired back by telling National Urban League (NUL) officials in New York that Afro-Americans' economic status had improved significantly by March of 1931. By April and May of the same year, according to Whitson, most of those out of work had been White. He argued that people of color found jobs as cotton pickers outside Houston and as compress laborers and landscapers. The bureau, according to historian Randy Sparks, discriminated against African Americans with impunity, refusing to serve them at commissaries and food pantries.[111]

Local social service efforts contrasted sharply with African American relief. Established residents and recent migrants in the community aided one another. Service sororities such as ZPB and AKA regularly raised money for the disabled and elderly, especially during the cold winter months. Organizations and institutions regularly helped others in need through fundraisers, direct self-help intervention, scholarships, and programs designed to assist those in need. Organizations such as the International Longshoreman's Association, churches, women's clubs, and fraternal societies raised thousands of dollars for the Community Chest. Ironically, these groups faithfully donated to the Community Chest even when the charity agency blatantly discriminated against people of color. Women's groups raised money, cooked for neighborhood soup kitchens or shelters, and offered further aid. Many welfare recipients regularly received food and donations from neighborhood churches. Church caregivers often faced harsh circumstances themselves, such as spousal layoffs or family illnesses. People aided one another until other solutions came to the forefront.[112]

One of the city's most ardent givers, Rev. L. H. Simpson of a Fifth Ward Baptist church, would give tens of thousands of dollars to members of his community until his death in 1967. Born in the East Texas town of Calvert in 1884, a young Rev. Simpson graduated from Conroe Industrial and Normal School in the early 1900s, before completing his doctorate work in seminary decades later. In the 1920s, he relocated once more, moving to Houston in the late 1920s, becoming pastor of Pleasant Hill Baptist Church in 1928.[113]

Over the next several years, the city's African American religious community would take notice of the young pastor, particularly during the Great Depression. During the difficult 1930s, Rev. Simpson reached out to others. Pastor L. H. Simpson and the Pleasant Hill Baptist Church in Fifth Ward, for example, every year raised hundreds of dollars for the city's chief charity agency, the Community Chest (fig. 46). He also gave thousands of dollars to colleges. In later years, Simpson headed the local NAACP branch, unsuccessfully ran for the Houston City Council, and chaired the Colored Baptist Minister's Association for thirty years. A caring soul, he also opened a nursing home in Walker County, near Huntsville. Simpson also gave to other local charities, UNCF, regional colleges such as Mary Allen Seminary, Prairie View College, and HCN. Thousands

FIGURE 46. One of the city's most ardent givers, Rev. L. H. Simpson (first row, seated second from the left), pastor of Pleasant Hill Baptist Church in Fifth Ward, would give tens of thousands of dollars to members of his community until his death in 1967. The pastor, a native of Calvert, Texas, graduated from Conroe College in the 1900s. He moved to Houston in the 1920s and became pastor in 1928. At a time when entrenched racism marginalized African Americans in need of assistance during the Great Depression, Rev. Lee Haywood Simpson chose to find ways to provide resources to church members, Fifth Ward residents as well as resident African Americans. Even while suffering themselves, church members still found ways to inspire others. Each year the church raised hundreds of dollars for the city's chief charity agency, the Community Chest. At the same time, Rev. Simpson donated thousands of dollars to colleges. In later years, Simpson headed the local NAACP branch, unsuccessfully ran for the Houston City Council, and chaired the Colored Baptist Minister's Association for thirty years. He also opened a nursing home for seniors in Walker County. The quintessential philanthropist and civic leader, even as a member of the NAACP, chose not to browbeat Whites. Instead, in his sermons and speeches, he emphasized those commonalities that made all Houstonians extraordinary. Even while taking a quasi-accommodating tone from time to time, as well as encouraging African American financial independence, he nevertheless supported the integration of the races. *(Courtesy Houston Metropolitan Research Center, Houston Public Library, Houston, Texas,* MSS 0239-0003*)*

benefited from his wisdom, generosity, and peaceful demeanor toward the city's often strained race relations.[114]

Community groups as well as overburdened local agencies received needed assistance from the federal government, beginning with the Hoover Administration in 1932. President Herbert Hoover, though deeply concerned about the economy's devastation on the poor, endorsed volunteerism, the idea that private philanthropy, not government intervention, had a responsibility to provide for the unemployed and destitute. He also endorsed balanced budgets over deficit spending, and he felt that by discouraging massive layoffs and wage shrinkages within the private sector, the government could encourage consumer spending. Ultimately, in 1932, as the economy continued to deteriorate, Congress and President Hoover endorsed direct relief. Hoover and Congress's relief initiatives, the Emergency Committee for Employment, the Emergency Committee for Unemployment, and the Federal Reconstruction Finance Corporation, assisted several million people through direct relief, public works projects, and loans to businesses and states, in an attempt to slow down layoffs, and provided temporary relief to thousands of Houstonians; however, the programs simply did not go far enough. The relief measures especially failed to reach African Americans, some of the president's most loyal supporters.[115]

Fortunately, for Afro-Americans, Hoover's successor had a different perspective. President Franklin Roosevelt's New Deal programs, which alleviated economic distress for some Houston African Americans, did much more relatively quickly. By mid-1933, federal dollars began pouring into the city. The paltry social service budgets of city and private agencies—perhaps several hundred thousand dollars annually—received as much as $6,000,000 from the state and federal governments over the next several years (federal monies and matching state social service funds). President Roosevelt modeled his massive stimulus program after similar endeavors implemented in New York while governor, projects that were born out of New York welfare initiatives and the Hoover Administration, as well as projects developed by senior staffers, commonly known as the Brains Trust. Soon his administration began implementing his historic New Deal programs for the unemployed.[116]

Blacks, like other Americans, responded favorably to the New Deal. African Americans—Houstonians as well as Americans as a whole—not only embraced Roosevelt's New Deal. Blacks, overwhelmingly Republicans in 1932, permanently changed their party affiliation. The country witnessed the widespread political migration of African Americans into the Democratic Party by 1936. Motivated by New Deal programs that directly affected their families and communities, African Americans, including Houstonians, abandoned the Republican Party.[117]

Federal aid usually came in two forms—direct relief checks and work programs. Direct relief checks usually came to the Harris County Social Service or Houston welfare offices by way of the Texas State Department of Welfare, which dispensed funds to county welfare agencies, while the Texas welfare department oversaw public works. Relief, undoubtedly, brought some comfort to Houston's ailing community.[118]

Black Texans saw a modicum of improvement due to New Deal programs. In the state, for example, the number of African Americans receiving aid on some occasions exceeded the proportion of the race in the state. Blacks, according to historian William Brophy, comprised the only Texas group in which the vast majority of females on relief—based on percentages—exceeded the proportion of males. This probably stemmed from the higher number of Afro-American single mothers as household heads who qualified for relief, compared to other groups. Of the estimated eighty-five thousand recipients of New Deal and state welfare, public works, long-term benefits, African Americans comprised perhaps as many as one-third or twenty-five thousand of this number. Thus, the New Deal did assist African Americans, even if for brief periods of time.[119]

Economically distressed Houston Afro-Americans benefited from federal relief in numerous ways. First, the federal government pumped money into local redress projects. Funded with federal dollars, the Harris County Board of Welfare and Employment opened nutrition and diet centers at three Houston locations. With the assistance of Afro-American and European American physicians, the centers provided free exams and food for babies and preschool-aged children. Next, New Deal public works programs, through the newly formed TDW, temporarily put to work thousands of unemployed men and women of African descent, thus, cutting unemployment, at least for a while, in the city. The overwhelming majority of African American relief recipients garnered assistance through New Deal programs like the FERA, National Recovery Administration (NRA), Civilian Conservation Corps (CCC), National Youth Administration (NYA), Civil Works Administration (CWA), and Works Progress Administration (WPA). Some of those receiving assistance had only recently left their small town and rural surroundings for Houston in search of help.[120]

Kile Wood moved his family to Houston in October 1937. A native of New Waverly, a small community fifty-five miles north of Houston, Wood for years farmed the land of George Peacock. The Great Depression of the 1930s, however, accelerated an agricultural revolution—one that began decades earlier and prompted by natural disasters, plunging agricultural prices, and increased global competition—in Texas and across the South—pushed millions of small farm owners, cash tenants, and croppers like Wood off the land. As a result, thousands of eastern Texas and Louisiana Black farm families trekked to urban industrial centers like Houston, Dallas, and Beaumont to rebuild their lives. Often, financial devastation came with other heartbreak. Wood, only months earlier, suffered the loss of his wife. The widower moved his family to a labor camp right outside of Houston and briefly secured employment at the Hines Realty Company. Wood and his eldest sons cut pulpwood for the business. Within weeks, however, the company laid off the Woods men. Unemployed with six children, Kile followed the suggestion of a White neighbor and applied for work with the WPA. Fortunately for the father, government assistance tided the family over for a period of time. In the midst of the Great Depression tragedy, recent migrants often readily received government relief in Houston.[121]

Even while New Deal programs hired and employed large numbers of out-of-work teens; young adults; and middle-aged, out-of-work African American adults, local agencies regularly discriminated against African Americans. According to historian Randy Sparks, the NRA mostly hurt people of African descent. The NRA proposed to solve the problem of economic instability by addressing competition, overproduction, price fluctuations, and labor-management squabbles. NRA boards were composed of business interests, labor leaders, and government officials. Aside from developing codes of fair competition to limit production, assigning quotas among producers, and imposing strict price guidelines, the NRA guaranteed laborers minimum wages, maximum working hours, and collective bargaining. Unfortunately, according to Sparks, the agency's embrace of unions curtailed African American's access to jobs. By 1935, federal support for closed shop unions allowed for sabotaging African Americans' employment by union locals and employers. In responding to the agency's wage regulations, some Houston businesspeople fired their Afro-American personnel and replaced them with Whites. The process of Black displacement happened continuously during the 1930s.[122]

Other agencies helped and hurt African Americans. The CCC employed young men between the ages of eighteen and twenty-five, males who built fire towers, stocked depleted streams with water, planted saplings, constructed monuments, and reforested historic battlefields like the San Jacinto Battleground. In the early 1930s, many local CCC offices banned

African Americans from registering. Houston ultimately formed specific registration sites for men of African descent. By 1935, three hundred African American Texas males participated in the program. Blacks who participated in the CCC, however, worked in segregated branches like the Walker County site near Huntsville. Hardly surprising, the CCC and all New Deal programs in the South conformed to the dictates of White supremacy and segregated all work and relief programs.[123]

Like the CCC, the CWA and NYA aided young people, even while discriminating. Nearly one thousand African American CWA laborers, mostly men, in Houston made forty cents an hour, five hours a day, six days a week building roads, privies, playgrounds, and schools. Other programs helped both males and females. Vivian Hubbard (Seals), the daughter of Independence Heights politician and East Texas migrant Oliphant Hubbard, worked for the NYA as an assistant in the registrar's office of HCN. The job put her through school in the 1930s, even though her wages differed from that of White students attending and working at the University of Houston and Rice Institute in 1934.[124]

Sometimes individuals employed with the NYA used their training to secure better employment opportunities in Houston. In doing so, these African American workers—skilled and unskilled—utilized conciliatory protest strategies in their daily battles with bigotry. Born in 1918 in the East Texas town of Huntsville, James Otis "Pap" Baker, a college junior, left Prairie View College in the late 1930s. His father, Jesse Baker, an aging Walker County landholder, could no longer assist him with his tuition. When the Houston Shipbuilding Company hired "Pap" Baker as a skilled artisan in 1940, he felt a sense of both relief and obligation.[125]

An upperclassman at Prairie View College, he dropped out of college in 1938 to take a position at the National Youth Administration's (NYA) Negro Division in Texas. Soon he headed the Northeast Texas office's African American division.[126] He eventually left the agency and moved to Houston, where he took a position at the Houston Shipbuilding Company two years later in order to earn higher wages; provide for his ailing parents in nearby Huntsville; and, of course, live in the big city. Unfortunately, Whites and Blacks at the new firm rejected Baker. Whites, because of his skills as a master welder, discredited and resented him; and older Blacks, because of his higher earnings, youth, good looks, superior skills, confident personality, and red Studebaker, enviously dubbed him a "sellout." Heated arguments, fights, and accusations motivated supervisors to move him to a separate building away from both Black and White coworkers. Only after the United States Navy drafted the young man in 1942 did Baker see an end to his nonstop harassment on the job. After the war, he moved to Los Angeles. Recent migrant Baker remained, nevertheless, determined to do his best as a first-rate welder. Accommodatingly, he looked inward, smiled at his envious peers, and only fought back with his fists when attacked.[127]

The WPA put people to work as well. The WPA's huge employment program, created in 1935 for working people and the educated alike, hired many African Americans. Wiley College alumna Lullelia Harrison, the daughter of Texas and Louisiana migrants, and a wife and mother of two, secured a teaching post with the WPA in Dayton, Texas, her mother's hometown. She taught at the African American schoolhouse, dividing her time between Dayton and Houston, where her husband found work at Southern Pacific Railroad as a redcap baggage handler and at the Warwick Hotel as a cook. The Harrisons only relocated to Houston in 1934, after spending two years in Chicago, where Lullelia could not find permanent work as an educator. They represented a small but influential group of college-educated, middle-class African Americans who returned to the city, usually in the 1930s and 1940s, after spending time away working or attending school out of state. Although some returned to Houston to find stable employment opportunities, others, like Lullelia Harrison, found stable employment and longed to return to family, friends, and Texas, despite the discrimination they routinely encountered.[128]

The number of Texas Afro-Americans employed by the WPA, at nearly 16 percent, exceeded the total state population of 14 percent. The WPA employed Afro-Americans like Harrison in a number of capacities, for example, building or renovating hospitals, schools, playgrounds, and airport fields. The WPA also sponsored a number of educational programs: health care, home nursing, literacy, adult education, and home demonstration classes. Others, like high school graduate and Galveston native Raynola Thomas, participated in academic and leadership development classes, photojournalism tasks, theatrical productions, artistic and decorative programs, research assignments, and writing projects like the oral history slave narratives.[129]

Randy Sparks, nevertheless, points out the deficiencies of the otherwise laudable WPA. For people of color, the number of participants never matched the number of African Americans in need. Furthermore, personal vendettas, misunderstandings, or carelessness could prevent African American workers from receiving pay. Finally, by 1936, the president, concerned about growing public expenses, ordered massive WPA layoffs, which adversely affected African Americans.[130]

Table 7 suggests that unemployed African Americans still sought employment in the wake of racism and economic despondency. African Americans also sought alternative measures in the midst of unemployment and poverty. The *Houston Informer* observed that people of color's increased interest in communism in the early 1930s stemmed from the fact that they searched for answers to alleviate their financial burdens. The Communist Party, according to the *Houston Informer*, would keep attracting a large body of African American followers because neither steady employment nor social justice seemed forthcoming.[131]

Full-time industrial workers saw an ounce of relief. One of the most far-reaching achievements of the New Deal era, with respect to African Americans, was the passage of the Wagner Act in 1935. The National Labor Relations Act (Wagner Act) built on the NRA Section 7a, guaranteeing laborers' right to bargain through the National Labor Relations Board (NLRB), which had power to prohibit labor practices deemed unfair to workers, determine bargaining units, and conduct worker elections. Most importantly for Afro-Americans, the act encouraged unprecedented labor organizing, especially among unskilled workers. In 1936, a conglomerate of workers' unions formed the Congress of Industrial Organizations (CIO) and developed a heavy recruitment campaign to organize Afro-American workers.[132]

In Houston, African American workers joined unions for a host of reasons. Some sought better pay. Others wanted economic parity with White peers. Most demanded self-respect. Blacks wanted something else as well. In time, these efforts effectively laid the groundwork for the major community-building strategies and the modern Civil Rights Movement among African Americans of the World War II and postwar eras. In Houston, thousands of African Americans, from railroaders, steelworkers, and oil refinery laborers to teamsters, theatrical artists, musicians, and mechanics, joined unions in the 1930s and 1940s to transform their workforces, communities, and their own lives. Members of the ILA, active in union organizing since the 1910s, even joined forces with their White peers in an attempt to negotiate wage increases. Sometimes racial factionalism ultimately broke up the efforts, although at times union efforts propelled victory for all workers.[133]

Nowhere is this plainer than among railroaders. Some thirty thousand African Americans worked in the railroad industry at the time of World War I, the height of railroading in America. In Houston, nearly one thousand African Americans worked in the industry in 1940. Blacks comprised one-third of all skilled railroaders in the city, hiring on as common switchmen, firemen, and brakemen. They represented a sizable majority of the city's railroad service workers as well, mostly serving as coach cleaners, dining car servers, cooks, porters, and redcaps. Many relied on temporary work as construction crew and repairmen. Mostly unskilled and nonunion, African Americans increasingly saw union organizing as a legitimate form of protest.[134]

Black railroaders utilized varying approaches in an effort to advance their cause of financial parity and respect. Service workers adopted the race-class trade union approach of A. Phillip Randolph. Randolph's Brotherhood of Sleeping Car Porters, founded in 1925, secured voting rights under the National Mediation Board in 1935, along with a bona fide contract with the Pullman Company for its eight thousand members in 1937, the first African American union to do so. Ishmael Flory and the Joint Council of Dining Car Employees, formed in 1937, followed suit; representing nine thousand employees, it organized fifty different contracts for Afro-American laborers. Organized by Willard Townsend, a third group, the International Brotherhood of Redcaps (later the United Transport Service Employees of America), formed in 1937, also secured contracts for its four thousand workers. Ultimately, these railroad trade unionists integrated their approach with mainstream and radical civil-rights organizations like the NAACP, NUL, and National Negro Congress. They established, according to scholar Eric Arnesen, a "New Crowd" activist approach that fused varying protest perspectives and set the stage for the postwar modern movement for civil rights.[135]

New Caney migrant Luther Stullivan and former San Antonio resident Judson Robinson Sr. helped form an International Brotherhood of Red Caps (IBRC) local in 1940 for African American redcaps at SP's downtown station. A return migrant from New Caney and nephew of railroader Tillie Stullivan, Luther Stullivan found permanent work in Houston in 1934 after a family friend put in a good word for him at SP. Earning just tips for three years, Stullivan, Robinson, and other redcaps finally secured union recognition in 1937, as an affiliate of the IBRC, which changed into the UTSEA in 1940. In addition, the company paid redcaps $20 weekly, a decision that prompted activist Luther Stullivan to purchase his first home in Fifth Ward. Stullivan became the organization's Houston president in 1940, as the head of Local 804, and combined forces with the NAACP to broaden the attack on racial segregation. Robinson and Stullivan often waged war with their employer on behalf of Blacks. Whites, of course, only fought back. The White man, according to Stullivan, "[j]ust figure you don't have no rights as far as he was concerned—the law don't mean nothing as far as you are concerned."[136]

Interestingly, skilled African American railroaders took a contradictory approach. Organizations like the Texas-based Association of Colored Trainmen and Locomotive Firemen (ACT), founded during World War I in Kingsville, Texas, formed independently of the CIO in the 1930s and often joined forces with White affiliates who were given the task of representing segregated African American unions as well as Whites. Often these White affiliates retained close ties with employer unions that also ignored the chief concerns of skilled craft workers of color. In both instances, African Americans fared poorly as White unionists and employers practiced discrimination. In the 1930s, Afro-American craftsmen in Houston and elsewhere formed the International Association of Railroad Employees (IARE) and remained outside the mainstream African American civil-rights–unionist perspective of Randolph, Stullivan, and others. Business owner, newspaperman, and Tennessee migrant C. W. Rice served as the chief spokesperson for independent African American unionists who opposed the CIO, believing the labor giant rarely acted in the best interests of African Americans. Still World War II, skilled railroaders would successfully rely on the civil-rights model of the NAACP and take their oppressors to court, witnessing huge victories for African American railroaders. Victories, however, did not put an end to lawful workplace racism, which only ceased in the wake of massive African American resistance to discrimination during the modern Civil Rights Movement.[137]

Nevertheless, for the time being, wage earners of color, as well as others desiring relief in the 1930s, had to come to terms with the real limits of local unionization efforts, the CIO, NLRA, and the New Deal. Although the New Deal in tangible terms aided a large body of African Americans in Houston, the government program did little to improve the overall conditions of African Americans, for whom unemployment remained high.[138] Expressing frustration at African Americans' unabashed loyalty to Roosevelt, a character in the novel *Lonely Crusade* cried, "Roosevelt! Roosevelt!

All He ever done for the nigger was to put him on relief. . . . How he done it I do not know—starve you niggers and make you love 'im [him]."[139]

Regrettably, Roosevelt and his administration consistently yielded to racism. Black gains monetarily were met with discrimination in New Deal agencies—pay differentials, inaccessibility to skilled jobs, abrupt layoffs, agency support of racist organizations that purposely blocked Black progress, poor treatment by relief workers, and complete exclusion. This and countless examples of willful neglect, discrimination, and insensitivity typified the period. Moreover, the administration refused to combat racism for fear of losing White southern political support.[140]

Nevertheless, New Deal programs encouraged internal migrations into the city, especially in the latter half of the 1930s. Cato and Hattie McKenzie moved to Houston in 1937 from Bellville, Texas, in Austin County, just west of the city. A native of nearby Waller County, Cato McKenzie toiled as a farm tenant for most of his life. His wife of twenty-one years, Hattie Sylvester McKenzie of Austin County, labored on the farm alongside her husband and raised the couple's children. They worked hard in the fields, growing cotton, corn, and legumes. Sharecropping served as a means to a crucial end, of course, because the McKenzies dreamed of owning the land they farmed. Unfortunately, they never reached this milestone. Like many African American sharecroppers in the years that followed World War I, they found it all but impossible to make ends meet. Declining revenues in a shrinking world market beset Texas cotton farmers—owners and tenants alike—by 1920. Revolving debt and the crop lien system also wreaked havoc on African American farmers like the McKenzies. The situation only worsened in the 1930s, as the value of Texas farms fell from $3.6 billion to $2.6 billion by 1940. African American sharecroppers in Texas, on average, rarely earned enough to sustain a family.[141]

Cotton farmers especially faced uncertainty as numerous factors exacerbated the crisis. Soil depletion as well as falling cotton prices worsened the cycle of desperation on Texas cotton farms. Government programs did not help matters. AAA allotment programs, for example, inadvertently dislocated African American tenants. In an attempt to raise cotton prices to pre-1920 parity levels, the AAA awarded acreage reduction contracts to farm owners. Although farmers saw the first steady profits in more than a decade and were expected to share some of their proceeds with tenants, many instead supplanted their tenant farmers and sharecroppers with Mexican migratory laborers. Growing reliance on migratory farm labor, along with mechanization, displaced tens of thousands of African American tenants in Texas, including the McKenzies. The number of Afro-American tenants in Texas dwindled from 50,941 to 23,878 between 1935 and 1945.[142]

Without formal education, Cato and Hattie McKenzie had few choices outside agriculture and baseline employment prospects. Throughout the 1930s, Cato McKenzie toiled as a farm laborer in and around Austin County and as a short-stint menial worker for the Works Progress Administration (WPA). Temporary work in the country, however, could no longer sustain his family, which included a granddaughter by the late 1930s. As the cost of cotton dropped from eighteen cents to six cents per pound between 1929 and 1933, the McKenzies and other African Americans increasingly saw rural-to-urban migration as their only means of defense.[143]

Troubled and frustrated, Cato McKenzie moved his wife and granddaughter to the community of Third Ward in Houston. Fortunately, like twenty million other Americans, the McKenzies, at least for the time being, found both reliable work and public relief in the city. Cato worked a number of odd jobs as a common laborer, while Hattie labored in the home of White families as a domestic. When they did not work, they received public assistance. Due to the family's slightly improved financial status, the McKenzie's granddaughter, Lela Edwards, remained in school. The high school student did not have to worry about working part-time to supplant the family's income. Even in the midst of the Depression, Houston gave the family hope.[144]

The decision to uproot their family to a larger city involved for Cato and Hattie McKenzie planning, determination, and hope. Although temporary work relief programs in the country gave the struggling family some relief, they knew the city would offer them more stability and autonomy. Only a city with a growing, dispersed African American population and fledgling economy could provide the family with a promising new start. The McKenzies, like millions of others in the first half of the twentieth century, opted for improved social freedoms and economic prosperity in cities and urban centers throughout the United States. Even if troublesome reminders of poverty and racism remained for generations to come, migration to Houston changed lives.[145]

Even while out-migration to California and the Midwest grew as an option for African Americans, Houston, like many cities during the decade, witnessed more sustained growth in the last half of the 1930s, prompting perhaps the onset of the Second Great Migration. Historians have studied the growing migration streams into cities in the mid- to late 1930s, as Americans searched for jobs, monetary relief, and federal services.[146] These slow-to-steady influxes shed light on what historian Luther Adams calls the start of the Second Great Migration. Fueled by the sharp decline of farm tenancy and lured by federal programs in cities, internal migrants poured into Houston. In Texas, the number of Afro-American tenants declined from 50,941 in 1935 to 23,878 in 1945. The number of tenant farms in the state declined by 32 percent between 1930 and 1940. Historians have also looked more closely at the high death rates among African Americans residing in rural Texas and Louisiana communities that surrounded Houston, in an effort to expose another explanation for the exoduses of the next decade, when twenty thousand African Americans moved to Houston and eighty thousand left the state. The Second Great Migration of the World War II era, according to Adams, in many ways began with the rise of federal intervention into the economy in the 1930s.[147]

Between 1935 and 1940, an estimated 6,362 non-Whites relocated to Houston from the surrounding Texas countryside and nearby states, namely Louisiana, with 29 percent entering the city from contiguous states. These migrants made up the overwhelming majority of the estimated 8,414 migrants who moved to Houston in the 1930s. If correct, the data show that the bulk of the depression-decade internal migrants flocked to the city in the second half of the decade, compared to the first half of the 1930s. Once again, the city attracted a steady flow of fourth-wave newcomers, especially after the start of the First New Deal, which overshadowed the efforts of local charities and agencies. Even while problems—economic, racial, or otherwise—persisted within New Deal agencies, on the job, and customarily throughout the city, African Americans, from the educated to the uneducated, continued to support Roosevelt's New Deal. Their continued internal migrations to cities confirm this observation. Nevertheless, the New Deal, in quantitative terms, failed Black America. In truth, neither the New Deal nor local efforts eliminated racial injustice and economic contraction. For African Americans in Houston—both migrants and established residents—other remedies would have to bring relief and respite.[148]

Conclusion

In conclusion, between 1900 and 1941, the Houston workforce witnessed enormous change. The migration of farmers into the area expanded the Afro-American labor force, especially in the common labor and personal service divisions. The migration of farmers to Houston and into the wage-earning labor force led to the creation of a viable industrial urban working class. This working-class proletariat more assertively and effectively sought racial equality on the job.[149]

Whereas African American men increasingly moved into industries, women found employment primarily in White households as maids. African American women, in particular, increased the number of Afro-American workers in Houston at a time when women primarily worked in the household as homemakers. Black women and men experienced racism and had difficulty abandoning the lower level job market. Although their numbers represented a small portion of the middle-class job divisions, they did in fact find limited but sustaining work as ministers, educators, physicians, attorneys, and librarians. They also owned businesses that catered to the community in numerous ways. Nevertheless, Whites primarily occupied the skilled and white-collar positions.[150]

During the Depression, when African Americans experienced underemployment and unemployment at huge levels, White men's labor status remained relatively unchanged. The Great Depression stimulated continued migration of rural refugees from surrounding counties in Texas and Louisiana. These people sought jobs and relief. Black farmers also found some relief in the aggressive union organizing strategies of the 1930s. The CIO, especially, emphasized social equality and improved conditions for African Americans. This new unionized, proletariat workforce worked with its middle-class allies like C. W. Rice and Carter Wesley to eradicate racial discrimination on the job and in the community.[151]

Although Afro-Americans found themselves still searching for social empowerment by the close of the depression, they relied heavily on themselves and their neighbors for assistance and aid. Whether giving to needy people in a soup line, collecting food and clothing for church members, or debating the best alternatives for the working classes, African Americans, borrowing from their tradition of social networks first developed in the country, relied more on themselves for answers. The end of the 1930s did not see dramatic changes in the economy resulting from the federal government's relief efforts and public work projects, but World War II and the Second Great Migration would usher in profound changes for Houston's Afro-American residents and migrants alike. If the workplace and Great Depression substantiated one idea in the psyches of African Americans, it was that racism remained a visible opponent in the face of economic adversity and financial uncertainty. The determined exclusionist policies and actions of White industrialists, supervisors, and unionists confirmed that racism would not disappear. Nor would the incorrect perception of African American inferiority, laziness, and savagery disappear from the psyches of White Houstonians.[152]

Conclusion

New Beginnings, New Institutions, New Migrations

Born in Carthage, Texas, a small community in Panola County just south of Marshall, in 1891, Anna Johnson, the eldest of six children, lived a typical East Texas life as the daughter of African-descent wage earners. The family moved in 1904 to Galveston, where Anna, a domestic, met her future husband, Clarence A. Dupree of Plaquemine, Louisiana. Orphaned at age seven, Clarence worked odd jobs at Galveston hotels and barbershops. White customers cared for Dupree by providing him with shelter, food, and clothing, probably in exchange for rendered services. Anna and Clarence soon met, fell in love, and married in 1918.[1]

The newlyweds moved to Houston shortly thereafter, although Clarence was subsequently drafted into the US Army and served as a cook during the remaining months of World War I. After returning home, Clarence worked as a porter at the Bender Hotel; his bride worked as a beautician in a White beauty salon. Anna soon joined a more exclusive establishment in the city's River Oaks subdivision, securing a prosperous clientele among River Oaks and Montrose housewives. Although the two struggled during the Depression years, residing in Fourth Ward and living off Clarence Dupree's meager earnings, they managed to save $20,000.[2]

By the late 1930s, they invested their savings in real estate ventures that provided important services to the Afro-American community. They reopened the Pastime Theater on McKinley in Third Ward, built the Eldorado business center at Elgin and Dowling Street, right across from Emancipation Park in Third Ward, opened a pharmacy, men's apparel shop, paint store, and nightclub. The Eldorado Ballroom for decades would host parties, dances, and social events. Dowling, the Lennox Avenue of Houston's African American Third Ward community, was an intelligent choice for the business center, which also made the Duprees a good deal of money.[3]

The Duprees made money and built lasting institutions. In the early 1940s, they opened the Negro Child Center on Solo Street in Fifth Ward, an orphanage for Black youths (fig. 47). Having lived as an orphan, Clarence realized the importance of a first-class orphanage in the community for African American children. During World War II and after the war, Anna also opened the Eliza Johnson Home for the Negro Aged at 10010 Cullen Boulevard. The facility, named for Anna's late mother, was home to ninety seniors. The community builders also donated $11,000 to Houston College for Negroes Negro Child Center and the construction of the Thorton M. Fairchild Building. They contributed annually to the United Negro College Fund (UNCF); formed the first Little League Baseball team for Black children; raised money for Camp Robinhood, the first Girl Scout Camp in the state for African American girls; and encouraged others to donate money and land for other causes, including the South Central YMCA and the St. Luke Episcopal Church, both on Wheeler Avenue near Texas University for Negroes.[4]

The wealthy Duprees formed a bridge between the poor and middle class. They never forgot where they came from and bettered the lives of thousands of African American college students, seniors, club members, youths, and church members, as well as the indigent. Without question, their activism came in the form of migration and community agency. Their protests rarely provoked criticism among Whites. Nor did they threaten their traditional White clientele by publicly denouncing Jim Crow segregation, although near the end of her life, Anna Dupree did speak out against regular injustices faced by Blacks. Nevertheless, they utilized segregation as a beneficial ploy to secure land, businesses, needed services for African Americans, and racial autonomy through the pocketbook and self-help programs. The Great Migrations of Clarence and Anna Dupree into the city not only shaped their destiny, but also inspired thousands.[5]

Between 1900 and 1941, an estimated thirty-two thousand Afro-Americans migrated to Houston from surrounding rural and small-town communities in Texas and Louisiana. Until now, their stories have largely gone untold. Interestingly, large numbers of African Americans remained in the South, deciding to refrain from interregional migration and instead invest in short-distance relocations to Houston from eastern Texas and Louisiana. Blacks emigrated from their hometowns and stepwise communities in search of opportunities.[6]

FIGURE 47. Anna and Clarence Dupree both came from impoverished backgrounds. Neither finished high school. Clarence spent a considerable amount of time on the streets in Galveston, living there as a child. Anna went to beauty school and soon developed a successful clientele among middle-class and upscale White women in Houston. Clarence worked as a porter at the Bender Hotel. During the difficult 1930s, the couple saved nearly every penny they earned. By the end of the decade, they had $20,000 to invest in real estate development. As both entered the world from meager means, they wanted to find ways to care for the poor, particularly children and the elderly. They opened the Anna Dupree Cottage of the Negro Child Care Center in Fifth Ward. They also invested in Texas State University for Negroes, UNCF, the South Central YMCA near TSUN, St. Luke's Episcopal Church, and the Girl Scouts, forming the first Girl Scout camp for African American girls in the Houston area. The couple also established the Eliza Johnson Home for the Negro Aged near Sunnyside. They remained committed to the idea of community building until their deaths, circa 1940. *(Courtesy Houston Metropolitan Research Center, Houston Public Library, Houston, Texas, Anna Dupree Collection, MSS 0110-0001)*

Four separate but similar migratory groups settled Houston between the turn of the century and the Japanese invasion of Pearl Harbor, the historic event that stimulated another migratory stream known to scholars as the Second Great Migration. Influenced by temporary migration patterns to nearby cities, towns, and rural manufacturing areas for work-related purposes, as well as by earlier nineteenth-century migratory streams of chattel slaves, freed people, and their descendents after the Civil War, migrants sought respite from socioeconomic travails, notably rural and small-town poverty. An estimated seven thousand five hundred newcomers poured into the city for jobs in the expanding labor market between 1900 and 1914, and another estimated one thousand individuals moved to Houston during World War I, from 1914 to 1918. Houston provided numerous jobs for migrants. Railroad expansion, the discovery of oil, the improvement of commercial transportation facilities (especially the newly expanded ship channel), the development of an oil refining industry, the abundance of inexpensive land, and the city's close proximity to the surrounding countryside attracted African Americans, Afro-Caribbeans, rural European Americans, European nationals, Mexican-descent immigrants, and Mexicans Americans to Houston.[7]

Continued migration immediately following World War I and into the next decade spurred a third migration. The city's economic boom of the 1920s particularly had an enormous impact on its population growth and the decline of the interior rural communities in eastern Texas and southern Louisiana, as an estimated fifteen thousand newcomers of African descent entered the Houston area.

Black internal migrants usually found entry-level, unskilled jobs, but, depending on their level of education and skills, occasionally found other options. Men worked as dockworkers, cotton compress workers, steel foundry laborers, store porters, sextons, teamsters, landscapers, construction laborers, railroad porters, railroad workers, and personal service employees to White families. These jobs allowed African American men to move into the permanent wage-earning class, with unskilled laborers constituting 70 percent of the African American male labor force between 1920 and 1930. A smaller percentage of men earned their living as artisans, technical professionals, and business owners. As more African Americans moved to the city, the number of professionals and retailers grew as their services became more vital to the segregated community.[8]

Black women, like men, played a primary role in the Houston workforce. Between 1920 and 1930, they comprised at least 35 percent of the Houston female workforce. During this time, they also comprised almost 40 percent of the entire African American labor force. African American men alone could not sustain their families on their incomes; they needed the assistance of their wives, daughters, and sisters. Black women primarily worked as domestics. However, a growing number held unskilled and semiskilled factory jobs as cotton picker workers at compresses, seamstresses in private homes, and laundry operators in laundries and dry cleaning establishments. Black women with college degrees generally found employment in

Houston's flourishing and segregated school district. Black women teachers outnumbered men by three to one. Black men, however, outnumbered African American females as administrators at an equal or higher ratio. Like the majority of workers, African American clerical and professional employees faced ongoing discrimination. For example, African American teachers and principals never enjoyed the salary levels of their White colleagues. Black educators earned 30 percent less than Whites. Although the Houston economy sustained both an African American workforce and migration, on-the-job discrimination continued.[9]

Families as well as individuals left their rural and small-town homes for other reasons also. Refugee families from southern Louisiana fled after unprecedented floods damaged the region's economy in 1927. An estimated ten thousand Afro-American Louisianans relocated to the Houston area. They mostly settled the community of Fifth Ward.[10]

Impoverished African Americans also fled social debasement and degradation on the farm and in the small town. African American farmers, like half of all White farmers and the majority of Mexican migratory workers, largely faced economic powerlessness, but their circumstances were rooted in a racist caste system. The social mechanisms that produced institutionalized racism—social-psychological subjugation, learning inequities, disfranchisement, legal segregation, violence, legal constraints in lending institutions, and job discrimination—prevented African Americans from finding economic fulfillment in rural eastern Texas and southern Louisiana. Although these problems existed in the city, increased social and economic freedoms challenged White supremacy in Houston, Dallas, and San Antonio. Therefore, migration to the Houston area offered people the promise of a better life. In truth, many—especially young people—preferred the North or West to even southern cities. They desired the chance at a better life free of Jim Crow subjugation in the rural and urban South. Still, Texans, in particular, decided to remain close to home, choosing nearby Houston to Chicago, Detroit, or Los Angeles, and keeping the channels of chain migration networks and community agency close by.[11]

Houston migrants used a sophisticated web of communication networks—also known as chain migration—in their search for jobs, churches, homes, schools, physicians, social clubs, and groceries. Family members and friends already in Houston provided most of this assistance. They offered shelter to migrant families until breadwinners could secure work and homes. Established residents also helped newcomers find jobs, and in some instances provided migrants with money, food, and clothing until they became economically self-sufficient, as did Trinity East Methodist Episcopal Church for the Rev. Wilbur Hayes family of East Texas in Third Ward. Sometimes husbands, like Oran Williams of Roans Prairie, migrated first to Houston, found permanent work, and then sent for their family after saving enough money to rent a house. Williams's wife took care of the remaining family business and boarded a train to Houston with her small children one year later. Once settled, migrants aided other newcomers seeking improvement. After migrating to Houston and investing in residential property, Lee Coleman rented inexpensive homes to newcomers in Third Ward. Migrants also employed other forms of chain migration networks, from newspapers, letter writing, recommendations from employers, and regular visits into the city for social purposes.[12]

Black Houstonians—migrants and established residents—also nurtured protest initiatives in the wake of lingering racism. To the disappointment of many, racism followed them to the city. Perhaps because of their growing economic clout, maybe due to their larger segregated communities that shielded them from perpetual discrimination, or due in part to the "New Negro" sociopolitical ideology of the post–World War I years, African-descent people found ways to circumvent their fears and stand up to racists. They opened institutions and organizations that fostered self-imposed community-building efforts; as well, migrants and established residents increasingly formed organizations like the NAACP and Third Ward Civic Club that sought more confrontational ways to halt racial exclusion, even while generally remaining deferential to Whites.[13]

Regrettably, the Great Depression eroded the minor political and economic gains made by Houston African Americans in the 1920s. Usually the "last hired," African Americans became the "first fired" when company layoffs increased in the wake of the economic calamity. Moreover, they faced growing competition for menial work from Whites and Mexicans, although Black women sometimes saw their status in the family improved as they became the only individuals bringing home paychecks. Out-of-work men often returned to rural areas to work as temporary farm laborers during the harvest season. Already hit hard by the economic crisis, African American communities continued to witness an influx of down-and-out tenants from the country. The fourth migratory group studied in this work traveled to the city in the 1930s. During the depressed 1930s, an estimated nine thousand African Americans moved to Houston, with most moving to the city between 1935 and 1940 for jobs and relief. For this reason, a growing number of scholars have begun to place the start of the Second Great Migration in the 1930s, when New Deal programs gave people of color, as well as other Americans, hope. Unfortunately, New Deal programs failed to reach the majority of those in need. High levels of unemployment and underemployment devastated African American families as late as 1940.[14]

World War II, The Second Great Migration, Civil Rights, and The New Great Migrations

Only with the coming of World War II did African Americans find some solace. World War II doubled the rate of migrants to Houston; it also propelled the decline of the rural interior. In 1940, 55 percent of Texas African Americans resided on farms; in 1950, 37 percent remained there. While eighty thousand two hundred African Americans left Texas between 1940 and 1950, twenty thousand moved to the Houston area during the war. The proliferation of industrial firms heightened the labor demand in the area. Black males secured employment in oil refineries, munitions plants, shipyards, railroads, cotton compresses, steel factories, and longshoremen businesses. An estimated ten thousand migrant men and women entered the Houston workforce in the 1940s. Many, like Desso Douglass of Onalaska in Polk County, moved into the industrial job sector for the first time upon arriving in the city. Others migrated to Houston before World War II but only secured industrial work in the 1940s. These industrial laborers comprised almost 70 percent of the African American male workforce during World War II. The proletarianization of African American workers fundamentally changed their lives. For many African American males, the war fostered pride and hope: they once again took the helm as the primary economic providers in their households. African American women, nonetheless, made significant gains in the workplace as well. Many remained in the domestic arena but demanded better wages and treatment. Others left the household workforce and moved into the industrial and institution service arena. Black working-class families, thereby increased their standard of living and improved their financial well-being. World War II thus ended the Depression and propelled, once again, heavy migration streams into the city.[15]

Desso Douglass of Onalaska, Texas, a rural community one hundred miles northeast of Houston, dreamed of attending college. Unfortunately, after completing high school in 1940 his father could not afford to send him to college. Devastated by his misfortunes, Douglass vowed to give his unborn children a college education. In 1941, he married Mary Durden, a childhood friend. Douglass, a sharecropper, often discussed migration to Houston with his wife. Mary had once lived in Houston and loved the city. In the late 1940s, the Douglasses left their rural farm and moved to the Bayou City. Douglass first worked for Southern Pacific Railroad and then at Sheffield Steel Company. He eventually bought a house in Kashmere Gardens and sent to college his five children, including former Texas Southern University President James O. Douglass.[16]

Black rural-to-urban migration to Houston during World War II helped transform the city into an international producer of petroleum goods and petrochemicals. According to a National Housing Agency report on the Houston area, between 1940 and 1945, approximately 18,500 African American women, children, and men from eastern Texas and Louisiana resettled in Houston. By 1950, the African American population reached 124,760, an increase of 34 percent since 1940. By 1950, the overwhelming majority of Texans lived in communities the Bureau of Census defined as urban. Much of this had to do with the wartime expansion that went on during World War II. Defense industries in the Houston-area provided job opportunities never before witnessed. Blacks like Desso Douglass moved into the industrial labor force. Men worked primarily as unskilled laborers for defense firms such as Hughes Tool Company, Shell Oil Company, Dickson Gun Plant, Brown Shipbuilding Company, Sheffield Steel Corporation, and Sinclair Refining Company. Farmers like Douglass moved into the wage earning class for the first time; their contemporaries, such as Lee Coleman and Oran Williams, left low-paying personal service and nonindustrial jobs and found unskilled work in Houston industries. Their wives and daughters found work in the domestic, personal service, institutional service, and war service employment sectors; these women also labored as dressmakers, seamstresses, semiskilled operatives, laundresses, and schoolteachers. As in the period before World War II, African American migrants mainly found bottom-rung, wage-earning positions in Houston. Unlike the pre-war era, however, they used their growing numbers in the military-industrial sector and the war itself as windows of opportunity to aggressively aim for racial equality. African Americans adopted the "Double V" slogan ("Democracy: Victory at Home, Victory Abroad") and recognized the urgent need for economic and social empowerment in their communities.[17]

World War II also promoted the growth of the African-descent middle class. Middle-class professionals, mainly teachers, saw increased employment opportunities as a result of the war. The rapid rise of the African American population opened new faculty positions at Houston-area schools. The expansion of the Afro-American economy also affected businesses throughout the community. As people of color acquired more money, they saw a rise in their disposable incomes. Increasingly, they ate out, tithed regularly in church, participated in community fundraisers, purchased cars, used automobile services more regularly, vacationed more often, and attended social gatherings. They also spent more money on fashionable clothes. Blacks could regularly afford to get teeth cleanings and physical examinations. As a way to build a stronger community, much of their money went to Black-owned businesses within the community.[18]

The booming African-descent economy during wartime did not propel the end of racial discrimination, of course. Continued job discrimination frustrated Afro-American workers during World War II. They continued to face wage differentials and problematic job classifications. White employers remained adamant about White employees receiving better wages, job titles, and job promotions. Hostile White workers made life difficult for those racial minorities who pursued change on the job. Black and White women too worked in tense environments. White women, like men, wanted to maintain segregation and Jim Crow debasement in the workplace, at all costs.[19]

Blacks, motivated by the *Pittsburgh Courier*'s "Double V" motto, sought assistance in their fight for equal justice and economic parity on the job. President Franklin Roosevelt formed the Committee on Fair Employment Practice—later named the Fair Employment Practice Committee (FEPC)—in June 1941, after threats of protest in Washington, DC, surfaced among the African American civil-rights community. The FEPC had the authority to investigate job discrimination in federally funded war defense agencies and unions. The agency could also recommend courses of action to the War Manpower Commission (WMC) and president. Unfortunately, from its inception the FEPC had limited power to implement real change. Nevertheless, African Americans sought the assistance of the FEPC, Afro-American elite, and local civil-rights groups in an effort to eradicate job discrimination. Common laborers especially reached out to members of the African American bourgeoisie—C. W. Rice, Lulu White,

Richard Randolph Grovey, and Carter Wesley—for encouragement and guidance. With the help of community leaders, workers made some gains. Significantly, Afro-American union membership increased in Houston. Wesley's support of the CIO especially pushed thousands of African American workers into the union movement. For Wesley and many others, a segregated union at the local level, practicing equality for all, represented a better alternative to nonunion activity and continued powerlessness. To African American workers' dismay, however, no real progress occurred in the way of overturning racism on the job, at least not until the postwar era in another generation.[20]

Black teachers, unlike working-class proletariat laborers, did win a monumental victory. For years, community leaders had challenged educators to demand pay equalization from the Houston Independent School District (HISD). Beginning in 1935, the NAACP sponsored a series of lawsuits on behalf of southern African American educators. Shortly after Dallas teachers secured pay equalization in January 1943, Houston teachers followed suit. The school board at first charged that most African American teachers did not possess equal qualifications as Whites and scored poorly on teacher examinations. Fearful of an expensive lawsuit, the board on April 12, 1943, gave in to the demands of African-descent teachers and principals. According to historian William H. Kellar, the victory represented the first decisive win for African Americans in their quest for racial equality in the city. The triumph especially boosted the credibility of women in the community, who represented the vast number of teachers, and paved the way for future civil-rights successes, including school desegregation. Teachers, mostly migrants themselves, and with the aid of other migrants and others, effectively achieved this decisive victory.[21]

In many ways, earlier periods of Afro-American protest nourished a new period of economic solidarity, racial pride, self-help, and a renewed commitment to challenging White supremacy. Relying less on White institutions, organizations, and the government, African Americans looked inward and found ways of improving their lives. At the same time, they expanded the "New Negro" creed of the post–World War I era and formulated new strategies for challenging racial discrimination. All these early efforts helped create the atmosphere of direct confrontation and massive resistance among people of color—migrants and their direct descendants.[22]

A second notable protest initiative was the dismantling of the all-White Democratic primary in 1944. In *Smith v. Allwright,* the Supreme Court declared the White primary unconstitutional. According to scholar Darlene Clark Hine, the decision represented the clear beginning of the modern Civil Rights Movement and gave legitimacy to a growing national coalition of social activists. Black migration—an important phenomenon that stimulated greater social and political awareness—fostered the first real impetus for this change.[23]

The Great Migration to Houston between 1900 and 1941 involved many overlapping facets of African American life such as emancipatory hope, rural and small-town poverty, racial injustice, temporary migrations, chain migration, urbanization, industrialization, proletarianization, cultural construction, agency, racial solidarity, political consciousness, and financial disaster. The Second Great Migration repeated these processes but also fueled new forms of community consciousness. World War II and the Second Great Migration both propelled the modern Civil Rights Movement and sparked unprecedented change within the African American community. Notably, the barriers to legal equity began disappearing as the last half of the twentieth century unfolded.[24]

Ironically, as the modern Civil Rights Movement reshaped southern society and ushered in the Black Power Movement, Houstonians, including recent migrants from the interior, along with their descendants, took a more cautious approach to racial justice. For example, immediately following the *Smith v. Allwright* decision, membership in the Houston NAACP, one of the largest in the United States in the early 1940s, declined, even as Houstonians continued to make national headlines and history. The *Sweatt v. Painter* decisions of 1947 and 1950 did propel continued activism and interest in African American protest, but only briefly. With few exceptions, 1960s Houston revealed a growing generational gap that separated the "New Negro" generation from the less patient, younger modern civil-rights/Black Power vanguard of the day (fig. 48). Whether due to apathy or patience, the "New Negro" generation in many ways mimicked the strategies of Emmett J. Scott of the previous generation.[25]

Younger Houstonians, certainly the beneficiaries of the "New Negro" protest initiatives, modeled their strategies after the modern Civil Rights Movement generation. The achievements of young college students like

FIGURE 48. In 1963, the Married Ladies Social, Art & Charity Club celebrated over sixty years of service to the Houston area. The organization, founded by Melissa Price and Mary Crawford in 1902, focused its efforts on charity and self-discovery. Having donated tens of thousands of dollars to the poor in Houston over the past sixty years, the women in this photograph, including individuals who had been with the group for over fifty years, knew their work had not ended. These women probably felt somewhat excited by the changes taking place within the African American community as a result of the Civil Rights movement, although a few perhaps thought the changes were happening too soon. *(Courtesy Houston Metropolitan Research Center, Houston Public Library, Houston, Texas, Covington Family Collection, MSS 0170-0034)*

Eldrewey Stearns, Naomi Ledé, Deloyd Parker, Lynne Eusan, Gene Locke, and others, in the orderly desegregation campaigns of downtown Houston and Third Ward in 1960, increasingly turned into violent tirades between young people and police, for example, the Texas State University (TSU) upheaval of 1967, with "New Negroes" and Martin King integrationists often siding with law enforcement officers. Of course, one of the chief preceptors of urban racial tensions during this time was the growing socioeconomic divide between the haves, who were mostly Whites, and the have-nots, who included the majority of the city's African Americans. Therefore, poverty as an indicator of wealth—or lack thereof—remained a hindrance for people of color. According to sociologist Robert Bullard, those communities with the largest concentration of African Americans remained among the poorest, most environmentally toxic, and less educated in the city.[26]

Ironically, the expansion of the Sunbelt economy, with Houston as the region's "golden buckle," precipitated continued migrations to the city. Blacks, along with other racial and ethnic groups, saw Houston as a popular destination in the last quarter of the twentieth century. Two interesting trends defined Houston's growth at this time. First, the New Great Migration has brought hundreds of thousands of internal migrants into the city from the disappearing hinterland and other parts of the country, especially the decaying Rust Belt.[27]

The author, for example, relocated to Texas in the mid-1980s, to attend Texas Southern University; after graduation, instead of returning to Detroit, she remained in Texas to attend graduate school. In fact, perhaps almost a quarter of TSU's fall semester 1984 freshman class comprised transplanted Midwesterners, Californians, and East Coasters from the North. Many of these individuals continue to live in the Houston area in the twenty-first century. The newest internal migrants, including return migrants, have found Houston attractive for numerous reasons. Young people moved to the city for college; urban professionals left the decaying industrial centers of the North for science and technology jobs. A good number of retirees have returned to the Houston area. Often, these retired groups include individuals whose parents or grandparents left Texas in the first half of the last century. According to historian Aferdteen Harrison, these migration schemes mirror those taken by their ancestors—only backwards.[28]

Newcomers have also left other parts of the world, namely Latin America, the Caribbean, Asia, and Africa. Several hundred thousand Afro-Latinos from Latin America, Caribbeans, and Africans, particularly West Africans and Ethiopians, have not only transformed Houston's economy but have fused with the larger African American community. They have intermarried American-born Blacks, sent children to American colleges, including HBCUs, and continue to enter the middle and upper-middle classes at a higher rate than US-born Afro-Americans. In fact, African immigrants are some of the most educated immigrants in the United States today. Therefore, the contributions of both recent internal migrants and immigrants of the African Diaspora to Houston's larger US-born African-descent community, as well as to the city's and region's social, cultural, and economic vitality, is significant.[29]

Scholars must widen their research net to determine the relationship between internal migration and community agency of the early

FIGURE 49. Thelma Scott Bryant (standing, far left) and dear friends celebrate her eighty-eighth birthday. Others include retired educator and local historian Willie Lee Gay (just right of Bryant); granddaughter of Rev. Jack Yates and retired educator Olee Yates McCullough (second from left); retired educator Lena Robinson (standing, far right); the daughter of Independence Heights second mayor, retired reading teacher, and local historian Vivian Hubbard Seals; an unidentified woman (sitting in the center); and retired educator Thelma Hainsworth Young. These women, all retired or former educators, had given so much to their beloved Houston, over the course of a century. *(Courtesy Houston Metropolitan Research Center, Houston Public Library, Houston, Texas, Thelma Scott and Ira Bryant Collection, MSS 0005-0002)*

twentieth century and the later historical developments that transpired after World War II. Historians must look more closely at the modern-day Civil Rights Movement as well as the New Great Migrations since 1970 to find commonality and divides (fig. 49). More importantly, any social science research that attempts to find solutions to lingering problems facing people of African descent—health challenges, poverty, drugs and crime, educational disparity, and structural racism—should excite historians and non-historians alike.[30]

NOTES

Preface

1. Bernadette Pruitt, "Challenging Whiteness and Celebrating Blackness: One Scholar's Journey," unpublished paper presented at the East Texas Historical Association, September 28, 2012, Nacogdoches, Texas.

2. Bertha Juanita Pruitt, December 8, 1984, Michigan Deaths, 1971–1996, Michigan Department of Vital and Health Records, Michigan Death Index, Lansing, Michigan, from Ancestry.com, http://search.ancestry.com/; Catherine Collins, telephone interview by Bernadette Pruitt, transcript, December 25, 2005, University Park, Illinois, in possession of the author; and Alice McPhereson, interview by Bernadette Pruitt, tape recording, April 16, 2009, Detroit, Michigan, in possession of the author.

3. "In Loving Memory of Bertha Pruitt," December 15, 1984, obituary; and Bertha Lively, Voter Registration List, Detroit, Michigan, May 30, 1940, in Voter Registration Lists, Public Record Filings, Historical Residential Records, and Other Household Database Listings, US Public Records Index, vol. 2, from Ancestry.com, http://search.ancestry.com/.

4. Gloria Ann Pruitt, high school diploma, Charles Chadsey High School, Detroit, Michigan, June 1, 1959; Malcolm Lively, diploma, Lewis Cass Technical High School, Detroit, Michigan, January 10, 1958; Gwendolyn Lively, diploma, Wilbur Wright High School, Detroit, Michigan, July 1, 1958; Catherine Collins, General Educational Development (GED) certificate, Thornton Community College, South Holland, Illinois, 1980; Malcolm Lively, interview by Bernadette Pruitt, tape recording, March 17, 1993, Detroit, Michigan, in possession of the author; and Bernadette Pruitt, diploma, Northwestern High School, Detroit, Michigan, June 6, 1984.

5. Clarence Edward Pruitt interviewed by Bernadette Pruitt, tape recording, Detroit, Michigan, August 23, 1999, in the possession of author; and "In Loving Memory of a Great Man: Clarence Edward Pruitt," obituary, January 6, 2001, Detroit, Michigan, in possession of the author.

6. Clarence Edward Pruitt interview; and Vera Hayden, telephone interview by Bernadette Pruitt, transcript, Meridian, Mississippi, December 25, 2010, in possession of the author.

7. Clarence Edward Pruitt interview; Vera Hayden interview; and Frank Pruitt,

telephone interview by Bernadette Pruitt, transcript, Detroit, Michigan, November 28, 2010, in possession of the author.

8. Family Reunion Booklet, "'A Family Is . . . One That Prays Together Stays Together': John and Lillian Stinson, "Stinson + Hicks Family Reunion, Detroit, Michigan, August 11–13, 2000," in possession of the author; Michael Shawn Stinson, interview by Bernadette Pruitt, transcript, July 10, 1996, Houston, Texas, in possession of the author; and Naomi Ledé, interview by Bernadette Pruitt, tape recording, Huntsville, Texas, February 1, 2003, in possession of the author. For thirty years, I have had close contact with a good number of my friends from college at Texas Southern University in Houston, Texas. During this period, I have been fortunate to meet my classmates' immediate and extended family members at barbeques, weddings, church services, graduations, and their homes during holiday celebrations continued these conversations on migration and kith/kin relationships. Our casual and intimate conversations about family, life, joy, sorrow, and society continue to this day.

9. This book not only builds on the work of scholars whose works precede mine but also continues my own work as a graduate student and professional historian. See Bernadette Pruitt, "The Urban Transformation of the MacGregor Area, 1950–1970" (master's thesis, Texas Southern University, 1991); Bernadette Pruitt, "'For the Advancement of the Race': African American Migration and Community Building in Houston, 1914–1945" (Ph.D. diss., University of Houston, 2001); Bernadette Pruitt, "In Search of Freedom: Black Migration to Houston, 1914–1945," *Houston Review of History and Culture* 3 (Fall 2005): 46–57, 85–86; and Bernadette Pruitt, "'For the Advancement of the Race': The Great Migrations to Houston, Texas, 1914–1941," *Journal of Urban History*, 31 (May 2005): 435–478.

Introduction

1. Annette Fields, "More Than a Survivor: Former Wiley President Reaches into His Past, Urges Students to Adapt to Changing World," *Longview News-Journal*, October 20, 1991; Lullelia Harrison interview by author, tape recording, Houston, Texas, September 23, 1999, in possession of the author; and Bruce A. Glasrud, "Black Texans, 1900–1930: A History" (Ph.D. diss., Texas Technical College, 1969), 224–26.

2. Manuscript Census of the United States, Orange County, Texas, 1910, roll 1582, Bureau of the Census, series T624, Heritage Quest Online, http://persi.heritagequestonline.com/; Manuscript Census of the United States, Harrison County, Texas, 1920, roll 1815, Bureau of the Census, series T625, Heritage Quest Online, http://persi.heritagequestonline.com/; Annette Fields, "More Than a Survivor"; and Robert Hayes Sr. interview by Bernadette Pruitt, tape recording, September 23, 1999, Houston, Texas, in possession of the author.

3. Robert Hayes Sr. interview.
4. Ibid.
5. Ibid.
6. Ibid.
7. Ibid.

8. Robert Hayes Sr. interview; and E. W. Hayes, Texas Death Index, 1903–2000, December 22, 1931, certificate number 56565, Texas Death Index, 1903–2000, from Ancestry.com, http://search.ancestry.com/.

9. Robert Hayes Sr. interview; and Hayes, Texas Death Index, 1903–2000, no. 56565.

10. Robert Hayes Sr. interview; Ira B. Bryant, *The History of Houston Negro Schools* (Houston: Informer, 1935); and Wiley College, "About Wiley College/History," http://www.wileyc.edu/history.asp.

11. Pruitt, "'For the Advancement of the Race,'" 2005, 435–44. In recent years, a growing body of works has challenged the notion that emigration represented the only plausible alternative to the harshness of farm tenancy for rural and small-town southerners of African descent. Some scholars have studied African American activism in the rural and small-town South. See John Dittmer, *Local People: The Struggle for Civil Rights in Mississippi* (Urbana: University of Illinois Press, 1996); Robin D. G. Kelley, *Hammer and Hoe: Alabama Communists during the Great Depression* (Chapel Hill: University of North Carolina, 1990); Glenda Elizabeth Gilmore, *Defying Dixie: The Radical Roots of Civil Rights, 1919–1950* (New York: W. W. Norton, 2008); Patricia Sullivan, *Days of Hope: Race and Democracy in the New Deal* (Chapel Hill: University of North Carolina Press, 1996); Steven Hahn, *A Nation Under Our Feet: Black Political Struggles in the Rural South, From Slavery to the Great Migration* (Cambridge: Harvard University Press, 2003); R. Douglas Hurt, *African American Life in the Rural South, 1900–1950* (Columbia: University of Missouri Press, 2003); and Greta de Jong, *A Different Day: African American Struggles for Justice in Rural Louisiana, 1900–1970* (Chapel Hill: University of North Carolina Press, 2002). The growing stream of internal migration to the North began in the 1890s. See "The Northern Migration," In Motion: The African-American Migration Experience, The Schomburg Center for Research in Black Culture, New York Library, New York, http://www.inmotionaame.org/migrations/landing.cfm?migration=7 (hereafter cited as Schomburg Center, In Motion).

12. Pruitt, "'For the Advancement of the Race,'" 2005, 435–75.

13. Bureau of the Census, *Twelfth Census of the United States Taken in the Year 1900*, vol. 1: *Population; Population of States and Territories* (Washington: US Government Printing Office, 1901), 132 (hereafter cited as *Twelfth Census of the United States, 1900*); Bureau of the Census, *Negro Population in the United States, 1790–1915* (1918; reprint, New York: Arno Press, 1969), 92, 205 (hereafter cited as *Negro Population in the United States, 1790–1915*); Bureau of the Census, *Fourteenth Census of the United States Taken in the Year 1920* (hereafter cited as *Fourteenth Census of the United States, 1920*), vol. 2, *Population: General Reports and Analytical Tables* (Washington: US Government Printing Office, 1923), 354; and Bureau of the Census, *Sixteenth Census of the United States, 1940: Population and Housing* (hereafter cited as *Sixteenth Census of the United States, 1940*), vol. 2: *Characteristics of the Population* (Washington: US Government Printing Office, 1943), 1044. The estimated migration figure of 32,000 for the 1900–1941 period comes from aggregate census figures in net intercensal age cohort tables. Net intercensal figures allow researchers to trace census population growth by the use of age cohorts. The cohort tables do not include the children below age 10 who may or may not have been migrants to the city. As a precautionary measure, I thought it best to omit this group

because it would be difficult to differentiate between those children born in Houston and those who migrated to the city with their parents. Birth records for the city remained faulty through the 1930s as the city did not always accurately document the births of African Americans. In truth, the elected figure of 32,000 is probably below the exact number, as the figure excludes young children under the age of ten. Earl Lewis, in his seminal study on Blacks in Norfolk, titled *In Their Own Interests: Race, Class, and Power in Twentieth Century Norfolk* (Berkeley: University of California Press, 1991), coined the use of age cohort tables to describe certain aspects of migration such as the age of newcomers. The intercensal net migration tables for the periods 1900–10, 1910–20, 1920–30, and 1930–40 are based on census figures. The numbers are derived from the census figures given in each age cohort in the general population census volumes on Houston. The former decennial year is subtracted from the later year in each cohort group. The figure given represents the possible migration number for that particular cohort. The numerical increase for each period reveals in-migration for those decennial periods. Although most African Americans arrived in the city as a result of in-migration, others such as residents of Independence Heights, moved to the city via annexation, even though the latter uprooted to the said community from the surrounding hinterland. For these reasons, the migration figure given in this study can only serve as a suggestive estimate and not an approximate number. There is no clear way of differentiating between migrants and others who came to the city through annexation. Most Afro-Americans were products of internal migration, but others such as the residents of Independence Heights entered Houston by way of annexation. For these reasons, the migration figure given here can only serve as a suggestive estimate and not an approximate number.

14. In recent years, scholars have tackled the controversial question of African immigration to the Americas prior to Spanish Conquest. For more on this subject, see Ivan Van Sertima, *They Came before Columbus: The African Presence in Ancient America* (New York: Random House, 1976). For more on coerced and voluntary migratory patterns among Africans and their descendents in Colonial, Antebellum, and Reconstruction America, see Gwendolyn Mildo Hall, *Slavery and African Ethnicities in the Americas: Restoring the Links* (Chapel Hill: University of North Carolina Press, 2005; Ernest Obadele-Starks, *Freebooters and Smugglers: The Foreign Slave Trade in the United States after 1900* (Fayetteville: University of Arkansas Press, 2007); Nell I. Painter, *Exodusters: Black Migration to Kansas after Reconstruction* (1977; reprint, Lawrence: University Press of Kansas, 1986); Schomburg Center, In Motion; Carter G. Woodson, *A Century of Migration* (1918; reprint, New York: Dover Publications, 2002); Ira Berlin, *The Making of African America: The Four Great Migrations* (New York: Penguin, 2010). Woodson's work is the first to discuss the varying facets of African American internal migrations prior to the First Great Migration of World War I. From the period of prehistory to the middle period of migratory interaction resulting from marriage, pilgrimages, warfare, and continental removal, Africans too have engaged in voluntary and coercive migratory patterns. For more on African migration and immigration, see Basil Davidson, *The African Genius: An Introduction to African Social and Cultural History* (London: Atlantic-Little, Brown Books, 1969); Toyin Falola, ed., *Africa: African History Before 1885*, vol. 1 (Durham: Carolina Academic Press, 2000); Hugh Thomas, *The Slave Trade: The Story of*

the Transatlantic Slave Trade, 1440–1870 (New York: A Touchtone Book—a division of Simon & Schuster, 1999); and Erik Gilbert and Jonathan T. Reynolds, *Africa in World History: From Prehistory to the Present* (Upper Saddle River, New Jersey: Pearson, 2004).

15. Like displaced Germans, Irish, Scandinavians, and English in the early seventeenth through nineteenth centuries; Italian, Mexican, Chinese, and Eastern European peasants of the late nineteenth and early twentieth centuries; impoverished and/or ambitious Puerto Ricans (internal migrants), Ethiopians, Nigerians, Vietnamese, Korean, Iranians, Syrians, Hondurans, Haitians, and Jamaicans of the late twentieth century; and Whites moving from the Appalachians or East Texas Cotton Belt into northern, western, and southern industrial centers, African Americans moved into urban-industrial settings throughout the United States. For comprehensive studies on United States immigration, see John Bodnar, *The Transplanted: A History of Immigrants in Urban America* (Bloomington: Indiana University Press, 1987); Thomas A. Guglielmo, *White on Arrival: Italians, Race, Color, and Power in Chicago, 1890–1945* (Press, 2003); Rodolfo Acuña, *Occupied America: A History of Chicanos* (New York: Longman, 2003), 135–306; Ronald Takaki, *A Different Mirror: A History of Multicultural America* (Boston: Little, Brown and Company, 1993); Ronald Takaki, *Strangers from a Different Shore: A History of Asians Americans* (1989; Boston: Little, Brown & Company, 1999); and Elliott Robert Barkan, *And Still They Came: Immigrants and American Society, 1920–1990s* (Arlington Heights, Ill.: Harlan Davidson, 1996), 1–6. For comprehensive studies that discuss rural-to-urban migrations within the United States, see James N. Gregory, *The Southern Diaspora: How the Great Migrations of Black and White Southerners Transformed America* (Chapel Hill: University of North Carolina Press, 2005), 11–41; *Encyclopedia of the Great Black Migration*, 3 vols., ed. Steven A. Reich (Westport: Connecticut: Greenwood Press, 2006); J. Trent Alexander, "'They're Never Here More Than a Year': Return Migration in the Southern Exodus, 1940–1970," *Journal of Social History* 38, no. 3 (2005): 653–71; and Blaine A. Brownell and David Goldfield, eds., *The City in Southern History: The Growth of Urban Civilization in the South* (Port Washington, N.Y.: Kennikat, 1977).

16. *Encyclopedia of the Great Black Migration*, vol. 1, s.v., "Introduction," xxxv–xlviii; Schomburg Center, In Motion; Carole Marks, *Farewell—We're Good and Gone: The Great Migration* (Bloomington: Indiana University, 1989), 1–13; Kenneth W. Goings and Raymond A. Mohl, eds., *The New African American Urban History* (Thousand Oaks, California: Sage Publications, 1996); Farah Jasmine Griffin, *"Who Set You Flowin'?": The African-American Migration Narrative* (New York: Oxford University Press, 1996); Joe William Trotter Jr., Earl Lewis, and Tera Hunter, "Introduction: Connecting African American Urban History, Social Science Research, and Policy Debates," in *The African American Urban Experience: Perspectives from the Colonial Period to the Present* (New York: Palegrave-Macmillan, 2004), 1–20; Emmett J. Scott, *Negro Migration During the War* (1920; reprint with an introduction by Thomas Cripps, New York: Arno Press and the *New York Times,* 1969); Woodson, *A Century of Negro Migration;* Joe William Trotter Jr., "Afro-American Urban History: A Critique of the Literature," in *Black Milwaukee: The Making of an Industrial Proletariat, 1915–45* (1985; Urbana: University of Illinois Press, 1988), 264–82; Joe William Trotter Jr., ed. *The Great Migration in Historical*

Perspective: New Dimensions of Race, Class, and Gender (Bloomington: Indiana University Press, 1991); Peter Gottlieb, *Making Their Own Way: Southern Blacks' Migration Experiences to Pittsburgh, 1916–30* (Urbana: University of Illinois Press, 1987); and Isabel Wilkerson, *The Warmth of Other Suns: The Epic Story of America's Great Migration* (New York: Random House, 2010). A growing number of historians have redefined the start of the Second Great Migration, placing it in the 1930s with the beginning of New Deal public assistance, which influenced flight to cities.

17. For works that discuss the Great Black Migrations as well as African-descent immigration within the South, see Bernadette Pruitt, "'For the Advancement of the Race': The Great Migrations to Houston, Texas, 1914–1945," *Journal of Urban History* 31 (May 2005): 435–78; Laurie B. Green, *Battling the Plantation Mentality: Memphis and the Black Freedom Struggle* (Chapel Hill: University of North Carolina Press, 2007); Luther Adams, *Way Up North in Louisville: African American Migration in the Urban South, 1930–1970* (Chapel Hill: University of North Carolina Press, 2010); Earl Lewis, *In Their Own Interests*, 22; George A. Devlin, *South Carolina and Black Migration, 1865–1940: In Search of the Promised Land* (New York: Garland, 1989); Tera Hunter, *To 'Joy My Freedom: Southern Black Women's Lives and Labors after the Civil War* (Cambridge: Harvard University Press, 1997); Susan D. Greenbaum, *More Than Black: Afro-Cubans in Tampa* (Gainesville: University Press of Florida, 2002); Hahn, *A Nation Under Our Feet*; Andrew Wiese, *Places of Their Own: African American Suburbanization in the Twentieth Century* (Chicago: University of Chicago Press, 2004); Elizabeth Anne Gessel, "Nowhere But Heaven: Savannah, Georgia during the Era of the First Great Migration" (Ph.D. diss., University of California at Berkeley, 2003); Tyina Leaneice Steptoe, "Dixie West: Race, Migration, and the Color Lines in Jim Crow Houston" (Ph.D. diss., University of Wisconsin at Madison, 2008); Jason Carl Digman, "Which Way to the Promised Land? Changing Patterns in Southern Migration, 1865–1920" (Ph.D. diss., University of Illinois at Chicago, 2001); and *Encyclopedia of the Great Black Migration*.

18. *Negro Population in the United States, 1790–1915*, 831–34; *Twelfth Census of the United States, 1900*, 40–42; *Fourteenth Census of the United States, 1920*, vol. 3: *Population: Composition and Characteristics of the Population by States*, 990–1004; *Sixteenth Census of the United States, 1940*, vol. 2, Part 6, 792–806; and Joseph A. Pratt, *The Growth of a Refining Region* (Westport, Connecticut: JAI Press, 1980), 20. For works that discuss in detail internal migration or immigration to Houston, see Steptoe, "Dixie West"; Fred R. von der Mehden, ed., *The Ethnic Groups of Houston* (Houston: Rice University Press, 1984); David G. McComb, *Houston: A History* (1969; Austin: University of Texas Press, 1981); Howard O. Beeth and Cary D. Wintz, eds., *Black Dixie: Afro-Texan History and Culture in the Bayou City* (College Station: Texas A&M University Press, 1992); Robert D. Bullard, *Invisible Houston: The Black Experience in Boom and Bust* (College Station: Texas A&M University Press, 1987); Arnoldo De León, *Ethnicity in the Sunbelt: Mexican Americans in Houston* (1989; College Station: Texas A&M University Press, 2001); James M. SoRelle, "The Darker Side of 'Heaven,': The Black Community in Houston, 1917–1945" (Ph.D. diss., Kent State University, 1980); Joseph A. Pratt, ed., "Coming to Houston," Special Issue, *Houston Review of History* 3, no. 1 (2005); Uzma Quraishi, "Educationally Empowered : The Indian and Pakistani Student Community

in Houston, Texas, 1960–1975" (master's thesis, University of Houston, 2008); Bela Thacker, "Homeward Bound: Asian-Indian Women Putting Down Roots in Houston, Texas" (Ph.D. diss., State University of New York, Buffalo, 2005); Afzal Ahmed, "Islam and the Making of Transnational Citizenship: Pakistani Immigrant Experience in Houston, Texas" (Ph.D. diss., Yale University, 2005); and Paul Alejandro Levengood, "For the Duration and Beyond: World War II and the Creation of Modern Houston, Texas" (Ph.D. diss., Rice University, 1999). For a detailed bibliography of historical works that concentrate on the history of Houston, see University of Houston, Center for Public History, "Bibliography of Works," unpublished bibliography, Houston, Texas, July 10, 2010, in the possession of author.

19. Lewis, *In Their Own Interests,* 30; Steptoe, "Dixie West"; Pruitt, "'For the Advancement of the Race,'" 2005, 435–44; Gilbert Osofsky, *Harlem: The Making of a Ghetto, 1890–1930,* 2nd ed. (New York: Harper Torchbooks, 1971), ix, 17–19, 128–35; Allan Spear, *Black Chicago: The Making of a Negro Ghetto, 1890–1920* (Chicago: University of Chicago Press, 1967), vii–x, 11–12, 129–31. For four essays that discuss in detail the literature of African American urban studies and the Great Migrations, see Trotter Jr., ed., "Introduction: A Review of the Literature," in *The Great Migration in Historical Perspective*; Griffin, "Who Set You Flowin'?"; Trotter Jr., *Black Milwaukee,* 264–82; and James S. Gregory, *The Second Migration: A Historical Overview in African American Urban History since World War II,* ed. Kenneth Kusmer and Joe Trotter (University of Chicago Press, 2009), 19-38.

20. Pratt, *The Growth of a Refining Region,* 23–60; and Pruitt, "'For the Advancement of the Race,'" 2005, 445–54. For works that discuss immigration and internal migrations within Texas, see Carlos Kevin Blanton, "Deconstructing Texas: The Diversity of People, Place, and Historical Imagination in Recent Texas History," in *Beyond Texas Through Time: Breaking Away from Past Interpretations* (College Station: Texas A&M University Press, 2011); Robert A. Calvert, "Agrarian Texas," in *Texas Through Time: Evolving Interpretations,* ed. Walter A. Buenger and Robert A. Calvert (College Station: Texas A&M University Press, 1991), 219–20; Terry G. Jordan, "A Century and a Half of Ethnic Change in Texas, 1836–1986," *Southwestern Historical Quarterly* 89 (April 1986): 385–417; Arnoldo De León, "Texas Mexicans: Twentieth Century Interpretations," in *Texas Through Time: Evolving Interpretations,* eds. Walter L. Buenger and Robert A. Calvert (College Station: Texas A&M University Press, 1991), 20–35; and Gary Clayton Anderson, *The Conquest of Texas: Ethnic Cleansing in the Promised Land, 1820–1875* (Norman: University of Oklahoma Press, 2005); and Steptoe, "Dixie West."

21. Historian W. D. Wright, in the work entitled *Black History and Black Identity,* makes a compelling case for the use of *Black,* over *black,* when defining people of African descent in the United States. According to Wright, middle-class and professional African Americans have in recent years urged society to capitalize the first letter in the word *black,* when describing African Americans of the United States. According to Wright, this use of *Black* designates ethnicity, whereas *black* defines race and color. Wright also argues that this designation must and should be determined by African Americans, and not others. The author agrees with this argument, although she would insist that using the capital "B" over the preferred use of the lowercase "b" when referring to the entire race or all people of the African Diaspora warrants discussion as well. Therefore, she

has decided to adopt *Black* when defining both the race of people of African descent and multiplicity of ethnicities represented in the African Diaspora, instead of *black*. To avoid controversy, the author has decided to use the word *White* when defining people of European descent and *Brown* when referring to people of Latin American ancestry. The use of *Black* over the standard *black* challenges mainstream sentiment around the definition of *black*. Although standard dictionaries define the word as a color, racial category, and so forth, in Western culture the term is largely—although not exclusively—associated with unpleasantness, evil, misfortune, negative consequences, sadness, and ugliness. Here, the author attempts to challenge society's negative association with Blackness, including Black people, as a depressing, damaging element. Elsewhere in the text, African American, Afro-American, or African-descent American defines people of African origin, whereas European American classifies individuals of European ancestry, and Mexican-origin, Mexican American, Mexican national, Hispanic or Latino defines people of Latin origin. See W. D. Wright, *Black History and Black Identity: A Call for a New Historiography* (Westport, Connecticut, 2001), 1–21; and John McWhorter, "Why I'm Black, not African-American," *Detroit News*, September 30, 2004.

22. Pruitt, "'For the Advancement of the Race,'" 2005, 445–57.

23. Beeth and Wintz, eds., *Black Dixie;* Cary D. Wintz, "Blacks," in *The Ethnic Groups of Houston*, ed. Fred von der Mehden (Houston: Rice University Press, 1984), 15–33; Pruitt, "'For the Advancement of the Race,'" 2005, 445–54; and Ernest Obadele-Starks, *Black Unionism in the Industrial South* (College Station: Texas A&M University, 1999), 3–30.

24. Pruitt, "'For the Advancement of the Race,'" 2005, 445–78; and Steptoe "Dixie West."

25. Beeth and Wintz, eds., *Black Dixie;* Wintz, "Blacks," 15–33; and Pruitt, "'For the Advancement of the Race,'" 2005, 445–54; and Steptoe "Dixie West," 49–122, 146–150, 206.

26. This work draws on the scholarship of several scholars who have attempted to redefine the parameters of modern Civil Rights. See Stephanie J. Shaw, "Black Club Women and the Creation of the National Association of Colored Women," in *"We Specialize in the Wholly Impossible": A Reader in Black Women's History*, ed. Darlene Clark Hine, Wilma King, and Linda Reed (New York: Carlson Publishing Inc., 1995).; Merline Pitre, *In Struggle against Jim Crow: Lula B. White and the NAACP, 1900–1957* (College Station: Texas A&M University Press, 1999); Jacqueline Ann Rouse, "Out of the Shadow of Tuskegee: Margaret Murray Washington, Social Activism, and Race Vindication," *Journal of Negro History* 81 (1996): 31–46; Obadele-Starks, *Black Unionism in the Industrial South*, 3–26; Darlene Clark Hine, *Black Victory: The Rise and Fall of the White Primary in Texas* (1979; new edition with essays by Darlene Clark Hine, Steven F. Lawson, and Merline Pitre (Columbia: University of Missouri Press, 2003), 43–45; Michael R. Botson, *Labor, Civil Rights, and the Hughes Tool Company* (College Station: Texas A&M University, 2005); Dwight Watson, *Race and the Houston Police Department, 1930–1990: A Change Did Come*. College Station: Texas A&M University Press, 2005; Amilcar Shabazz, *Advancing Democracy: African Americans and the Struggle for Access and Equity in Higher Education in Texas* (Chapel Hill: University of North Carolina Press, 2004); Amilcar Shabazz, "Carter Wesley and the Making of Houston's Civic Culture before the Second Reconstruction," in *Houston Review of History and Culture* 1

(Summer 2004): 2–12; Eric Arnesen, *Brotherhoods of Color: Black Railroad Workers and the Struggle for Equality* (Cambridge: Harvard University Press, 2002), 1–13; Steven A. Reich, "Soldiers of Democracy: Black Texans and the Fight for Citizenship, 1917–1921," *Journal of American History* 82, no. 4 (1996): 1478–1504; and Robin D. G. Kelley, *Race Rebels: Politics, Culture and the Black Working Class* (New York: Free Press, 1996).

27. James C. Scott, *Weapons of the Weak: Everyday Forms of Peasant Resistance* (New Haven: Yale University Press, 1987), vxv–xix; James C. Scott, *Domination and the Arts of Resistance: Hidden Transcripts* (New Haven: Yale University Press, 1990), ix–xiii; and Pruitt, "In Search of Freedom," 48–57, 85–86.

28. Pruitt, "'For the Advancement of the Race,'" 2005, 445–60; and Steptoe "Dixie West."

29. Steptoe, "Dixie West"; and Pruitt, "'For the Advancement of the Race,'" 2005, 445–60.

30. Steptoe, "Dixie West"; and Pruitt, "'For the Advancement of the Race,'" 2005, 445–60.

31. See *Negro Population in the United States, 1790–1915*, 205; *Fourteenth Census of the United States, 1920*, vol. 2, 354; *Sixteenth Census of the United States, 1940*, vol. 2, Part 3: *Kansas-Michigan—New York*; Marvin Hurley, *Decisive Years for Houston* (Houston, Tex.: Houston Chamber of Congress, 1966), 43–47, 53–59, 415–17; Pruitt, "'For the Advancement of the Race,'" 2005, 444–60; *Texas Almanac, 2002–2003: 2000 Census Data* (Dallas: Dallas Morning News, 2001), 125–27, 287, 383–99; Pratt, *The Growth of a Refining Region*, 19–23; 46–50, 83–85, 109–17; and Randolph Campbell, *Gone to Texas: A History of the Lone Star State* (New York: Oxford University Press, 2004), 324–29, 260–64, 402–10. For a broader discussion on the development, specific features, and impact of Jim Crow segregation in the South, see C. Vann Woodward, *The Strange Career of Jim Crow*, 3rd rev. ed. (New York: Oxford University Press, 1974); John W. Cell, *The Highest Stage of White Supremacy: The Origins of Segregation in South Africa and the American South* (1982; New York: Cambridge University Press, 1989); Charles S. Johnson, *Patterns of Segregation* (New York: Harper and Brothers, 1943); Rayford W. Logan, *The Betrayal of the Negro: From Rutherford B. Hayes to Woodrow Wilson* (New York: New York: MacMillan, 1969); I. E. Newby, *Jim Crow's Defense: Anti-Negro Thought in America, 1900–1930* (Baton Rouge: Louisiana University Press, 1969); Joel Williamson, *The Crucible of Race: Black-White Relations in the American South since Emancipation* (New York: Oxford University Press, 1984); George M. Fredrickson, *White Supremacy: A Comparative Study in American and South African History* (New York: Oxford University Press, 1981); Leon Litwack, *North of Slavery: The Negro in the Free States, 1790–1860*, First Phoenix ed. (Chicago: University of Chicago Press, 1965); Samuel C. Hyde Jr., ed., *Sunbelt Revolution: The Historical Progression of the Civil Rights Struggle in the Gulf Coast, 1866–2000* (Gainesville: University Press of Florida, 2003); Neil McMillen, *Dark Journey: Black Mississippians in the Age of Jim Crow* (Urbana: University of Illinois Press, 1990); Donald E. Lively, *The Constitution and Race* (New York: Preger, 1992), 61–108; James D. Anderson, *The Education of Blacks in the South, 1860–1935* (Chapel Hill: University of North Carolina Press, 1988); and John Hope Franklin and Elizabeth Brooks Higginbotham, *From Slavery to Freedom: A History of African-Americans* (New York: Macmillan, 2010).

32. Pruitt, "'For the Advancement of the Race,'" 2005, 443–51; Pruitt, "In Search of Freedom," 46–57, 85–86; *Encyclopedia of the Great Black Migration*, vol. 1, s.v., "Houston, Texas," 408–11, and "Chain Migration," 168–70; and Steptoe, "Dixie West."

33. Pruitt, "'For the Advancement of the Race,'" 2005, 441–63.

34. Pitre, *In Struggle against Jim Crow*; Hine, *Black Victory*; and Jon R. Wilson, "Origins: The Houston NAACP, 1915–1918" (master's thesis, University of Houston, 2005).

35. Pruitt, "'For the Advancement of the Race;'" 2005, 435–444; and Steptoe, "Dixie West."

36. *Fourteenth Census of the United States*, vol. 4: *Population: Occupations*, 1114–15; Bureau of the Census, *Fifteenth Census of the United States, 1930: Population and Housing* (hereafter cited as *Fifteenth Census of the United States, 1930*), vol. 4: *Occupations, by States* (Washington: US Government Printing Office, 1933), 1593–95; Bureau of the Census, *Negro Population of the United States, 1790–1915*, 812–13, 831–34; *Sixteenth Census of the United States, 1940*, vol. 2, 362–65, 792–806, 1044; *Sixteenth Census of the United States, 1940*, vol. 3: *The Labor Force*, Part 5: *Pennsylvania–Wyoming*, 906–7; and Pruitt, "'For the Advancement of the Race,'" 2005, 451–60.

37. Robert Hayes Sr. interview.

38. Ibid.

39. Robert Hayes Sr. interview; and "Bishop Robert E. Hayes Jr.," The United Methodist Church Online, accessed July 2, 2011, http://www.umc.org/site/apps/nlnet/content2.aspx?c=lwL4KnN1LtH&b=6387671&ct=7269843.

40. Manuscript Census of the United States, Harris County, Texas, 1930, roll 2347, Bureau of the Census, series T626, Heritage Quest Online, http://persi.heritagequestonline.com/; Annette Fields, "More Than a Survivor"; Lullelia Harrison interview, September 23, 1999; "Bishop Robert E. Hayes Jr."; and Glasrud, "Black Texans, 1900–1930," 224–26.

41. Robert Hayes Sr. interview; and Robert E. Hayes, Florida Marriage Collection, 1822–1875 and 1927–2001, 1945, vol. 992, certificate number 11009, from Ancestry.com, http://search.ancestry.com/.

42. Robert Hayes Sr. interview.

43. Ibid.

44. Manuscript Census, Harris County, 1930, roll 2347, series T626; Annette Fields, "More Than a Survivor"; Lullelia Harrison interview, September 23, 1999; Wiley College, "About Wiley College/History"; and Glasrud, "Black Texans, 1900–1930," 224–26.

Chapter 1

1. Photo Identification Sheet, Jeff Collins Family Collection, Houston Metropolitan Research Center, Houston Public Library, Julia Ideson Building, Houston, Texas, MSS 184, box 1, folder 2–1R (hereafter cited as Jeff Collins Family MSS); "Edward Collins," Jeff Collins Family MSS, 184, box 1, folder 2–21R; and Pruitt, "'For the Advancement of the Race,'" 2005, 444–445.

2. Jeff Collins Family History, Jeff Collins Family MSS, 184, box 1, folder 1.

3. Ibid.

4. Ibid.
5. Ibid.
6. Ibid.
7. Ibid.
8. Ibid.
9. Photo Identification Sheet, Jeff Collins Family MSS, 184, box 1, folder 2–1R; "Edward Collins," Jeff Collins Family MSS, 184, box 1, folder 2–21R; and Pruitt, "'For the Advancement of the Race,'" 2005, 444–445.
10. Robert S. Maxwell and Robert D. Baker, *Sawdust Empire: The Texas Lumber Industry, 1830–1940* (College Station: Texas A&M University Press, 1983); *The Handbook of Texas Online,* s.v., "Lumber Industry," accessed January 3, 2011, http://www.tshaonline.org/handbook/online/articles/LL/dr12.html; *The Handbook of Texas Online,* s.v., "Brotherhood of Timber Workers," accessed January 3, 2011, http://www.tshaonline.org/handbook/online/articles/BB/ocbbb.html/; *The Handbook of Texas Online,* s.v., "Kirby, John Henry," accessed January 3, 2011, http://www.tshaonline.org/handbook/online/articles/KK/fki33.html; and *The Handbook of Texas Online,* s.v., "Walker County," http://www.tshaonline.org/handbook/online/articles/WW/hcw1.html; de Jong, *A Different Day;* William P. Jones, *The Tribe of Black Ulysses: African American Lumber Workers in the Jim Crow South* (Urbana: University of Illinois Press, 2005); John C. Howard, *The Negro in the Lumber Industry in America* (Philadelphia: University of Pennsylvania Press, 1970); and Steven A. Reich, "The Making of a Southern Sawmill World: Race, Class, and Rural Transformation in the Piney Woods of East Texas, 1830–1930" (Ph.D. diss., Northwestern University, 1998).
11. Photo Identification Sheet, Jeff Collins Family MSS, 184, box 1, folder 2–1R; "Edward Collins," Jeff Collins Family MSS, 184, box 1, folder 2–21R; and Pruitt, "'For the Advancement of the Race,'" 2005, 444–45.
12. Photo Identification Sheet, Jeff Collins Family MSS, 184, box 1, folder 2–1R; "Edward Collins," Jeff Collins Family MSS, 184, box 1, folder 2–21R:1; and Pruitt, "'For the Advancement of the Race,'" 2005, 444–45.
13. Jeff Collins Family History, Jeff Collins MSS, 184, box 1, folder 1.
14. Photo Identification Sheet, Jeff Collins Family MSS, 184, box 1, folder 2–1R; "Geneva Mae Justice," Jeff Collins Family MSS, 184, box 1, folder 2–9R, 184, box 1, folder 2–17R; "Arma Collins," Jeff Collins Family MSS, 184, box 1, folder 2–20R; "Ellison Collins," Jeff Collins Family MSS, 184, box 1, folder 2–24R; "John H. Gay," Jeff Collins Family MSS, 184, box 1, folder 2–28R; "Ernest Johnson," Jeff Collins Family MSS, 184, box 1, folder 2–29R; "Horace Williams," Jeff Collins Family MSS, 184, box 1, folder 2–36R; "Homer Collins," Jeff Collins Family MSS, 184, box 1, folder 2–37R; "Robert Johnson," Jeff Collins Family MSS, 184, box 1, folder 2–42R; "Mary Collins," Jeff Collins Family MSS, 184, box 1, folder 2–44R; "John Marion Gay," Jeff Collins Family MSS, 184, box 1, folder 2–57R; *Negro Population in the United States, 1790–1915,* 92, 205; *Fourteenth Census of the United States, 1920,* vol. 2, 354; *Sixteenth Census of the United States, 1940,* vol. 2, 1044; Pruitt, "'For the Advancement of the Race,'" 2005, 444–45; and Gottlieb, *Making Their Own Way,* 44–45.
15. Jeff Collins Family History, Jeff Collins MSS 184, box 1, folder 1.

16. Ibid.

17. Photo Identification Sheet, Jeff Collins Family MSS, 184, box 1, folder 2–1R; "Geneva Mae Justice," Jeff Collins Family MSS, 184, box 1, folder 2–9R, 184, box 1, folder 2–17R; "Arma Collins," Jeff Collins Family MSS, 184, box 1, folder 2–20R; "Ellison Collins," Jeff Collins Family MSS, 184, box 1, folder 2–24R; "John H. Gay," Jeff Collins Family MSS, 184, box 1, folder 2–28R; "Ernest Johnson," Jeff Collins Family MSS, 184, box 1, folder 2–29R; "Horace Williams," Jeff Collins Family MSS, 184, box 1, folder 2–36R; "Homer Collins," Jeff Collins Family MSS, 184, box 1, folder 2–37R; "Robert Johnson," Jeff Collins Family MSS, 184, box 1, folder 2–42R "Mary Collins," Jeff Collins Family MSS, 184, box 1, folder 2–44R; "John Marion Gay," Jeff Collins Family MSS, 184, box 1, folder 2–57R; *Negro Population in the United States, 1790–1915,* 92, 205; *Fourteenth Census of the United States, 1920,* vol. 2, 354; *Sixteenth Census of the United States, 1940,* vol. 2, 1044; and Pruitt, "'For the Advancement of the Race,'" 2005, 444–45.

18. Pruitt, "'For the Advancement of the Race,'" 2005, 435–78.

19. Pruitt, "'For the Advancement of the Race,'" 2005, 435–78; Schomburg Center, *In Motion;* Trotter Jr., ed., "Introduction," in *Black Migration in Historical Perspective;* Quintard Taylor and Shirley Ann Wilson Moore, ed., *African American Women Confront the West* (Norman: University of Oklahoma, 2003); Quintard Taylor, *In Search of the Racial Frontier: African Americans in the West, 1528–1990* (New York: W. W. Norton, 1998); Trotter Jr. et al., "Introduction: Connecting African American Urban History, Social Science Research, and Policy Debates," 1–20; Kimberly Phillips, *Alabama North: African-American Migrants, Community, and Working-Class Activism in Cleveland, 1915–1945* (Urbana: University of Illinois Press, 1999); Goings and Mohl, eds., *The New African American Urban History;* Trotter Jr., *Black Milwaukee,* 264–82; Adams, *Way North in Louisville;* and Marks, *Farewell—We're Good and Gone,* 1–13.

20. Pruitt, "'For the Advancement of the Race,'" 2005, 435–78; Schomburg Center, *In Motion;* Trotter Jr., ed., "Introduction," in *Black Migration in Historical Perspective;* Taylor and Moore, ed., *African American Women Confront the West;* Taylor, *In Search of the Racial Frontier;* Trotter Jr. et al., "Introduction: Connecting African American Urban History, Social Science Research, and Policy Debates," 1–20; Phillips, *Alabama North;* Goings and Mohl, eds., *The New African American Urban History;* and Trotter Jr., "Afro-American Urban History: A Critique of the Literature," in *Black Milwaukee,* 264–82; see also Luther Adams, "African American Migration to Louisville in the Mid Twentieth Century," *Register of the Kentucky Historical Society* 99, no. 4 (2001): 363–84; Adams, *Way Up North in Louisville,* 2010; and Marks, *Farewell—We're Good and Gone,* 444–45. The nickname "Bayou City" refers to Houston, Texas, mainly as a point of reference, recognizing the city's twenty bayou waterways or streams that have both propelled the metropolis's economic growth and shielded the low-lying, flat urban center from torrential floods.

21. Woodward, *The Strange Career of Jim Crow;* Cell, *The Highest Stage of White Supremacy;* Johnson, *Patterns of Segregation;* Logan, The Betrayal of the Negro; Newby, *Jim Crow's Defense;* Williamson, *The Crucible of Race;* Fredrickson, *White Supremacy;* Litwack, *North of Slavery;* McMillen, *Dark Journey;* Lively, *The Constitution and Race,*

61–108; Anderson, *The Education of Blacks in the South, 1860–1935;* and Alwyn Barr, *Black Texans: A History of African Americans in Texas, 1528–1995* (Norman: University of Oklahoma Press, 1996).

22. Pruitt, "'For the Advancement of the Race,'" 2001, 1–44; Obadele-Starks, *Black Unionism in the Industrial South,* 3–26; Hine, *Black Victory,* 43–45; Scott, *Weapons of the Weak,* xv–xix; and Scott, *Domination and the Arts of Resistance,* ix–xiii. These historians argue that the African American struggle for equality began when kidnapped Africans challenged the authority of slavers and Whites on West African coasts and on slave ships. Most African Americans rejected Africa as a safe haven against institutionalized racism, even though their African ancestors—those kidnapped and taken to the Americas—adhered to an opposite cultural, spiritual mentality. Regardless of their circumstances, they saw themselves as Americans. See Michael A. Gomez, *Exchanging Our Country Marks: The Transformation of African Identities in the Colonial and Antebellum South* (Chapel Hill: University of North Carolina Press, 1998); Craig Steven Wilder, *In the Company of Black Men: The African Influence on African American Culture in New York* (New York: New York University Press, 2001); Darlene Clark Hine, William C. Hine, and Stanley Harrold, *African-American Odyssey,* 5th ed. (Upper Saddle River, New Jersey: Prentice Hall, 2011); Barbara Blair, "Though Justice Sleeps, 1880–1900," in *To Make Our World Anew: A History of African Americans from 1880,* vol. 2, ed. Robin D. G. Kelley and Earl Lewis (New York: Oxford University Press, 2000), 281–344; and "Colonization and Emigration," Schomburg Center, In Motion, http://www.inmotion aame.org/migrations/landing.cfm?migration=4.

23. For general and specific works on Reconstruction in Texas and Louisiana, see Eric Foner, *Reconstruction: America's Unfinished Revolution, 1863–1877* (New York: Harper and Row, 1988); *The Handbook of Texas Online,* s.v., "Reconstruction," http://www.tshaonline.org/handbook/online/articles/RR/mzr1.html; Charles William Ramsdell, *Reconstruction in Texas* (New York: Columbia University Press, 1910); Carl H. Moneyhon, *Texas After the Civil War: The Struggle of Reconstruction* (College Station: Texas A&M University Press, 2004); Randolph Campbell, *Grass-Roots Reconstruction in Texas, 1865–1880* (Baton Rouge: Louisiana State University, 1997), 1–22; Merline Pitre, *Through Many Dangers, Toils and Snares, Black Leadership in Texas, 1870–1890,* 2nd ed. (Austin: Eakin Press, 1997), vii–viii; Kenneth W. Howell, *Still in the Arena of the Civil War: Violence and Turmoil in Reconstruction Texas, 1865–1874* (Denton: University of North Texas Press, 2012). Barry A. Crouch, *The Freedmen's Bureau and Black Texans* (Austin: University of Texas Press, 1999); Charles Vincent, ed., *The African American Experience in Louisiana: From the Civil War to Jim Crow, The Louisiana Purchase Bicentennial series in Louisiana History,* vol. 11, (Lafayette: Center for Louisiana Studies, 1999); and John W. Blassingame, *Black New Orleans, 1860–1880* (Chicago: University of Chicago Press, 1976).

24. Hine et al., *The African-American Odyssey,* 302–6, 366–70; and Blair, "Though Justice Sleeps, 1880–1900," 281–344.

25. Blair, "Though Justice Sleeps, 1880–1900," 281–344; Kelley, *Race Rebels,* 1–54; Hine et al., *African-American Odyssey,* 259–304; Eric Foner, *A Short History of Reconstruction* (New York: Harper and Row, 1990), 40–52, 69–81, 168–81; Neil Foley, *The White Scourge: Mexicans, Blacks, and Poor Whites in Texas Cotton Culture* (Berkeley:

University of California Press, 1997), 64–71; Campbell, *Gone to Texas*, 310–313; William Joseph Brophy, "The Black Texan, 1900–1950: A Quantitative History" (Ph.D. diss., Vanderbilt University, 1974), 4, 13, 63–64; and Glasrud, "Black Texans, 1900–1930," 101–7.

26. *Negro Population in the United States, 1790*–1915, 789–94; Henry Coleman, interview by author, tape recording, February 13, 1998, in possession of author; Jacqueline Jones, *The Dispossessed: America's Underclass from the Civil War to the Present* (New York: BasicBooks, 1992), 13–17; William Cohen, *At Freedom's Edge: Black Mobility and the Southern White Quest for Racial Control, 1861–1915* (Baton Rouge: Louisiana State University Press, 1991), 1–22; Evans, "Texas Agriculture, 1880–1930" (Ph.D. diss., University of Texas, Austin, Texas, 1960), iv, 1–2; Randolph Campbell, *An Empire for Slavery: The Peculiar Institution in Texas, 1821–1865* (College Station: Texas A&M University, 1989), 2; Forest Garrett Hill, "The Negro in the Texas Labor Supply" (master's thesis, University of Texas, 1946), 9, 67, 81–84; Glasrud, "Black Texans, 1900–1930," 2, 97–101; Barr, *Black Texans*, 88–89, 147–48; and Brophy, "The Black Texan, 1900–1950," 4, 15–20.

27. *Negro Population in the United States, 1790–1915*, 789–94; Henry Coleman interview; Jones, *The Dispossessed*, 13–17; Cohen, *At Freedom's Edge*, 1–22; Evans, "Texas Agriculture, 1880–1930," iv, 1–2; Campbell, *An Empire for Slavery*, 2; Hill, "The Negro in the Texas Labor Supply," 9, 67, 81–84; Glasrud, "Black Texans, 1900–1930," 2; 97–101, Barr, *Black Texans*, 70–98, 147–48; Brophy, "The Black Texan, 1900–1950," 4, 15–20; and Campbell, *Gone to Texas*, 268–74, 310–323.

28. Bureau of the Census, *Negro Population of the United States, 1790–1915*, 393; and Anderson, *The Education of Blacks in the South, 1860–1935*, 1–2, 184–237.

29. Glasrud, "Black Texans, 1900–1930," 173–77; McMillen, *Dark Journey*, 4–7; and Cell, *The Highest Stage of White Supremacy*, 82–92, 103–4.

30. Gregg Cantrell, "Racial Violence and Reconstruction Politics in Texas, 1867–1868," *Southwestern Historical Quarterly* 93, no. 3 (1990): 333–55; Glasrud, "Black Texans, 1900–1930, 173–77; Campbell, *Grass-Roots Reconstruction in Texas, 1865–1880;* McMillen, *Dark Journey*, 4–7; Cell, *The Highest Stage of White Supremacy*, 82–92, 103–4; Charles Vincent, ed., *The African American Experience in Louisiana: From the Civil War to Jim Crow, The Louisiana Purchase Bicentennial series in Louisiana History*, vol. 12 (Lafayette: Center for Louisiana Studies, 1999); and *Know LA: Encyclopedia of Louisiana*, s.v., "Reconstruction" (by Nystrom, Justin A.), http://www.knowla.org/entry.php?rec=463.

31. Grace Elizabeth Hale, *Making Whiteness: The Culture of Segregation in the South, 1890–1940* (New York: Vintage Book, 1999).

32. Pruitt, "'For the Advancement of the Race,'" 2005, 435–478.

33. Pratt, *The Growth of a Refining Region*, 3–11, 13–30, 33–55; McComb, *Houston: A History*, 65–82; Frederick Law Olmstead, *A Journey Through Texas* (1857; Lincoln: University of Nebraska Press, 2004); HoustonHistory.com, "From a Troubled Beginning," http://www.houstonhistory.com/decades/history5.htm; and James L. Glass, compiler, "The Actualization of Houston, Texas: 1823–42," in *Surveys, Field Notes, Documents and Maps* (Houston: N.P.), 16–28.

34. Pratt, *The Growth of a Refining Region*, 3–11, 13–30, 33–55; McComb, *Houston: A History*, 65–82; *The Handbook of Texas Online*, s.v., "Houston, Texas," http://www

.tshaonline.org/handbook/online/articles/HH/hdh3.html; and *Handbook of Texas Online*, s.v., "Railroads," http://www.tshaonline.org/handbook/online/articles/eqr01.

35. Pratt, *The Growth of a Refining Region*, 3–11, 13–30, 33–55; McComb, *Houston: A History*, 65–82; *The Handbook of Texas Online*, s.v., "Houston, Texas"; and Marilyn McAdams Sibley, *The Port of Houston: A History* (Austin: University of Texas, 1968).

36. *The Handbook of Texas Online*, s.v., "Galveston Island," http://www.tshaonline.org/handbook/online/articles/rrg02; Pratt, David G. McComb, *Galveston: A History* (Austin: University of Texas, 1986); McComb, *Houston: A History*, 65–82; *The Handbook of Texas Online*, "Houston, Texas"; and *The Handbook of Texas Online*, s.v., "Galveston Hurricane of 1900," http://www.tshaonline.org/handbook/online/articles/ydg02.

37. The first major oilfield discovery took place in Navarro County near Corsicana in 1894. *The Handbook of Texas Online*, s.v., "Oil and Gas Industry," http://www.tshaonline.org/handbook/online/articles/OO/doogz.html; and *The Handbook of Texas Online*, s.v., "Spindletop Oilfield," http://www.tshaonline.org/handbook/online/articles/SS/dos3.html.

38. Pratt, *The Growth of a Refining Region*, 42–56.

39. McComb, *Houston: A History*, 65–82; Obadele-Starks, *Black Unionism in the Industrial South*, 3–6; Jessie O. Thomas, *A Study of the Social Welfare Status of Negroes in Houston, Texas* (Houston: Webster Richardson, 1929), 7–8; Bruce A. Beaubouef, "War and Change: Houston's Economic Ascendancy during World War I." *Houston Review: History and Culture of the Gulf Coast* 14 (Fall 1992): 89–112; Pruitt, "'For the Advancement of the Race,'" 2001, x–xi, 21–26, 70–71; Pratt, *The Growth of a Refining Region*, 3–11, 13–30, 33–56, 69–75; Howard O. Beeth, "Historians, Houston, and History," in *Black Dixie*, 3–5; Trotter, "Great Migration in Historical Perspective," 14–17; Robert Zeigler, "The Workingman in Houston, Texas, 1865–1914" (Ph.D. diss., Texas Tech, 1972); 1–42; Campbell, *Gone to Texas*, 360–437; Lewis, *In Their Own Interests*, 1–7; Suzanne L. Summers, "Banking in Houston, 1840–1914," in *Houston Review: History and Culture of the Gulf Coast* 12 (Fall 1990):40–41; and Pruitt, "'For the Advancement of the Race,'" 2005, 443–44.

40. *Negro Population in the United States, 1790–1915*, 205; *Fourteenth Census of the United States, 1920*, vol. 2, 354; *Sixteenth Census of the United States, 1940*, vol. 2, 1044; Robert Calvert, Gregg Cantrell, and Arnoldo De León, *The History of Texas*, 3rd ed. (Wheeling, Illinois: Harlan-Davidson, 2002); Marvin Hurley, *Decisive Years for Houston*, 43–47, 53–59, 415–17; Pruitt, "'For the Advancement of the Race': The Great Migrations to Houston, Texas, 1914–1945," 2001, 59–60, 142; *Texas Almanac, 2004–2005* (Dallas: Dallas Morning News, 2001), 125–27, 287, 383–99; Pratt, *The Growth of a Refining Region*, 19–23; 46–50, 83–85, 109–17; Campbell, *Gone to Texas*, 324–29, 260–64, 402–10; and Pruitt, "'For the Advancement of the Race,'" 2005, 443–44.

41. Calvert et al., *The History of Texas*; Hurley, *Decisive Years for Houston*, 43–47, 53–59, 415–417; Pruitt, "'For the Advancement of the Race,'" 2001, 59–60, 142; *Texas Almanac, 2004–2005*, 125–27, 287, 383–399; Pratt, *The Growth of a Refining Region*, 19–23; 46–50, 83–85, 109–17; Campbell, *Gone to Texas*, 324–29, 260–64, 402–10; and Pruitt, "'For the Advancement of the Race,'" 2005, 443–44.

42. Bureau of the Census, *Negro Population of the United States, 1790–1915*, 205; and

Bureau of the Census, *Negroes in the United States, 1920–1932* (1935; New York: Arno Publishing Co., 1969), 141 (hereafter cited as *Negroes in the United States, 1920–1932*).

43. "The Wright Company," in "Independence Heights, Texas: The First Black City in Texas, 1915–1928," researched and compiled by Vivian Hubbard Seals, Texas Room, Houston Public Library, Houston, Texas; W. H. Ward, County Judge to M. P. Hammond, Sheriff, Harris County, Texas, "Order Calling Election on Independence Heights Incorporation," January 25, 1915, in "Independence Heights, Texas"; and "Growth of Houston," Houston—Annexation—Chronological Listing—Vertical Files, Texas Room, Houston Public Library, Houston, Texas (all Vertical Files hereafter cited are in same location).

44. Bureau of the Census, *Negroes in the United States, 1920–1932*, 23; *The Handbook of Texas Online*, s.v., "Chinese," http://www.tshaonline.org/handbook/online/articles/CC/pjc1.html; Donna Collins, "Greeks," in *The Ethnic Groups of Houston*, ed. Fred von der Mehden (College Station: Texas A&M University), 113–25; "Jews," *The Handbook of Texas Online*, s.v., "Jews," http://www.tshaonline.org/handbook/online/articles/JJ/pxj1.html; *The Handbook of Texas Online*, s.v., "Italians," http://www.tshaonline.org/handbook/online/articles/II/ppi1.html; *The Handbook of Texas Online*, s.v., "Czechs," http://www.tshaonline.org/handbook/online/articles/CC/plc2.html; and *The Handbook of Texas Online*, s.v., "Poles," http://www.tshaonline.org/handbook/online/articles/PP/plp1.html. The word *Creole or Criollo* [Spanish] once exclusively defined Whites of French or Spanish ancestry born in the Colonial Caribbean, New France, especially French Louisiana, or New Spain. The term identified a distinct group of native-born local residents in Colonial America who largely traced their bloodline to Europe exclusively, although the Spanish caste system did permit Criollos to have one Amerindian ancestor. Today the term *Creole* also refers to Americans of African descent with mixed-race ancestry, particularly Americans who trace their linage to colonial Louisiana. The term, however, continues to evolve. In popular usage, *Black Creoles* descend from "Frenchmen" and African or African-descent women of early Louisiana. A broader definition also common includes Blacks with White fathers who lived prior to the Civil War: French or Spanish Creoles, indigenous Louisiana natives, French or Spanish immigrants, Anglo-Americans, Acadians/Cajuns, and other White ethnics as transplanted Americans of the United States.

45. De León, *Ethnicity in the Sunbelt*, 3–56, 110, 147; Guadalupe San Miguel, *Brown Not White: School Integration and the Chicano Movement in Houston* (College Station: Texas A&M University Press, 2001), 4–6, 23, 55, 99, 110, 147; Emilio Zamora, *The World of the Mexican Worker in Texas* (College Station: Texas A&M University Press, 1993), 10–54; Acuña, *Occupied America: A History of Chicanos*, 151–235; *The Handbook of Texas Online*, s.v., "Mexican Americans," http://www.tshaonline.org/handbook/online/articles/MM/pqmue.html; and Margarita Melville, "Mexicans," in *The Ethnic Groups of Houston*, ed. Fred von der Mehden (Houston: Rice University Press, 1984), 41–62.

46. Fred R. von der Mehden, ed., *The Ethnic Groups of Houston*; Pratt, *The Growth of a Refining Region*; Pratt, "Coming to Houston," 4–9; McComb, *Houston: A History*, 56–114; Campbell, *Gone to Texas*, 327–28, 361–65; Betty Trapp Chapman, *Houston Women: Invisible Threads in the Tapestry* (Virginia Beach: Donning, 2000), 15–26;

The Handbook of Texas Online, s.v., "Houston, Texas"; *The Handbook of Texas Online,* s.v., "San Antonio, Texas," http://www.tshaonline.org/handbook/online/articles/SS/hds2.html; *The Handbook of Texas Online,* s.v., "Fort Worth, Texas," http://www.tshaonline.org/handbook/online/articles/FF/hdf1.html; *The Handbook of Texas Online,* s.v., "Galveston County, Texas," http://www.tshaonline.org/handbook/online/articles/GG/hcg2.html; *The Handbook of Texas Online,* s.v., "Urbanization," http://www.tshaonline.org/handbook/online/articles/UU/hyunw.html; and *The Handbook of Texas Online,* s.v., "Dallas, Texas," http://www.tshaonline.org/handbook/online/articles/DD/hdd1.html.

47. Pratt, *The Growth of a Refining Region,* 19–23, 77–80; Pratt, "Coming to Houston," 4–9; McComb, *Houston: A History;* and Chapman, *Houston Women,* 15–26.

48. *Negro Population in the United States, 1790–1915,* 205; *Fourteenth Census of the United States, 1920,* vol. 2, 354; *Sixteenth Census of the United States, 1940,* vol. 2, 1044; Calvert, *History of Texas,* 3rd ed.; Hurley, *Decisive Years for Houston,* 43–47, 53–59, 415–17; Pruitt, "'For the Advancement of the Race,'" 2001, 59–60, 142; *Texas Almanac, 2002–2003,* 125–27, 287, 383–99; and Pratt, *The Growth of a Refining Region,* 19–23; 46–50, 83–85, 109–17.

49. Bureau of the Census, *Negroes in the United States, 1920–1932,* 41–42.

50. Pruitt, "'For the Advancement of the Race,'" 2005, 439–44.

51. Milton Larkin, interview by Louis Marchiafava, tape recording, January 5, 1988, Milton Larkin Collection, 252:1, Houston Metropolitan Research Center, Houston Public Library, Julia Ideson Building, Houston, Texas (hereafter, cited as Milton Larkin interview); Lorenzo Thomas, "Milt Larkin: Houston Jazz Bandleader," paper presented at the Texas State Historical Association Annual Meeting, Austin, March 5, 1998, 6–2; Photo Identification Sheet, Jeff Collins Family Collection, 184–1R:1; *The Handbook of Texas Online,* s.v., "Covington, Jennie Belle Murphy," http://www.tshaonline.org/handbook/online/articles/CC/fcoyp.html; *The Handbook of Texas Online,* s.v., "Covington, Benjamin Jesse," http://www.tshaonline.org/handbook/online/articles/CC/fcocp_print.html; "Funeral Service: Mrs. Jennie B. Covington," obituary, 1966, Dr. Benjamin Covington Papers, 170:1, folder 1, Houston Metropolitan Research Center, Houston Public Library, Houston, Texas (hereafter cited as Dr. Benjamin Covington MSS); Jean Walsh, "Dr. Covington, at 90, Is Still Practicing," *Houston Post,* March 12, 1961, Dr. Benjamin Covington MSS, 170:1, folder 1; Henry Coleman interview; Vivian Hubbard Seals, Historian, "Three Generations of Hubbards and Room for More . . ." in Hubbard Family Reunion Book, Hubbard Family Reunion: Getting to Know You, June 19–21, 1992," in possession of author; and Vivian Hubbard Seals, interview by author, tape recording, May 17, 1999, Houston, Texas, in possession of the author.

52. Census data along with other evidence suggest that most Houston Black migrants traveled from nearby farms and small towns in eastern Texas and Louisiana prior to 1945. See *Negro Population in the United States, 1790–1915,* 305; *Fourteenth Census of the United States, 1920,* vol. 3, 990–1014; *Sixteenth Census of the United States, 1940,* vol. 2, 792–806; Brophy, "The Black Texan, 1900–1950," 4, 15, 20; Campbell, *An Empire for Slavery,* 2; Hill, "The Negro in the Texas Labor Supply," 9, 67, 81–84; Pruitt, "'For the Advancement of the Race,'" 2005, 442–43; and Everett S. Lee, Ann Ratner Miller, Carol P. Brainerd, and Richard A. Easterlin, *Methodological Considerations and Reference*

Tables, vol. 1, *Population Redistribution and Economic Growth: United States, 1870–1950,* ed. Simon Kuznets and Dorothy Swaine Thomas (Philadelphia: American Philosophical Society, 1957–1964), 88–90.

53. Pruitt, "'For the Advancement of the Race,'" 2005, 435–45. Along with general census data, welfare applications and census manuscript schedules suggest that Houston migrants came from surrounding areas in Texas. Selected Harris County Social Service Client Case Files represented in this study are taken from the nonrandom sampling of 400 families—or 2,100 individuals—that applied for and received public assistance between 1917 and 1960 (primarily during the Great Depression). Texas-born applicants—1,368 persons—comprised 71 percent of the sample group, whereas persons born in Louisiana—466 persons—made up 24 percent. Individuals born in Houston comprised 38 percent (527 people) of the total Texas sample population. Only 3 percent—or 61 individuals—came to Houston from other southern states, and less than 1 percent, or 9 persons, came from outside the South. The birthplaces of 196 persons—mainly lodgers or landlords—could not be determined. See Social Service Department Client Case Files, Harris County Archives, boxes 24–1674, 1882–6600, 11851–12651, 12984–15153, 15170–16536, and 17041–17821, and WPA files, Harris Criminal Justice Center, Harris County, Texas (hereafter cited as Social Service Department Client Case Files); and Pruitt, "'For the Advancement of the Race,'" 2005, 435–78.

54. The 1920 Houston Manuscript Census figures used in this study are based on the nonrandom sampling of 3,400 persons totaling 10 percent of Houston's African American population for the year 1920. Some 2,764 Texas-born migrants comprised 81 percent of the surveyed group, and 409 individuals from Louisiana made up 12 percent of the sampled persons selected from the 1920 census manuscript schedules. In-migrants born in other southern places totaled 196, or 5 percent, of the entire sample pool. Less than 1 percent moved from other communities in the United States or places outside the country. See Manuscript Census of the United States, Harris County, Texas, 1920, rolls 1812–1814, Bureau of the Census, series T625, Clayton Genealogy Library, Houston Public Library, Houston, Texas; and Pruitt, "'For the Advancement of the Race,'" 2005, 435–78. The manuscript census of 1920 and the Harris Country welfare applications do not document the entire estimated migrant community for a number of reasons. First, the manuscript census only determines the state of birth and cannot distinguish between those persons born in Houston and those born in other Texas communities. Second, these records were not randomly sampled. None of the records selected for this book come from random samples. Third, the welfare applicants only represented a miniscule number of migrants, because most African American Houstonians did not receive public assistance at the time of the Great Depression. Taking these limitations into account, these sources nevertheless give researchers a glimpse into the world of Houston Black migrants in the first half of the twentieth century.

55. Manuscript Census, Harris County, 1920, rolls 1812–1814, series T625; Social Service Department Client Case Files, box 24–1674; Photo Identification Sheet, Jeff Collins Family MSS, 184–1R:1; Joseph Williams, interviewed by Bernadette Pruitt, tape recording, Houston, Texas, February 13, 1998, in possession of the author; Walsh, "Dr.

Covington, at 90, Is Still Practicing"; Pratt, *The Growth of a Refining Region*, 20; and Pruitt, "'For the Advancement of the Race,'" 2005, 442–43.

56. The intercensal net migration table (see table 3) for the periods 1900–10, 1910–20, and 1920–30 is based on census figures. See note 13 in the introduction for a thorough description of the table. See Bureau of the Census, *Negroes in the United States, 1920–1932*, 54–55, 141; *Fourteenth Census of the United States, 1920*, vol. 3, 1–26; *Sixteenth Census of the United States, 1940*, vol. 2, part 6: *Pennsylvania–Texas*, 1044; and Pruitt, "'For the Advancement of the Race,'" 2001, 143–45.

57. *Negro Population in the United States, 1790–1915*, 205; *Fourteenth Census of the United States, 1920*, vol. 2, 354; and *Sixteenth Census of the United States, 1940*, vol. 2, part 4, 1044.

58. *Negro Population in the United States, 1790–1915*, 92; Bureau of the Census, *Negroes in the United States, 1920–1932*, 53; Bureau of the Census, *Sixteenth Census of the United States*, vol. 2, part 3: *Kansas–Michigan*, 763; *Twelfth Census of the United States, 1900*, 40–42; *Fourteenth Census of the United States, 1920*, vol. 3, 990–1004; Brophy, "The Black Texan: 1900–1950," 13–14; Hill, "The Negro in the Texas Labor Supply," 82–84, 112–13; Lee et al., *Methodological Considerations and Reference Tables*, vol. 1, 88–90; and Pruitt, "'For the Advancement of the Race,'" 2005, 442–43.

59. Bureau of the Census, *Mortality Statistics, 1920: Twenty-First Annual Report* (Washington: US Government Printing Office, 1922), 91–92; Bureau of the Census, *Mortality Statistics, 1921: Twenty-Second Annual Report* (Washington: US Government Printing Office, 1924), 137–38; Bureau of the Census, *Mortality Statistics, 1922: Twenty-Third Annual Report* (Washington: US Government Printing Office, 1924), 109–11; Bureau of the Census, *Mortality Statistics, 1923: Twenty-Fourth Annual Report* (Washington: US Government Printing Office, 1925), 110; Bureau of the Census, *Mortality Statistics, 1924: Twenty-Fifth Annual Report* (Washington: US Government Printing Office, 1926), 102; Bureau of the Census, *Mortality Statistics, 1925: Twenty-Sixth Annual Report* (Washington: US Government Printing Office, 1927), 14–15; Bureau of the Census, *Mortality Statistics, 1926: Twenty-Seventh Annual Report* (Washington: US Government Printing Office, 1929), 14–15; Bureau of the Census, *Mortality Statistics, 1927: Twenty-Eighth Annual Report* (Washington: US Government Printing Office, 1929), 11–12; Bureau of the Census, *Mortality Statistics, 1928, 1929, Thirtieth Annual Report* (Washington: US Government Printing Office, 1932), 33–34; *Bureau of the Census, Mortality Statistics, 1930: Thirty-First Annual Report* (Washington: US Government Printing Office, 1934), 88–89; Bureau of the Census, *Mortality Statistics, 1931 and 1932: Thirty-Second Annual Report* (Washington: US Government Printing Office, 1934), 10; Bureau of the Census, *Mortality Statistics, 1933 and 1934: Thirty-Third Annual Report* (Washington: US Government Printing Office, 1936), 24–25; Bureau of the Census, *Mortality Statistics, 1935 and 1936: Thirty-Fourth Annual Report* (Washington: US Government Printing Office, 1938), 91–92; Bureau of the Census, *Vital Statistics of the United States, 1937* (Washington: US Government Printing Office, 1939), 50–51; Bureau of the Census, *Vital Statistics of the United States, 1938* (Washington: US Government Printing Office, 1940), 50–51; Bureau of the Census, *Vital Statistics of the United States, 1939* (Washington: US Government Printing Office, 1941), 50–51; Bureau of the Census, *Vital Statistics of the United States,*

1941 (Washington: US Government Printing Office, 1943), 79–81; *Fourteenth Census of the United States, 1920,* vol. 3, 393–98; and *Sixteenth Census of the United States, 1940,* vol. 2, part 3, 362–65.

60. Bureau of the Census, *Mortality Statistics, 1920,* 91–92; Bureau of the Census, *Mortality Statistics, 1921,* 137–38; Bureau of the Census, *Mortality Statistics, 1922,* 109–11; Bureau of the Census, *Mortality Statistics, 1923,* 110; Bureau of the Census, *Mortality Statistics, 1924,* 102; Bureau of the Census, *Mortality Statistics, 1925,* 14–15; Bureau of the Census, *Mortality Statistics, 1926,* 14–15; Bureau of the Census, *Mortality Statistics, 1927,* 11–12; Bureau of the Census, *Mortality Statistics, 1928, 1929, Thirtieth Annual Report,* 33–34; and Bureau of the *Census, Mortality Statistics, 1930,* 88–89.

61. Bureau of the Census, *Mortality Statistics, 1920,* 91–92; Bureau of the Census, *Mortality Statistics, 1921,* 137–38; Bureau of the Census, *Mortality Statistics, 1922,* 109–11; Bureau of the Census, *Mortality Statistics, 1923,* 110; Bureau of the Census, *Mortality Statistics, 1924,* 102; Bureau of the Census, *Mortality Statistics, 1925,* 14–15; Bureau of the Census, *Mortality Statistics, 1926,* 14–15; Bureau of the Census, *Mortality Statistics, 1927,* 11–12; Bureau of the Census, *Mortality Statistics, 1928, 1929, Thirtieth Annual Report,* 33–34; and Bureau of the Census, *Mortality Statistics, 1930,* 88–89.

62. *Negro Population in the United States, 1790–1915,* 78; *Fourteenth Census of the United States, 1920,* vol. 2, 639; Bureau of the Census, *Negroes in the United States, 1920–1932,* 30; Social Service Department Client Case Files, boxes 24–1674, 1882–6600, 11851–12651, 12984–15153, 15170–16536, 17041–17282, and 17286–17435, WPA box, and Finding Aid, Harris County Social Services, Harris County Archives, Harris County Courthouse, Houston, Texas, CR08; Manuscript Census, Harris County, 1920, rolls 1812–1814, series T625; Carol Rust, "Frenchtown," *Houston Chronicle,* February 23, 1992, Houston—Subdivisions—Frenchtown—Vertical Files; Robert C. Giles, Curtis M. Dowell, and Vivian J. Zermeno, "Josephites Have Logged 90 Years in the Diocese," A Tribute to the Josephites, Supplement to the *Texas Catholic Herald,* September 10, 1993; "A Tribute to Ellis Montgomery Knight Jr.," in possession of J. R. Knight, Houston, Texas; Luther Stullivan, *Roots of the Stullivan Family* (Houston, N.P.), 18–20; and Pruitt, "'For the Advancement of the Race,'" 2005, 442–43.

63. Glenn R. Conrad and Carl A. Brasseaux, *Crevasse! The 1927 Flood in Acadiana* (Lafayette: the Center for Louisiana Studies, the University of Southwestern Louisiana, 1994), 21–31; John M. Barry, "After the Deluge: In the Wake of Hurricane Katrina, a Writer Looks Back at the Repercussions of Another Great Disaster—the Mississippi Flood of 1927," Smithsonian Magazine.Com, November 2005, http://www.smithsonianmag.com/history-archaeology/pom.html; Gary Rotstein, "The Next Great Diaspora? Many Scattered by Katrina May Never Return Home," *Pittsburgh Post-Gazette,* September 11, 2005; *Fatal Flood: A Story of Greed, Power, and Race,* directed and produced by Chana Gazit, 60 minutes, A Steward/Gazit Productions, Inc. film for American Experience, 2001; and Pruitt, "'For the Advancement of the Race,'" 2005, 442–43.

64. *Fatal Flood;* Barry, "After the Deluge"; Conrad and Brasseaux, *Crevasse!* 21–41; Rothstein, "The Next Great Diaspora?"; and Pruitt, "'For the Advancement of the Race,'" 2005, 442–43."

65. John S. MacDonald and Leatrice D. MacDonald, "Chain Migration, Ethnic

Neighborhood Formation and Social Networks," *Millbank Memorial Fund* 42 (1964): 82–97; and Lewis, "Expectations, Economic Opportunities, and Life in the Industrial Age," 24; and Reich, ed., *Encyclopedia of the Great Black Migration*, vol. 1, s.v., "Chain Migration," 168–70.

66. Stullivan, *Roots of the Stullivan Family*, 1–10; Luther Stullivan, interviewed by Bernadette Pruitt, tape recording, Houston, Texas, July 23, 1996, in possession of the author.; Joseph Williams interview; Henry Coleman interview; and Pruitt, "'For the Advancement of the Race,'" 2001, 56, 83–116.

67. Joseph Williams interview; Henry Coleman interview; and Pruitt, "'For the Advancement of the Race,'" 2001, 83–116, 55.

68. "News from Texas Towns," *Houston Informer*, June 17, 1919; Joseph Williams interview; Calvin L. Rhone to Lucia J. Rhone, December 20, 1920, Rhone Family Papers, 1886–1971, 3U171:2, Afro-American Collection, Dolph Briscoe Center for American History, University of Texas at Austin, Austin, Texas (hereafter cited as Rhone Family MSS); and "News from Texas Towns," *Houston Informer*, January 23, 1932.

69. William M. Tuttle Jr., *Race Riot: Chicago in the Red Summer of 1919* (New York: Antheneum, 1970), 208–14; Spear, *Black Chicago*, 134–35; Cary D. Wintz, *Black Culture and the Harlem Renaissance* (Houston: Rice University Press, 1988), 30–31; James M. SoRelle, "The Emergence of Black Business in Houston, Texas: A Study of Race and Ideology, 1919–45," in *Black Dixie*, 105–8; Beeth and Wintz, "Segregation, Violence and Civil Rights: Race Relations in Twentieth Century Houston," in *Black Dixie*, 160–61; James M. SoRelle, "Race Relations in 'Heavenly Houston,' 1919–45," 178–81; Robert V. Haynes, "Black Houstonians and the White Democratic Primary, 1920–45," in *Black Dixie*, 198–99, 202; and *Houston Informer*, October 6, 1923.

70. "Biographical Note," C. F. Richardson Sr. Papers, MSS 1457, Houston Metropolitan Research Center, Houston Public Library, Julia Ideson Building, Houston, Texas, Texas Archival Resources Online, http://www.lib.utexas.edu/taro/houpub/00191/hpub-00191.html (hereafter cited as C. F. Richardson Sr. MSS); Luther Stullivan interview. For *Houston Informer* articles and editorials that promoted the "New Negro" philosophy of the post–World War I era and that were written largely by Clifton F. Richardson Sr., see "South's Idea of a Good Negro," *Houston Informer*, July 28, 1928; "Leaders and Lackeys," *Houston Informer*, March 5, 1927; "An Open Letter to City Fathers," *Houston Informer*, February 23, 1924; "Condition of Houston Negro Schools," *Houston Informer*, March 15, 1924; Kelly Miller, "Rescinding Jim Crow Laws," *Houston Informer*, May 7, 1927; "Upholding White Man's Primary Law," *Houston Informer*, April 26, 1924; "Colored Men and Women! Pay Your Poll Tax Now! Get Ready for 1921!" *Houston Informer*, January 8, 1921; "Republican Council's Jim-Crowism—Will Colored Voters Stand for Such?" *Houston Informer*, March 13, 1920; "Race Leaders' Selling Out the Race," *Houston Informer*, July 24, 1926; "Texas Negroes' Political Apathy," *Houston Informer*, October 1, 1927; and "Report Reveals Lynching of Two Colored Boys and One Colored Girl Planned and Executed by Ku Klux Klan—Officers Played Prominent Part in Orgy—Reputable White Citizens Heavily Armed and Living in Terror—Governor's Kinsman Member of Mob," *Houston Informer*, November 6, 1926.

71. "Biographical Note," C. F. Richardson Sr. MSS, 1457; "Colored Americans in

Walker County Victims of Wholesale Depredations," *Houston Informer,* June 7, 1919; and Ellis Elizabeth Newell, "The Life and Works of C. F. Richardson" (senior thesis, Houston College for Negroes, 1941), 5.

72. "Biographical Note," C. F. Richardson Sr. MSS, 1457; "Colored Americans in Walker County Victims of Wholesale Depredations"; and Ellis Elizabeth Newell, "The Life and Works of C. F. Richardson" (senior thesis, Houston College for Negroes, 1941), 5.

73. "Colored Americans in Walker County Victims of Wholesale Depredations," *Houston Informer,* June 7, 1919.

74. "Dyer Mob-Violence Killed," *Houston Informer,* June 11, 1919; and Howard Jones, *The Red Diary: A Chronological History of Black Americans in Houston and Some Neighboring Harris County Communities* (Austin: Nortex Press, 1991), 54–55, 61.

75. "Dyer Mob-Violence Killed"; Obadele-Starks, *Black Unionism in the Industrial South,* 8.

76. "Dyer Mob-Violence Killed."

77. Black newspapers and community and civic activists used the term *race* when referring to African Americans—communities, churches, schools, and businesses. The word suggested dignity, pride, and loyalty on the part of African Americans.

78. SoRelle, "Race Relations in 'Heavenly Houston,' 1919–45," 175–80.

79. Lorenzo J. Greene, *Selling Black History for Carter G. Woodson: A Diary, 1930–1933,* edited and with an introduction by Arvarh E. Strickland (Columbia: University of Missouri Press, 1996), 130.

80. Thomas, *A Study of the Social Welfare Status of Negroes in Houston, Texas,* 102.

81. SoRelle, "Race Relations in 'Heavenly Houston,' 1919–45," 175–80.

82. "News from Texas Towns," *Houston Informer,* June 28, 1919; June 17, 1919; March 13, 1920; SoRelle, "Race Relations in 'Heavenly Houston,' 1919–45," 175–80; and Thomas, *A Study of the Social Welfare Status of Negroes in Houston, Texas,* 102–3.

83. "News and Views from Texas Towns," *Houston Informer,* January 23, 1932; "News and Views from Texas Towns," *Houston Informer,* June 10, 1933; and "The Catholic Circle," *Houston Informer,* November 24, 1934.

84. Kenneth Kusmer, *A Ghetto Takes Shape: Black Cleveland, 1870–1930* (Urbana: University of Illinois Press, 1980), 206; Trotter, *Black Milwaukee,* 80–83; and Spear, *Black Chicago,* 167–68.

85. Beeth and Wintz, "Economic and Social Development in Black Houston during the Era of Segregation," in *Black Dixie,* 88–90.

86. Joseph Williams interview; William H. Harris, *The Harder We Run: Black Workers since the Civil War* (New York: Oxford University Press, 1982), 77–78; and William H. Harris, *Keeping the Faith: A. Philip Randolph, Milton P. Webster, and the Brotherhood of Sleeping Car Porters, 1925–37* (Urbana: University of Illinois Press, 1977), 2–15.

87. Joseph Williams interview.

88. Ibid.

89. Ibid.

90. Ibid.

91. Ibid.

92. Ibid.

93. Ibid.
94. Ibid.
95. Ibid.
96. Ibid.
97. Ibid.
98. Joseph Williams interview; William H. Harris, *The Harder We Run,* 77–78; and William H. Harris, *Keeping the Faith,* 2–15.
99. Joseph Williams interview; William H. Harris, *The Harder We Run,* 77–78; and William H. Harris, *Keeping the Faith,* 2–15.
100. Joseph Williams interview.
101. Joseph Williams interview; William H. Harris, *The Harder We Run,* 77–78; and William H. Harris, *Keeping the Faith,* 2–15.
102. Joseph Williams interview; Raymond Lewis, interview by Bernadette Pruitt, tape recording, February 14, 1998, Houston, Texas, in possession of the author; and Lewis, *In Their Own Interests,* 22–33, 40–42.
103. Joseph Williams interview; Henry Coleman interview; and Pruitt, "'For the Advancement of the Race,'" 2001, 83–116, 55.
104. Joseph Williams interview; Henry Coleman interview; and Pruitt, "'For the Advancement of the Race,'" 2001, 83–116, 55.
105. Joseph Williams interview; Henry Coleman interview; and Luther Stullivan interview.
106. Joseph Williams interview; Henry Coleman interview; Luther Stullivan interview; Gottlieb, *Making Their Own Way,* 45–59; Phillips, *Alabama North,* 50–56; Lullelia Harrison interview, September 23, 1999; and Catherine Collins interview.
107. Joseph Williams interview; Henry Coleman interview; Luther Stullivan interview; Gottlieb, *Making Their Own Way,* 45–59; Phillips, *Alabama North,* 50–56; Lullelia Harrison interview, September 23, 1999; Lullelia Harrison interview, March 8, 2000; and Rick Mitchell, "Houston Jazz Legend Larkin Dies at 65."
108. Taylor, George, and Ethel, Case Record of Family Referred to Works Progress Administration, Case No. 5006, 1937, Social Service Department Client Case Files, Case No. W-5006, and WPA box CR08.
109. Ibid.
110. "News from Texas Towns," *Houston Informer,* January 23, 1932.
111. "News from Texas Towns," *Houston Informer,* January 23, 1932; "News from Texas Towns," *Houston Informer,* June 10, 1933; Luther Stullivan interview; and Marks, *Farewell—We're Good and Gone,* 19–48.
112. Calvin L. Rhone to Lucia J. Rhone, December 20, 1920, Rhone Family MSS, 3U171:2; and Obituary of Calvin L. Rhone Sr., *Western Star,* January 29, 1921, Rhone Family MSS, 3U180:1.
113. Calvin L. Rhone to Lucia J. Rhone, December 20, 1920, Rhone Family MSS, 3U171:2; Obituary of Calvin L. Rhone Sr., Rhone Family MSS, 3U180:1.
114. Pruitt, "'For the Advancement of the Race,'" 2005, 438–39.
115. Ibid.

Chapter 2

1. "The Rev. George B. Orviss, Grandfather of Constance Houston Thompson," photograph, in Naomi Ledé, *Precious Memories of a Black Socialite: A Narrative of the Life and Times of Constance Houston Thompson* (Houston: D. Armstrong Co., 1991), 40; "Mrs. George B. (Mary) Orviss, mother of Georgia C. Orviss Houston, photograph, in Ledé, *Precious Memories of a Black Socialite*, 40; David Williams, "A Brief History of St. James Methodist Church," 1934, in possession of Wendell H. Baker, Huntsville, Texas; Houston Family, 1898, Joshua Houston Family Collection, 437–6, Houston Metropolitan Research Center, Houston Public Library, Julia Ideson Building, Houston, Texas (hereafter cited as Houston Family MSS); Sisters and Sisters-in-Law Cornelia Orviss Houston and Georgia C. Orviss Houston, Houston Family MSS, 437–3; Ledé, *Precious Memories of a Black Socialite*, 40–106; Patricia Smith Prather and Jane Clements Monday, *From Slave to Statesman: The Legacy of Joshua Houston, Servant to Sam Houston* (Denton: University of North Texas Press, 1993), 29–175; *The Handbook of Texas Online*, s.v., "Houston, Samuel," http://www.tshaonline.org/handbook/online/articles/HH/fho73.html; *The Handbook of Texas Online*, s.v., "Houston, Joshua," http://www.tshaonline.org/handbook/online/articles/fhohq; and *African American National Biography*, s.v., "Houston, Joshua," ed. Henry Louis Gates Jr. and Evelyn Brooks Higginbotham (New York: Oxford University Press, 2005), 336–337.

2. Ledé, *Precious Memories of a Black Socialite*, 70–73.

3. Ibid., 71.

4. Ibid., 70–73.

5. Quoted in Ledé, "Constance Houston Thompson," in *Precious Memories of a Black Socialite*, 71. The probable lynching death Constance Houston Thompson referred to more than likely involved the Cabaness family of Huntsville. In a span of four days, White vigilantes killed seven family members, including children. Black farm owner George Cabaniss's refusal to register for the draft sparked the bloodshed. See "Six Negroes Slain for Alleged Plot to Wipe Out Family," *San Antonio Express*, June 1, 1918; "Six Negroes Die After Battle with Citizens Posse," *San Antonio Express*, June 2, 1918; Christine's Genealogy Website, "Six Negroes Die After Battle with Citizens Posse," http://ccharity.com/content/six-negroes-dead-after-battle-citizens-posse; and Ralph Ginzburg, *100 Years of Lynchings* (Baltimore: Black Classic Press, 1988), 269.

6. "The Rev. George B. Orviss, Grandfather of Constance Houston Thompson," photograph, in Ledé, *Precious Memories of a Black Socialite*, 40; "Mrs. George B. (Mary) Orviss, mother of Georgia C. Orviss Houston," photograph, in Ledé, *Precious Memories of a Black Socialite*, 40; Williams, "A Brief History of St. James Methodist Church"; Houston Family, 1902, Houston Family MSS, 437–6; Sisters and sisters-in-law Cornelia Orviss Houston and Georgia C. Orviss Houston, Houston Family MSS, 437–3; Ledé, *Precious Memories of a Black Socialite*, 40–106; Smith Prather and Clements Monday, *From Slave to Statesman*; *The Handbook of Texas Online*, s.v., "Houston, Samuel"; *The Handbook of Texas Online*, s.v., "Houston, Joshua"; Zellar, "Rogersville," 2–12; and *African American National Biography*, s.v., "Houston, Joshua," 336–337.

7. Ledé, *Precious Memories of a Black Socialite*, 40–106; Prather Smith and

Monday Clements, *From Slave to Statesman*, 200–38; Ledé, ed., "Constance Houston Thompson," in *Pathfinders: A History of the Pioneering Efforts of African Americans—Huntsville, Walker, County, Texas* (Virginia Beach, Virginia: Donning Company Publishers, 2004), 70–72; and Ledé, "Hortense Houston Young," in *Pathfinders*, 84–86.

8. Ledé, *Precious Memories of a Black Socialite*, 109–17, 144–48; Prather Smith and Clements Monday, *From Slave to Statesman*, 200–38; and Ledé, "Hortense Houston Young," in *Pathfinders*, 84–86. Hortense Houston, the youngest child of Joshua and Georgia Houston, was actually the couple's third child. Joshua and Georgia Houston's second daughter, Maxine Houston, died of cholera at the age of six months in late 1902.

9. Ledé, "Hortense Houston Young," in *Pathfinders*, 84–86; and Ledé, *Precious Memories of a Black Socialite*, 109–17, 144–48.

10. "Educator, Wife, and Mother Hortense Houston Young," Houston Family MSS, 437–9; Ledé, *Precious Memories of a Black Socialite*, 109–17, 144–48; Ledé, "Hortense Houston Young," in *Pathfinders*, 84–86; and University of Louisville Louis Brandeis School of Law, Black History Month, Louis D. Brandeis School of Law, http://www.law.louisville.edu/node/1300; K. Dawn Rutledge-Jones, "Minority Engineer Watched Evolution of Industry," *Nashville Business Journal*, February 20, 1998; and Young, C. Milton Jr., Oral History Index: Y&Z, University Archives and Records, University Libraries, University of Louisville, http://library.louisville.edu/uarc/ohc/ohYZ.html; Civil Rights Digital Library, Digital Library of Georgia, University of Georgia, s.v., "C. Milton (Coleman Milton) Young," http://crdl.usg.edu/; Walter Reuther Library, "One Giant Leap for Womankind," Wayne State University, Detroit, Michigan, http://www.reuther.wayne.edu/node/7948; and Yvonne Clark, Irene Sharpe interview, Society for Women Engineers, accessed October 17, 2012, http://societyofwomenengineers.swe.org/index.php/employers-q1-2010-career-center-408/963-swe-women-clark. Hortense Young became the first African American woman accepted into the University of Louisville Louis Brandeis School of Law; however, sexism and racism precluded her from graduating. Because of Young's courage, her children would excel in their chosen professions. Yvonne Young Clark, the first woman graduate of Howard University's mechanical engineering department in 1951 or 1952, first Black woman mechanical engineer in the United States, first African American member of the Society of Women Engineers, and first woman graduate from Vanderbilt's Engineering Management program in 1972, served as head of Tennessee State University's Department of Mechanical Engineering for several decades and has served as associate professor of mechanical engineering for fifty years. The 1957 Society of Women Engineer's annual convention at the Houston Sheraton Hotel. Segregationist management barred Clark from staying overnight on the premises A life member and fellow of the professional society, Clark had a more pleasant experience in the city while attending another meeting in 1998. In 1969, Clark helped design the case Apollo 11 astronauts used as a transport carrier for rocks they lifted from the surface of the moon. C. Milton and Hortense Young's youngest child, physician C. Milton Young III, still practices internal medicine in Louisville.

11. Patricia Smith Prather, "The Houston Place," *Houston Chronicle*, June 19, 1986, Houston—Subdivisions—Fifth Ward—Vertical Files; The Wedding of Tracy Thompson and Constance Houston, June 18, 1928, Houston Family MSS, 437–20;

Ledé, *Precious Memories of a Black Socialite*, 40–142, 144–48, 152–77; Smith Prather and Clements Monday, *From Slave to Statesman*, 200–38; and Ledé, "Constance Houston Thompson," in *Pathfinders*, 70–72.

12. MacDonald and MacDonald, "Chain Migration," 82–97; Earl Lewis, "Expectations, Economic Opportunities, and Life in the Industrial Age," 24–25; Pruitt, "'For the Advancement of the Race,'" 2005, 435–36, 445–47; Schomburg Center, "The Great Migration," *In Motion*, http://www.inmotionaame.org/migrations/landing.cfm?migration=8; and in *Encyclopedia of the Great Black Migration*, vol. 1, s.v., "Chain Migration," 168–70; and Claudia Feldman, "Historic Fourth Ward Called 'Living Coffin,'" *Houston Chronicle*, September 23, 1976, Houston—Subdivisions—Fourth Ward—Vertical Files; and *The Handbook of Texas Online*, s.v., "Fourth Ward, Houston," http://www.tshaonline.org/handbook/online/articles/FF/hpf1.html.

13. "Houston Ward Boundaries, From Houston City Directory[,] 1879–1880, 20," Houston—Wards—Vertical Files; Feldman, "Historic Fourth Ward Called 'Living Coffin'"; "Where Were the 6 Wards?" *Houston Post*, Sound Off, February 28, 1965; Houston—Growth of Houston, Incorporated Area City of Houston, Texas, Houston—Annexation—Chronological List, Texas Room, Houston Public Library, Houston, Texas; *Negro Population in the United States, 1790–1915*, 831–34; *Twelfth Census of the United States, 1900*, 40–42; *Fourteenth Census of the United States, 1920*, vol. 3, 990–1004; and *The Handbook of Texas Online*, s.v., "Fourth Ward, Houston."

14. Growth of Houston, Incorporated Area City of Houston, Texas; *The Handbook of Texas Online*, s.v., "Fifth Ward, Houston" (by Cary D. Wintz), http://www.tshonline.org/handbook/online/articles/FF/hpfhk.html; *The Handbook of Texas Online*, s.v., "Acres Homes, Texas," http://www.tshaonline.org/handbook/online/articles/AA/hrazv.html; *The Handbook of Texas Online*, s.v., "Acres Homes Transit Authority," http://www.tshaonline.org/handbook/online/articles/AA/dgama.html; Roger Townsend Ward, "Acres Shakers: The Solution to Public Transportation Needs in a Black Community" (master's thesis, University of Houston, 1993), 1–17; "Historic Acres Homes Poised for Economic Progress," *Houston Business Journal*, November 3, 2002, http://www.bizjournals.com/houston/stories/2002/11/04/story5.html?t=printable; City Savvy: Online Edition, "Sunnyside Up: Residents Preserve Community's Heritage," August 30, 2007, in possession of the author. Seals, "Oliphant Lockwood Hubbard Sr., 1880–1968: Educator—Mayor—Real Estate Dealer," in "Independence Heights, Texas"; Sunnyside Working Plan, Sunnyside Area Study Area and Sections, Houston's Neighborhood Improvement Planning Program, September 1973, City of Houston Planning and Development Department, City of Houston Annex, Houston, Texas; and Acres Homes Neighborhood Improvement Plan, City of Houston Planning and Development Department, City of Houston Annex, Houston, Texas.

15. Thelma Scott Bryant, *Pioneer Families of Houston (Early 1900s) as Remembered by Thelma Scott Bryant* (Houston: N. P., 1991); Knight Family Reunion Book, "Our History." 1997. In possession of J. R. Knight. Houston, Texas; Luther Stullivan interview; Dan Plesa, "Revitalize: Third Ward Pushing Change," *Houston Post*, July 21, 1993, Houston—Subdivisions—Third Ward—Vertical Files; Museum of Fine Arts Houston,

Eye on Third Ward: Historical Reflections on The Third Ward, August 2, 2009, http://www.mfah.org/exhibitions/past/eye-third-ward-2012-yates-high-school-photography/; Thelma Scott Bryant, interview by Bernadette Pruitt, tape recording, July 24, 1996, Houston, Texas, in possession of the author; Lullelia Harrison interview, March 8, 2000, in possession of author; Lullelia Harrison interview, September 23, 1999, in possession of author; Who's Who in American Education, vol. 21, 1963–64, Olee Yates McCullough Papers, 370:1, Houston Metropolitan Research Center, Houston Public Library, Julia Ideson Building, Houston, Texas (hereafter cited as Olee Yates McCullough MSS); obituary of Olee Yates McCullough, Olee Yates McCullough MSS, 370:9; and Precious Memories, an autobiographical portrait, Olee Yates McCullough MSS, 370:9.

16. Emmett J. Scott, ed., *The Red Book of Houston: A Compendium of Social, Professional, Religious, Educational, and Industrial Interests of Houston's Colored Population* (Houston: Sotex Publishing Co., 1915); Bryant, *Pioneer Families of Houston,* 3–35; Pruitt, "'For the Advancement of the Race,'" 2005, 435–45; Beeth and Wintz, "Slavery and Freedom: Blacks in Nineteenth-Century Houston," in *Black Dixie,* 25; and Cary D. Wintz, "The Emergence of a Black Neighborhood: Houston's Fourth Ward, 1865–1915," in *Urban Texas: Politics and Development,* eds., Char Miller and Heywood Sanders (College Station: Texas A&M University Press, 1990), 96–100.

17. Louise Passey Maxwell, "Freedmantown: The Origins of a Black Neighborhood in Houston, 1865–1880," in *Bricks Without Straw: A Comprehensive History of African Americans in Texas,"* written and ed. David A. Williams (Austin: Eakin Press, 1997), 139–52; and Beeth and Wintz, "Economic and Social Development in Black Houston during the Era of Segregation," 87–88.

18. Scott, *The Red Book of Houston;* Beeth and Wintz, "Economic and Social Development in Black Houston during the Era of Segregation," 88–90; and Pruitt, "'For the Advancement of the Race,'" 2005, 453–459

19. Bryant, *Pioneer Families of Houston;* Olee Yates McCullough obituary, Olee Yates McCullough MSS, 370:9; and "Funeral Service: Mrs. Jennie B. Covington," obituary, 1966, Dr. Benjamin Covington MSS, 170:1, folder 1.

20. Carmen Keltner, "Economics and Historic Roots on Collision Course in Fourth Ward," Houston Downtown Magazine, November 5, 1984, Houston—Subdivisions—Fourth Ward—Vertical Files; National Urban League, *A Review of the Economic and Cultural Problems of Houston, Texas: As They Relate to Conditions of the Negro Population. N. P., 1945,* 17; Cary D. Wintz, *Blacks in Houston* (Houston: Houston Center for the Humanities and the National Endowment for the Humanities), 17–19; *The Handbook of Texas Online,* s.v., "Fourth Ward, Houston"; *The Handbook of Texas Online,* s.v., "Poles"; Maxwell, "Freedmantown," 139–52; and Beeth and Wintz, "Slavery and Freedom: Blacks in Nineteenth-Century Houston," 25.

21. Keltner, "Economics and Historic Roots on Collision Course,"—Houston—Subdivisions—Fourth Ward—Vertical Files; National Urban League, *A Review of the Economic and Cultural Problems of Houston, Texas,* 17; Wintz, *Blacks in Houston,* 17–19; Wintz, "Fourth Ward, Houston," 1141–42; Wintz, "The Emergence of a Black Neighborhood," 96–100; and Glass, "The Actualization of Houston, Texas," 16–28.

22. Bureau of the Census, *Ninth Census of the United States, 1870: Population, part 1* (Washington: US Government Printing Office, 1872), 272–73 (hereafter cited as *Ninth Census of the United States, 1870*); Bureau of the Census, *Eleventh Census of the United States, 1890: Population, part 1* (Washington: US Government Printing Office, 1895), 540–79 (hereafter cited as *Eleventh Census of the United States, 1890*); Wintz, "The Emergence of a Black Neighborhood," 99–104; and *Twelfth Census of the United States, 1900*, 132.

23. *Ninth Census of the United States, 1870*, 272; *Fourteenth Census of the United States, 1920*, vol. 3, 1026; Social Service Department Client Files, boxes 24–24–1674, 1882–6600, 11851–12651, 12984–15153, 15170–16536, 16551–17036, 17041–17282, and 17286–17435; Houston—Subdivisions—Fourth Ward—Vertical Files; National Urban League, *A Review of the Economic and Cultural Problems of Houston, Texas*, 17; and SoRelle, "The Darker Side of 'Heaven,'" 217–18.

24. Manuscript Census of the United States, Travis County, Texas, 1880, roll 1329, Bureau of the Census, series T9, Heritage Quest Online, http://persi.heritagequestonline.com/; Martha A. Sneed, Texas Death Index, 28135, 1958, from Ancestry.com, http://search.ancestry.com/; Manuscript Census of the United States, Galveston, Texas, 1900, roll 1637, Bureau of the Census, series T623, Heritage Quest Online, http://persi.heritagequestonline.com/; Glenn O. Sneed, Houston, Texas City Directory, 1917, from Ancestry.com, http://search.ancestry.com/; and Sneed Family Collection, Historical Context Sheet, Sneed Family Collection, 293–1:1, Houston Metropolitan Research Center, Houston Public Library, Houston, Texas (hereafter cited as Sneed Family MSS). The Galveston Hurricane of 1900 killed more than six thousand Galveston residents and cost the city millions of dollars. Although the city built a seventeen-foot-high seawall to protect itself from future hurricanes, Galveston never recovered financially from the disaster. Businesses and families, like the Sneeds, fled the city for more inland communities like Houston.

25. Historical Context, Sneed Family MSS; Photo Identification Sheet 12C, Sneed Family MSS, 293–12C:1; Photo Identification Sheet 13, Sneed Family MSS, 293–13:1; Photo Identification Sheet 16, Sneed Family MSS, 293–16:1; Photo Identification Sheet 23, Sneed Family MSS, 293–23:1; Photo Identification Sheet 24, Sneed Family MSS, 293–24:1; Photo Identification Sheet 26, Sneed Family MSS, 293–26:1; Photo Identification Sheet 27, Sneed Family MSS, 293–27:1; Photo Identification Sheet 27, Sneed Family MSS, 293–27:1; Photo Identification Sheet 28, Sneed Family MSS, 293–28:1; Photo Identification Sheet 31, Sneed Family MSS, 293–32:1; Photo Identification Sheet 31, Sneed Family MSS, 293–32:1; Photo Identification Sheet 34, Sneed Family MSS, 293–34:1; and Manuscript Census, Harris County, 1930, roll 2348, series T626.

26. Dorothy Knox Howe Houghton, Katherine S. Howe, and Sadie Gwyn Blackburn, *Houston's Forgotten Heritage: Landscape, Houses, Interiors, 1824–1914* (Houston: Rice University Press, 1991), 33–44, 52. US survey textbooks define the "Walking City" as an early nineteenth-century city that stretched not far from the central downtown business district. Before the advent of urban transportation, most urban dwellers lived very close to their businesses and jobs. Only with the formation of urban transportation did the walking city in which neighborhoods that encircled downtown

disappear. Like New York, Detroit, Chicago, and Philadelphia, Houston wards represented the first neighborhoods of those Houstonians who lived and worked in the city. Prior to 1906, persons elected aldermen to represent individual districts also known as wards. At the turn of the century, the city covered only sixteen square miles, and the wards never expanded far beyond the intersection of Main and Congress. See Houston—Wards—Vertical Files.

27. *Ninth Census of the United States, 1870; Fourteenth Census of the United States, 1920*, vol. 3, 1026; National Urban League, *A Review of the Economic and Cultural Problems of Houston, Texas,* 17; SoRelle, "The Darker Side of 'Heaven,'" 217–18. For the development of White subdivisions near Third Ward, see, Bernadette Pruitt, "The Urban Transformation of the MacGregor Area, 1950–1970"; Robert Fisher, "Protecting Community and Property Values: Civic Clubs in Houston, 1909–70," in *Urban Texas: Politics and Development,* ed. Char Miller and Heywood Sanders (College Station: Texas A&M University Press, 1990), 134–37; and *This Is My Home, It Is Not For Sale,* directed and produced by Jon Schwartz, 194 min., Riverside Productions, Videocassette, 1987. At present, the original boundaries of Third Ward have changed to include the subdivisions directly north of Brays Bayou, such as Riverside and Riverside Terrace. During the time being discussed, however, these subdivisions were not considered part of Third Ward. See Houston—Subdivisions—Third Ward—Vertical Files.

28. *Ninth Census of the United States,* 272; *Fourteenth Census of the United States, 1920*, vol. 3, 1026; Social Service Department Client Case Files, boxes 24–1674, 1882–6600, 11851–12651, 12984–15153, 15170–16536, 17041–17282, and 17286–17435, and WPA box; Harris County Social Services Finding Aids, CR08, Harris County Archives, Houston, Texas; Thelma Scott Bryant interview; Joseph Williams interview; Pitre, *In Struggle against Jim Crow,* 13–16; and Betty T. Chapman, "Third Ward: Silk Stocking Seat of County Government," in "Houston Heritage," *Houston Business Journal,* n. d., Houston—Subdivisions—Wards—Vertical Files.

29. Thelma Scott Bryant interview; Bryant, *Pioneer Families of Houston;* and Thelma Scott Bryant, *Our Journey through Houston and US History,* 2nd ed. (Houston: N. P., 1997). Ira Bryant's publications include *Andrew Jackson Young, Mr. Ambassador: United States Ambassador to the United Nations* (Houston: Armstrong, 1979).

30. Thelma Scott Bryant interview; "Funeral Service: Mrs. Jennie B. Covington"; Walsh, Dr. Covington, at 90, Is Still Practicing"; *The Handbook of Texas Online,* s.v., "Covington, Benjamin"; Thelma Scott Bryant, *Pioneer Families of Houston,* 1–36; Bryant, *Our Journey through Houston and US History,* 10–13; Seals, "Oliphant Lockwood Hubbard Sr., 1880–1968: Educator—Mayor—Real Estate Dealer"; Vivian Hubbard Seals interview; and Hine et al., *The African-American Odyssey,* 420–75.

31. Betty T. Chapman, "Old City Wards Developed Unique Economic and Political Identities," in "Houston Heritage," *Houston Business Journal,* March 15–21, 1988, Houston—Subdivisions—Wards—Vertical Files; Betty T. Chapman, "Fifth Ward: Ethnic Melting Pot and Industrial Business District," in "Houston Heritage," *Houston Business Journal,* n.d., Houston—Subdivisions—Wards, Vertical Files; *The Handbook of Texas Online,* s.v., "Fifth Ward, Houston"; De León, *Ethnicity in the Sunbelt,* 22–31; The Handbook of Texas Online, s.v., "Jews"; *The Handbook of Texas Online,* s.v., "Poles";

A. Alexander, Houston Street Guide, 1913, Map, (Houston: J. M. Kelsen), Texas State Library and Archives Division, Historic Maps of Texas Cities, Map Collection, Perry-Castañeda Library, University of Texas Libraries, University of Texas at Austin, Austin, Texas; Houston Northeast, 1922, Map, Historical Maps of Texas Cities, Map Collection, Perry-Castañeda Library, University of Texas Libraries, University of Texas at Austin, Austin, Texas; R. L. Polk and Co., Polk's Houston City Directory (Houston: R. L. Polk and Co, 1917); and Clyde McQueen, *Black Churches in Texas: A Guide to Historic Congregations* (College Station: Texas A&M University Press, 2000), 151–57.

32. Chapman, "Fifth Ward: Ethnic Melting Pot and Industrial Business District"; *The Handbook of Texas Online*, s.v., "Fifth Ward"; De León, *Ethnicity in the Sunbelt*, 22–31; *The Handbook of Texas Online*, s.v., "Jews,"; *The Handbook of Texas Online*, s.v., "Poles"; and A. Alexander, Houston Street Guide, 1913.

33. Although scholars are unable to determine the approximate number of migrants in Houston's wards/census tracts in the first half of the century, supporting evidence—De León, demographic migration patterns, oral histories, manuscript collections, church records, memoirs and autobiographies, and secondary sources—suggest that recent in-migrants and established residents living in Fifth Ward trekked to the community from East Texas and Louisiana. Census manuscript schedules for 1920 and 1930 also provide researchers with evidence supporting this claim. Residents did give census enumerators their state of birth. Although this does not enable scholars to distinguish between those Texans born in Houston and elsewhere in the state, it does substantiate the claim that Louisiana migrants comprised the greatest number of interstate migrants. For examples of such sources, see Houston—Wards—Vertical Files; Social Service Department Client Case Files, boxes 24–1674, 1882–6600, 11851–12651, 12984–15153, 15170–16536, 17041–17282, and 17286–17435, and WPA box CR08; *The Handbook of Texas Online*, s.v., "Fifth Ward"; Hazel Young, interviewed by Bernadette Pruitt, tape recording, Houston, Texas, August 7, 1996, in possession of the author; and Thelma Scott Bryant, *Pioneer Families of Houston,* 49.

34. Hazel Young interview; Thelma Scott Bryant, *Pioneer Families of Houston,* 437–54; Lullelia Harrison interview, September 23, 1999; Stullivan, *Roots of the Stullivan Family,* 1–10; Luther Stullivan interview, July 23, 1996; *The Handbook of Texas Online*, s.v., "Fifth Ward"; Jones, *The Red Diary,* 67; McQueen, *Black Churches in Texas,* 156; Beeth and Wintz, "Economic and Social Development in Black Houston during the Era of Segregation," 87–88"; and Houston Firefighters' Relief and Retirement Fund, "1912—The Great Fifth Ward Fire of," https://www.hfrrf.org/admin_History_19125thWardFire.asp.

35. McBride, Luther, and Louise, Face Sheet, Record No. 17381, Social Services Department Client Case Files, CR08; Social Service Department Client Case Files, boxes 24–1674, 1882–6600, 11851–12651, 12984–15153, 15170–16536, 17041–17282, and 17286–17435, and WPA box CR08.

36. Hazel Young interview; Lullelia Harrison interview, September 23, 1999; Stullivan, *Roots of the Stullivan Family;* Knight Family Reunion Book; Luther Stullivan interview; and Beeth and Wintz, "Economic and Social Development in Black Houston during the Era of Segregation," 87–88.

37. Manuscript Census of the United States, Grimes County, Texas, 1910, roll 1555,

Bureau of the Census, series T624, Heritage Quest Online, http://persi.heritagequestonline.com/; Manuscript Census of the United States, Grimes County, Texas, 1920, roll 1806, Bureau of the Census, series T625, Heritage Quest Online, http://persi.heritagequestonline.com/, Manuscript Census, Harris County, 1920, roll 1812, series T625; Larkin interview; Thomas, "Milt Larkin: Houston Jazz Bandleader," 1–26; Lorenzo Thomas, *Don't Deny My Name: Words and Music and the Black Intellectual Tradition,* ed. and with an introduction by Aldon Lynn Nielson (Ann Arbor: University of Michigan Press, 2008), 64–73; Mitchell, "Houston Jazz Legend Larkin Dies at 85"; Roger T. Wood, *Down in Houston: Bayou City Blues* (Austin: University of Texas Press, 2003), 82, 85; *The Handbook of Texas Online,* s.v., "Jazz" (by Dave Oliphant), http://www.tshaonline.org/handbook/online/articles/xbjyb; *The Handbook of Texas Online,* s.v., "Blues" (by Alan Govenar), http://www.tshaonline.org/handbook/online/articles/xbb01; Glen Alyn, "Fight, Flight, or Blues: Mance Lipscomb, Musician, Farmer, Storyteller, Philosopher, Legend, Gatekeeper of the Centuries," 1995, Lipscomb-Alyn Collection, 2.325:A112, Dolph Briscoe Center for American History, University of Texas, Austin, Texas (hereafter cited as Lipscomb-Alyn MSS); and Illinois Jacquet, interview by Louis Marchiafava and Charles Stephenson, tape recording, Houston, Texas, June 1, 1990, Illinois Jacquet Collection, 403:1, folder 2, Houston Metropolitan Research Center, Houston Public Library, Houston, Texas (hereafter cited as Illinois Jacquet interview). Interestingly, Ella Larkin, a widow in 1920, is listed in both the Harris County and Grimes County manuscript censuses. Both households also include two of her children, Nora and Milton. The census lists her as the owner of the Grimes County farm, whereas it names her as a renter in Harris County.

38. Cyprian Davis, *The History of Black Catholics in the United States* (New York: Crossroads, 1995), 238–39; Sister Frances Jerome Woods, *Marginality and Identity: A Colored Creole Family through Ten Generations* (Baton Rouge: Louisiana State University Press, 1972), 20–22; Carl A. Brasseaux, Claude F. Oubre, and Keith P. Fontentot, *Creoles of Color in the Bayou Country* (Jackson: University Press of Mississippi, 1994), xi; Kathy Russell, Midge Wilson, and Ronald Hall, *The Color Complex: The Politics of Skin Color Among African Americans* (New York: Doubleday, 1990), 2–7, 16–18; and Pruitt, "'For the Advancement of the Race,'" 2005, 442–43.

39. Marie Lee Phelps, "Frenchtown," *Houston Post,* May 22, 1955; David Kaplan, "Houston's Creole Quarter," *Houston Post,* March 19, 1989; Patricia Smith Prather, "A Unique Houston Neighborhood Called Frenchtown," *Houston Chronicle,* September 15, 1986, Houston—Subdivisions—Fifth Ward—Vertical Files; Davis, *The History of Black Catholics in the United States,* 238–39; Woods, *Marginality and Identity,* 20–22; Brasseaux et al., *Creoles of Color in the Bayou County,* xi; Russell et al., *Color Complex,* 2–7, 16–18; Pruitt, "'For the Advancement of the Race,'" 2005, 442–43; and SoRelle, "The Darker Side of 'Heaven,'" 222.

40. Brasseaux et al., *Creoles of Color in the Bayou Country,* xi–xii, 40–67, 113–20; Carole Rust, "Frenchtown"; "In Loving Memory of Ellis Montgomery Knight"; Luther Stullivan, *Roots of the Stullivan Family,* 1–10; and Pruitt, "'For the Advancement of the Race,'" 2005, 442–43.

41. Davis, *The History of Black Catholics in the United States,* 238–39; Woods,

Marginality and Identity, 20–22; Brauseaux et al., *Creoles of Color in the Bayou County,* xi; Russell et al., *The Color Complex,* 2–7, 16–18; and Pruitt, "'For the Advancement of the Race,'" 2005, 442–43.

42. Kaplan, "Houston's Creole Quarter"; Smith Prather, "A Unique Houston Neighborhood Called Frenchtown"; and Rust, "Frenchtown."

43. Raymond Lewis interview.

44. *Fourteenth Census of the United States, 1920,* vol. 3, 1026; *Sixteenth Census of the United States, 1940,* vol. 2, 1044; and *The Handbook of Texas Online;* s.v., "Fifth Ward."

45. Smith Prather, "The Houston Place"; Ledé, *Precious Memories of a Black Socialite,* 40–142, 144–48, 152–77; Smith Prather and Clements Monday, *From Slave to Statesman,* 200–38; and Ledé, "Constance Houston Thompson," in *Pathfinders,* 70–72.

46. On materials that discuss the histories of surrounding African American communities near early twentieth-century Houston, see *The Handbook of Texas Online,* s.v., "Acres Homes, Texas"; *The Handbook of Texas Online,* s.v., "Acres Homes Transit Authority"; Ward, "Acres Shakers," 1–17; Houston Business Journal, "Historic Acres Homes poised for economic progress"; City Savvy: Online Edition, s.v., "Sunnyside Up"; Vivian Hubbard Seals, "Oliphant Lockwood Hubbard Sr."; Vivian Hubbard Seals interview; Vivian Hubbard Seals, "Independence Heights, Texas"; and *The Handbook of Texas Online,* s.v., "Barrett Station, Texas," http://www.tshaonline.org/handbook/online/articles/hgbo3.

47. Vivian Hubbard Seals, "Three Generations of Hubbards and Room for More," Hubbard Family Reunion Book; and Vivian Hubbard Seals interview.

48. Vivian Hubbard Seals, "Three Generations of Hubbards and Room for More"; and Vivian Hubbard Seals interview.

49. Vivian Hubbard Seals, "Three Generations of Hubbards and Room for More; and Vivian Hubbard Seals interview.

50. Vivian Hubbard Seals, "Oliphant Lockwood Hubbard Sr."; and Vivian Hubbard Seals interview.

51. Vivian Hubbard Seals, "Oliphant Lockwood Hubbard Sr., 1880–1968"; Vivian Hubbard Seals interview; and Vivian Hubbard Seals, "Independence Heights, Texas."

52. B. G. Gaffney to Mrs. Leona Walls, July 22, 1988, in "Independence Heights, Texas"; and "The Wright Company," in "Independence Heights, Texas."

53. W. H. Ward, County Judge to M. P. Hammond, Sheriff, Harris County, Texas, "Order Calling Election on Independence Heights Incorporation," January 25, 1915, in "Independence Heights, Texas"; and Vivian Hubbard Seals interview.

54. J. Spencer, "'Our Neighbor," Houston Flame, January 31, 1987, in Vivian Hubbard Seals, "Independence Heights, Texas."

55. Ibid.

56. Seals, "Oliphant Lockwood Hubbard Sr., 1880–1968"; and Vivian Hubbard Seals interview.

57. Vivian Hubbard Seals, "Independence Heights, Texas."

58. Vivian Hubbard Seals, "Oliphant Lockwood Hubbard Sr., 1880–1968"; Vivian Hubbard Seals interview; and Vivian Hubbard Seals, "Independence Heights, Texas."

59. Manuscript Census, Harris County, 1920, roll 1812, series T625; Hazel Young

interview; Manuscript Census, Harris County, 1930, roll 2351, series T626; and Christia Adair Collection, 109:4, folder 1, Houston Metropolitan Research Center, Houston Public Library, Julia Ideson Building, Houston, Texas (hereafter referred to as Christia Adair MSS).

60. Howard N. Rabinowitz, *Race Relations in the Urban South, 1865–1890,* rev. ed. (1977; reprint, Athens: University of Georgia Press, 1996), 97–124; Brownell and Goldfield, "Southern Urban History," in *The City in Southern History,* 5–22; Brownell, "The Urban South Comes of Age, 1860–1900," in *The City in Southern History,* 123–58; and Joel Williamson, *A Rage for Order: Black-White Relations in the American South since Emancipation,* New York: Oxford University Press, 1986, vii–x.

61. SoRelle, "The Darker Side of 'Heaven,'" 238–41; HoustonHistory.com, "Blacks in Houston Today" (by Cary D. Wintz), in *169 Years of Houston History,* www.houstonhistory.com; Cary D. Wintz, "The Emergence of a Black Neighborhood," 99–104; Cary D. Wintz, "Blacks," 16–23; Beeth and Wintz, "Economic and Social Development in Black Houston during the Era of Segregation," 88–91; and De León, Ethnicity in the Sunbelt, 3–56.

62. Lullelia Harrison interview, September 23, 1999.

63. Maxwell, "Freedmantown," 139–52.

64. Influenced by NAACP litigators, the Supreme Court, in *Buchanan v. Warley* (1917), ruled that a Louisville, Kentucky, ordinance that required the residential segregation of the races violated the Fourteenth Amendment of the Constitution, thereby invalidating restrictive covenants. Cities nevertheless continued to pass residential racial ordinances well into the 1940s. Dallas, for example, unsuccessfully attempted to reinstate residential restrictions based on race. In every instance following the *Buchanan* decision, lower courts, based on the 1917 ruling, struck down these ordinances. See *Buchanan v. Warley,* 245 US 60 (1917).

65. For works that discuss de facto housing discrimination in Houston, see *Buchanan v. Warley,* 245 US 60 (1917); *Shelley v. Kraemer,* 334 US 1, (1948); Robert Fisher, "Protecting Community and Property Values," 128–31; McComb, *Houston: A History,* 107–14; De León, *Ethnicity in the Sunbelt,* 9–16; Pruitt, "The Urban Transformation of the MacGregor Area"; *This Is My Home, It Is Not For Sale;* Sam Felt interview; Kevin Fox Gotham, "Urban Space, Restrictive Covenants and the Origins of Racial Residential Segregation in a US City, 1900–1950," *International Journal of Urban and Regional Research,* 24, no. 3 (2000): 616–29; Roger L. Rice, "Residential Segregation by Law, 1910–1917," *Journal of Southern History* 34, no. 2 (1968): 179–94; James D. Saltzman, "Houston Says No to Zoning," *The Freeman: Ideas on Liberty* 44, no. 8 (1994), http://www.thefreemanonline.org/columns/houston-says-no-to-zoning/; Sherry Thomas, "Houston: A City Without Zoning," *USA Today,* October 30, 2003, http://www.usatoday.com/travel/destinations/cityguides/houston/2003-10-07-spotlight-zoning_x.htm; Michael Lewyn, "Zoning Without Zoning," Planetizen: *The Planning and Development Network,* November 23, 24, 2003, http://www.planetizen.com/node/109; Robert Reinhold, "FOCUS: Houston; A Fresh Approach to Zoning," *New York Times,* August 17, 1986, http://query.nytimes.com/gst/fullpage.html?res=9A0DEFDB103FF934A2575BC0A9609 48260; Barry J. Kaplan, "Urban Development, Economic Growth, and Personal

Liberty: The Rhetoric of the Houston Anti-Zoning Movements, 1847–1962," *Southwestern Historical Quarterly* 84, no. 2 (1980): 133–156; and Archie Henderson, "City Planning in Houston, 1920–1930," *Houston Review: History and Culture of the Gulf Coast* 9, no. 3 (1987): 107–29.

66. Fisher, "Protecting Community and Property Values," 126–25.

67. *Shelley v. Kraemer*, 334 US, 1 (1948); SoRelle, "The Darker Side of 'Heaven,'" 216–26; Rabinowitz, *Race Relations in the Urban South, 1865–1890*, 97–124; Brownell and Goldfield, "Southern Urban History," 5–22; Brownell, "The Urban South Comes of Age, 1900–1940," 123–58; Hunter, *To 'Joy My Freedom*, 44–50; Lewis, *In Their Own Interests*, 67–68, 80–81; and Fisher, "Protecting Community and Property Values," 128–31.

68. SoRelle, "The Darker Side of 'Heaven,'" 238–41; Wintz, "The Emergence of a Black Neighborhood," 99–104; Wintz, "Blacks," 16–23; Beeth and Wintz, "Economic and Social Development in Black Houston during the Era of Segregation," 88–91; and De León, *Ethnicity in the Sunbelt*, 3–56; and Scott, *The Red Book of Houston*.

69. Marks, *Farewell—We're Good and Gone*, 1–13; Trotter, *Black Milwaukee*, 264–82; Trotter et al., "Introduction: Connecting African American Urban History, Social Science Research, and Policy Debates," 1–20; and Richard B. Pierce, "Something Old, Something New, Something Borrowed, Some Things Black? African American Urban History," *Journal of Urban History* 31 (November 2004): 106–14.

70. Thomas, *A Study of the Social Welfare Status of Negroes in Houston, Texas*, 19–30; National Urban League, *A Review of the Economic and Cultural Problems of Houston, Texas*, 95–114; SoRelle, "The Darker Side of 'Heaven,'" 238–41; and Beeth and Wintz, "Economic and Social Development in Black Houston during the Era of Segregation," 89–90.

71. Thomas, *A Study of the Social Welfare Status of Negroes in Houston, Texas*, 19–30; National Urban League, *A Review of the Economic and Cultural Problems of Houston, Texas*, 95–114; SoRelle, "The Darker Side of 'Heaven,'" 238–41; Beeth and Wintz, "Economic and Social Development in Black Houston during the Era of Segregation," 89–90; and Henderson, "City Planning in Houston, 1920–1930," 107–35.

72. Thomas, *A Study of the Social Welfare Status of Negroes in Houston, Texas*, 19–30, 45–51; National Urban League, *A Review of the Economic and Cultural Problems of Houston, Texas*, 95–114; SoRelle, "The Darker Side of 'Heaven,'" 238–41; Beeth and Wintz, "Economic and Social Development in Black Houston during the Era of Segregation," 89–90; and Dr. H. E. Lee, "Negro Health Problem," in *The Red Book of Houston: A Compendium of Social, Professional, Religious, Educational, and Industrial Interests of Houston's Colored Population*, ed. Emmett J. Scott, Houston: Sotex, 1915, 148–51.

73. National Urban League, *A Review of the Economic and Cultural Problems of Houston, Texas*, 95–114; SoRelle, "The Darker Side of 'Heaven,'" 238–41; and Beeth and Wintz, "Economic and Social Development in Black Houston during the Era of Segregation," 89–90.

74. Pitre, *In Struggle against Jim Crow*, 20–26; Beeth and Wintz, "Economic and Social Development in Black Houston during the Era of Segregation," 88–100; Thelma Scott Bryant, *Pioneer Families of Houston*, 9–46; and Thomas, *A Study of the Social Welfare Status of Negroes in Houston, Texas*, 19–30.

75. SoRelle, "The Darker Side of 'Heaven,'" 238–41; and "Growth of Houston" Houston—Subdivisions—Vertical Files.

76. SoRelle, "The Darker Side of 'Heaven,'" 238–41; and "Growth of Houston," Houston—Subdivisions—Vertical Files; and Pruitt, "The Urban Transformation of the MacGregor Area."

77. Scott, "Efficiency," in *The Red Book of Houston*, 9–11; Thomas, *A Study of the Social Welfare Status of Negroes in Houston, Texas*, 5–73; Bryant, *Pioneer Families of Houston*, 1–36; and Beeth and Wintz, "Economic and Social Development in Black Houston during the Era of Segregation," 88–100.

78. Scott, "Efficiency," in *The Red Book of Houston*, 9–11; Thomas, *A Study of the Social Welfare Status of Negroes in Houston, Texas*, 5–73; Bryant, *Pioneer Families of Houston*, 1–36; and Beeth and Wintz, "Economic and Social Development in Black Houston during the Era of Segregation," 88–100.

79. *Encyclopedia of the Great Black Migration*; Thomas, *A Study of the Social Welfare Status of Negroes in Houston, Texas*, 5–73; 9–19; Thelma Scott Bryant, *Pioneer Families of Houston*, 1–36; Beeth and Wintz, "Economic and Social Development in Black Houston during the Era of Segregation," 1–37, 88–100; Stullivan, *Roots of the Stullivan Family*, 1–8; Luther Stullivan interview; Wintz, "Blacks"; Pruitt, "'For the Advancement of the Race,'" 2005, 445–68; SoRelle, "The Darker Side of 'Heaven,'" 152–82, 339–92; Trotter, *Black Milwaukee*; and Hine, *Black Victory*, 43–45.

80. Scott L. Stabler, "Free Men Come to Houston: Blacks During Reconstruction," *Houston Review of History and Culture* 3 (Fall 2005): 40–43, 73–76; Beeth and Wintz, "Slavery and Freedom," 19–24; Wintz, "The Emergence of a Black Neighborhood," 96–106; Jones, *The Red Diary*, 15–40; Rev. W. H. Logan, "Progress of Negro Churches in Houston Since Emancipation or the Civil War," in *The Red Book of Houston: A Compendium of Social, Professional, Religious, Educational, and Industrial Interests of Houston's Colored Population*, ed. Emmett J. Scott (Houston: Sotex, 1915), 21–23; *The Handbook of Texas Online*, s.v., "Yates, John Henry" accessed October 17, 2012, http://www.tshaonline.org/handbook/online/articles/fya07; Blackpast.org, s.v., "Antioch Missionary Baptist Church," http://www.blackpast.org/?q=aaw/antioch-missionary-baptist-church-houston-texas-1868; Rev. Lights, "Brief Sketch of Houston Baptists," in *The Red Book of Houston: A Compendium of Social, Professional, Religious, Educational, and Industrial Interests of Houston's Colored Population*, ed. Emmett J. Scott (Houston: Sotex, 1915), 24–25; and McQueen, *Black Churches in Texas*, 151–57.

81. Stabler, "Free Men Come to Houston," 40–43; Wintz, "Blacks"; Beeth and Wintz, "Slavery and Freedom," 19–24; Wintz, "The Emergence of a Black Neighborhood," 96–106; Jones, *The Red Diary*, 15–40; Logan, "Progress of Negro Churches in Houston Since Emancipation or the Civil War," 21–23; *The Handbook of Texas Online*, s.v., "Yates, John Henry," 1113; Rev. Lights, "Brief Sketch of Houston Baptists," 24–25; and McQueen, *Black Church in Texas*, 151–57.

82. Stabler, "Free Men Come to Houston," 40–43; Wintz, "Blacks"; Beeth and Wintz, "Slavery and Freedom," 19–24; Wintz, "The Emergence of a Black Neighborhood," 96–106; Jones, *The Red Diary*, 15–40; Logan, "Progress of Negro Churches in Houston Since Emancipation or the Civil War," 21–23; *The Handbook of Texas Online*,

s.v., "Yates, John Henry," 1113; Rev. Lights, "Brief Sketch of Houston Baptists," 24–25; and McQueen, *Black Church in Texas*, 151–57.

83. *Fourteenth Census of the United States, 1920*, vol. 4, 1114–15; *Fifteenth Census of the United States, 1930*, vol. 4, 1593–95; Luther Stullivan interview; Kaplan, "Houston's Creole Quarter"; SoRelle, "The Darker Side of 'Heaven,'" 152–82, 339–92; Beeth and Wintz, "Economic and Social Development in Black Houston during the Era of Segregation," 88–100; Pruitt, "'For the Advancement of the Race,'" 2005, 447–66; and Thomas, *A Study of the Social Welfare Status of Negroes in Houston, Texas*, 9–19.

84. Lullelia Harrison interview, March 8, 2000.

85. SoRelle, "The Darker Side of 'Heaven,'" 152–82; Beeth and Wintz, "Economic and Social Development in Black Houston during the Era of Segregation," 88–100; and Pruitt, "'For the Advancement of the Race,'" 2005, 447–66.

86. SoRelle, "The Darker Side of 'Heaven,'" 152–82; Beeth and Wintz, "Economic and Social Development in Black Houston during the Era of Segregation," 88–100; and Pruitt, "'For the Advancement of the Race,'" 2005, 447–66.

87. SoRelle, "The Darker Side of Heaven,'" 152–82; Beeth and Wintz, "Economic and Social Development in Black Houston during the Era of Segregation," 88–100; and Pruitt, "'For the Advancement of the Race,'" 2005, 447–66.

88. Harper, Nathaniel, and Mary (Carter), Face Sheet, State Department of Public Welfare, No. 946, Social Service Department Client Case Files, box 24–1674, and WPA box CR08.

89. Ibid.

90. MacDonald and MacDonald, "Chain Migration," 82–97; Lewis, "Expectations, Economic Opportunities, and Life in the Industrial Age," 24–25; Pruitt, "'For the Advancement of the Race,'" 2005, 435–36, 445–47; Schomburg Center, "The Great Migration," *In Motion;* and *Encyclopedia of the Great Migration*, vol. 1, s.v., "Chain Migration," 168–70.

91. Pruitt, "'For the Advancement of the Race,'" 2005, 445–47.

92. Pruitt, "'For the Advancement of the Race,'" 2005, 445–47; Vivian Hubbard Seals interview; Joseph Williams interview; Henry Coleman interview; Luther Stullivan interview; and Lullelia Harrison interview, March 8, 2000.

93. Pruitt, "'For the Advancement of the Race,'" 2005, 445–47; Vivian Hubbard Seals interview; Joseph Williams interview; Henry Coleman interview; Luther Stullivan interview; and Lullelia Harrison interview, September 23, 1999.

Chapter 3

1. *The Handbook of Texas Online*, s.v., "Covington, Jennie Belle Murphy"; *The Handbook of Texas Online*, s.v., "Covington, Benjamin Jesse"; "Funeral Service: Mrs. Jennie B. Covington"; and Walsh, "Dr. Covington, at 90, Is Still Practicing."

2. *The Handbook of Texas Online*, s.v., "Covington, Jennie Belle Murphy"; *The Handbook of Texas Online*, s.v., "Covington, Benjamin Jesse"; "Funeral Service: Mrs. Jennie B. Covington"; and Walsh, "Dr. Covington, at 90, Is Still Practicing."

3. "Funeral Services: Mrs. Jennie B. Covington."

4. *The Handbook of Texas Online*, s.v., "Covington, Jennie Belle Murphy"; *The*

Handbook of Texas Online, s.v., "Covington, Benjamin"; "Funeral Service: Mrs. Jennie B. Covington"; Walsh, "Dr. Covington, at 90, Is Still Practicing"; and "Marian Anderson to be Guest of Dr. and Mrs. B. J. Covington," newspaper unknown, n.d., Dr. Benjamin Covington MSS, 170:1, folder 1.

5. *The Handbook of Texas Online,* s.v., "Covington, Jennie Belle Murphy"; "Funeral Service: Mrs. Jennie B. Covington"; "Seventeen Years with the YWCA in Houston," newspaper unknown, N.D., Dr. Benjamin Covington MSS, 170:1, folder 1; Ira Bryant, *Houston's Negro Schools* (Houston: Informer, 1935), 58–63; Shaw, "Black Club Women and the Creation of the National Association of Colored Women," 10–25; Rufus E. Clement, "Educational Programs for the Improvement of Race Relations: Interracial Committees," *Journal of Negro Education* 13, no. 3 (1944), 316–20; Pamela Faith Wille, "More Than Classes in Swimming and Making Hats: The YWCA and Social; Reform in Houston, Texas, 1907–1977" (Ph.D. diss., Texas Tech University, 2004), 54–91; Alice Dunbar-Nelson, "Negro Women in War Work," in *Scott's Official History of the American Negro in the World War,* ed. Emmett J. Scott (Washington: Emmett J. Scott, 1919), http://net.lib.byu.edu/estu/wwi/comment/Scott/SCh27.htm; Historical Context Sheet, Sneed Family MSS, 293–1:1; Lullelia Harrison interview, March 8, 2000; "History of the Blue Triangle Branch," Houston Young Women's Christian Association Collection, RG F 017, box 1:5, Houston Metropolitan Research Center, Houston Public Library, Julia Ideson Building, Houston, Texas (hereafter cited as Houston YWCA RGF 017); "*YWCA Chronological Highlights and Leaders*" [Houston], YWCA RG 017, box 1, folder 3; Thelma Scott Bryant interview; and Thelma Scott Bryant, *Pioneer Families of Houston,* 7.

6. "Travesty of Justice, Says Mrs. Covington," *Houston Post,* n.d., Dr. Benjamin Covington MSS 170:1, folder 1; Ann Lundy, "Pioneer Concert Pianist: Anne Lundy and Ernestine Jessie Covington Dent," *The Black Perspective* in Music 12, no. 2 (1984): 245–65; "Jessie C. Dent, 96, Pianist, Teacher and Community Leader Who Inspired the Creation of the Ebony Fashion Fair, Dies," *Jet Magazine,* April 2, 2001; Brief Biographies: African American Biographies, vol. 4, s.v., "Thomas Covington Dent Biography: From Academia to Activism, Worked with Free Southern Theater, Oral Historian, Selected Writings," http://biography.jrank.org/pages/2514/Dent-Thomas-Covington.html; Chickenbones: A Journal for Literary & Artistic African-American Themes, s.v., "Thomas Covington Dent, 1932–1998: New Orleans Writer and Cultural Activist," www.nathanielturner.com/tomdentbio.htm; Black Collegian Online, "Tom Dent: New Orleans Writer, May 26, 2008, http://www.black-collegian.com/african/dent9.shtml; *The Handbook of Texas Online,* s.v., "Covington, Jennie Belle Murphy"; and *The Handbook of Texas Online,* s.v., "Covington, Benjamin Jesse." Writer and activist Tom Dent graduated from Morehouse College and Syracuse University. Stirred by the modern Civil Rights Movement, he wrote for African American newspapers, sponsored Black Nationalist arts groups, oral history projects and local theaters throughout the South. He also served as executive director of the New Orleans Jazz and Heritage Foundation. He died in 1998 from complications of a heart attack. His works can be found in the Dent Collections at the Amistad Research Center at Tulane and Will W. Alexander Library, Dillard University, New Orleans, Louisiana.

7. Clarence Edward Pruitt interview.

8. Pruitt, "'For the Advancement of the Race,'" 2005, 439–43.

9. Pruitt, "'For the Advancement of the Race,'" 2005, 439–43; Richard W. Thomas, *Life for Us Is What We Make It: Building Black Community in Detroit, 1915–1945* (Bloomington: Indiana University Press, 1992), xiii, 175; and Andrew Webster Jackson, *A Sure Foundation* (Houston: Webster-Richardson, 1940).

10. Beeth and Wintz, "Economic and Social Development in Black Houston during the Era of Segregation," 88–89; and Pitre, *In Struggle against Jim Crow,* 455–67.

11. Pruitt, "'For the Advancement of the Race,'" 435–78, 2005; Walter Johnson, "On Agency," *Journal of Social History* 37, no. 3 (2003): 113–24; and Hale, *Making Whiteness,* 2–35.

12. Pruitt, "'For the Advancement of the Race,'" 2005, 439–43; Steptoe, "Dixie West"; and Pruitt, "In Search of Freedom," 46–57, 85–86.

13. "A Life Sketch of Dr. M. L. Price," Rev. Moses L. Price Papers, 277:1, folder 1, Houston Metropolitan Research Center, Houston Public Library, Houston, Texas (hereafter cited as Rev. Moses L. Price MSS, 277); "Funeral Service: Mrs. Jennie B. Covington"; Photo Identification Sheet, Sneed Family Collection, 293-1:1, Houston Metropolitan Research Center, Houston Public Library, Houston, Texas; Lullelia Harrison interview, March 8, 2000; Hazel Young interview; Vivian Hubbard Seals interview; Thelma Scott Bryant interview; Thomas, *Life for Us Is What We Make It,* xiii, 175; Jones, *The Red Diary,* 83–153; Jackson, *A Sure Foundation,* 45–46, 116–17, 238, 264–65, 385–86; Beeth and Wintz, "Economic and Social Development in Black Houston during the Era of Segregation," 88–89; Pitre, *In Struggle against Jim Crow;* and Hine, *Black Victory.*

14. Beeth and Wintz, eds., *Black Dixie,* 13–86; Barr, *Black Texans;* and Ruth Winegarten, *Black Texas Women: 150 Years of Trial and Triumph* (Austin: University of Texas Press, 1995), 1–86.

15. Rutherford B. H. Yates Sr. and Paul L. Yates, The Life and Efforts of Jack Yates (Houston: Texas Southern University Press, 1985), 4–13; *The Handbook of Texas Online,* s.v., "Yates, John Henry"; Maxwell, "Freedmantown," 139–52; and Stabler, "Free Men Come to Houston," 40–43.

16. *The Handbook of Texas Online,* s.v., "Allen, Richard," http://www.tshaonline.org/handbook/online/articles/AA/fa124.html; Jackson, *A Sure Foundation*"; "Biography of J. B. Bell, Capitalist," in *The Red Book of Houston,* 80–84; and Audrey Crawford, "'To Protect, to Feed, and to Give Momentum to Every Effort': African American Clubwomen in Houston, 1880–1910," *Houston Review of History and Culture* 1, no. 1 (2003): 15–23.

17. Thelma Scott Bryant interview; Bryant, *Pioneer Families of Houston,* 58–59, 63–67; and Maceo C. Dailey Jr., "Neither 'Uncle Tom' Nor 'Accommodationist': Booker T. Washington, Emmett J. Scott, and Constructionalism," *Atlanta History* 38, no. 4 (1995): 20–33.

18. Jackson, *A Sure Foundation,* 45–46, 116–17, 238, 264–65, 385–86; Jones, *The Red Diary;* Scott, *The Red Book of Houston;* and Beeth and Wintz, eds., *Black Dixie.*

19. Scott, *The Red Book of Houston,* 96–98; Barr, *Black Texans,* 106–7; Crawford, "'To Protect, to Feed, and to Give Momentum to Every Effort,'" 15–17; and Wilder, *In the Company of Black Men,* 1–5.

20. Scott, *The Red Book of Houston,* 96–98; Barr, *Black Texans,* 106–7; and Crawford, "'To Protect, to Feed, and to Give Momentum to Every Effort,'" 15–17.

21. Scott, *The Red Book of Houston,* 96–98; Barr, *Black Texans,* 106–7; Crawford, "'To Protect, to Feed, and to Give Momentum to Every Effort,'" 15–17; Thomas, *A Study of the Social Welfare Status of Negroes in Houston, Texas,* 68–69; Jones, *The Red Diary,* 48–99; Bryant, *Pioneer Families of Houston,* 7; Theda Skocpol and Jennifer Lynn Oser, "Organization Despite Adversity: The Organization and Development of African American Fraternal Associations," *Social Science History* 28, no. 3 (2004): 377; and sloangallery.com, "Historic and Vintage Houston Architecture," http://www.sloanegallery.com/newpage44.htm; and virtualtourist.com, "Unique/Unusual/One-Of-A-Kind: Ancient Order of Pilgrims," http://www.virtualtourist.com/travel/North_America/United_States_of_America/Texas/Houston-878298/Off_the_Beaten_Path-Houston-Unique_Unusual_One_Of_A_Kind-BR-1.html.

22. Crawford, "'To Protect, to Feed, and to Give Momentum to Every Effort,'" 15–17; and Cheryl Knott Malone, "Autonomy and Accommodation: Houston's Colored Carnegie Library, 1907–1922," *Libraries & Culture* 34, no. 2 (1999): 95–112.

23. Jones, *The Red Diary,* 72, 81–98; Thomas, *A Study of the Social Welfare Status of Negroes in Houston, Texas,* 68–69; Skocpol and Oser, "Organization Despite Adversity," 373–84; Malone, "Autonomy and Accommodation," 94–97; Merah Steven Stuart, *An Economic Detour: A History of Insurance in the Lives of American Negroes* (1940; College Park: McGrath, 1969), 11–34, 190–94; and SoRelle, "The Emergence of Black Business in Houston, Texas," 108.

24. Crawford, "'To Protect, to Feed, and to Give Momentum to Every Effort,'" 15–17; Greene, *Selling Black History for Carter G. Woodson,* 124–28; Winegarten, *Black Texas Women,* 186–87; and Pitre, *In Struggle against Jim Crow,* 134.

25. Greene, *Selling Black History for Carter G. Woodson,* 124–28; Winegarten, *Black Texas Women,* 186–87; and Pitre, *In Struggle against Jim Crow,* 134.

26. Minutes, Knights of Phythias, Court of Calanthe, Omega Tent #26, 1952," Helen G. Perry Family Collection, 276, box 1: folder 3, Houston Metropolitan Research Center, Houston Public Library, Julia Ideson Building, Houston, Texas (hereafter cited as Perry Family MSS); "Club Matinee, Lyons Avenue, 5th Ward, Houston, Members of the Princes of Omar, Court of Calanthe," Perry Family MSS, 276, box 2, folder 1–R54; Greene, *Selling Black History for Carter G. Woodson,* 124–28; Winegarten, *Black Texas Women,* 186–87; and Pitre, *In Struggle against Jim Crow,* 134.

27. Minutes, Knights of Phythias, Court of Calanthe, Omega Tent #26, 1952," Perry Family MSS, 276-box 1: folder 3; and "Club Matinee, Lyons Avenue, 5th Ward, Houston, Members of the Princes of Omar, Court of Calanthe," Perry Family MSS, 276, box 2, folder 1–R54.

28. Crawford, "'To Protect, to Feed, and to Give Momentum to Every Effort,'" For other works that discuss African-descent women's self-help activism in women's clubs, anti-lynching and suffrage organizations, charities, community and cultural institutions, and civil-rights organizations, see Winegarten, *Black Texas Women,* 186–87; Bruce Glasrud and Merline Pitre, *Black Women in Texas History* (College Station: Texas A&M University Press, 2008); Glenda Elizabeth Gilmore, *Gender and Jim Crow: Women and*

the Politics of White Supremacy in North Carolina, 1896–1920. (Chapel Hill: University of North Carolina Press, 1996); Jacqueline A. Rouse, *Luginia Burns Hope: A Black Southern Reformer* (Athens: University of Georgia Press, 1989); Cynthia Neverdon-Morton, Afro-American Women of the South and the Advancement of the Race, 1895–1925 (Knoxville: University of Tennessee Press, 1998); Stephanie Shaw, *What a Woman Out to Be and Do: Black Professional Workers during the Jim Crow Era* (Chicago: University of Chicago Press, 1996); Ida B. Wells Barnett, Southern Horrors and Other Writings: The Antilynching Campaign of Ida B. Wells, 1892–1931, edited and with an introduction by Jacqueline Jones Royster (New York: Bedford/St. Martin's, 1997); Rosalyn Terbourg-Penn, African American Women in the Struggle for the Vote, 1850–1920 (Bloomington: Indiana University Press, 1998); Paula Giddings, *"When and Where I Enter": The Impact of Black Women on Race and Sex in America* (New York: William Morrow, 1984); Ann D. Gordon et. al., African American Women and the Vote, 1937–1965 (Amherst: University of Massachusetts Press, 1997); and Darlene Clark Hine, Kathleen Thompson, Elsa Barkley Brown, and Rosalyn Terborg-Penn, eds. *Black Women in America: An Historical Encyclopedia,* 2nd ed. (New York: Oxford University Press, 2005).

29. "Jennie Belle Murphy Covington"; "Funeral Service: Mrs. Jennie B. Covington"; "Seventeen Years with the YWCA in Houston," newspaper unknown, N.D., Dr. Benjamin Covington Papers, 170:1, folder 1; "Agency History," Harris County Social Services, CR08; and Charles W. Leavens, "Historical Development of the Harris County Welfare Department in Houston, Texas" (master's thesis, Sam Houston State University, 1971), 19–25.

30. "Agency History," Harris County Social Services CR08; and Leavens, "Historical Development of the Harris County Welfare Department in Houston, Texas," 19–25.

31. "Funeral Service: Mrs. Jennie B. Covington"; Thomas, *A Study of the Social Welfare Status of Negroes in Houston, Texas,* 10, 77–92; and Leavens, "Historical Development of the Harris County Welfare Department in Houston, Texas," 22–24.

32. Historical Context, Married Ladies Social, Art & Charity Club Records, Record Group E 46, Houston Metropolitan Research Center, Houston Public Library, Julia Ideson Building, Houston, Texas; Historical Context, Vivian Hubbard Seals interview; "Zeta Phi Betas Stage Their 1st Public Affair," *Houston Informer,* May 12, 1934; and Unidentified group photograph of Constance Houston Thompson and others with Mary McLeod Bethune—probably an annual convention of the National Council of Negro Women, circa late 1930s–1940s, Joshua Houston Family MSS, 437–1.

33. "Mrs. Melissa Price Active 61 Years in Married Ladies Social Club," Dr. Benjamin Covington MSS, 170:1, folder 1; and Crawford, "'To Protect, to Feed, and to Give Momentum to Every Effort,'" 20.

34. "Mrs. Melissa Price Active 61 Years in Married Ladies Social Club," Dr. Benjamin Covington MSS, 170:1, folder 1; and Crawford, "'To Protect, to Feed, and to Give Momentum to Every Effort,'" 20.

35. A Musical Panorama, 42nd Anniversary of the Married Ladies Social, Art and Charity Club," General and Mary L. Jones Johnson, MSS 119: 4—Programs, Houston Metropolitan Research Center, Houston Public Library, Julia Ideson Building, Houston, Texas (hereafter referred to as Johnson MSS); Thelma Scott Bryant interview; and

Historical Context, "Mrs. Melissa Price Active 61 Years in Married Ladies Social Club," Dr. Benjamin Covington MSS, 170:1, folder 1.

36. Thelma Scott Bryant interview; Bryant, *Our Journey through Houston and US History*, 34–35; Winegarten, *Black Texas Women*, 187–93; Historical Context, Ethel Ransom Art and Literary Club Records, RG E59, Houston Metropolitan Research Center, Houston Public Library, Julia Ideson Building, Houston, Texas; "Who's Who in American Education," Olee Yates McCullough MSS, 370:1, folder 9; and Crawford, "'To Protect, to Feed, and to Give Momentum to Every Effort.'"

37. Photo Identification Sheet, "Youth Council Competition Sponsor by the Houston Chapter of the National Association for the Advancement of Colored People, 1946," Perry Family MSS, 276–2: R63; "Funeral Service: Mrs. Jennie B. Covington"; Winegarten, *Black Texas Women*, 97; "Who's Who in American Education," Olee Yates McCullough MSS, 370:1, folder 9; "'To Protect, to Feed, and to Give Momentum to Every Effort,'" 15–23; "A Musical Panorama, 42nd Anniversary of the Married Ladies Social, Art and Charity Club," Johnson MSS, 119: 4—Programs; Vivian Hubbard Seals interview; Photo identification sheet, Alpha Kappa Alpha Sorority, Inc., Alpha Kappa Omega Alumnae Chapter, circa 1942, Sneed Family, MSS 293–26; Photo identification sheet, Members of the Houston Chapter of The Links, Inc., Sneed Family MSS, 293–33; Ledé, *Precious Memories of a Black Socialite*, 124–66; Ledé, "Constance Houston Thompson," in *Pathfinders*, 70–72; Ledé, "Hortense Houston Young," in *Pathfinders*, 82–84; Bryant, *Pioneer Families of Houston*, 1–366; "'To Protect, to Feed, and to Give Momentum to Every Effort,'" 20–21; Pitre, *In Struggle against Jim Crow*, 88; Teresa Tomkins-Walsh, "Thelma Scott Bryant: Memories of a Century in Houston's Third Ward," *Houston Review of History and Culture* 1, no. 1 (2003): 53–54; "Biographical Directory of Zeta Women, Zeta Women Bicentennial, 1976," Zeta Amicae Collection, RG E 50, box 2, Houston Metropolitan Research Center, Houston Public Library, Julia Ideson Building, Houston, Texas; Zeta Phi Betas Stage Their 1st Public Affair"; Lullelia Harrison interview, September 23, 1999; Lullelia Harrison interview, March 8, 2000; and Hundreds Honor Lifelong Civil-Rights Fight," Christia Adair MSS, 109, box 4, folder 1.

38. Winegarten, *Black Texas Women*, 4–13, 20–22; Cindy Bland Verheyden, "They Danced Until Dawn and Other Untold Texas Legends," in Bricks Without Straw, 105–7; Scott, *The Red Book of Houston*, 21–22; The Handbook of Texas Online, s.v., "African-American Churches," http://www.tshaonline.org/handbook/online/articles/AA/pkatz.html; McQueen, *Black Churches in Texas*, 150–51; C. Eric Lincoln, "The Radical Factor in the Shaping of Religion in America," in African American Religious Studies, in *African American Religious Thought: An Anthology*, ed. by Cornel West and Eddie S. Glaude Jr. (Louisville, Kentucky: Westminster John Knotts Press, 2003), 156–69, 171–74; Jones, *The Red Diary*, 15, 16–17, 28–30; and William E. Montgomery, "The Formation of African American Churches," introduction to *Under Their Own Vine and Fig Tree: The African-American Church in the South, 1865–1900* (Baton Rouge: Louisiana State University Press, 1993), 5–11. The Freedmen's Bureau established two of the city's three Freedmen's Bureau schools at Trinity Methodist Episcopal and Antioch Baptist Churches.

39. Thomas, *A Study of the Social Welfare Status of Negroes in Houston, Texas*, 72–77;

National Urban League, *A Review of the Economic and Cultural Problems of Houston, Texas*, 160–65; Barr, *Black Texans*, 165–66. Although Thomas's study puts the number of Black churches at ninety-five, Barr gives a higher number for the year 1930—160. It is hardly likely that sixty-five churches sprang up in the city between 1929 and 1930. In his work, Thomas probably omitted church services held in homes. It is also possible that, given Thomas's bias against smaller congregations, he simply ignored numbers of storefront churches and ad hoc gatherings. On the other hand, Barr does not reveal his source materials, making it difficult to corroborate his higher number.

40. Thomas, *A Study of the Social Welfare Status of Negroes in Houston, Texas*, 72–77; Rev. W. H. Logan, "Progress of Negro Churches in Houston Since Emancipation or the Civil War," in *The Red Book of Houston*, 21–23; and Rev. Lights, "Brief Sketch of Houston Baptists," in *The Red Book of Houston*, 24–25.

41. Karen Kossie-Chernyshev, "A 'Grand Old Church' Rose in the East: The Church of God in Churst (COGIC) in East Texas," *East Texas Historical Journal* 31 (Winter 2003), 26–33; Gary B. McGee, "William Seymour and the Azusa Street Revival," in "A Century of Pentecostal Vision," *Enrichment Journal: A Journal for Pentecostal Ministry, Assemblies of God* (Fall 1999), http://enrichmentjournal.ag.org/199904/026_azusa.cfm; *Dictionary of Pentecostal and Charismatic Movements*, s.v., "Azusa Street Revival," (by Cecil M. Robeck Jr.), ed. Stanley M. Burgess and Gary B. McGee (Grand Rapids, Michigan: Zondervan Publishing House, 1988), 31–36; and Karen Lynell Kossie, "The Move Is On: African American Pentecostals/Charismatics in the Southwest" (Ph.D. diss., Rice University, 1998), 50–57, 60–61, 71–82.

42. Kossie, "The Move Is On," 60–82. The phrase, "shotgun houses" usually describes small row houses built for working-class and poor families at the turn of the century. The small wood frame houses, very common in Houston's older neighborhoods like Third Ward, were narrow, and comprised two to three rooms, including the kitchen. These homes rarely provided indoor plumbing. People compared these homes to a shotgun barrel: so narrow and small that one could see straight through the house when standing directly in front of it. See Houghton, *Houston's Forgotten Heritage*, 145.

43. Kossie, "The Move Is On," 50–57, 71–82; and Thomas, *A Study of the Social Welfare Status of Negroes in Houston, Texas*, 77.

44. Robert C. Giles, "St. Nicholas Church, Houston," in 125th Anniversary: Diocese of Galveston-Houston, 1847–1972 (Houston: The Most Reverend John L. Morkovsky, S.T.D., The Diocese of Galveston-Houston, 1972), 104–6; Father Peter E. Hogan, S. S. J., "The Catholic Church and African Americans in Texas" (unpublished paper presented at the Texas Catholic Historical Society, Austin, Texas, 1993, in possession of the author), 1–2; Davis, *The History of Black Catholics in the United States*, 238–39; Robert C. Giles, Curtis, M. Dowell, and Vivian J. Zermeno, "Josephites Close Centennial Year"; and Giles et al., "Josephites Have Logged 90 Years in the Diocese."

45. Smith Prather, "A Unique Houston Neighborhood Called Frenchtown"; Brasseaux et al., *Creoles of Color in the Bayou Country*, 115, 117–20; Woods, *Marginality and Identity*, 44; Robert C. Giles, "Our Mother of Mercy Church, Houston," in 125th Anniversary: Diocese of Galveston-Houston, 1847–1972 (Houston: The Most Reverend John L. Morkovsky, S.T.D., The Diocese of Galveston-Houston, 1972), 141–42;

Robert C. Giles, "St. Nicholas Church, Houston"; Kaplan, "Houston's Creole Quarter"; Raymond Lewis interview; and "St. Joseph's Society of the Sacred Heart, Inc., Parish Annual Report by Year, St. Nicholas," Archives, Diocese of Galveston-Houston, Houston Texas.

46. "Catholics and Negroes," *Houston Informer and Texas Freeman,* May 5, 1934.

47. Crawford, "'To Protect, to Feed, and to Give Momentum to Every Effort,'" 16–17; Karen Kossie-Chernyshev, "A 'Grand Old Church' Rose in the East," 29–34; Winegarten, *Black Texas Women,* 86–89, 129–34, 220; Evelyn Brooks Higginbotham, *Righteous Discontent: The Women's Movement in the Black Baptist Church, 1880–1920.* Cambridge: Harvard University Press, 1993, 1–19; and Montgomery, *Under Their Own Vine and Fig Tree,* 94, 114, 139, 320–22. Black men too were cognizant of their contradictory, sexist actions. Nevertheless, as Zora Neale Hurston argues, African American men felt compelled to control African-descent women. The church is the one place where African American men work in leadership roles. See Higginbotham, *Righteous Discontent,* 1–19.

48. "A Service of Christian Worship in Memory of Sister Kathleen Stewart, Saturday, October 10, 1981," obituary, in possession of the author.

49. Ibid.

50. Bryant, *Houston's Negro Schools,* 64–93; Kellar, *Make Haste Slowly: Moderates: Conservatives, and School Desegregation in Houston* (College Station: Texas A&M University Press), 1999, 30–33; Robert Hayes Sr. interview; Lullelia Harrison interview, March 8, 2000; and Glasrud, "Black Texans, 1900–1930," 224–26.

51. Clifton Richardson Sr., "Condition of Houston Colored Schools," *Houston Informer,* March 15, 1924; Kellar, *Make Haste Slowly,* 23–30; Winegarten, *Black Texas Women,* 93–95; Beeth and Wintz, "Economic and Social Development in Black Houston during the Era of Segregation," 95–98; Thomas, *A Study of the Social Welfare Status of Negroes in Houston, Texas,* 63–68; National Urban League, *A Review of the Economic and Cultural Problems of Houston, Texas,* 63–68; Johnny Johnson, "African-American Leadership from 1876–1954: A Study of an Urban School District," (Ed.D. diss., Texas Southern University, 1993), 1–31; Karen Benjamin, "Progressivism Meets Jim Crow: Curriculum Revision and Development in Houston, Texas, 1924–1929," *Paedagogica Historica* 39 (August 2003): 457–60; and Amilcar Shabazz, "One for the Crows, One for the Crackers: The Strange Career of Public Higher Education in Houston, Texas," *Houston Review: History and Culture of the Gulf Coast* 28 (Fall 1996): 124–28.

52. San Miguel, *Brown Not White,* 21–34.

53. Richardson Sr., "Condition of Houston Colored Schools"; "Not Only in Asia," *Houston Informer and Texas Freeman,* February 13, 1932; "Handbook for Instructors," Booker T. Washington High School, Houston, Texas, 1947–1948," Johnson MSS, 119-4—Programs; Benjamin, "Progressivism Meets Jim Crow," 460–65; Shabazz, "One for the Crows, One for the Crackers," 124–28; Kellar, *Make Haste Slowly,* 30–34; *The Handbook of Texas Online,* s.v., "Oberholtzer, Edison Ellisworth," http://www.tshaonline.org/handbook/online/articles/OO/fob2.html; Beeth and Wintz, "Economic and Social Development in Black Houston during the Era of Segregation," 95–98; Thomas, *A Study of the Social Welfare Status of Negroes in Houston, Texas,* 63–68; Anderson, *The*

Education of Blacks in the South, 1860–1935, 1–2, 184–237; Fredrickson, *White Supremacy,* 268–77; and Williamson, *A Rage for Order,* 174–75.

54. Shabazz, "One for the Crows, One for the Crackers," 124.

55. "Graduate Class, Master in Education Degree, 1946, University of Houston," Hicks Family Collection, 190: 122:3, Houston Metropolitan Research Center, Houston Public Library, Houston, Texas; Crawford, "'To Protect, to Feed, and to Give Momentum to Every Effort,'" 17; Nancy Ruth Eckols Bessent, "The Publisher: A Biography of Carter W. Wesley" (master's thesis, University of Texas, 1981), 1–4; Bryant, *Houston's Negro Schools,* 195–214; Ira B. Bryant Jr., *Texas Southern University and Its Antecedents, Political Origins, and Future* (Houston: Bryant, 1975), 35–110; and Shabazz, "One for the Crows, One for the Crackers," 128–30.

56. Thomas, *A Study of the Social Welfare Status of Negroes in Houston, Texas,* 63–66; and Kellar, *Make Haste Slowly,* 35–45.

57. Kellar, *Make Haste Slowly,* 27; Hazel Young interview; Thelma Scott Bryant interview; and Lullelia Harrison interview, March 8, 2000.

58. Thelma Scott Bryant interview; Special Nominee, Dr. Fredda Witherspoon, Iota Phi Lambda Sorority, Inc., Essence Awards Luncheon; and Daughter of Vanita Crawford, Vanita Crawford and Antioch Baptist Church Collection, 192, box 1, File 29, Houston Metropolitan Research Center, Houston Public Library, Houston, Texas.

59. Jackson, *A Sure Foundation,* 116–17; Bryant, *Pioneer Families of Houston,* 9–56; Bryant, *Houston's Negro Schools,* 115–20; and *The Handbook of Texas Online,* s.v., "Bryant, Ira Babington, Jr.," http://www.tshaonline.org/handbook/online/articles/BB/fbrdt.html.

60. Jackson, *A Sure Foundation,* 116–17; Bryant, *Houston's Negro Schools,* 115–20; Bryant, *Pioneer Families of Houston,* 9–56; and *The Handbook of Texas Online,* s.v., "Ryan, James Delbridge," http://www.tshaonline.org/handbook/online/articles/RR/fry5.html.

61. Jackson, *A Sure Foundation* (Houston: N. P., 1939), 116–17; and Bryant, *Pioneer Families of Houston,* 9–56; Bryant, *Houston's Negro Schools,* 115–20.

62. Thelma Scott Bryant interview; Bryant, *Houston's Negro Schools;* and *The Handbook of Texas Online,* s.v., "Bryant, Ira Babington, Jr."

63. Thelma Scott Bryant interview; Bryant, *Houston's Negro Schools;* and *The Handbook of Texas Online,* s.v., "Bryant, Ira Babington, Jr."

64. "Jack Yates High School," Johnson MSS, 119, box 1, Miscellaneous; "First Jack Yates Faculty," photograph, Johnson, MSS 119–1: Miscellaneous; Pioneer Citizen and Church Worker, Mary Lou Jones, Antioch, 1895–1935," Johnson MSS, 119–1: Programs; "Antioch Baptist Church General Mission Society, Mary Lou Jones Circle in Charge, Sister Mary Lou Jones," Johnson, MSS 119–1: Miscellaneous; and Bryant, *Pioneer Families of Houston,* 33–34, 39, 49.

65. "Jack Yates High School," Johnson Collection, 119, box 1, Miscellaneous; and Bryant, *Houston's Negro Schools,* 79–8979–89,123–30.

66. "Jack Yates High School," Johnson Collection, 119, box 1, Miscellaneous; Program, Negro History Club of the University of Houston College for Negroes Observing Negro History Week, Sunday, February 17, 1935, St. Johns Baptist Church, Houston, Texas, Johnson Collection, MSS 119, box 4; Syllabus, Houston Colored Junior College,

R. O'Hara, Dean, Department of Social Science, Syllabus in American History, Mary L. Jones, Instructor, First Semester, 1933–1934, Johnson Collection, MSS 119, box 4; and Play, *The Life of Mirabeau Lamar,* performed in 1936, Johnson Collection, MSS 119, box 4.

67. "Jack Yates High School," General and Mary L. Jones Johnson Collection, 119, box 1, Miscellaneous; and Bryant, *Pioneer Families of Houston,* 1–8.

68. National Urban League, *A Review of the Economic and Cultural Problems of Houston, Texas,* 147–48; Jackson, *A Sure Foundation,* 71–72; Bryant, *Our Journey through Houston and US History,* 60; and Crawford, "To Protect, to Feed, and to Give Momentum to Every Effort."

69. Thelma Scott Bryant interview; Hazel Young interview; Pioneer Families of Houston, 10; Morrison & Fourmy's Directory of the City of Galveston, 1898, from Ancestry.com, http://search.ancestry.com/; Manuscript Census, Harris County, 1920, roll 1813, series T625; and Manuscript Census, Harris County, 1930, roll 2347, series T626.

70. Thelma Scott Bryant interview; Hazel Young interview; Bryant, *Houston's Negro Schools,* 58–65, 104–20; Kellar, *Make Haste Slowly,* 28–33; and Bessent, "The Publisher," 4.

71. Henry E. Lee, "Negro Health Problem," in *The Red Book of Houston,* 148–51.

72. Ibid., 149.

73. Henry E. Lee, "Negro Health Problem," in *The Red Book of Houston,* 148–51; Thomas, *A Study of the Social Welfare Status of Negroes in Houston, Texas,* 45–51; National Urban League, A *Review of the Economic and Cultural Problems of Houston, Texas,* 67–87; and SoRelle, "The Darker Side of 'Heaven,'" 226–38.

74. Lee, "Negro Health Problem," in *The Red Book of Houston,* 148–51; Thomas, *A Study of the Social Welfare Status of Negroes in Houston, Texas,* 45–51; and SoRelle, "The Darker Side of 'Heaven,'" 226–38.

75. Lee, "Negro Health Problem," in *The Red Book of Houston,* 148–51; and Scott, "Efficiency," in *The Red Book of Houston,* 5–11.

76. Lee, "Negro Health Problem," in *The Red Book of Houston,* 148–51; and Scott, "Efficiency," in *The Red Book of Houston,* 5–11.

77. Lee, "Negro Health Problem," in *The Red Book of Houston,* 148–51.

78. Lee, "Negro Health Problem," in *The Red Book of Houston,* 148–51; and Scott, "Efficiency," in *The Red Book of Houston,* 5–11.

79. Thomas, *A Study of the Social Welfare Status of Negroes in Houston, Texas,* 45–51.

80. Thomas, *A Study of the Social Welfare Status of Negroes in Houston, Texas,* 45–51; and Bryant, *Pioneer Families of Houston,* 9–56.

81. Thomas, *A Study of the Social Welfare Status of Negroes in Houston, Texas,* 30–51; Wintz, "The Emergence of a Black Neighborhood," 106; Bryant, *Pioneer Families of Houston,* 10–13; Thelma Scott Bryant interview; Scott, *The Red Book of Houston,* 170; Mary Jane Schier, "Golden Anniversary of Black Hospital's Founding Tonight," *Houston Post,* October 30, 1975," Benjamin Covington Papers, 170:1, folder 1; *The Handbook of Texas Online,* "Covington, Jennie Belle Murphy"; *The Handbook of Texas Online,* "Covington, Benjamin"; "Funeral Service: Mrs. Jennie B. Covington"; Walsh, Dr. Covington, at 90, Is Still Practicing"; "Seventeen Years with the YWCA in Houston," 1937, Benjamin Covington Papers, 170:1, folder 1; "Marian Anderson to be Guest of Dr.

and Mrs. B. J. Covington," Benjamin Covington Papers, 170:1, folder 1; Mr. Read to Dr. and Mrs. B. J. Covington, "John Hope Memorial Fund Committee," Benjamin Covington Papers, 170:1, folder 4; *The Handbook of Texas Online,* "Lone Star State Medical, Dental, and Pharmaceutical Association," http://www.tshaonline.org/handbook/online/articles/sa101; and *The Handbook of Texas Online,* "Majors, Monroe Alpheus," http://www.tshaonline.org/handbook/online/articles/fmacq.

82. Thomas, *A Study of the Social Welfare Status of Negroes in Houston, Texas,* 30–51; Wintz, "The Emergence of a Black Neighborhood," 106; Bryant, *Pioneer Families of Houston,* 10–13; Thelma Scott Bryant interview; Scott, *The Red Book of Houston,* 170; Schier, "Golden Anniversary of Black Hospital's Founding Tonight," Benjamin Covington MSS, 170:1, folder 1; *The Handbook of Texas Online,* "Covington, Jennie Belle Murphy"; *The Handbook of Texas Online,* "Covington, Benjamin"; and "Funeral Service: Mrs. Jennie B. Covington"; Walsh, Dr. Covington, at 90, Is Still Practicing."

83. A. Fletcher, M.D., to Whom It May Concern, October 30, 1923, Houston Negro Hospital, 1923–25, Houston Negro Hospital, Joseph Stephen Cullinan Family Papers, 69, box 22, folder 1, Houston Metropolitan Research Center, Julia Ideson Building, Houston Public Library, Houston, Texas (hereafter cited as Houston Negro Hospital, Joseph S. Cullinan Family MSS); O. M. Terrell to Mr. J. S. Cullinan, 30 October 1923, Houston Negro Hospital, 1923–25, Joseph S. Cullinan MSS 69, box 22, folder 1; "Houston Negro Hospital Offered to the City: Unknown Philanthropist Donates $75,000 Through Dr. Slaughter," *Houston Post-Dispatch,* January 1, 1925, Houston Negro Hospital, Joseph S. Cullinan Family MSS 69, box 22, folder 1; Oscar F. Holcombe to Mr. J. S. Cullinan, 24 January 1925, Houston Negro Hospital, Joseph S. Cullinan MSS 69, box 22, folder 1; Center for Public History, University of Houston, To Bear Fruit for Our Race: A History of African-American Physicians in Houston (hereafter cited as To Bear Fruit for Our Race), s.v., "Houston's Union Hospital (1900–1926, Section 8)," http://www.history.uh.edu/cph/tobearfruit/story_1900–1926_section8.html; Betty L. Martin, "Fourth Ward Freedmen's Town Minister's Home Gets Historical Marker," *Houston Chronicle,* April 2, 2009; Bryant, *Pioneer Families of Houston,* 10–13, 55; Scott, *The Red Book of Houston,* 171; Wintz, "The Emergence of a Black Neighborhood," 106; Schier, "Golden Anniversary of Black Hospital's Founding Tonight," MSS 170:1, folder 1; Walsh, "Dr. Covington, at 90, Is Still Practicing"; and Dan Gerig, "Joseph Stephen Cullinan and the Houston Negro Hospital, 1925–1937" (unpublished paper presented at the East Texas Historical Association Fall Meeting, September 25, 2008, Nacogdoches, Texas).

84. Charter of Incorporation, Houston Negro Hospital, November 10, 1926, Houston Negro Hospital, Joseph S. Cullinan Family MSS 69, box 22, folder 3; HNH, Colored Medical Staff, n.d., Houston Negro Hospital, Joseph S. Cullinan Family MSS 69, box 22, folder 4; Houston Negro Hospital Advisory Committee, Houston Negro Hospital, Joseph S. Cullinan Family MSS 69, box 22, folder 4; Houston Negro Hospital: List of Negro Citizens, Furnished by O. M. Terrell, as Being Capable and Willing to Cooperate, Houston Negro Hospital, Joseph S. Cullinan Family MSS 69, box 22, folder 4; To Bear Fruit for Our Race s.v., "Houston's Union Hospital (1900–1926, Section 8)"; Betty L. Martin, "Fourth Ward Freedmen's Town Minister's Home Gets

Historical Marker"; Bryant, *Pioneer Families of Houston,* 10–13, 55; Scott, *The Red Book of Houston,* 171; Wintz, "The Emergence of a Black Neighborhood," 106; Schier, "Golden Anniversary of Black Hospital's Founding Tonight," MSS 170:1, folder 1; Walsh, "Dr. Covington, at 90, Is Still Practicing"; and Gerig, "Joseph Stephen Cullinan and the Houston Negro Hospital, 1925–1937."

85. Published death record of Thelma Patton Law, November 15, 1968, PublicRecordsNow, Privateeye.com, http://www.privateeye.com; Winegarten, *Black Texas Women,* 158–60, 332;"Dr. Thelma Patten and daughter, [sic] Pauline Anna Taking a Night Out to See 'Angel Street' [sic] at TSU," *Houston Informer,* October 30, 1948; Houston Chapters of Zeta Phi Beta Sorority Honor Dr. Thelma Patten-Law [sic], Mrs. Jayne Robinson, and Miss Nancy Smith at the Finer Woman Observance, Texas Southern University Music Center Auditorium, March 25, 1962, Houston, Texas, in possession of the author; Manuscript Census of the United States, Walker County, Texas, 1900, roll 1676, Bureau of the Census, series T623, Heritage Quest Online, http://persi.heritagequestonline.com/=; Larissa Lindsay, "Capstone Introduction by Larissa Lindsay of Dr. Thelma Patten, given March 12, 2009" (unpublished paper presented at an unknown venue, March 12, 2009, Houston, Texas, in possession of the author), 3–7; and To Bear Fruit for Our Race, s.v., "Thelma Patten Law," http://www.history.uh.edu/cph/tobearfruit/resources_bios_pattenlaw.html.

86. Bureau of the Census, *Negroes in the United States, 1920–1932,* 357; To Bear Fruit for Our Race, s.v., "Thelma Patten Law"; Lindsay, "Capstone Introduction," 7–10; and Sigma Pi Phi Fraternity, "James H. Law, Nu Boulé," *The Boulé Journal* 16, no. 4 (1951), http://www.sigmapiphi.org/home/james-h.-law.php; *Black Women in America* vol. 2, s.v., "Physicians, Nineteenth Century" (by Darlene Clark Hine), ed. Darlene Clark Hine, Elsa Barkley Brown, and Rosalyn Terborg Penn (Bloomington: Indiana University Press, 1994), 923–26; *Black Women in America,* vol. 2, s.v. "Physicians, Twentieth Century" (by Vanessa Gamble), 926–28; and *Black Women in America,* vol. 2, 2nd ed., s.v., "Physicians" (by Vanessa Northington Gamble), ed. Darlene Clark Hine (New York: Oxford University Press, 2005), 488–99.

87. To Bear Fruit for Our Race, s.v., "Thelma Patten Law"; and Mariah H. Anderson, "Private Choices vs. Public Voices: The History of Planned Parenthood in Houston" (master's thesis, Rice University, 1998), 59–74.

88. To Bear Fruit for Our Race, s.v., "Thelma Patten Law"; Anderson, "Private Choices vs. Public Voices," 59–74; "Capstone Introduction," 7–10; To Bear Fruit for Our Race, s.v., "Dr. Edith Irby Jones," http://www.history.uh.edu/cph/tobearfruit/resources_bios_jones.html; and To Bear Fruit for Our Race, s.v., "Catherine J. Roett," http://www.history.uh.edu/cph/tobearfruit/resources_bios_roett.c.html.

89. *Black Women in America,* vol. 2, s.v., "Nursing" (by Darlene Clark Hine), 887–91; *Black Women in America,* vol. 2, s.v., "Nursing, World War I" (by Darlene Clark Hine), 891–94; *Black Women in America,* vol. 2, 2nd ed., s.v., "Nursing," (by Darlene Clark Hine), 441–49; *The Handbook of Texas Online,* s.v., "Prairie View A&M. University College of Nursing," http://www.tshaonline.org/handbook/online/articles/PP/kcp8.html; *The Handbook of Texas Online,* s.v., "Nursing Education," http://www.tshaonline.org/handbook/online/articles/NN/shn1.html; *The Handbook of Texas Online,* "Nursing,"

http://www.tshaonline.org/handbook/online/articles/NN/shn2_print.html; and Peggy J. Hardman, "The Anti-Tuberculosis Crusade and the Texas African American Community, 1900–1950" (Ph.D. diss., Texas Tech University, 1997), 99–134.

90. Webster, *A Sure Foundation,* 410; Hardman, "The Anti-Tuberculosis Crusade," 99–134; and *Black Women in America,* vol. 2, 2nd ed., s.v., "Nursing," 441–49.

91. Webster, *A Sure Foundation,* 410; Hardman, "The Anti-Tuberculosis Crusade," 99–134; and Black Women in America, vol. 2, 2nd ed., s.v., "Nursing," 441–49.

92. Pruitt, "'For the Advancement of the Race,'" 2005, 439–43;

93. Steptoe, "Dixie West," 52–73; and Pruitt, "In Search of Freedom, 46–57, 85–86.

Chapter 4

1. "Construction of Camp Logan Will Start Tomorrow," *Houston Post,* July 23, 1917; Robert V. Haynes, *A Night of Violence: The Houston Riot of 1917* (Baton Rouge: Louisiana State University Press, 1976), 47–52; Garna L. Christian, *Black Soldiers in Jim Crow Texas, 1899–1917* (College Station: Texas A&M University Press, 1985), 145–272; and C. Calvin Smith, "The Houston Riot of 1917, Revisited," *Houston Review: History and Culture on the Gulf Coast* 13 (Fall 1991): 85–88. For three interpretations of the Houston Race Riot, see the above works. On July 28, 1866, the Thirty-ninth Congress passed the Army Reorganization Act, later signed into law by President Andrew Johnson. The Act created six African American regiments—four infantry and two cavalry units as part of the army's overall sixty-regiment force. Three years later, in an effort to streamline the military, the 1869 army appropriation act consolidated the six African American regiments into four—the Twenty-fourth and Twenty-fifth Infantries and the Ninth and Tenth Cavalries. Through 1898, the Twenty-fourth Infantry mostly served in the Indian Wars, performing numerous tasks, including constructing and maintaining post roads, protecting the building of the transcontinental railroads, safeguarding travelers along wagon trails, regularly patrolling the Mexican border, and policing Indian reservations. This experienced regiment also saw fighting in the Spanish American War, the Philippines, and later in Mexico as part of the Punitive Expedition in 1916.

2. Gail Buckley, *American Patriots: The Story of Blacks in the Military from the Revolution to Desert Storm* (New York: Random House, 2001), xvii–xxii, 163–64; Haynes, *A Night of Violence,* 51–53; Smith, "The Houston Riot of 1917, Revisited," 85–102; and Christian, *Black Soldiers in Jim Crow Texas, 1899–1917,* 145–72. Under Secretary of War Newton Baker, the United States Army banned African Americans from fighting in the American Expeditionary Force. The War Department also issued a directive to French officers, warning them about the supposed dangers of fraternizing with and befriending African American officers and noncommissioned troops. See Scott, *Scott's Official History of the American Negro in the World War.*

3. W. E. B. Du Bois, "Close Ranks," *Crisis,* July 16, 1918, in *W. E. B. Du Bois: A Reader,* ed. David Levering Lewis (New York: H. Holt, 1995): 697; Mark Ellis, "'Closing Ranks' and 'Seeking Honors': W. E. B. Du Bois in World War I," *Journal of American History* 79 (January 1992): 76–124; and Shane A. Smith, "The Crisis in the Great War:

W. E. B. Du Bois and His Perception of African American Participation in the Great War," *Historian* 70, no. 2 (Summer 2008): 239–62.

4. Hine et al., *The African-American Odyssey,* 428–43; Jones et al., *Created Equal: A Social and Political History of the United States,* 5th ed. (New York: Pearson-Longman, 2009), 632–649; Stephen L. Harris, *Harlem's Hell Fighters: The African-American 369th Infantry in World War I,* with a Foreword by Ron Paschall (Washington: Brassey's, 2003), 137–68; Buckley, *American Patriots,* 163–221; John Hope Franklin and Evelyn Brooks Higginbotham, *From Slavery to Freedom: A History of African Americans,* 9th ed. (New York: McGraw-Hill, 2011), 327–46; Chad L. Williams, *Torchbearers: African American Soldiers in the World War I Era* (Chapel Hill: University of North Carolina Press, 2010), 105–86; and Arthur E. Barbeau and Florette Henri, *The Unknown Soldier: Black American Troops in World War I,* with a new introduction from Bernard C. Nalty (Philadelphia: Temple University Press, 1974; New York: Da Capo of Perseus Publishing, 1996), 70–163.

5. Haynes, *A Night of Violence,* 51–89; Smith, "The Houston Riot of 1917, Revisited," 87–91; and Christian, *Black Soldiers in Jim Crow Texas, 1899–1917,* 147–52; and Edgar A. Schuler, "The Houston Race Riot, 1917," *Journal of Negro History* 29, no. 3 (1944), 300–301. Although the Brownsville and Houston tragedies have garnered the most attention among historians, numerous racial skirmishes involving African American soldiers and White or Latino residents occurred in several Texas cities between 1881 and 1917. For works that examine these clashes, see Christian, *Black Soldiers in Jim Crow Texas, 1899–1917;* John B. Weaver, *The Brownsville Raid* (New York: W. W. Norton, 1992); and James N. Leiker, *Racial Borders: Black Soldiers Along the Rio Grande* (College Station: Texas A&M University Press, 2002).

6. Haynes, *A Night of Violence,* 63–89.

7. *Africana,* vol. 3, s.v., "Harrison, Hubert Henry" (by Jeffrey B. Perry), 171–73; and Alain Locke, *The New Negro: An Interpretation,* with an introduction by Arnold Rampersad (New York: A & C. Boni, 1925; New York: Simon & Schuster, 1992), 3–18. For a comprehensive list of works about the "New Negro" Movement, including the evolution of the term, see Franklin and Higginbotham, *From Slavery to Freedom,* 660–62; *Encyclopedia of the Harlem Renaissance,* 2 vols., ed., Cary D. Wintz and Paul Finkelman (New York: Routledge, 2004); and *Encyclopedia of the Great Black Migration,* vol. 2, s.v., "New Negro," 614. Alain Locke (the first Black Rhodes Scholar to study at Oxford University, the Howard University professor of philosophy, and the noted scholar/artist of the Harlem Renaissance) popularized the use of the term "New Negro" in 1925 to describe a cultural and social movement among Blacks after World War I. The "New Negro" combined Booker T. Washington's self-help and accommodation philosophy, Marcus Garvey's Pan-Africanism, and Du Bois's social and political integrationist creed with economic radicalism. See Cary D. Wintz, *Black Culture and the Harlem Renaissance,* 1, 30–31; Cary D. Wintz, *The Harlem Renaissance: A History and An Anthology* (Upper Saddle River, New Jersey, 2003), 1–18; and Tuttle, *Race Riot,* 2–41.

8. Scott, *The Red Book of Houston;* Jackson, *A Sure Foundation;* Wilson, "Origins: The Houston NAACP, 1915–1918"; Jones, *The Red Book of Houston;* and Beeth and Wintz, eds., *Black Dixie.*

Notes to Pages 144–147

9. Wilson, "Origins: The Houston NAACP, 1915–1918," 71–77; and Steptoe, "Dixie West," 19–75. Twenty people lost their lives in the events of August 23, 1917.

10. *In the Name of Colored High, '04*, produced by Angenita Davis, 95 minutes, Houston, self-produced, DVD, 1993.

11. Hazel Young interview; Vivian Hubbard Seals interview; Thelma Scott Bryant interview; Jones, *Red Diary*, 72–79; and Haynes, *A Night of Violence*, 41–45.

12. Hazel Young interview.

13. Hazel Young interview; Vivian Hubbard Seals interview; Thelma Scott Bryant interview; and Haynes, *A Night of Violence*, 69.

14. Haynes, *A Night of Violence*, 92–103; Smith, "The Houston Riot of 1917, Revisited," 91–94; and Christian, *Black Soldiers in Jim Crow Texas, 1899–1917*, 150–51.

15. Haynes, *A Night of Violence*, 96–108; Smith, "The Houston Riot of 1917, Revisited," 90–91; and Christian, *Black Soldiers in Jim Crow Texas, 1899–1917*, 151–152.

16. Haynes, *A Night of Violence: The Houston Riot of 1917*, 108–126; Christian, *Black Soldiers in Jim Crow Texas, 1899–1917*, 151–152; and Smith, "The Houston Riot of 1917, Revisited," 91–94. Some scholars continue to argue that legitimate fear provoked the heinous crime spree that led to the deaths of twenty people. See Smith, "The Houston Riot of 1917, Revisited."

17. Haynes, *A Night of Violence: The Houston Riot of 1917*, 108–126; Christian, *Black Soldiers in Jim Crow Texas, 1899–1917*, 151–152; and Smith, "The Houston Riot of 1917, Revisited," 91–94."

18. Haynes, *A Night of Violence*, 123.

19. Haynes, *A Night of Violence*, 123, 143–70; Sullivan, *Lift Every Voice: The NAACP and the Making of the Civil Rights Movement.* (New York: The Free Press, 2008), 71–72. According to historian Patricia Sullivan in *Lift Every Voice*, two African American civilians died in the melée as well. No other scholarly source makes this claim, however.

20. "16 Dead—22 Injured from Riot," *Houston Press*, August 24, 1917; "Martial Law Declared—Result of Riot Started by Negro Regulars Who Mutinied, Fired Upon Their Officers and Left Camp, Slaying 13, Wounding 19: One Officer of Illinois Regiment Slain and 9 Policemen are Dead or Wounded," *Houston Post*, August 24, 1917; "17 Killed; 21 are Injured in Wild Night," *Houston Chronicle*, August 24, 1917; "Murderous Riot Replaces Negro Watermelon Party," *Houston Chronicle*, August 24, 1917; "The Effects of Martial Law: Mad Riot Clouds Disappear Before Shining Guns of Regulars," *Houston Chronicle*, August 25, 1917; "Peace Restored Throughout the Riot Zone," *Houston Chronicle*, August 26, 1917; Haynes, *A Night of Violence*, 143–75; and Christian, *Black Soldiers in Jim Crow Texas, 1899–1917*, 152–54.

21. Haynes, *A Night of Violence*, 208–96; Smith, "The Houston Riot of 1917, Revisited," 96–102; and Christian, *Black Soldiers in Jim Crow Texas, 1899–1917*, 153–72.

22. *In the Name of Colored High, '04*.

23. Ibid.

24. Haynes, *A Night of Violence*, 305.

25. Smith, "The Houston Riot of 1917, Revisited," 88–93, 100–2; Wilson, "Origins: The Houston NAACP, 1915–1918," 71–77; Steptoe, "Dixie West"; Schomburg Center, *In Motion*. According to tribunal testimonials and other eyewitness accounts, Officer Lee

Sparks prided himself on his contempt and hatred for African Americans. For these officers, police brutality toward African Americans had its place, especially in maintaining the racial status quo. For more about Sparks, see Haynes, *A Night of Violence*, 208–96; Smith, "The Houston Riot of 1917, Revisited," 96–102; and Christian, *Black Soldiers in Jim Crow Texas, 1899–1917*, 150–51.

26. Louis Harlan, *Booker T. Washington: The Making of a Black Leader, 1856–1901* (New York: Oxford University Press, 1972), 115–210; and Louis Harlan, *Booker T. Washington: The Wizard of Tuskegee, 1901–1915* (New York: Oxford University Press, 1983).

27. Booker T. Washington, "The Standard Printed Version of the Atlanta Exposition Address," in *Souls of Black Folk: A Norton Critical Reader*, ed. by Henry Lewis Gates Jr. and Terri Hume Oliver (1903; reprint, New York: Norton, 2000), 169.

28. Ibid., 170.

29. John W. Blassingame, *The Slave Community* (New York: Oxford University Press, 1974); Campbell, *An Empire for Slavery;* Akbar Na'im, *Breaking the Chains of Psychological Slavery* (Tallahassee: Mind Productions & Associates, 1993); and Alex Bontemps, *The Punished Self: Surviving Slavery in the Colonial South* (Ithaca: Cornell University Press, 2001). For works that discuss the evolution of slave resistance and acquiescence, see Franklin and Higginbotham, *From Slavery to Freedom*, 641–55.

30. An Act to Amend Section 58 of Chapter 122 of the General Laws Enacted by the Twenty-third Legislature, entitled An Act to Provide for a More Efficient System of Public Free Schools for the State of Texas, *General Laws of the State of Texas*, 23rd Leg, Chapter 24—C. S. for H. Bs. Nos. 3 and 7, §58, from *The Laws of Texas, 1822–1897*, vol. 10, part 2(Texas State Library and Archives Commission, Austin, Texas, 1895); An Act to provide for the survey of lands to be set apart as a permanent endowment fund for the Branch University for colored people of this state, General Laws of the State of Texas, 23rd Leg, Chapter 109—H. B. No. 124, from The Laws of Texas, 1822–1897, vol. 10, part 3(Texas State Library and Archives Commission, Austin, Texas, 1895); An Act to provide for the organization and support of a Normal School at Prairie View (formally called Alta Vista), in Waller County, for the preparation and training of colored teachers, Special Laws of the State of Texas, 15th Leg, Chapter 159—from The Laws of Texas, 1822–1897, vol. 8, part 3(Texas State Library and Archives Commission, Austin, Texas, 1895); Railroads—Separate Coaches Required, *General Laws of the State of Texas*, 22nd Leg, Chapter 41—S. B. No. 97, §1, from *The Laws of Texas, 1822–1897*, vol. 10, part 1, (Texas State Library and Archives, 1891); Public Schools, Chapter 61, Art 949, Public Charter and Revised Codes of Ordinances of the City of Houston, Texas, 1904 (Texas Room, Houston Public Library, Houston, Texas, 1904) (passed October 31, 1904); An Act Guaranteeing Street Railways Must Provide Separate Compartments, Houston Revised Codes, Ch. XLVIII, Art 1029, Street Railways (Texas Room, 1904); and Public Morals and Decency, Ch. XXX, § 1583b, Revised Codes of Ordinances of the City of Houston, Texas, 1922 (Texas Room, Houston Public Library, Houston, Texas, 1922); Forever Free: Nineteenth Century African-American Legislators and Constitutional Delegates of Texas, from the Texas State Library and Archives Commission, http://www.tsl.state.tx.us/exhibits/forever/index.html; The History of Jim Crow; and An Educators Site Made Possible by New York Life, http://www.pbs.org/wnet/jimcrow/.

31. Emmett J. Scott, "Introductory," in *The Red Book of Houston*, 1.

32. *The Handbook of Texas Online*, s.v., "Allen, Richard"; Jackson, *A Sure Foundation*, 287; "Biography of J. B. Bell, Capitalist," in *The Red Book of Houston*, 80–84; Crawford, "'To Protect, To Feed, and to Give Momentum to Every Effort.'" For works that discuss the evolution of the African American elite, see Lawrence O. Graham, *Our Kind of People: Inside America's Upper Class* (New York: Harper Collins, 1999); E. Franklin Frazier, *Black Bourgeoisie: The Rise of a New Middle Class* (New York: The Free Press, 1957); and Kusmer, *A Ghetto Takes Shape*; Ledé, *Precious Memories*; Spear, *Black Chicago*.

33. Emmett J. Scott, "Introductory," in *The Red Book of Houston*, 1; Jackson, *A Sure Foundation*, 219–20; Bryant, *Houston's Negro Schools*, 169–70; and Bessent, "The Publisher," 3–5; Crawford, "To Protect, to Feed, and to Give Momentum to Every Effort."

34. Joseph A. Pratt, "8F and Many More: Business and Civic Leadership in Modern Houston," *The Houston Review of History and Culture* 4, no. 2 (2004), 2–7, 31–42.

35. "Uplift Society is Rebuffed by Hobby," *Dallas Morning News*, August 24, 1919. Executive Director of the NAACP, John R. Shillady traveled to Austin, Texas, in August 1919 to assist the city's chapter in its effort to derail the attorney general's plans to ban the organization in the state. The Hobby administration posited the view that the "Bolshevik" organization wanted to prompt African American attacks on Whites. See Sullivan, *Lift Every Voice*, 86–87. For an assessment of the beating from the victim, John R. Shillady, see John R. Shillady, "NAACP Secretary Says Attack on Him Unwarranted: Has Stirred Up Hornet's Nest," Houston Informer, September 6, 1919.

36. Emmett J. Scott, "Introductory," in *The Red Book of Houston*, 1; Jackson, *A Sure Foundation*; and Beeth and Wintz, eds., *Black Dixie*.

37. For a few studies that address race relations in Houston and Texas, see SoRelle, "'The Darker Side of Heaven,'"; Haynes, *A Night of Violence*; Pitre, *In Struggle against Jim Crow*; Hine, *Black Victory*; Michael Phillips, *White Metropolis: Race, Ethnicity, and Religion in Dallas, 1841–2001* (Austin: University of Texas Press, 2008); Obadele-Starks, *Black Unionism in the Industrial South*; Bullard, *Invisible Houston*; De León, *Ethnicity in the Sunbelt*; Botson, *Labor, Civil Rights, and the Hughes Tool Company*; San Miguel, *Brown Not White*; Foley, *White Scourge*; Gary Hartman, *The History of Texas Music* (College Station: Texas A.&M. University, 2008); Kellar, *Make Haste Slowly*; Watson, *Race and the Houston Police Department*; Zamora, *The World of the Mexican Worker in Texas*; Joseph A. Pratt, ed., "Coming to Houston"; Joseph A. Pratt, ed., "Houston Remembers World War II," *The Houston Review of History and Culture* 2, no. 2, Special Issue (2005); Joseph A. Pratt, ed., "Civic Leadership in Houston," *The Houston Review of History and Culture* 1, no. 2, Special Issue (2004); Joseph A. Pratt, ed., "Confronting Jim Crow." Houston History 8, no. 1, Special Issue (2010); Joseph A. Pratt, ed., Houston Women in Texas and US History"; Glasrud and Pitre, *Black Women in Texas History*; Shabazz, "One for the Crows and One for the Crackers"; Barr, *Black Texans*; Roger R. Wood, *Down in Houston: Bayou City Blues* (Austin: University of Texas Press, 2003); Boston, Labor, Civil Rights, and the Hughes Tool Co.; and Shabazz, *Advancing Democracy*.

38. Jackson, *A Sure Foundation*, 219–20; Bryant, *Houston's Negro Schools*, 169–70; Bessent, "The Publisher," 3–5; and Crawford, "To Protect, to Feed, and to Give Momentum to Every Effort."

39. Pitre, *In Struggle against Jim Crow*, 9–36; and Darlene Hine, *Black Victory*, 95–110.

40. Clifton Richardson Sr. "Watch Your Step, Waco!" *Houston Informer*, January 20, 1923.

41. Biographical Note, C. F. Richardson Sr., Papers, MSS 1457; Newell, "The Life and Works of C. F. Richardson"; and Mary M. Cronin, "C. F. Richardson and the *Houston Informer*'s Fight for Racial Equality in the 1920s," *American Journalism* 23, (Summer 2006): 79–103. Migrant newspaperman Clifton Richardson embodied the "New Negro" of the interwar era, someone conscious of economic independence, racial unity, intellectual genius, cultural creativity, political radicalism as well as realpolitik. Nothing makes this observation more real than his newspapers'—*Houston Informer* (1919–30) and *Houston Defender* (1930–39)—editorials and articles under his leadership. For over a decade, the *Houston Informer*, under the direction of founder and editor Clifton Richardson, provoked thought, rage, pain, and hope in his readers. The paper's editorials, columns, and articles on racial segregation especially enlightened the masses of Black Houstonians, including those newcomers who recently entered the city. For stories/editorials on racism and Black unity at the start of the "New Negro Movement," see "Informer Editorial Policy Endorsed by Real Race Men Here and Elsewhere," *Houston Informer*, September 6, 1919; Colored Passenger Assaulted on Franklin Street Car by Conductor and White Civilian," *Houston Informer*, June 7, 1919; "A Lesson from the Jewish Race," editorial, *Houston Informer*, June 7, 1919; "Full Text Anti-Lynch Measure Introduced in Present Congress," *Houston Informer*, June 14, 1919; "Is Watermelon To Be Our Only Reward For Great Service in Democracy's Martial Conflict?" *Houston Informer*, June 28, 1919; "Riot Spirit Rampant in America," *Houston Informer*, August 9, 1919; and "Two Young Girls Are Victims of Hunnish Kultur At Hands of Marshall Police," *Houston Informer*, July 24, 1920. For more on Houston's "New Negro," including discussions around church work, clubwomen activism, fraternal orders, politics, labor unions, social welfare reform, and education, see *Houston Informer*, June 7, 1919–27, December 1929.

42. Robert A. Hill, ed., *The Marcus Garvey and Universal Improvement Association Papers*, 10 vols. (Berkeley: University of California Press, 2006); Amy Jacques, *Garvey and Garveyism*, with an introduction by John Henrik Clarke (New York: Octagon Books, 1978); *Encyclopedia of the Great Black Migration;* Trotter, *The Great Migration in Historical Perspective;* and Judith Stein, *The World of Marcus Garvey: Race and Class in Modern Society* (Baton Rouge: Louisiana State University, 1991). For a detailed bibliography on the period, see Franklin and Higginbotham, *From Slavery to Freedom*, 659–61; and Hine et al., *African American Odyssey*, 432–460.

43. Sullivan, *Lift Every Voice;* Kevin K. Gaines, *Uplifting the Race: Black Leadership, Politics, and Culture in the Twentieth Century* (Chapel Hill: University of North Carolina Press, 1996); Cary D. Wintz, ed., *African American Political Thought, 1890–1930: Washington, Du Bois, Garvey, and Randolph* (New York: M. E. Sharpe, 1996); and David Levering Lewis, *Du Bois: A Biography of Race, 1868–1919* (New York: H. Holt, 1994).

44. May Childs Nerny to Henry Mims, February 6, 1915, reel 19 of 20, Papers of the National Association for the Advancement of Colored People, Part 12: Selected Branch Files, 1913–1939, States A: The South, ed. John H. Bracey Jr. and August Meier,

Bethesda, Maryland, University Publications of America, located at M. D. Anderson Library, University of Houston, Houston, Texas (hereafter cited as Part 12, Reel 19 of 20, Papers of the NAACP); Martha Gruening, "National Association for the Advancement of Colored People—Houston: An NAACP Investigation," *The Crisis*, November 15, 1917, 14–19; Martha Gruening to James Weldon Johnson, n.d., reel 19 of 20, Papers of the National Association for the Advancement of Colored People, Part 1: Meetings of the Board of Directors, Records of Annual Conferences, and Special Reports, Special Correspondence, 1910–1919, Group I, Series C, Reel 17 of 28, Correspondence of James Weldon Johnson, ed. John H. Bracey Jr. and August Meier, Bethesda, Maryland, University Publications of America, located at M. D. Anderson Library, University of Houston, Houston, Texas (hereafter cited as Part 1, Reel 17 of 28, Papers of the NAACP); Walter F. White to Mr. M. B. Patton, May 11, 1918, Part 12, Reel 19 of 20, Papers of the NAACP; Martha Gruening, "Houston: An Investigation," Crisis 15 (November 1917), in *Black Protest and The Great Migration: A Brief History with Documents*, ed. Eric Arnesen (New York: Bedford/St. Martin's, 2003), 94–96; and Pitre, *In Struggle against Jim Crow*, 25–26.

45. For specific examples of African American political mobilization in Houston in the early twentieth century, see Director of Branches to E. O. Smith, June 19, 1923, Part 12, Reel 19 of 20, Papers of the NAACP; Wilson, "Origins: The Houston NAACP, 1915–1918"; "Constitution and By-Laws, Civic Betterment League of Houston and Harris County, 1918," Reel 19 of 20, Papers of the NAACP; "Miscellaneous," Rev. Lee Haywood Simpson & Pleasant Hill Baptist Church Collection, 239:6, folder 6, Houston Metropolitan Research Center, Houston Public Library, Julia Ideson Building, Houston, Texas (hereafter cited as Rev. L. H. Simpson & Pleasant Hill Baptist Church MSS); "Membership Cards, Third Ward Civic Club, 1946–1948," Harrison Family Collection, 182:1, file 10, Houston Metropolitan Research Center, Houston Public Library, Julia Ideson Building, Houston, Texas (hereafter cited as Harrison Family MSS, 182); "Membership Cards, NAACP, 1945, 1967," Harrison Family MSS, 182:1, file 9; Stullivan, *Roots of the Stullivan Family;* Luther Stullivan interview; "Constance Houston Thompson and National Council of Negro Women Photograph, circa 1940s," Joshua Houston Family Collection, 437:1; William L. Sherrill, "We the Negro," Opinions, *Houston Informer*, January 17, 1942; "Biography of J. B. Bell, Capitalist," in *The Red Book of Houston*, 35–80–85; Jackson, *A Sure Foundation;* Pitre, *In Struggle against Jim Crow*, 13–24; and Hine, *Black Victory,* 95–103.

46. Minutes of the Annual Meeting of the Texas Commission on Interracial Cooperation, Houston, Texas, November 26, 1926, Presbyterian Church, Houston, Texas, Texas Commission on Interracial Cooperation Records, RG E-12, box 1, folder 1, Houston Metropolitan Research Center, Houston Public Library, Houston, Texas (hereafter cited as TCIRC, RG E 12); M. W. Dogan to Texas Commission on Interracial Cooperation, November 5, 1926, TCIRC, RG E-12, box 1, folder 1; The Texas Commission on Inter-Racial Cooperation, 1920–1940: A Southern Organization for the Promotion of Racial Goodwill," Dr. Benjamin Covington MSS 170:1, folder 1; "Jennie Belle Murphy Covington"; "Funeral Service: Mrs. Jennie B. Covington"; "Seventeen Years with the YWCA in Houston," newspaper unknown, N.D., Dr. Benjamin Covington Papers,

170:1, folder 1; and Wille, "More Than Classes in Swimming and Making Hats," 54–91. For works that discuss interracial coalition building in early twentieth-century Houston, see Kellar, Make Haste Slowly; Botson, Labor, Civil Rights, and the Hughes Tool Company; Wille, "More Than Classes in Swimming and Making Hats"; and Pitre, In Struggle against Jim Crow.

47. "The Texas Commission on Inter-Racial Cooperation, 1920–1940: A Southern Organization for the Promotion of Racial Goodwill," Dr. Benjamin Covington MSS 170:1, folder 1; The Handbook of Texas Online, s.v., "Covington, Jennie Belle Murphy"; Rufus E. Clement, "Educational Programs for the Improvement of Race Relations; and William E. Cole, "The Role of the Commission on Interracial Cooperation in War and Peace," *Social Forces* 21, No. 4 (May 1943), 456–63.

48. Minutes of the Annual Meeting of the Texas Commission on Interracial Cooperation, November 6, 1926, TCIRC, RG E 12, box 1, folder 1; M. W. Dogan to Texas Commission on Interracial Cooperation, November 5, 1926, TCIRC, RG E-12, box 1, folder 1; Minutes of the Annual Meeting of the Texas Commission on Interracial Cooperation, November 1 and 2, 1929, TCIRC, RG E 12, box 1, folder 1; Minutes of the Annual Meeting of the Texas Commission on Interracial Cooperation, November 3 and 4, 1933, TCIRC, RG E 12, box 1, folder 1; Minutes of the Annual Meeting of the Texas Commission on Interracial Cooperation, December 7 and 8, 1934, TCIRC, RG E 12, box 1, folder 2; and Minutes of the Annual Meeting of the Texas Commission on Interracial Cooperation, December 6 and 7, 1940, TCIRC, RG E 12, box 1, folder 2.

49. Finding Aid, Jesse Daniel Ames Papers, 1866–1972, 3686, Louis Round Wilson Special Collections Library, University of North Carolina at Chapel Hill, Chapel Hill, North Carolina, http://www.lib.unc.edu/mss/inv/a/Ames,Jessie_Daniel.html#; *The Handbook of Texas Online*, s.v., "Ames, Jessie Harriet Daniel," http://www.tshaonline.org/handbook/online/articles/fam06; *The Handbook of Texas Online*, s.v., "Association of Southern Women for the Prevention of Lynching," http://www.tshaonline.org/handbook/online/articles/via01; Henry E. Barber, "Association of Southern Women for the Prevention of Lynching," *Phylon* 34, no. 4 (1973): 378–89; Jacqueline Dowd Hall, "The 'Mind That Burns in Each Body': Women, Rape, and Racial Violence," *Southern Exposure* 12, no. 6 (1984): 61–71; Laura Lynn Gray, "Women and the American Interracial Movement: A Rhetorical Analysis" (Ph.D. diss., Texas Women's University, 2002), 113–35, 165–80, 201–4; Jacqueline Dowd Hall, Carol Ruth Berkin, and Mary Beth Norton, "A Truly Subversive Affair: Women Against Lynching in the Twentieth-Century South," in *Women of America: A History*, written by Carol Ruth Berkin, and Mary Beth Norton (New York: Houghton Mifflin, 1979), 360–88; *The Handbook of Texas Online*, s.v., "Clark, Joseph Lynn," http://www.tshaonline.org/handbook/online/articles/fcl11; and Jeffrey Littlejohn, "Historian and Activist: Joseph Lynn Clark and the Texas Commission on Interracial Cooperation," an unpublished paper presented at East Texas Historical Association Spring Meeting, Waco, Texas, February 18, 2011.

50. Presbyterian Church—Afternoon Session, November 5, 1926, TCIRC, RG E 12, box 1, folder 1.

51. Ibid.

52. Ibid.

53. A Report of Experience with the Scholarship and Appropriation, Minutes of the Annual Meeting of the Texas Commission on Interracial Cooperation, December 6 and 7, 1940, TCIRC, RG E 12, box 1, folder 2; and Shabazz, *Advancing Democracy,* 27–33.

54. The Fourth Report of the Houston Commission on Interracial Cooperation to the State Commission Which Convenes at Houston, Texas, November 6, 1926, TCIRC, RG E 12, box 1, folder 1.

55. Ibid.

56. Minutes of the Annual Meeting of the Texas Commission on Interracial Cooperation, November 1 and 2, 1929, TCIRC, RG E 12, box 1, folder 1.

57. The Fourth Report of the Houston Commission on Interracial Cooperation to the State Commission Which Convenes at Houston, Texas, November 6, 1926, TCIRC, RG E 12, box 1, folder 1.

58. Minutes of the Annual Meeting of the Texas Commission on Interracial Cooperation, November 3 and 4, 1933, TCIRC, RG E 12, box 1, folder 1; Minutes of the Annual Meeting of the Texas Commission on Interracial Cooperation, December 7 and 8, 1934, TCIRC, RG E 12, box 1, folder 2; Hardman, "The Anti-tuberculosis Crusade and the Texas African-American Community, 1900–1950," 99–134; and J. L. Clark, chairman, to members of the Texas Commission of Inter-Racial Commission, April 11, 1934, TCIRC, RG E 12, box 1, folder 3.

59. Minutes of the Annual Meeting of the Texas Commission on Interracial Cooperation, November 6, 1926, TCIRC, RG E 12, box 1; Minutes of the Annual Meeting of the Texas Commission on Interracial Cooperation, December 7 and 8, 1934, TCIRC, RG E 12, box 1, folder 2; "The Texas Commission on Inter-Racial Cooperation, 1920–1940: A Southern Organization for the Promotion of Racial Goodwill," brochure, Dr. Benjamin Covington MSS 170:1, folder 1; *The Handbook of Texas Online,* s.v., "Association of Southern Women for the Prevention of Lynching"; "'Travesty of Justice,' Says Mrs. Covington"; and Gray, "Women and the American Interracial Movement," 165–80, 193–204.

60. "Travesty of Justice, Says Mrs. Covington."

61. Like Covington, NAACP and NACW founder Mary Church Terrell in later years increasingly denounced racism.

62. "Henry L. Mims," in *The Red Book of Houston,* 132; Henry L. Mims, "The Call," National Alliance of Postal Employees (NAPFE), August 24, 1913, http://www.napfe.com/home.php, 132–33; Jackson, *A Sure Foundation,* 29–30; Cronin, "C. F. Richardson and the *Houston Informer*'s Fight for Racial Equality in the 1920s," 79–87; Wilson, "Origins: The Houston NAACP, 1915–1918," 56–108; Walter F. White to Mr. M. B. Patton, May 11, 1918, Part 12, Reel 19 of 20, Papers of the NAACP; W. L. Davis to W. E. B. Du Bois, May 21, 1918, Part 12, Reel 19 of 20, Papers of the NAACP; W. L. Davis and E. O. Smith, "Why Not? The Civic Betterment League Officials Speak Out," *Western Star,* May 10, 1918, Part 12, Reel 19 of 20; National Alliance of Postal and Federal Employees, 132–33; Hine, *Black Victory,* 100; and Melvin James Banks, "In the Pursuit of Equality: The Movement for First Class Citizenship among Negroes in Texas, 1920–1950" (Ph.D. diss., Syracuse University, 1962), 101. Although William Leonard Davis was born in Lavaca County in southeastern Texas, his family later moved the family to nearby La

Grange in adjacent Fayette County, where he attended school with future educator and farmer Calvin Rhone Sr. The two remained close friends until Rhone's death in the early 1920s. See Jackson, *A Sure Foundation*, 29–; Calvin L. Rhone to Lucia J. Rhone, December 20, 1920, Rhone Family MSS, 3U171:2; and Obituary of Calvin L. Rhone Sr., Western Star, January 29, 1921, Rhone Family MSS, 3U180:1

63. E. O. Smith to Walter F. White, May 22, 1918, Part 12, Reel 19 of 20, Papers of the NAACP; Walter F. White to E. O. Smith, June 3, 1918, Part 12, Reel 19 of 20, Papers of the NAACP; E. O. Smith to Walter F. White, June 10, 1918, Part 12, Reel 19 of 20, Papers of the NAACP; Civic Betterment League to Board of Directors, NAACP, June 8, 1918, Part 12, Reel 19 of 20, Papers of the NAACP; and C. F. Richardson to Mr. Shillady, June 17, 1918, Part 12, Reel 19 of 20, Papers of the NAACP. For the complete correspondence between Houston leaders and the NAACP National Office, see Part 12, Reel 19 of 20, Papers of the NAACP.

64. For a complete analysis of the NAACP letter-writing campaign of 1918, see Wilson, "Origins: The Houston NAACP, 1915–1918."

65. Walter White to E. O. Smith, July 28, 1918, Part 12, Reel 19 of 20, Papers of the NAACP.

66. Mims, "The Call," NAPFE.

67. Mims, "The Call," NAPFE; "History of NAPFE," NAPFE; Mims," *The Red Book of Houston*, 132; and National Alliance of Postal Employees, 132–33.

68. *Love v. Griffith*, 266 US 32, 45 Sup. Ct. 12 (1924); Pitre, *In Struggle against Jim Crow*, 25–26; Michael Lowery Gillette, "The NAACP in Texas" (Ph.D. diss., University of Texas, 1984), 1; and Hine, *Black Victory*, 95–110.

69. *Love v. Griffith*, 266 US 32, 45 Sup. Ct. 12 (1924); Pitre, *In Struggle against Jim Crow*, 25–26; Gillette, "The NAACP in Texas," 1; Hine, *Black Victory*, 95–110; Reich, "Soldiers of Democracy"; "The Waco Horror: A Report of a Lynching," in The Waco Horror, supplement, *The Crisis: A Record of the Darker Races* 12 (July 1916): 1–8; "Lynching in Temple, Texas," Crisis, XI (January, 1916), 145; *Dallas Morning News*, "Uplift Society is Rebuffed by Hobby; *Dallas Morning News*, "Judge Threshes Man Organizing Negroes: J. R. Shillady, White, Secretary of Organization, Is Beaten in Austin," August 23, 1919; James SoRelle, "The 'Waco Horror': The Lynching of Jesse Washington," *Southwestern Historical Quarterly* 86 (April 1983): 517–36; William M. Tuttle Jr., "Violence in the 'Heathen Land': The Longview Race Riot of 1919," *Phylon* 33, no. 4 (1972): 324–33; "Six Negroes Dead After Battle with Citizen's Posse: Entire Family Wiped Out as a Result of Resistance to Draft Call," *San Antonio Express,* June 2, 1918; "Six Negroes Slain for Alleged Plot to Wipe Out Family: Wholesale Execution Sequel to Killing of Draft Evader in Dodge, Texas," June 1, 1918, from Christine's Genealogy Website, *San Antonio Light,* http://ccharity.com/contents/transcriptions-wills-property-tax-rolls-inventory-lists-and-newspaper-clippings-contributed-website/six-negroes-dead-after-battle-citizens-posse/; Cynthia Skove Nevels, *Lynching to Belong: Claiming Whiteness Through Racial Violence* (College Station: Texas A&M University Press, 2007); Henry Coleman interview; Ralph Ginzburg, *100 Years of Lynching*, 269–70; Edward Hake Phillips, "The Sherman Courthouse Riot of 1930," *East Texas Historical Journal* 25, no. 2 (1987): 12–19; Patricia Hale, "Violence in Small Town Texas: The Documentation of East Texas'

Lynching Culture" (master's thesis, Sam Houston State University, 2012), 9–10; and David Chapman, "Lynching in Texas" (master's thesis, Texas Tech University, 1973). For a detailed listing of Texas lynching victims in the late nineteenth and early twentieth centuries, see Ralph Ginzburg, *100 Years of Lynching*.

70. Nancy Maclean, *Behind the Mask of Chivalry: The Making of the Second Ku Klux Klan* (New York: Oxford University Press, 1994); and Kathleen Blee, *Women of the Klan: Racism and Gender in the 1920s* (Berkeley: University of California Press, 1991).

71. Walter White to E. O. Smith, July 22, 1925, Reel 19 of 20, Papers of the NAACP; Casey Greene, "Guardians Against Change: The Ku Klux Klan in Houston and Harris County, 1920–1925," *Houston Review*, 10 (Fall 1988), 3–18; Danny Lee Ahlfield, "Fraternalism Gone Awry: The Ku Klux Klan in Houston, 1920–1925" (master's thesis, University of Texas at Austin, 1984), 1–7, 18–32, 63–68, 732–73; Charles Comer Alexander, "Invisible Empire in the Southwest: The Ku Klux Klan in Texas, Louisiana, Oklahoma, and Arkansas, 1920–1930" (Ph.D. diss., University of Texas at Austin, 1962); SoRelle, "Race Relations in 'Heavenly Houston,'" 177–80; Dwight Watson, "In the Name of Progress and Decency: The Response of Houston's Civic Leaders to the Lynching of Robert Powell in 1928," *Houston Review of History and Culture*, 1, no. 2 (2005), 26–28; and SoRelle, "Race Relations in 'Heavenly Houston,' 1919–1945," 175–91.

72. Texas Citizen League, n.d., flyer, Part 12, Reel 19 of 20, Papers of the NAACP; Texas Citizenship League to John M. Adkins, March 27, 1923, Reel 19 of 20, Papers of the NAACP; Ahlfield, "Fraternalism Gone Awry," 68, 98–109; Greene, "Guardians Against Change," 3–18; Dan S. Gerig, "The Ku Klux Klan, Invisible Government, and Joseph Stephen Cullinan," unpublished paper presented at the East Texas Historical Association, September 26, 2009, Nacogdoches, Texas, 4–12; *The Handbook of Texas Online*, s.v., "Wortham, Gus Sessions," http://www.tshaonline.org/handbook/online/articles/fwo34; *The Handbook of Texas Online*, s.v., "Kirby, John Henry"; The Handbook of Texas Online, s.v., "Cullinan, Joseph Stephen," http://www.tshaonline.org/handbook/online/articles/fcu07; and Pratt, "8F and Many More," 2–7, 31–42.

73. Texas Citizen League, n.d., flyer, Part 12, Reel 19 of 20, Papers of the NAACP.

74. Ibid.

75. Texas Citizenship League to John M. Adkins, March 27, 1923, Part 12, Reel 19 of 20, Papers of the NAACP; Gerig, "The Ku Klux Klan, Invisible Government," 1–12; Greene, "Guardians Against Change," 3–18; Pratt, "8F and Many More," 2–7, 31–42; Watson, "In the Name of Progress and Decency," 26–28; and Wilson, "Origins: The Houston NAACP, 1915–1918," 56–108.

76. E. O. Smith, "An Open Letter to Colored People of Houston," *Texas Freeman*, April 12, 1922, Part 12, Reel 19 of 20, Papers of the NAACP; Joel E. Spingarn, "Why the NAACP," 1923, brochure, Part 12, Reel 19 of 20, Papers of the NAACP; Robert W. Bagnall to John M. Adkins, March 14, 1923, Part 12, Reel 19 of 20, Papers of the NAACP; J. E. Armistead to unknown recipient, April 12, 1923, Part 12, Reel 19 of 20, Papers of the NAACP; E. O. Smith to Robert W. Bagnall, April 4, 1923, Part 12, Reel 19 of 20, Papers of the NAACP; and Reich, "Soldiers of Democracy," 1490–1501.

77. Thelma Scott Bryant interview.

78. John Lafayette Cockrell, 1918, US Selective Service System, World War I Selective

Service Draft Registration Cards, 1917–1918 (Washington: National Archives and Records Administration, M1509, 4,582 rolls), from Ancestry.com, http://search.ancestry.com/; Clifton Richardson, "'Heavenly Houston' Turns Hellish and Hunish as Mobbists Stage Pastime," *Houston Informer,* June 23, 1928; Watson, "In the Name of Progress and Decency," 26–28; SoRelle, "Race Relations in 'Heavenly Houston,' 1919–1945," 175–91; and Gerig, "The Ku Klux Klan, Invisible Government, 4–12.

79. "Crimes in Houston and Lufkin Contrasted," *Houston Informer,* March 8, 1928.

80. E. O. Smith, "An Open Letter to Colored People of Houston"; Joel E. Spingarn, "Why the NAACP," 1923, brochure, Part 12, Reel 19 of 20, Papers of the NAACP; Robert W. Bagnall to John M. Adkins, 14 March 1923, Part 12, Reel 19 of 20, Papers of the NAACP; J. E. Armistead to unknown recipient, April 12, 1923, Part 12, Reel 19 of 20, Papers of the NAACP; E. O. Smith to Robert W. Bagnall, April 4, 1923, Part 12, Reel 19 of 20, Papers of the NAACP; and Reich, "Soldiers of Democracy," 1490–1501.

81. "O. L. Hubbard Takes Oath of Office as Mayor," Independence Heights Department, *Houston Informer,* June 28, 1919, in Vivian Hubbard Seals, "Independence Heights, Texas"; Seals, "Oliphant Lockwood Hubbard Sr., 1880–1968"; Vivian Hubbard Seals interview; and J. Spencer, "Our Neighbor."

82. Vivian Hubbard Seals interview.

83. *Houston Informer,* "O. L. Hubbard Takes Oath of Office as Mayor," Independence Heights Department, Houston Informer, June 28, 1919, in Vivian Hubbard Seals, "Independence Heights, Texas"; Seals, "Oliphant Lockwood Hubbard Sr., 1880–1968"; Vivian Hubbard Seals interview; J. Spencer, "Our Neighbor"; Kimberly McCullough, "The First All-Black City in Texas," *Touchstone* 22, no. 1 (2003).

84. Glasrud, "Black Texans, 1900–1930," 59, 91; Newell, "The Life and Works of C. F. Richardson," 5; "Republican Primary Election Pure Farce," editorial, *Houston Informer,* July 31, 1926; "Colored Americans in Walker County Victims of Wholesale Depredations"; SoRelle, "Race Relations in 'Heavenly Houston,' 1919–45"; and Thelma Scott Bryant interview.

85. Thelma Scott Bryant interview.

86. *Houston Informer,* September 8, 1923, quoted in SoRelle, "'The Darker Side of Heaven: The Black Community in Houston, Texas," 74.

87. Clifton Richardson Jr., interview by Louis Marchiafava and Veronica Perry, digitized tape recording, Houston Oral History Project, Houston Metropolitan Research Center, Houston, Texas, 9 June 1975, http://digital.houstonlibrary.org/oral-history/cliff-richardson.php (hereafter cited as Richardson interview).

88. Ibid.

89. SoRelle, "Race Relations in 'Heavenly Houston,' 1919–45," 175–80; Thomas, *A Study of the Social Welfare Status of Negroes in Houston, Texas,* 102–6.

90. Thelma Scott Bryant interview.

91. Ibid.

92. Ibid.

93. SoRelle, "Race Relations in 'Heavenly Houston,' 1919–45," 175–80.

94. "Houston, Texas NAACP Wins Fight Freeing Condemned Negro," no date, Press Release, Part 12, Reel 19 of 20, Papers of the NAACP; "Houston, Texas NAACP

Saves Luther Collins from Death Penalty," November 7, 1924, Press Release, Part 12, Reel 19 of 20, Papers of the NAACP; Walter White to John M. Atkins, October 15, 1923, Part 12, Reel 19 of 20, Papers of the NAACP; E. O. Smith to Walter White, December 18, 1922, Part 12, Reel 19 of 20, Papers of the NAACP; Walter White to E. O. Smith, December 18, 1922, Part 12, Reel 19 of 20, Papers of the NAACP; "NAACP, Houston Branch[,] Secures Third Trial for Luther Collins," July 10, 1925, Press Release, Part 12, Reel 19 of 20, Papers of the NAACP; Walter White to John M. Atkins, October 2, 1924, Part 12, Reel 19 of 20, Papers of the NAACP; Clifton Richardson, "Collins Case a Double Loss to State," *Houston Informer,* September 25, 1926; SoRelle, "The Darker Side of 'Heaven,'" 368–70; Steptoe, "Dixie West," 97–100; and Pitre, *In Struggle against Jim Crow,* 27.

95. Jackson, *A Sure Foundation,* 385–86; O. P. DeWalt to Walter White, December 1, 1926, Part 12, Reel 19 of 20, Papers of the NAACP; and *The Handbook of Texas Online,* s.v., "DeWalt, O. P.," http://www.tshaonline.org/handbook/online/articles/DD/fdeaf.html.

96. William Pickens to C. F. Richardson, October 4, 1938, Part 12, Reel 19 of 20, Papers of the NAACP; William Pickens to C. F. Richardson, November 30, 1938, Part 12, Reel 19 of 20, Papers of the NAACP; NAACP, 89 Fifth Avenue, New York City, Officers of Texas Branches, n.d., Part 12, Reel 19 of 20, Papers of the NAACP; E. Frederic Morrow to C. F. Richardson, January 24, 1939, Part 12, Reel 19 of 20, Papers of the NAACP; E. Frederic Morrow to A. Maceo Smith, February 15, 1939, Part 12, Reel 19 of 20, Papers of the NAACP; E. Frederic Morrow to A. Maceo Smith, February 20, 1939, Part 12, Reel 19 of 20, Papers of the NAACP; A. Maceo Smith to E. Frederic Morrow, February 27, 1939, Part 12, Reel 19 of 20, Papers of the NAACP; E. Frederic Morrow to A. Maceo Smith, February 28, 1939, Part 12, Reel 19 of 20, Papers of the NAACP; E. Frederic Morrow to C. F. Richardson, June 9, 1939, Part 12, Reel 19 of 20, Papers of the NAACP; E. Frederic Morrow to C. F. Richardson, August 25, 1939, Part 12, Reel 19 of 20, Papers of the NAACP; E. L. Snyder to Walter White, September 7, 1939, Part 12, Reel 19 of 20, Papers of the NAACP; E. L. Snyder to Walter White, September 7, 1939, #11781, Part 12, Reel 19 of 20, Papers of the NAACP; E. L. Snyder to Members and Friends, Memorial Service Date, September 17, 1939, n.d., Part 12, Reel 19 of 20, Papers of the NAACP; Pitre, *In Struggle against Jim Crow,* 25–26; Hine, *Black Victory,* 95–102; Reich, "Soldiers of Democracy," 1478–83, 1494–1497; Haynes, "Black Houstonians and the White Democratic Primary, 194–208; Gillette, "The Rise of the NAACP in Texas," *Southwestern Historical Quarterly* 81 (June 1978), 393–402; and Reich, "Soldiers of Democracy," 1480–1504.

97. "Resolution Passed by School Board on Pay Equalization," *Houston Informer,* April 17, 1943; "Nearly 1,000 Negroes Given Work: Mostly Assigned to Fine White Sections of the City," *Houston Informer,* December 2, 1933; "Relief in Houston Goes 'Jim Crow,'" *Houston Informer,* March 31, 1934; "Negroes on the Outer Rims of Employment, "*Houston Informer,* February 7, 1942; Thelma Scott Bryant interview; Lullelia Harrison interview, March 8, 2000; *In the Name of Colored High,* '04; Pitre, *In Struggle against Jim Crow,* 56–80; Hine, *Black Victory,* 22–24, 164; Obadele-Starks, *Black Unionism in the Industrial South,* 24–36; Shabazz, "Carter Wesley," 2–12; Botson,

Labor, Civil Rights, and the Hughes Tool Company; Kellar, *Make Haste Slowly,* 26–44; Ramona Houston, "The NAACP State Conference in Texas: Intermediary and Catalyst for Change, 1937–1957," *The Journal of African American History* 94 (Fall 2009): 510–11; Shabazz, *Advancing Democracy,* 18–33; and Randy J. Sparks, "'Heavenly Houston' or 'Hellish Houston'?" Black Unemployment and Relief Efforts, 1929–1936," *Southern Studies* 25 (Winter 1986): 356–64.

98. Richard Grovey, World War I Draft Registration Card, Precinct 13, June 5, 1917, Houston, Texas, Military Records, from Ancestry.com, http://content.ancestry.com/; Manuscript Census of the United States, Brazoria County, Texas, 1900, roll 1614, Bureau of the Census, series T623, Heritage Quest Online, http://persi.heritagequestonline.com/; Manuscript Census of the United States, Brazoria County, Texas, 1910, roll 1534, Bureau of the Census, series T624, Clayton Genealogy Library, Houston Public Library, Houston, Texas; Manuscript Census, Harris County, 1930, roll 2347, series T626; Hine, *Black Victory,* 164–67; and *The Handbook of Texas Online,* s.v., "Grovey, Richard Randolph," http://www.tshaonline.org/handbook/online/articles/fgrat.

99. Nell Grovey Cole. Interviewed by Bernadette Pruitt, tape recording, Houston, Texas, April 19, 2008, in possession of the author; Kelley, *Race Rebels,* 11–13, 37–51; Scott, *Domination and the Arts of Resistance,* 5–16; Darlene Clark Hine, *Hine Sight: Black Women and the Reconstruction of American History* (Bloomington: Indiana University Press, 1994), 37–57; and Jacqueline Jones, *Labor of Love, Labor of Sorrow: Black Women, Work, and the Family, From Slavery to the Present* (New York: Vintage, 1985). Although these works largely discuss protest imagination in the context of poor wage earners, the actions of the Groveys, an educated working-class couple, do speak to the multitude of ways African Americans resisted White racism.

100. Nell Grovey Cole interview.

101. Grovey, World War I Draft Registration Card; Manuscript Census, Brazoria County, 1900, roll 1614, series T623; Manuscript Census, Brazoria County, 1910, roll 1534, series T624; Manuscript Census, Harris County, 1930, roll 2547, series T626; Hine, *Black Victory,* 164–67; and *The Handbook of Texas Online,* s.v., "Grovey, Richard Randolph."

102. Membership Cards, Third Ward Civic Club, 1946–1948," Harrison Family MSS, 182:1, file 10; "Third Ward Civic Club," letterhead, Carroll P. Blue Collection, Houston, Texas, in possession of author; Grovey, World War I Draft Registration Card; Manuscript Census, Brazoria County, 1900, roll 1614, series T623; Manuscript Census, Brazoria County, 1910, roll 1534, series T624; Manuscript Census, Harris County, 1930, roll 2547, series T626; Hine, *Black Victory,* 164–67; and *The Handbook of Texas Online,* s.v., "Grovey, Richard Randolph."

103. Submitting Constitutional Amendment to Vote of the People, *The Laws of Texas, 1897–1902,* vol.11, S.J.R. No. 3, Joint Resolution (Austin: Texas State Library, 1902); Elections—Manner of Holding and Making Returns, *General Laws of the State of Texas,* 28th Leg, S.H.B. Nos. 45 and 170 (Austin: Texas State Library, 1903), 133–59; Elections—Manner of Holding and Making Returns, *General Laws of the State of Texas,* 29th Leg, H.B. No. 8, § 103 (Austin: Texas State Library, 1905), 543; Hine, *Black Victory,* 69–94; and SoRelle, "The Darker Side of 'Heaven,'" 169–72.

104. *Love v. Griffith*, 236, S.W. 239 (Texas Civ. App, 1922); *Love v. Griffith*, 266 US 32 (1924); and SoRelle, "The Darker Side of 'Heaven,'" 169–72, 173–76.

105. Qualifications in Voting in Democratic Primaries, *General Laws of the State of Texas*, 38th Leg., First, Second, and Third Called Sessions, S. B. No. 44, Ch. 32 (Austin: Texas State Library, 1923); Hine, *Black Victory*, 91–94; Haynes, "Black Houstonians and the White Democratic Primary," 194–96; Reich, "Soldiers of Democracy," 480–504; and SoRelle, "The Darker Side of 'Heaven,'" 172–73.

106. Authorizing Political Parties Through State Executive Committees to Prescribe Qualifications of Their Members, *General Laws of the State of Texas*, 40th Leg, H.B. No. 57, Chapter 67 (Austin: Texas State Library, 1927), 193–94; *Nixon v. Herndon*, 273 US 536 (1927); *Nixon v. Condon*, 286 US 73 (1932); Manuscript Census, Harrison County, 1920, roll 1813, series T625; Hine, *Black Victory*, 111–72; Will Guzman, "Border Physician: The Life of Lawrence A. Nixon, 1883–1966 (Ph.D. diss., University of Texas at El Paso), 128–64; and SoRelle, "The Darker Side of 'Heaven,'" 176–84. Black migrants and business owners James B. Grigsby of Mississippi and O. P. DeWalt of Polk County in the East Texas Pine Belt lost their case in 1928 when Judge Joseph C. Hutcheson Jr. ruled in favor of the defendants in *Grigsby v. Harris*, 27 F.2d 945 (1928), arguing the petition had no basis, as the new law was contrived by a private political organization and not the state. The Houston branch of the NAACP did aid Nixon once again challenge Texas, although DeWalt, who later served as president of the local NAACP, died prematurely from gunshot wounds during an argument with a dissatisfied employee at his business, the Lincoln Theater, in 1930. Nightclub owner and Victoria, Texas, native Julius White, the spouse of civil-rights activist Lulu White, also filed a writ of mandamus in federal court to force Harris County Democratic Party Committee chair J. B. "Shorty" Lubbock to comply with the Supreme Court ruling in *Nixon v. Herndon*. Federal Judge Joseph C. Hutcheson, not surprisingly, in *White v. Lubbock*, 30 SW 2d 722 (Tex. Civ. App. 1930), denied the request. Black migrants, like established residents of Houston, remained undaunted by these disappointments and continued pressing forward.

107. Nell Grovey Cole interview; "R. R. Grovey on the Air," photograph, n.d., Grovey Family Collection, Houston, Texas, in possession of Claude Cole, the son-in-law of Mr. Grovey; Hine, *Black Victory*, 164–92; Haynes, "Black Houstonians and the White Democratic Primary," 194–210; *The Handbook of Texas Online*, s.v., "National Association for the Advancement of Colored People," http://www.tshaonline.org/handbook/online/articles/ven01; David Montejano, *Anglos and Mexicans in the Making of Texas, 1836–1986* (1987; Austin: University of Texas Press, 1992), 143–52; Alwyn Barr, *Reconstruction to Reform: Texas Politics, 1876–1906* (1971; Dallas: Southern Methodist University Press, 2000), 193–208; *The Handbook of Texas Online*, s.v., "African Americans and Politics," http://www.tshaonline.org/handbook/online/articles/wmafr; *The Handbook of Texas Online*, s.v., "Grovey, Richard Randolph," http://www.tshaonline.org/handbook/online/articles/fgrat; *The Handbook of Texas Online*, s.v., "White, Julius," http://www.tshaonline.org/handbook/online/articles/fwh91; "NAACP to Test Newest Attempt to Disfranchise Blacks," *Houston Informer*, August 4, 1928; and NAACP papers.

108. *White v. Lubbock, 30 SW 2d 722 (Tex. Civ. App. 1930)*; Haynes, "Black Houstonians and the White Democratic Primary," 194–210; *The Handbook of Texas Online*, s.v.,

"White, Julius"; *The Handbook of Texas Online,* s.v., "Richard Randolph Grovey"; and Pitre, *In Struggle against Jim Crow,* 19–24.

109. Hine, *Black Victory,* 185–92; Guzman, "Border Physician," 128–65; and Haynes, "Black Houstonians and the White Democratic Primary," 194–210.

110. Hine, *Black Victory,* 193–209.

111. *Grovey v. Townsend,* 295 US 45 (1935); "Demos Propose Resolution to Bar Negro Vote," unknown newspaper, n.d., Reel 5 of 13, Papers of the National Association for the Advancement of Colored People, Part 4: Voting Rights Campaign, 1916–1950, ed. John H. Bracey Jr. and August Meier, Bethesda, Maryland, University Publications of America, located at M. D. Anderson Library, University of Houston, Houston, Texas (hereafter cited as Part 4, Reel 5 of 13, Papers of the NAACP); R. D. Evans to Walter White, May 1, 1935, Part 4, Reel 5 of 13, Papers of the NAACP; Fred C. Knollenberg to Walter White, April 4, 1935, Part 4, Reel 5 of 13, Papers of the NAACP; Fred C. Knollenberg to J. Alston Atkins, April 4, 1935, Part 4, Reel 5 of 13, Papers of the NAACP; Lawrence A. Nixon to Clifton F. Richardson Sr., April 5, 1935, Part 4, Reel 5 of 13, Papers of the NAACP; "White Primaries Sanctioned," *National Juridical Association* 3, no. 11 (April 1935): 5; Jack Alston Atkins to Charles Hamilton Houston, May 12, 1935, Part 4, Reel 5 of 13, Papers of the NAACP; and Hine, *Black Victory,* 193–209. For more correspondences and newspaper clippings regarding the national response to the Grovey decision, see Part 4: Voting Rights Campaign, 1916–1950, Reel 5 of 13, Papers of the NAACP.

112. *Smith v. Allwright,* 321 US 649 (1944); "Dr. L. E. Smith Files Petition in Primary Case," *Houston Informer,* April 24, 1943; Carter Wesley, "Historic Decision Removes All Bars Against Race Voting," Editorial, *Houston Informer,* April 8, 1944; Carter Wesley, "The Right to Vote," *Houston Informer,* April 8, 1944; and Hine, *Black Victory,* 231–48.

113. Nell Grovey Cole interview.

114. National Urban League, *A Review of the Economic and Cultural Problems of Houston, Texas,* 166–76; Jackson, *A Sure Foundation;* Pitre, *In Struggle against Jim Crow,* 13–80; and Hine, *Black Victory,* 95–110, 193–209. Most African American Houston residents were between the ages of twenty and forty in 1930 and 1940. For specific data, see Sixteenth Census of the United States, 1940, vol. 2, 1044.

115. Newell, "The Life and Works of C. F. Richardson," 19; Shabazz, "Carter Wesley," 2–12; and Greene, *Selling Black History for Carter G. Woodson.* For the names of younger second and third-wave migrants, see Jackson, *A Sure Foundation.*

116. A Life Sketch, Rev. M. L. Price MSS, 277:1; Jackson, *A Sure Foundation,* 157.

117. Ibid.

118. Ibid., 157.

119. Ibid., 157.

120. Ibid., 157.

121. Ibid., 157.

122. Ibid., 157.

123. For two examples of manhood consciousness, see Scott, *The Red Book of Houston;* Jackson, *A Sure Foundation.* For more on African American manhood, see Darlene Clark Hine and Ernestine Jenkins, ed., *A Question of Manhood: A Reader in Black Men's History and Masculinity,* 2 vols. (Bloomington: Indiana University Press, 1999); and

Angela Hornsby-Gutting, *Black Manhood and Community Building in North Carolina, 1890–1930* (Gainesville: University Press of Florida, 2009); and Steptoe, "Dixie West," 72–100.

124. Houstonians, including recent migrants, celebrated Afro-American manhood in their actions, viewpoints, and writings. For concrete examples, see *Houston Informer and Texas Freeman,* January 1919–December 1941; Scott, *The Red Book of Houston;* and Jackson, *A Sure Foundation.*

125. Manuscript Census of the United States, Burleson County, Texas, 1900, roll 1615, Bureau of the Census, series T623, Heritage Quest Online, http://persi.heritagequestonline.com/; Manuscript Census of the United States, Montgomery County, Texas, 1920, roll 1834, Bureau of the Census, series T625, Heritage Quest Online, http://persi.heritagequestonline.com/; *Houston Informer,* March 23, 1940; *Houston Informer,* November 18, 1940; Church Anniversary Program, "Good Hope Missionary Baptist church Celebrates 100 Years of Service," Houston, Texas, 1972, in possession of author; Church Anniversary Program, "Vision 2000: The Hope of the Future: Good Hope Missionary Baptist Church Celebrating and Building on 123 Years of Faithful Christian Service," Houston, Texas, 1995, in possession of author; Jackson, *A Sure Foundation,* 45–46; Pitre, *In Struggle against Jim Crow,* 33–34; and Hine, *Black Victory,* 230–31.

126. Church Anniversary Program, "Good Hope Missionary Baptist church Celebrates 100 Years of Service"; Jackson, *A Sure Foundation,* 45–46; Spear, *Black Chicago,* 192–93; Pitre, *In Struggle against Jim Crow,* 33–34; and Hine, *Black Victory,* 230–31.

127. Hine and Jenkins, ed., *A Question of Manhood,* vol. 1, *The Construction of Black Man's History and Manhood,* 1750–1870, 1–61; and Steptoe "Dixie West".

128. For works that discuss moderately radical African American women activists, see Pitre, *In Struggle against Jim Crow;* Stephanie Decker, "Women in the Civil Rights Movement: Juanita Craft versus the Dallas Elite," *East Texas Historical Journal* 39 (Spring 2001): 33–42. Melba Joyce Boyd, "A Review Essay: Canon Configuration for Ida B. Wells-Barnett," *Black Scholar* 24, no. 1 (1994): 8–13; Mia Bay, "The Improbable Ida B. Wells," *Reviews in American History* 30, no. 3 (2002): 439–44; Patricia A. Schechter, *Ida B. Wells-Barnett and American Reform, 1880–1930* (Chapel Hill: University of North Carolina Press, 2001); Paula Giddings, *"When and Where I Enter";* and Hine, *Hine Sight.*

129. Pitre, *In Struggle against Jim Crow,* 28–36, 37–129.

130. Minutes of the Annual Meeting of the Texas Commission on Interracial Cooperation, 3 and November 4, 1933, TCIRC, RG E 12, box 1, folder 1; Minutes of the Annual Meeting of the Texas Commission on Interracial Cooperation, December 7 and 8, 1934, TCIRC, RG E 12, box 1, folder 2; "The Texas Commission on Inter-Racial Cooperation, 1920–1940: A Southern Organization for the Promotion of Racial Goodwill," Dr. Benjamin Covington MSS, 170:1, folder 1; Historical Context, Married Ladies Social, Art & Charity Club Records, RG 46; Historical Context, Ethel Ransom Art and Literary Club Records, RG E 59; and Pitre, *In Struggle against Jim Crow,* 19–23.

131. Pitre, *In Struggle against Jim Crow,* 28–128.

132. Alicia Davis, "Christia V. Adair: A Servant of Humanity," *Texas Historian* 38, no. 1 (1977), 1, Christia Adair MSS, 109:4, folder 1; Manuscript Census of the United

States, Jackson County, Texas, 1900, roll 1648, Bureau of the Census, series T623XXX, Heritage Quest Online, http://persi.heritagequestonline.com/; Bureau of the Census, series T623; ND *The Handbook of Texas Online*, s.v., "Adair, Christia V. Daniels," http://www.tshaonline.org/handbook/online/articles/AA/fad19.html.

133. Davis, "Christia V. Adair: A Servant of Humanity."

134. Diploma, Prairie View State Normal and Industrial College, 1916, Christia Adair MSS, 109:4; Certification, "American School of Home Economics, Chicago, Illinois, Matriculation Certificate, 1916, Christia Adair MSS, 109:4, folder 1; Barbara Karkabi, "'Fire in Her Belly'": Hundreds Honor Lifelong Civil-Rights Fight," *Houston Chronicle*, January 8, 1990, Christia Adair MSS, 109:4, folder 1; The Handbook of Texas Online, s.v., "Adair, Christia V. Daniels"; and Davis, "Christia V. Adair: A Servant of Humanity," 2. Adair also attended Samuel Huston College as a young girl, where her godfather, J. W. Frazier, served as a member of the school's first faculty.

135. Davis, "Christia V. Adair: A Servant of Humanity," 3.

136. Manuscript Census of the United States, Jackson County, Texas, 1910, roll 1567, Bureau of the Census, series T624, Heritage Quest Online, http://persi.heritagequestonline.com/; Davis, "Christia V. Adair: A Servant of Humanity," 3; and Karkabi, "'Fire in Her Belly.'" Unlike the women's movement in Kingsville, most White southerners avoided reaching out to African American women. For a discussion on women's suffrage in Houston, see Janelle D. Scott, "Local Leadership in the Woman's Suffrage Movement: Houston's Campaign for the Vote 1917–1918," *The Houston Review: History and Culture of the Gulf Coast* 12, no. 1 (1990): 3–22.

137. Karkabi, "'Fire in Her Belly'"; and Davis, "Christia V. Adair: A Servant of Humanity," 4.

138. Davis, "Christia V. Adair: A Servant of Humanity," 4.

139. Ibid.

140. Manuscript Census, Harris County, 1930, roll 2351, series T626; Davis, "Christia V. Adair: A Servant of Humanity," 4; and Adair, Elbert H., h3620 Bremond Avenue, Houston City Directory (Houston: Morrison & Fourmy, 1939), 32.

141. "Christian Social Relations and Local Church Activities, Texas Conference Women Society of Christian Service," Christia Adair MSS, 109: 2, folder 1; "A Manual for the Local Church Commission on Christian Social Concerns"; assorted pamphlets folder, Christia Adair MSS, 109:2, folder 2; Notes on church activities folder, Christia Adair MSS, 109:2, folder 3; Davis, "Christia V. Adair: A Servant of Humanity," 4–7; Karkabi, "'Fire in Her Belly'"; *The Handbook of Texas Online*, s.v., "Adair, Christia V. Daniels"; and Pitre, *In Struggle against Jim Crow*, 105–26.

142. Photo Identification Sheet 30, Sneed Family MSS, 293-30:1, Houston Metropolitan Research Center, Houston Public Library, Houston, Texas; Luther Stullivan interview; Lullelia Harrison interview, March 8, 2010; *In the Name of Colored High*, '04; Pitre, *In Struggle against Jim Crow*, 16–24; Hine, *Black Victory*, 59–61, 127–31; SoRelle, "The Darker Side of 'Heaven,'" 337–49; Obadele-Starks, *Black Unionism in the Industrial South*, 1–36; Botson, *Labor, Civil Rights, and the Hughes Tool Company*, 82–107; Jackson, *A Sure Foundation*, 417–18; Ellis Elizabeth Newell, "The Life and Works of C. F. Richardson," 4–5; and Hunter, *To 'Joy My Freedom*, 224. Taylor was the

first African American millionaire in Texas. See Larry J. Jackson, "The Development of Black Business in Texas, 1919–1969: From a Houston Perspective" (master's thesis, Texas Tech University, 1979), 8; and Harlan, *The Wizard of Tuskegee*, vii–xii. Although Washington is often cited for fostering the African American accommodation, or "Uncle Tom," philosophy of the twentieth century, behind the scenes he financed legal battles against disfranchisement, peonage, lynchings, and educational racism. He saw himself as the "axis" between Blacks and Whites, and more than likely hoped to one day move more in the direction of publicly attacking discrimination as King did some fifty years later.

143. Clifton Richardson, "Pussyfooting Pulpit Pimps," *Houston Informer*, September 6, 1919.

144. Photo Identification Sheet 30, Sneed Family MSS, 293–30:1; Luther Stullivan interview; Lullelia Harrison interview, March 8, 2010; *In the Name of Colored High, '04*; Pitre, *In Struggle against Jim Crow*, 16–24; Hine, *Black Victory*, 59–61, 127–31; SoRelle, "The Darker Side of 'Heaven,'" 337–49; Obadele-Starks, *Black Unionism in the Industrial South*, 1–36; Botson, *Labor, Civil Rights, and the Hughes Tool Company*, 82–107; Jackson, *A Sure Foundation*, 417–18; Jackson, "The Development of Black Business in Texas," 8; Newell, "The Life and Works of C. F. Richardson," 4–5; and Hunter, *To 'Joy My Freedom*, 224.

145. SoRelle, "Race Relations in 'Heavenly Houston,'" 175–80; Elgin Hychew, "M. L. Price . . . the Man," Rev. M. L. Price MSS, 277:1, folder 1; "A Life Sketch of Dr. M. L. Price," Rev. M. L. Price MSS, 277:1, folder 1; Obadele-Starks, "The Road to Jericho: Black Workers, the Fair Employment Practice Commission, and the Struggle for Racial Equality in the Upper Gulf Coast, 1941–1947" (Ph.D. diss., University of Houston, 1996), 40–42, 166–67; and Pitre, *In Struggle against Jim Crow*, 22–23, 33–34, 43, 92–93.

146. Greene, *Selling Black History for Carter G. Woodson*, 131.

147. Ibid.

148. Gerig, "Joseph Stephen Cullinan and the Houston Negro Hospital," 7–20; Houston Negro Hospital, January–May 1926 folder, Joseph Stephen Cullinan MSS, 69:22, folder 2; Houston Negro Hospital, June–December 1926 folder, Joseph Stephen Cullinan Collection, 69:22, folder 3; Houston Negro Hospital, 1927–28 folder, Joseph Stephen Cullinan Collection, 69:22, folder 4; "When Will Houston Negro Hospital Open?" *Houston Informer*, October 23, 1926; "Our Hospital Attitude Further Explained," *Houston Informer*, October 30, 1926; "What's Wrong With Negro Hospital?" *Houston Informer*, September 14, 1929; "Naming of Chairman Settles Hospital Affair," *Houston Sentinel*, February 1, 1929, Houston Negro Hospital, 1929 folder, Joseph Stephen Cullinan Collection, 69:22, folder 5; William Drake to Joseph Cullinan, January 16, 1929, Houston Negro Hospital, 1929 folder, Joseph Stephen Cullinan Collection, 69:22, folder 5; J. W. Slaughter to Judge W. W. Moore, April 11, 1929, Houston Negro Hospital, 1929 folder, Joseph Stephen Cullinan Collection, 69:22, folder 5; W. W. Moore to J. S. Cullinan, June 9, 1926; and Houston Negro Hospital, 1926, June-December 1926 folder, Joseph Stephen Cullinan Collection, 69:22, folder 3.

149. "Hospital Staff Being Selected; PV Nurse Here," *Houston Informer*, May 14, 1927,

Houston Negro Hospital, 1927–28 folder, Joseph Stephen Cullinan MSS, 69: 22, folder 4; and SoRelle, "The Darker Side of 'Heaven': The Black Community in Houston, Texas, 1919–1945," 332–35.

150. H. H. Lee and B. J. Covington to the Honorable Board of Directors and Advisory Committee of the Houston Negro Hospital, December 8, 1928, Houston Negro Hospital, 1927–28 folder, Joseph Stephen Cullinan MSS, 69: 22, folder 4.

151. Ibid.; Dr. H. H. Lee to J. W. Slaughter, November 28, 1928, Houston Negro Hospital, 1927–28 folder, Joseph Stephen Cullinan MSS, 69: 22, folder 4; Margaret H. Bright to W. T. Sinclair, October 23, 1932, Houston Negro Hospital, 1930–32 folder, Joseph Stephen Cullinan MSS, 69: 22, folder 6; Margaret H. Bright to Miss P. A. Newby, June 10, Houston Negro Hospital, 1929 folder, Joseph Stephen Cullinan MSS, 69: 22, folder 5; Margaret H. Bright to W. T. Sinclair, October 23, 1932, Houston Negro Hospital, 1930–32 folder, Joseph Stephen Cullinan MSS, 69: 22, folder 6; W. W. Moore to W. C. Hogg, June 27, 1929, Houston Negro Hospital, 1929 folder, Joseph Stephen Cullinan MSS, 69: 22, folder 6; Margaret H. Bright to W. T. Sinclair, January 28, 1937, Houston Negro Hospital, 1934–37 folder, Joseph Stephen Cullinan MSS, 69: 22, folder 8; W. W. Moore to Joseph S Cullinan, October 9, 1928, Houston Negro Hospital, 1927–28 folder, Joseph Stephen Cullinan MSS, 69: 22, folder 4; and William Drake to Joseph Cullinan, January 16, 1929, Houston Negro Hospital, 1929 folder, Joseph Stephen Cullinan Collection, 69:22, folder 5.

152. W. W. Moore to W. C. Hogg, June 27, 1929, Houston Negro Hospital.

153. Gerig, "Joseph Stephen Cullinan and the Houston Negro Hospital"; Houston Negro Hospital, January–May 1926 folder, Joseph Stephen Cullinan Collection, 69:22, folder 2; Houston Negro Hospital, June–December 1926 folder, Joseph Stephen Cullinan Collection, 69:22, folder 3; Houston Negro Hospital, 1927–28 folder, Joseph Stephen Cullinan Collection, 69:22, folder 4; "When Will Houston Negro Hospital Open?"; "Our Hospital Attitude Further Explained"; and "What's Wrong With Negro Hospital?"

154. Thelma Scott Bryant interview.

155. SoRelle, "Race Relations in 'Heavenly Houston,'" 175–80.

156. Luther Stullivan interview.

157. Ibid.

158. Washington Phillips, "Take Your Burden to the Lord and Leave It There," recorded December 2, 1927, Dallas, Texas, 145305–1, Columbia Phonograph Co., January 21, 1973, New York, New York, LP, RE 16588, 14277-D, and on *The Keys to the Kingdom*, B0006TR054, March 2005, Yazoo, compact disc, www.fretlesszithers.com.

159. Romans 12: 17, Holy Bible.com, http://www.holybible.com/; and R. H. Boyd, accessed July 2, 2011, http://www.rhboydpublishing.com/index.php.

160. Greene, *Selling Black History for Carter G. Woodson*, 130–31; SoRelle, "The Darker Side of 'Heaven,'" 106–68, 213–15; and SoRelle, "Race Relations in 'Heavenly Houston,' 1919–45," 175–91.

161. Richardson, "Texas Negros' Political Apathy"; and Beeth and Wintz, eds., *Black Dixie*, 157–61.

162. Scott, *Weapons of the Weak*, vxv–xix; Scott, *Domination and the Arts of Resistance*,

ix–xiii, 5–16; Kelley, *Race Rebels*, 1–19, 35–53; Hine, *Hine Sight*, 37–57; and Jones, *Labor of Love, Labor of Sorrow.*

163. "Girl Is Raped and Slain: Dead Body Found in Second Ward; One Arrest Made," *Houston Informer*, January 27, 1923; and Thomas, *A Study of the Social Welfare Status of Negroes in Houston, Texas*, 55–61. For more on Black-on-Black crime in Houston during the interwar period, see the *Houston Informer* and the *Houston Defender*.

164. Du Bois, *The Philadelphia Negro: A Social Study*, 1899, reprint with a new introduction by Elijah Anderson, Philadelphia: University of Pennsylvania Press, 1996, 235–36.

165. Thelma Scott Bryant interview.

166. Nell Grovey Cole interview; Kelley, *Race Rebels*, 1–19, 35–53; J. Jerome Zolten, "Black Comedians: Forging an Ethnic Identity," *Journal of American Ethnic Culture* 16, no. 2 (1993): 65–76; Alan Schaffer, *On the Real Side: Laughing, Lying, and Signifying—The Underground Tradition of African-American Humor That Transformed American Culture from Slavery to Richard Pryor* (New York: Simon and Schuster, 1994), 169–235, 412–54, 620; and Lynn Domina, "Protection in My Mouf: Self, Voice, and Community in Zora Neale Hurston's Dusk Tracks on a Road . . . ," *African American Review* 31, no. 2 (1997): 197–209.

167. Richardson interview.

168. Stullivan interview.

169. Lee, "Negro Health Problem," 148–51; Scott, "Efficiency," 5–11; Scott, *Weapons of the Weak*, vxv–xix; Scott, *Domination and the Arts of Resistance*, ix–xiii; Domina, "Protection in My Mouf," 197–209; Brewer, *American Negro Folklore* (1968; Chicago: Quadrangle Books, 1972); and Kelley, *Race Rebels*, 1–19, 35–53. For recent scholarship addressing African American health challenges and initiatives, see The National Medical Association Online, accessed July 3, 2011, http://www.nmanet.org/.

170. Jesse O. Thomas, *Negro Participation in the Texas Centennial Exposition* (University of Wisconsin—Madison: Christopher, 1938), p. A. Maceo Smith's quote about the Negro Hall of Life representing a second revolution is an important unofficial starting point for the modern Civil Rights Movement in Texas.

171. SoRelle, "The Darker Side of 'Heaven,'" 137–49; SoRelle, "Race Relations in 'Heavenly Houston,' 1919–1945," 177, 189; Greene, *Selling Black History for Carter G. Woodson*, 131; and Clifton Richardson, "Houston's Colored Citizens: Activities and Conditions among the Negro Population in the 1920s," in *Black Dixie: Afro-Texan History and Culture in Houston*, ed. Howard Beeth and Cary D. Wintz (College Station: Texas A&M University Press, 1992), 128–33.

Chapter 5

1. Manuscript Census, Waller County, Texas, 1910, roll 1593, Bureau of the Census, series T624, Heritage Quest Online, http://persi.heritagequestonline.com/; Manuscript Census, Waller County, 1900, roll 1676, series T623, Heritage Quest Online, http://persi.heritagequestonline; *Galveston-Dallas News, Texas Almanac and Industrial Guide* (Galveston: Clarke & Courts, 1904), 384–85, from The Portal to Texas History, The

University of North Texas, crediting The Texas State Historical Association, http://texas history.unt.edu/ark:/67531/metapth123779/m1/396/?q; Robert L. Campbell, Leonard J. Bukowski, and Armin Büttner, *The Tom Archia Discography*, 2011, http://hubcap.clemson.edu/~campber/archia.html; and *The Handbook of Texas Online*, s.v., "Sunny Side, Texas (Waller County)," http://www.tshaonline.org/handbook/online/articles/hls85.

2. Manuscript Census, Harris County, 1930, roll 2352, series T626; Archie, Ernest A. (Henrietta), Houston, Texas, City Directory, 1926, from Ancestry.com, http://search.ancestry.com; Ernest Alvin Archie, World War I Draft Registration Card, Registration No. 4-100, June 2, 1917, Hempstead, Texas, Military Records, from Ancestry.com, http://search.ancestry.com; and Campbell, Bukowski, and Büttner, *The Tom Archia Discography*.

3. Manuscript Census, Harris County, 1930, roll 2352, series T626; The Handbook of Texas Online, "Sunny Side, Texas (Waller County)"; and Campbell, Bukowski, and Büttner, *The Tom Archia Discography*.

4. Thomas, "Milt Larkin," 6–26; Rick Mitchell, "Houston Jazz Legend Larkin Dies at 85," *Houston Chronicle*, August 31, 1996; Thomas, *Don't Deny My Name*, 69–73; Robb Walsh, "The Nickel Burger: How is a Falling-Apart Fifth Ward Joint Turning Out the Best Burgers in Town? Adrian's Has History," *Houston Press*, October 31, 2002; Reginald Buckner, "A History of Music Education in the Black Community Kansas City, Kansas, 1905–1954," *Journal of Research in Music Education* 30, no. 2 (1982): 94–100; Campbell, Bukowski, and Büttner, *The Tom Archia Discography*; Wood, *Down in Houston*, 35, 82, 85,; *The Handbook of Texas Online*, s.v., "Jazz"; The Handbook of Texas Online, s.v., "Blues"; and Campbell, Bukowski, and Büttner, *The Tom Archia Discography*.

5. Campbell, Bukowski, and Büttner, *The Tom Archia Discography*.

6. For works that examine the broadening meaning of the Harlem Renaissance as well as the construction of an Africana cultural aesthetic in the United States, the African Diaspora, including Texas, see Davarian Baldwin, *Chicago's New Negroes: Modernity, the Great Migration & Black Urban Life* (Chapel Hill: University of North Carolina Press, 2007; Tim Brooks, *Lost Sounds: Blacks and the Birth of the Recording Industry, 1890–1919* (Urbana: University of Illinois Press, 2004); George Chauncey, *Gay New York: Gender, Urban Culture, and the Making of the Gay Male World, 1890–1940* (New York: Basic Books, 1994); Thomas Cripps, *Making Movies Black: The Hollywood Message Movie from World War II to the Civil Rights Era* (New York: Oxford University Press, 1993); Thomas Cripps, *Slow Fade to Black: The Negro in American Film, 1900–1942* (New York: Oxford University Press, 1993); *African American National Biography*, s.v. "Harlem Renaissance Lives: From the African American National Biography", Henry Louis Gates and Elizabeth Brooks Higginbotham, eds. (New York: Oxford University Press, 2009); Nathan I. Huggins, *Harlem Renaissance* (New York: Oxford University Press, 2007); Martha Jane Nadell, *Enter the New Negroes: Images of Race in American Culture* (Cambridge: Harvard University Press, 2004); Tyrone Tillery, *Claude McKay: A Black Poet's Struggle for Identity* (Amherst: University of Massachusetts Press, 2004); Steven A. Reich, "The Great Migration and the Historical Imagination," *The Historical Society* 9, no. 1 (2009): 87–128; Anne Meis Knupfer, Chicago Black Renaissance and Women's Activism (Urbana: University of Illinois Press, 2011); Wintz and Finkelman,

Encyclopedia of the Harlem Renaissance; Lillian B. Horace, Angie Brown, eds., *Karen Kossie-Chernyshev* (Acton, Massachusetts: Copley Press), 2008; Lillian B. Horace, *The Diary of Lillian B. Horace,* ed. Karen Kossie-Chernyshev (Boston: Pearson, 2007); Wood, *Down in Houston;* Bruce A. Glasrud, "From Griggs to Brewer: A Review of Black Texas Culture, 1899–1940," *The Journal of Big Bend Studies* 15 (2003):195–212; Joe W. Specht, "Oil Well Blues: African Americans Oil Patch Songs," *East Texas Historical Association* 49, no. 1 (2011): 86–108; Alan Govenar, *Texas Blues: The Rise of a Contemporary Sound* (College Station: Texas A&M University Press, 2008); Francis E. Abernathy, Patrick B. Mullen, and Alan B. Govenar, eds., *Juneteenth Texas: Essays in African-American Folklore* (Denton, Texas: University of North Texas, 1996); Bernice Love Wiggins, *tuneful tales (in the remote desert of 1925 el paso bloomed a bit of Harlem Renaissance),* ed., Maceo Dailey Jr. and Ruthe Wingarten (Lubbock: Texas Tech University Press, 2002); Franklin and Higginbotham, *From Slavery to Freedom;* and Hine, *The African American Odyssey.*

7. Material about Mr. Williams is scarce. Information about newspaperman and educator S. B. Williams is possibly lost. Published and nonpublished records do mention a Simmie B. Williams of Fourth Ward, dating back to the 1900 Manuscript Census for Harris County. The names Cimbee, Simmie, and Simeon could possibly refer to the same individual. See Manuscript Census of the United States, Harris County, 1900, roll 1642, Bureau of the Census, series T623, Heritage Quest Online, http://persi.heritagequestonline.com/; Manuscript Census of the United States, Harris County, Texas, 1910, roll 1560, series T624; Manuscript Census, Harris County, 1920, roll 1813, series T625; Simmie Bartholomew Williams, World War I Draft Registration Card, 1917–1918, from Ancestry.com, http://search.ancestry.com/; Bryant, *Houston's Negro Schools,* 135; Cronin, "C. F. Richardson and the *Houston Informer*'s Fight for Racial Equality in the 1920s," 86, 100; John P. Morgan, "Reading Race into the Scopes Trial: African American Elites, Science, and Fundamentalism," *Journal of American History* 90, no. 3 (2003): 899; and SoRelle, "The Darker Side of 'Heaven.'"

8. "Cimbee's Ramblings," *Houston Informer,* September 6, 1919.

9. W. E. B. Du Bois, *Souls of Black Folk: A Norton Critical Reader.* Ed. Henry Lewis Gates Jr. and Terri Hume Oliver (1903; New York: Norton, 2000); and *Houston Informer* (psychological effects of racism).

10. *Houston Informer;* The Handbook of Texas Online, s.v., "Brewer, John Mason, http://www.tshaonline.org/handbook/online/articles/fbrbb; Brewer, *American Negro Folklore;* Sapper, "Black Culture in Urban Texas," 69–73; and Lorenzo Thomas, "The African American Folktale and J. Mason Brewer," in *Juneteenth Texas,* 223–34. Houstonians of color also enjoyed other musical art forms, including classical music. Marion Anderson held multiple concerts in Houston during her career. The Houston Symphony began giving concerts to Black schoolchildren in 1946. In addition, a local Houstonian, Ernestine Jessie Covington Dent (1904–2001), earned a master's degree in classical music from Oberlin College in 1934, even garnering four $1,000 fellowships from the Julliard Foundation, the precursor to the famed music school. A pianist and educator, serving as head of Piano Department at Bishop College from 1929–31, she married hospital administrator Albert Dent, the future president of Dillard University, in 1931. In later

years, she founded Ebony Fashion Show as a fundraiser for Flint-Goodrich Hospital in New Orleans. Her parents, migrants Benjamin and Jennie Covington, also played musical instruments. See Biographical Notes and series Notes, Covington Family MSS, 170; and Lundy, "Pioneer Concert Pianist, 245–65.

11. Wilder, *In the Company of Black Men*, 1–15; de Jong, *A Different Day*, 41–60; Kelley, *Race Rebels*, 1–19, 35–55; *The Handbook of Texas Online*, s.v., "Blues"; *The Handbook of Texas Online*, s.v., "Jefferson, Blind Lemon," accessed July 31, 2010, http://www.tshaonline.org/handbook/online/articles/JJ/fje1.html; Alan Govenar, *Texas Blues*, vii–37, 335; Gary Hartman, *The History of Texas Music* (College Station: Texas A&M University Press, 2008), 56–99; *Africana*, 2nd ed., vol. 3, s.v., "Gospel Music," 23–29; *Africana*, 2nd ed., vol. 3, s.v., "Gospel Quartets," 29; *Africana*, 2nd ed., vol. 1, s.v., "Blues: Growth of a Genre (by Paul Oliver)," 547–50, 550–56; *Africana*, 2nd ed., vol. 3, s.v., "Jazz," 353–361; and *Africana*, 2nd ed., vol. 5, s.v. "Zydeco," 516–17.

12. For works that trace the genesis of Black music to West African culture and American slavery, see Robert Darden, "People Get Ready": *A New History of Black Gospel Music* (New York: Continuum, 2011); Burton W. Peretti, *"Lift Every Voice": The History of African American Music* (Latham, Maryland: Rowan & Littlefield, 2011); Joyce Marie Jackson, "The Changing Nature of Gospel Music: A Southern Case Study," *African American Review* 29, no. 2 (1995): 185–201; Paul Oliver, *Story of the Blues* (1969; reprint, Boston: Northeastern University, 1998); Richard Wright and Edwin Rosham, *Twelve Million Voices: A Folk History of the Negro in the United States* (1941; reprint, Athens: Thunder's Mouth, 1988); Alan Lomax, *The Land Where Blues Began* (New York: Pantheon, 1993); and Hartman, *The History of Texas Music*.

13. Alyn, "Fight, Flight, or Blues: Mance Lipscomb, Lipscomb-Alyn CMSS, 2.325:A112; Lipscomb-Alyn MSS, 2K201:1; "Bossman Kills Blackman and Jim Crow Laws," September 2, 1973, Lipscomb-Alyn MSS, 2K198:1; Kaplan, "Houston's Creole Quarter"; Smith Prather, "A Unique Houston Neighborhood Called Frenchtown"; Rust, "Frenchtown"; The Handbook of Texas Online, s.v., "Blues"; Hartman, *The History of Texas Music*, 56–75; *Africana*, 2nd ed., vol. 1, s.v., "Blues: Growth of a Genre," 550–56; and Mance Lipscomb, Glenn A. Myers, and Don Gardner, "Out of the Bottoms and Into the Big City," *Southern Exposure* 8, no. 2 (1980):4–11.

14. Schomburg Center, "The Great Migration," *In Motion;* Amiri Baraki. *Blues People* (New York: Morrow Quill, 1963); Lawrence Levine. *The Unpredictable Past: Explorations of American Cultural History* (New York: Oxford University Press, 1993); The Handbook of Texas Online, s.v., "Blues"; and Hartman, *The History of Music in Texas*, 50–66.

15. Milton Larkin interview; Thomas, "Milt Larkin," 6–26; Mitchell, "Houston Jazz Legend Larkin Dies at 85"; R. Wood, *Down in Houston*, 82, 85; in The Handbook of Texas Online, s.v., "Jazz"; *The Handbook of Texas Online*, s.v., "Blues"; Alyn, "Fight, Flight, or Blues," Lipscomb-Alyn MSS, 2.325:A112; The Handbook of Texas Online, s.v., "Blues"; Illinois Jacquet interview; Garna L. Christian, "Texas Beginnings: Houston in the World of Jazz," *Houston Review: History and Culture of the Gulf Coast* 12, no. 2 (1990): 144–54; Charles Stephenson, "Jazz Images: A Sampling from the Texas Jazz Archive," *Houston Review: History and Culture of the Gulf Coast* 12, no. 2 (Winter 1990): 157–66; John Minton, "Creole Community and 'Mass' Communication: Houston

Zydeco As a Mediated Tradition," *Journal of Folklore Research* 35 (Fall 1995), 1–12; and Jackson, *The Changing Nature of Gospel Music*, 187–92.

16. Calvin L. Rhone to Lucia J. Rhone, January 20, 1920, Rhone Family MSS, 3U171:1; Alyn, "Flight, Fight, or Blues," Lipscomb-Alyn MSS, 2.325:A112; Pearson Jr., "Mance Lipscomb," Lipscomb-Alwyn MSS, 2K201:1; "Bossman Kills Blackman and Jim Crow Laws," Lipscomb-Alyn MSS, 2K198:1; Gottlieb, *Making Their Own Way*, 20–22; and Glasrud, "Black Texans: 1900–1930," 260–75.

17. "Big Boss Man," Lipscomb-Alyn MSS, 2K201:3.

18. Calvin L. Rhone to Lucia J. Rhone, January 20, 1920, Rhone Family MSS, 3U171:1; Alwyn, "Flight, Fight, or Blues," Lipscomb-Alyn MSS, 2.325:A112; Nathan W. Pearson Jr., "Mance Lipscomb: An American Musician" (master's thesis, Wesleyan University, 1974, Lipscomb-Alyn MSS, 2K201:1); "Bossman Kills Blackman and Jim Crow Laws," September 2, 1973, Lipscomb-Alyn MSS, 2K198:1; Gottlieb, *Making Their Own Way*, 20–22; and Glasrud, "Black Texans: 1900–1930," 260–75.

19. Milton Larkin interview; Thomas, *Don't Deny My Name*, 64–73; and Thomas, "Milt Larkin."

20. Milton Larkin interview; Thomas, "Milt Larkin," 6–26; Thomas, *Don't Deny My Name*, 64–73; Mitchell, "Houston Jazz Legend Larkin Dies at 85"; Wood, *Down in Houston*, 82, 85; The Handbook of Texas Online, s.v., "Jazz"; The Handbook of Texas Online, s.v., "Blues"; Alyn, "Fight, Flight, or Blues," Lipscomb-Alyn MSS, 2.325:A112; and Illinois Jacquet interview.

21. Milton Larkin interview; Thomas, "Milt Larkin," 6–26; Thomas, *Don't Deny My Name*, 6973; Mitchell, "Houston Jazz Legend Larkin Dies at 85"; Wood, *Down in Houston*, 82, 85; *The Handbook of Texas Online*, s.v., "Jazz"; *The Handbook of Texas Online*, s.v., "Blues"; Alyn, "Fight, Flight, or Blues," Lipscomb-Alyn MSS, 2.325:A112; and Illinois Jacquet interview.

22. Milton Larkin interview; Thomas, "Milt Larkin," 6–26; Mitchell, "Houston Jazz Legend Larkin Dies at 85"; Thomas, *Don't Deny My Name*, 69–73; Wood, *Down in Houston*, 82, 85; *The Handbook of Texas Online*, s.v., "Jazz"; s.v., "Blues"; Alyn, "Fight, Flight, or Blues," Lipscomb-Alyn MSS, 2.325:A112; Illinois Jacquet interview; and Kelso B. Morris, "The Wiley Collegians: Reminiscences of a Black College Bandleader, 1925–1935," *Annual Review of Jazz Studies* 1, 17–20.

23. Milton Larkin interview; Thomas, *Don't Deny My Name*, 64–73; Thomas, "Milt Larkin," 6–26; Mitchell, "Houston Jazz Legend Larkin Dies at 85"; Wood, *Down in Houston*, 82, 85; *The Handbook of Texas Online*, s.v., "Jazz"; *The Handbook of Texas Online*, s.v., "Blues"; Alyn, "Fight, Flight, or Blues," Lipscomb-Alyn MSS, 2.325:A112; Illinois Jacquet interview; George McElroy, "Anna Dupree Looks with Pride on Her Life" *The Informer and Texas Freeman*, December 9, 1972, Anna Dupree Collection, 110:1, folder 5, Houston Metropolitan Research Center, Houston Public Library, Julia Ideson Building, Houston, Texas (hereafter cited as Anna Dupree MSS); Photo Identification Sheet, Anna Dupree MSS, 110: 1, folder 1; Photo Identification Sheet, "The Bronze Peacock in the Firth Ward, Houston," Perry Family MSS, 276-box 2: 22R; Photo Identification Sheet, "Ennigan Park Recreation Center in Fifth Ward," Perry Family MSS, 276-2:R19; 26; Jackson, "The Development of Black Business in Texas,"

58; National Urban League, *A Review of the Economic and Cultural Problems of Houston, Texas,* 177–78; and Schomburg Center, "The Great Migration: Migration Resources: Maps: The Great Blues Migration," *In Motion,* http://www.inmotionaame.org/gallery/index.cfm?migration=8&topic=1&type=map.

24. Milton Larkin interview, 252:1; Thomas, *Don't Deny My Name,* 64–73; Thomas, "Milt Larkin," 6–24; Mitchell, "Houston Jazz Legend Larkin Dies at 85"; Wood, *Down in Houston,* 82, 85; and *The Handbook of Texas Online,* s.v., "Jazz."

25. Illinois Jacquet interview; and "Illinois Jacquet: Jazz At The Philharmonic Crowd Favorite in the 1940s and 1950s," Legends of Jazz History, Swingmusic.net, http://www.swingmusic.net/Illinois_Jacquet_Big_Band_And_Jazz_Legend_Biography.html (hereafter cited as "Illinois Jacquet: Jazz at the Philharmonic").

26. Illinois Jacquet interview; and "Illinois Jacquet: Jazz At The Philharmonic."
27. Illinois Jacquet interview; and "Illinois Jacquet: Jazz At The Philharmonic."
28. Illinois Jacquet interview; and "Illinois Jacquet: Jazz At The Philharmonic."
29. Illinois Jacquet interview; and "Illinois Jacquet: Jazz At The Philharmonic."
30. Illinois Jacquet interview; and "Illinois Jacquet: Jazz At The Philharmonic."
31. Illinois Jacquet interview; and "Illinois Jacquet: Jazz At The Philharmonic."
32. Illinois Jacquet interview; and "Illinois Jacquet: Jazz At The Philharmonic."

33. Manuscript Census of the United States, Bastrop County, 1880, roll 1290, Bureau of the Census, series T90, Heritage Quest Online, http://persi.heritagequestonline.com/; Manuscript Census, Harris County, 1910, roll 1559, series T624; Manuscript Census, Harris County, 1930, roll 2379, series T626; "Season's Greetings," Afro-American Medical, Dental, Pharmaceutical Association of Houston and Harris County, advertisement, *Houston Informer,* December 25, 1926; Fountain L. McDavid, physician, 611 Robin, in R. L. Polk and Company, Polk's Houston City Directory, 1917 (Houston: R. L. Polk, 1917). From Ancestry.com, http://search.ancestry.com/; McDavid, Fountain L., Texas Death Index, Harris County, July 14, 1934, certificate number 32621, from Ancestry.com, http://search.ancestry.com/; and Campbell, Bukowski, and Büttner, *The Tom Archia Discography.*

34. Buckner, "A History of Music Education"; Campbell et al, *The Tom Archia Discography*; and Matthew Duersten, "The Arkivists: Unearthing the treasure of Horace Tapscott," *LA Weekly,* April 5, 2006.

35. Buckner, "A History of Music Education"; Duersten, "The Arkivists"; YouTube, Tom Archia; Walsh, "The Nickel Burger"; "Negroes Protest Ouster of Negro Bandleader," *Jet* Magazine, July 9, 1953; "The Amalgamation of Local 47 and 647," Professional Musicians Local 47, http://www.promusic47.org/amalgamation.htm; Russell McDavid, California Death Index, 1940–1997, Los Angeles, October 28, 1969, California Department of Health Services, Center for Health Statistics, from Ancestry.com, http://search.ancestry.com/; Dennis McLellan, "Marl Young Dies at 92; Pianist Was Key in Desegregating LA Musicians Union," *New York Times,* May 3, 2009; Percy H. McDavid, California Death Index, 1940–1997, Los Angeles, May 2, 1975, California Department of Health Services, Center for Health Statistics, from Ancestry.com, http://search.ancestry.com/; and Horace Tapscott, *Songs of the Unsung: The Musical and Social Journey of Horace Tapscott,* ed. Steven L. Isoardi (Durham: Duke University Press, 2001),

25–29, 90–95. Tapscott partook in the mid-twentieth-century Great Music Migration of Texas and Louisiana artists who ended up in Los Angeles. Other jazz greats originally from Texas and Louisiana were Ornette Coleman, John Carter, and Bobby Bradford.

36. Quoted from Campbell, Bukowski, and Büttner, *The Tom Archia Discography*.

37. Walsh, "The Nickel Burger"; Aimee L'Heureux, "Illinois Jacquet: Integrating Houston Jazz Audiences . . . Lands Ella Fitzgerald and Ella Fitzgerald in Jail," *Houston History* 8, no. 1 (2010): 6–8, 49; Illinois Jacquet interview; "Illinois Jacquet: Jazz At The Philharmonic"; and Buckner, "A History of Music Education."

38. Illinois Jacquet interview; L'Heureux, "Illinois Jacquet," 6–8, 49; "Illinois Jacquet: Jazz At The Philharmonic"; Buckner, "A History of Music Education"; Milton Larkin interview, 252:1; Thomas, "Milt Larkin," 6–26; Mitchell, "Houston Jazz Legend Larkin Dies at 85"; Wood, *Down in Houston*, 82, 85; and "Jazz," in The Handbook of Texas Online, s.v., "Jazz."

39. Illinois Jacquet interview; L'Heureux, "Illinois Jacquet," 6–8, 49; "Illinois Jacquet: Jazz At The Philharmonic"; Buckner, "A History of Music Education"; Milton Larkin interview, 252:1; Thomas, "Milt Larkin," 6–26; Mitchell, "Houston Jazz Legend Larkin Dies at 85"; Wood, *Down in Houston*, 82, 85; and "Jazz," in The Handbook of Texas Online, s.v., "Jazz."

40. Paul J. McArthur, "One for All: Sax Giant Helped Desegregate Houston Audiences," *Houston Press*, November 18, 1999.

41. Illinois Jacquet interview; L'Heureux, "Illinois Jacquet," 6–8, 49; "Illinois Jacquet: Jazz At The Philharmonic"; Buckner, "A History of Music Education"; Milton Larkin interview, 252:1; Thomas, "Milt Larkin," 6–26; Mitchell, "Houston Jazz Legend Larkin Dies at 85"; Wood, *Down in Houston*, 82, 85; and "Jazz," in The Handbook of Texas Online, s.v., "Jazz."

42. Milton Larkin interview, 252:1; Thomas, "Milt Larkin," 6–26; Mitchell, "Houston Jazz Legend Larkin Dies at 85"; Wood, *Down in Houston*, 82, 85; "Jazz," in The Handbook of Texas Online, s.v., "Jazz"; Illinois Jacquet interview; and "Illinois Jacquet: Jazz At The Philharmonic."

43. The Handbook of Texas Online, s.v., "Robey, Don Deadric," July 31, 2010, http://www.tshaonline.org/handbook/online/articles/RR/fropc.html; The Handbook of Texas Online, s.v., "Eldorado Ballroom," July 31, 2010, http://www.tshaonline.org/handbook/online/articles/EE/xde2.html; Leigh H. Cuttler, "'We Really Just Wanted to Dance': The Rise and Decline of Houston's Eldorado Ballroom," unpublished paper written for Twentieth Century African American History, Professor Gerald Horne, Instructor, December 2005, University of Houston, Houston, Texas, 1–11; McElroy, "Anna Dupree Looks with Pride on Her Life"; Jackson, "The Development of Black Business in Texas," 58; and National Urban League, *A Review of the Economic and Cultural Problems of Houston, Texas*, 177–78.

44. Thelma Scott Bryant interview.

45. Thelma Scott Bryant interview; and Hazel Young interview.

46. "Ennington Park Recreation Center in 5th Ward," Photo Identification Sheet, Perry Family MSS, 276–19; "Bronze Peacock in 5th Ward, Houston," Photo Identification Sheet, Perry Family MSS, 276–22; "Houston Club, in Houston," Photo

Identification Sheet, Perry Family MSS, 276–33; Wood, *Down in Houston,* 50, 86–97, 188–205; and The Handbook of Texas Online, s.v., "Robey, Don Deadric."

47. The Handbook of Texas Online, s.v., "Robey, Don Deadric"; To Bear Fruit for Our Race, s.v., "Dr. Louis R. Robey," http://www.history.uh.edu/cph/tobearfruit/resources_bios_robey.1.html; Jessie Simon, "Funeral Director Althea Antoinette Robey Laid to Rest," *African-American News & Issues,* July 23, 2003; and Don Deadric Robey II, obituary, *Houston Chronicle,* January 4, 2007.

48. McElroy, "Anna Dupree Looks with Pride on Her Life"; Historical Context Sheet, Anna Dupree MSS, 110: 1, folder 1; Manuscript Census, Harris County, 1920, roll 1813, series T625; Manuscript Census, Harris County, 1930, roll 2347, series T626; National Urban League, *A Review of the Economic and Cultural Problems of Houston, Texas,* 177–78; The Handbook of Texas Online, s.v., "Dupree, Anna Johnson," http://www.tshaonline.org/handbook/online/articles/fdu39; The Handbook of Texas Online, s.v., "Eldorado Ballroom"; "Eldorado Ballroom on Dowling and Elgin in Houston's 3rd Ward," Photo Identification Sheet, Perry Family MSS, 276–31; and Cutler, "'We Really Just Wanted to Dance,'" 1–7.

49. Shelby Hodge, "Eldorado Ballroom Back in the Swing," *Houston Chronicle,* May 19, 2003; Alan Turner, "'Home of Happy Feet': Eldorado's Rebirth Will Showcase Music of the Past, Present," *Houston Chronicle,* February 5, 2001; Betty L. Martin, "Spirit of Jazz: Event Held to Fund Eldorado Restoration," *Houston Chronicle,* May 1, 2003; Cynthia Thomas, "Lowe and Behold," *Houston Chronicle,* October 13, 1996; Mike McDaniel, "Channel 8 History is Just for Fun," *Houston Chronicle,* May 22, 1999; and Cutler, "'We Really Just Wanted to Dance,'" 2–11.

50. Cutler, "'We Really Just Wanted to Dance,'" 16. Escaping from reality was perhaps a constant rite of passage for African Americans—migrants as well as established residents. Blacks, like other Houstonians, took pleasure in outdoor celebrations, from Juneteenth parades and De-Ro-Loc carnivals during Mardi Gras season, to amusement attractions and circuses. Emancipation Park, for example, hosted Juneteenth celebrations, De-Ro-Loc festivals, movies, concerts, amusements, and sporting events such as the Prairie View and Bishop College football games, the latter ultimately paving the way for the establishment of the Southwestern Athletic Conference (SWAC). Always segregated, these events provided African Americans with a modicum of pleasure, peace, and thrills. For more on African American amusements in twentieth-century Houston, see Archaeological Commission and City of Houston Planning and Development, Protected Landmark Designation Report, Emancipation Park, 2007, http://blog.chron.com/bayoucityhistory/files/legacy/EmancipationPark3018DowlingStreetR.pdf.

51. For more on Harlem Renaissance artists, see Lisa Gail Collins, *The Art of History: African American Women Artists Engage the Past* (New Brunswick: Rutgers University Press, 2002); Lisa E. Farrington, *Creating Their Own Image: The History of African American Women Artists* (New York: Oxford University Press, 2004); Huggins, *Harlem Remembered;* Nadell, *Enter the New Negroes; Africana,* 2nd ed., vol. 3, s.v., "Lawrence, Jacob Armstead," 534–36; and *Africana,* 2nd ed., vol. 2, s.v., "Douglas, Aaron," 434–35.

52. Sapper, "Black Culture in Urban Texas," 67–71.

53. Photo Identification Sheet, Samuel Albert Countee, Rev. Jack Yates Family and

Antioch Baptist Church Collection, 281–7:65R, Houston Metropolitan Research Center, Houston Public Library. Julia Ideson Building. Houston, Texas (hereafter cited as Rev. Jack Yates Family and Antioch Baptist Church MSS); "Dedicated, July 15, 1982[,] to Samuel Albert Countee," Rev. Jack Yates and Antioch Baptist Church MSS, 281–1:11; "BTW Commencement, 1928," Rev. Jack Yates and Antioch Baptist Church MSS, 281–3:5; "The Eagle, 1928," Rev. Jack Yates and Antioch Baptist Church MSS, 281–3:5; and Steven Smith, US Army Corps of Engineers Construction Engineering Research Laboratories and US Department of Defense Legacy Resource Management Program, *A Historic Context Statement for a World War II Era Black Officers' Club at Fort Leonard Wood, Missouri,* November 1998, http://www.cas.sc.edu/sciaa/PDFdocs/military-research/FLWBlackOfficersClub.pdf, 87–99.

54. Photo Identification Sheet, Samuel Albert Countee, Rev. Jack Yates Family and Antioch Baptist Church MSS, 281–7:65R; "Dedicated, July 15, 1982[,] to Samuel Albert Countee," Rev. Jack Yates and Antioch Baptist Church MSS, 281–1:11; and Smith, *A Historic Context Statement,* 87–99. Today, Bishop College is closed. The Museum of African American History now occupies many of Bishop College's buildings ever since the school moved to Dallas in the 1970s.

55. Photo Identification Sheet, Samuel Albert Countee, Rev. Jack Yates Family and Antioch Baptist Church MSS, 281–7:65R; "Dedicated, July 15, 1982[,] to Samuel Albert Countee," Rev. Jack Yates and Antioch Baptist Church MSS, 281–1:11; and Smith, *A Historic Context Statement,* 87–99.

56. Photo Identification Sheet, Samuel Albert Countee, Rev. Jack Yates Family and Antioch Baptist Church MSS, 281–7:65R; "Dedicated, July 15, 1982[,] to Samuel Albert Countee," Rev. Jack Yates and Antioch Baptist Church, MSS 281–1:11; BTW Commencement, 1928," Rev. Jack Yates and Antioch Baptist Church, MSS 281–3:5; "The Eagle, 1928," Rev. Jack Yates and Antioch Baptist Church, MSS 281–3:5; Thomas, *Negro Participation in the Texas Centennial Exposition,* 39–40, 131; The Handbook of Texas Online, s.v., "Negro Hall of Life," http://www.tshaonline.org/handbook/online/articles/HH/pkh1.html; Alain Locke, *The Negro in Art* (New York: Association in Negro Folk Education, 1940), 110, 131; "Dedication of Mosaic Head of Christ by Samuel Albert Countee," The Lutheran Church of the Epiphany, March 27, 1966, Jack Yates Family and Antioch Baptist Church, MSS 281–1:11; and Smith, *A Historic Context Statement,* 87–99.

57. Pvt. Countee, Samuel, Army of the United States promotion certificate, Camp Claiborne, Louisiana, July 1, 1942, Jack Yates Family and Antioch Baptist Church, MSS 281–1:11; and Smith, *A Historic Context Statement,* 87–99.

58. Pvt. Countee, Samuel, Army of the United States promotion certificate; and Smith, *A Historic Context Statement,* 87–99.

59. Pvt. Countee, Samuel, Army of the United States promotion certificate; and Smith, *A Historic Context Statement,* 87–99. Historian Steven Smith tells readers in his Fort Leonard Wood book that his next project will highlight the life of Countee.

60. James VanDerZee, photographer, "The Barefoot Prophet," Harlem, New York, 1929, from *The African American Odyssey,* 5th ed., 748; and *Africana,* vol. 5, s.v., "VanDerZee, James Augustus," 300–301.

61. Scott, *The Red Book of Houston*, 171; Dannehl M. Twomey, "Into the Mainstream: Early Black Photography in Houston," *Houston Review: History and Culture of the Gulf Coast* 9, no. 1 (1987), 39–48; Alan Govenar, "The Photographs of Benny Joseph," in *Folklife Annual 90: A Publication of the American Folklife Center at the Library of Congress*, ed. James Hardin, (Washington: Library of Congress, 1991), 82; and Alan Govenar, *Portraits of Community: African American Photography in Texas* (Austin: Texas State Historical Association, 1996), 1–30, 164–70, 201–3.

62. Scott, *The Red Book of Houston*, 171; Twomey, "Into the Mainstream," 39–48; Govenar, "The Photographs of Benny Joseph," 82; Alan Govenar, *Portraits of Community*, 1–30, 164–70, 201–3.

63. Twomey, "Into the Mainstream," 42–48.

64. *Negroes in the United States, 1920–1932*, 324; Twomey, "Into the Mainstream," 42–48; and The Handbook of Texas Online, "Teal Portrait Studio," http://www.tshaonline.org/handbook/online/articles/kjtwc.

65. Twomey, "Into the Mainstream," 42–48.

66. "Photographer A. C. Teal is Beaten by Police," *Houston Informer*, March 9, 1940.

Chapter 6

1. Luther Stullivan interview; and Stullivan, *Roots of the Stullivan Family*, 1–10.

2. Manuscript Census of the United States, Montgomery County, Texas, 1900, roll 1660, Bureau of the Census, series T623, Heritage Quest Online, http://persi.heritagequestonline.com/; Luther Stullivan interview; and Stullivan, *Roots of the Stullivan Family*, 1–10.

3. Luther Stullivan interview; Stullivan, *Roots of the Stullivan Family*, 1–10; Beaubouef, "War and Change, 89–112; Pratt, *The Growth of a Refining Region*, 3–11, 13–30, 33–56, 69–75; and Zeigler, "The Workingman in Houston," 1–42.

4. It is difficult to ascertain the exact number of railroad employees in the city from the Bureau of the Census manufacturer and occupation reports because the breakdown of railroad manufacturers and railroad workers are not inclusive of all persons employed in the industry. See Bureau of the Census, Thirteenth Census of the United States Taken in the Year 1910 (hereafter cited as Thirteenth Census of the United States, 1910), vol. 9: Manufacturers 1909 (Washington: US Government Printing Office, 1912–1914), 1220; Thirteenth Census of the United States, 1910, vol. 4: Population 1910: Occupational Statistics, 232–37; Luther Stullivan interview; Stullivan, *Roots of the Stullivan Family*, 1–10; Beaubouef, "War and Change, 89–112; Pratt, *The Growth of a Refining Region*, 3–11, 13–30, 33–56, 69–75; Zeigler, "The Workingman in Houston," 1–42; Campbell, *Gone to Texas*, 360–437; and Thomas, *A Study of the Social Welfare Status of the Negro in Houston, Texas*, 7–8.

5. Stullivan, *Roots of the Stullivan Family*, 1–10; Luther Stullivan interview; and Manuscript Census, Montgomery County, 1900, roll 2345, series T626; Manuscript Census of the United States, Montgomery County, Texas, 1910, roll 1579, Bureau of the Census, series T624, Heritage Quest Online, http://persi.heritagequestonline.com/; and Manuscript Census, Montgomery County, 1920, roll 1834, series T625.

6. Stullivan, *Roots of the Stullivan Family*, 1–10; Luther Stullivan interview; *Negro Population in the United States, 1790–1915*, 205; *Fourteenth Census of the United States, 1920*, vol. 2, 354; *Sixteenth Census of the United States, 1940*, vol. 2, 1044; *Fourteenth Census of the United States, 1920*, vol. 4, 1114–16; Beeth and Wintz, "Economic and Social Development in Black Houston during the Era of Segregation," 87–94; Pratt, *The Growth of a Refining Region*, 83–85; Obadele-Starks, *Black Unionism in the Industrial South*, 7–12; and Pruitt, "'For the Advancement of the Race,'" 2005, 448–50.

7. Stullivan, *Roots of the Stullivan Family*, 1–10; Luther Stullivan interview; *Negro Population in the United States, 1790–1915*, 205; *Fourteenth Census of the United States, 1920*, vol. 2, 354; *Sixteenth Census of the United States, 1940*, vol. 2, 1044; *Fourteenth Census of the United States, 1920*, vol. 4, 1114–16; Beeth and Wintz, "Economic and Social Development in Black Houston during the Era of Segregation," 87–94; Pratt, *The Growth of a Refining Region*, 83–85; Obadele-Starks, *Black Unionism in the Industrial South*, 7–12; Pruitt, "'For the Advancement of the Race,'" 2005, 448–50; De León, *Ethnicity in the Sunbelt*, 22–24, 45–55, San Miguel, *Brown, Not White*, 15–17; and Zamora, *The World of the Mexican Worker in Texas*, 12, 26, 49–50.

8. Wintz, "Blacks," 12–14; Tamara Miller Haygood, "Use and Distribution of Slave Labor in Harris County, Texas, 1830–60," in *Black Dixie: Afro-Texan History and Culture in Houston*, eds. Howard Beeth and Cary D. Wintz (College Station: Texas A&M University Press, 1992), 32–38; and Andrew Forest Muir, "The Free Negro in Harris County, Texas," *Southwestern Historical Quarterly* 46, no. 3 (1943): 214–238.

9. Wintz, "Blacks," 12–14; Haygood, "Use and Distribution of Slave Labor in Harris County, Texas, 1830–60," 38–53; and Muir, "The Free Negro in Harris County, Texas," 220–238.

10. *Ninth Census of the United States, 1870*, 272–73; *Eleventh Census of the United States, 1890*, 540–79; Zeigler, "The Workingman in Houston," 3–12; and SoRelle, "The Darker Side of 'Heaven,'" 33–36. The author's workforce numbers come from Zeigler's data taken from the Harris County Manuscript Census for 1870 and 1880.

11. *Thirteenth Census of the United States, 1910*, vol. 3: *Reports by States, Nebraska–Wyoming, Alaska, Hawaii and Puerto Rico*, 859; and Cary D. Wintz, "Blacks," 21–23.

12. Wintz, "Blacks," 21–23; SoRelle, "The Darker Side of 'Heaven,'" 36–38; Zeigler, "The Workingman in Houston," 3–12; and Botson, *Labor, Civil Rights, and the Hughes Tool Company*, 14–33.

13. Botson, *Labor, Civil Rights, and the Hughes Tool Company*; and Zeigler, "The Workingman in Houston," 32–43.

14. *Ninth Census of the United States, 1870*, 272–73; *Eleventh Census of the United States, 1890*, 540–79; *Thirteenth Census of the United States, 1910*, vol. 3, 859; Zeigler, "The Workingman in Houston," 3–12; and *Fifteenth Census of the United States, 1930*, vol. 4, 1593–95; *Thirteenth Census of the United States, 1910*, vol. 9, 1220, and vol. 4, 232–37.

15. Cohen, *At Freedom's Edge*; Jones, *The Dispossessed*; Hunter, *To 'Joy My Freedom*; Robin D. G. Kelley, "We Are Not What We Seem": Rethinking Black Working-Class Opposition in the Jim Crow South, *The Journal of American History* 80, no. 1 (June 1993): 75–112; Scott, *Domination and the Arts of Resistance*, ix–xiii; Maxwell and Baker,

Sawdust Empire; The Handbook of Texas Online, s.v., "Lumber Industry"; The Handbook of Texas Online, s.v., "Brotherhood of Timber Workers"; The Handbook of Texas Online, s.v., "Kirby, John Henry"; The Handbook of Texas Online, s.v., "Walker County"; Jones, *The Tribe of Black Ulysses;* Howard, *The Negro in the Lumber Industry in America;* Reich, "The Making of a Southern Sawmill World"; and de Jong, *A Different Day,* 28–30.

16. Cohen, *At Freedom's Edge,* 76–147, 248–98.

17. Ibid., xi–xvi, 248–98.

18. Ibid.

19. Offenses Against Public Morals, Decency and Chastity, The Penal Code of the State of Texas, 16th Leg. § 11.7 (Galveston: A. H. Belo & Co. 1879); Offenses Against Public Policy, The Penal Code of the State of Texas, 32nd Leg. § 11.11 (Austin: Austin Printing Co., 1911); Donald R. Walker, *Penology for Profit: A History of the Texas Prison System, 1867–1912* (College Station: Texas A&M University Press, 1988), 1–12, 114; Thomas Michael Parrish, "'The Species of Slave Labor': The Convict Lease System in Texas, 1871–1914 (master's thesis, Texas Tech University, 1976), 71–83; and Cohen, *At Freedom's Edge,* xi–xvi, 248–98. Harris County Client Case Files provide researchers with a rich laboratory of temporary migration patterns in the early twentieth century. Most migrants shared with caseworkers their labor history, which often included temporary migrations between the country and town. Migrants also routinely traveled back and forth between the country and Houston in search for work. For specific examples, see State Department of Public Welfare, Social Service Department Client Case Files, boxes 24–1674, 1882–6600, 11851–12651, 12984–15153, 15170–16536, 17041–17821, and 17286–17455, and WPA box CR08.

20. Phillips, *Alabama North,* 15–56; Gottlieb, Making Their Own Way, 12–38; and Neil McMillen, "The Migration and Black Protest in Jim Crow Mississippi," in *Black Exodus: The Great Migration from the American South,* ed. Alferdteen Harrison (Jackson: University Press of Mississippi, 1991), 83–101; and James R. Grossman, "A Chance to Make Good, 1900–1929," in *To Make Our World Anew: A History of African Americans,* ed. Robin D. G. Kelley and Earl Lewis (New York: Oxford University Press, 2000).

21. Luther Stullivan interview; Lullelia Harrison interview, September 23, 1999; Raymond Lewis interview; and Joseph Williams interview.

22. Lullelia Harrison interview, September 23, 1999.

23. Ibid.

24. Luther Stullivan interview; Stullivan, *Roots of Stullivan Family,* 9; Raymond Lewis interview; Joseph Williams interview; Gottlieb, *Making Their Own Way,* 101–3, 121–22, 126; Trotter Jr., "Introduction," 1–17; and Shirley Ann Moore, "Getting There, Being There: African-American Migration in Richmond, California, 1910–1945," in *The Great Migration in Historical Perspective,* ed. Joe William Trotter Jr. (Bloomington: Indiana University Press, 1991), 106–23; Thomas, *Life for Us Is What We Make It,* 24–48; and Pruitt, "'For the Advancement of the Race,'" 2005, 452–55.

25. Fourteenth Census of the United States, 1920, vol. 4, 1114–15; Fifteenth Census of the United States, 1930, vol. 4, 1593–95; Bureau of the Census, Negro Population of the United States, 1790–1915, 812–13, 831–34; Sixteenth Census of the United States, 1940,

vol. 2, 362–65, 792–806, 1044; and Sixteenth Census of the United States, 1940, vol. 3: The Labor Force, 906–7.

26. Zamora, *The World of the Mexican Worker in Texas*, 10–30, 211; Melville, "Mexicans," 43–45; San Miguel, *Brown Not White*, 4–6, 23, 55, 99, 110, 147; and De León, *Ethnicity in the Sunbelt*, 6–18, 25–38. I have chosen to use the term *Mexican* to refer to immigrants from Mexico and Mexican Americans. In the period under discussion, Whites refused to differentiate between Mexican Americans and Mexicans, and interchangeably used the word *Mexican*, which confused nationality with race/ethnicity. Scholars today also use the term when referring to both groups. To many scholars like Zamora, *Mexican* best describes both groups because each identified with a particular indigenous Mexican culture and both faced similar forms of discrimination. The figures used here are an estimate because Mexican Americans and Mexican immigrants before 1930 were classified as White. The researcher cannot correctly ascertain the number of Mexican-origin workers in the United States because the occupation breakdowns do not distinguish Houstonians by country of origin. People of Mexican ancestry but born in the United States, with two parents also born in the United States, were classified as White. Only in 1970 did the Bureau of the Census formulate a new category for people of Latin American ancestry—Hispanic. The word *colonia(s)* refers to community.

27. Thomas, *A Study of the Social Welfare Status of Negroes in Houston, Texas*, 15–20; and Foley, *The White Scourge*, 2–10.

28. Zamora, *The World of the Mexican Worker in Texas*, 10–30, 211; and De León, *Ethnicity in the Sunbelt*, 8–43.

29. Foley, *The White Scourge*, 5; Johnson, *Patterns of Negro Segregation*, 118; Cell, *The Highest Stage of White Supremacy*, 131–70; and Pruitt, "'For the Advancement of the Race,'" 2005, 452–55.

30. Johnson, *Patterns of Negro Segregation*, 89–103, 117–23, 294–302; Cell, *The Highest Stage of White Supremacy*, 131–40; and Pruitt, "'For the Advancement of the Race,'" 2005, 452–55.

31. Eric Arnesen, *Black Waterfront Workers of New Orleans: Race, Class, and Politics, 1863–1923* (Urbana: University of Illinois Press, 1994), 160–252; Obadele-Starks, *Black Unionism in the Industrial South*, 3–8; and Rebecca Montes, "Working for American Rights: Black, White, and Mexican American Dockworkers in Texas during the Great Depression," in *Sunbelt Revolution: The Historical Progression of the Civil Rights Struggle in the Gulf South, 1865–2000*, ed. Samuel C. Hyde Jr. (Gainesville: University Press of Florida, 2003), 102–32; Clifford Farrington, *Biracial Unions on Galveston's Waterfront, 1865–1925* (College Station: Texas A&M University Press, 2003), 1–80; and The Handbook of Texas Online, s.v., "International Longshoremen's Association," http://www.tshaonline.org/handbook/online/articles/oci01.

32. Obadele-Starks, *Black Unionism in the Industrial South*, 9–35; The Handbook of Texas Online, s.v., "International Longshoremen's Association"; and Montes, "Working for American Rights," 102–32.

33. Obadele-Starks, *Black Unionism in the Industrial South*, 9–35.

34. Obadele-Starks, *Black Unionism in the Industrial South*, 9–35; Pruitt, "'For the Advancement of the Race,'" 2005, 452–55.

35. Lewis, *In Their Own Interests*, 32.

36. Lewis, *In Their Own Interests*, 32; Fourteenth Census of the United States, 1920, vol. 4, 1114–15; Fifteenth Census of the United States, 1930, vol. 4, 1593–95; Bureau of the Census, Negro Population of the United States, 1790–1915, 812–13, 831–34; Sixteenth Census of the United States, 1940, vol. 2, 362–65, 792–806, 1044; Sixteenth Census of the United States, 1940, vol. 3, 906–7; National Urban League, *A Review of the Economic and Cultural Problems of Houston, Texas*, 24; Obadele-Starks, "The Road to Jericho," 180–205. Although the census classified stevedores as unskilled workers, Thomas refers to the members of the International Longshoremen's Association (ILA) as skilled laborers. See Thomas, *A Study of the Social Welfare Status of Negroes in Houston, Texas*, 9–18; and Pruitt, "'For the Advancement of the Race,'" 2005, 452–55.

37. Lewis, *In Their Own Interests*, 32; Fourteenth Census of the United States, 1920, vol. 4, 1114–15; Fifteenth Census of the United States, 1930, vol. 4, 1593–95; Bureau of the Census, *Negro Population of the United States, 1790–1915*, 812–13, 831–34; Sixteenth Census of the United States, 1940, vol. 2, 362–65, 792–806, 1044; Sixteenth Census of the United States, 1940, vol. 3, 906–7; National Urban League, *A Review of the Economic and Cultural Problems of Houston, Texas*, 24; and Obadele-Starks, *Black Unionism in the Industrial South*, 180–205. Although the census classified stevedores as unskilled workers, Thomas refers to the members of the International Longshoremen's Association (ILA) as skilled laborers. See Thomas, *A Study of the Social Welfare Status of Negroes in Houston, Texas*, 9–18; and Pruitt, "'For the Advancement of the Race,'" 2005, 452–55.

38. Fourteenth Census of the United States, 1920, vol. 4, 1114–15; Fifteenth Census of the United States, 1930, vol. 4, 1593–95; Manuscript Census, Harris County, 1920, roll 1812, series T625; Lewis, *In their Own Interests*, 1–42; Arnesen, *Black Waterfront Workers of New Orleans*, 160–252; Obadele-Starks, *Black Unionism in the Industrial South*, 3–8; and Montes, "Working for American Rights," 102–32. Galveston longshoremen applied for one of the first ILA charters in the South in 1900. See also Pruitt, "'For the Advancement of the Race,'" 2005, 452–55.

39. Fourteenth Census of the United States, 1920, vol. 4, 1114–15; Fifteenth Census of the United States, 1930, vol. 4, 1593–95; Manuscript Census, Harris County, 1920, roll 1812, series T625; Lewis, *In their Own Interests*, 1–42; Arnesen, *Black Waterfront Workers of New Orleans*, 160–252; Obadele-Starks, *Black Unionism in the Industrial South*, 3–8; and Montes, "Working for American Rights," 102–32; and Pruitt, "'For the Advancement of the Race,'" 2005, 452–55.

40. Fourteenth Census of the United States, 1920, vol. 4, 1114–15; Fifteenth Census of the United States, 1930, vol. 4, 1593–95; Manuscript Census, Harris County, 1920, rolls 1812–1814, series T625; and Social Service Department Client Case Files, boxes 24–1674, 1882–6600, 11851–12651, 12984–15153, 15170–16536, 17041–17821, and 17286–17455, and WPA box CR08. Although this book relies on sample welfare applicants who received public assistance in the first half of the twentieth century, it primarily concentrates on those persons who did not receive assistance. Census materials and supporting sources such as oral histories, manuscript collections, church records, biographies, and memoirs point to the vast majority of Blacks in Houston who did not receive public aid from federal and local governments.

41. Fourteenth Census of the United States, 1920, vol. 4, 1114–15; Fifteenth Census of the United States, 1930, vol. 4, 1593–95; Luther Stullivan interview; Kaplan, "Houston's Creole Quarter"; Smith Prather, "A Unique Houston Neighborhood Called Frenchtown"; Rust, "Frenchtown"; and Pruitt, "'For the Advancement of the Race,'" 2005, 452–55.

42. Fourteenth Census of the United States, 1920, vol. 4, 1114–15; Fifteenth Census of the United States, 1930, vol. 4, 1593–95; and Pruitt, "'For the Advancement of the Race,'" 2005, 452–55.

43. Thomas, *A Study of the Social Welfare Status of Negroes in Houston, Texas*, 18–19; Lewis, *In Their Own Interests*, 32–46; and Pruitt, "'For the Advancement of the Race,'" 2005, 452–55.

44. Hazel Young interview; Bryant, *Pioneer Families of Houston*, 49; Pruitt, "'For the Advancement of the Race,'" 2005, 452–55; and Manuscript Census, Harris County, 1930, roll 2345, Bureau of the Census, series T626.

45. Hazel Young interview; Bryant, *Pioneer Families of Houston*, 49; and Pruitt, "'For the Advancement of the Race,'" 2005, 452–55.

46. Fourteenth Census of the United States, 1920, vol. 4, 1114–15; Fifteenth Census of the United States, 1930, vol. 4, 1593–95; Sixteenth Census of the United States, 1940, vol. 3, 506–7; and Pruitt, "'For the Advancement of the Race,'" 2005, 452–55.

47. Jones, *Labor of Love, Labor of Sorrow*, 110–34, 147; E. Franklin Frazier, *The Negro Family in the United States*, rev. and abr. ed. with foreword by Nathan Huggins (Chicago: University of Chicago Press, 1969), 281–91; SoRelle, "The Darker Side of 'Heaven,'" 110–27; Brophy, "The Black Texan, 1900–1950," 107–10; Winegarten, *Black Texas Women*, 156–57; Thomas, *A Study of the Social Welfare Status of Negroes in Houston, Texas*, 16–17; and Pruitt, "'For the Advancement of the Race,'" 2005, 456–59.

48. Brophy, "The Black Texan: 1900–1950," 107–10; Fourteenth Census of the United States, 1920, vol. 4, 1116; Fifteenth Census of the United States, 1930, vol. 4, 1595–96; Sixteenth Census of the United States, 1940, vol. 3, 511; Fourteenth Census of the United States, 1920, vol. 3, 1026; Sixteenth Census of the United States, 1940, vol. 2, 791; and Pruitt, "'For the Advancement of the Race,'" 2005, 456–59. Because of the strong presence of African American female laborers, especially in the personal service classification, White women, compared to their percentage in the overall Texas population, had a smaller showing in the Houston labor force. In 1920, for example, they were 40.37 percent of the overall Texas population and 54.92 percent of the Houston female workforce. In 1940, White women comprised 42.39 percent of the entire Texas population and 63.86 percent of the Houston female workforce. Although they dominated Houston's female labor force, Black women had a stronger presence when compared to their overall smaller numbers in the state's population. In truth, White females' numbers in the Houston female labor force are actually much smaller because Mexican and Mexican American women were categorized in the White female labor category.

49. Jones, *Labor of Love, Labor of Sorrow*, 3–10, 110–51, 160–90.

50. Fourteenth Census of the United States, 1920, vol. 4, 1116; Fifteenth Census of the United States, 1930, vol. 4, 1595–96; Sixteenth Census of the United States, 1940, vol. 3, 510; Jones, *Labor of Love, Labor of Sorrow*, 110–51; Zamora, *The World of the Mexican*

Worker in Texas, 26–29; 30–54; and Pruitt, "'For the Advancement of the Race,'" 2005, 456–59.

51. Manuscript Census, Harris County, 1920, rolls 1812–1813, series T625.

52. Manuscript Census, Houston, 1920, roll 1814, series T625; Social Service Department Client Case Files, boxes 24–1674, 1882–6600, 11851–12651, 12984–15153, 15170–16536, 17041–17821, and 17286–17455; Fourteenth Census of the United States, 1920, vol. 4, 1116; Fifteenth Census of the United States, 1930, vol. 4, 1595–96; Sixteenth Census of the United States, 1940, vol. 3, 510; and Zamora, *The World of the Mexican Worker in Texas,* 26–52.

53. Mexican women's entry into the domestic and personal service job sector began in the early twentieth century; however, their numbers did not peak or pass those of Black women in Texas for some decades after World War II. See Zamora, *The World of the Mexican Worker in Texas,* 26–28, 40–53; Winegarten, *Black Texas Women,* 262; and Pruitt, "'For the Advancement of the Race,'" 2005, 456–59.

54. Jones, *Labor of Love, Labor of Sorrow,* 127–34; Winegarten, *Black Texas Women,* 175–78; and Pruitt, "'For the Advancement of the Race,'" 2005, 456–59.

55. Social Service Department Client Case Files, box 15170–16536; Jones, *Labor of Love, Labor of Sorrow,* 127–34; Winegarten, *Black Texas Women,* 175–78; Frazier, *The Negro Family in the United States,* 268–91; Gunnar Myrdal, *An American Dilemma: The Negro Problem and Modern Democracy,* 2 vols. (1943; New York: Pantheon Books, 1975), 930–31, 1086; and Pruitt, "'For the Advancement of the Race,'" 2005, 456–59.

56. Jones, *Labor of Love, Labor of Sorrow,* 127–34; SoRelle, "The Darker Side of 'Heaven,'" 118–23; and Pruitt, "'For the Advancement of the Race,'" 2005, 456–59.

57. Social Service Department Client Files, box 24–1674 and WPA box CR08; Jones, *Labor of Love, Labor of Sorrow,* 127–34; Louis Tuffly Ellis, "The Texas Cotton Compress Industry: A History" (Ph.D. diss., University of Texas, 1964), 263–64; and Pruitt, "'For the Advancement of the Race,'" 2005, 456–59.

58. Fourteenth Census of the United States, 1920, vol. 4, 1116; Fifteenth Census of the United States, 1930, vol. 4, 1595–96; and Pruitt, "'For the Advancement of the Race,'" 2005, 456–59.

59. Kaplan, "Houston's Creole Quarter"; Smith Prather, "A Unique Houston Neighborhood Called Frenchtown"; and Rust, "Frenchtown."

60. Manuscript Census, Harris County 1930, roll 2345, series T626; Robert Hayes Sr. interview; Thelma Scott Bryant interview; Bryant, *Pioneer Families of Houston,* 76–83. Following her husband's death in 1989, Thelma Bryant began several writing projects about the African American community in Houston. Since 1989, she has authored five local history works, including the one mentioned above.

61. Fourteenth Census of the United States, 1920, vol. 4, 1116; Fifteenth Census of the United States, 1930, vol. 4, 1595–96; Sixteenth Census of the United States, 1940, vol. 3, 510; and Pruitt, "'For the Advancement of the Race,'" 2005, 456–59.

62. Winegarten, *Black Texas Women,* 85, 101–2; Jones, *Labor of Love, Labor of Sorrow,* 142–46; Bryant, *Houston's Negro Schools,* 93–97; Kellar, *Make Haste Slowly,* 26–40; and Shabazz, "One for the Crows, One for the Crackers," 124–28.

63. Winegarten, *Black Texas Women,* 85, 101–2; Jones, *Labor of Love, Labor of Sorrow,*

142–46; Bryant, *Houston's Negro Schools*, 93–97, 122; and Kellar, *Make Haste Slowly*, 26–40.

64. Kellar, *Make Haste Slowly*, 26–40. The field of education still attracts a large segment of the Black collegiate population. Today, 50 percent of Blacks holding advanced doctorate degrees have them in education.

65. Julia Kirk Blackwelder, *Styling Jim Crow: African American Beauty Training during Segregation* (College Station: Texas A&M University Press, 2003), 3–53.

66. Ibid.

67. Blackwelder, *Styling Jim Crow*, 64–67; and Biographical Note, Franklin Beauty School Collection, RG 44, Houston Metropolitan Research Center, Houston Public Library, Julia Ideson Building, Houston, Texas.

68. Blackwelder, *Styling Jim Crow*, 67–87.

69. Blackwelder, *Styling Jim Crow*, 67–87; Ayanda D. Byrd and Lori T. Tharps, *Hair Story: Untangling the Roots of Black Hair in America* (New York: St. Martin's Press, 2001), 17–42; and Tracy Owens Patton, "'Hey Girl, Ain't I More Than My Hair?' African American Women and the Struggles with Beauty, Body Image, and Hair," *NWSA (National Women's Studies Association) Journal* 18, no. 2 (2006): 24–51.

70. Blackwelder, *Styling Jim Crow*, 113–42.

71. Blackwelder, *Styling Jim Crow*, 69–134; "God, Politics & Love: The Example of Rev. L. H. Simpson and Pleasant Hill Baptist Church," Rev. L. H. Simpson & Pleasant Hill Baptist Church MSS, 239, box 1, folder 1, "Bios"; "Board Meeting of General Central District Association and Auxiliaries. Convening at the Old Folks Home and Campus, New Waverly, Texas, Thursday and Friday[,] October 6th and 7th[,] 1960," Rev. L. H. Simpson & Pleasant Hill Baptist Church MSS, 239: 4, folder 15; "Old Folks Home, New Waverly, Texas, 1958–1964," Rev. L. H. Simpson & Pleasant Hill Baptist Church MSS, 239 box 4, folder 15; McElroy, "Anna Dupree Looks with Pride on Her Life"; Walsh, "Dr. Covington, at 90, Is Still Practicing"; and "Biographical Note," C. F. Richardson Sr., Papers, MSS 1457.

72. J. Spencer, "Our Neighbor," in Vivian Hubbard Seals, "Independence Heights, Texas"; Vivian Hubbard Seals interview; Vivian Hubbard Seals, "Independence Heights, Texas"; "Independence Heights: A Portrait of a Historic Neighborhood," Hogg Middle School, Burrus Elementary School, and the Historic Independence Heights Neighborhood Council, along with Rice University, Center for Technology in Teaching and Learning, http://indepheights.rice.edu/; Scott, *The Red Book of Houston;* and Jackson, "The Development of Black Business in Texas," 1–27, 50–70, 94–101.

73. J. Spencer, "Our Neighbor," in Vivian Hubbard Seals, "Independence Heights, Texas"; Vivian Hubbard Seals interview; Vivian Hubbard Seals, "Independence Heights, Texas: The First Black City in Texas, 1915–1928"; "Independence Heights: A Portrait of a Historic Neighborhood; Scott, *The Red Book of Houston;* and Jackson, "The Development of Black Business in Texas," 1–27, 50–70, 94–101.

74. Morrison & Fourmy's General Directory of the City of Houston, 1900–1901; Beeth and Wintz, eds., *Black Dixie*, 16–27; and Wintz, "The Emergence of a Black Neighborhood," 100–1.

75. Scott, *The Red Book of Houston*, 152–73; Thomas, *A Study of the Social Welfare*

Status of Negroes in Houston, Texas, 68–73; and National Urban League, *A Review of the Economic and Cultural Problems of Houston, Texas,* 59–66.

76. *Negroes in the United States, 1920–1932,* 518–23; Wintz, "The Emergence of a Black Neighborhood," 99–104; Cary D. Wintz, "Black Business in Houston, 1910–1930," 30–38; Beeth and Wintz, eds., *Black Dixie,* 90–98; SoRelle, "The Emergence of Black Business in Houston, Texas," 103–15.

77. *Negroes in the United States, 1920–1932,* 518–23; Wintz, "Black Business in Houston, 1910–1930," 30–38; and Jackson, "The Development of Black Business in Texas," 1–27, 50–70, 94–101.

78. Jackson, *A Sure Foundation,* 416–18, 424–25; The Handbook of Texas Online, s.v., "Taylor, Hobart T., Sr.," (by Richard Allen Burns), http://www.tshaonline.org/handbook/online/articles/fta30.

79. Jackson, *A Sure Foundation,* 416–18, 424–25; Hine, *Black Victory,* 97–98, 102–110, 167, 210–39; Haynes, "Black Houstonians and the White Democratic Primary, 1920–45," 202–7; Gillette, "The Rise of the NAACP in Texas," 393–410; The Handbook of Texas Online, s.v, "Taylor, Hobart T., Sr."; and Pruitt, "'For the Advancement of the Race,'" 2005, 452–55.

80. Richard L. Zweigenhaft and G. William Domhoff, *Diversity in the Power Elite: How it Happened, Why it Matters* (New York: Rowman & Littlefield, 2006), 95–96–132; Historic Boston-Edison Association, "Politicians and Public Servants of the Boston-Edison Historic District," accessed November 6, 2010, http://www.historicbostonedison.org/history/people_pol.shtml; Hobart Taylor Jr., "Untrained Negro Youths Constitute the Wasted Reservoir," *The Negro Digest,* June 1963, 44–48; J. Clay Smith Jr., *Emancipation: The Making of the Black Lawyer, 1844–1944* (Philadelphia: University of Pennsylvania Press, 1999), 40; BlackPast.org: An Online Reference Guide to African American History, s.v., "Taylor, Hobart Jr.," http://www.blackpast.org/?q=aah/taylor-hobart-jr-1920–1981.

81. Jackson, *A Sure Foundation,* 416–18, 424–25; The Handbook of Texas Online, s.v., "Taylor, Hobart T., Sr."; and Pruitt, "'For the Advancement of the Race,'" 2005, 452–55.

82. Jackson, "The Development of Black Business in Texas," 1–27, 50–70, 94–101; Wintz, "Black Business in Houston, 1910–1930," 28–38; HoustonHistory.com, "Blacks in Houston Today"; Jackson, *A Sure Foundation,* 385–86, 417–18, 423–24, 588–89; SoRelle, "The Emergence of Black Business in Houston, Texas," 103–7; Hine, *Black Victory,* 97–98, 102–10; Scott, *The Red Book of Houston;* Blackwelder, *Styling Jim Crow,* 64–117; and Pruitt, "'For the Advancement of the Race,'" 2005, 452–55.

83. Jackson, "The Development of Black Business in Texas," 1–27, 50–70, 94–101; Wintz, "Black Business in Houston, 1910–1930," 30–38; Jackson, *A Sure Foundation,* 385–86, 417–18, 423–24, 588–89; Henderson, *Atlanta Life Insurance Company: Black Economic Dignity* (Tuscaloosa: University of Alabama Press, 1990), 1–65; SoRelle, "The Emergence of Black Business in Houston, Texas," 103–7; Hine, *Black Victory,* 97–98, 102–110, 167, 210–41; Scott, *The Red Book of Houston;* Blackwelder, *Styling Jim Crow;* and Pruitt, "'For the Advancement of the Race,'" 2005, 452–55.

84. Jackson, "The Development of Black Business in Texas, 1919–1969," 1–27, 50–70, 94–101; Blackwelder, *Styling Jim Crow;* Cary D. Wintz, "Black Business in

Houston, 1910–1930," 30–38; Jackson, *A Sure Foundation,* 385–86, 417–18, 423–24, 588–89; Henderson, *Atlanta Life Insurance Company,* 1–65; SoRelle, "The Emergence of Black Business in Houston, Texas," 103–7; Hine, *Black Victory,* 97–98, 102–110, 167, 210–41; Scott, *The Red Book of Houston;* and Pruitt, "'For the Advancement of the Race,'" 2005, 452–55.

85. Fifteenth Census of the United States, vol. 4, 1595–96; Sixteenth Census of the United States, 1940, vol. 3, 510; Fifteenth Census of the United States, 1930, vol. 1: Unemployment, 953; Fifteenth Census of the United States, 1930, vol. 2: General Report: Statistics by Subjects, 490–91; Sparks, "'Heavenly Houston' or 'Hellish Houston'?" 353–66; The Handbook of Texas Online, s.v., "Great Depression," http://www.tshaonline.org/handbook/online/articles/npg01; Raymond Wolters, *Negroes and the Great Depression: The Problem of Economic Recovery* (Westport, Connecticut: Greenwood Publishing Corporation, 1970), 113–24; Harvard Sitkoff, *A New Deal for Blacks: The Emergence of Civil Rights as a National Issue, The Depression Decade* (1978; New York: Oxford University Press, 2009), 44–76; and WPA surveys.

86. Williams, Charlie, and Martha, Face Sheet, Record No. 12384, Social Service Department Client Files, box 11851–12651, and WPA, box CR08; and Pruitt, "In Search of Freedom," 48–49.

87. Williams, Charlie, and Martha, Face Sheet, Record No. 12384, Social Service Department Client Files, box 11851–12651, and WPA box, CR08; and Pruitt, "In Search of Freedom," 48–49.

88. Williams, Charlie, and Martha, Face Sheet, Record No. 12384, Social Service Department Client Files, box 11851–12651, and WPA box CR08; *Encyclopedia of the Great Depression,* s.v., "Domestic Workers," ed. Robert McElvaine (New York: Macmillan), 241–44; Mary Romero, *Maid in the USA,* Tenth Anniversary Edition (New York: Routledge, 2002), 65–142; Julia Kirk Blackwelder, *Now Hiring: The Feminization of Work in the United States, 1900–1995* (College Station: Texas A&M University Press, 1997), 65–166; Pruitt, "'For the Advancement of the Race,'" 2005, 435–478; and Pruitt, "In Search of Freedom," 48–49.

89. Williams, Charlie, and Martha, Face Sheet, Record No. 12384, Social Service Department Client Files, box 11851–12651, and WPA box CR08; *Encyclopedia of the Great Depression,* s.v., "Domestic Workers," 241–44; Romero, *Maid in the USA,* 65–142; Blackwelder, *Now Hiring,* 65–166; and Pruitt, "In Search of Freedom," 48–49.

90. Williams, Charlie, and Martha, Face Sheet, Record No. 12384, Social Service Department Client Files, box 11851–12651, and WPA box CR08; *Encyclopedia of the Great Depression,* s.v., "Domestic Workers," 241–44; Romero, Maid, 65–142; Blackwelder, *Now Hiring,* 65–166; and Pruitt, "In Search of Freedom," 48–49.

91. Texas Department of Health, Bureau of Vital Statistics, Texas Mortality, 1930–1950, Austin, Texas; Texas Department of Health, Bureau of Vital Statistics, Texas Births, 1930–1950, Austin, Texas.

92. Texas Department of Health, Bureau of Vital Statistics, Texas Mortality, 1930–1950; Vivian Hubbard Seals interview; and Henry Coleman interview.

93. Texas Department of Health, Bureau of Vital Statistics, Texas Mortality, 1930–1950; Vivian Hubbard Seals interview; and Henry Coleman interview.

94. Fourteenth Census of the United States, 1920, vol. 3, 393–98; Sixteenth Census of the United States, 1940, vol. 2, part 3, 362–65; Bureau of the Census, Mortality Statistics, 1930, 88–89; Bureau of the Census, Mortality Statistics, 1931 and 1932, 10; Bureau of the Census, Mortality Statistics, 1932, 10; Bureau of the Census, Mortality Statistics, 1934 and 1935, 91–92; Bureau of the Census, *Vital Statistics of the United States, 1937*, 50–51; Bureau of the Census, *Vital Statistics of the United States, 1938*, 50–51; Bureau of the Census, *Vital Statistics of the United States, 1939*, 50–51; and Bureau of the Census, *Vital Statistics of the United States, 1941*, 79–81.

95. "Boyd, Emily, and Archie," Face Sheet, Record No. 16116, Social Service Department Client Files, box 15170–16536, and WPA box CR08; Pruitt, "'For the Advancement of the Race,'" 2005, 460–63; and Sparks, "'Heavenly Houston' or 'Hellish Houston'?" 356–57.

96. Shives, Rosie Lee, and Willie, Face Sheet, Record No. 17276, Social Service Department Client Files, box 17041–17282, and WPA box CR08.

97. Boyd, Emily, and Archie, Face Sheet, Record No. 16116, Social Service Department Client Files, box 15170–16536, and WPA box CR08.

98. Illinois Jacquet interview; "Illinois Jacquet: Jazz At The Philharmonic"; Buckner, "A History of Music Education"; Manuscript Census, Harris County, 1910, roll 1559, series T624; Duersten, "The Arkivists"; and Walsh, "The Nickel Burger."

99. The intercensal-net-migration table (see table 12) for the period 1930–40 comes from census figures. The numbers are derived from the census figures given in each age cohort in the general population census volumes on Houston. The former decennial year is subtracted from the later year in each cohort group. The figure given represents the probable migration number for that particular cohort. The numerical increase for each period suggests in-migration for those decennial periods. There is, however, no clear way of differentiating between those individuals who came into the city as migrants and others who came to the city through annexation. While most Blacks arrived to the city as a result of in-migration, others, like residents of Independence Heights, came to the city through annexation. For this reason, the migration figure given for this work can only serve as a suggestive estimate and not an approximate number. See Sixteenth Census of the United States, 1940, vol. 2, part 3, 1044; Rev. Robert Hayes Sr. interview; Luther Stullivan interview; Henry Coleman interview; Earl Lewis, "Expectations, Economic Opportunities, and Life in the Industrial Age," 23–24; Edwards, Buss, Case Record of Family Referred to Works Progress Administration, Case No. 16191, Social Service Department Client Files, boxes 24–1674, 1882–6600, 11851–12651, 12984–15153, 15170–16536, 17041–17821, and WPA box CR08.

100. Illinois Jacquet interview; "Illinois Jacquet: Jazz At The Philharmonic"; Buckner, "A History of Music Education"; Manuscript Census, Harris County, 1910, roll 1559, series T624; Duersten, "The Arkivists"; and Walsh, "The Nickel Burger."

101. Carl M. Rosenquiest, and Walter Gordon Browder, *Family Mobility in Houston, Texas, 1922–1938* (Austin: University of Texas Press, 1942), 13–25; and *Houston Informer* article(s) of 1931 and Black jobless percentage.

102. Fifteenth Census of the United States, 1930, vol. 1, 953; Fifteenth Census of the United States, 1930, vol. 5: General Report on Occupations and vol. 2, 490–91.

103. Thomas, *A Study of the Social Welfare Status of Negroes in Houston, Texas*, 45–51; National Urban League, *A Review of the Economic and Cultural Problems of Houston, Texas*, 26–52; Rosenquiest and Browder, *Family Mobility in Houston, Texas*, 13–25; Sparks, "'Heavenly Houston' or 'Hellish Houston'?" 353–66; and James D. SoRelle, "'An De Po Cullud Man Is in De Wuss Fix Uv Awl': Black Occupational Status in Houston, 1920–1940," *The Houston Review: History and Culture of the Gulf Coast* 1 (Spring 1979): 20–22.

104. Thomas, *A Study of the Social Welfare Status of Negroes in Houston, Texas*, 45–51; National Urban League, *A Review of the Economic and Cultural Problems of Houston, Texas*, 26–52; "Odd Fellows Plug Ahead," *Houston Informer and Texas Freeman*, February 13, 1932; "Odd Fellows Have the Greatest Thanksgiving in Their History, *Houston Informer and Texas Freeman*, May 20, 1933; and Sparks, "'Heavenly Houston' or 'Hellish Houston'?" 353–66.

105. Thomas, *A Study of the Social Welfare Status of Negroes in Houston, Texas*, 45–51; National Urban League, *A Review of the Economic and Cultural Problems of Houston, Texas*, 26–52; De León, *Ethnicity in the Sunbelt*, 45–59; Jackson, "The Development of Black Business in Texas," 3–5, 40–45; and Sparks, "'Heavenly Houston' or 'Hellish Houston'?" 353–66. Each week the *Houston Informer* reported on depression-driven abuse toward African Americans across the country. For newspaper coverage on discrimination in the midst of the Great Depression, see The Associate Negro Press, "White Firemen Crowd Negroes from Their Job," *Houston Informer and Texas Freeman*, February 6, 1932; "It Happens to the Voteless," *Houston Informer and Texas Freeman*, February 13, 1932; and "'Jim Crow' Moves Up a Notch," *Houston Informer and Texas Freeman*, April 7, 1934. In 1932, Carter Wesley merged his newspaper with the owners of the Texas Freeman, the city's first newspaper for African Americans. The newspaper for a period of time became the *Houston Informer and Texas Freeman*.

106. Caffey, Etta, Case Record of Family Referred to Works Progress Administration, State Department of Public Welfare, No. 372, Social Service Department Client Case Files, box 24–1674, and WPA box CR08; Jackson, "The Development of Black Business in Texas," 3–5, 40–45; and Pruitt, "'For the Advancement of the Race,'" 2005, 460–63.

107. Caffey, Etta, Case Record; Jackson, "The Development of Black Business in Texas," 3–5, 40–45; SoRelle, "'An De Po Cullud Man Is in De Wuss Fix Uv Awl'"; National Urban League, *A Review of the Economic and Cultural Problems of Houston, Texas*, 26–52; and Pruitt, "'For the Advancement of the Race,'" 2005, 460–63.

108. "Jennie Belle Murphy Covington"; "Funeral Service: Mrs. Jennie B. Covington"; "Seventeen Years with the YWCA in Houston," newspaper unknown, N.D., Dr. Benjamin Covington MSS, 170:1, folder 1; "Agency History," Harris County Social Services, CR08; and Leavens, "Historical Development of the Harris County Welfare Department in Houston," 19–25.

109. "Agency History," Harris County Social Services CR08; and Leavens, "Historical Development of the Harris County Welfare Department in Houston," 19–25.

110. Sparks, "'Heavenly Houston' or 'Hellish Houston'?" 356–63; and *Houston Informer*.

111. "Mexicans Put With Negroes in Bread Line Apart from Whites," *Houston Informer and the Texas Freeman* March 31, 1934; "Mexicans Get White Again," *Houston*

Informer and Texas Freeman, May 5, 1934; and Sparks, "'Heavenly Houston' or 'Hellish Houston'?" 356–63.

112. "Wiley College Offers Year's Schooling Free," *Houston Informer and Texas Freeman,* June 23, 1934; "Funeral Service: Mrs. Jennie B. Covington"; "Zeta Phi Betas Stage Their 1st Public Affair"; Sparks, "'Heavenly Houston' or 'Hellish Houston'?" 355–62; Hazel Young interview; Thelma Scott Bryant interview; Lullelia Harrison interview, March 8, 2000; Hazel Young interview; "God, Politics & Love," Rev. L. H. Simpson & Pleasant Hill Baptist Church MSS, 239, box 1; "The Houston Community Chest: A Description of Nine Months Working with a Statement of Accounts and List of Subscribers with Amounts Pledged, 1930, Annual Report, Houston Community Chest, 1930," Rev. L. H. Simpson & Pleasant Hill Baptist Church MSS, 239, box 4, folder 5; Jackson, *A Sure Foundation,* 284–85; and Pruitt, "'For the Advancement of the Race,'" 2005, 460–63.

113. "God, Politics & Love," Rev. L. H. Simpson & Pleasant Hill Baptist Church MSS, 239; "Annual Statement, Financial Department, Pleasant Hill Baptist Church, 1934," box 1, folder 3, 1930," MSS 239; Jackson, *A Sure Foundation,* 284–85; and Pruitt, "'For the Advancement of the Race,'" 2005, 460–63.

114. Hazel Young interview; Thelma Scott Bryant interview; Lullelia Harrison interview, March 8, 2000; Hazel Young interview; "God, Politics & Love," Rev. L. H. Simpson & Pleasant Hill Baptist Church MSS, 239; "Annual Statement, Financial Department, Pleasant Hill Baptist Church, 1934"; "Annual Report, Houston Community Chest, 1930," MSS 239: box 4, folder 5; Jackson, *A Sure Foundation,* 284–85; and Pruitt, "'For the Advancement of the Race,'" 2005, 460–63.

115. Leavens, "Historical Development of the Harris County Welfare Department in Houston, Texas," 34, 39; *Encyclopedia of the Great Depression,* vol. 1 s.v., "Emergency Relief and Construction Act" (by Jeff Singleton), 295–96; *Encyclopedia of the Great Depression,* vol. 2, s.v., "Reconstruction Finance Corporation" (by James S. Olson), 804–6; *Encyclopedia of the Great Depression,* vol. 1, s.v., "Herbert Hoover," (by Susan E. Kennedy), 462–63; and Sitkoff, *A New Deal for Blacks,* 26–32.

116. Sparks, "'Heavenly Houston' or 'Hellish Houston'?" 362–66; and Sitkoff, *A New Deal for Blacks,* 44–62.

117. "Roosevelt Not to Neglect the Needy Negroes," *Houston Informer and Texas Freeman,* May 20, 1933; "Early 1000 Negroes Given Work," *Houston Informer and Texas Freeman,* December 2, 1933; "Negroes Back NRA," *Houston Informer and Texas Freeman,* August 5, 1933; "Negroes and National Recovery, *Houston Informer and Texas Freeman,* July 29, 1933; "Negro University is Possible"; Nancy Weiss, *Farewell to the Party of Lincoln: Black Politics in the Age of FDR* (Princeton: Princeton University Press, 1983), 296–301; and Sitkoff, *A New Deal for Blacks,* 44–76.

118. Sparks, "'Heavenly Houston' or 'Hellish Houston'?" 362–66.

119. Social Service Department Client Case Files, WPA box CR08; Weiss, *Farewell to the Party of Lincoln,* 296–301; Leavens, "Historical Development of the Harris County Welfare Department in Houston, Texas," 34, 39; William J. Brophy, "Black Texan, 1900–1950: A Quantitative History" (Ph.D. diss., Vanderbilt University, 1974), 221–22;' Sparks, "'Heavenly Houston' or 'Hellish Houston'?" 221–22; and Pruitt, "'For the Advancement of the Race,'" 2005, 460–63. In Texas, the percentage of Mexican

Americans on federal relief exceeded that of both Blacks and Whites. There is no way of knowing the approximate number of African American migrants living in Houston who applied for and received public assistance during the depression, without examining the entire collection of case files.

120. "Lee, Martha Barnett," Case Record of Family Referred to Works Progress Administration, Case No. 6516, Social Service Department Client Case Files, WPA box CR08; Leavens, "Historical Development of the Harris County Welfare Department in Houston, Texas," 30–39; Leavens, "Historical Development of the Harris County Welfare Department in Houston, Texas," 34, 39; and Sparks, "'Heavenly Houston' or 'Hellish Houston'?" 361–62.

121. "Wood, Kile," Case Record of Family Referred to Works Progress Administration, Case No. W-8079, Social Service Department Client Case Files, WPA box CR08; and Pruitt, "'For the Advancement of the Race,'" 2004, 460–63.

122. *Houston Informer;* James M. SoRelle, "The Darker Side of 'Heaven,'" 138–41; Sparks, "'Heavenly Houston' or 'Hellish Houston'?" 362–63; Barton J. Bernstein, ed., "The New Deal: The Conservative Achievements of Liberal Reform," in *Twentieth Century America: Recent Interpretations,* 2nd ed. (San Diego: Harcourt Brace Jovanovich, 1972), 260–61; Wolters, *Negroes and the Great Depression,* 113–24; and Pruitt, "'For the Advancement of the Race,'" 2005, 460–63.

123. Leavens, "Historical Development of the Harris County Welfare Department in Houston, Texas," 26–53; James M. SoRelle, "The Darker Side of 'Heaven,'" 130–39; Sparks, "'Heavenly Houston' or 'Hellish Houston'?" 362–63; and The Handbook of Texas Online, s.v., "Great Depression."

124. "Nearly 1,000 Negroes Given Work"; Sparks, "'Heavenly Houston' or 'Hellish Houston'?" 361–64; Pruitt, "'For the Advancement of the Race,'" 2005, 460–63; and Vivian Hubbard Seals interview.

125. James Baker, interview by author, tape recording, November 27, 2004, Huntsville, Texas, in possession of author.

126. Lullelia Harrison interview, March 8, 2000; Vivian Hubbard Seals interview; Sparks, "'Heavenly Houston' or 'Hellish Houston'?" 362; Brophy, "The Black Texan, 1900–1950," 218–21; Weiss, *Farewell to the Party of Lincoln,* 168–73; James Baker interview; and Pruitt, "'For the Advancement of the Race,'" 2005, 460–63.

127. James Baker interview; Obadele-Starks, *Black Unionism in the Industrial South,* 3–26; and Pruitt, "'For the Advancement of the Race,'" 2005, 460–63.

128. Lullelia Harrison interview, March 8, 2000.

129. Thomas, Robert and Anna, Case Record of Family Referred to Works Progress Administration, Case No. 12384, Social Service Department Client Files, WPA box CR08; and Lullelia Harrison interview, March 8, 2000.

130. Thomas, Robert and Anna, Case Record of Family Referred to Works Progress Administration, Case No. 12384, Social Service Department Client Files, WPA box CR08; and Lullelia Harrison interview, March 8, 2000.

131. Weiss, *Farewell to the Party of Lincoln,* 167–68; Sparks, "'Heavenly Houston' or 'Hellish Houston'?" 362–63; Bernstein, "The New Deal," 260–61; Wolters, *Negroes and the Great Depression,* 113–24; and Pruitt, "'For the Advancement of the Race,'" 2005, 460–63.

132. "Mob Strikes Longshoreman's Home," *Houston Informer and Texas Freeman*, May 12, 1934; "Port Arthur CIO Hears Editor on 'Labor's' Stake," *Houston Informer and Texas Freeman*, March 6, 1943; Harris, *The Harder We Run*, 95–113; and Robert Korstad and Nelson Lichtenstein, "Opportunities Found and Lost: Labor, Radicals, and the Early Civil Rights Movement," in *The Black Worker: A Reader*, ed. Eric Arnesen (Urbana: University of Illinois Press, 2007), 222–65.

133. Sixteenth Census of the United States, 1940, vol. 3, 506–7; Weiss, *Farewell to the Party of Lincoln*, 163–66; Botson, *Labor, Civil Rights, and the Hughes Tool Company*, 108–27; Obadele-Starks, "The Road to Jericho," 26–39; and Pruitt, "'For the Advancement of the Race,'" 2005, 460–63.

134. Arnesen, *Brotherhoods of Color*, 84–115, 151–202; and Obadele-Starks, *Black Unionism in the Industrial South*, 53, 61–63.

135. Arnesen, *Brotherhoods of Color*, 84–115, 151–180.

136. Luther Stullivan interview.

137. Articles of Incorporation of the Colored Trainmen of America, 1918, RG R3, box 1, folder 1, Union Charter, Colored Trainmen Union, Houston Metropolitan Research Center, Houston Public Library, Julia Ideson Building, Houston, Texas; "In Loving Memory of Ellis Montgomery Knight"; Jackson, *A Sure Foundation*, 54, 24–65; Brophy, "The Black Texan: 1900–1950," 151–52; Obadele-Starks, *Black Unionism in the Industrial South*, 49–52; Obadele-Starks, "Black Struggle, White Resistance, and the Upper Texas Gulf Coast Railroads, 1900–1945," *Houston Review* 18 (Fall 1996): 104–6; Pruitt, "'For the Advancement of the Race,'" 2005, 460–63; and Arnesen, *Brotherhoods of Color*, 116–50, 203–29.

138. Bernstein, "The New Deal," 260–62.

139. Chester Himes, *The Lonely Crusade* (1947; reprint with a foreword by Graham Hodges, New York: Thunder's Month Press, 1986), 55.

140. Himes, *The Lonely Crusade*, 55; Bernstein, "The New Deal," 260–62; Weiss, *Farewell to the Party of Lincoln*, 296; and Pruitt, "'For the Advancement of the Race,'" 2005, 460–63.

141. "McKenzie, Hattie, and Cato," Face Sheet, State Department of Public Welfare, No. 3121, Social Service Department Client Case Files, box 1662–6600, and WPA box CR08; and Campbell, *Gone to Texas*, 360–64, 378.

142. E. J. Kyle, "The Tragic Plight of Cotton and Its Effect Upon the State and Nation," June 27, 1940, Texas Agriculture Extension Service Collection, 9:104, Cushing Memorial Library and Archives, Texas A&M University, College Station, Texas; Campbell, *Gone to Texas*, 376–79; Forrest Garrett Hill, "The Negro in the Texas Labor Supply," 120–23; Brophy, "The Black Texan, 1900–1950," 63–67; Foley, *The White Scourge*, 40–91, 163–82; Zamora, *The World of the Mexican Worker in Texas*, 15–26; *Africana*, vol. 4, s.v., "Sharecropping," 739–40; *Encyclopedia of the Great Depression*, vol. 2, s.v., "Sharecroppers," 877–880; *Encyclopedia of the Great Depression*, vol. 1, s.v., "African Americans, Impact of Great Depression on," 8–13; Steve Volanto, *Texas, Cotton, and the New Deal* (College Station: Texas A&M University Press, 2004), 125–41; and Hine et al., *African-American Odyssey*, 481.

143. "McKenzie, Hattie, and Cato," Face Sheet, State Department of Public Welfare, No. 3121, Social Service Department Client Case Files, box 1662–6600; Kyle, "The

Tragic Plight of Cotton and Its Effect Upon the State and Nation"; Hill, "The Negro in the Texas Labor Supply," 120–23; Brophy, "The Black Texan, 1900–1950," 63–67; Foley, *The White Scourge*, 40–91, 163–82; Zamora, *The World of the Mexican Worker in Texas*, 15–26; and *Encyclopedia of the Great Depression*, s.v., "African Americans, Impact of Great Depression on," 8–13.

144. "McKenzie, Hattie, and Cato," Face Sheet, State Department of Public Welfare, No. 3121; Hill, "The Negro in the Texas Labor Supply," 120–23; Brophy, "The Black Texan, 1900–1950," 63–67; and *Africana*, vol. 4, s.v., "African Americans, Impact of Great Depression on," 8–13. Houston was far from perfect. Many newcomers and established residents alike found themselves traveling from place to place even after settling in Houston, largely because New Deal programs were temporary and permanent work was scarce.

145. Pruitt, "'For the Advancement of the Race,'" 2005, 435–444.

146. Beeth and Cary D. Wintz, eds., *Black Dixie;* Wintz, "Blacks," 15–33; Pruitt, "'For the Advancement of the Race,'" 2005, 445–54; and Obadele-Starks, *Black Unionism in the Industrial South*, 3–30.

147. Adams, *Way Up North in Louisville*, 13–36; Foley, *The White Scourge*, 1997, 163–78; James H. Street, *The New Revolution in the Cotton Economy: Mechanization and Its Consequences* (Chapel Hill: University of North Carolina Press, 1957), 50–66; Brophy, "The Black Texan, 1900–1950," 65–66; Forest Garrett Hill, "The Negro in the Texas Labor Supply," 161–62; Texas Department of Health, Bureau of Vital Statistics, Texas Mortality, 1930–1950; Texas Department of Health, Bureau of Vital Statistics, Texas Births, 1930–1950; Bureau of the Census, A Report of the Seventeenth Decennial Census of the United States: Census of Population: 1950, vol. 2: Characteristics of the Population, part 43: Texas (Washington: US Government Printing Office, 1953), 509–510 (hereafter cited as A Report of the Seventeenth Decennial Census,1950); National Housing Agency, Office of the Administrator, "Locality Analysis," War Housing Program, WHP No. H-2, A2, Records of the War Housing Agency, Locality Program Operating Files, General Records of the Department of Housing and Urban Development, Record Group 207, National Archives at College Park, College Park, Maryland; "War Activities," War Housing Program, WHP No. 5-Q3-C4, June 21, 1943; and Lee et al., *Methodological Considerations and Reference Tables*, vol. 1.

148. Sixteenth Census of the United States, 1940, vol. 2, 1040; and Sixteenth Census of the United States, 1940, vol. 4, 22.

149. Fourteenth Census of the United States, 1920, vol. 4, 1116; Fifteenth Census of the United States, vol. 4, 1595–96; Sixteenth Census of the United States, vol. 3, 510; Luther Stullivan interview; Obadele-Starks, *Black Unionism in the Industrial South*, 3–8; and Montes, "Working for American Rights," 102–32.

150. Fourteenth Census of the United States, 1920, vol. 4, 1116; Fifteenth Census of the United States, vol. 4, 1595–96; and Sixteenth Census of the United States, vol. 3, 510.

151. *Houston Informer* articles on employment racism; Luther Stullivan interview; Sparks, "'Heavenly Houston' or 'Hellish Houston'?" 355–56; Obadele-Starks, *Black Unionism in the Industrial South*, 3–8; "In Loving Memory of Ellis Montgomery

Knight"; Jackson, *A Sure Foundation*, 54, 24–65; and Arnesen, *Brotherhoods of Color*, 84–115, 151–80.

152. Luther Stullivan interview; Thelma Scott Bryant interview; Michael R. Botson Jr., "Jim Crow Wearing Steel-Toed Shoes and Safety Glasses: Duel Unionism at the Hughes Tool Company," *Houston Review: History and Culture of the Gulf Coast* 16 (Winter 1994)," 110–16; Sparks, "'Heavenly Houston' or 'Hellish Houston'?" 355–56; and Pratt, *The Growth of a Refining Region*, 89–90.

Conclusion

1. McElroy, "Anna Dupree Looks with Pride on Her Life"; Photo Identification Sheet, Anna Dupree MSS, 110: 1, folder 1; and Manuscript Census, Harris County, 1920, roll 1813, series T625.

2. McElroy, "Anna Dupree Looks with Pride on Her Life"; Photo Identification Sheet, Anna Dupree MSS, 110: 1, folder 1; and Manuscript Census, Harris County, 1920, roll 1813, series T625.

3. McElroy, "Anna Dupree Looks with Pride on Her Life"; Photo Identification Sheet, Anna Dupree MSS, 110: 1, folder 1; Manuscript Census, Harris County, 1920, roll 1813, series T625; and Jackson, "The Development of Black Business in Texas," 58.

4. McElroy, "Anna Dupree Looks with Pride on Her Life"; Historical Context Sheet, Anna Dupree MSS, 110: 1, folder 1; Manuscript Census, Harris County, 1920, roll 1813, series T625; Manuscript Census, Harris County, 1930, roll 2347, series T626; and National Urban League, *A Review of the Economic and Cultural Problems of Houston*, 177–78.

5. "Anna Dupree Looks with Pride on Her Life," Historical Context Sheet, Anna Dupree MSS, 110:1, folder 5.

6. Twelfth Census of the United States, 1900, 132; *Negro Population in the United States, 1790–1915*, 92, 205; *Fourteenth Census of the United States, 1920*, vol. 2, 354; *Sixteenth Census of the United States*, vol. 2, 1044; *A Decennial Report of the Seventeenth Census of the United States: Census of Population: 1950*, vol. 2, part 43, 43–63, 43–358; Social Service Department Client Case Files, boxes 24–1674, 1882–6600, 11851–12651, 12984–15153, 15170–16536, 17041–17821, and WPA box CR08; and Trotter, "Introduction," 15–17.

7. *Twelfth Census of the United States, 1900*, 132; *Negro Population in the United States, 1790–1915*, 205; *Fourteenth Census of the United States, 1920*, vol. 2, 354.

8. *Fourteenth Census of the United States, 1920*, vol. 4, 1114–15; *Fifteenth Census of the United States*, vol. 4, 1593–95; *Sixteenth Census of the United States*, vol. 3, 506–7, 510; and Pratt, *The Growth of a Refining Region*, 61–85.

9. *Fourteenth Census of the United States, 1920*, vol. 4, 1114–16; *Fifteenth Census of the United States*, vol. 4, 1593–95; *Sixteenth Census of the United States*, vol. 3, 506–7, 510; and Kellar, *Make Haste Slowly*, 35–46.

10. Rust, "Frenchtown."

11. Robert Hayes Sr. interview; and Scott, *Negro Migration during the War*, 3–6.

12. Joseph Williams interview; Robert Hayes Sr. interview; Henry Coleman

interview; Luther Stullivan interview; "Colored Americans in Walker County Victims of Wholesale Depredations"; "News from Texas Towns," *Houston Informer,* January 23, 1932; and "News From Texas Towns," *Houston Informer,* January 29, 1919.

13. "Constitution and By-Laws, Civic Betterment League of Houston and Harris County, 1918," Reel 19 of 20, Papers of the NAACP; "Miscellaneous," Rev. Lee Haywood Simpson and Pleasant Hill Baptist Church MSS, 239:6, folder 6; and "Membership Cards, Third Ward Civic Club, 1946–1948," Harrison Family MSS, 182:1, file 10.

14. *Fourteenth Census of the United States, 1920,* vol. 2, 354; *Sixteenth Census of the United States,* vol. 2, 1040; *Sixteenth Census of the United States,* vol. 4, *1935–1940,* 22; Sparks, "'Heavenly Houston' or 'Hellish Houston'?" 353–62; Foley, *The White Scourge,* 163–78; and Karen Tucker Anderson, "Last Hired, First Fired: Black Women Workers during World War II," *Journal of American History* 69 (June 1982): 82–97.

15. James Douglass, interview by author, tape recording, Houston, Texas, June 30, 1998, in possession of author; Henry Coleman interview; Hill, "The Negro in the Texas Labor Supply," 161–62; Pratt, *The Growth of a Refining Region,* 94–95; Obadele-Starks, "Road to Jericho," 71, 98, 127, 184; A Report of the Seventeenth Decennial Census,1950, vol. 2, part 43, 509–510; and McComb, *Houston: A History,* 232.

16. James Douglass interview.

17. Housing and Urban Development, "Locality Analysis," WHP No. H-2, A2; Housing and Urban Development, War Housing Program, WHP No. 5-Q3-C4; Trotter, Black Milwaukee, 226–38; and Richard M Dalfiume, "The 'Forgotten Years' of the Negro Revolution," *Journal of American History* 55 (June 1968): 95–96. On February 14, 1942, the Pittsburgh Courier initiated the "Double V" crusade—"victory over our enemies at home and victory over our enemies abroad." A month later the *Chicago Defender* coined another slogan after a brutal lynching in Sikeston, Missouri, "Remember Pearl Harbor . . . and Sikeston too" in the March 14, 1942 issue.

18. "Analysis of Houston, Texas Housing Market," Research and Statistics Division, Reports of Housing Market Analysis, Dallas, Texas—Port Arthur, Texas, 3–4, Records of the Federal Housing Administration, RG 31, National Archives II, College Park, Maryland; Pitre, *In Struggle against Jim Crow,* 16–17; and Hine, *Black Victory,* 54–56.

19. Obadele-Starks, *Black Unionism in the Industrial South,* 62–67, 79–81, 100–111, 154–79; Emilio Zamora, "The Failed Promise of Wartime Opportunity for Mexicans in the Texas Oil Industry," *Southwestern Historical Quarterly* 95 (Winter 1992): 323–40; and Winegarten, *Black Texas Women,* 233–39.

20. "First Report, Fair Employment Practice Committee," Records of the Information Service, Records of the Office of the Director of General Records, 1942–1945, Records of the War Manpower Commission, Record Group 211, National Archives at College Park, College Park, Maryland; Obadele-Starks, "Road to Jericho," 71, 98, 127, 154–79; Zamora, "The Failed Promise of Wartime Opportunity," 323–40; Winegarten, *Black Texas Women,* 233–39; Dalfiume, "The 'Forgotten Years' of the Negro Revolution,"90–106; Obadele-Starks, *Black Unionism in the Industrial South,* 35, 64–67, 76–81, 91–100, 101–111; Botson, *Labor, Civil Rights, and the Hughes Tool Company,* 108–145; and Arnesen, *Brotherhoods of Color,* 116–150,181–229.

21. Kellar, *Make Haste Slowly,* 35–46.

22. Walsh, "Dr. Covington, at 90, Is Still Practicing"; Hine, *Black Victory,* 123–37, 185–203, 207–23; Bessent, "The Publisher," 3–7; Bryant, *Houston's Negro Schools,* 157–61; Kaplan, "Houston's Creole Quarter"; Smith Prather, "A Unique Houston Neighborhood Called Frenchtown"; SoRelle, "The Darker Side of 'Heaven,'" 337–49; and Pitre, *In Struggle against Jim Crow,* 19–44.

23. Hine, *Black Victory,* iv–vi.

24. Pruitt, "'For the Advancement of the Race,'" 2001, 317–42; and Pruitt, "'For the Advancement of the Race,'" 2005, 463–65.

25. *The Strange Demise of Jim Crow,* produced by Thomas R. Cole, 56 minutes, California Newsreel, DVD, 1998; Pitre, *In Struggle against Jim Crow,* 117–28; Shabazz, *Advancing Democracy,* 98–108; Watson, *Race and the Houston Police Department,* 62–93; and Thomas Cole, *No Color Is My Kind: The Life of Eldrewey Stearns and the Integration of Houston* (Austin: University of Texas, 1997), 14–99.

26. Cole, *The Strange Demise of Jim Crow;* Pitre, *In Struggle against Jim Crow,* 63–104; Watson, *Race and the Houston Police Department,* 62–93; Cole, *No Color Is My Kind,* 14–99; and Bullard, *Invisible Houston,* 3–13.

27. Bullard, *Invisible Houston,* 3–13; David Goldfield, "Writing the Sunbelt," *OAH (Organization of American Historians) Magazine of History* 18, no. 1 (October 2003): 5–10; Carl Abbott, "Urbanizing the Sunbelt," *OAH Magazine* 18, no. 1 (2003):6–16; and Quintard Taylor, "Seeking the Sunbelt Freedom: African Americans in the Urban Southwest, 1866–1970," *OAH (Organization of American Historians) Magazine of History* 18, no. 1: 5–10:4–21.

28. *Texas Southern University Alumni Directory, 1947–1999* (Houston: Texas Southern University, 2000).

29. Schomburg Center, *In Motion.*

30. Schomburg Center, *In Motion;* Pruitt, "'For the Advancement of the Race,'" 2001, 317–42; and Pruitt, "'For the Advancement of the Race,'" 2005, 463–65.

BIBLIOGRAPHY

Case Studies, Reports, and Surveys

Greater Houston partnership. *Houston Facts 2000.* Houston: Houston partnership, 1999.

National Urban League. *A Review of the Economic and Cultural Problems of Houston, Texas: As They Relate to Conditions of the Negro Population.* N. P., 1945.

Pruitt, Bertha Juanita. December 8, 1984. Michigan Deaths, 1971–1996. Michigan Department of Vital and Health Records. Michigan Deaths, 1971–1996. Ancestry.com. http://search.ancestry.com/.

Rosenquist, Carl M., and Walter Gordon Browder. *Family Mobility in Houston, Texas, 1922–1938.* Austin: University of Texas Press, 1942.

Thomas, Jessie O. *A Study of the Social Welfare Status of Negroes in Houston, Texas.* Houston: Webster-Richardson, 1929.

Court Cases

Buchanan v. Warley, 245 US 60 (1917)
Grigsby v. Harris, 27 F.2d 945 (1928)
Grovey v. Townsend, 295 US 45 (1935)
Love v. Griffith, 236, S.W. 239 (Texas Civ. App., 1922)
Love v. Griffith, 266, US 32 (1923)
Nixon v. Herndon, 273 US 536 (1927)
Nixon v. Condon, 286 US 73 (1932)
Shelley v. Kraemer, 334 US 1, (1948)
Smith v. Allwright, 321 US 649 (1944)
Sweatt v. Painter, 339 US 629 (1950)
United States v. Classic, 313 US 299 (1941)
White v. Lubbock, 30 SW 2d 722 (Tex. Civ. App. 1930)

Government Documents

"Analysis of Houston, Texas, Housing Market." Research and Statistics Division. Reports of Housing Market Analysis, Dallas, Texas—Port Arthur, Texas, 3–4.

Records of the Federal Housing Administration. RG 31. National Archives II. College Park, Maryland.

Archaeological Commission and City of Houston Planning and Development, Protected Landmark Designation Report. Emancipation Park, 2007. http://blog.chron.com/bayoucityhistory/files/legacy/EmancipationPark3018DowlingStreetR.pdf.

Archie, Ernest Alvin. World War I Draft Registration Card. Registration No. 4–100. June 2, 1917. Hempstead, Texas. Military Records. Ancestry.com. http://search.ancestry.com/.

Bureau of the Census. 1950 United States Census of Population. Houston, Texas: Census Tracts. Washington: US Government Printing Office, 1953.

Bureau of the Census. 1980 Census of Population and Housing. Census Tracts. Houston, Texas. Standard Metropolitan Statistical Area. Washington: US Government Printing Office, 1983.

Bureau of the Census. 1990 Census of Population and Housing: Population and Housing Characteristics for Census Tracts and Block Numbering Areas. Houston-Galveston-Brazoria, Texas CMSA. Washington: US Government Printing Office, 1993.

Bureau of the Census. A Report of the Seventeenth Census of the United States: Census of Population, vol. 2, part 18. Louisiana. Washington: US Government Printing Office, 1953.

Bureau of the Census. A Report of the Seventeenth Decennial Census of the United States: 1950. Population, vol. 2: Characteristics of the Population. Part 43: Texas. Washington: US Government Printing Office, 1953.

Bureau of the Census. Fifteenth Census of the United States, 1930: Population and Housing. Vol. 1: Unemployment; vol. 2: General Report: Statistics by Subjects; vol. 4: Occupations, by States; and vol. 5: General Report on Occupations. Washington: US Government Printing Office, 1932.

Bureau of the Census. Fifteenth Census of the United States, 1930: Population and Housing, vol. 3: Composition and Characteristics: Composition of Population by Counties. Washington, DC: US Government Printing Office, 1932.

Bureau of the Census. Fourteenth Census of the United States Taken in the Year 1920: Population, vol. 2. Population: General Reports and Analytical Tables; vol. 3: Population: Composition and Characteristics of the Population by States; and vol. 4: Population: Occupations. Washington: US Government Printing Office, 1923.

Bureau of the Census. Mortality Statistics, 1920: Twenty-First Annual Report. Washington: Government Printing Office, 1922.

Bureau of the Census. Mortality Statistics, 1921: Twenty-Second Annual Report. Washington: Government Printing Office, 1924.

Bureau of the Census. Mortality Statistics, 1922: Twenty-Third Annual Report. Washington: Government Printing Office, 1924.

Bureau of the Census. Mortality Statistics, 1923: Twenty-Fourth Annual Report. Washington: Government Printing Office, 1925.

Bureau of the Census. Mortality Statistics, 1924: Twenty-Fifth Annual Report. Washington: Government Printing Office, 1926.

Bureau of the Census. Mortality Statistics, 1925: Twenty-Sixth Annual Report. Washington: Government Printing Office, 1927.

Bureau of the Census. Mortality Statistics, 1926: Twenty-Seventh Annual Report. Washington: Government Printing Office, 1929.
Bureau of the Census. Mortality Statistics, 1927: Twenty-Eighth Annual Report. Washington: Government Printing Office, 1929.
Bureau of the Census. Mortality Statistics, 1928 and 1929: Thirtieth Annual Report. Washington: Government Printing Office, 1932.
Bureau of the Census. Mortality Statistics, 1930: Thirty-First Annual Report. Washington: Government Printing Office, 1934.
Bureau of the Census. Mortality Statistics, 1931 and 1932: Thirty-Second Annual Report Washington: Government Printing Office, 1934.
Bureau of the Census. Mortality Statistics, 1933 and 1934: Thirty-Third Annual Report Washington: Government Printing Office, 1936.
Bureau of the Census. Mortality Statistics, 1935 and 1936: Thirty-Fourth Annual Report Washington: Government Printing Office, 1938.
Bureau of the Census. Negro Population in the United States, 1790–1915. 1918. Reprint. New York: Arno Press, 1969.
Bureau of the Census. Negroes in the United States, 1920–1932. 1935. Reprint. New York: Greenwood Publishers, 1969.
Bureau of the Census. Ninth Census of the United States, 1870: Population, part 1. Washington: US Government Printing Office, 1872.
Bureau of the Census. Seventh Census of the United States, Texas. Washington: Robert Armstrong Public Printer, 1853.
Bureau of the Census. Sixteenth Census of the United States, 1940. Population, vol. 2 (Population: Characteristics of the Population; Part 3: Kansas-Michigan and Part 6: Pennsylvania—Texas); vol. 3 (The Labor Force: Part 5: Pennsylvania–Wyoming); and vol. 4 (Internal Migration: 1935–940). Washington: US Government Printing Office, 1943.
Bureau of the Census. Thirteenth Census of the United States Taken in the Year 1910, vol. 3: Manufacturers 1909. Washington: US Government Printing Office, 1913.
Bureau of the Census. Thirteenth Census of the United States Taken in the Year 1910, vol. 4: Population 1910: Reports by States, Nebraska-Wyoming, Alaska, Hawaii and Puerto Rico. Washington: US Government Printing Office, 1913.
Bureau of the Census. Thirteenth Census of the United States Taken in the Year 1910, vol. 9: Population. Washington: US Government Printing Office, 1913.
Bureau of the Census. Twelfth Census of the United States Taken in the Year 1900, vol. 1: Population. Washington: US Government Printing Office, 1901.
Bureau of the Census. Vital Statistics of the United States, 1937. Washington: US Government Printing Office, 1939.
Bureau of the Census. Vital Statistics of the United States, 1938. Washington: US Government Printing Office, 1940.
Bureau of the Census. Vital Statistics of the United States, 1939. Washington: US Government Printing Office, 1941.
Bureau of the Census. Vital Statistics of the United States, 1941. Washington: US Government Printing Office, 1943.
Bureau of the Census. Vital Statistics of the United States, 1942. Washington: US Government Printing Office, 1943.

Bureau of the Census. Vital Statistics of the United States, 1943. Washington: US Government Printing Office, 1945.
Bureau of the Census. Vital Statistics of the United States, 1944. Washington: US Government Printing Office, 1946.
Bureau of the Census. Vital Statistics of the United States, 1945. Washington: US Government Printing Office, 1947.
Bureau of the Census. Vital Statistics of the United States, 1947. Washington: US Government Printing Office, 1949.
Bureau of the Census. Vital Statistics of the United States, 1948. Washington: US Government Printing Office, 1950.
Bureau of the Census. Vital Statistics of the United States, 1949. Washington: US Government Printing Office, 1951.
Bureau of the Census. Vital Statistics of the United States, 1950. Washington: US Government Printing Office, 1953.
Bureau of the Census Library. Population of the United States Compiled from the Original Returns of the Eighth Census under the Direction of the Secretary of the Interior, Classified Population. Washington: Government Printing Office, 1864.
Cockrell, John Lafayette. 1918. US Selective Service System, World War I Selective Service Draft Registration Cards, 1917–1918. Washington: National Archives and Records Administration, M1509, 4,582 rolls. From Ancestry.com, http://search.ancestry.com/.
"First Report, Fair Employment Practice Committee." Records of the Information Service. Records of the Office of the Director of General Records, 1942–1945. Records of the War Manpower Commission. Record Group 211. National Archives at College Park, College Park, Maryland.
General Laws of the State of Texas. 28th Leg., S.H.B. Nos. 45 and 170, § 103. Austin: Texas State Library, 1903.
—. 29th Leg., S.H.B. Nos. 45 and 170, § 103. Austin: Texas State Library, 1905.
—. 38th Leg., First, Second, and Third Called Sessions, S.B. No. 44, Ch. 32. Austin: Texas State Library, 1923.
—. 40th Leg., S.H.B. Nos. 45 and 170, § 103. Austin: Texas State Library, 1927.
General Records of the Department of Housing and Urban Development. Record Group 207. National Archives II. College Park, Maryland.
Grovey, Richard. World War I Draft Registration Card. Precinct 13. June 5, 1917. Houston, Texas. "Military Records. From Ancestry.com, http://content.ancestry.com/.
Harris County Social Services Finding Aids, Harris County Archives, Harris County Courthouse, Houston, Texas.
Hayes, E. W. Texas Death Index, 1903–2000. December 22, 1931. Houston, Texas. Certificate number 56565. Ancestry.com. http://search.ancestry.com/.
Hayes, Robert. Florida Marriage Collection, 1822–1875 and 1927–2001, 1945. Palm Beath, Florida. Vol. 992. Certificate number 11009. From Ancestry.com, http://search.ancestry.com/.
The Laws of Texas, 1822–1897, vol. 8, part 3. Austin: Texas State Library and Archives, 1891, 1897.
—. *1822–1897*, vol. 10, part 1. Austin: Texas State Library and Archives, 1891, 1897.
—. *1822–1897*, Vol. 10, part 2. Austin: Texas State Library and Archives, 1891, 1897.

—. *1822–1897,* Vol. 10, part 3. Austin: Texas State Library and Archives, 1891, 1897.

—. *1897–1902,* V.11, S.J.R. No. 3, Joint Resolution. Austin: Texas State Library, 1902.

Manuscript Census of the United States: Bastrop County, Texas, 1880. Roll 1290. Bureau of the Census. Series T90. Heritage Quest Online. http://persi.heritagequestonline.com/.

Manuscript Census of the United States: Brazoria County, Texas, 1880. Heritage Quest Online. http://persi.heritagequestonline.com/.

Manuscript Census of the United States: Brazoria County, Texas, 1900. Roll 1614. Bureau of the Census. Series T623. Heritage Quest Online. http://persi.heritagequestonline.com/.

Manuscript Census of the United States: Brazoria County, Texas, 1910. Roll 1534. Bureau of the Census. Series T624. Clayton Genealogy Library. Houston Public Library, Houston, Texas.

Manuscript Census of the United States: Burleson County, Texas, 1900. Roll 1615. Bureau of the Census. Series T623. Heritage Quest Online. http://persi.heritagequestonline.com/.

Manuscript Census of the United States: Galveston County, Texas, 1900. Heritage Quest Online. http://persi.heritagequestonline.com/.

Manuscript Census of the United States: Grimes County, Texas, 1910. Roll 1555. Bureau of the Census. Series T624. Heritage Quest Online. http://persi.heritagequestonline.com/.

Manuscript Census of the United States: Grimes County, Texas, 1920. Roll 1806. Bureau of the Census. Series T625. Heritage Quest Online. http://persi.heritagequestonline.com/.

Manuscript Census of the United States: Harris County, Texas, 1870. Roll M593. Bureau of the Census Series. Series 1589. http://persi.heritagequestonline.com/.

Manuscript Census of the United States: Harris County, Texas, 1880. Bureau of the Census Series. Series T9. http://persi.heritagequestonline.com/.

Manuscript Census of the United States: Harris County, Texas, 1900. Roll 1309/ Bureau of the Census Series. Series T623. Heritage Quest Online. http://persi.heritagequestonline.com/.

Manuscript Census of the United States: Harris County, Texas, 1910. Roll 1560. Bureau of the Census. Series T624. Heritage Quest Online, http://persi.heritagequestonline.com/.

Manuscript Census of the United States: Harris County, Texas. 1920. Rolls 1812–1814. Bureau of the Census. Series T625. Clayton Genealogy Library. Houston Public Library. Houston, Texas.

Manuscript Census of the United States: Harris County, Texas, 1930. Roll 2347. Bureau of the Census. Series T626. Heritage Quest Online. http://persi.heritagequestonline.com/.

Manuscript Census of the United States: Jackson County, Texas, 1900. Roll 1648. Bureau of the Census. Series T623XXX. Heritage Quest Online. http://persi.heritagequestonline.com/.

Manuscript Census of the United States: Jackson County, Texas, 1910. Roll 1567. Bureau of the Census. Series T624. Heritage Quest Online. http://persi.heritagequestonlin.com/.

Manuscript Census of the United States: Montgomery County, Texas, 1900. Roll 1660. Bureau of the Census. Series T623; and Roll 2345, Series T626. Heritage Quest Online. http://persi.heritagequestonline.com.

Manuscript Census of the United States: Montgomery County, Texas, 1910. Roll 1579. Bureau of the Census. Series T624. Heritage Quest Online. http://persi.heritagequestonline.com/.

Manuscript Census of the United States: Montgomery County, Texas, 1920. Roll 1834. Bureau of the Census. Series T625. Heritage Quest Online. http://persi.heritagequestonline.com/.

Manuscript Census of the United States: Orange County, Texas, 1910. Roll 1582. Bureau of the Census. Series T624. Heritage Quest Online. http://persi.heritagequestonline.com/.

Manuscript Census of the United States: Travis County, Texas, 1880. Roll 1329. Bureau of the Census. Series T9. Heritage Quest Online. http://persi.heritagequestonline.com/.

Manuscript Census of the United States: Walker County, Texas, 1900. Roll 1676. Bureau of the Census. Series T623. Heritage Quest Online. http://persi.heritagequestonline.com/.

Manuscript Census of the United States: Waller County, Texas, 1910. Roll 1593. Bureau of the Census. Series T624. Heritage Quest Online. http://persi.heritagequestonline.com/.

McDavid, Fountain L. Texas Death Index. Harris County. July 14, 1934. certificate number 32621. Texas Death Index. Ancestry.com. http://search.ancestry.com/.

McDavid, Percy H. California Death Index, 1940–1997. Los Angeles. May 2, 1975. California Department of Health Services. Center for Health Statistics. Ancestry.com. http://search.ancestry.com/.

McDavid, Russell. California Death Index, 1940–1997. Los Angeles. October 28, 1969. California Department of Health Services. Center for Health Statistics. Ancestry.com. http://search.ancestry.com.

Michigan Deaths, 1971–1996. Michigan Department of Vital and Health Records. Michigan Death Index. Lansing, Michigan. Ancestry.com. http://search.ancestry.com/.

Offenses Against Public Morals, Decency and Chastity. The Penal Code of the State of Texas. 16th Leg. § 11.7. Galveston: A. H. Belo, 1879.

Offenses Against Public Policy. The Penal Code of the State of Texas, 32nd Leg. § 11.11. Austin: Austin Printing Co., 1911.

Public Charter and Revised Codes of Ordinances of the City of Houston, Texas, 1904. Texas Room, Houston Public Library, Houston, Texas 1904.

Public Morals and Decency, Ch. 30 XXX, § 1583b, Revised Codes of Ordinances of the City of Houston, Texas, 1922. Houston: Texas Room, Houston Public Library, 1922.

Public Schools. Chapter 61, Art 949. Public Charter and Revised Codes of Ordinances of the City of Houston, Texas, 1904. Texas Room, Houston Public Library, Houston, Texas, 1904.

Social Service Department Client Case Files. Boxes 24–1674, 1882–6600, 11851–12651, 12984–15153, 15170–16536, 17041–17821. Harris County Records Center. Harris County, Texas. Harris County subsequently transferred this Collection to the Harris County Archives, Harris County Criminal Justice Center, Houston, Texas.

Sunnyside Working Plan, Sunnyside Area Study Area and Sections. Houston's Neighborhood Improvement Planning Program. September 1973. City of Houston Planning and Development. City of Houston Annex. Houston, Texas.

Texas Death Index, 1903–2000. Ancestry.com. http://www.ancestry.com/.

Texas Department of Health, Bureau of Vital Statistics, Texas Births, 1930–1950. Texas Department of Health, Bureau of Vital Statistics, Austin, Texas.

Texas Department of Health, Bureau of Vital Statistics, Texas Mortality, 1930–1950. Texas Department of Health, Bureau of Vital Statistics, Austin, Texas.

United States Census Bureau, Campbell Gibson, and Kay Jung, *Historical Census Statistics On Population Totals By Race, 1790 to 1990, and by Hispanic Origin, 1970 to 1990, for Large Cities and Other Urban Places in the United States.* http://www.census.gov/population/www/documentation/twps0076/twps0076.html#intro.

United States Census Bureau, Sonya Rastogi, Tallese D. Johnson, Elizabeth M. Hoeffel, and Malcolm P. Drewery Jr. *The Black Population: 2010,* http://www.census.gov/population/race/publications/.

United States Census Bureau, *United States Census 2010,* http://2010.census.gov/2010census/# [this site changes to 2010.census.gov Jan 1, 2013].

United States Department of Labor, Division of Negro Economic. *Negro Migration in 1916–1917.* 1918. Reprint. Negro Universities Press, 1969.

Voter Registration List, Detroit, Michigan, May 30, 1940. In Voter Registration Lists, Public Record Filings, Historical Residential Records, and Other Household Database Listings. US Public Records Index, vol. 2. Ancestry.com. http://search.ancestry.com/.

Williams, Simmie Bartholomew. World War I Draft Registration Card, 1917–1918. Ancestry.com. http://search.ancestry.com/.

Works Progress Administration files. Harris County Archives. Harris County Criminal Justice Center. Houston, Harris County, Texas.

Manuscript Collections

Adair, Christia Collection. Houston Metropolitan Research Center. Houston Public Library. Julia Ideson Building. Houston, Texas.

Ames, Jesse Daniel. Papers, 1866–1972. 3686. Louis Round Wilson Special Collections Library. University of North Carolina at Chapel Hill. Chapel Hill, North Carolina. http://www.lib.unc.edu/mss/inv/a/Ames,Jessie_Daniel.html.

Bryant, Thelma Scott Collection. African American Library at the Gregory School. Houston Public Library. Julia Ideson Building. Houston. Texas.

Collins, Jeff. Family Collection. Houston Metropolitan Research Center. Houston Public Library. Julia Ideson Building. Houston, Texas.

Colored Trainmen Union. Houston Metropolitan Research Center. Houston Public Library. Julia Ideson Building. Houston, Texas.

Covington, Dr. Benjamin. Papers. Houston Metropolitan Research Center. Houston Public Library. Julia Ideson Building. Houston, Texas.

Crawford, Vanita E & Antioch Baptist Church Collection. Houston Metropolitan Research Center. Houston Public Library. Julia IdlesonIdeson Building. Houston, Texas

Cullinan, Joseph Stephen Collection. Houston Metropolitan Research Center. Houston Public Library. Julia Ideson Building. Houston, Texas.

University. New Orleans, Louisiana.

Dupree, Anna Collection. Houston Metropolitan Research Center. Houston Public Library. Julia Ideson Building. Houston, Texas.

Franklin Beauty School Collection. Houston Metropolitan Research Center. Houston Public Library. Julia Ideson Building. Houston. Texas.

Harrison Family Collection. Houston Metropolitan Research Center. Houston Public Library. Julia Ideson Building. Houston, Texas.

Hicks Family Collection. Houston Metropolitan Research Center. Houston Public Library. Houston, Texas.

HMRC Photograph Collection. Houston Metropolitan Research Center. Houston Public Library, Julia Ideson Building. Houston, Texas.

Houston, Joshua. Family Collection. Houston Metropolitan Research Center. Houston Public Library. Julia Ideson Building. Houston, Texas.

Houston Young Women's Christian Association Collection. Houston Metropolitan Research Center. Houston Public Library. Julia Ideson Building. Houston, Texas.

Insurance Surveys. Archives of the Archdiocese of Galveston-Houston. Archdiocese of Galveston-Houston. Houston, Texas.

Jacquet, Illinois S. Collection. Houston Metropolitan Research Center. Houston Public Library. Julia Ideson Building. Houston, Texas.

Johnson, General and Mary L. Jones Collection. Houston Metropolitan Research Center. Houston Public Library. Julia Ideson Building. Houston, Texas.

Josephite Collection. Archdiocese of Galveston-Houston Archives. Archdiocese of Galveston-Houston. Houston, Texas.

Larkin, Milton Collection. Houston Metropolitan Research Center. Houston Public Library. Julia Ideson Building. Houston, Texas.

Lipscomb-Alyn Collection. Dolph Briscoe Center for American History. University of Texas. Austin, Texas.

Married Ladies Social, Art & Charity Club Records. Houston Metropolitan Research Center. Houston Public Library. Julia Ideson Building. Houston, Texas.

McCullough, Olee Yates. Papers. Houston Metropolitan Research Center. Houston Public Library. Julia Ideson Building. Houston, Texas.

National Association for the Advancement of Colored People Papers. Reel 19 of 20. part 12: Selected Branch Files, 1913–1939. Series A: The South. Edited by John H. Bracey Jr. and August Meier. Bethesda, Maryland: University Publications of America, 1991, located at M. D. Anderson Library, University of Houston, Houston, Texas.

Perry, Helen G. Family Collection. Houston Metropolitan Research Center. Houston Public Library, Julia Ideson Building. Houston, Texas.

Photograph Collection. Archives of the Archdiocese of Galveston-Houston. Archdiocese of Galveston-Houston. Houston, Texas.

Photograph Collection. Houston Metropolitan Research Center. Houston Public Library, Julia Ideson Building. Houston, Texas.

Price, Rev. Moses L. Papers. Houston Metropolitan Research Center. Houston Public Library. Julia Ideson Building. Houston, Texas.
Ransom, Ethel. Art and Literary Club Records. Houston Metropolitan Research Center. Houston Public Library. Julia Ideson Building. Houston, Texas.
Rhone Family. Papers, 1886–1971. Afro-American Collection. Center for American History. University of Texas. Austin, Texas.
Rice, C. W., Family and *Negro Labor News* Collection. Houston Metropolitan Research Center. Houston Public Library. Julia Ideson Building. Houston, Texas.
Richardson Sr., C. F. Papers. Houston Metropolitan Research Center. Houston Public Library. Julia Ideson Building. Houston, Texas.
Robinson Sr., Judson. Family Collection. Houston Metropolitan Research Center, Houston Public Library. Julia Ideson Building. Houston, Texas.
Simpson, L. H., Rev., & Pleasant Hill Baptist Church Collection. Houston Metropolitan Research Center, Houston Public Library. Julia Ideson Building. Houston, Texas
Selected African American Collections. Houston Metropolitan Research Center. Houston Public Library. Houston, Texas.
Sneed Family Collection. Houston Metropolitan Research Center. Houston Public Library. Julia Ideson Building. Houston, Texas.
St. Joseph's Society of the Sacred Heart, Inc. Parish Annual Report by Year. St. Nicholas. Archives, Diocese of Galveston-Houston, Houston Texas.
Sullivan, Maurice J., Papers. Houston Metropolitan Research Center. Houston Public Library. Julia Ideson Building. Houston, Texas.
Sutton Family File. University of Texas at San Antonio. Texas Women's History Project. Archives for Research on Women and Gender Project. University of Texas at San Antonio Library. San Antonio, Texas.
Texas Commission on Interracial Cooperation Papers. Houston Metropolitan Research Center. Houston Public Library. Houston, Texas.
Yates, Rev. Jack. Family and Antioch Baptist Church Collection. Houston Metropolitan Research Center. Houston Public Library. Julia Ideson Building. Houston, Texas.
Zeta Amicae Records. Houston Metropolitan Research Center. Houston Public Library. Julia Ideson Building. Houston, Texas.

Maps

Alexander, A. Houston Street Guide, 1913. Map. (Houston: J. M. Kelsen). Texas State Library and Archives Division. Historic Maps of Texas Cities, Map Collection. Perry-Castañeda Library. University of Texas Libraries. University of Texas at Austin. Austin, Texas.
Department of Public Works, City of Houston. *Super Neighborhood Map of Houston, Texas.* Houston: Department of Public Works, 2004.
Gallo, Rafael. *Louisiana Points of Departure, 1900–1941.* Houston: NP, 2011.
Glass, James L. Compiler. "The Actualization of Houston, Texas: 1823–42." In *Surveys, Field Notes, Documents and Maps.* Houston: N.P., N.D.

Houston Northeast. 1922, Map, Historical Maps of Texas Cities, Map Collection, Perry-Castañeda Library, University of Texas Libraries, University of Texas at Austin, Austin, Texas Nierth, Larry, *City of Houston Select Super Neighborhood Boundaries*. Houston: Department of Planning and Development, GIS Division, 2011.

—. *Texas Places of Departure, 1900–1941*. Houston: Department of Planning and Development, GIS Division, 2011.

Memoirs, Autobiographies, Obituaries, City Directories, and Miscellaneous

"A Service of Christian Worship in Memory of Sister Kathleen Stewart. Saturday, October 10, 1981." Obituary. In possession of the author.

Annual Report, Houston Community Chest, 1930." Box 4, Folder 5. Simpson, L. H., Rev., & Pleasant Hill Baptist Church Collection. Houston Metropolitan Research Center, Houston Public Library. Julia Ideson Building. Houston, Texas.

Baker, Wendell. *"If Not Me, Who?" What One Man Accomplished in His Battle for Equality*. Huntsville: N.P., 2004.

Bryant, Thelma Scott. *Pioneer Families of Houston (Early 1900s) as Remembered by Thelma Scott Bryant*. Houston: N.P., 1991.

—. *Our Journey through Houston and U.S. History*, 2nd ed. Houston: N. P., 1997.

Church Anniversary Program. "Vision 2000: The Hope of the Future: Good Hope Missionary Baptist Church Celebrating and Building on 123 Years of Faithful Christian Service," Houston, Texas, 1995. In possession of the author.

"'A Family Is . . . One That Prays Together Stays Together': John and Lillian Stinson; "Stinson + Hicks Family Reunion. Detroit, Michigan. August 11–13, 2000." In possession of the author.

Giles, Robert C. *Changing Times: The Story of the Diocese of Galveston-Houston in Commemoration of Its Founding*. Houston: The Most Reverend John L. Morkovsky, S. T. D., 1972.

Giles, Robert C. "St. Nicholas Church, Houston." In 125th Anniversary: Diocese of Galveston-Houston, 1847–1972. Houston: The Most Reverend John L. Morkovsky, S.T.D. The Diocese of Galveston-Houston, 1972, 104–106.

Giles, Robert C. "Our Mother of Mercy Church, Houston." In 125th Anniversary: Diocese of Galveston-Houston, 1847–1972. Houston: The Most Reverend John L. Morkovsky, S.T.D. The Diocese of Galveston-Houston, 1972, 141–42.

Giles, Robert C., Curtis M. Dowell, and Vivian J. Zermeno. "Josephites Close Centennial Year." A Tribute to the Josephites. Supplement to the *Texas Catholic Herald*, September 10, 1993.

Giles, Robert C., Curtis M. Dowell, and Vivian J. Zermeno. "Josephites Have Logged 90 Years in the Diocese." A Tribute to the Josephites. *The Texas Catholic Herald*, September 10, 1993.

"Homecoming Celebration in Memory of Reverend Elisha Reginald Green." 1999. Obituary. In possession of Vivian Hubbard Seals. Houston, Texas.

"Homecoming Service Honoring Lela A. Robinson." 1999. Obituary. In possession of Vivian Hubbard Seals.

"Houston Chapters of Zeta Phi Beta Sorority Honor Dr. Thelma Patten-Law, MRs. Jayne Robinson, and Miss Nancy Smith at the Finer Woman Observance," Texas Southern University Music Center Auditorium, March 25, 1962, Houston, Texas. In possession of the author.

"Independence Heights, Texas: The First Black City in Texas, 1915–1928." 1997. Researched and compiled by Vivian Hubbard Seals. Texas Room. Houston Public Library. Houston, Texas.

"In Loving Memory of Bertha Pruitt," December 15, 1984. Obituary. Detroit, Michigan. "In Loving Memory of Ellis Montgomery Knight." March 6, 1997. Obituary. Houston, Texas. In possession of J. R. Knight.

"In Loving Memory of a Great Man: Clarence Edward Pruitt." January 6, 2001. Obituary. Detroit, Michigan, in possession of the author.

"In Loving Memory of Lucille Knight Lewis." October 6, 1989. Obituary. Houston, Texas. In possession of J. R. Knight.

Knight Family Reunion Book. "Our History." 1997. In possession of J. R. Knight. Houston, Texas.

Morrison & Fourmy's General Directory of the City of Houston, 1900–1901. Galveston: Morrison & Fourmy, 1900. Ancestry.com. http://search.ancestry.com/.

Morrison & Fourmy's General Directory of the City of Houston, Texas, City Directory. Houston: Morrison & Fourny Directory Co. 1926. *Ancestry.com. http://search.ancestry.com.*

Morrison & Fourmy's General Directory of the City of Houston, 1939. Houston: Morrison & Fourmy, 1939. Ancestry.com, http://search.ancestry.com/.

Polk, R. L., and Company. Polk's Houston City Directory. Houston, TX, USA: R. L. Polk, 1917. Ancestry.com. http://www.ancestry.com/.

Robey, Don Deadric, II. Obituary. *Houston Chronicle.* January 4, 2007.

Rhone, Calvin L., Sr. Obituary. *Western Star,* January 29, 1921. Rhone Family Papers, 1886–1971. 3U180:1. Afro-American Collection. Center for American History. University of Texas. Austin, Texas.

Richardson Jr., Clifton. Interview by Louis Marchiafava and Veronica Perry. Digitized tape recording. Houston Oral History Project. Houston Metropolitan Research Center. Houston, Texas, 9 June 1975, http://digital.houstonlibrary.org/oral-history/cliff-richardson.php.

Scott, Emmett J. Editor. *The Red Book of Houston: A Compendium of Social, Professional, Religious, Educational, and Industrial Interests of Houston's Colored Population.* Houston: Sotex, 1915.

Seals, Vivian Hubbard. "Three Generations of Hubbards and Room for More . . ." Hubbard Family Reunion Book. "Hubbard Family Reunion: Getting to Know You." 1992. In possession of Vivian Hubbard Seals. Houston, Texas.

"A Service of Christian Worship in Memory of Sister Kathleen Stewart." Saturday, October 10, 1981." Obituary. In possession of author.

Simon, Jessie. "Funeral Director Althea Antoinette Robey Laid to Rest." *African-American News & Issues.* July 23, 2003.

Stullivan, Luther. *Roots of the Stullivan Family.* Houston: N. P., 1981.

Texas Southern University Alumni Directory, 1947–1999. Houston: Texas Southern University, 2000.

University of Houston. Center for Public History. "Bibliography of Works." Unpublished Bibliography. Houston, Texas, July 10, 2010. In the possession of author.

Williams, David. "A Brief History of St. James Methodist Church." N. P. 1934. In possession of Wendell H. Baker. Huntsville, Texas.

Sound Recordings

Phillips, Washington. "Take Your Burden to the Lord and Leave It There." Recorded December 2, 1927, Dallas, Texas, 145305–1. Columbia Phonograph Co. January 21, 1973. New York, New York. LP, RE 16588, 14277-D. And on *The Keys to the Kingdom*, B0006TR054. March 2005. Yazoo, compact disc. www.fretlesszithers.com; http://www.wirz.de/music/philwfrm.htm, April 26, 2012.

Speeches

Washington, Booker T. "The Atlanta Compromise." The Cotton States and International Exposition, Atlanta, Georgia, September 18, 1895.

Vertical Files Collection

Houston. Annexation. Chronological Listing. Vertical Files. Texas Room. Houston Public Library. Houston, Texas.

Houston. Charter of Communities. Research Publication. Vertical Files. Texas Room. Houston Public Librar. Houston, Texas

Houston. Population. Vertical Files. Texas Room. Houston Public Library. Houston, Texas.

Houston. Subdivisions. Fifth Ward. Vertical Files. Texas Room. Houston Public Library. Houston, Texas.

Houston. Subdivisions. Fourth Ward. Vertical Files. Texas Room. Houston Public Library. Houston, Texas.

Houston. Subdivisions. Frenchtown. Vertical Files. Texas Room. Houston Public Library. Houston, Texas.

Houston. Subdivisions. Third Ward. Vertical Files. Texas Room. Houston Public Library. Houston, Texas.

Houston. Subdivisions. Wards. Vertical Files. Texas Room. Houston Public Library. Houston, Texas.

Videocassettes and Digital Video Disks

Eyes on the Prize: America's Civil Rights Years, Vol. 2. "Ain't Scared of Your Jails, 1960–1961." Directed and produced by Orlando Bagwell, 120 min. Blackside Inc. Videocassette, 1987.

Fatal Flood: A Story of Greed, Power, and Race. Directed and produced by Chana Gazit,

60 minutes, A Steward/Gazit Productions, Inc. film for *American Experience*. Videocassette and digital video disk, 2001.
In the Name of Colored High, '04. Produced by Gretchen Hollingsworth, 95 minutes. Houston: Self-Produced. DVD, 1993.
Sankofa. Directed and produced by Haile Gerima, 120 minutes. Mypheduh Films, Inc. Videocassette and DVD, 1993.
The Strange Demise of Jim Crow. Produced by Thomas R. Cole, 56 minutes. California Newsreel. DVD, 1998.
This Is My Home, It Is Not For Sale. Directed and produced by Jon Schwartz, 194 min., Riverside Productions. Videocassette, 1987.
When the Levees Broke: A Requiem in Four Acts. Directed and produced by Spike Lee, 270 minutes. HBO Documentary Films. Televised production.

Books, Book Chapters, Scholarly Periodicals, and Newspapers

Abbott, Carl. "Urbanizing the Sunbelt." *OAH Magazine* 18, no. 1 (2003): 6–16.
Abernathy, Francis E., Patrick B. Mullen, and Alan B. Govenar, eds. *Juneteenth Texas: Essays in African-American Folklore*. Denton, Texas: University of North Texas, 1996.
Acuña, Rodolfo. *Occupied America: A History of Chicanos* (New York: Longman, 2003).
Adams, Luther. *Way Up North in Louisville: African American Migration in the Urban South, 1930–1970*. Chapel Hill: University of North Carolina Press, 2010.
—. "African American Migration to Louisville in the Mid Twentieth Century" *Register of the Kentucky Historical Society* 99, nol 4 (2001): 363–384.
Akbar, Na'im. *Breaking the Chains of Psychological Slavery*. Tallahassee: Mind Productions & Associates, 1993.
Alexander, J. Trent. "'They're Never Here More Than a Year': Return Migration in the Southern Exodus, 1940–1970," *Journal of Social History* 38, no. 3 (2005): 653–71.
"The Amalgamation of Local 47 and 647." Professional Musicians Local 47. http://www.promusic47.org/amalgamation.htm.
Anderson, Gary Clayton. *The Conquest of Texas: Ethnic Cleansing in the Promised Land, 1820–1875*. Norman: University of Oklahoma Press, 2005.
Anderson, James D. *The Education of Blacks in the South, 1860–1935*. Chapel Hill: University of North Carolina Press, 1988.
Anderson, Karen Tucker. "Last Hired, First Fired: Black Women Workers during World War II." *Journal of American History* 69 (June 1982): 82–97.
Arbingast, Stanley A. *Atlas of Texas*. Austin: Bureau of Business Research, University of Texas, 1963.
Arnesen, Eric. *Brotherhoods of Color: Black Railroad Workers and the Struggle for Equality*. Cambridge: Harvard University Press, 2002.
—. *Black Waterfront Workers of New Orleans: Race, Class, and Politics, 1863–1923*. Urbana: University of Illinois Press, 1994.
Baldwin, Davarian. *Chicago's New Negroes: Modernity, the Great Migration & Black Urban Life*. Chapel Hill: University of North Carolina Press, 2007.

Barbeau, Arthur E., and Florette Henri. *The Unknown Soldier: Black American Troops in World War I*. With a new introduction from Bernard C. Nalty. Philadelphia: Temple University Press, 1974; New York: Da Capo Press of Perseus Publishing, 1996; Philadelphia: Temple University Press, 1974.

Barber, Henry E. "Association of Southern Women for the Prevention of Lynching." *Phylon* 34, no. 4 (1973): 378–89.

Bardin, James T. "Science and the 'Negro Problem.'" In *The Development of Segregationist Thought*. Edited by I. E. Newby. Homewood, Illinois: Dorsey Press, 1968.

Baraki, Amiri. *Blues People*. New York: Morrow Quill, 1963.

Barkan, Elliott Robert. *And Still They Came: Immigrants and American Society, 1920–1990s*. Arlington Heights, Ill.: Harlan Davidson, 1996.

Barr, Alwyn. *Black Texans: A History of African Americans in Texas, 1528–1995*. Norman: University of Oklahoma Press, 1996.

—. *Reconstruction to Reform: Texas Politics, 1876–1906*. 1971. Reprint Dallas: Southern Methodist University Press, 2000.

Barry, John M. *Rising Tide: The Great Mississippi Flood of 1927 and How It Changed America*. New York: Simon and Schuster, 1998.

—. "After the Deluge: In the Wake of Hurricane Katrina, A Writer Looks Back at the Repercussions of Another Great Disaster—the Mississippi Flood of 1927." Smithsonian Magazine.Com. November 2005. http://www.smithsonianmag.com/history-archaeology/pom.html

Bay, Mia. "The Improbable Ida B. Wells." *Reviews in American History* 30, no. 3 (2002): 439–44.

Beauboeuf, Bruce Andre. "War and Change: Houston's Economic Ascendancy during World War I." *Houston Review: History and Culture of the Gulf Coast* 14 (Fall 1992): 89–112.

Beeth, Howard. "Historians, Houston, and History." In *Black Dixie: Afro-Texan History and Culture in Houston*. Edited by Howard Beeth and Cary D. Wintz. College Station: Texas A&M University Press, 1992.

Beeth, Howard, and Cary D. Wintz, eds. *Black Dixie: Afro-Texan History and Culture in Houston*. College Station: Texas A&M University Press, 1992.

—, eds. "Economic and Social Development in Black Houston during the Era of Segregation." In *Black Dixie: Afro-Texan History and Culture in Houston*. Edited by Howard Beeth and Cary D. Wintz. College Station: Texas A&M University Press, 1992.

—. eds. "Segregation, Violence and Civil Rights: Race Relations in Twentieth Century Houston." In *Black Dixie: Afro-Texan History and Culture in Houston*. Edited by Howard Beeth and Cary D. Wintz. College Station: Texas A&M University Press, 1992.

—. eds. "Slavery and Freedom: Blacks in Nineteenth-Century Houston." In *Black Dixie: Afro-Texan History and Culture in Houston*. Edited by Howard Beeth and Cary D. Wintz. College Station: Texas A&M University Press, 1992.

Benjamin, Karen. "Progressivism Meets Jim Crow: Curriculum Revision and Development in Houston, Texas, 1924–1929." *Paedagogica Historica* 39 (August 2003): 457–76.

Bernstein, Barton J., ed. "The New Deal: The Conservative Achievements of Liberal

Reform." In *Twentieth Century America: Recent Interpretations,* 2nd ed. San Diego: Harcourt Brace Jovanovich, 1972.

Blackwelder, Julia Kirk . *Now Hiring: The Feminization of Work in the United States, 1900–1995.* College Station: Texas A&M University Press, 1997.

—. *Styling Jim Crow: African-American Beauty Training during Segregation.* College Station: Texas A&M University Press, 2003.

Blair, Barbara. "Though Justice Sleeps, 1880–1900." In *To Make Our World Anew: A History of African Americans from 1880,* vol. 2. Edited by Robin D. G. Kelley and Earl Lewis. New York: Oxford University Press, 2000.

Blanton, Carlos Kevin. "Deconstructing Texas: The Diversity of People, Place, and Historical Imagination in Recent Texas History." *In Beyond Texas Through Time: Breaking Away from Past Interpretations.* College Station: Texas A.& M. University Press, 2011.

Blassingame, John W. *The Slave Community.* New York: Oxford University Press, 1974.

—. *Black New Orleans, 1860–1880* (Chicago: University of Chicago Press, 1976).

Blee, Kathleen. *Women of the Klan: Racism and Gender in the 1920s.* Berkeley: University of California Press, 1991.

Bodnar, John. *The Transplanted: A History of Immigrants in Urban America.* First Midland Book Edition. Bloomington: Indiana University Press, 1987.

Bontemps, Alex. *The Punished Self: Surviving Slavery in the Colonial South.* Ithaca: Cornell University Press, 2001.

Borchert, James. *Alley Life in Washington: Family, Community, Religion, and Folklife in the City, 1850–1970.* Urbana: University of Illinois Press, 1980.

Botson Jr., Michael R. "Jim Crow Wearing Steel-Toed Shoes and Safety Glasses: Duel Unionism at the Hughes Tool Company." *Houston Review: History and Culture of the Gulf Coast* 16 (Winter 1994): 101–16.

—. *Labor, Civil Rights, and the Hughes Tool Company.* College Station: Texas A&M University Press, 2005.

Boutwell, Bryant. "Two Bachelors, a Vision and the Texas Medical Center," *The Houston Review of History and Culture* 2, no. 1 (Fall 2004): 9–14.

Boyd, Melba Joyce. "A Review Essay: Canon Configuration for Ida B. Wells-Barnett." *Black Scholar* 24, no. 1 (1994): 8–13.

Brasseaux, Carl A., Keith P. Fontenot, and Claude F. Oubre. *Creoles of Color in the Bayou Country.* Jackson: University Press of Mississippi, 1994.

Brewer, J. Mason. *American Negro Folklore.* 1968. Reprint Chicago: Quadrangle Books, 1972.

Brooks, Tim. *Lost Sounds: Blacks and the Birth of the Recording Industry, 1890–1919.* Urbana: University of Illinois Press, 2004).

Broussard, Albert. *Black San Francisco: The Struggle for Racial Equality in the West,1900–1954.* Lawrence: University of Kansas Press, 1993.

Brown, Tamara L., Gregory S. Parks, Clarenda M. Phillips, ed., *African American Fraternities And Sororities: The Legacy And The Vision.* Knoxville: University of Tennessee Press, 2005.

Brownell, Blaine A. "The Urban South Comes of Age, 1900–1940," in *The City in*

Southern History: The Growth of Urban Civilization in the South. Edited by Blaine A. Brownell and David R. Goldfield. Port Washington: Kennikat, 1977.

Brownell, Blaine, and David R. Goldfield. "Southern Urban History." In *The City in Southern History: The Growth of Urban Civilization in the South.* Port Washington, N.Y.: Kennikat, 1977.

Brownell, Blaine A., and David Goldfield, eds. *The City in Southern History: The Growth of Urban Civilization in the South.* New York: National University Publication, 1977.

Bryant, Ira. *Houston's Negro Schools.* Houston: Informer, 1935.

Bryant Jr., Ira B. *Texas Southern University and Its Antecedents, Political Origins, and Future.* Houston: Bryant, 1975.

———. *Andrew Jackson Young, Mr. Ambassador: United States Ambassador to the United Nations.* Houston: Armstrong, 1979.

Buckner, Reginald. "A History of Music Education in the Black Community Kansas City, Kansas, 1905–1954." *Journal of Research in Music Education* 30, no. 2 (1982): 94–100.

Bullard, Robert. *Invisible Houston: The Black Experience in Boom and Bust.* College Station: Texas A&M University Press, 1987.

Bullock, Henry Allan. "Some Readjustments of the Texas Negro Family to the Emergency of War." *Southwestern Social Science Quarterly* 25 (June 1944–March 1945): 101–17.

Byrd, Ayanda D., and Lori T. Tharps, *Hair Story: Untangling the Roots of Black Hair in America.* New York: St. Martin's Press, 2001.

Calvert, Robert A. "Agrarian Texas." In *Texas Through Time: Evolving Interpretations.* Edited by Walter A. Buenger and Robert A. Calvert. College Station: Texas A&M University Press, 1991.

———, Gregg Cantrell, and Arnoldo DeLeón, *The History of Texas.* 3rd ed. Wheeling, Illinois: Harlan-Davidson, 2002.

Campbell, Randolph. *An Empire for Slavery: The Peculiar Institution in Texas, 1821–1865.* College Station: Texas A&M University Press, 1989.

———. *Grass-Roots Reconstruction in Texas, 1865–1880.* Baton Rouge: Louisiana State University, 1997.

———. *Gone to Texas: A History of the Lone Star State.* New York: Oxford University Press, 2004.

Cantrell, Gregg. and Barton D. Scott, "Texas Populists and the Failure of Biracial Politics. *Journal of Southern History* 55 (November 1989): 659–92.

———. "Racial Violence and Reconstruction Politics in Texas, 1867–1868." *Southwestern Historical Quarterly* 93, no. 3 (1990): 333–55.

———. *Kenneth and John B. Rayner and the Limits of Southern Dissent.* Urbana: University of Illinois Press, 1993.

———. *Feeding the Wolf: John B. Rayner and the Politics of Race, 1850–1918.* College Station: 2001.

Carlton, Don. *Red Scare! Right-wing Hysteria, Fifties Fanaticism, and Their Legacy in Texas.* Austin: University of Texas Press, 1985.

Carrigan, William D. *The Making of a Lynching Culture: Violence and Vigilantism in Central Texas, 1836–1916.* Urbana: University of Illinois Press, 2004.

Cell, John W. *The Highest Stage of White Supremacy: The Origins of Segregation in South Africa and the American South.* 1982. Reprint. New York: Cambridge University Press, 1989.
Chapman, Betty Trapp. *Houston Women: Invisible Threads in the Tapestry.* Virginia Beach: Donning, 2000.
——. "Fifth Ward: Ethnic Melting Pot and Industrial Business District," in "Houston Heritage," *Houston Business Journal,* n.d., Houston—Subdivisions—Wards, Vertical Files
Chauncey, George. *Gay New York: Gender, Urban Culture, and the Making of the Gay Male World, 1890–1940.* New York: Basic Books, 1994.
Christian, Garna L. *Black Soldiers in Jim Crow Texas, 1899–1917.* College Station: Texas A&M
University Press, 1985.
——. "Texas Beginnings: Houston in the World of Jazz," *Houston Review: History and Culture of the Gulf Coast* 12, no. 2 (1990): 144–55.
Clement. Rufus E. "Educational Programs for the Improvement of Race Relations: Interracial Committees." *Journal of Negro Education* 13, no. 3 (1944), 316–20.
Cohen, William. *At Freedom's Edge: Black Mobility and the Southern White Quest for Racial Control, 1861–1915.* Baton Rouge: Louisiana State University Press, 1994.
Cole, Thomas R. *No Color Is My Kind: The Life of Eldrewey Stearns and the Integration of Houston.* Austin: University of Texas, 1997.
Cole, William E. "The Role of the Commission on Interracial Cooperation in War and Peace." *Social Forces* 21, no. 4 (May 1943), 456–63.
Collins, Donna. "Greeks." In *The Ethnic Groups of Houston.* Edited by Fred von der Mehden. College Station: Texas A&M University.
Collins, Lisa Gail. *The Art of History: African American Women Artists Engage the Past.* New Brunswick: Rutgers University Press, 2002.
Conrad, Glenn R., and Carl A. Brasseaux. *Crevasse! The 1927 Flood In Acadiana.* Lafayette: Center for Louisiana Studies, 1994.
Couvares, Frances G., Martha Saxton, Gerald N. Grob, George Athan Billias, eds. *Interpretations of American History,* vol. 2, 8th ed. Boston: Bedford/St. Martin's, 2009.
Crawford, Audrey. "'To Protect, to Feed, and to Give Momentum to Every Effort': African American Clubwomen in Houston, 1880–1910," *Houston Review of History and Culture* 1 (Fall 2003): 15–23.
Crew, Spencer R. *Black Life in Secondary Cities: Comparative Analysis of the Black Communities of Camden and Elizabeth, New Jersey, 1860–1920.* New York: Garland, 1993.
Cripps, Thomas. *Making Movies Black: The Hollywood Message Movie from World War II to the Civil Rights Era.* New York: Oxford University Press, 1993.
——. *Slow Fade to Black: The Negro in American Film, 1900–1942* (New York: Oxford University Press, 1993).
Cronin, Mary M. "C. F. Richardson and the *Houston Informer*'s Fight for Racial Equality in the 1920s." *American Journalism* 23, no. 3 (Summer 2006): 79–103.
Crouch, Barry A. *The Freedmen's Bureau and Black Texans* (Austin: University of Texas Press, 1999).

Dailey, Maceo C. "Neither 'Uncle Tom' Nor 'Accommodationist': Booker T. Washington, Emmett Jay Scott, and Constructionalism." *Atlanta History* 38, no. 4 (1995): 20–33.

Dalfiume, Richard. "The 'Forgotten Years' of the Negro Revolution." *Journal of American History* 55 (June 1968): 90–106.

Darden, Robert. "People Get Ready": A New History of Black Gospel Music. New York: Continuum, 2011.

Davidson, Basil. *The African Genius: An Introduction to African Social and Cultural History* (London: Atlantic-Little, Brown Books, 1969).

Davis, Alicia. "Christia V. Adair: A Servant of Humanity," *Texas Historian* 38, no. 1 (1977): 1–7.

Davis, Cyprian, OSB. *The History of Black Catholics in the United States*. New York: Crossroads, 1990.

Davis, Francis. *The History of the Blues: The Roots, the Music, the People*. Cambridge, Mass.: De Capo Press, 1995.

Davis, W. L., and E. O. Smith, "Why Not? The Civic Betterment League Officials Speak Out," *Western Star*, May 10, 1918.

De Graaf, Lawrence B., Kevin Mulroy, Quintard Taylor, eds. *Seeking El Dorado: African Americans in California*. Seattle: University of Washington Press, 2004.

de Jong, Greta. *A Different Day: African American Struggles for Justice in Rural Louisiana, 1900–1970*. Chapel Hill: University of North Carolina Press, 2002.

De León, Arnoldo. *Ethnicity in the Sunbelt: Mexican Americans in Houston*, 2nd ed. College Station: Texas A&M University Press, 2003.

—. "Texas Mexicans: Twentieth Century Interpretations," in *Texas Through Time: Evolving Interpretations*, eds. Walter L. Buenger and Robert A. Calvert (College Station: Texas A&M University Press, 1991), 20–35.

Decker, Stephanie. "Women in the Civil Rights Movement: Juanita Craft versus the Dallas Elite." *East Texas Historical Journal* 39 (Spring 2001): 33–42.

Devlin, George A. *South Carolina and Black Migration, 1865–1940*. New York: Garland, 1989.

Diop, Cheikh Anta. *The African Origin of Civilization: Myth or Reality*. Edited and translated by Mercer Cook. 1955. Reprint. Chicago: Lawrence Hill Books, 1974.

Dittmer, John. *Local People: The Struggle for Civil Rights in Mississippi*. Urbana: University of Illinois Press, 1996.

Domina, Lynn, "Protection in My Mouf: Self, Voice, and Community in Zora Neale Hurston's Dusk Tracks on a Road . . . ," *African American Review* 31, no. 2 (1997): 197–209.

Dressman, Frances. "'Yes, We Have No Jitneys!' Transportation Issues in Houston's Black Community, 1914–1924." In *Black Dixie: Afro-Texan History and Culture in Houston*. Edited by Howard Beeth and Cary D. Wintz. College Station: Texas A&M University Press, 1992.

Du Bois, W. E. B. "Close Ranks," *Crisis*, July 16, 1918. In *W. E. B. Du Bois: A Reader*, ed. David Levering Lewis (New York: Owl Books, 1995), 697.

Du Bois, W. E. B. *The Philadelphia Negro: A Social Study*. 1899. Reprint. with a new introduction by Elijah Anderson. Pennsylvania: University of Pennsylvania Press, 1996.

———. *Souls of Black Folk: A Norton Critical Reader.* Edited by Henry Lewis Gates Jr. and Terri Hume Oliver. 1903. Reprint New York: Norton, 2000.

Duersten, Matthew, "The Arkivists: Unearthing the treasure of Horace Tapscott." *LA Weekly,* April 5, 2006.

Dunbar-Nelson, Alice. "Negro Women in War Work. In *Scott's Official History of the American Negro in the World War.* Edited by Emmett J. Scott. Washington: Emmett J. Scott, 1919. http://net.lib.byu.edu/estu/wwi/comment/Scott/SCh27.htm.

Falola, Toyin, ed. *Africa: African History Before 1885,* vol. 1 (Durham: Carolina Academic Press, 2000).

Farmer, James. *Lay Bare the Heart: An Autobiography of the Civil Rights Movement.* New York: Penguin Books, 1985.

Farrington, Clifford. *Biracial Unions on Galveston's Waterfront, 1865–1925.* College Station: Texas A&M University Press, 2003.

Farrington, Lisa E., *Creating Their Own Image: The History of African American Women Artists* (New York: Oxford University Press, 2004).

Feldman, Claudia. "Historic Fourth Ward Called 'Living Coffin.'" *Houston Chronicle.* September 23, 1976. Houston—Subdivisions—Fourth Ward—Vertical Files. Texas Room, Houston Public Library. Houston, Texas.

Ferrell Jr., Henry C. "Migratory Workers." In *Encyclopedia of the Great Depression.* Edited by Robert McElvaine. New York: Macmillan, 2003, 629–35.

Finkle, Lee. "The Conservative Aims of Militant Rhetoric: Black Protest during World War II. *Journal of American History* 60 (December 1973): 692–713.

Fields, Annette. "More Than a Survivor: Former Wiley President Reaches into His Past, Urges Students to Adapt to Changing World." *Longview News-Journal,* October 20, 1991.

Fisher, Robert. "Protecting Community and Property Values: Civic Clubs in Houston, 1909–1970." In *Urban Texas: Politics and Development.* Edited by Char Miller and Heywood Sanders. College Station: Texas A&M University Press, 1990.

Foley, Neil. *The White Scourge: Mexicans, Blacks, and Poor Whites in Texas Cotton Culture.* Berkeley: University of California Press, 1997.

Foner, Eric. *Reconstruction: America's Unfinished Revolution, 1863–1877.* New York: Harper and Row, 1988.

Foner, Eric. *A Short History of Reconstruction* (New York: Harper and Row, 1990).

Foner, Nancy, and George M. Frederickson. Editor. *Not Just Black and White: Historical and Contemporary Perspectives on Immigration, Race, and Ethnicity in the United States.* New York: Russell Sage Foundation, 2004.

Foner, Phillip S., and Ronald L. Lewis, eds. *The Black Worker: A Documentary History from Colonial Times to the Present.* Philadelphia: Temple University Press, 1980.

Franklin, John Hope, and Elizabeth Brooks Higginbotham. *From Slavery to Freedom: A History of African-Americans.* 9th ed. New York: McGraw Hill, 2011.

Frazier, E. Franklin. *Black Bourgeoisie: The Rise of a New Middle Class.* New York: The Free Press, 1957.

———. *The Negro Family in the United States.* 1948. Rev. and abr. ed. with a foreword by Nathan Huggins. Chicago: University of Chicago Press, 1969.

Frear, Yvonne Davis, "Juanita Craft and the Struggle to End Racial Segregation in Dallas, 1945–1955," in *Major Problems in Texas History*, ed., Sam Haynes and Cary D. Wintz (New York: Houghton-Mifflin, 2002

Fredrickson, George M. *White Supremacy: A Comparative Study in American and South African History.* New York: Oxford University Press, 1981.

Gaines, Kevin K. *Uplifting the Race: Black Leadership, Politics, and Culture in the Twentieth Century.* Chapel Hill: University of North Carolina Press, 1996.

Gamble, Vanessa. "Physicians, Twentieth Century." In *Black Women in America*, vol. 2, 1st ed. Edited by Darlene Clark Hine, Elsa Barkley Brown, and Rosalyn Terborg-Penn. Bloomington: Indiana University Press, 1994.Giddings, Paula. *"When and Where I Enter": The Impact of Black Women on Race and Sex in America.* New York: William Morrow, 1984.

—. *In Search of Sisterhood: Delta Sigma Theta and the Challenge of the Black Sorority Movement.* New York: Quill, 1988.

Gilbert, Erik, and Jonathan T. Reynolds. *Africa in World History: From Prehistory to the Present* (Upper Saddle River, New Jersey: Pearson, 2004).

Gillette, Michael L. "The Rise of the NAACP in Texas," *Southwestern Historical Quarterly,* 81 (June 1978), 393–402.

Gilmore. Glenda Elizabeth. *Gender and Jim Crow: Women and the Politics of White Supremacy in North Carolina, 1896–1920.* Chapel Hill: University of North Carolina Press, 1996.

Gilmore, Glenda Elizabeth. *Defying Dixie: The Radical Roots of Civil Rights, 1919–1950.* New York: W. W. Norton, 2008.

Ginzburg, Ralph. *100 Years of Lynchings.* 1962. Reprint Baltimore: Black Classic Press, 1988.

Glasrud, Bruce A. "From Griggs to Brewer: A Review of Black Texas Culture, 1899–1940." *The Journal of Big Bend Studies* 15 (2003): 195–212.

Glasrud, Bruce, and Merline Pitre. *Black Women in Texas History.* College Station: Texas A&M University Press, 2008.

Glasrud, Bruce A. "Blacks and Texas Politics during the Twenties." *Red River Valley Historical Review,* 7 (1982): 39–53.

Goings, Kenneth W., and Raymond A. Mohl, eds., *The New African American Urban History.* Thousand Oaks, California: Sage Publications, 1996.

Goldfield, David. *Region, Race, and Cities: Interpreting the Urban South.* Baton Rouge: Louisiana University Press, 1997.

—."Writing the Sunbelt," *Organization of American Historians Magazine of History* 18, no. 1 (October 2003): 5–10.

Gomez, Michael. *Exchanging Our Country Marks: The Transformation of African Identities in the Colonial and Antebellum South.* Chapel Hill: University of North Carolina, 1998.

Goodwin, E. Marvin. *Black Migration to America from 1915–1960: An Uneasy Exodus.* Studies in Twentieth Century American History. London: Edwin Mellen Press, 1990.

Gotham, Kevin Fox. "Urban Space, Restrictive Covenants and the Origins of Racial Residential Segregation in a US City, 1900–1950." *International Journal of Urban and Regional Research* 24, no. 3 (2000): 616–29.

Gottlieb, Peter. *Making Their Own Way: Southern Blacks' Migration Experience to Pittsburgh, 1916–30.* Urbana: University of Illinois Press, 1987.
Govenar, Alan. "The Photographs of Benny Joseph." In *Folklife Annual 90: A Publication of the American Folk Center at the Library of Congress.* Edited by James Hardin. Washington: Library of Congress, 1991, 82–99.
—. *Portraits of Community: African American Photography in Texas.* Austin: Texas State Historical Association, 1996.
—. *Texas Blues: The Rise of a Contemporary Sound.* College Station: Texas A&M University Press, 2008.
Graham, Lawrence O. *Our Kind of People: Inside America's Upper Class.* New York: Harper Collins, 1999.
Green, Laurie B. *Battling the Plantation Mentality: Memphis and the Black Freedom Struggle.* Chapel Hill: University of North Carolina Press, 2007.
Greene, Casey. "Guardians Against Change: The Ku Klux Klan in Houston and Harris County, 1920–1925," *Houston Review* 10 (Fall 1988), 3–18.
Greene, Lorenzo. *Selling Black History for Carter G. Woodson: A Diary, 1930–1933.* Edited and with an introduction by Arvarh E. Strickland. Columbia: University of Missouri Press, 1996.
Gregory, James N. *The Southern Diaspora: How the Great Migrations of Black and White Southerners Transformed America.* Chapel Hill: University of North Carolina Press, 2005.
Griffin, Farah Jasmine *"Who Set You Flowin'?": The African-American Migration Narrative.* New York: Oxford University Press, 1996.
Grob, Gerald N. and George Athan Billias, eds. *Interpretations of American History: Patterns and Perspectives,* 2nd ed. 2 vols. New York: The Free Press, 1992.
Grossman, James R. *Land of Hope: Chicago, Black Southerners, and the Great Migration.* Chicago: University of Chicago Press, 1989.
—. "The White Man's Union: The Great Migration and the Resonance of Race and Class in Chicago, 1916–1922." In *The Great Migration in Historical Perspective: New Dimensions of Race, Class, and Gender.* Edited by Joe William Trotter Jr. Bloomington: Indiana University Press, 1991.
—. "A Chance to Make Good, 1900–1929." In *To Make Our World Anew: A History of African Americans.* Edited by Robin D. G. Kelley and Earl Lewis. New York: Oxford University Press, 2000.
Gruening, Martha. "National Association for the Advancement of Colored People—Houston: An NAACP Investigation," *The Crisis,* Nov. 15, 1917.
Haas, Edward F., "The Southern Metropolis." In *The City in Southern History: The Growth of Urban Civilization in the South.* Edited by Blaine A. Brownell and David R. Goldfield. Fort Washington, New York: National University Publications, 1977.
Hahn, Steven. *A Nation Under Our Feet: Black Political Struggles in the Rural South, From Slavery to the Great Migration.* Cambridge: Harvard University Press, 2003.
Hale, Grace Elizabeth. *Making Whiteness: The Culture of Segregation in the South, 1890–1940.* New York: Vintage Book, 1999.

Hales, Douglas. *A Southern Family in White and Black: The Cuneys of Texas*. College Station: Texas A&M University Press, 2003.

Hall, Gwendolyn Midlo. *Africans in Colonial Louisiana: The Development of Afro-Creole Culture in the Eighteenth Century*. Baton Rouge: Louisiana University Press, 1992.

Hall, Gwendolyn Midlo. *Slavery and African Ethnicities in the Americas: Restoring the Links*. Chapel Hill: University of North Carolina Press, 2005.

Hall, Jacqueline Dowd. "The 'Mind That Burns in Each Body": Women, Rape, and Racial Violence," *Southern Exposure* 12, no. 6 (1984): 61–71.

Hall, Jacqueline Dowd, Carol Ruth Berkin, and Mary Beth Norton. "A Truly Subversive Affair: WomenAgainst Lynching in the Twentieth-Century South." In *Women of America: A History*. Written by Carol Ruth Berkin, and Mary Beth Norton. New York: Houghton Mifflin, 1979.

Handlin, Oscar. *The Newcomers: Negroes and Puerto Ricans in a Changing Metropolis*. 1959. Reprint. Garden City, New York: Doubleday, 1962.

Harlan, Louis. *Booker T. Washington: The Making of a Black Leader, 1856–1901*. New York: Oxford University Press, 1972.

—. *Booker T. Washington: The Wizard of Tuskegee, 1901–1915*. New York: Oxford University Press, 1983.

Harris, Stephen L. *Harlem's Hell Fighters: The African-American 369th Infantry in World War I*. Foreword by Ron Paschall. Washington: Brassey's, 2003.

Harris, William H. *Keeping the Faith: A. Philip Randolph, Milton P. Webster, and the Brotherhood of Sleeping Car Porters, 1927–1937*. Urbana: University of Illinois Press, 1977.

—. *The Harder We Run: Black Workers since the Civil War*. New York: Oxford University Press, 1982.

Harrison, Alferdteen, ed. *Black Exodus: The Great Migration from the American South*. Jackson: University Press of Mississippi, 1991.

Hartman, Gary. *The History of Texas Music*. College Station: Texas A&M University Press, 2008.

Haygood, Tamara Miller. "Use and Distribution of Slave Labor in Harris County, Texas, 1830–60." In *Black Dixie: Afro-Texan History and Culture in Houston*. Edited by Howard Beeth and Cary D. Wintz. College Station: Texas A&M University Press, 1992.

Haynes, Robert V. *A Night of Violence: The Houston Riot of 1917*. Baton Rouge: Louisiana State University Press, 1976.

—. "Black Houstonians and the White Democratic Primary, 1920–1945." In *Black Dixie: Afro-Texan History and Culture in Houston*. Edited by Howard Beeth and Cary D. Wintz. College Station: Texas A&M University Press, 1992.

Heintze, Michael R. *Private Black Colleges in Texas, 1865–1954*. College Station: Texas A&M University Press, 1985.

Henderson, Alexa Benson. *Atlanta Life Insurance Company: Black Economic Dignity*. Tuscaloosa: University of Alabama Press, 1990.

Henderson, Archie. "City Planning in Houston, 1920–1930." *Houston Review: History and Culture of the Gulf Coast* 9, no. 3 (1987): 107–29.

Henri, Florette. *Black Migration: Movement North, 1900–1920.* Garden City, New York: Doubleday, 1975.

Herskovits, Melville J. *Myth of the Negro Past.* 1941. Reprint. Boston: Beacon Press, 1990.

Higginbotham, Evelyn Brooks. *Righteous Discontent: The Women's Movement in the Black Baptist Church, 1880–1920.* Cambridge: Harvard University Press, 1993.

—, ed. *Harlem Renaissance Lives: From the African American National Biography* (New York: Oxford University Press, 2009).

Hill, Robert A. Editor. The *Marcus Garvey and Universal Improvement Association Papers,* 10 vols. Berkeley: University of California Press, 2006.

Hine, Darlene Clark. "Black Migration to the Urban Midwest: The Gender Dimension." In *The Great Migration in Historical Perspective: New Dimensions of Race, Class, and Gender.* Edited by Joe William Trotter Jr. Bloomington: Indiana University Press, 1991.

—. *Hine Sight: Black Women and the Reconstruction of American History.* Bloomington: Indiana University Press, 1994.

—. *Black Victory: The Rise and Fall of the White Primary in Texas.* 1979. New edition with essays by Darlene Clark Hine, Steven F. Lawson, and Merline Pitre. Columbia: University of Missouri Press, 2003.

Hine, Darlene Clark, William C. Hine, and Stanley Harrold. *The African-American Odyssey,* 5th ed. Upper Saddle River, New Jersey: Prentice Hall, 2011.

Hine, Darlene Clark, and Ernestine Jenkins, eds. *A Question of Manhood: A Reader in Black Men's History and Masculinity,* 2 vols. Bloomington: Indiana University Press, 1999.

Hine, Darlene Clark, and Kathleen Thompson. *A Shining Thread of Hope: The History of Black Women in America.* New York: Broadway Books, 1998.

Hine, Darlene Clark, and Ernestine Jenkins, ed., Hine, *A Question of Manhood: A Reader in Black Men's History and Masculinity,* 2 vols. Bloomington: Indiana University Press, 1999.

Hine, Darlene Clark, Kathleen Thompson, Elsa Barkley Brown, and Rosalyn Terborg-Penn, eds. *Black Women in America: An Historical Encyclopedia,* 2nd ed. 2, 3 vols. New York: Oxford University Press, 2005.

Himes, Chester. *The Lonely Crusade.* 1947. Reprint with a foreword by Graham Hodges. New York: Thunder's Mouth Press, 1997.

Hodge, Shelby. "Eldorado Ballroom Back in the Swing." *Houston Chronicle.* May 19, 2003.

Hollandsworth, James G. "'Damned Sons of Bitches': The First Demonstrations for Black Civil Rights in the Gulf South." In *Sunbelt Revolution: The Historical Progression of the Civil Rights Struggle in the Gulf South, 1866–2000.* Edited by Samuel C. Hyde Jr. Gainesville: University of Florida Press, 2004.

Honey, Michael K. *Southern Labor and Black Civil Rights: Organizing Memphis Workers.* Urbana: University of Illinois Press, 1993.

Horace, Lillian B. *The Diary of Lillian B. Horace.* Edited by Karen Kossie-Chernyshev. Boston: Pearson, 2007.

Horace, Lillian B., *Angie Brown*. Edited by Karen Kossie-Chernyshev. Acton, Massachusetts: Copley Press. 2008.

Hornsby-Gutting, Angela. *Black Manhood and Community Building in North Carolina, 1890–1930*. Gainesville: University of Florida Press, 2009.

Houghton, Dorothy Knox Howe, Katherine S. Howe, and Sadie Gwyn Blackburn. *Houston's Forgotten Heritage: Landscape, Houses, Interiors, 1824–1914*. Houston: Rice University Press, 1991.

Houston, Ramona. "The NAACP State Conference in Texas: Intermediary and Catalyst for Change, 1937–1957," *The Journal of African American History* 94 (Fall 2009): 509–28.

Howard, John C. *The Negro in the Lumber Industry in America*. Philadelphia: University of Pennsylvania Press, 1970.

Howard, Vicki. "The Courtship Letters of an African-American Couple: Race, Gender, Class, and the Cult of True Womanhood." *Southwestern Historical Quarterly* 100 (July 1996): 65–80.

Huggins, Nathan I. *Harlem Remembered*. New York: Oxford, 2007.

Hunt, Annie Mae. *I Am Annie Mae: An Extraordinary Woman in Her Own Words*. Collected and edited by Ruthe Winegarten and Frieda Werden. Austin: Rosegarden Press, 1983.

Hunter, Tera. *To 'Joy My Freedom: Southern Black Women's Lives and Labors after the Civil War*. Cambridge: Harvard University Press, 1997.

Hurley, Marvin. *Decisive Years for Houston*. Houston: Houston Magazine, 1996.

Hurt, R. Douglass, ed. *African American Life in the Rural South*. Columbia: University of Missouri Press, 2003.

Hyde Jr., Samuel C., ed. *Sunbelt Revolution: The Historical Progression of the Civil Rights Struggle in the Gulf South, 1865–2000*. Gainesville: University of Florida Press, 2003.

"Illinois Jacquet: Jazz At The Philharmonic Crowd Favorite in the 1940s and 1950s." Legends of Jazz History. Swingmusic.net. http://www.swingmusic.net/Illinois_Jacquet_Big_Band_And_Jazz_Legend_Biography.html.

Jackson, Joyce Marie. "The Changing Nature of Gospel Music: A Southern Case Study." *African American Review* 29, no. 2 (Summer 1995), 185–200.

Jackson, Andrew Webster. *A Sure Foundation*. Houston: Webster-Richardson, 1940.

Jacques, Amy. *Garvey and Garveyism*. With an introduction by John Henrik Clarke. New York: Octagon Books, 1978.

Janken, Kenneth Robert. *White: The Biography of Walter White, Mr. NAACP.* New York: The New Press, 2001.

Jensen, F. Kenneth. "The Houston Sit-In Movement of 1960–61." In *Black Dixie: Afro-Texan History and Culture in Houston*. Edited by Howard O. Beeth and Cary D. Wintz. College Station: Texas A&M University Press, 1992.

Johnson, Charles S. *Patterns of Segregation*. New York: Harper and Brothers, 1943.

Johnson, Daniel M. and Rex Campbell. *Black Migration in America: A Social Demographic History*. Durham: Duke University Press, 1981.

Johnson, Walter. "On Agency." *Journal of Social History* 37, no. 1 (2003): 113–124.

Jones, Howard. *The Red Diary: A Chronological History of Black Americans in Houston and Some Neighboring Harris County Communities.* Austin: Nortex Press, 1991.

Jones, Jacqueline. *Labor of Love, Labor of Sorrow: Black Women, Work, and the Family from Slavery to the Present.* New York: Basic Books, 1986.

———. *The Dispossessed: America's Underclass from the Civil War to the Present.* New York: BasicBooks, 1992.

Jones, Jacqueline, Peter H. Wood, Thomas Borstelmann, Elaine Tyler May, and Vicki L. Ruiz. *Created Equal: A History of the United States,* 3rd ed. New York: Pearson-Longman, 2009.

Jones, Ricky L. *Black Haze: Violence, Sacrifice, and Manhood in Black Greek-Letter Fraternities.* Stony Brook, New York: State University of New York Press, 2004.

Jones, William P. *The Tribe of Black Ulysses: African American Lumber Workers in the Jim Crow South.* Urbana: University of Illinois Press, 2005.

Jordan, Terry G. "A Century and a Half of Ethnic Change in Texas, 1836–1986." *Southwestern Historical Quarterly* 89 (April 1986): 385–417.

Jordan, Winthrop D. *White Over Black: American Attitudes toward the Negro,* 1968. Reprint. New York: W. W. Norton, 1977.

Kaplan, Barry J. "Urban Development, Economic Growth, and Personal Liberty: The Rhetoric of the Houston Anti-Zoning Movements, 1847–1962." *Southwestern Historical Quarterly* 84, no. 2 (1980): 133–156.

Kaplan, David. "Houston's Creole Quarter." *Houston Post,* March 19, 1989.

Karenga, Maulana. *Introduction to Black Studies,* 3rd ed. Los Angeles: University of Sankore Press, 2002.

Karkabi, Barbara. "'Fire in Her Belly'": Hundreds Honor Lifelong Civil-Rights Fight." *Houston Chronicle.* January 8, 1990. Christia Adair Collection, 109:4, folder 1. Houston Metropolitan Research Center. Houston Public Library. Julia Ideson Building. Houston, Texas.

Katzman, David. *Before the Ghetto: Black Detroit in the Nineteenth Century.* Urbana: University of Illinois Press, 1972.

Kellar, William Henry. "Alive With a Vengeance: Houston's Black Teachers and Their Fight for Equal Pay." *Houston Review: History and Culture on the Gulf Coast* 18, no. 2 (1996): 89–103.

———. *Make Haste Slowly: Moderates, Conservatives, and School Desegregation in Houston.* College Station: Texas A&M University Press, 1999.

Kelley, Robin D. G. *Hammer and Hoe: Alabama Communists during the Great Depression.* Chapel Hill: University of North Carolina, 1990.

———. "'We Are Not What We Seem': Rethinking Black Working-Class Opposition in the Jim Crow South." *The Journal of American History* 80, no. 1 (June 1993): 75–112.

———. *Race Rebels: Culture, Politics, and the Black Working Class.* New York: The Free Press, 1996.

Kelley, Robin D. G., and Earl Lewis. *To Make Our World Anew: A History of African Americans.* New York: Oxford University Press, 2000.

Knupfer, Anne Meis. *Chicago Black Renaissance and Women's Activism.* Urbana: University of Illinois Press, 2011.

Korstad, Robert, and Nelson Lichtenstein. "Opportunities Found and Lost: Labor, Radicals, and the Early Civil Rights Movement." In *The Black Worker: A Reader*. Edited by Eric Arnesen. Urbana: University of Illinois Press, 2007.

Kossie-Chernyshev, Karen. "A 'Grand Old Church' Rose in the East: The Church of God in Churst (COGIC) in East Texas." *East Texas Historical Journal* 31 (Winter 2003), 26–33.

Kraut, Alan. *The Huddled Masses: The Immigrant in American Society*, 2nd ed. Arlington Heights: Harlan Davidson, 2001.

Kusmer, Kenneth. *A Ghetto Takes Shape: Black Cleveland, 1870–1930*. Urbana: University of Illinois Press, 1980.

Kyle, E. J. "The Tragic Plight of Cotton and Its Effect Upon the State and Nation." June 27, 1940. Texas Agriculture Extension Service Collection. Cushing Memorial Library. Texas A&M University. College Station, Texas.

Lawrence-Brown, Annie Lea, Evelyn Hawkins Hood, Katie Kinnard White, and Lillie Wilkes. *The Legacy Continues: The History of Sigma Gamma Rho Sorority, 1974–1994*, vol. 2. Chicago: Sigma Gamma Rho Sorority, Inc., 1994.

Ledé, Naomi. *Samuel W. Houston and His Contemporaries: A Comprehensive History of the Origin, Growth, and Development of the Black Educational Movement in Huntsville and Walker* County. Houston: Pha Green Printing, 1981.

—. *Precious Memories of a Black Socialite: A Narrative of the Life and Times of Constance Houston Thompson*. Houston: N. W. Ledé, 1991.

—, ed. *Pathfinders: A History of the Pioneering Efforts of African Americans—Huntsville, Walker, County, Texas*. Virginia Beach, Virginia: Donning Company Publishers, 2004.

Lee, Everett S., Ann Ratner Miller, Carol P. Brainerd, and Richard A. Easterlin, *Methodological Considerations and Reference Tables*, vol. 1. *Population Redistribution and Economic Growth: United States, 1870–1950*. Edited by Simon Kuznets and Dorothy Swaine Thomas. Philadelphia: American Philosophical Society, 1957–1964.

Lee, Henry E., Dr. "Negro Health Problem." In *The Red Book of Houston: A Compendium of Social, Professional, Religious, Educational, and Industrial Interests of Houston's Colored Population*. Edited by Emmett J. Scott. Houston: Sotex, 1915, 148–51.

Leiker, James N. *Racial Borders: Black Soldiers Along the Rio Grande*. College Station: Texas A&M University Press, 2002.

Lemann, Nicholas. *The Promised Land: The Great Black Migration and How It Changed America*. New York: Knopf, 1991.

Lemke-Santangelo, Gretchen. *Abiding Courage: African American Migrant Women and the East Bay Community*. Chapel Hill: University of North Carolina Press, 1996.

Levine, Lawrence. *The Unpredictable Past: Explorations of American Cultural History*. New York: Oxford University Press, 1993.

Lewis, David Levering. *W. E. B. Du Bois: A Biography of a Race, 1868–1919*. New York: H. Holt, 1994.

—. *W. E. B. Du Bois: A Reader*. New York: H. Holt, 1995.

Lewis, Earl. "Expectations, Economic Opportunities, and Life in the Industrial Age: Black Migration to Norfolk, Virginia, 1910–1945." In *The Great Migration in*

Historical Perspective: New Dimensions of Race, Class, and Gender. Edited by Joe William Trotter Jr. Bloomington: Indiana University Press, 1991.

—. *In Their Own Interests: Race, Class, and Power in Twentieth Century Norfolk.* Berkeley: University of California Press, 1991.

Lewyn, Michael. "Zoning Without Zoning." Planetizen: *The Planning and Development Network.* November 24, 2003. Accessed September 3, 2005, http://www.planetizen.com/about. L' Heureux, Aimee. "Illinois Jacquet: Integrating Houston Jazz Audiences . . . Lands Ella Fitzgerald and Ella Fitzgerald in Jail." *Houston History* 8, no. 1 (2010): 6–8, 49.

Lights, Rev. "Brief Sketch of Houston Baptists." In *The Red Book of Houston: A Compendium of Social, Professional, Religious, Educational, and Industrial Interests of Houston's Colored Population.* Edited Emmett J. Scott. Houston: Sotex, 1915, 24–25

Lipscomb, Mance, Glenn A. Myers, and Don Gardner. "Out of the Bottoms and into the Big City." *Southern Exposure* 8, no. 2 (1980): 4–11.

Litwack, Leon. *North of Slavery: The Negro in the Free States, 1790–1860.* First Phoenix ed. Chicago: University of Chicago Press, 1965.

Lively, Donald. *The Constitution and Race.* New York: Praeger, 1992.

Locke, Alain. *The New Negro: An Interpretation.* New York: A. & C. Boni, 1925.

—. *The New Negro: An Interpretation,* with an introduction by Arnold Rampersad. New York: A & C. Boni, 1925; New York: Touchstone Press of Simon & Schuster, 1992)

—. *The Negro in Art.* New York: Association in Negro Folk Education, 1940.

Logan, Rayford. *The Betrayal of the Negro: From Rutherford B. Hayes to Woodrow Wilson.* New York: MacMillan, 1969.

Logan, W. H., Rev. "Progress of Negro Churches in Houston Since Emancipation or the Civil War." In *The Red Book of Houston: A Compendium of Social, Professional, Religious, Educational, and Industrial Interests of Houston's Colored Population.* Edited by Emmett J. Scott. Houston: Sotex, 1915, 21–23.

Lomax, Alan. *The Land Where Blues Began.* New York: Pantheon, 1993.

Lucko, Paul M. "Dissertations and Theses in African American Studies in Texas: A Selected Bibliography, 1904–1990." *Southwestern Historical Quarterly* 96 (April 1993): 347–73.

Lundy, Ann. "Pioneer Concert Pianist: Anne Lundy and Ernestine Jessie Covington Dent." *The Black Perspective* in Music 12, no. 2 (1984): 245–65.

MacDonald, John S., and Leatrice D. MacDonald. "Chain Migration, Ethnic Neighborhood Formation and Social Networks." *Millbank Memorial Fund* 42 (1964): 82–97.

Maclean, Nancy. *Behind the Mask of Chivalry: The Making of the Second Ku Klux Klan.* New York: Oxford University Press, 1994.

Malone, Cheryl Knott. "Autonomy and Accommodation: Houston's Colored Carnegie Library, 1907–1922." *Libraries & Culture* 34, no. 2 (1999): 95–112.

Marks, Carole. *Farewell, We're Good and Gone: The Great Black Migration.* Bloomington: Indiana University Press, 1989.

Martin, Betty L. "Spirit of Jazz: Event Held to Fund Eldorado Restoration." *Houston Chronicle.* May 1, 2003.

Martin, Betty L. "Fourth Ward Freedmen's Town Minister's Home Gets Historical Marker." *Houston Chronicle*. April 2, 2009.

Maxwell, Louise Passey. "Freedmantown: The Origins of a Black Neighborhood in Houston, 1865–1880." In *Bricks Without Straw: A Comprehensive History of African Americans in Texas*." Written and edited by David A. Williams. Austin: Eakin Press, 1997.

Maxwell, Robert S., and Robert D. Baker, *Sawdust Empire: The Texas Lumber Industry, 1830–1940*. College Station: Texas A&M University Press, 1983.

McArthur, Paul J. "One for All: Sax Giant Helped Desegregate Houston Audiences." *Houston Press*. November18, 1999.

McDaniel, Mike. "Channel 8 History is Just for Fun." *Houston Chronicle*. May 22, 1999.

McGee, Gary B. "William Seymour and the Azusa Street Revival." In "A Century of Pentecostal Vision." *Enrichment Journal: A Journal for Pentecostal Ministry, Assemblies of God*. (Fall 1999). http://enrichmentjournal.ag.org/199904/026_azusa.cfm.

McComb, David. *Houston: A History*. 1969. Reprint. Austin: University of Texas Press, 1981.

McCullough, Kimberly, "The First All-Black City in Texas," *Touchstone* 22 (2003):54–64:

McLellan, Dennis. "Marl Young Dies at 92; Pianist Was Key in Desegregating LA Musicians Union." *New York Times*. May 3, 2009.

McMillen, Neil. *Dark Journey: Black Mississippians in the Age of Jim Crow*. Illini Edition. Urbana: University of Illinois Press, 1990.

—. "The Migration and Black Protest in Jim Crow Mississippi." In *Black Exodus: The Great Migration from the American South*. Edited by Alferdteen Harrison. Jackson: University Press of Mississippi, 1991.

McQueen, Clyde. *Black Churches in Texas: A Guide to Historic Congregations*. College Station: Texas A&M University Press, 2001.

McWhorter, John. "Why I'm Black, not African-American." *Detroit News*, September 30, 2004.

Melville, Margarita. "Mexicans." In *The Ethnic Groups of Houston*. Edited by Fred von der Mehden. Houston: Rice University Press, 1984, 1–62.

Mehden, Fred, von der. *The Ethnic Groups of Houston*. Houston: Rice University Press, 1984.

Minton, John. "Creole Community and 'Mass' Communication: Houston Zydeco as a Mediated Tradition." *Journal of Folklore Research* 35 (Fall 1995), 1–12.

Mitchell, Rick. "Houston Jazz Legend Larkin Dies at 85." *Houston Chronicle*. August 31, 1996.

Moneyhon, Carl H. *Texas After the Civil War: The Struggle of Reconstruction*. College Station: Texas A&M University Press, 2004.

Montejano, David. *Anglos and Mexicans in the Making of Texas, 1836–1986*. 1987. Reprint Austin: University of Texas Press, 1992.

Montes, Rebecca. "Working for American Rights: Black, White, and Mexican American Dockworkers in Texas during the Great Depression." In *Sunbelt Revolution: The Historical Progression of the Civil Rights Struggle in the Gulf South, 1865–2000*. Edited by Samuel C. Hyde Jr. Gainesville: University of Florida Press, 2003.

Montgomery, David. *Workers' Control in America: Studies in the History of Work, Technology, and Labor Struggles.* 1979. Reprint, New York: Cambridge University Press, 1981.

Montgomery, William E. *Under Their Own Vine and Fig Tree: The African-American Church in the South, 1865–1900.* Baton Rouge: Louisiana State University Press, 1993.

Moore, Shirley Ann. "Getting There, Being There: African-American Migration to Richmond, California, 1910–1945." In *The Great Migration in Historical Perspective: New Dimensions of Race, Class, and Gender.* Edited by Joe William Trotter Jr. Bloomington: Indiana University Press, 1991.

—. *To Place Our Deeds: The African American Community in Richmond,* California. Berkeley: University of California Press, 2000.

Morgan, John P. "Reading Race into the Scopes Trial: African American Elites, Science, and Fundamentalism." *Journal of American History* 90, no. 3 (2003): 891–911.

Morris, Kelso B. "The Wiley Collegians: Reminiscences of a Black College Bandleader, 1925–1935." *Annual Review of Jazz Studies* 1, 17–20.

Muir, Andrew Forest. "The Free Negro in Harris County, Texas." *Southwestern Historical Quarterly* 46, no. 3 (1943): 214–238.

Mullin, Michael. *Africa in America: Slave Acculturation and Resistance in the American South and the British Caribbean, 1736–1831.* Urbana: University of Illinois Press, 1992.

Myrdal, Gunnar. *An American Dilemma: The Negro Problem and Modern Democracy.* 2 vols. 1944. Reprint. New York: Harper & Row Publishers, 1969.

Nadell, Martha Jane. *Enter the New Negroes: Images of Race in American Culture.* New York: Cambridge, 2007.

"Negroes Protest Ouster of Negro Bandleader." *Jet* Magazine. July 9, 1953.

Nevels, Cynthia Skove. *Lynching to Belong: Claiming Whiteness Through Racial Violence.* College Station: Texas A&M University Press, 2007.

Newby, I. E., ed. *Segregationist Thought in America.* Homewood, Illinois: Dorsey Press, 1968.

—. *Jim Crow's Defense: Anti-Negro Thought in America, 1900–1930.* Baton Rouge: Louisiana State University Press, 1969.

Obadele-Starks, Ernest. "Black Struggle, White Resistance, and the Upper Texas Gulf Coast Railroads, 1900–1945." *Houston Review* 18 (Fall 1996): 104–06.

—. *Black Unionism in the Industrial South.* College Station: Texas A&M University Press, 1999.

—. *Freebooters and Smugglers: The Foreign Slave Trade in the United States after 1900.* Fayetteville: University of Arkansas Press, 2007.

Oliver, Paul. *Story of the Blues.* 1969. Reprint. Boston: Northeastern University, 1998.

Olmstead, Frederick Law. *A Journey Through Texas.* 1857. Reprint Lincoln: University of Nebraska Press, 2004.

Osofsky, Gilbert. *Harlem: The Making of a Ghetto, 1890–1930,* 2nd ed. New York: Harper Torchbooks, 1971.

Painter, Nell I. *Exodusters: Black Migration to Kansas after Reconstruction.* New York: Knopf, 1977. Reprint. Lawrence: University Press of Kansas, 1986.

Patton, Tracy Owens. "Hey Girl, Ain't I More Than My Hair?" African American

Women and the Struggles with Beauty, Body Image, and Hair." *NWSA (National Women's Studies Association) Journal* 18, no. 2 (2006): 24–51.

Peretti, Burton W. *"Lift Every Voice": The History of African American Music.* Latham, Maryland: Rowan & Littlefield, 2011.

Phillips, Edward Hake. "The Sherman Courthouse Riot of 1930." *East Texas Historical Journal* 25, no. 2 (1987): 12–19.

Phillips, Kimberly. *Alabama North: African-American Migrants, Community, and Working-Class Activism in Cleveland, 1915–1945.* Urbana: University of Illinois Press, 1999.

Phillips, Michael. *White Metropolis: Race, Ethnicity, and Religion in Dallas, 1841–2001.* Austin: University of Texas, 2006.

Pierce, Richard B. "Something Old, Something New, Something Borrowed, Some Things Black? African American Urban History." *Journal of Urban History* 31 (November 2004): 106–14.

Pickens, William. "Every Effort to Punish Lynchers." Houston Informer. October 17, 1925

Pitre, Merline. *In Struggle against Jim Crow: Lulu B. White and the NAACP, 1900–1957.* College Station: Texas A&M University Press, 1999.

—. *Through Many Dangers, Toils, and Snares: The Black Leadership of Texas, 1868–1900.* 1986. Austin: Eakin Press, 2006.

Plesa, Dan. "Revitalize: Third Ward Pushing Change." *Houston Post*, July 21, 1993. Houston—Subdivisions—Third Ward—Vertical Files. Texas Room. Houston Public Library. Julia Ideson Building. Houston, Texas.

Pratt, Joseph A. *The Growth of a Refining Region.* Greenwich, Connecticut: JAI Press, 1980.

—. "8F and Many More: Business and Civic Leadership in Modern Houston." *The Houston Review of History and Culture* 4, no. 2 (2004), 2–7, 31–42.

—, ed. "Coming to Houston." *Houston Review of History* 3, no. 1, Special Issue (2005).

—, ed. "Houston Remembers World War II." *The Houston Review of History and Culture* 2, no. 2, Special Issue (2005).

—, ed. "Civic Leadership in Houston." *The Houston Review of History and Culture* 1, no. 2, Special Issue (2004).

—, ed. "Confronting Jim Crow." *Houston History* 8, no. 1, Special Issue (2010).

—, ed. "Houston Women in Texas and US History." *The Houston Review of History and Culture* 1, no. 1, Special Issue (2003).

Pruitt, Bernadette. "'For the Advancement of the Race': The Great Migrations to Houston, Texas, 1914–1941." *Journal of Urban History*, 31 (May 2005): 435–478.

—. "In Search of Freedom: Black Migration to Houston, 1914–1945." *Houston Review of History and Culture* 3 (Fall 2005): 46–57, 85–86.

Quraishi, Uzma, "Educationally Empowered : the Indian and Pakistani Student Community in Houston, Texas, 1960–1975." Master's Thesis, University of Houston, 2008.

Rabinowitz, Howard N. "Continuity and Change: Southern Urban Development, 1860–1900. In *The City in Southern History: The Growth of Urban Civilization in the South.* Edited by Blaine A. Brownell and David R. Goldfield. Fort Washington: New York, 1977.

—. *Race Relations in the Urban South, 1865–1890.* 1977. Rev. ed. Athens: University of Georgia Press, 1996.

Rainwater, Lee, and William Yancy. *The Moynihan Report and the Politics of Controversy.* New York: MIT Press, 1967.

Ramsdell, Charles William. *Reconstruction in Texas.* New York: Columbia University Press, 1910.

Reed, Merl E. "Black Workers, Defense Industries, and Federal Agencies in Pennsylvania, 1941–1945." In *African Americans in Pennsylvania: Shifting Historical Perspectives.* Edited by Joe William Trotter Jr. and Eric Ledell Smith. Philadelphia: Pennsylvania State Historical and Museum Commission and the Pennsylvania State University Press, 1997.

Reich, Steven A. "Soldiers of Democracy: Black Texans and the Fight for Citizenship." *Journal of American History* 82 (March 1996): 1478–1504.

—. "The Great Migration and the Historical Imagination." *The Historical Society* 9, no. 1 (2009): 87–128.

Reinhold, Robert. "FOCUS: Houston; A Fresh Approach to Zoning." *New York Times.* August 17, 1986. http://query.nytimes.com/gst/fullpage.html?res=9A0DEFDB103FF934A2575BC0A960948260.

Rice, Roger L. "Residential Segregation by Law, 1910–1917." *Journal of Southern History* 34, no. 2 (1968): 179–94.

Richardson, Clifton F. "Houston's Colored Citizens: Activities and Conditions among the Negro Population in the 1920s." In *Black Dixie: Afro-Texan History and Culture in Houston.* Edited by Howard Beeth and Cary D. Wintz. College Station: Texas A&M University Press, 1992.

Robeck Jr., Cecil M. "Azusa Street Revival." In *Dictionary of Pentecostal and Charismatic Movements.* Edited by Stanley M. Burgess and Gary B. McGee. Grand Rapids, Michigan: Zondervan Publishing House, 1988, 31–36.

Roberson, Houston B. ""Accommodating Activism: Dexter Avenue Baptist Church and Robert Chapman Jenkins, Workers That Needeth Not Be Ashamed, 1883–1920." In *Sunbelt Revolution: The Historical Progression of the Civil Rights Struggle in the Gulf South, 1866–2000.* Edited by Samuel C. Hyde Jr. Gainesville: University Press of Florida, 2003.

Rodrigue, John C. *Reconstruction in the Cane Fields: From Slavery to Free Labor in Louisiana's Sugar Parishes, 1862–1880.* Baton Rouge: Louisiana University Press, 2001.

Romero, Mary. *Maid in the USA,* Tenth Anniversary Edition. New York: Routledge, 2002.

Ross Jr., Lawrence C. *The Divine Nine: The History of African American Fraternities and Sororities.* New York: Kensington, 2002.

Rotstein, Gary. "The Next Great Diaspora? Many Scattered by Katrina May Never Return Home." *Pittsburgh Post-Gazette.* September 11, 2005.

Rouse, Jacqueline A. *Luginia Burns Hope: A Black Southern Reformer.* Athens: University of Georgia Press, 1989.

—. "Out of the Shadow of Tuskegee: Margaret Murray Washington, Social Activism, and Race Vindication." *Journal of Negro History* 81 (1996): 31–46.

Russell, Kathy, Midge Wilson, and Ronald Hall. *The Color Complex: The Politics of Skin Color Among African Americans*. New York: Doubleday, 1990.

Rust, Carol. "Frenchtown." *Houston Chronicle*. February 23, 1992. Houston—Subdivisions—Frenchtown—Vertical. Texas Room, Houston Public Library. Houston, Texas.

Rutledge-Jones, K. Dawn. "Minority Engineer Watched Evolution of Industry." *Nashville Business Journal*. February 20, 1998.

Safa, Helen I., and Bran M. Du Toit. *In Migration and Development: Implications for Ethnic Identity and Political Conflict*. The Hague: Mouton Publishers, 1975.

Saltzman, James D. "Houston Says No to Zoning." *The Freeman: Ideas on Liberty* 44, no. 8 (1994), http://www.fee.org/the_freeman/detail/houston-says-no-to-zoning/#axzz2E2 8eTCNo

San Miguel, Guadalupe. *Brown Not White: School Integration and the Chicano Movement in Houston*. College Station: Texas A&M University Press, 2001.

Sapper, Neil. "Black Culture in Urban Texas: A Lone Star Renaissance." *Red River Valley Historical Review* 6, no. 1 (1981): 69–73.

Schaffer, Alan. *On the Real Side: Laughing, Lying, and Signifying—The Underground Tradition of African-American Humor That Transformed American Culture from Slavery to Richard Pryor*. New York: Simon and Schuster, 1994.

Schechter. Patricia A. *Ida B. Wells-Barnett and American Reform, 1880–1930*. Chapel Hill: University of North Carolina Press, 2001.

Schier, Mary Jane. "Golden Anniversary of Black Hospital's Founding Tonight." *Houston Post*, October 30, 1975." Dr. Benjamin Covington Papers, 170:1, folder 1. Houston Metropolitan Research Center. Houston Public Library. Julia Ideson Building. Houston, Texas.

Schuler, Edgar A. "The Houston Race Riot, 1917." *Journal of Negro History* 29, no. 3 (1944): 300–338.

Scott, Emmett J., ed., *The Red Book of Houston: A Compendium of Social, Professional, Religious, Educational, and Industrial Interests of Houston's Colored Population*. Houston: Sotex, 1915.

—, ed. *Scott's Official History of the American Negro in the World War*. Washington: Emmett J. Scott, 1919.

—. *Negro Migration during the War*. 1920. Reprint with an introduction by Thomas Cripps. New York: Arno Press, 1969.

Scott, James C. *Weapons of the Weak: Everyday Forms of Peasant Resistance*. New Haven: Yale University Press, 1987.

—. *Domination and the Arts of Resistance: Hidden Transcripts*. New Haven: Yale University Press, 1990.

Scott, Janelle D. "Local Leadership in the Woman's Suffrage Movement: Houston's Campaign for the Vote 1917–1918." *The Houston Review: History and Culture of the Gulf Coast* 12, no. 1 (1990): 3–22.

Sernett, Milton C. *Bound for the Promised Land: African American Religion and the Great Migration*. Durham: Duke University Press, 1997.

Shabazz, Amilcar. "One for the Crows, One for the Crackers: The Strange Career of Public Higher Education in Houston, Texas." *Houston Review: History and Culture of the Gulf Coast* 28 (Fall 1996): 124–43.

—. "Sounding the Ram's Horn for Human Rights." In *The Human Tradition in Texas*. No. 9, *The Human Tradition in America*. Edited by Ty Cashion and Jesús F. De La Teja. Wilmington, Del.: SR Books, 2001.

—. *Advancing Democracy: African Americans and the Struggle for Access and Equity in Higher Education in Texas*. Chapel Hill: University of North Carolina Press, 2004.

—. "Carter Wesley and the Making of Houston's Civic Culture before the Second Reconstruction." *Houston Review of History and Culture* 1 (Summer 2004): 2–12.

Shaw, Stephanie J. "Black Club Women and the Creation of the National Association of Colored Women." In *"We Specialize in the Wholly Impossible": A Reader in Black Women's History*. Edited by Darlene Clark Hine, Wilma King, and Linda Reed. New York: Carlson Publishing Inc., 1995.

—. *What a Woman Ought to Be and to Do: Black Professional Women Workers during the Jim Crow Era*. Chicago: University of Chicago Press, 1996.

Shiflett, Mary. "The Second Downtown." *The Houston Review of History and Culture*, vol. 2, no. 1 (Fall 2004): 3–7, 47–49.

Sibley, Marilyn McAdams. *The Port of Houston: A History*. Austin: University of Texas, 1964.

Sitkoff, Harvard. "Racial Militancy and Interracial Violence in the Second World War." *Journal of American History* 58 (December 1971): 661–81.

—. *A New Deal for Blacks: The Emergence of Civil Rights as a National Issue, The Depression Decade*. 1978. Reprint. New York: Oxford University Press, 2009.

Sitton, Thad, and James H. Conrad. *Freedom Colonies: Independent Black Texans in the Time of Jim Crow*. Austin: University of Texas at Austin, 2003.

Skocpol, Theda, and Jennifer Lynn Oser. "Organization Despite Adversity: The Organization and Development of African American Fraternal Associations." *Social Science History* 28, no. 3 (2004): 367–477.

Smallwood, James. *Time of Hope, Time of Despair: Black Texans during Reconstruction*. Port Washington, NY: Kennekat, 1981).

Smith, J. Clay, Jr. *Emancipation: The Making of the Black Lawyer, 1844–1944*. Philadelphia: University of Pennsylvania Press, 1999.

Smith, C. Calvin. "The Houston Riot of 1917, Revisited." *The Houston Review: History and Culture on the Gulf Coast* 13 (Fall 1991): 85–102.

Smith, Steven. US Army Corps of Engineers Construction Engineering Research Laboratories, and US Department of Defense Legacy Resource Management Program. *A Historic Context Statement for a World War II Era Black Officers' Club at Fort Leonard Wood, Missouri*. November 1998. http://www.cas.sc.edu/sciaa/PDFdocs/military-research/FLWBlackOfficersClub.pdf.

Smith Prather, Patricia. "The Houston Place." *Houston Chronicle*. June 19, 1986. Houston—Subdivisions—Fifth Ward—Vertical Files. Texas Room, Houston Public Library. Houston, Texas.

—. "A Unique Houston Neighborhood Called Frenchtown." *Houston Chronicle*. September 15, 1986. Houston—Subdivisions—Fifth Ward—Vertical Files. Texas Room, Houston Public Library. Houston, Texas.

Smith Prather, Patricia, and Jane Clements Monday. *From Slave to Statesman: The*

Legacy of Joshua Houston, Servant to Sam Houston. Denton: University of North Texas Press, 1993.

SoRelle, James M. "'An De Po Cullud Man Is in De Wuss Fix Uv Awl': Black Occupational Status in Houston, 1920–1940." *The Houston Review: History and Culture of the Gulf Coast* 1 (Spring 1979): 20–22.

—. "The 'Waco Horror': The Lynching of Jesse Washington." *Southwestern Historical Quarterly* 86 (April 1983): 517–36.

—. "The Emergence of Black Business in Houston, Texas: A Study of Race and Ideology." In *Black Dixie: Afro-Texan History and Culture in Houston*. Edited by Howard Beeth and Cary D. Wintz. College Station: Texas A&M University Press, 1992.

—. "Race Relations in 'Heavenly Houston,' 1919–1945." In *Black Dixie: Afro-Texan History and Culture in Houston*. Edited by Howard Beeth and Cary D. Wintz. College Station: Texas A&M University Press, 1992.

Sparks, Randy J. "'Heavenly Houston' or 'Hellish Houston'?" *Southern Studies* 25 (Winter 1986): 353–66.

Specht, Joe W. "Oil Well Blues: African Americans Oil Patch Songs." *East Texas Historical Association* 49, no. 1 (2011): 86–108.

Spear, Allan. *Black Chicago: The Making of a Negro Ghetto, 1890–1920*. Chicago: University of Chicago Press, 1967.

Spero, Sterling D. and Abram L. Harris. *The Black Worker: The Negro and the Labor Movement*. 1931. Reprint with a new preface from Herbert G. Gutman. New York: Atheneum, 1968.

Stabler, Scott L. "Free Men Come to Houston: Blacks During Reconstruction." *Houston Review of History and Culture* 3 (Fall 2005): 40–43, 73–76.

Stein, Judith. *The World of Marcus Garvey: Race and Class in Modern Society*. Baton Rouge: Louisiana State University, 1991.

Stephenson, Charles. "Jazz Images: A Sampling from the Texas Jazz Archive." *Houston Review: History and Culture of the Gulf Coast* 12, no. 2 (1990): 157–66.

Street, James H. *The New Revolution in the Cotton Economy: Mechanization and Its Consequences*. Chapel Hill: University of North Carolina Press, 1957.

Stuart, Merah Steven. *An Economic Detour: A History of Insurance in the Lives of American Negroes*. 1940. Reprint. College Park: McGrath, 1969.

Sullivan, Patricia. *Days of Hope: Race and Democracy in the New Deal*. Chapel Hill: University of North Carolina Press, 1996.

Sullivan, Patricia. *Lift Every Voice: The NAACP and the Making of the Civil Rights Movement*. New York: The Free Press, 2008.

Summers, Suzanne. "Banking in Houston, 1840–1914." In *Houston Review: History and Culture of the Gulf Coast* 12 (Fall 1990): 37–41.

Takaki, Ronald. *A Different Mirror: A History of Multicultural America*. Boston: Little, Brown, 1993.

—. *Strangers From a Different Shore: A History of Asian Americans*. Updated and rev. ed. Boston: Little, Brown, 1998.

Tapscott, Horace. *Songs of the Unsung: The Musical and Social Journey of Horace Tapscott*. Edited by Steven L. Isoardi. Durham: Duke University Press, 2001.

Taylor, Hobart, Jr. "Untrained Negro Youths Constitute the Wasted Reservoir." *The Negro Digest,* June 1963, 44–48.

Taylor, Quintard. *The Forging of a Black Community: Seattle's Central District from 1870 through the Civil Rights Era.* Seattle: University of Washington Press, 1994.

—. *In Search of the Racial Frontier: African Americans in the West, 1528–1990.* New York: W. W. Norton, 1999.

—. "Seeking Sunbelt Freedom: African Americans in the Urban Southwest, 1866–1970," *OAH (Organization of American Historians) Magazine of History* 18, no. 1 (October 2003): 17–20.

—, and Shirley Ann Wilson Moore, ed. *African American Women Confront the West.* Norman: University of Oklahoma, 2003.

Thomas, Jesse O. *Negro Participation in the Texas Centennial Exposition.* University of Wisconsin—Madison: Christopher, 1938.

Thomas, Cynthia. "Lowe and Behold." *Houston Chronicle.* October 13, 1996.

Thomas, Lorenzo. *Don't Deny My Name: Words and Music and the Black Intellectual Tradition.* Edited and with an Introduction by Aldon Lynn Nielson. Ann Arbor: University of Michigan Press, 2008.

—_. "The African American Folktale and J. Mason Brewer." In *Juneteenth Texas: Essays in African American Folklore.* Edited by Abernathy, Francis E., Patrick B. Mullen, and Alan B. Govenar. Denton, Texas: University of North Texas, 1996.

Thomas, Richard W. *Life for Us Is What We Make It: Building Black Community in Detroit, 1915–1945.* Bloomington: Indiana University Press, 1992.

Thomas, Sherry. "Houston: A City Without Zoning." *USA Today,* October 30, 2003. http://www.usatoday.com/travel/destinations/cityguides/houston/2003-10-07-spotlight-zoning_x.htm.

Tillery, Tyrone. *Claude McKay: A Black Poet's Struggle for Identity.* Amherst: University of Massachusetts Press, 2004.

Tolnay, Stewart E., and E. M. Beck. "Black Flight: Lethal Violence and the Great Migration, 1900–1930." *Social Science History* 14 (Fall 1990): 347–70.

Trotter Jr., Joe William. *Black Milwaukee: The Making of an Industrial Proletariat, 1915–1945.* Urbana: University of Illinois Press, 1988.

—. *Coal, Class, and Color: Blacks in Southern West Virginia, 1915–1932.* Urbana: University of Illinois Press, 1990.

—, ed. *The Great Migration in Historical Perspective: New Dimensions of Race, Class, and Gender.* Bloomington: Indiana University Press, 1991.

Trotter Jr., Joe William, Earl Lewis, and Tera Hunter. "Introduction: Connecting African American Urban History, Social Science Research, and Policy Debates." In *The African American Urban Experience: Perspectives from the Colonial Period to the Present.* New York: Palgrave-Macmillan, 2004.

Tomkins-Walsh, Teresa. "Thelma Scott Bryant: Memories of a Century in Houston's Third Ward." *Houston Review of History and Culture* 1 (Fall 2003): 48–58.

Tucker, Karen Anderson. "Last Hired, First Fired: Black Women Workers during World War II." *Journal of American History* 69 (June 1982): 82–97.

Tucker, Robert C., ed., *The Marx-Engels Reader,* 2nd ed. New York: W. W. Norton, 1978.

Turner, Alan. "'Home of Happy Feet': Eldorado's Rebirth Will Showcase Music of the Past, Present." *Houston Chronicle,* February 5, 2001.

Tuttle, William. *Race Riot: Chicago in the Red Summer of 1919.* New York: Atheneum, 1970.

—. "Violence in the 'Heathen Land': The Longview Race Riot of 1919." *Phylon* 33, no. 4 (1972): 324–33.

Twomey, Dannehl M. "Into the Mainstream: Early Black Photography in Houston." *Houston Review: History and Culture of the Gulf Coast* 9, no. 1 (1987): 39–48.

Van Sertima, Ivan. *They Came Before Columbus: The African Presence in Ancient America.* New York: Random House, 1976.

Vincent, Charles, ed. *The African American Experience in Louisiana: From Africa to the Civil War. The Louisiana Purchase Bicentennial Series in Louisiana History,* vol. 11. Lafayette: Center for Louisiana Studies, 1999.

—, ed. *The African American Experience in Louisiana: From the Civil War to Jim Crow. The Louisiana Purchase Bicentennial Series in Louisiana History,* vol. 12. Lafayette: Center for Louisiana Studies, 1999.

—, ed. *The African American Experience in Louisiana: From Jim Crow to Civil Rights. The Louisiana Purchase Bicentennial Series in Louisiana History,* vol. 13. Lafayette: Center for Louisiana Studies, 1999.

Volanto, Steve. *Texas, Cotton, and the New Deal.* College Station: Texas A&M University Press, 2004.

Walker, Donald R. *Penology for Profit: A History of the Texas Prison System, 1867–1912.* College Station: Texas A&M University Press, 1988.

Walsh, Jean. "Dr. Covington, at 90, Is Still Practicing." *Houston Post.* March 12, 1961. Dr. Benjamin Covington Collection. 184–1R:1. Houston Metropolitan Research Center. Houston Public Library. Julia Ideson Building. Houston, Texas.

Walsh, Robb. "The Nickel Burger: How is a Falling-Apart Fifth Ward Joint Turning Out the Best Burgers in Town? Adrian's Has History." *Houston Press.* October 31, 2002.

Watson, Dwight. "In the Name of Progress and Decency: The Response of Houston's Civic Leaders to the Lynching of Robert Powell in 1928." *Houston Review of History and Culture,* 1, no. 2 (2005), 26–28.

—. *Race and the Houston Police Department, 1930–1990: A Change Did Come.* College Station: Texas A&M University Press, 2005.

Weare, Walter B. *Black Business in the New South: North Carolina Mutual Life Insurance Company.* Urbana: University of Illinois Press, 1975.

Weaver, John B. *The Brownsville Raid* (New York: W. W. Norton, 1992)

Weiss, Nancy J. *Farewell to the Party of Lincoln: Black Politics in the Age of FDR.* Princeton: Princeton University Press, 1983.

Welsing, Francis Cress. *The Isis Papers: The Keys to the Colors.* Chicago: Third World Press, 1991.

West, Cornel, and Eddie S. Glaude Jr. Editors. *African American Religious Thought: An Anthology.* Louisville, Kentucky: Westminster John Knotts Press, 2003.

"Where Were the 6 Wards?" *Houston Post,* Sound Off, February 28, 1965.

Wiggins, Bernice Love. *Tuneful Tales (In the Remote Desert of 1925 El Paso Bloomed a Bit of Harlem Renaissance).* Edited by Maceo Dailey Jr. and Ruthe Wingarten. Lubbock: Texas Tech University Press, 2002.
Wilder, Craig Steven. *In the Company of Black Men: The African Influence on African American Culture in New York.* New York: New York University Press, 2001.
Wilkerson, Isabel. *The Warmth of Other Suns: The Epic Story of America's Great Migration.* New York: Random House, 2010.
Williams, Chad L. *Torchbearers: African Americans in the World War I Era.* Chapel Hill: University of North Carolina Press, 2010.
Williamson, Joel. *The Crucible of Race: Black-White Relations in the American South Since Emancipation.* New York: Oxford University Press, 1984.
—. *A Rage for Order: Black-White Relations in the American South since Emancipation.* New York: Oxford University Press, 1986.
Winegarten, Ruthe. *Black Texas Women: 150 Years of Trial and Triumph.* Austin: University of Texas Press, 1995.
Wintz, Cary D., ed., *African American Political Thought, 1890–1930: Washington, Du Bois, Garvey, and Randolph.* New York: M. E. Sharpe, 1996.
—. "Black Business in Houston, 1910–1930." *Essays in Economic and Business History* 10 (1992), 30–38.
—. *Blacks in Houston.* Houston: Houston Center for the Humanities and the National Endowment for the Humanities, 1982.
—. "Blacks." In *The Ethnic Groups of Houston.* Edited by Fred von Der Mehden. Houston: Rice University Press, 1984.
—. *Black Culture and the Harlem Renaissance.* Houston: Rice University Press, 1988.
—. "The Emergence of a Black Neighborhood: Houston's Fourth Ward, 1865–1915." In *Urban Texas: Politics and Development.* Edited by Char Miller and Heywood Sanders. College Station: Texas A&M University Press, 1990.
—. *The Harlem Renaissance: A History and An Anthology.* Upper Saddle River, New Jersey: Brandywine Press, 2003.
Woodward, C. V. *The Strange Career of Jim Crow,* 3rd rev. ed. New York: Oxford University Press, 1974; Commemorative 6th ed. New York: Oxford University Press, 2001.
Wolters, Raymond. *Negroes and the Great Depression: The Problem of Economic Recovery.* Westport, Conn.: Greenwood, 1970.
Wood, Peter. "'I Did the Best That I Could for My Day': The Study of Early Black History during the Second Reconstruction, 1960–1976." *William and Mary Quarterly* 35 (January 1978): 166–99.
Wood, Roger R. *Down in Houston: Bayou City Blues.* Austin: University of Texas Press, 2003.
Woods, Sister Frances Jerome. *Marginality and Identity: A Colored Creole Family through Ten Generations.* Baton Rouge: Louisiana State University Press, 1972.
Woodson, Carter G. *A Century of Negro Migration.* 1918. Reprint. New York: Dover Publications, 2002.
Woodward, C. Vann. *The Strange Career of Jim Crow.* 3rd rev. ed. New York: Oxford University Press, 1974.

Wright, Richard, and Edwin Rosham. *Twelve Million Voices: A Folk History of the Negro in the United States.* 1941. Reprint. Athens: Thunder's Mouth, 1988.

Wright, W. D. *Black History and Black Identity: A Call for a New Historiography.* Westport, Connecticut, 2001.

Zamora, Emilio. "The Failed Promise of Wartime Opportunity for Mexicans in the Texas Oil Industry." *Southwestern Historical Quarterly* 95 (Winter 1992): 323–50.

—. *The World of the Mexican Worker in Texas.* College Station: Texas A&M University Press, 1993.

Zangrando, Robert L. *The NAACP Crusade Against Lynching, 1909–1950.* Philadelphia: Temple University Press, 1980.

Zweigenhaft, Richard, and G. William Domhoff. *Diversity in the Power Elite: How it Happened, Why it Matters.* New York: Rowman & Littlefield, 2006.

Zolten, J. Jerome. "Black Comedians: Forging an Ethnic Identity." *Journal of American Ethnic Culture* 16, no. 2 (1993): 65–76.

Reference Books and Digital Sources

African American National Biography. Edited by Henry Louis Gates Jr. and Evelyn Brooks Higginbotham. New York: Oxford University Press, 2005.

Africana: The Encyclopedia of the African and African American History. Edited by Kwame Anthony Appiah and Henry Louis Gates Jr. New York: Oxford University Press, 2005.

The Black Collegian Online. http://www.black-collegian.com/.

Black Women in America, 3 vols. 2nd ed. Edited by Darlene Clark Hine. New York: Oxford University Press, 2005.

Black Women in America, 2 vols. Edited by Darlene Clark Hine, Elsa Barkley Brown, and Rosalyn Terborg-Penn. Bloomington: Indiana University Press, 1994.

Brief Biographies: African American Biographies. http://biography.jrank.org/.

Blackpast.org: An Online Reference Guide to African American History. http://www.blackpast.org/.

Campbell, Robert L., Leonard J. Bukowski, and Armin Büttner, The Tom Archia Discography, 2011, Accessed October 1, 2012. http://hubcap.clemson.edu/~campber/archia.html.

ChickenBones: A Journal for Literary & Artistic African American Themes. http://www.nathanielturner.com/jessecovingtondent.htm.

Christine's Genealogy Website. *San Antonio Light.* http://ccharity.com/content/six-negroes-dead-after-battle-citizens-posse.

City Savvy: Online Edition, "Sunnyside Up: Residents Preserve Community's Heritage." http://www.houstontx.gov/savvy/archives/sum05/sum05_sunnyside.htm

Dictionary of Pentecostal and Charismatic Movements. Edited by Stanley M. Burgess and Gary B. McGee. Grand Rapids, Michigan: Zondervan Publishing House, 1988.

Encyclopedia of Black Studies. Edited by Asante, Molfi Kete and Ama Mazama. Thousand Oaks, California: Sage Publications, 2005.

Encyclopedia of the Great Black Migration. Edited by Steven A. Reich. Westport, Connecticut: Greenwood Publishing, 2006.

Encyclopedia of the Great Depression. Edited by Robert McElvaine. New York: Macmillan.

Forever Free: Nineteenth Century African-American Legislators and Constitutional Delegates of Texas, from the Texas State Library and Archives Commission. from http://www.tsl.state.tx.us/exhibits/forever/index.html.

Encyclopedia of the Harlem Renaissance, 2 vols. Edited by Cary D. Wintz and Paul Finkelman New York: Routledge, 2004.

Historic Boston-Edison Association, "Politicians and Public Servants of the Boston-Edison Historic District." http://www.historicbostonedison.org/history/people_pol.shtml.

The History of Jim Crow; An Educators Site Made Possible by New York Life. http://www.pbs.org/wnet/jimcrow/education.html.

Holy Bible.com, accessed July 2, 2011. http://www.holybible.com/.

Houston Business Journal, https://secure.bizjournals.com/subscribe/selectTerm?market=houston&csrc=6325.

Houstonhistory.com. http://houstonhistory.com/.

Handbook of Texas Online. http://www.tshaonline.org/handbook/online/.

"Independence Heights: A Portrait of a Historic Neighborhood." Hogg Middle School, Burrus Elementary School, and the Historic Independence Heights Neighborhood Council along with Rice University, Center for Technology in Teaching and Learning Houston, Texas. Accessed July 14, 2011, http://indepheights.rice.edu/.

In Motion: The African-American Migration Experience. The Schomburg Center for Research in Black Culture. New York Library. http://www.inmotionaame.org/.

Know LA: Encyclopedia of Louisiana. http://www.knowla.org/index.php.

Museum of Fine Arts Houston. *Eye on Third Ward 2012. Historical Reflections on The Third Ward.* http://www.mfah.org/exhibitions/past/eye-third-ward-2012-yates-high-school-photography/.

National Alliance of Postal and Federal Employees (NAPFE), August 24, 1913. http://www.napfe.com/home.php.

The National Medical Association Online. Accessed July 3, 2011. http://www.nmanet.org/.

The Negro Digest.

The Negro World

Oxford Dictionary of Modern Slang. New York: Oxford University Press, 1991.

Professional Musicians Local 47. http://www.promusic47.org/.

R.H. Boyd Publishing Corporation, http://www.rhboydpublishing.com/index.php.

Sigma Pi Phi Fraternity. *The Boulé Journal.* http://www.sigmapiphi.org.

sloangallery.com. http://www.sloanegallery.com.

Smith, Steven. US Army Corps of Engineers Construction Engineering Research Laboratories and US Department of Defense Legacy Resource Management Program. A Historic Context Statement for a World War II Era Black Officers' Club at Fort Leonard Wood, Missouri. http://www.cas.sc.edu/sciaa/PDFdocs/military-research/FLWBlackOfficersClub.pdf.

Swingmusic.net. http://www.swingmusic.net.

Texas Almanac, 2002–2003: 2000 Census Data. Dallas: Dallas Morning News, 2001.
Texas Almanac, 2004–2005. Dallas: Dallas Morning News, 2004.
The United Methodist Church online. http://www.umc.org/site/c.lwL4KnNiLtH/b.1353935/k.4713/Our_mission_is_to_make_disciples_of_Jesus_Christ_for_the_transformation_of_the_world.htm.
University of Louisville. Louis Brandeis School of Law. Black History Month, Louis D. Brandeis School of Law. http://www.law.louisville.edu/node/.
University of Georgia. Civil Rights Digital Library. Digital Library of Georgia. http://crdl.usg.edu/?Welcome/.
University of Houston. Center for Public History. To Bear Fruit for Our Race: A History of African-American Physicians in Houston. http://www.history.uh.edu/cph/tobearfruit/index.html.
University of Louisville. Oral History Index: Y&Z, University Archives and Records, University Libraries, University of Louisville. http://library.louisville.edu/uarc/ohc/ohYZ.html.
Virtualtourist.com. http://www.virtualtourist.com.
Walter Reuther Library, "One Giant Leap for Womankind," Wayne State University, Detroit, Michigan. http://www.reuther.wayne.edu/node/7948.
Wikipedia: The Free Encyclopedia, http://en.wikipedia.org/wiki/Main_Page.
Wiley College. http://www.wileyc.edu/.
Wintz, Cary D., and Paul Finkelman. *Encyclopedia of the Harlem Renaissance.* New York: Routledge, 2004.
YouTube. http://www.youtube.com.

Unpublished Materials

Ahlfield, Danny Lee. "Fraternalism Gone Awry: The Ku Klux Klan in Houston, 1920–1925." Master's thesis, University of Texas at Austin, 1984.
Alexander, Charles Comer. "Invisible Empire in the Southwest: The Ku Klux Klan in Texas, Louisiana, Oklahoma, and Arkansas, 1920–1930." PhD diss., University of Texas at Austin, 1962.
Alexander, J. Trent. "'They're Never Here More Than a Year': Return Migration in the Southern Exodus, 1940–1970." Journal of Social History 38, no. 3 (2005): 653–71.
Anderson, Mariah H. "Private Choices vs. Public Voices: The History of Planned Parenthood in Houston." Master's thesis, Rice University, 1998.
Banks, Melvin James. "In the Pursuit of Equality: The Movement Toward First Class Citizenship among Negroes in Texas, 1920–1950." PhD diss., Syracuse University, 1962.
Bessent, Nancy Ruth Eckols. "The Publisher: A Biography of Carter W. Wesley." Master's thesis, University of Texas, 1981.
Botson, Michael. "The Labor History of Houston's Hughes Tool Company, 1901–1964: From Autonomy and Jim Crow to Industrial Democracy and Civil Rights." PhD diss., University of Houston, 1999.
Brophy, William Joseph. "The Black Texan, 1900–1950: A Quantitative History." PhD diss., Vanderbilt University, 1974.

Campbell, Robert L., Leonard J. Bukowski, and Armin Büttner. *The Tom Archia Discography*. March 29, 2011. http://hubcap.clemson.edu/~campber/archia.html.

Chapman, David L. "Lynching in Texas." Master's thesis, Texas Tech University, 1973.

Codwell, John E., Jr. "Biographical Sketch of John E. Codwell Sr." Unpublished paper presented to Dr. Margaret Ford-Fisher, president, Houston Community College-Northeast, August 30, 2011. In possession of the author.

Cuttler, Leigh H. "'We Really Just Wanted to Dance': The Rise and Decline of Houston's Eldorado Ballroom." Unpublished paper written for Twentieth Century African American History. Professor Gerald Horne, Instructor. December 2005. University of Houston, Houston, Texas.

Digman, Jason Carl. "Which Way to the Promised Land? Changing Patterns in Southern Migration, 1865–1920." PhD diss., University of Illinois at Chicago, 2001.

Ellis, Louis Tuffly. "The Texas Cotton Compress Industry: A History." PhD diss., University of Texas, 1964.

Evans, Samuel Lee. "Texas Agriculture, 1880–1930." PhD diss., University of Texas, 1960.

Gerig, Dan. "Joseph Stephen Cullinan and the Houston Negro Hospital, 1925–1937." Unpublished paper presented at the East Texas Historical Association Fall Meeting, September 25, 2008, Nacogdoches, Texas. In the possession of the author.

—. "The Ku Klux Klan, Invisible Government, and Joseph Stephen Cullinan." Unpublished paper presented at the East Texas Historical Association. September 26, 2009. Nacogdoches, Texas.

Gillette, Michael Lowery. "The NAACP in Texas." PhD diss., University of Texas, 1984.

Glasrud, Bruce Alden. "Black Texans, 1900–1930: A History." PhD diss., Texas Technical College, 1969.

Gray, Laura Lynn. "Women and the American Interracial Movement: A Rhetorical Analysis." PhD diss., Texas Women's University, 2002.

Guzman, Will. "Border Physician: The Life of Lawrence A. Nixon, 1883–1966." PhD diss., University of Texas at El Paso.

Patricia Hale, "Violence in Small Town Texas: The Documentation of East Texas' Lynching Culture." Master's thesis, Sam Houston State University, 2012.

Hardman, Peggy J. "The Anti-Tuberculosis Crusade and the Texas African American Community, 1900–1950." PhD diss. Texas Tech University, 1997.

Hill, Forrest Garrett. "The Negro in the Texas Labor Supply." Master's thesis, University of Texas, 1946.

Hogan, Father Peter, S. S. J. "The Catholic Church and African Americans in Texas." Unpublished paper presented at the Texas Catholic Historical Society. Austin, Texas, 1993. In possession of the author.

Jackson, Larry J. "The Development of Black Business in Texas, 1919–1969: From a Houston Perspective." Master's thesis, Texas Technical University, 1979.

Johnson, Johnny. "African-American Leadership from 1876–1954: A Study of an Urban School District." Ed.D. diss., Texas Southern University, 1993.

Kirven, Lamar L. "A Century of Warfare: Black Texans." PhD diss., Indiana University, 1974.

Kossie, Karen Lynell. "The Move Is On: African-American Pentecostals/Charismatics in the Southwest." PhD diss., Rice University, 1998.

Kossie-Chernyshev, Karen. "Black Educators and Political Activism: The Case of Lillian B. Horace." Unpublished conference paper read at the Texas State Historical Association Annual Meeting, March 5, 2004.

Leavens, Charles W. "Historical Development of the Harris County Welfare Department in Houston, Texas. Master's thesis, Sam Houston State University, 1971, 19–25.

Larissa Lindsay. "Capstone Introduction by Larissa Lindsay of Dr. Thelma Patten." Given March 12, 2009." Unpublished paper presented at an unknown venue, March 12, 2009, Houston, Texas. In possession of the author.

Littlejohn, Jeffrey. "Historian and Activist: Joseph Lynn Clark and the Texas Commission on Interracial Cooperation." An unpublished paper presented at East Texas Historical Association Spring Meeting, Waco, Texas, February 18, 2011.

Murphy, Leonard Brewster. "A History of Negro Segregation Practices in Texas, 1865–1958." Master's thesis, Southern Methodist University, 1958.

Newell, Ellis Elizabeth. "The Life and Works of C. F. Richardson." Senior thesis, Houston College for Negroes, 1941.

Obadele-Starks, Ernest. "The Road to Jericho: Black Workers, the Fair Employment Practice Commission, and the Struggle for Racial Equality in the Upper Gulf Coast, 1941–1947." PhD diss., University of Houston, 1996.

Parrish, Thomas Michael. "'The Species of Slave Labor': The Convict Lease System in Texas, 1871–1914. Master's thesis, Texas Tech University, 1976.

Passie, M. Louise. "Freedmantown: The Evolution of a Neighborhood in Houston, 1865–1880." Master's thesis, Rice University, 1993.

Pruitt, Bernadette. "The Urban Transformation of the MacGregor Area, 1950–1970." Master's thesis, Texas Southern University, 1991.

—. "'For the Advancement of the Race': African American Migration and Community Building in Houston, 1914–1945," PhD diss., University of Houston, 2001.

—. "Challenging Whiteness and Celebrating Blackness: One Scholar's Journey," unpublished paper presented at the East Texas Historical Association, September 28, 2012, Nacogdoches, Texas.

Reich, Steven A. "The Making of a Southern Sawmill World: Race, Class, and Rural Transformation in the Piney Woods of East Texas, 1830–1930." PhD diss., Northwestern University, 1998.

SoRelle, James M. "The Darker Side of 'Heaven': The Black Community in Houston, 1917–1945." PhD diss., Kent State University, 1980.

Steptoe, Tyina Leaneice. "Dixie West: Race, Migration, and the Color Lines in Houston, Texas." PhD diss., University of Wisconsin, 2008.

Thomas, Lorenzo. "Milt Larkin: Houston Jazz Bandleader." Unpublished paper presented at the Texas State Historical Association Annual Meeting, Austin, Texas, 1998. In possession of the author.

Ward, Roger Townsend, "Acres Shakers: The Solution to Public Transportation Needs in a Black Community." Master's thesis, University of Houston, 1993.

Wille, Pamela Faith. "More Than Classes in Swimming and Making Hats: The YWCA and Social; Reform in Houston. Texas, 1907–1977." PhD diss., Texas Tech University, 2004, 54–91.
Wilson, Jon. Ralph. "Origins: The Houston NAACP, 1915–1918." Master's thesis, University of Houston, 2005.
Zeigler, Robert E. "The Workingman in Houston, Texas, 1865–1914." PhD diss., Texas Tech University, 1972.
Zellar, Gary. "Rogersville: The Historic Legacy of a Neighborhood," unpublished paper presented to the Huntsville Arts Commission, February 1, 2003, Huntsville, Texas, 2–12.

Oral Histories and Interviews

Note: Tape recordings and transcripts in possession of the author.

Adams, Leola Baker—September 21, 2005
Baker, James—November 27, 2004
Baker, Wendell—Various interviews between February 1, 2003, and April 5, 2008
Bryant, Thelma Scott—July 24, 1996
Clark, Yvonne—Accessed September 27, 2011; interview with Society for Women Engineers, http://societyofwomenengineers.swe.org/index.php?option=com_content&task=view&id.=963&Itemid=55.
Codwell, John E. Jr.—May 3, 2012
Cole, Nell Grovey—April 19, 2008
Coleman, Henry—February 13, 1998
Collins, Catherine—December 25, 2005
Douglas, James—June 30, 1998
Felt, Sam—July 23, 1991
Hayes, Robert, Sr.—July 30, 1996
Harrison, Lullelia—September 23, 1999, March 8, 2000
Hayden, Vera—December 25, 2010
Johnson, London—June 12, 1999
Ledé, Naomi—February 1, 2003
Lewis, Raymond—February 14, 1998
Lively, Malcolm— March 17, 1993
McPhereson, Alice—April 13, 2007
Pruitt, Clarence Edward—August 23, 1999, July 16, 1999
Pruitt, Frank— November 28, 2010
Richardson Jr., Clifton—June 9, 1975; interview by Louis Marchiafava and Veronica Perry, http://digital.houstonlibrary.org/oral-history/cliff-richardson.php.
Seals, Vivian Hubbard—May 17, 1999
Stinson, Michael Shawn—July 10, 1996
Stullivan, Luther—July 23, 1996
Williams, Joseph—February 13, 1998
Young, Hazel—August 7, 1996

INDEX

Note: Page numbers in *italics* indicate figures and tables; those in **bold** indicate maps.

Abiding Courage (Lemke-Santangelo), 257
Abner, David, Jr., 95
absentee landlords, 85–86, 130
accommodationism
    Booker T. Washington on, 147
    and culture of slavery, 147–48, 149–50
    healthcare professionals, 131
    in "New Negro" movement, 177–78, 182
    and political apathy, 181–82
    and self-help in public schools, 120–25
    v. integration, 97
    and White hegemony, 148–49
Acres Homes, 65, 80, 81, 91–92
Adair, Christia (nee Daniels), *23*, 82, 110, 176–77
Adair, Elbert, *23*, 82, 176
Adams, Luther, 9, 274
advertisements and migration appeal, 42, 44–45, 51
Africa, identification with, 21–22, *112*, 188
African American Pentecostal (AAP) sect, 112–13
African Americans. *See* Blackness, culture of; racial consciousness; racial identity
Afro-American Baptist Church, 101
age of migrants, overviews, 34–35, *229*, 257–58
agency. *See* community agency
Agricultural Adjustment Administration (AAA), 253, 272, 273–74
agriculture
    Depression era effects on, 265–66, 272, 274
    rural hardships and migration, 11, 30, 53, 77, 281
    tenant farming, 22–24, 272, 274, 293*n* 11
    See also cotton industry
Alabama, migration from, 30, *54*, 82, 103
Alexander, Alfred, 81
Alfred, James g., 168
Allen, Richard, 100
Allen brothers (Augustus Chapman and John Kirby), 25
Alpha Kappa Alpha Sorority (AKA), 70, *71*, 107, 262
American Federation of Labor (AFL), 217
American Mutual Benefit Association building, 204
American Woodmen, 103
Ames, Jesse Harriet Daniels, 153
Ancient Order of Pilgrims, 102, *243*, 259
    See also Pilgrim Building/Temple

Anderson, L. C., 58
Andrews, R. T., 43
annexation of communities, 28, 82, 85, 86, 160, 377n 99
Antioch (Missionary) Baptist Church, 100, 107, 111, *112*, 144
anti-Semitism, 29, 84
Apollo Theater Band, 197
Apostolic Faith movement, 113
Aragon Ballroom, 189, 196
Archia, Richie Dell, 188–89, 190, 202–3
Archia, Tom, 187–91
Archie/a, Ernest Alvin, Jr. (and family), 187–88
See also Archia, Tom
Aristocrat Records, 190
Army, US and Houston Riot, 141–42
Army Reorganization Act, 338n 1
Arnesen, Eric, 270
1906 Art and Literary Club, 109
arts, visual, 207–12
arts and culture. *See* cultural Renaissance and "New Negro" movement
Association of Colored Trainmen and Locomotive Firemen (ACT), 271
Association of Railway Trainmen, 19
Association of Southern Women for the Prevention of Lynching (ASWPL), 153–54
At Freedom's Edge (Cohen), 219
Atchison, Topeka and Santa Fe Railway, 25
Atkins, Jasper Alston, 167
Austin, Bertha Lee, 76
Austin County, migration from, 1, 272
Azusa Street Revival, 113

B. B. King, 206
Bailey, Ernestine Mae, 182
Baker, James Addison, Sr., 72, 149
Baker, James Otis "Pap," 267–68
Baker, Newton, 141–42
Baltimore, Charles, 145–46
Banks, W. R., 153

Baptist Association for African Americans, 100
Baptist religion and churches, overview, 111–12
See also individual churches
Baptist university, support for, 171–72
Barclay, DeWitt Farris, *62*
Baron Rouge, Louisiana, 91
Barr, Alwyn, 32
beauty industry, 56, 239–40, 241, 277
bebop, 190
bed and breakfast inns, 79–80
Bell, John Brown, 100, 149, 244
Bellville (Texas), migration from, 1–2, 46, 272
benefits organizations, 102–3, 104–5, 245, 259, 260
benevolent societies, 101–6
See also service organizations
Benjamin, Karen, 118
Bethel Baptist Church, 107
Bethlehem Center, 107
Bethune, Mary McLeod, 60, *63*
"Big Boss Man," 195–96
"big-foot swing," 197
bigotry, defense strategies, 55–56
Bilbo, Theodore, 190
"Bilbo is Dead," 190
Bill Pinkard quartet, 189
binary migration, 50
Birth of a Nation (film), 159
Bishop College, 55, 208–9
Black Brains Trust, *63*
Black Cabinet (Federal Council of Negro Affairs), *63*
Black History and Black Identity (Wright, W. D.), 297–98n 21
"Black" terminology issues, 297–98n 21
Black Urban Professionals (BUPPIES), 247
Blackness, culture of
activism for, *43*
embracing under accommodation stance, 87

emergence, 12, 98
fear of and White supremacy, 219
and music/arts, influence of, 187, 188, 191, 192, 207, 212
physical beauty and Black/White dichotomy, 239, 240
Black-on-Black crime, 182–83
Blackwelder, Julia, 239
Blair, Barbara, 22
Blue Triangle branch of YWCA, 96, 107
blues culture, 195–96
Booker T. Washington High School, 58–59, 73, 123, *124*, 238
Boy Scouts of America, 19, 107
Boyd, Archie and Emily, 256–57
Boze, Calvin, 189
Bradford, Bobby, 364*n* 35
Brazoria County, migration from, 69, 163
Brazos County, migration from, 173
Brazos River, 67
Brewer, John Mason, 193
bridges, cultural, 53, 78, 89, 109, 175, 191, 278
Bright, Margaret H., 179–80
Bronze Peacock, 198, 205
Brooks, Carrie Jane (nee Sutton), *135, 136*
Brophy, William, 265
Brotherhood of Sleeping Car Porters, 270
Brotherhood of Timber Workers, 17
Brown, Tony Russell (Charles), 189
"Brown" terminology issues, 297–98*n* 21
Brownsville Raid, 143
Bryant, Ira Babington, 72–73, 123–25, 237, 238
Bryant, Thelma Scott, *128, 290*
on Black crime, 183
on dance halls, 204
and family, priority of, 237
family profile, 72–73
on Houston Riot, 146–47
on Klan violence, 160, 161
on physicians, 180
on Southern segregationist culture, 162
on teachers and discrimination, 120
Buchanan v. Warley, 84, 353*n* 64
Buffalo Bayou, 25–26
Bukowski, Leonard J., 187
Burleson County, migration from, 35–36, 173
businesses/business owners, African American
1929 profile and value, *247–48*
beauty industry, 239–41
civic involvement and community agency, 241–45, 249
Depression era, effects of, 259, 260
Fifth Ward business district, 244
Fourth Ward business district, 67, *242,* 243–44
growth and success of, 245–46
office space for, 102, 243–44, 259
racial unity, lack of, 250
temporary work and financial opportunities, 218
Third Ward business district, 244
Büttner, Armin, 187

C. U. Luckie Elementary School Mothers' Club, 107
Cab Calloway Band, 203, 204
Cabaness family, murder of, 158, 314*n* 5
Caffey, Etta, 260
Callaloo, 97
Calloway, Cab, 198, 203, 204
Camp Logan, 141, 142–43
See also Houston Riot of 1917
Campbell, Randolph, 32
Campbell, Robert L, 187
Caribbean immigrants, 28–29, 102, 134, 143, 306*n* 44
Carlee, Kendall, 211
Carnegie, Andrew, 103–4
Carnegie Colored Library, 103–4

Carroll Dickerson band, 189
Carter, H. P., 122
castration as punishment, 160
Catholic religion and churches, 78, 113–16, 236–37
chain migration
    definition/overviews, 53, 76, 92–93, 281–82
    and job mobility, 219–20
    networks, 20–21, 51–53
    newspapers as aid to, 42–44
    rental housing, 49–50
    women's roles, 50–51
    See also community agency; step wise migration
Chamber of Commerce, Houston, 44–45, 250
charitable works. *See* service organizations
Charles, Ray, 206
Chicago music scene, 190–91
child labor, 2–3, 225
Christian, Garna, 147
Christian principle and accommodationism, 181
Chrysler Motor Corporation, 246
Church of God in Christ (COGIC), 112–13
churches
    and chain migration support, 42
    church women, influence of, 116–17
    community building, 100
    denominations and profiles, 111–16
    Depression era aid by, 262
    Fourth Ward, 69
    See also individual churches, religions
"Cimbee's Ramblings" (column), 192–93
CIO (Congress of Industrial Organizations), 49, 269, 271, 275, 286
city services and health issues, 82, 85–86, 129–30
City Wide Beauticians Association, 241
Civic Betterment League (CBL), 156–57
civic organizations and migration appeal, 44–45
Civil Right Movement (modern), roots of, 97, 269–71, 285–87
Civil Works Administration (CWA), 167, 265, 267
Civilian Conservation Corps (CCC), 265, 266–67
"C-Jam Blues," 204
The Clansman (Dixon), 159
Clark, Joseph Lynn, 154
Clark, William F., Jr., *59*
Clark, Yvonne (nee Young), *59, 60*
Clarke, Juanita, 137–38
class divisions among African Americans, 66, 87–92, 108–9
    See also stratification of African American community
classical music, *201*
clerical occupations, 231
Clinton, Bill, 203–4
clustering, 84–85
Cobb, Arnett, *127,* 189, 205
Cockrell, John Lafayette, 160
Cohen, William, 218–19
Cole, Nell, 164–65, 170, 183
Coleman, Lee and Richard, 49, 282
Coleman, Robert, 158
colleges/universities, inequities in, 119
    See also higher education
Collins, Arma, 18–20
Collins, J. D. and J. T., *112*
Collins, Jefferson E. "Jeff" and Ella, 15–17
Collins, Luther, 163
Colonel Mayfield's Weekly, 159
"the color line," 193
Colored Carnegie Library, 103–4
Colored High School, 59, 122, 231
    See also Booker T. Washington High School
Colored Teachers State Association of Texas (CTSAT), *58,* 122

Commission on Interracial Cooperation. *See* TCIRC (Texas Commission on Interracial Cooperation)
Committee on Fair Employment Practice, 285
community agency
    definition/overviews, 10, 53, 97, 138–39
    evolution of, 98–101
    and musical culture, 194
    and self-sufficiency, 22
    and slavery, legacy of, 88–89, 98–100, 147–48
    See also businesses/business owners, African American; chain migration; self-help strategies and community building
community building
    churches, 100, 111–17
    community pride, 82
    overview, 10–12, 282
    and unions, 269
    women's organizations, 106–10
    See also community agency
community centers, 109, 127–28, 205–7
Community Chest, Houston, 105, 106–7, 261, 262
conciliatory approach. *See* accommodationism
Congress of Industrial Organizations (CIO), 49, 269, 271, 275, 286
constructionalism, 147–48, 153, 157
    See also accommodationism
convict-labor laws, 219
coping mechanisms, 182–83, 206–7
    See also cultural Renaissance and "New Negro" movement
cosmetology profession, 239–40
    See also beauty industry
Costigan-Wagner anti-lynching bill, 154
cotton industry
    boll weevils, 30
    Depression era, effects of, 272–73
    farming regions, 32
    job opportunities, 16, 218, 236
    migration from, 35–36
Countee, Samuel Albert, 207–10
Countee, Thomas and family, 207
Covington, Benjamin Jesse "B. J.," 31–32, *74*, 95–96, 133, 178–79
Covington, Ernestine Jessie, *31, 128–29, 201*
Covington, Jennie Belle (nee Murphy), 31–32, *74*, 87, 95–97, 105, 106–7, 129
    activism of, 152–53, 156, 175
Crawford, Audrey Y., 106
Crawford, Fredda, 120, *121*
Crawford, Mary, 108, *288*
Crawford, R. E. and Vanita, *121*
Creole settlers and culture, 77–79, 306*n* 306
criminal activity as coping mechanism, 182–83
Criollo. *See* Creole settlers and culture
The Crisis: A Record of the Darker Races, 151
Crockett (Texas), migration from, 15, 55, 72, 123
Cruise, Andrew, *112*
cuisine, Creole, 78–79, 244
Cullinan, Joseph S., 133–34, 149, 159, 178–79
cultural constructs, and Southern racial identity, 11, 21–22
    See also Blackness, culture of; Southern culture of segregation
cultural Renaissance and "New Negro" movement
    cultural awareness and racial consciousness, 191–92, 212
    overview, 187
    print media, 192–93
    Tom Archia, 187–91
    visual arts, 207–12
    See also musical Renaissance and cultural consciousness
culture and arts, 56, 58, 69
    See also cultural Renaissance and "New Negro" movement

Cuney, Norris Wright, 101
customary segregation, 83, 84–85
Cutler, Leigh H., 205, 207

Dallas (Texas), industrialization of, 27, 266
dance halls/clubs, 204–7
Daniels, Christia and family, 176–77
Daniels, Rufus, 146
Darcus Home for Delinquent Girls, 107
Daughters of Czar, 103
Davis, John, 70
Davis, William Leonard, 52, 156–57, 158, 166
Davis Robinson, Martha Francis (nee Sneed), 69–70
Day, Etta and family, 220
de facto/de jure segregation, 83, 84, 148
deaf, rights of, 116–17
deaths of African Americans
 Depression era, 36, 39, 252–53, 254–55
 and poor health issues, 130, 131, 132
Delta Sigma Theta Sorority, 107, *135*, 136
Democratic Party, 166–70, 264
Dent, Albert Thomas, *31*, 96
Dent, Ernestine Jessie (nee Covington), *31*, 96, 128–29
Dent, Thomas, 96–97
Department of Welfare, Texas (TDW), 265
Depression. *See* Great Depression
desegregation efforts, resistance to, 84, 154–55
 See also NAACP (National Association for the Advancement of Colored People)
The Development of Houston Negro Schools (Bryant), 124
Dewalt/DeWalt, O. P., 163
DeWitt County, migration from, 32, 95
Dibble, Elias, 100
Dickerson, Carroll. *See* Carroll Dickerson band

diet and health issues, 39, 130
disabled, rights of, 116–17
discrimination
 gender inequalities, 116, 131, 136, 155, 173–75, 238
 in healthcare, 129, 132
 in medical profession, 132–33, 134–36, 137–38, 178–80
 schools/teachers/faculty, 24, 119–20, 225, 238, 281, 285–86
 by social service/welfare organizations, 262, 266–67
 in unions, 17, 215, 217, 271
 See also segregation
disease, 56, 85–86, 129–30, 131–32
disenfranchisement of Blacks, 24, 165–70
Dixon, Thomas, 159
dockworkers, 90–91, 223–24
domestic/service occupations, 216, 230, 233–34, 280
"Double V" slogan, 284–85
Douglass, Desso, 283–84
Du Bois, W. E. B., 97, 125, 142, 151, 183, 193
Dupree, Clarence A. and Anna, 205–6, 241, 277–78
Durden, Mary, 284
Dyett, Walter Henry, 200

East Texas, migration from, overviews, 5, 15, 17–18, 32
Eastern Star, 175
Edna (Texas), migration from, *23*, 176
education and health/lifestyle improvement, 130
educational inequity, 24, 118–19, 225
educators, African American, *58*
 salaries, inequities in, 119–20, 238, 281, 285–86
 self-help exemplars, 120–25, 126–29
 women as, 237–39, 280–81
Edwards, Alonzo, 144–45
Edwards, Lela, 273
Eldorado Ballroom, 198, 205–7, 277–78

Eldridge, Roy, 189
elite Afro-Americans, 65, 72, 73–74, 88–89, 108–9, 257
    See also class divisions among African Americans
Eliza Johnson Home for the Negro Ages, 278
Ellington, Duke, *127*, 202–3, 204
Ellington Field, 141
Emancipation Park, 100, 365n 50
Emergency Committee for Employment, 264
Emergency Committee for Unemployment, 264
employment participation rates, 225–32, 233
    See also workforce
equal protection clause of Fourteenth Amendment, 166
Ethel Ransom Art and Literary Club, 107
European immigrants
    Afro-American relations, 47–48
    Fifth Ward, 75–76, 79
    internal migrations, 29–30
    and population growth, 28–29
    and residential segregation patterns, 83
    in skilled workforce, 216
    Third Ward, 72
Exodus of 1879, 100
Exodusters, 9

Fair Employment Practice Committee (FEPC), 285
Falls, H. W., 113
Falls County, migration from, 95
family, importance of
    connections and proximity, importance of, 9–11, 42, 49, 50, 51–53
    working mothers *v.* homemakers, 234–35, 236–37
    See also chain migration
farm tenancy, 22–24, 272, 274, 293n 11
Farrow, Lucy F., 113
Fats Domino, 206
Fayette County, migration from, 52–53
Federal Council of Negro Affairs, *63*
Federal Emergency Relief Administration (FERA), 252, 265
Federal Reconstruction Finance Corporation, 264
Ferguson, Miriam, 159
Fifteenth Amendment rights, 170
    See also voting rights
Fifth Ward
    business district, 244
    churches in, 113, 114–15
    Louisiana-born migrants in, 65, 77–78, 79–80, 281
    map, **64**
    Mexican-origin Texans in, 75
    migrants coming to, profiles, 57–60, 127–28, 188
    nightclubs, 205, 244
    profile of, 65, 75–80
    Southern Pacific Railroad, 75, 214
    See also Wheatley High School
Fifth Ward Civic Club, *169*
First Great Migration
    African Diaspora and migration theme, 3–4
    and community building, overview, 10
    overviews, 53, 279–83, 287, 289
    stages of, 20
    urban development and motivations for, 4–5, 9, 11
    See also chain migration; internal migration
Fisher, Robert, 84
Fitzgerald, Ella, 203
flooding and health issues, 130
floods, 39–40, 77, 130
    See also Great Mississippi Flood (1927)
Flory, Ishmael, 270
Fluellen, Marie, 1
"Flying Home," 203

folklore and racial consciousness, 193
food, Depression era relief, 265
food safety issues, 130
Forde, George Patrick Alphonse, 134
Foster, Marcellus, 72, 149, 159
Fourteenth Amendment rights, 166
Fourth Ward
    business district, *242*, 243–44
    hospitals in, 133
    map, **64**
    Pilgrim Building, 102
    profile, 66–71, *73*
    riot of 1917, 144–47
Franklin, John Hope, 124
Franklin, Nobia A., 239–40
Franklin, Sonny Boy, 197
Franklin Beauty School, 239–40
fraternal orders, 101–4
    See also individual organizations
Frazier, J. W., 176
Freedmantown, 67
Freedmen's Aid Society, 102
Freedmen's Bureau, 15, 67
Freemasons, 102
French Army, Black soldiers in, 142
Frenchtown, 77–78, *115*, 236–37
Friskin, James, *201*
From Slavery to Freedom (Franklin), 124

Galveston (Texas), migration from, 26, *28*, 68, 268, 277
Garvey, Marcus, 151
Garza, Pauline B., 136
Gay, Willie Lee, *290*
gender discrimination, 116, 131, 136, 155, 173–75, 238
generational activism, 99
generational activism/gap, 287–88
Georgia natives, migration of, 30, 100, 127
Gillespie, Dizzy, 190, 203
Gilmore, Campbell A., 43
Gladys City Oil, Gas and Manufacturing Company, 26

glossolalia, 113
Good Hope Baptist Church, 173–74
Goodall, T. J., *112*
Goodman, Benny, 203
Gottlieb, Peter, 219
gradualism approach, 155
Grand Court Order of Calanthe, 103, 105, 175
Grand Lodge of the Knights of Pythias, 102, 104–5
Grand United Order of Odd Fellows (GUOOF), 259, 260
    See also Odd Fellows
Grantz, Norman, 189–90, 203
Gray, Willie Lee, 124
Great Depression
    economic/social effects, overview, 250–52, 260, 282–83
    hardship overviews, 2–3
    and job competition, 215
    and migration, effect on, 252–53, 256–58, 260, 273–74, 275
    relief programs, federal, 263–69
    relief programs, local and state, 260–63
    and women's organizations, 105–6
Great Flood. *See* Great Mississippi Flood (1927)
Great Migrations, origins and background, 21–28
    See also First Great Migration; Second Great Migration
Great Mississippi Flood (1927), 39–40, 65, 77, 114–15, 253, 281
Greater Zion Baptist Church, 171
Greene, Lorenzo, 45
Gregory Institute, 100
Griffith, D. W., 159
Grigsby v. Harris, 352n 106
Grimes County, migration from, 31, 47–49, 50, 77, 82, 122
Grovey, Richard Randolph, 163–65, 167, 168–70, 178
Grovey v. Townsend, 168–69, 175, 249

Gruening, Martha, 152
Guess, Richard, 178
Guillory, Alice, 235
Gunnel, Octavia, *63*
gynecology/obstetrics, 135–36

Hagan, William, *112*
Hainsworth, Harry and Beatrice and family, 82, *112*, 231, 237
Hainsworth, Hazel (nee Young), *71, 112,* 120, *124, 125,* 126
Hainsworth, Thelma, 128–29, *290*
hair and grooming. *See* beauty industry
Hale, Grace Elizabeth, 24, 98–99
Hampton, Lionel, 203
The Handbook of Texas Online, 211
Harding, Warren G., 176–77
Hardman, Peggy, 137–38
Hardy, Henry Cohen, 102, *243*
Harlem Renaissance, 191, 207, 208
Harmon, William E., 209
Harmon Collection, 207
Harper, Nathaniel and Mary, 91–92
Harris County Board of Welfare and Employment, 265
Harris County Democratic Executive Committee (HCDEC), 166
Harris County Department of Public Welfare (HCDPW), 252
Harris County Medical Society, 136–37
Harris County Negro Democratic Club (HCNDC), 167
Harris County Social Service, 265
Harrison, Alexander, 90
Harrison, Edwin, *18*
Harrison, Hubert H., 143
Harrison, Lullelia, 83, 110, 120, 268
Harrison, Stafford, *242*
Harrison County, migration from, 1, 15
Hawkins, Coleman, 190
Hayes, Edward Wilbur, 1–2, 32, 282
Hayes, Marie (nee Fluellen), 1–2
Hayes, Robert, 2, 3
Haynes, Ella, 15–17

Haynes, George, 189
Haynes, Rovert V., 147
health insurance, 102, 104, 105
health issues
    Depression era assistance, 265
    disease, *56,* 85–86, 129–30, 131–32
    healthcare, lack of, and discrimination, 129, 132
    hospitals, 132–33, 133–36, 178–80
    and inadequate housing/services, 85–86, 129–30
    insurance, 102, 104, 105
    nurses, African American, 20, 137–38
    post-WWII improvements, 285
    self-help strategies, 130–31
healthcare. *See* health issues
healthcare professionals
    and bigotry, 132–35
    nurses, African American, 20, 137–38
    physicians, African American, 132–33, 134–36, 178–80
    See also health issues
hearing-impaired, rights of, 116–17
"Heavenly Houston," 45
Helen Humes and Her Allstars, 189–90
Henry, Georgina, 203
Henry, V. C., *112*
Henry, Vida, 146
Hermann, George H., 72
Hermann Hospital, 132, 133
Hermione Lodge, 104–5
Heroines of Jericho, 103
Hester, Julia C., 126–28
Hester House, 127–28
Higginbotham, Elizabeth Brooks, 116
higher education
    activism for, 171–72
    Baptist university, support for, 171–72
    desegregation efforts, 154
    importance of, 187
    inequities in, 119

Highland Heights, 81
Hine, Darlene Clark, 22, 136, 138, 169, 173
Hines, Chester, 271–72
Historically Black Colleges and Universities (HBCUs), *110*, 155, 171–72
Hobby, William P., 149
Holy and Noble Order of the Knights of Labor, 217
homemakers, 236–37
homeownership, importance of, 67, 130
honking, 197, 203
Hoover, Herbert, 263–64
Horton, "Big" Walter, 195
hospitals, 132–33, 133–36, 178–80
Household of Ruth, 103
housing
    homeownership, importance of, 67, 130
    inadequacy of, 85–86, 129–30
    new developments, 86–87
    projects, federal, 60
    projects, municipal, 87
    temporary boarding, 82
Houston, Constance Eloise, *56*, 60, *61*, *62*, *63*, 79–80
Houston, Georgia (nee Orviss), 54, 55–60, *61*
Houston, Harold, *54*
Houston, Hortense Cordelia, 58–60, *62*
Houston, Joshua, Jr., Martha and family, *54*, 55–60
Houston, Sam, *54*, 55
Houston, Samuel Walker, *54*, 55, *62*, 153
Houston, Texas
    industrial growth and development, 26–28
    origins of, 25
    settlement highlights, 55–60, 55–66
    settlement patterns, 60, 62–66
    settlement profiles, 66–82
    See also wards (Houston neighborhoods)
Houston Baptist Academy, 100
Houston Chronicle, 159
Houston College for Negroes, 119, 278
Houston Colored Junior College (HCJC), 119
Houston Commission on Interracial Cooperation. *See* TCIRC (Texas Commission on Interracial Cooperation)
Houston County, migration from, 15, 237, 253
Houston Defender, 43
Houston Foundation, 106, 260
Houston Housing Authority, 87
Houston Independent School District, 118, 286
Houston Informer, 135
    anti-racial activism, 150
    and chain migration support, 42, 44
    on Communism, appeal of, 269
    founding of, 43–44
    and rural coverage, 11
    satire and racial consciousness, 192–93
    on solidarity of segregation, 249
    on unemployment, Depression era, 258
    on White violence, 160
    See also Richardson, Clifton F.
Houston Informer and Texas Freeman, 116
    See also Houston Informer
Houston Junior College (HJC), 119
Houston Junior College for Negroes, 100
Houston Lyceum and Carnegie Library, 103
Houston Methodist Church, 100
Houston Museum of Fine Arts, 207
Houston Music Hall, 203
Houston Mutiny. *See* Houston Riot of 1917
Houston Negro Community Center, 127
Houston Negro Hospital, 132, 133–36, 178–80

INDEX 441

Houston Observer, 43
The Houston Place, 79–80
Houston Press, 202
Houston Public School System
    racial segregation/discrimination, 117–18
    self-help exemplars, 120–25, 126–29
    women educators, impact of, 125–29, 237–39
    See also educators, African American; *individual schools*
Houston Riot of 1917, *43,* 84, 141–47, 150, 159
Houston Settlement Association, 107
Houston Ship Channel, 9, 25–26, 223–24
Houston Unemployment Aid Committee, 261
Houstonian Normal Institute, 55
HT Taxicab Co., 246, 249
Hubbard, Ella K. (nee Kyle), 31, 80–82
Hubbard, Oliphant Lockwood, 31, 80–82, 160
Huggins, William O., 168
Huggins Plan, 168
Hughes, George, 158
Humes, Helen, 189–90
Huntsville (Texas), migration from, 55–57, 105, 135, 149
hurricanes, 26, 68

Ideson, Julia, 103–4
immigration and population growth, 28–29
In the Name of Colored High, '04 (Jefferson, R.), *69*
Independence Heights, 28, 65, 80–82, 244
Independent Colored Voters Leagues (ICVL), 158, 167
Indians, American, 199
industrial development and migration, 4–6, 213–15, 217, 280, 283
inferiority myth, engaging, 148, 180, 182–83

"infrapolitics," 164–65
institution building and women's organizations, 106–10
institutionalized racism, 118, 235–36
insurance benefits through service organizations. *See* benefits organizations
internal migration
    Depression era, effects of, 252–53, 256–58, 260, 273–74, 275
    East Texas overview, 32
    and New Deal programs, 272
    overviews and description, 1–14, 20, 53, 278–80, 289
    Texas profile, 32–36
    White immigrants, 29–30
    See also Louisiana-born African American migrants
internalization of oppression, 180–84
International Association of Railroad Employees (IARE), 271
International Brotherhood of Redcaps (IBRC), 270–71
International Longshoremen's Association (ILA), 52, 223–24
interracial cooperation
    and activism, 87, 153–54, 156, 176–77
    and culture of accommodation, 149–50
    See also bridges, cultural
interracial relationships, 47–48, 190
intraregional migration. *See* internal migration

Jack Yates High School. *See* Yates High School
Jackson County, migration from, *23,* 176
Jacquet, Gilbert and family, 198–200
Jacquet, Illinois (Jean-Baptiste), *127,* 189, 198–200, 203–4, 205
Jacquet, Russell, 189, 203
James D. Ryan Middle School, *125,* 126
Jammin' the Blues (film), 203

jazz
    emerging culture of, 196–200
    Wheatley High School program, 127, 188–89, 196, 200, 202–3
Jazz at the Philharmonic (JATP), 190, 203
Jemison, James H., 239–41
Jewish immigrants, 29, 72, 75, 84
Jim Crow culture, 24
job discrimination
    Louisiana-born migrants, 90, 214, 220, 230
    overviews, 281
    post-WWII profile, 285–87
    in teaching, 237–38
    and unions, 17, 215–17, 224, 271
    for women, 234–36
    See also salaries/wages
Johnson, Andrew, 338*n* 1
Johnson, Anna, 277–78
Johnson, Conrad, 205
Johnson, Frank, 145
Johnson, G. S., *112*
Johnson, James Weldon, 152
Johnson, Lyndon Baines, 249
Johnson, Mary L. (nee Jones), 96, 105, *125*, 126, *127*
Johnson, S. W., 155
Johnson, Walter, 98
Johnson, William "Billie," 116
Joint Council of Dining Car Employees, 270
Jones, Edith Irby, 137
Jones, Jacqueline, 233, 234–35
Jones, Jesse H., 149
Jones, Mary L., 96, 105, *125*, 126, *127*
Jones, Will J., 122
Jordan, Barbara, *127*, *169*, 176
Josephites, 114–15
Julia C. Hester House, 127–28
Julliard Musical Foundation, *201*
"Jump Through the Window," 189
Justice, Geneva Mae, 20

Kashmere Gardens High School, *123*, 124
Kaufman County, migration from, 175
Kellar, William H., 117, 286
Kelley, Robin D. G., 10, 164, 182, 183
Kelln, Fredda, 190
Kennedy, John F., 249
kidnappings, 160
King, B. B., 206
King, Wallace and Cleopatra, 258
Kirby, John H., 159
Kirby Lumbering Company, 5
Knights and Daughters of Tabor, 102–3
Knights of Peter Claver, 114
Knights of Pythias, 102, 104–5
Kossie-Chernyshev, Karen, 112–13, 116
Ku Klux Klan (KKK), Second, 159–62
Kyle, Ella K., 31, 80–82

La Grange (Texas), migration from, 52
La Porte (Texas), migration from, 116
labor agents and control of workforce, 51, 219
labor market. *See* workforce
labor organizations, 165
    See also unions
Ladies Symphony Orchestra, *128*, 129
landownership, importance of, 22
Langham, Emily, *208*, 209
Larkin, Ella, 77, 82
Larkin, Milton, 50, 77, 196–98, 205
    See also Milton Larkin band
Latinos. *See* Mexican-origin Texans
Lavaca County, migration from, 156
Law, James, 136
Law, Thelma Adele (nee Patten), 135–37, 237
Lea, Margaret M., *54*
Ledé, Naomi, 56, *61*
Lee, Henry E., 85, 129–32
Lee, Herbert, 179–80
Lemke-Santangelo, Gretchen, 257
Leon County, migration from, 176
Lewis, Bertha Marie (nee Thomas), 79
Lewis, Charles E., 49, 79

Lewis, Earl, 41, 225
Lewis, Hazel, 3
Liberty County, migration from, 220
libraries, African American, 103–4
life insurance, 102, 104
    See also benefits organizations
The Links, Inc., *69,* 70, 107
Lionel Hampton Orchestra, 203
Lipscomb, Mance, 195–96
Little Brown Boy (painting), 209
living conditions. *See* housing
loans to African Americans, 81, 100, 104, 105, 264
Locke, Alain, 143, 209
Lockett, R. G., 122
lodges, fraternal, 101–4
Logan, John A., 141
logging. *See* timber industry
Lomax, John, 202
Lone Star State Medical Association, 133, *135,* 136
Lonely Crusade (Hines), 271–82
longshoremen, 90–91, 223–24
Longview Riot 1919, 158
Louisiana-born African American migrants
    and class stratification in Houston, 93
    Creole settlers and culture, 77–79, 306*n* 306
    Depression era patterns, 251, 253, 256
    Fifth Ward settlement, 65, 77–78, 79–80, 281
    Illinois Jacquet, 199
    and job mobility, 49, 220
    mortality figures, 36, 39, *255,* 256
    pre-Depression era patterns, 20, 21–22, 24, 30, 32, 36, 39–41
    profiles of, 3–4, 10–12, 91, 113, 114–15
    and skilled-labor dichotomy, 90, 214, 220, 230
Louisville, Kentucky, *59,* 60
Love, Charles Novell, 44, 166

Love v. Griffith 1922 and 1924, 166
Loyal Friends of America, 103
Lucas, Albert Anderson, 172, 173, 178
Lucas, Anthony, 26
lumber industry. *See* timber industry
lynching, 49, 57, 153–54, 158–59, 160

MacDonald, John, 41
MacDonald, Leatrice, 41
Macomba Lounge, Chicago, 190
Making Whiteness (Hale), 24
male leadership and manhood concept, 173
Mandell, Arthur J., *174*
manhood concept and male leadership, 173
Married Ladies Social, Art & Charity Club, 69, 107, 108–9, *288*
Marshall, Thurgood, 170
Marshall (Texas), migration from, 1, 43, 136, 169, 208, 277
Mason, Charles H., 113
Masons (Freemasons), 102
Masterson, Martha Emma, 68–69
Matagorda County, migration from, 100
Maternal Health Center, 136
Maxwell, Louise Passey, 83
Mayfield, Billie, 159
McBride, Luther and Louise, 76
McCullough, Olee Yates, *290*
McDade family, 187
McDavid, Fountain L. and family, 200, 202
McDavid, Percy, *127,* 189, 196, 200, 202–3, 257
McDavid, Russell, *127,* 257
McGhee, Howard, 189
McKenzie, Cato and Hattie, 272–73
meatpacking industry, 17, 27
medical care. *See* health issues; hospitals
Memorial Park, 141
Methodist religion and churches, overview, 1–2, 100, 111–12

Metropolitan Council of Negro Women, 175
Mexican-origin Texans
   in Covington family, *31*
   Depression era, effects of, 259, 379–80*n* 119
   in Fifth Ward, 75
   health issues, 132
   immigration overview, 29
   jobs, competition for, 215, 221–22, 234
   migratory farm labor, 272–73
   schools, discrimination in, 118
   in Second and Third Wards, 72
   terminology issues, 297–98*n* 21, 370*n* 26
   and voting rights, 165
middle-class elites, profile of, 88–89
migration figures, overviews
   1930–1940, 229
   First Great Migration overviews, 3–4, 279–80
   Second Great Migration overview, 283–98
Milam County, migration from, 188
Milton Larkin band, 189, 197
Mims, Henry L., 156, 157
Miner, Mary, 210
Mingus, Charles, 203
Mississippi, migration from, 30, 240
   See also Great Mississippi Flood (1927)
Missouri, Kansas and Texas (MKT) Railway, 17, 47
mobility, importance of, 49, 217–20, *219*
Monteith, Walter E., 261
Montgomery County, migration from, 75, 213
mortality rates of African Americans. *See* deaths of African Americans
Mosley, W. L., *112*
Mothers' Clubs, 129
Mouton, Lena, 77
Murphy, Jennie Belle "Ladybelle," 31–32, 95–97

music
   Covington family, *31*, 128–29
   in schools, self-help exemplars, 122
   teacher Corrilla Rochon, 128–29
   Yates High School, 3
   See also musical Renaissance and cultural consciousness
musical Renaissance and cultural consciousness
   blues culture, 195–96
   classical, *201*
   jazz culture, 196–200
   nightclubs and dance halls, 204–7
   overview, 194–95
   urban evolution and protest agency, 204–7
   Wheatley High School jazz program, *127*, 200, 202–3
   See also individual musicians
mutual aid societies, 101–6
My Guitar, 209

NAACP (National Association for the Advancement of Colored People), 163
   1930s profiles, 163, 172
   and escalation of violence post-Word War I, 158–59, 160
   founding of, 52, 151
   Houston branch formation challenges, 152, 156–59
   violence against, 149
   and voting rights activism, 169–70
   on White supremacy, 159–60
   women in, 177
Nabrit, James, 167
Nathan, Ethel, 163
National Alliance of Postal Employees (NAPE), 157
National Association of Colored Graduate Nurses, 137
National Association of Colored Women (NACW), *63*, 109, 153
National Baptist Convention, 52

National Council of Negro Women
    (NCNW), 60, *62, 63,* 153–54
National Guard, Army, 141
National Labor Relations Act, 269
National Labor Union (NLU), 216–17
National Medical Association, 136, 137
National Negro Business League
    (NNBL), 100
National Recovery Administration
    (NRA), 265, 266, 269
National Urban League (NUL), 85, 162
National Youth Administration (NYA),
    63, 265, 267–68
natural disasters
    Great Mississippi Flood (1927),
        39–40, 65, 77, 114–15, 253, 281
    hurricanes, 26, 68
Navasota (Texas), migration from, 50,
    77, 119, 120, 122, 195, 231
Negro Chamber of Commerce, 250
Negro Child Center, 278, *279*
The Negro Genius (Locke), 209
Negro World, 151
neighborhoods
    early settlement profiles, 60,
        62–66, *63,* **64**
    intragroup stratification, 87–92, 93
    See also Acres Homes;
        Independence Heights; wards
        (Houston neighborhoods)
New Caney (Texas), migration from,
    42, 213
"New Crowd" activism, 270
New Deal programs, *63,* 264–69, 271–
    72, 274
New Great Migration, 5
The New Negro: An Interpretation
    (Locke), 143
"New Negro" movement
    cultural Renaissance, overview,
        191–92
    evolution of, 143–44, 147–52
    generational shifts, 170–71, 287,
        289

Houston Informer on, 42
Houston profile, overview, 152
male dominance in, 173–75
oppression, internalization of,
    180–84
strategy profiles, 177–78
women's activism, 175–77
See also cultural Renaissance and
    "New Negro" movement; NAACP
    (National Association for the
    Advancement of Colored People)
New Waverly (Texas), migration from,
    265
New Willard (Texas), migration from,
    17, 31
newspapers. *See Houston Informer;* print
    media; Richardson, Clifton F., Jr.
Niagara Movement, 151
Nickerson, William N., Jr., 43
nightclubs, 204–7
1906 Art and Literary Club, 109
Nixon, Lawrence, 166–67, 168
Nixon v. Condon, 166, 168
Nixon v. Herndon, 166, 352n 106
Nixon v. McCann, 168
Nobia A. Franklin Beauty School,
    239–40
Northern migration, 5–6, 20, 46
nurses, African American, 20, 137–38
nursing homes, 241, 262, 278

Oberholtzer, Edison Ellsworth, 118, 119,
    120
Oberlin Conservatory of Music, *31,* 128,
    201
obstetrics/gynecology, 135–36
Odd Fellows order and building, 102,
    204, 239, 243
office space for African Americans, 102,
    243–44, 259
oil industry, 5, 9, 26–27, 251, 284
"Old Colored High," *124*
Onalaska (Texas), migration from,
    283–84

Orviss, Georgia C. and family, *54,* 55–60, *61*
Osborn, Bessie, 129
Our Mother of Mercy, 115
out-migration, Depression era, 252–53, 257, 273–74
overcrowding, *58, 63,* 67, 86, 129, 130
Ovington, Mary White, 149

Pan-Africanism, 151
Parent Teacher Association (PTA), 129
parents' roles in education, 125–26, 129
Parham, Charles F., 113
Parker, Charlie "Bird," 189
passive resistance strategies, 10, 147–48, 183
    See also coping mechanisms
paternalism, White, 224
Patten, Mason Barnett, 136
Patten, Pauline B. (nee Garza), 136
Patten Law, Thelma Adele, 135–37, 237
Peacock Records, 205
Pemberton, Charles Whittaker, 136
Pendleton, R. H., 120
Pentecostalism, 112–13
People's Sanitarium, 133
Perry, Helen, *169*
personal service jobs. *See* service/domestic occupations
petroleum industry, 5, 9, 26–27, 251, 284
pharmacists, African American
Phi Beta Sigma, 173, 174
Phi Delta Kappa, 125
The Philadelphia Negro (Du Bois), 125
philanthropists, African American, 262–63
    See also service organizations
Phillips, Kimberly, 219
photographers, 210–11
Phyllis Wheatley High School. *See* Wheatley High School
physicians, African American, 132–33, 134–36, 178–80
Pilgrim Building/Temple, 102, 204, 243–44

Pilgrim Congregational Church and Library Association, 103–4
Pinkard, Bill, 189
Pitre, Merline, 173, 175
Pittsburgh Courier, 285
Planned Parenthood, 136
Platt, Sarah, 77
Pleasant Hill Baptist Church, 262, *263*
police brutality, 145
political mobilization, emergence of, 152, 172
Polk County, migration from, 76, 163
poll taxes, 165–66
    See also primary election laws
population decline, Depression era, 252–53
population density in housing, 86
population growth, Black
    Fifth Ward, 76, 79
    Fourth Ward, 67–68
    Houston, 28, 30
    major US cities 1900–1950, 6–8
    Third Ward, 72
population growth, Houston, 27–28
Porter, Roy, 197
Powell, Robert, 160
Prairie View (College) A&M University, *58*
Price, Britain and Alice, 171
Price, Melissa, 108, *288*
Price, Moses L., 171–73, 178
primary election laws, 165–67, *172,* 174
print media
    and chain migration, 42–44, 45–46
    Houston's cultural image, 45
    job advertisements, 42, 44, 51
    and racial consciousness, 43–44, 191, 192–93
    support of Black military members, 142
professional occupations, 231–32, 233, 237–38
    See also businesses/business owners, African American; educators,

African American; nurses,
African American; physicians,
African American
"Professor Jimmie" (James Ryan), 119, 120, 121
Progressive Order of Pilgrims, 259
See also Ancient Order of Pilgrims
Progressive Voters League (PVL), 158
protest initiatives, evolution of, 150–52, 282, 285–87
proximity and migration, 10–11, 42, 49, 50, 51–52
public assistance, 92, 252, 273
See also social welfare organizations
public health programs, 106
public works programs (New Deal), 265–69

Rabinowitz, Howard, 83
"race" communities, 42
racial consciousness
    in Houston Afro-Americans, 185
    and Houston Riot of 1917, 147
    and print media, 43–44
    and rise of radicalism, 147, 170–71
    and women's service organizations, 108, 109
    See also cultural Renaissance and "New Negro" movement
racial identity
    and Southern culture, 11, 20, 21–22, 24–25, 148–49, 162
    terminology issues, 297–98n 21
    Whiteness, rejecting, 188
    See also Blackness, culture of
racism. See discrimination; disenfranchisement of Blacks; Mexican-origin Texans; segregation; violence against African Americans
radicalism, rise of and racial consciousness, 147, 170–71
railroad industry
    early Houston, 25
    importance to migration, 42, 46–47, 49, 213–14
    and job opportunities, 9
    passenger segregation, 162
    unions, 270–71
Randolph, A. Phillip, 270
rape. See sexual abuse
real estate investment, 89, 102, 105, 246, 277
Red Book of Houston, 129, 148, 210
Red Summer 1919, 147
Reese, Della, 206
refineries, oil, 5, 9, 26–27
relief, disaster, and discrimination, 41
relief, social. See social welfare organizations
religion and political apathy, 181
religious denominations, 111–16
    See also churches
religious leaders and racial activism, 173–74, [maybe]
Republican Party, 264
resident Afro-American resentment to migrants, 46, 65
re-step migrations, 256–57
return migration patterns, 256–57
Rhone, Calvin L. and Lucia, 52
Rhumboogie Club/Café, 189
Rice, C. W., 178, 271
Rice, H. Baldwin, 149
Rice, Ruby Leola, 43
Rice, William Marsh, 25
Rice Hotel, 203
Richardson, Charlie and Bettie, 43
Richardson, Clifton F., Jr., 161–62, 183–84
Richardson, Clifton F., Sr.
    on accommodationism, 177–78, 182
    activism of, 150, 179
    community agency of, 241
    on inequitable school facilities, 119
    and NAACP, 156, 157–58
    profile and influence of, 43–44
    residence, *73*
    threats and violence against, 161–62, 178

Richardson, Ruby, 68, *73*
riots, 151
    See also Houston Riot of 1917
Rivers and Harbors Act, 25
Roans Prairie (Texas), migration from, 31, 47, 48
Robertson County, 256
Robey, Don D. and Lena, 145, 205
Robinson, Judson, Sr., 49, *70*, 270–71
Robinson, Lena, *290*
Rochon, Corrilla, 128–29
Roett, Catherine J., 137
Roman Catholic religion. *See* Catholic religion and churches
Roosevelt, Franklin D., *63*, 264, 271–72, 285
Roy Eldridge "Little Jazz" Orchestra, 189
rural hardships and migration, 11, 30, 53, 77, 281
Ryan, James Delbridge "Professor Jimmie," 119, 120, 121, 123, *125*
Ryan Middle School, *125*, 126

St. John's Baptist Church, 116–17
St. Nicholas Catholic Church, 114
salaries/wages
    Depression era effects, 250–52, 260, 282–83
    inequality in, 17, 47, *58*, 90–91, 199, 230
    teachers/faculty, 119–20, 238, 281, 285–86
    See also job discrimination; unskilled/semiskilled workers
Sally, Zack, *112*
Sam Houston Industrial and Training School, 55
Samaroff, Olga, *201*
San Antonio, Texas, 27, 136
San Jacinto County, migration from, 253
San Miguel, Guadalupe, 118
sanitation. *See* city services
satire and racial consciousness, 191, 192–93
schools, Houston. *See* Houston Public School System
Scott, Emmett Jay, 44, 73, 101, 103–4, 148, 182, 287
Scott, James C., 10
Scott, Thelma. *See* Bryant, Thelma Scott
Seals, Vivian (nee Hubbard), 80, 81–82, 160, 267, *290*
seasonal employment, 16, 47, 91, 218–20, 261–62, 282
Second Great Migration, 5, 9, 274, 279, 283–87, 289
Second Ku Klux Klan (KKK). *See* Ku Klux Klan (KKK), Second
Second Ward, 72
segregation
    and the arts, 207
    in public works programs, 267
    residential, 83–87
    in schools, 117–18
    solidarity benefits of, 66, 88, 148–49, 151, 245, 249–50, 278
    Southern culture of, 11, 20, 21–22, 24–25, 148–49, 162
    See also discrimination
self-help strategies and community building
    evolution of, 99–100, 138–39
    exemplars, 120–25, 126–29
    groups and societies, 22, 53, 101–6
    health professionals, 130–31
    See also accommodationism; community agency
self-preservation *v.* racial backlash, 98–99
semiskilled workers, profile of. *See* unskilled/semiskilled workers
service organizations, 96–97, 101–6, 260–63
    See also sororities, service; women's clubs
service/domestic occupations, 216, 230, 233–34, 280
Services of Supply (SOS) units, 142
sex, interracial, 24, 160

sex ratio of migrants, 34–35
sexism, 116, 131, 136, 155, 173–75, 238
sexual abuse, 48, 51, 159, 160, 182
sexual promiscuity and disease, 131, 132
Seymour, William J., 113
Shabazz, Amilcar, 119
sharecropping, 15, 22–24, 47, 272
Sharkie, Mariah, 100–101
Shelley v. Kraemer, 84, 120, *121*
Shillady, John R., 149, 158
ship channel. *See* Houston Ship Channel
shipping industry, development of in Houston, 25–27
Shives, Willie and Rosie Lee, 256
shotgun house, 113
Sigma Gamma Rho Sorority, 107
sign language, 117
Simpson, Lee Haywood, 172, 241, 262–63
Sisters of the Holy Family, 114
Sisters of the Incarnate Word, 114
Sisters of the Mysterious Ten, 103
skill divisions of labor force, 216
skilled workers and racial dichotomy, 90, 214
slavery
    and agency, evolution of, 88–89, 98–100, 147–50
    and culture of accommodation, 147–48, 149–50
    and labor force, evolution of, 215–16
    and music culture, 194
    social conditioning of, 21–22
The Smart Set Club, *69,* 70, 107
Smith, Ernest O., 103, 119, 156–57, 158
Smith, Lonnie, 169–70
Smith, Ruby, 235–36
Smith, Walter, *112*
Smith v. Allwright, 170, 287
Sneed, Glenn Owen, 68–69
Sneed, Martha Emma (nee Masterson), 68–69, 96
Sneed, Martha Francis and Ruth, 69–70

Snow, Kneeland S., 146
Social Darwinism, 224
Social Service Bureau (SSB), 106–7, 261–62
social welfare organizations, 106–7, 260–63, 263–69
    See also public assistance; service organizations
Society of St. Joseph (Josephites), 114–15
socioeconomic class divisions, 66
soldiers, African American, 141–43, 151, [riot of 1917]
Sons and Daughters of Mercy, 103
SoRelle, James M., 84, 158, 177–78, 249
sororities, service, 70, *71,* 106, 107, 110, *135,* 136, 262
South, identification with, 11, 21–22
Southern culture of segregation, 11, 20, 21–22, 24–25, 148–49, 162
Southern interregional migration, 30–31
Southern Pacific Railroad, 19, 25, 75, 213–14
Southwestern Athletic Conference (SWAC), 365*n* 50
Sparks, Lee, 145
Sparks, Randy, 262, 266, 268–69
"speaking in tongues," 113
Spindletop Oilfield, 26–27
Spivey, L. H., *112*
Stanley, Will, 158
stepwise migration, 17, 18–19, 50, 188, 220, 251, 278
sterotyping of African Americans, 108, 180, 182, 207, 211, 276
Stewart, Kathleen Evans, 116–17
Stewart, W. H., 116
stonings, 160
storefront (working-class) churches, 112–13
Stormy Weather, 203
stratification of African American community, 87–92, 93
    See also class divisions among African Americans

Stullivan, Isam, 213
Stullivan, Luther, 42–43, 49, 181, 184, 257, 270–71
Stullivan, Tillie, 42, 213–14
Sunbelt economy, 289
Sunnyside, 80
Sutton, Carrie Jane, *135*, 136
Sweatt, Erma, *71*, *125*, 126
Sweatt, Heman, *71*, 126
Sweatt v. Painter, 71, *125*, 287
Sylvester, Hattie, 272

Tapscott, Horace, 363–64*n* 35
tarring incidents, 160
taxi services, 246, 249
Taylor, George and Ethel, 51
Taylor, Hobart, Sr. and family, 246–47, 249, 355–56*n* 142
Taylor, Ida Lee, 51
TCIRC (Texas Commission on Interracial Cooperation), 153–56, 158, 175–76
teaching. *See* educators, African American
Teal, Arthur Chester and Elnora, 211–12
Teal Studios/School of Photography, 211
temporary migrations
    Depression era, 253, 256–57, 261–62, 282
    mobility and labor empowerment, 217–20
    and railroads, importance of, 47, 49
    and seasonal employment, 16
tenant farming, 22–24, 272, 274, 293*n* 11
Terrell, Alexander W., 165
Terrell, Mary Church, 156
"territory bands," 196–97
Texaco Oil, 133
Texas Baptist State Sunday School Convention (TBSSSC), 52
Texas Board of Hairdressers and Cosmetologists, 241
Texas Centennial Central Exposition, 209
Texas Citizenship League, 159–60
Texas Federation of Negro Women's Clubs, 109
Texas Freeman, 44, 101
Texas Pacific Railway, 25
Texas Southern University (TSU), 100, 119
Texas State Department of Welfare (TDW), 265
Texas State Federation of Labor (TSFL), 217
Texas State University for Negroes (TSUN), 60
Third Ward
    business district, 244
    churches in, 113, 114, 116, 171
    hospitals, 133–36
    map, **64**
    migrants coming to, profiles, 2, 49–50
    nightclubs, 205
    profile of, 65, 71–75
    schools, influence of, 126
    See also Yates High School
Third Ward Civic Club (TWCC), 165, 167–68
Thomas, Bertha Marie, 79
Thomas, Jesse O., 45, 85, 113, 131–32, 162, 222, 261
Thomas, Lorenzo, 193, 197
Thomas, Rachel, 95
Thomas, Raynola, 268
Thompson, Constance Eloise (nee Houston), *56*, 60, *61*, *62*, *63*, 79–80
Thompson, Tracy, 60, *61*, *62*, 79–80
Tibbett, J. S., 44
Tibbs, Andrew, 190
timber industry, overview, 5, 17, 32
Tom Archia and His All Stars, 190
Townsend, Albert, 168
Townsend, Willard, 270
Townsend, William, *112*
transportation industry, 25–26, 25–27, 230
    See also railroad industry; shipping industry

Travers, Sara, 144–45
Trinity (Texas), migration from, 15
Trinity County, migration from, 18, 49, 76, 187
Trinity East Methodist Episcopal Church, 2
Trinity Methodist Episcopal Church, 100, 111
Trotter, Joe William, 4
tuberculosis, 131–32
Turner, Zelda, *71*
Twomey, Dannehl M., 210–11

"Uncle Tom" philosophy, 356n 142
  See also accommodationism
unemployment, 90, 91, 252–53, 258–59
unincorporated communities, 80
Union Hospital, 133
Union-Jeremiah Hospital, 133
unions
  Black participation in, 19, 269–71
  Depression era Black displacement, 266
  discrimination in, 17, 215, 217, 271
  exclusions from, 90, 217
  International Longshoremen's Association (ILA), 223–24
  musician's, 190, 191, 202
  National Alliance of Postal Employees (NAPE), 157
  National Labor Union (NLU), 216–17
  railroad workers, 270–71
United Brothers of Friendship, 103
United Charities, 106, 260
United Transport Service Employees of America (UTSEA), 270–71
United Way, 106, 260
Universal Negro Improvement Association and African Communities League (UNIA-ACL), 151
University of Houston, 119
unsafe community conditions, 85–86

unskilled/semiskilled workers
  Depression era profile, 275
  profiles of, 90–91, 216, 280
  women, 236
  workforce share, 228–30
Upper Texas Gulf Coast (UTGC) manufacturing region, 26–27
Upshur County, migration from, 1, 32
urbanization, 27–28, 30, 35–36, *37*

VanDerZee, James, 210
veiled resistance. *See* passive resistance strategies
violence against African Americans
  and accommodation strategy, 178
  against Black activists, 149, 161–62
  domestic, cycle of, 51
  lynching, 49, 57, 153–54, 158–59, 160
  as means of "social control," 24
  post World War I escalation, 24, 158–59, 160
  riot of 1917, 141–47
visual arts and racial consciousness, 207–12
vocational training, 124–25
volunteerism, 264
voting rights, activism for, 165–70, 287

Waco (Texas), migration from, 211
wages. *See* salaries/wages
Wagner Act, 269
Walker, Franklin Pierce, 220
Walker, Lullelia Harrison, 90
Walker County, migration from, 76
"Walking City" era, 71–72
Wallace, Erma (nee Sweatt), *71, 125, 126*
Waller County, migration from, 163–64, 187–88, 272
Walton, Johnnie Mae, 189
War Manpower Commission (WMC), 285
Ward, R. H., 160

wards (Houston neighborhoods), 63, **64,** 65
  See also Fifth Ward; Fourth Ward; Second Ward; Third Ward
Washington, Booker T. and accommodationism, 97, 147, 150
Washington, Jesse, 158
Washington, Margaret Murray, 109
water supplies and health issues, 130
waterway transportation, 25–26
Webster, George, 44
Webster-Richardson Publishing Company, 44
welfare organizations, 260–63
  See also social welfare organizations
Wesley, Carter and Mamie, 150, 167, 170, 178, 241
Wharton County, migration from, 32, 246
Wheatley High School, *124,* 125, 127
  music program, *127,* 188–89, 196, 200, 202–3
White, Julius, 167, 168, 175, 249
White, Lulu B., 105, 168, 175–76, 177, 178
White, Walter, 157, 163
White Democratic Primary law, 166, 287
  See also voting rights
White out-migration, 79
White Sisters of the Incarnate Word, 114
White supremacy, 159–62, 267
"White" terminology issues, 297–98n 21
White v. Lubbock, 168, 352n 106
Whiteness concept, 24–25, 89, 93, 188, 240
Whitson, Walter W., 261–62
Wilder, Craig, *112*
Willard (Texas), migration from, 17
Williams, Charlie and Martha, 251–52
Williams, Oran and family, 31, 47–49, 49–50, 257, 282
Williams, Simeon B., 192–93
Willis (Texas), migration from, 46
Wilson, Jon, 156–57, 158

Winters, Joe, 158
Wintz, Cary D., 67, 216–17, 245
Witherspoon, Fredda (nee Crawford), 120
Witherspoon, Robert, 120
women
  as business owners, 239–40, 250
  church women, influence of, 116
  and domestic violence, 51
  as educators, impact of, 125–29, 237–39
  Fifth Ward profiles, 77
  as homemakers, 236–37
  middle-class Black profiles, 57–58
  and moral responsibility, 131
  notable accomplishments of, *59,* 68–69
  photographers, 211
  physicians, 135–38
  political activism of, 175–77
  role in migration scenarios, 50–51, 257–58
  in workforce, 218, 225, 226–28, 232–39, 280–81, 283
  See also women's clubs/groups
women's clubs/groups
  community building, 87, 101, 106–10
  Depression era service, 262
  fraternal and service organizations, 104–6
  political/social activism, 60, 69–70, 175–76
  See also individual organizations
women's rights advocacy, 153, 157
Wonderful Workers of the World, 103
Wood, Kyle, 265–66
Wood County, migration from, 1
Woodley, Albert E., 114
Woodmen Union, 103
workforce
  employment participation rates, 225–32, 233
  Mexican-origin workers, competition from, 221–22

origins and 1800s profile, 215–20
overviews, 213–15, 221, 280
permanent jobs and 1900s overview, 221
post-WWII profile, 284–86
racial dichotomy and marginalization of non-Whites, 222–23, 224–25, 233–34
women in, 218, 225, 226–28, 232–39, 280–81, 283
See also businesses/business owners, African American; unions

working class
churches, 112–13
and elites, racial solidarity with, 183–84
and political apathy, 182–83
profile of, 88, 89–90, 275
See also class divisions among African Americans

Works Progress Administration (WPA), 265, 266, 268–69

World War I
African American support in, 142
labor shortages, 5
and urban/economic growth, 9, 251

World War II and Second Great Migration, 283–87, 289

Wortham, John Lee, 159
Wright, Sarah, 81
Wright, W. D., 297–98n 21
Wright Land Company, 81
Wright Loan and security, 81

xenophobia, 159

Yates, John Henry "Jack," 100, *112*
Yates High School, 3, 122, *125*, 126
Young, C. Milton, Jr., *59*, 60
Young, Hazel, *71, 112,* 120, *124, 125,* 126, 144, 145, 146
Young, Hortense Cordelia (nee Houston), 58–60, *62,* 126
Young, Milton III., *59*
Young, Thelma (nee Hainsworth), 128–29, *290*
Young (Clark), Yvonne, *59,* 60
Young Men's Benevolent Club, 102
Young Women's Christian Association (YWCA), 96, 107, 175

Zeigler, Robert, 216–17
Zeta Phi Beta Sorority (ZPB), 107, 110, 262
zoning, indifference to, 83–84, 85
zydeco music, 199

www.ingramcontent.com/pod-product-compliance
Lightning Source LLC
Chambersburg PA
CBHW070124080526
44586CB00015B/1541